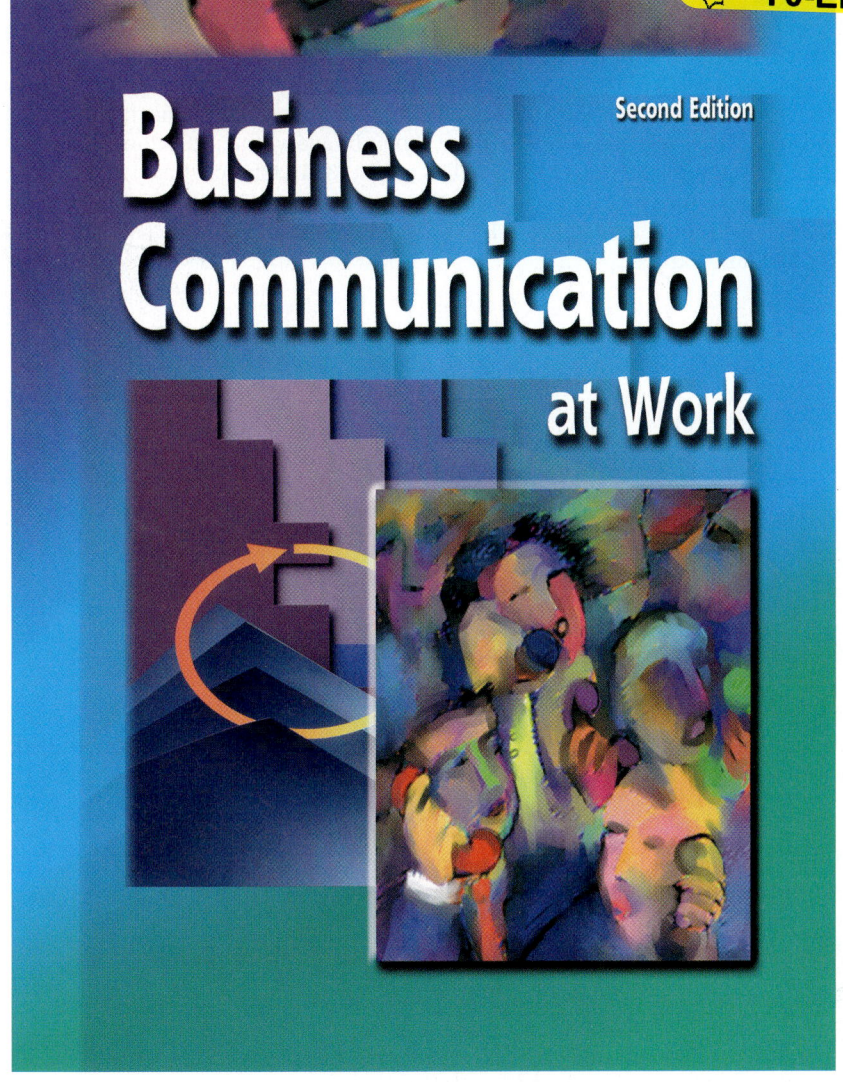

Marilyn L. Satterwhite
Business Division
Danville Area Community College
Danville, Illinois

Judith Olson-Sutton, Ph.D.
Associate Dean
Business Division
Madison Area Technical College
Madison, Wisconsin

Boston   Burr Ridge, IL   Dubuque, IA   Madison, WI   New York   San Francisco   St. Louis
Bangkok   Bogotá   Caracas   Kuala Lumpur   Lisbon   London   Madrid   Mexico City
Milan   Montreal   New Delhi   Santiago   Seoul   Singapore   Sydney   Taipei   Toronto

PHOTO CREDITS

Cover: Phototake (image), SuperStock (illustration); **2** Dave Teel/Corbis; **22** Digital Vision/PictureQuest; **46** Sanford Agliolo/Corbis; **72** Rachael Mackey; **73** Mary Kaufmann; **73** The Longaberger® Company; **80** Digital Vision/Getty Images; **102** Ken Davies/Masterfile; **132** Ken Davies/Masterfile; **154** Digital Vision/PictureQuest; **188** Anne Williams; **196** Susan Le Yan/Artville/PictureQuest; **228** elektraVision AG/Index Stock Imagery, Inc.; **264** Jon Allen/Illustration Works, Inc.; **290** Steve Allen/Brand X Pictures/PictureQuest; **326** Corbis; **351** Allisun Kale Marshall; **360** Mauritius Die Bildagentur/Index Stock Imagery, Inc.; **382** Danny Izumi; **388** Robin Jareaux/Artville/PictureQuest; **405** Ray Durazo; **408** Joe Bator/Corbis; **442** Digital Vision/PictureQuest; **458** Michael Gunn; **464** Boden/Ledingham/Masterfile; **496** Chris McElcheran/Masterfile; **520** Jane Kappler.

Library of Congress Cataloging-in-Publication Data

Satterwhite, Marilyn L.
    Business communication at work / Marilyn L. Satterwhite, Judith Olson-Sutton.-- 2nd. ed.
      p. cm.
    Includes index.
    ISBN 0-07-829080-5 (softcover)
    1. Business communication. I. Olson-Sutton, Judith, 1944- II. Title.

HF5718 .S26 2002
658.4'5--dc21

                                                                                                              2002068989

The McGraw·Hill Companies

Published by McGraw-Hill, a business unit of The Mcgraw-Hill Companies, Inc., 1221 Avenue of the Americas, New York, NY, 10020. Copyright © 2003 by The McGraw-Hill Companies, Inc. All rights reserved. No part of this publication may be reproduced or distributed in any form or by any means, or stored in a database or retrieval system, without the prior written consent of The McGraw-Hill Companies, Inc., including, but not limited to, in any network or other electronic storage or transmission, or broadcast for distance learning.
Some ancillaries, including electronic and print components, may not be available to customers outside the United States.

Printed in the United States of America.

ISBN 0-07-293015-2

3 4 5 6 7 8 9 0 DOW/DOW 0 9 8 7 6 5

Table of Contents

Introduction vii
Acknowledgments x

Unit 1 — The Process and Challenge of Communication 1

Chapter 1: Setting the Stage for Effective Communication 2
- **Workplace Applications:** *Writer's Block* 3
- The Importance of Business Communication Skills 4
- The Changing Workplace Environment 5
- Using Business Communication at Work 6
- Principles of Written Communication 9
- **Worksheets** 19

Chapter 2: Choosing the Right Words 22
- **Workplace Applications:** *Standard American English* 23
- The Writing Process 24
- The Meanings of Words 24
- Proper Word Choices 26
- **Worksheets** 41

Chapter 3: Developing Sentences and Paragraphs 46
- **Workplace Applications:** *Prewriting* 47
- Writing Sentences and Paragraphs 48
- Sentence Structures 48
- Constructing Sentences 51
- Developing and Arranging Paragraphs 65
- **Communication at Work** 72
- **Worksheets** 75

Unit 2 — Basics for Communicating Effectively 79

Chapter 4: Developing Listening Skills 80
- **Workplace Applications:** *Cultural Diversity* 81
- Understanding the Importance of Listening 82
- The Process of Active Listening 84
- Interpreting Nonverbal Communication 87
- Barriers to Effective Listening 90
- Active Listening Techniques 92
- **Worksheets** 96

Table of Contents   iii

Chapter 5: Planning and Organizing Business Messages 102
Workplace Applications: *Time Management* 103
Oral and Written Communication 104
Planning for Effective Communication 104
Organizing the Message 107
Worksheets 123

Chapter 6: Using Technology to Improve Communication . . . 132
Workplace Applications: *Brainstorming* 133
Technology in the Office 134
The Internet: Keeping the World Connected 139
Using Application Technology 143
Using Technology to Improve Your Writing 148
Worksheets 152

Chapter 7: Formatting Business Messages 154
Workplace Applications: *Etiquette* 155
Formatting Memos 156
Other Types of Internal Messages 163
Parts of a Business Letter 167
Letter Styles 179
Addressing Envelopes 183
Communication at Work 188
Worksheets 190

Unit 3 | Effective Messages 195

Chapter 8: Messages That Promote Goodwill 196
Workplace Applications: *Conflict Management* 197
Promoting Goodwill 198
Projecting a Positive Tone 198
Promoting a Service Attitude 205
Writing Goodwill Messages 208
Thank-You Messages 210
Messages of Congratulations 210
Letters That Invite, Announce, or Welcome 212
Get-Well Wishes and Sympathy Letters 215
Letters That Maintain or Reactivate Business 216
Applying Principles for Goodwill Letters 217
Worksheets 220

Chapter 9: Messages for Inquiries and Requests 228
Workplace Applications: *Customer Service* 229
Handling Routine Correspondence 230
Preparing Routine Communications 232

Inquiries and Requests 239
Replies to Inquiries and Requests 245
Form Replies to Inquiries 251
Evaluating Your Writing 254
Worksheets 257

Chapter 10: Claim and Adjustment Messages 264
Workplace Applications: *Decision Making* 265
Claim Letters 266
Adjustment Letters 273
Worksheets 283

Chapter 11: Persuasive Messages 290
Workplace Applications: *Problem Solving* 291
Writing to Public Officials and the Media 292
Persuasive Requests 299
Sales Letters 303
Worksheets 321

Chapter 12: Order, Credit, and Collection Messages 326
Workplace Applications: *Constructive Criticism* 327
Sending Order Messages 328
Acknowledging Order Messages 332
Order Acknowledgment Letters 335
Credit Letters 339
Collection Messages 344
Communication at Work 351
Worksheets 353

Unit 4 — Reports and Media Communications 359

Chapter 13: Developing Memos and Memo Reports 360
Workplace Applications: *Team Building* 361
Internal Communications 362
Routine Memos 363
Memo Reports 370
Communication at Work 382
Worksheets 385

Chapter 14: Creating Press Releases and Newsletters 388
Workplace Applications: *Ethical Behavior* 389
Press Releases 390
Newsletters 398
Communication at Work 405
Worksheets 407

Table of Contents

Chapter 15: Constructing and Presenting Reports 408
Workplace Applications: *Plagiarism* 409
Approaches to Writing Reports 410
Organizational Patterns for Reports 411
Guidelines for Writing Reports 414
Letter Reports 414
Formal Reports 416
Parts of a Formal Report 421
Proposals 430
Using Visuals in a Report 432
Worksheets 437

Chapter 16: Preparing Meeting Communications 442
Workplace Applications: *Telecommuting and Teleconferencing* 443
Types of Meetings 444
Preparing Meeting Notices 445
Preparing Meeting Agendas 446
Preparing Minutes 451
Communication at Work 458
Worksheets 460

Unit 5 Employment Communication 463

Chapter 17: Conducting the Job Search 464
Workplace Applications: *Stress Management* 465
Starting the Employment Process 466
Conducting a Job Search 469
Preparing A Résumé 471
Completing an Employment Application 484
Developing a Portfolio 487
Worksheets 490

Chapter 18: Selling Yourself to Employers 496
Workplace Applications: *Styles of Leadership* 497
Preparing a Cover Letter 498
Guidelines for Writing an Effective Cover Letter 500
Interviewing 506
Guidelines for Follow-Up Letters 515
Resignation Letters 518
Communication at Work 520
Worksheets 522

Appendix A: References 525
Appendix B: Dictation Techniques 540
Index 543

INTRODUCTION

Welcome to the *Business Communication at Work, Second Edition* text and the wonderful world of communication in action. Getting and holding a job requires the ability to communicate effectively in many different types of situations. You will be provided the foundations you need for developing sentences and paragraphs and for capturing the message, whether you are communicating orally or by letter, memorandum, report, e-mail, or voice mail.

Each chapter opens with learning Objectives to guide your study of the chapter material.

Workplace Applications features offer opportunities to consider real-world facets of the challenges you will face when you are communicating in the workplace.

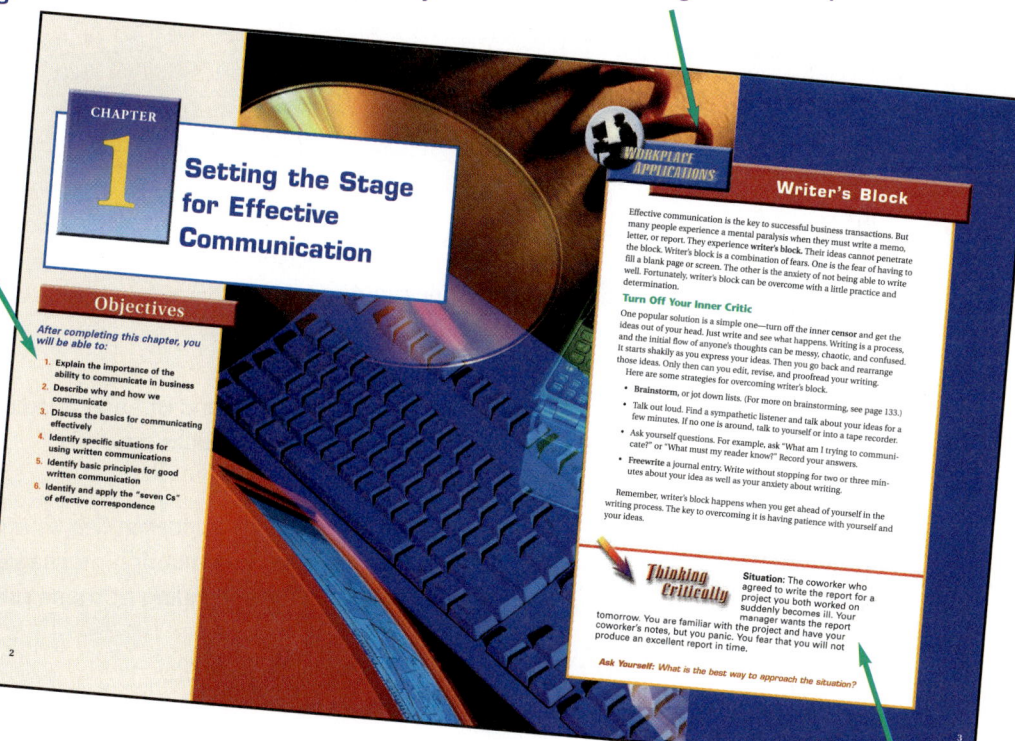

Thinking Critically questions challenge you to apply your personal experiences to the chapter content.

Components of the Program

The second edition of *Business Communication at Work* is a complete, well-rounded program that includes the following components:

- **Text-Workbook** with instruction, examples, Checkpoint exercises, and Worksheets for practice.

- **CD-ROM** with additional exercises and practices, providing hands-on completion of editing and proofreading exercises, composition of letters, memos, reports, and containing the Glencoe Interactive Grammar program for refreshing your grammar skills.

- **Web site** with a separate section reserved for students. This section contains online practice tests, crossword puzzles, additional learning exercises, and other World Wide Web links. Access is gained by entering the following Internet address: bcw.glencoe.com

Each chapter begins with a short **Introduction** to the chapter concepts.

Quotations get you thinking about the themes of each chapter.

Legal & Ethical scenarios tie the content of each chapter to legal/ethical concepts, inviting you to voice your opinion based on the information provided.

Special notes reminders stress important points relating to the information in the chapter.

Checkpoints provide chances to assess your understanding of the topics covered in the previous sections.

The **Summary** at the end of each chapter recaps for you the basic concepts covered.

Checklists provide opportunities to apply principles in the text to a communication message and then to check your understanding of these principles.

Worksheets at the end of each chapter provide myriad opportunities for you to increase your skills in the concepts and principles of letter and memo writing, report research and composition, sentence and paragraph construction, and employment communications.

The **Appendices** contain a review of the parts of speech, sentence and paragraph construction, punctuation, letter formats, and **Dictation Techniques.** In addition, a thorough **Index** is provided to help locate concepts and principles that you may want to review.

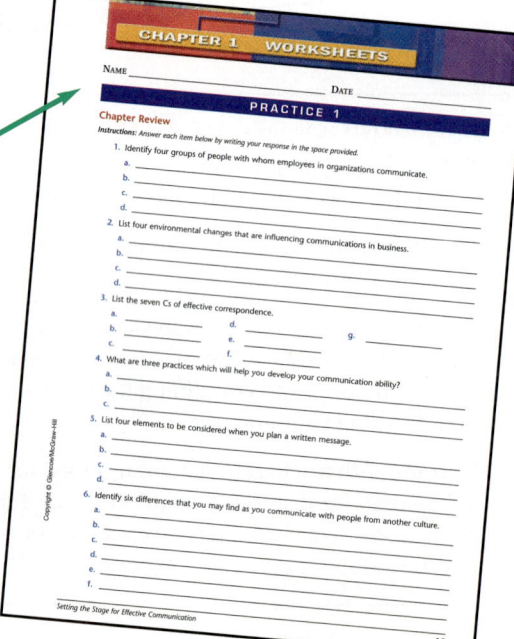

viii   Introduction

FEATURES

THINKING CAP icons lead you to challenging puzzlers that relate to the information studied in the chapters. Featured questions guide your thinking as you conceptualize these special communication situations.

GLOBAL DIVERSITY logos direct you to scenarios that describe how people in another part of the country or another culture may view communication in a different way. Probing questions direct your attention to the specifics of the situations.

GO TO CD-ROM prompts point you to the *Business Communication at Work* **STUDENT CD-ROM** to give you additional practice exercises covering chapter concepts. The CD-ROM is optional but highly recommended.

INTERNET margin notes direct you to the World Wide Web for additional research if you have access to the Internet.

Each unit features a Communication at Work profile focusing on a professional who provides insight into the use of communication principles in the process of doing his or her job.

Online Exercises presented in each chapter direct you to the *Business Communication at Work* Web site at bcw.glencoe.com for illuminating tours of various Internet sites.

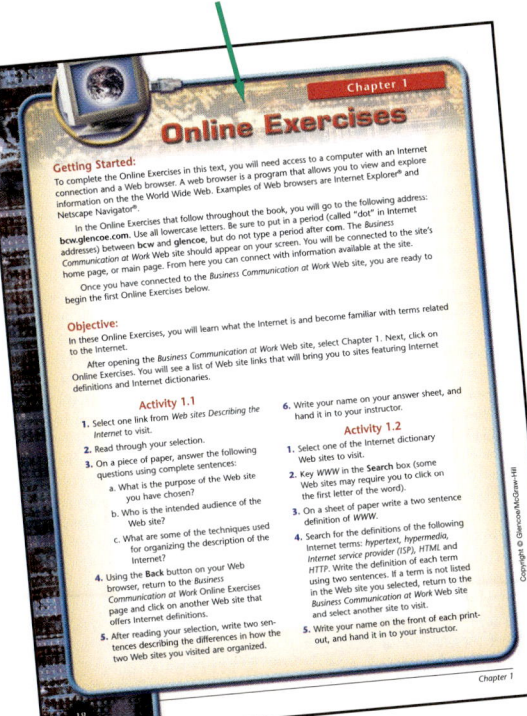

Discussion questions further exploration into the communication challenges these individuals describe.

Introduction

Acknowledgments

Special thanks to **Karen Schneiter**, Rochester, Minnesota, for her contributions in developing the special student CD-ROM activities.

Special thanks to **Nelda Shelton**, Tarrant County Junior College, Fort Worth, Texas, and **Sharon Burton**, Brookhaven College, Dallas, Texas. Their contributions to several chapters have brought timely content to this textbook.

The following educators have contributed significantly to the development of this text with their reviews and valuable comments. We thank them for their input.

George Pierre Asselin
South Texas Educational Technologies, Inc.
Weslaco, Texas

Carol Bennet
Santa Rosa College
Santa Rosa, California

Nancy J. Cann
Western Business College
Vancouver, Washington

Janet Caruso
Briarcliffe College
Bethpage, New York

Kathryn L. Cid
Lincoln Technical Institute
West Orange, New Jersey

Barbara Cluft
Northern Virginia Community College
Annandale, Virginia

Kelly Donahue
Globe College
Oakdale, Minnesota

Phyllis J. Donovan
Bryant & Stratton Business Institute
Buffalo, New York

Christine Foster
Grand Rapids Community College
Grand Rapids, Michigan

Donna Hines
Palo Alto College
San Antonio, Texas

Edna Jellesed
Lane Community College
Eugene, Oregon

Carol H. Jordan
Chemeketa Community College
Salem, Oregon

Elizabeth Kerbey
San Jacinto College Central
Pasadena, Texas

Jan Louthan
Lake Land College
Mattoon, Illinois

Diane Penn-Mickey
Northern Virginia Community College
Woodbridge, Virginia

Kay D. Post
Community College of Allegheny County-North Campus
Pittsburgh, Pennsylvania

Connianne Pugh
San Antonio College
San Antonio, Texas

Dean C. Rehm
Skadron College
San Bernardino, California

Alice Smith
Indiana Business College
Lafayette, Indiana

Carol A. Straka
Moraine Valley Community College
Palos Hills, Illinois

Peggy J. Thomsen
Heald Business College
San Francisco, California

Jane D. Williams
J. Sargeant Reynolds Community College
Richmond, Virginia

x Acknowledgments

unit 1

The Process and Challenge of Communication

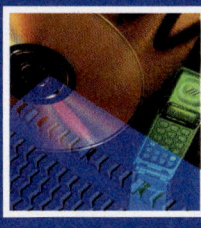

- **Chapter 1**
  Setting the Stage for Effective Communication

- **Chapter 2**
  Choosing the Right Words

- **Chapter 3**
  Developing Sentences and Paragraphs

CHAPTER 1

Setting the Stage for Effective Communication

Objectives

After completing this chapter, you will be able to:

1. Explain the importance of the ability to communicate in business
2. Describe why and how we communicate
3. Discuss the basics for communicating effectively
4. Identify specific situations for using written communications
5. Identify basic principles for good written communication
6. Identify and apply the "seven Cs" of effective correspondence

Workplace Applications

Writer's Block

Effective communication is the key to successful business transactions. But many people experience a mental paralysis when they must write a memo, letter, or report. They experience **writer's block.** Their ideas cannot penetrate the block. Writer's block is a combination of fears. One is the fear of having to fill a blank page or screen. The other is the anxiety of not being able to write well. Fortunately, writer's block can be overcome with a little practice and determination.

Turn Off Your Inner Critic

One popular solution is a simple one—turn off the inner **censor** and get the ideas out of your head. Just write and see what happens. Writing is a process, and the initial flow of anyone's thoughts can be messy, chaotic, and confused. It starts shakily as you express your ideas. Then you go back and rearrange those ideas. Only then can you edit, revise, and proofread your writing.

Here are some strategies for overcoming writer's block.

- **Brainstorm,** or jot down lists. (For more on brainstorming, see page 133.)
- Talk out loud. Find a sympathetic listener and talk about your ideas for a few minutes. If no one is around, talk to yourself or into a tape recorder.
- Ask yourself questions. For example, ask "What am I trying to communicate?" or "What must my reader know?" Record your answers.
- **Freewrite** a journal entry. Write without stopping for two or three minutes about your idea as well as your anxiety about writing.

Remember, writer's block happens when you get ahead of yourself in the writing process. The key to overcoming it is having patience with yourself and your ideas.

Situation: The coworker who agreed to write the report for a project you both worked on suddenly becomes ill. Your manager wants the report tomorrow. You are familiar with the project and have your coworker's notes, but you panic. You fear that you will not produce an excellent report in time.

Ask Yourself: What is the best way to approach the situation?

3

> **" *If I went back to college again, I'd concentrate on two areas: learning to write and to speak before an audience. Nothing in life is more important than the ability to communicate effectively.* "**
>
> —**Gerald R. Ford, 38th President of the United States**

The ability to communicate is important in all aspects of life. Looking at classified advertisements and job descriptions, you will find the majority of companies specifying that a successful applicant should have excellent communication skills, both oral and written. The ability to communicate effectively with others is named by many employers as a top attribute of the successful businessperson.

Your communication skills are vital to your success in the workplace. The ability to communicate effectively with customers, coworkers, subordinates, and supervisors may be the determining factor in your career advancement.

The Importance of Business Communication Skills

In obtaining a job, your technical skills are important. Employers want to hire the best candidate and will screen résumés and job application forms for evidence of applicants' job-related knowledge and experience. Equally important are your communication skills, both written and oral. To assist them in evaluating written communication skills, many employers include essay-type questions on their application forms. The applicants have an opportunity to demonstrate effective communication skills in their responses. At the interview, the employer may ask the applicants to respond orally to questions about a specific situation, such as a case study. Employers use this opportunity to evaluate applicants' oral communication skills.

Once you are employed, job skills alone will not ensure your success in business. If you lack the ability to communicate well with supervisors, customers, and coworkers, you are unlikely to be promoted to higher positions.

How Your Communication Skills Represent You and Your Company

Your communication skills are readily apparent whether they are in the form of a written document or a conversation. They reflect on both you and your organization. The impressions customers and business associates form of you and your organization are important and lasting. Many of these impressions are based solely upon the way you communicate.

Reflection on You

How you communicate with others determines their opinion of your overall competence and integrity. You may be an extremely intelligent, talented, and knowledgeable individual. If your communication skills are poor, however, others tend to question your abilities.

Whether you like it or not, many people judge your abilities and intelligence specifically by the quality of your writing, which includes the accuracy of your spelling, punctuation, and grammar. The memos, letters, and reports you write demonstrate your ability to communicate.

Rocky Top Farms, a supplier of farm and garden supplies, is seeking candidates for the position of Customer Service Representative. The successful candidate will handle customer questions and problems over the phone, develop and maintain a customer database, and provide support to District Sales Managers. Minimum job requirements include 1-3 years experience in Purchasing/Management, negotiation skills, strong communication skills, and the ability to interact with suppliers and customers.

Figure 1-1
Job placement ads such as this show that strong communication skills are important qualifications for employment.

Not only are others evaluating your competence, but they may be judging your integrity. Being ethical in your communications, oral or written, is very important. If you promise to do things but fail to do so, if you make statements that are not factual, if you make untruthful comments about others, or if you are careless in your writing, others will not trust you and will become hesitant to work with you.

Reflection on Your Company

When you communicate as an employee of your company, you represent the company. Customers will evaluate your company based on their interaction with you. **Goodwill** is the positive feeling or attitude that you show or that customers have about a business that encourages customer loyalty. As an employee, you can strengthen or you can destroy that goodwill based on the manner in which you communicate.

Your written communications are a permanent record of your ability to write. People who read these communications form an opinion of both you and your organization. Presenting yourself well in writing means that you will project a favorable image of your organization as well as promote successful business operations both internally and externally.

> **"** Communication is the most important skill in life. We spend most of our waking hours communicating. **"**
> —Stephen R. Covey,
> *The Seven Habits of Highly Effective People*

Thinking Cap 1.1

Discuss: Do you agree with Covey that communication is the most important skill in life? Why do you agree with him? or Why do you disagree with him?

THE CHANGING WORKPLACE ENVIRONMENT

Communication skills have always been important in the workplace. As the business world changes, the importance of these skills increases. Workers today are faced with the following challenges:

- Increased use of technology
- Increased global competition
- Restructured management and/or product lines
- Increased quality emphasis and customer focus
- Increased focus on legal and ethical problems

All of these changes influence the communication process within organizations. Technology, however, has had the greatest impact on how we communicate. Electronic mail, voice mail, teleconferences, computer networks, fax machines, and the Internet have expanded our methods of communicating. More employees are talking to each other and sharing data as they use the various technologies to search for, collect, prepare, and report information. Computer communication is also used for activities such as group problem solving, consensus building, and group projects.

These technological advances have also changed the world in which businesses operate. We now live in a global economy. To be successful, businesses need to compete in the global marketplace. Since English is the international business language, translations have become important;

Thinking Cap 1.2

Discuss: How does global competition affect the way we communicate?

Setting the Stage for Effective Communication

correct grammar is vital since the information communicated will be based on a literal translation of the original message. Slang, jargon, and acronyms need to be eliminated. In addition, you must become aware of different cultures and their unique communication processes.

As companies have restructured and invested in increased technology, more employees at all levels are having to create their own written communications. In addition, the emphasis on quality, whether total quality management (TQM) or continuous improvement, has put increased importance on employees doing work correctly the first time, working in teams, and being more customer focused. All of these changes in the environment have resulted in increased emphasis on ethical and legal concerns for all employees throughout the organization.

As the use of teams and groups expands within companies, the ability to work cooperatively and collaboratively becomes more important. Working together adds a new dimension to the communication skills needed in business. Previously, most communications were developed individually. Now, several individuals may work together in creating various documents and communications, a process requiring additional written and oral skills.

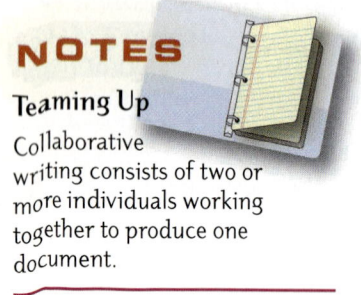

NOTES

Teaming Up
Collaborative writing consists of two or more individuals working together to produce one document.

USING BUSINESS COMMUNICATION AT WORK

The real challenge is to make good communication a handy and well-used tool. Then you are likely to pick it up and use it without thinking.

—**Max DePree,**
Leadership Is an Art

Communication is a vital part of our world today. You may be a very well-educated, talented individual who has much to offer your company. If you cannot get your ideas across to others, you will not be able to share your knowledge and skills. Ideas are commonplace, but the ability to communicate ideas clearly to others is rare. Learning to communicate your ideas is the major thrust of this book.

Business Communication at Work is designed to provide you with the background and skills needed to enter the business world and achieve success. Simply listening to a concert will not teach you to play the guitar, nor will strolling through an art museum teach you to paint pictures. Similarly, reading good business letters or reading about how to write good business letters won't teach you to write them, and hearing good reports won't teach you to create them.

To develop your communication ability, you must do three things:

1. Analyze good and bad examples of communication.
2. Use the principles and techniques of good communication.
3. Practice creating your own communications.

Both planning and composing effective messages require that you study and put into practice certain principles and techniques of effective communication. At first you will have to concentrate deliberately on using these principles and techniques; after practice, you will be able to master them and use them with ease. *Business Communication at Work* will offer you many opportunities for practice as you respond to the realistic communication situations presented. The major focus of this textbook will be on written business communication.

The principles and techniques presented can also be applied to your personal business affairs. They can be used to assist you in communicating effectively in non-work related areas of your life, whether you are writing a letter to your insurance company or preparing a report for a community group.

Why We Communicate

As you communicate, your goal may be one or more of the following:

- To inform
- To request
- To persuade
- To build goodwill

The purposes of communication may involve the sharing and exchange of information, such as:

- Ideas
- Facts
- Recommendations
- Proposals

Business communication is functional and useful. Without the ability to exchange information, business as we know it could not exist.

How We Communicate

Normally, we think of communication skills as talking and writing. We communicate, however, in several important ways, including:

- Written communications—letters, memos, reports, e-mail, faxes
- Oral communications—one-on-one meetings, phone conversations, speeches, video conferencing, group meetings
- Nonverbal communications—eye contact, facial expressions, body language, physical appearance
- Active listening—listening with a high level of concentration; listening for information

This text will expand your expertise in communicating in each of these important ways.

Saving Face

In some cultures, the concept of "having face" refers to the perceived status a person holds. In countries such as China or Thailand, "face" refers also to the entire organization the person represents. Criticizing an employee in public can result in the employee losing face, thereby disrupting the business relationship. *Suppose your company works closely with a Chinese manufacturing firm. How would you approach the manufacturing firm's representative with a complaint about the quality of the product?*

Words Unspoken

What we say nonverbally may communicate more than our spoken words.

Setting the Stage for Effective Communication

Thinking Cap 1.3

Discuss: How might hostility be apparent in written communications, in oral communications, in nonverbal communications, and in listening?

Notes

Legal Terms
- Ethics: moral principles or standards
- Slander: orally defaming an individual's character
- Libel: defaming an individual's character in writing

Basics for Communicating Effectively

When you are communicating, regardless of the purpose or situation, you should remember and make use of certain basics for communicating effectively. You should:

- Determine the purpose of your communication.
- Identify your "audience"—the person(s) who will receive the communication.
- Consider what your audience needs to "hear" in order for your communication to be effective.
- Develop your message in a clear, concise, and logical manner.
- Maintain a positive attitude throughout your communication.

In addition, being an effective business communicator requires you to be aware of your ethical and legal responsibilities and to be sensitive to language bias and cultural diversity. If you use the following as your guide, you will be on your way to meeting these responsibilities:

- Be honest in your communications.
- Give the correct information.
- Use gender-neutral language. Use words that reflect nonbias, such as *police officer* instead of *policeman*. Avoid using occupational phrases that indicate gender. For example, a manager should discuss the budget with *his or her* staff instead of *his* staff or *her* staff. You'll learn more about how to avoid these situations later in the text.
- Do not intentionally misrepresent or mislead others in your communications.
- Include all vital information that is relevant to the situation.
- Guard against damaging another person's name and reputation by making false accusations.
- Familiarize yourself with the laws pertaining to any communications for which you are responsible.

The people you will communicate with may be very different from you. They may be from another part of the world, and their ways of doing things as well as the way they think may be different. This difference in people is referred to as **cultural diversity**. As you recognize and become sensitive to cultural diversity, you will see that different groups of people communicate in different ways. When you communicate in a global community, remember that different meanings are often attached to the ways people communicate. Not only do people around the world have diverse values and beliefs and use different languages, but their written and oral communication styles and formats vary. For example, some styles are more formal than others.

Nonverbal communication also varies widely—gestures, body language, eye contact, and touch are all used in diverse ways by different cultures.

As you communicate with people in other cultures, you will need to learn about the specifics of communication for those cultures. Those who have learned English as their second language have been taught formal English. You, too, should use formal English and eliminate slang, jargon, acronyms, and other informal language in your writing and speaking. Remember to keep your communication brief, clear, and simple.

Checkpoint 1.1

1. Explain the significance of goodwill in a business situation.

2. Consider the following concepts in the light of business communications: *cultural awareness, efficiency, factual truth, goodwill,* and *integrity.* Arrange the ideas in the order of importance, and explain your choice of arrangement.

3. You must prepare a business letter to a potential customer, and you only have time to cover three of the following four concepts: *goodwill, awareness of cultural diversity, gender neutral language,* and *good grammar.* Which three would you choose and why?

PRINCIPLES OF WRITTEN COMMUNICATION

The principles and techniques you'll learn to use to prepare effective written communication can be applied to oral communication as well. You should know, however, when written communication is more appropriate than oral communication.

Using Written Communication

You may choose to use written communication for a variety of reasons. Among the reasons are the following:

- **Conveying complex information.** You may need to communicate technical, statistical, or detailed information. Your reader may find it easier to comprehend written material than material presented orally. You may also need to include charts, graphs, diagrams, or other visual data when presenting complex information.

- **Reaching your intended receiver.** You may find it is easier to reach your intended receiver through written communication. A person who may not be available by phone will eventually read a written correspondence.

66 *Dishonest or careless communication tells us as much about the people involved as it does about anything else. Communication is an ethical question. Good communication means a respect for individuals.* 99
—**Max DePree,**
Leadership Is an Art

Discuss: Do you agree with DePree? If yes, why? If no, why?

Setting the Stage for Effective Communication

- **Providing proof of the communication.** A written communication provides proof of the communication and becomes a document that may be legally acceptable as a binding contract or as evidence in a court of law.

- **Ensuring confidentiality of information.** You may want to convey information in writing that would be unsuitable to communicate in a telephone conversation. You may indicate "confidential" or "personal" on the communication if you want it to remain confidential.

- **Providing convenience for your reader.** A written communication allows your reader to review the material at a convenient time and place without interruptions.

- **Expediting the response to the communication.** A written communication allows the reader to refer to the original correspondence when responding. This will assist in developing a complete reply.

- **Planning your message.** A written communication allows you to spend time on the content of your message and to word it in the most advantageous way. A telephone or personal contact, however carefully planned, is subject to the events of the moment.

- **Saving time and money.** A written communication may be less expensive and time-consuming than a personal visit or a telephone call.

- **Stressing the importance of the communication.** People may attach greater importance to a letter than to a phone call. You may use a special mail service such as registered or certified mail that will attach greater importance to the message. A letter sent by a courier service in a special envelope may also attract attention and show impatience or urgency.

- **Aiding in the distribution of information to several individuals.** Using a written communication is a fast method of sending the same information to a number of individuals and ensuring that they receive the identical information.

- **Translating international communications.** A written communication allows the reader time to translate the information at an appropriate pace.

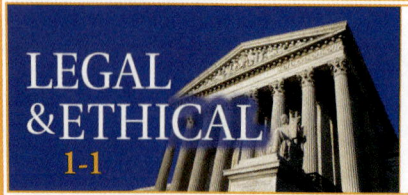

Listening In. You overhear a coworker at the coffee machine discussing a client who then states that the client is "a thief." Is this ethical conduct? What are the legal implications?

Good Letter Writing Techniques

Writing effective business correspondence is a many-sided challenge. Through practicing the principles and techniques in *Business Communication at Work*, you will be able to achieve two goals in producing written messages:

(1) a message that is structurally complete, and (2) a message that achieves its purpose quickly, clearly, and effectively.

The techniques you will learn will help you compose written communication that will impress the reader and accomplish your purpose. You should not expect to master all the techniques at once. As you develop your writing skills, you will quickly see that writing is a combination of activities going on at the same time. Writing is not a disconnected series of steps.

The Impact of a Unified Message

As you write, think of the overall effect of the whole message instead of individual parts of your message or individual writing principles. Be aware that by overlooking even one principle that is important to the reader, you may weaken or destroy the effectiveness of your message.

In planning your message, you will need to consider the following:

- The purpose of the communication
- Your intended audience
- The content of the communication
- The organization of the message

NOTES
Focus on Results
The real test of good written communication is the total effect it has on the reader.

You will determine the important points to include and the best method of organizing and presenting them. After your first draft, you will need to review and edit what you have written. Then, if you believe the reader's response will be positive, you will have succeeded.

The Total Effect on the Reader

Most people respond favorably to a letter that flows naturally and exhibits courtesy, friendliness, and sincerity. Picture your reader receiving your letter. Will he or she be receptive to its message? Try to visualize the receiver's reactions in reading the letter. For example, a reader may stiffen at the sentence, "We give every request full consideration," but the same reader may relax when the sentence is rewritten as, "Your request will be given full and prompt consideration."

Your letter's total effect on the reader determines whether he or she will react the way you want. If you have done your job properly, you'll be able to answer *yes* to the following three questions:

- Will the reader understand the message?
- Is the tone of the letter positive?
- Will the letter do its specific job and also build goodwill?

NOTES
Ask Yourself
How would you react to the message you have written?

Question 1: Will the reader understand the message?

Writing must be simple to be clear. The simple sentence is the most useful tool in business correspondence. The simple sentence is a single clause

Setting the Stage for Effective Communication   11

NOTES

Keep It Simple

Simple words and sentences will aid the understanding of your message.

containing a subject and a predicate (verb). Resist the temptation to join a single idea to another idea with a conjunction such as *and, but, nor,* and *or* unless using a conjunction will make the sentence easier to understand. To keep your sentences simple, avoid overuse of terms such as *therefore, moreover, however,* and *accordingly.*

While simple sentences will be used often in your writing, you will want to have a balance in your sentence structure. Some compound sentences as well as complex and compound-complex sentences will add variety to your writing. If you need to review sentence structure now, the references in Appendix A will provide a good review for you.

Avoid using complex and vague words. Ornate or difficult words won't impress the reader. Use simple words your reader will easily understand without having to consult a dictionary. Be correct and natural in your use of words and in the construction of sentences. This will help your writing flow smoothly—your reader will understand your message and be grateful to you as well. The highest compliment a reader can pay you, the writer, is to say, "Your letter was simple, clear, and easy to read."

Question 2: Is the tone of the letter positive?

How you say something may influence your reader just as much as what you say. Your letter will appeal to the reader if you use a conversational, informal writing style and stress positive rather than negative ideas. Be sure to emphasize a "you" viewpoint throughout the letter. The "you attitude" means that you put the reader first in your communication and emphasize the reader's wants and needs and how you can meet them. Using certain words and phrases—"you failed," "you don't understand," "you can't"—are not what we mean by the "you attitude." Use words and phrases that say to the reader that you care and want to help. For example, "Your order will be filled promptly and will be on the way to you by Express Mail tomorrow" does show the "you attitude."

NOTES

Keep It Friendly

The tone of your written message should be as friendly as the tone of your spoken message.

Thinking Cap 1.5

Discuss: "How you say something may influence your reader just as much as what you say." Do you agree with this statement? If yes, why? If no, why not?

Use a friendly tone that suggests that your attitude is positive and that you are interested in the reader. Naturalness, courtesy, friendliness, and sincerity are all essential to a positive tone in a letter. You will learn more about how to use the "you attitude" as you continue in your studies of effective business communication.

Question 3: Will the letter do its specific job and also build goodwill?

The easy readability and friendly tone of your message will attract and impress your reader. In addition, your letter should accomplish its specific job and increase goodwill.

Go to CD-ROM

Activity 1-1
To test your skills.

One of the main objectives of all business correspondence is to encourage the reader to react favorably to the message. You cannot always do all that the reader wants, but you can communicate to the reader that you understand her or his problems and that you want to do something about them.

12 Chapter 1

Effective business letters build or retain goodwill for a business, a priceless commodity that is hard-earned and easily lost. Writers who recognize this purpose of business letters strive to sharpen their understanding of psychology as well as English composition. Because the exchange of written communication is vital to business and essential for promoting goodwill, perfecting the art of creating effective correspondence will help ensure your success in business.

The Seven Tests of Effective Correspondence

To communicate easily and effectively with your reader, apply the following "seven Cs" to your correspondence. Is your communication (1) courteous, (2) considerate, (3) clear, (4) complete, (5) concise, (6) correct, and (7) consistent?

Courteous

A courteous communication is polite, tactful, friendly, and "reader-centered." Successful writers carefully choose the words they use, avoiding words to which they themselves would react unfavorably. In short, they put themselves in the reader's place by trying the words out on themselves before writing them to others. The expression, "It's not what you say, it's how you say it," applies.

The people who read your letters will judge you and your organization by your friendliness and courtesy. Friendliness is evident when you write informally and in a natural, conversational style. Use "please" and "thank you"—good manners are good business.

NOTES

Good Vibrations

If a word produces a negative feeling for you, do not use it when writing to others.

Considerate

Conserve the reader's time and effort by expressing yourself with words that are easily understood.

Through your writing, project an attitude that focuses on the reader—the "you attitude." Show the reader you are genuinely interested in communicating. The tone (the attitude your words express to the reader) of your letter should also show your sincerity and desire to be of service.

Clear

Clear writing is easy to understand. The exact meaning intended by the writer should be clear in the reader's mind.

That your message can be understood isn't enough—you must strive to write so that your message cannot possibly be misunderstood. The keys to clarity include the use of the following:

- **Logical, coherent arrangement.** Words should flow appropriately.

- **Specific, concrete words instead of general terms.** Calling a car "a red vehicle" would be less concrete than calling the vehicle "a red Ford."

Setting the Stage for Effective Communication 13

Table 1	Trite Phrases and Their Substitutes
Trite or Vague Phrase	**Substitute Phrase**
acknowledge receipt of	thank you for
as per your request	as you requested
at an early date	by Thursday, April 27
at this point in time	now
attached please find	attached is
due to the fact that	because
enclosed please find	enclosed is
in due course	in ten days
in receipt of	have received
regarding the matter	(omit this phrase from usage)
take under consideration	consider
this is to acknowledge	thank you for
under separate cover	separately
we are pleased to note	(omit this phrase from usage)

- **Directness.** Save the reader's time by staying on the main points of the message.

- **Consistency.** Use similar formats so that the reader understands the purpose of the messages; don't use one style in one part of the message and then switch to another style.

- **Balance.** Use a variety of sentence structures to provide balance and interest.

- **Comparison and contrast.** Use words that show how other words are similar or different from each other.

- **Unification.** Paragraphs should have one topic sentence and all other sentences should support that main idea; the message should be unified around a single topic.

Activity 1-2
To test your skills.

Trite, vague phrases are the enemy of clear writing and should be avoided. See Table 1 above for suggested substitutions for some trite phrases that are frequently used.

Verbs may be active or passive. Active verbs make writing forceful and more interesting to read or to hear. In the **active voice,** the subject of the sentence performs the action described by the verb.

The postal <u>carrier</u> <u>delivered</u> the packages.

(The *carrier* is performing the action.)

Our administrative <u>assistant</u> <u>prepares</u> the check requests to pay the reviewers of the manuscript.

(The *assistant* performs the action to request the checks.)

In the **passive voice**, the subject receives the action described by the verb.

> **The packages were delivered by the postal carrier.**
> (The *packages* receive the action performed by the carrier.)

> **The <u>check requests were processed</u> by the accounting department personnel.**
> (The *check requests* receive the action performed by the accounting personnel.)

The active voice creates the illusion of movement; the passive voice limits movement. While the active voice is used more often, there are situations in which the passive voice may be preferred. One such instance is in the presentation of negative information. You will study negative or bad news messages later in the text.

A frequent enemy of forceful writing is the participial phrase. Words such as *hoping, assuring, believing,* and the like introduce the participial phrase. As these phrases may be the weakest verbal construction in the English language, you should not use them to introduce sentences. Compare these two sentences:

Activity 1-3
To test your skills.

WEAK: Assuring us that Plan A was the best deal, the sales representative wrote the order.

STRONG: The sales representative wrote the order as she assured us that Plan A was the best deal.

The most important advantage of clear writing is that the reader can grasp the essential message quickly. Preparing and following a plan or outline will help you organize your thoughts and present a clear structure that will aid the reader in understanding and retention.

Complete

A complete communication contains all the essential information needed by the reader for action. Completeness is closely related to clarity; a written message will be unclear if essential information has been omitted. Unlike in oral communication, a reader is unable to ask for clarification, additional information, or interpretation. For example, the request, "Please send me some paper," cannot be acted upon with any degree of accuracy because it is incomplete. The reader needs to know how much, what size, what type, and other specifications of the paper before supplying it. A good way to test for completeness is to ask whether your message answers the five **W**s and one **H:** Who? What? Where? When? Why? How?

NOTES

Right the First Time

A complete communication eliminates the need for follow-up communication. Anticipate additional information the reader may need.

When you are replying to an inquiry or request, be thorough in answering all questions asked. You may even anticipate the reader's reaction by providing other relevant information. Writing a complete message will show your genuine interest in the reader and your wish for a favorable reaction. A complete message will also save you the expense and possible embarrassment of a follow-up message.

Setting the Stage for Effective Communication

Concise

A concise communication uses as few words as possible to communicate the message in a clear, courteous manner. Conciseness doesn't necessarily mean brevity. Instead, being concise is saying what you have to say in the fewest possible words. You are concise when you pare down your communication to essentials, stripping it of unnecessary words.

Teaming up two or more words of the same or similar meaning robs letters of conciseness. For example:

We are <u>grateful</u> and <u>appreciative</u> . . . .

We stand <u>ready</u>, <u>willing</u>, and <u>able</u> to be of <u>assistance</u> and <u>service</u> . . . .

We <u>look forward</u> with <u>anticipation</u> to . . . .

Being concise means saying all that needs to be said and no more. Do not leave out important facts, but do increase effectiveness by omitting irrelevant details and by giving complete, pertinent information. To achieve conciseness in your writing, you will need to edit and rewrite your message, eliminating unnecessary words, phrases, and sentences.

Correct

A correct communication is accurate in every way. Even a small error in a date or an amount of money may result in loss of time, money, or goodwill—or all three. Verifying facts and paying attention to details are vital to being an effective communicator. Dates, times, places, amounts, and other facts need to be confirmed. In order to produce communications that are error-free and consistent, you will want to proofread and verify all information.

In most instances, errors in correctness fall into two categories:

- **Typographical:** Errors in spelling, capitalization, and punctuation; insertion of extra words; omission of important words; and errors in spacing and alignment.

- **Failure to check reference sources:** Names spelled incorrectly; dates and figures not verified; information incomplete; capitalization and punctuation misapplied.

Consistent

Consistency is closely related to correctness. You would not list the date of a convention as *June 31* because June has 30 days. Likewise, you would not write a letter to *Miss John Jones* when you can verify that John is a male.

Too Many Zeros. You fail to proofread carefully and verify the numbers in a price quotation—you type in $500 instead of $5,000 in the quotation for a painting contract. It was "just a typo" and the client certainly realizes that you could not do the job for $500. What are the possible legal ramifications of your error?

When you give a person *a three-day grace period*, you would specify the dates chronologically, rather than a day here or there. To be consistent, you would also check to be sure that the information you provide is consistent each time you provide it. Saying something one way one time and another way the next time violates the element of consistency.

Checkpoint 1.2

1. Identify the advantages and disadvantages of written communication.
2. Explain why you agree or disagree that the following statement is a compliment: "Your letter was simple, clear, and easy to read."
3. How does written communication, in particular, promote goodwill? Give an example from your own experience if possible.

Chapter 1 Summary

The ability to communicate effectively in business is essential to both the individual and the organization. For the individual, effective communication skills are necessary in getting the job initially, accomplishing assigned tasks, and advancing to higher positions within an organization. For the organization, effective communication results in developing and maintaining goodwill among employees, customers, and business associates while getting the job done efficiently.

Communication skills can be developed through the process of analyzing communication, using the principles and techniques of good writing, and practicing the creation of different forms of communication. In all types of communication, it is important to determine the purpose of the communication, the intended audience, and the content. As you organize your message in a clear, concise, correct, and logical manner, you need to maintain a positive tone. When your written message passes the seven tests of effective correspondence (the seven Cs), you have reached your goal of building goodwill. You will also have achieved your purpose to request, inform, or persuade your receiver to respond positively. The techniques of composing business correspondence presented in this text will help you to produce letters, memos, e-mail messages, and reports that achieve their purpose.

66 There may be no single thing more important in our efforts to achieve meaningful work and fulfilling relationships than to learn and practice the art of communication. 99
— **Max DePree,**
Leadership Is an Art

✔ CHECKLIST FOR COMMUNICATION

Check Your "Cs" for Communicating:

Courteous _____	Complete _____	Correct _____
Considerate _____	Concise _____	Consistent _____
Clear _____		

Setting the Stage for Effective Communication

Chapter 1
Online Exercises

Getting Started:

To complete the Online Exercises in this text, you will need access to a computer with an Internet connection and a Web browser. A Web browser is a program that allows you to view and explore information on the the World Wide Web. Examples of Web browsers are Internet Explorer® and Netscape Navigator®.

In the Online Exercises that follow throughout the book, you will go to the following address: **bcw.glencoe.com**. Use all lowercase letters. Be sure to put in a period (called "dot" in Internet addresses) between **bcw** and **glencoe**, but do not type a period after **com**. The *Business Communication at Work* Web site should appear on your screen. You will be connected to the site's home page, or main page. From here you can connect with information available at the site.

Once you have connected to the *Business Communication at Work* Web site, you are ready to begin the first Online Exercises below.

Objective:

In these Online Exercises, you will learn what the Internet is and become familiar with terms related to the Internet.

After opening the *Business Communication at Work* Web site, select Chapter 1. Next, click on Online Exercises. You will see a list of Web site links that will bring you to sites featuring Internet definitions and Internet dictionaries.

Activity 1.1

1. Select one link from *Web Sites Describing the Internet* to visit.
2. Read through your selection.
3. On a piece of paper, answer the following questions using complete sentences:
   a. What is the purpose of the Web site you have chosen?
   b. Who is the intended audience of the Web site?
   c. What are some of the techniques used for organizing the description of the Internet?
4. Using the **Back** button on your Web browser, return to the *Business Communication at Work* Online Exercises page and click on another Web site that offers Internet definitions.
5. After reading your selection, write two sentences describing the differences in how the two Web sites you visited are organized.
6. Write your name on your answer sheet, and hand it in to your instructor.

Activity 1.2

1. Select one of the Internet dictionary Web sites to visit.
2. Key *WWW* in the **Search** box (some Web sites may require you to click on the first letter of the word).
3. On a sheet of paper write a two sentence definition of *WWW*.
4. Search for the definitions of the following Internet terms: *hypertext, hypermedia, Internet service provider (ISP), HTML,* and *HTTP*. Write the definition of each term using two sentences. If a term is not listed in the Web site you selected, return to the *Business Communication at Work* Web site and select another site to visit.
5. Write your name on the front of each printout, and hand it in to your instructor.

18   Chapter 1

CHAPTER 1 WORKSHEETS

NAME _____ DATE _____

PRACTICE 1

Chapter Review

Instructions: Answer each item below by writing your response in the space provided.

1. Identify four groups of people with whom employees in organizations communicate.
    a. Customers
    b. Co workers
    c. Subordinates
    d. Supervisors

2. List four environmental changes that are influencing communications in business.
    a. technology
    b. gobel competition
    c. Resturcted management & product lines
    d. Quaily emphasis & costomer focus

3. List the seven Cs of effective correspondence.
    a. Courteours
    b. Considerate
    c. Clear
    d. Complete
    e. Concise
    f. Correct
    g. Consistent

4. What are three practices that will help you develop your communication ability?
    a. Analyze good & bad examples of communication
    b. Use the principles & techniques of good communication
    c. Practice creating your own communications

5. List four elements to be considered when you plan a written message.
    a. The purpose of the communications
    b. Your intended audience
    c. The content of the communication
    d. The organization of the message

6. Identify six differences that you may find as you communicate with people from another culture.
    a. Be honest
    b. Give the correct information
    c. Use gender-neutrel language
    d. Don't intentionally mislead others
    e. Include all vital information
    f. Guard against damaging others ppl's name

Setting the Stage for Effective Communication 19

CHAPTER 1 WORKSHEETS

NAME _____ DATE _____

7. Describe six reasons for choosing written communications.
   a. *Providing proof of the communication*
   b. *Ensuring confidentiality of information*
   c. *Providing convenience for your reader*
   d. *Expediting the response to the communication*
   e. *Planning your message*
   f. *Saving time & money*

8. Give five techniques you will use to improve the clarity of your writing.
   a. *Directness*
   b. *Balance*
   c. *Unification*
   d. *Consistency*
   e. *Comparison and contrast*

PRACTICE 2

Seven Cs

Instructions: Each of the following sentences lacks one of the "C" qualities. On the line provided, write the "C" quality that is lacking and the word or phrase that improves the italicized word(s).

1. Please *advise me as to the date on which* you plan to visit our organization.
   Courteous

2. The personnel manager reviews all the impressive résumés and calls *them* for interviews.
   _____

3. We *demand* payment now.
   _____

4. The supporting documents will be mailed in a *seperate* envelope.
   _____

5. *You didn't send* your check.
   _____

6. Please send me *some black computer ribbons.*
   Courteous

7. The student told the instructor that *she* did not have time to review the homework assignment.
   _____

8. *I am writing to take this opportunity to say* thank you for representing me at the meeting last week.
   _____

20 Chapter 1

CHAPTER 1 WORKSHEETS

NAME _____ DATE _____

9. The confirmation of your *accomodations* was mailed this morning.
   _____

10. *We are in receipt* of your check for $120.
    _____

11. You can attend the conference during the three-day period *June 10, 11, and 13.*
    Consistent _____

PRACTICE 3

Business Letter Analysis

Instructions: In developing your communication skills, it is important to analyze examples of good and bad communication. For this course, it will be beneficial to start collecting various business communications for analysis. Keep a file of the materials collected. You will be able to analyze them for different principles as you progress through Business Communication at Work.

Obtain a business letter. Analyze the business letter according to the principles and techniques presented in this chapter. As you analyze your letter, answer the following questions, which emphasize the principles and techniques stressed in this chapter.

a. What is the purpose of the letter?
   _____

b. Who is the intended audience of the letter?
   _____

c. Is the tone of the letter positive? If it is not positive, what changes should be made?
   _____

d. Did the writer practice the seven Cs of effective correspondence?

	Yes	No	If no, explain why
Courteous	___	___	_____
Considerate	___	___	_____
Clear	___	___	_____
Concise	___	___	_____
Complete	___	___	_____
Correct	___	___	_____
Consistent	___	___	_____

e. Did the message achieve its purpose?
   _____

f. What is your reaction as the receiver of the message?
   _____
   _____

Setting the Stage for Effective Communication

CHAPTER

Choosing the Right Words

Objectives

After completing this chapter, you will be able to:

1. Describe the writing process.
2. Evaluate various meanings of words in order to select appropriate words for intended meaning.
3. Identify and use available references to facilitate the communication process.
4. Evaluate incorrect word usage and select correct word usage.

Standard American English

Language is the primary tool of communication. The problem with language, however, is that often our meanings are misunderstood. The English language in particular has millions of vocabulary words, and they often have several meanings and can be combined in different ways. The best way to ensure that people understand what you are saying is to use **Standard American English.**

Standard American English, also known as standard English, is a form of the English language that follows the rules set down in grammar and composition books. It is the English language at its most correct. Standard American English does not include informal or specialized language, and it does not use words or expressions that reflect particular cultures, backgrounds, or interests. The advantage of Standard American English is that it allows English-speaking people from all backgrounds to communicate with each other.

The Challenge Everyone Faces

Some people have argued that the use of standardized American English in business and other situations is a form of snobbery. The argument goes that requiring people to write and speak in a standardized way forces those who use a particular **dialect,** or regional way of speaking, to give up part of themselves and their cultures. In fact, the opposite is true. Few people in any country or culture speak their own language perfectly. Almost no one is raised to speak perfect standard English. Everyone faces the challenge of writing and speaking English well. The reward of meeting that challenge is that everyone understands one another.

Reference books, such as dictionaries and grammar and usage handbooks, can help you standardize the language in your business communications. Do not hesitate to consult them. After all, even professional writers, editors, and copy editors rely on reference books on a regular basis.

Situation: You receive the following communication from a coworker.

Hey, everybody! The buzz from the powers-that-be is that there'll be a gathering in the mess hall at three o'clock sharp to talk up the new ad campaign. Be there!

Your coworker wants to send the message to the whole department.

Ask Yourself: What changes or strategies would you suggest to help your coworker express himself in standard English?

" Kind words can be short and easy to speak, but their echoes are truly endless. "

—Mother Teresa, Catholic Nun

You now have an overview of the principles of business communication that apply to written messages. In this chapter, we will begin to examine the actual writing process and look at specific techniques that will help you choose the appropriate words in your writing.

The Writing Process

Writing is a building process during which the writer follows several steps to compose a message. Writing takes place when a writer:

1. Chooses words.
2. Assembles the words into phrases.
3. Connects the phrases to form sentences.
4. Groups the sentences into paragraphs.
5. Organizes the paragraphs into a coherent message.

NOTES

Words as Tools

The most basic tools of writing are words.

As simple as this sounds, the writing process is complex. The steps in this sequence overlap, and many things happen at the same time. We will start our examination of this complex process by looking at the simplest parts of language—words—and how the words you choose relate to and influence the interpretation of your writing.

The Meanings of Words

The fundamental element of any message is the **word.** The ability to choose the words that most precisely express your thoughts is essential in both written and oral communication. To communicate well, you need to choose words that are familiar and easy to understand. Further, you will want to choose words that accurately reflect your meaning and the attitude you desire to convey. You need to consider, for example, that although a single word can have various meanings, usually one of the meanings is more appropriate to use than the others.

Semantics is the study of word meanings. In short, it is the study of what you mean by what you say.

Types of Meanings

The two basic types of meanings are denotative meanings and connotative meanings. **Denotative** meanings are the definitions of words given in dictionaries, while **connotative** meanings are the subtle and often emotional meanings that become associated with the words.

Writers must be very careful when choosing the connotative meaning of words. Often the meanings of these words vary from one person to another depending on factors such as personal bias and experience. Without seeing things from each reader's unique perspective, you cannot be sure of each reader's reaction to your communication.

When you consider your reader you can often foresee that a particular word will evoke a negative image in the reader's mind. You should then choose a less antagonizing word that has the same denotative meaning without a negative connotation. Compare these sentences:

Discuss: People attach different meanings to the same words. Within one group the word *compromise* was used. Group members had various reactions to the word. What may have been some of the interpretations?

    Our furniture is <u>cheap</u>.   Our furniture is <u>inexpensive</u>.

The words *cheap* and *inexpensive* have the same denotative (dictionary) meaning, but their connotative meanings are much different. *Cheap* implies poor quality, whereas *inexpensive* implies a low price.

Word References

In developing your communication skills, word references are invaluable tools to help you choose words that reflect the meanings you intend. You will find that the two most helpful reference tools are a dictionary and a thesaurus.

The **dictionary** is a word reference book consisting of an alphabetical listing of words. Each word entry may contain the following information about each word as applicable to the word:

- Definitions and meanings
- Hyphenation (syllabic division)
- Acceptable and preferred spellings
- Pronunciation
- Parts of speech
- Capitalization
- Synonyms
- Antonyms

NOTES

Looking Up Words

Use the **dictionary** to verify a word's exact meaning.

Use the **thesaurus** to choose the word that best conveys your meaning.

Dictionaries are either abridged or unabridged. An **unabridged** dictionary is the most comprehensive edition of a given dictionary; definitions of all words are included. An **abridged** dictionary is condensed—that is, it contains fewer words and definitions.

A **thesaurus** is a word reference work containing synonyms (words that mean the same) and antonyms (words that are opposite in meaning) for each word listed. A thesaurus provides alternative words from which to select the precise word you need for expressing your ideas. Using a thesaurus will not only improve the quality of your writing, but it will also assist you in expanding your vocabulary.

Other helpful tools such as versions of electronic dictionaries and thesauri may be purchased as independent software programs; they are often

 **2.2**

Discuss: Why is it still necessary to proofread a document after you have used the spell check? What types of errors may occur to make the communication incorrect even though the words are spelled correctly? What are some examples of these errors?

included in your word processing software. Through an electronic thesaurus, you can access synonyms and antonyms right at your keyboard.

In addition, most word processing programs have a spell-check program, with which you can find and correct spelling errors at your computer. The spell-check software does exactly what the name implies—it checks the *spelling* of words used in the sentences, though Microsoft® Word's spell-check program includes the option "check grammar with spelling." The spell-check program cannot identify words used incorrectly or check grammar. You will also need to proofread your communication for correctness. For more detailed information on spell checkers, see Chapter 6, page 144.

Interpreting Meanings

When a word is read or heard, the word goes into the reader's or listener's **word bank**—that part of the mind where all the words the person has ever heard or read in all their contexts are stored. The reader, or listener, then matches that word with others in his or her word bank. Based on context, the reader then chooses the meaning for that word—hoping that it is the meaning intended by the writer. Miscommunication occurs in many instances, however, when the meaning selected by the recipient of the message is not necessarily the meaning the writer, or speaker, intended.

One of the strengths of English is that a single word can have multiple related meanings. Unfortunately, this strength can also become a weakness—you must be very careful to choose the word that means what your reader expects it to mean. For example, consider these varied meanings for the word *remote*:

a *remote* country	far away
the *remote* future	distant in time
a *remote* cousin	having only a slight relationship
a *remote* manner	aloof or distant
remote control	without physical contact (usually electronic)

Suppose, however, the word *remote* did not fit your sentence precisely or you had just used the word in the previous sentence and did not want to repeat it. By using a thesaurus, you could find synonyms such as *distant*, *removed*, and *far* to use instead. Finding synonyms illustrates another advantage of the English language—many words can have the same meaning or closely related meanings.

 PROPER WORD CHOICES

Consider the words *get* and *maize*. A student once counted more than 220 meanings of *get*. On the other hand, *maize*, which means "corn," has no other meanings. Between *get* and *maize* lies the difference between familiar and unfamiliar words. *Maize* is a word seldom heard or read. When you think

26   Chapter 2

of *maize,* you have only one meaning to attach to it. For the word *get,* you have an abundance of meanings to choose from, depending on the context in which it is used.

You can make your writing clearer and more effective for your reader by using these kinds of words:

- Simple words that the reader will understand
- Concise words that do not waste the reader's time
- Conversational words that avoid trite expressions
- Appropriate words that reflect common business usage
- Correct words that transmit the message accurately
- Specific words that make writing more precise
- Positive words that eliminate negative connotations

Let's look at each of these types of words in more detail.

Simple Words

In selecting your words, your goal is to choose words that are both understandable to your receiver and appropriate for the situation. Short, familiar words make your writing easy to read and to understand. Simple words are far more effective in business writing than complex words.

Short words usually have more clarity and power than long words. When short words will convey your meaning quickly and clearly, use them instead of longer, less familiar words.

Simple words are not always short and formal-sounding words are not always long. In conversation, for instance, the longer nouns *displeasure* and *irritation* are used more often than the shorter noun *pique,* which expresses the same meaning. As a rule, choose longer words only when they express the meaning more clearly or more naturally than their shorter synonyms.

The following example shows how short, familiar words can make reading easier. The original paragraph reads:

> Consideration of your request leads us to believe that of several alternative courses of action open at the present time the maximum effect will accrue if standard procedures are amended to permit actualization toward realization of the goals of our mission. (42 words)

The revision using short, familiar words is far more effective:

> We agree with you that we can best realize our mission goals by modifying our standard procedures. (17 words)

Table 1 on page 28 contains a list of complex words and phrases and some simple, direct alternatives. Most of these formal-sounding, complicated words are often found in business letters, but each of them can be stated in simpler terms that will allow for more effective communication.

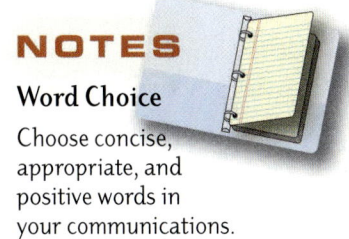

NOTES

Word Choice
Choose concise, appropriate, and positive words in your communications.

Go to CD-ROM

Activity 2-1
To test your skills.

Table 1	Alternatives for Complex Words
Complex Words	**Simpler Words**
approximately	about
ascertain	find out
assistance	help
commence	start *or* begin
converse	talk
endeavor	try
enumerate	list
equitable	fair
finalize	finish *or* complete
It has been a great pleasure to be the recipient of your generosity.	Thank you.
interrogate	ask
it is requested that	please
negligible	small *or* slight
numerous	many
peruse	read *or* study
procure	get
pursuant to your request	as you asked
render services	serve
sufficient	enough
terminate	end *or* finish
utilize	use
unavoidably detained	delayed
verbalize	say
viable option	choice

NOTES

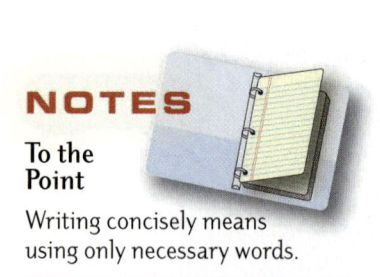

To the Point

Writing concisely means using only necessary words.

You can also make your own reference list of words and phrases and their simple alternatives. Look for complex, unfamiliar words and phrases both in your own writing and in communications that you receive. Try to replace these words and phrases with simpler, more familiar ones that will make the communications more understandable and useful.

Concise Words

Strive for conciseness in your writing—use only as many well-chosen words as you need to convey your message. Each word in the message should help make the meaning clear or the tone friendly. Conciseness helps the reader by:

- Saving the reader time
- Aiding in the understanding of the message
- Making the communication more interesting

According to recent estimates, an average of three out of ten words in the typical letter are unneeded. Your reader is likely to lose interest in a message if he or she must wade through wordiness to get to the main point. Why use two or more words when one will do the job well?

Look at this sentence from a business letter:

> In reply to your request for the status of the accounting proposal, the proposal for the new program of study for the accounting program was sent to the Board for their perusal and discussion, after which they accepted it as presented with all members voting in favor of the proposal to be implemented during the year. (56 words)

Three-fourths of the words in the sentence can be eliminated and the message stated concisely:

> The Board unanimously accepted the proposal for the new accounting program to begin in August. (15 words)

Notice that none of the necessary information is omitted and that the message is now actually clearer and easier to read. Table 2 on page 30 lists some examples of how word economy saves the reader time and effort.

To achieve further conciseness in your writing, avoid using repetitive, or **redundant,** words. In the following examples, the italicized words are unnecessary and should be omitted:

absolutely free	*first* began	refer *back*
adequate *enough*	*honest* truth	repeat *again*
advance warning	*kind* courtesy	right-*hand* turn
attached *hereto*	later *on*	*same* identical
basic essentials	lose *out*	seldom *ever*
both alike	*new* changes	*still* remains
continue *on*	*past* experience	*true* facts
cooperate *together*	*past* history	*up* above
customary practice	*perfectly* clear	*very* latest
dollar amount	*personal* opinion	*vitally* essential
end result	*proposed* plan	
finish *up*	*quite* unique	

Thinking Cap 2.3

Discuss: Redundancy is one of the main obstacles to clear, precise writing. Redundant phrases are a needless repetition of ideas. Analyze the following:
> combine together
> bisect in two
> fellow colleague
> continue to persist

Are they redundant phrases? If so, explain the redundancy.

You should also avoid using doublets. A **doublet** is created when two words that have nearly the same meaning are joined by the word *and*. In the following examples of doublets, use either the first or third word, omit the other, and drop the word *and*:

basic and fundamental	help and cooperation
each and every	pleased and delighted
fair and equitable	prompt and immediate
first and foremost	ready and willing
free and clear	wish and desire

When you write concisely, you use only necessary words to convey your message.

Go to CD-ROM
Activity 2-2
To test your skills.

Choosing the Right Words

Table 2 — Substituting Time Savers for Time Wasters

Time Wasters	Time Savers
according to our records	our records indicate
any one of the two	either
arrived at the conclusion	concluded
at a later date	later
at the present time *or* at this moment in time	now
costs a total of $50	costs $50
despite the fact that	although
do not hesitate to call me	call me
due to the fact that	because
during that time	while
I want to take this opportunity to tell you that we are grateful to you	thank you
I wish to say *or* permit me to say *or* may I say . . . that we are glad	we are glad
in a manner similar to	like
in a satisfactory manner	satisfactorily
in order to	to
in the amount of	for
in the event that	if
in the near future	soon
in this day and time	today
inasmuch as	since *or* because
is a matter of	is
may or may not	may
put in an appearance	appeared
self-addressed envelope	addressed envelope *or* return envelope
until such time as you can	until you can
venture a suggestion	suggest
whether or not	whether
with reference to	about
with the exception of	except
within the course of the next week	next week *or* within a week
would appear that	seems

Checkpoint 2.1

1. Why do people include unnecessary words in their writing?
2. How would you revise the language in the following sentences? *It is with much regret that we endeavor to draw your attention to your overdrawn checking account at First National. Your prompt and immediate attention to this important affair is requested and will be deeply and truly appreciated.*
3. How would you persuade the writer of the sentences in question 2 to change his or her writing style?

Conversational Words

In attempting to be conversational, communicators can fall into the habit of using outdated or trite expressions and clichés in their communications. Many expressions that were fashionable in business communications years ago sound lifeless, insincere, stilted, or even boring when used in today's communications. A message filled with worn-out words sounds awkward and unnatural, detracting from the personal tone of the message. Because word usage trends change, correct usage should be *current* usage. Do not go to out-of-date business letters to find words to use in letters today. Instead, use words that knowledgeable businesspeople currently use in well-organized communications.

Trite Expressions

The trite expressions in Table 3 often appear in business communications. As you study them, notice how simply and naturally the suggested conversational words convey the same meanings.

Table 3 — Trite Expressions With Conversational Words

Instead of These Trite Words . . .	. . . Choose These Conversational Words
acknowledge receipt of	thank you for
aforementioned	as stated previously
at the earliest possible date	as soon as (you) can
at the present writing	now
at your earliest convenience	as soon as you can *or* when you are ready
attached herewith	attached
due to the fact that	because
enclosed herewith *or* enclosed herein *or* enclosed please find	here *or* here are *or* enclosed is
in receipt of	have
in the amount of	for
in view of the fact that	because
kindly advise me *or* kindly inform me	please write me *or* please call me
please do not hesitate to	please
please find enclosed	enclosed
pursuant to	according to
regret to inform you that	am sorry that
thanking you in advance	I shall appreciate
under date of	on
under separate cover	separately
we will thank you to	please

NOTES

Natural Flow

Conversational communication is straightforward and natural.

GLOBAL DIVERSITY 2.1

Straight Talking

The use of clichés in communications creates problems and barriers for those individuals for whom English is a second language. A businessperson meeting with an individual from another culture may want to *lay the cards on the table* and not *beat around the bush* or *steal one's thunder,* but if they worked together, they would have *a land office business* and *one leg up on the competition.* How would the individual from another culture interpret this? *How could this be rephrased to allow for a meaningful translation?*

Choosing the Right Words

Clichés

Clichés are trite, stereotyped expressions that tend to resemble plays on words, or puns. Many of today's clichés come from TV programs or commercials and advertisements. Because they may not be understood or they may not convey the same meaning to all individuals, you should exercise care when and if you use them in business correspondence.

Although clichés might appear to be the perfect phrases to use in specific instances, good business communicators are careful to use them sparingly. Using clichés calls for a thorough knowledge of the recipient of the communication; however, you cannot always be sure who will read a memo or letter after the initial recipient passes it on. Use a cliché only if you are sure any reader will understand your intended meaning. Some of the more common clichés are shown in Table 4.

Many other trite expressions are also in current use. In analyzing your own communications and those of others, identify these expressions and their impact on the communications. Usually, avoiding such expressions will keep your writing clear, dynamic, and natural.

Go to CD-ROM
Activity 2-3
To test your skills.

Table 4 Clichés and Overused Expressions

Avoid These Clichés

all things being equal	break the ice
business as usual	by leaps and bounds
down to the last detail	draw the line at
finishing touch	from bad to worse
from start to finish	give and take
in due course	in a nutshell
in a word	in no uncertain terms
keep the ball rolling	lay the cards on the table
light at the end of the tunnel	missing link
needs no introduction	on the cutting edge
state of the art	step in the right direction
unwritten law	ups and downs
wishful thinking	

Avoid These Overused Expressions

a done deal	beat around the bush
crystal clear	dragging one's feet
drastic action	goes without saying
honest truth	in the final analysis
last but not least	leave no stone unturned
lion's share	needless to say
powers that be	reading between the lines
stands to reason	touch base
turn the corner	

Appropriate Words

By using the appropriate word for every circumstance, you help the reader understand exactly what you mean. You also build the reader's confidence in you and your ideas.

Errors that might go unnoticed in conversation are far more likely to be noticed in written communications. If you use an incorrect word or one that is not right for the context, the reader may misinterpret your intended meaning and form an unfair or inaccurate opinion of your ability and expertise. You must pay special attention to the use of homonyms, antonyms, synonyms, misused words, technical jargon, and bias-free and gender-neutral words in the communication process. Let's look at each of these categories of words more closely.

> **NOTES**
>
> **Say What You Mean**
>
> Appropriate words are words that convey the intended meaning.

Homonyms

Words that sound alike but have different meanings and spellings are called **homonyms,** or **homophones.** Because errors often occur when using homonyms, careful attention needs to be given to their proper use.

coarse, course	hear, here
meat, meet	principal, principle
stationary, stationery	their, there, they're
to, too, two	wood, would

Even more confusing are **pseudohomonyms**—words that are similar in sound but different in meaning and spelling, such as:

adapt, adept, adopt	affect, effect
allusion, illusion	

> **NOTES**
>
> **Types of Words**
>
> **Homonyms** are words that sound alike but have different meanings and spellings.
>
> **Antonyms** are words with opposite meanings.
>
> **Synonyms** are words that are similar in meaning.

Antonyms

Words that have opposite meanings are called **antonyms.** A thesaurus will give you a list of antonyms in addition to synonyms for each entry. Some words with opposite meanings can be confusing to writers.

anxious: Worried about.
confident: Certain.

Linda is <u>anxious</u> about her final exam but is <u>confident</u> that she will receive a passing grade for the semester.

eager: Looking forward to.
indifferent: Lacking interest, enthusiasm, or concern.

Mark is <u>eager</u> to help, but Sharon is <u>indifferent</u> about the situation.

Synonyms

Words that are similar in meaning are called **synonyms.** These words can also be confusing. Choose carefully the word that says exactly what you want to say. For example, "the balance of your shipment" is not quite accurate; the word *balance* usually refers to an amount of money. The word *remainder* or *rest* would be more appropriate in this situation. Similarly, "You can *obtain* the report from Jane" is more appropriate than "You can *secure* the report from Jane."

Choosing the Right Words

Misused Words

To avoid confusing your reader, choose carefully between each word in the sets of words shown in Table 5 below. These words are often misused and misunderstood. Use the dictionary to verify a word's exact meaning or a thesaurus to help you choose the word that best conveys your meaning.

Look at the groups of words shown in Table 5. Which of the groups of words give you trouble? Use your dictionary or thesaurus to learn their meanings. Practice using the words in sentences until you can use them confidently. Then choose another group and do the same until you are comfortable with the entire list of words.

Technical Vocabulary or Jargon

In choosing appropriate words, you must also consider your reader's experiences and interests. Every occupational or professional group has its own technical vocabulary or jargon. For example, people who work with computers understand such terms as *CPU, 60 Meg, client server, cursor, mouse,*

Table 5 — Words Often Misunderstood and Misused

accept—except	good—well
access—excess	hear—here
adapt—adept—adopt	human—humane
addition—edition	its—it's
advice—advise	later—latter
affect—effect	lay—lie
all ready—already	leased—least
assure—ensure—insure	leave—let
attendance—attendants	lessen—lesson
berth—birth	loose—lose
beside—besides	moral—morale
can—may	passed—past
canvas—canvass	patience—patients
capital—capitol	personal—personnel
cereal—serial	precede—proceed
choose—chose	principal—principle
cite—sight—site	recent—resent
complement—compliment	respectfully—respectively
confidentially—confidently	right—write
correspondence—correspondents	statue—stature—statute
council—counsel	suit—suite
credible—creditable	than—then
discreet—discrete	that—which
eminent—imminent	thorough—through
farther—further	who—whom
fiscal—physical	who's—whose
formally—formerly	your—you're

hard drive, macros, directories, modem, networking, and *laser printer.* These terms might be meaningless or might have very different meanings to someone not familiar with computers.

Technical words that are familiar to you may be the right choice when writing to a specialist in your area, but they may be useless to nearly everyone else. Use special terms with care to avoid creating rather than solving a communication problem. The successful business communicator learns and uses words that fit the vocabulary of the listener or reader.

NOTES
Write for Your Audience
Use words that fit the listener's or reader's vocabulary.

Bias-Free Language

Another important principle of proper business communication is the use of bias-free language. **Bias-free words** are words that do not discriminate against people on the basis of race, culture, gender, age, religion, physical or mental condition, socioeconomic level, or any other classification.

Avoid any possibility of offending your reader or discriminating on the basis of gender by choosing **gender-neutral terms,** nonsexist terms that treat both sexes neutrally. Historically, the word *man* and masculine pronouns were used generically to represent both males and females. Now, to avoid being regarded as one who is sexist, avoid using masculine pronouns unless you are specifically referring to males.

NOTES
Eliminate Bias
Treat both sexes equally by using nonsexist language.

Look at the following example:

The <u>manager</u> is responsible for the evaluations of <u>his</u> staff.

This sexist wording can be eliminated in one of the following ways:

The <u>managers</u> are responsible for the evaluations of <u>their</u> staffs.

<u>You</u> are responsible for the evaluations of <u>your</u> staff.

The manager is responsible for <u>the</u> staff's evaluations.

The manager is responsible for the evaluations of <u>his or her</u> staff.

In the last example, *his or her* is known as a pronoun pair. Excessive use of pronoun pairs results in awkward writing, so it is important to use a variety of strategies to eliminate sexist pronouns.

In addition to pronouns, look for gender bias in your writing by verifying that words and phrases, job titles and descriptions, and courtesy titles are bias-free and gender-neutral. See Table 6 on page 36 for a list of sexist terms and some gender-neutral alternatives.

It is important to avoid using stereotypes and discriminatory language. Unless relevant to your message, do not refer to someone's race, religion, age, disability, or disease. Try to stay current with preferred usage. Always use language that emphasizes the individual or group first, rather than the condition; for example, use the phrase *people with hearing disabilities* instead of *the deaf.*

Never use terms that could evoke negative images of any group of people. Choose words that do not offend or denigrate others. Try to see your writing through the reader's viewpoint. If there is a possibility that a word or phrase will offend your reader, rewrite it.

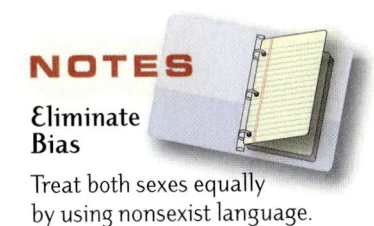

Choosing the Right Words 35

Table 6 Using Bias-Free Language

Instead of These Gender-Specific Words...	...Choose These Bias-Free Words
businessman	businessperson *or* business worker
chairman	chair, chairperson
fellow worker	coworker *or* colleague
fireman	firefighter
foreman	supervisor
housewife	homemaker
insurance salesman	insurance agent
landlord *or* landlady	owner
mailman	mail carrier *or* postal worker
newsman	newscaster *or* reporter *or* journalist
office boy	messenger *or* office helper
policeman *or* policewoman	police officer
salesman	salesperson *or* sales representative *or* sales associate *or* sales assistant
spokesman	spokesperson
stewardess	flight attendant
waitress	waitperson *or* food server
weatherman	weather reporter *or* meteorologist
workman	worker

GLOBAL DIVERSITY 2.2

Meaningful Gestures

Some gestures that are commonplace in the United States can carry hidden meaning in other cultures. Colombian women, for example, will often substitute the gesture of holding forearms for a handshake. In Chile, holding the palm of the hand upward with fingers spread signals that someone is "stupid." In England, using your fingers to form the peace sign, or "V" for Victory sign, but with the palm facing yourself, is considered a very offensive gesture. *Identify common gestures used in the workplace that might lead to confusion when communicating with people from other cultures.*

Correct Words

Careful business writers are aware of the skill involved in using words correctly. Avoid using words that are not recognized by language experts as usable words. For example, *irregardless* is not recognized by language experts; a better choice is *regardless*. Another type of nonexistent word may result from words pronounced incorrectly, such as *revelant* for *relevant; irrepairable* for *irreparable;* and *relator* for *realtor.*

Among additional errors in business writing are grammatical errors in the use of prepositions, conjunctions, adverbs, adjectives, and articles; mistakes in spelling; errors in abbreviations and contractions; and errors in expression of numbers.

Look over the list of misused words and phrases shown in Table 7. Are any of them mistakes you make? If so, learn to recognize and avoid them. You may add other errors and their replacements to this list for your reference.

Specific Words

You can make your writing more precise by using specific words rather than general words. Specific words present a clearly defined picture in a reader's mind. General words present a hazy, indefinite picture to the reader. For

Table 7	Using Correct Words and Phrases
Instead of These Frequently Misused Words and Phrases . . .	**. . . Choose These Correct Words and Phrases**
all but I	all but me
a lot of	many *or* much
and etc.	etc. *or* and so on
between us three	among us three
between we two	between us two
between you and I	between you and me
dep't	dept.
different than	different from
don't have but	have only
equally as good	equally good *or* just as good
had less errors	had fewer errors
if you will	whether you will
inside of	inside
insight of	insight into
irregardless	regardless
irrepairable	irreparable
like I do	as I do
long ways	long way
might of	might have
neither . . . or	neither . . . nor
real pleased	really pleased *or* very pleased
these kind	this kind *or* these kinds
try and	try to

example, what do you see in your mind when you hear the word *sweater*? Now, suppose we make it *red sweater*—has the picture in your mind changed? Let's be even more specific: *red, plaid, v-neck sweater*. What do you see in your mind now? How does it differ from what you thought of when we said only *sweater*?

As just illustrated, being specific sometimes means using more words. It can also mean using fewer but more precise words in order to paint an accurate picture in the reader's mind. Being specific is often a matter of choosing one word over another to create just the right image.

Being specific also means knowing exactly what you want to say. Whenever you can supply an exact fact, figure, or description to make your writing more concrete and convincing, do so. See Table 8 on page 38.

Positive Words

Positive words create a pleasant aura around your message. They impart enthusiasm and confidence, while negative words tend to trigger unpleasant feelings. That is why the effective business writer knows and deliberately uses positive

Choosing the Right Words

Table 8 Using Specific Words and Phrases

Instead of These General Words and Phrases . . .	. . . Choose These Specific Words and Phrases
fair response	34 percent response
fast	in one hour
for the full amount	for $655.39
gigantic loss	$9.2 million loss
low rating	C rating
often	25 out of 30 times
soon	on or before April 1

words to help stimulate the desired response from the reader. Positive words emphasize to the reader what can be done rather than what cannot be done, and will help you develop and maintain favorable relationships and goodwill. The following words help to produce this desirable psychological effect:

advantage	agreeable
benefit	can
comfortable	encourage
enjoy	fortunate
generous	help
opportunity	pleasure
profit	progress
recommend	satisfaction
success	thank you
valuable	welcome

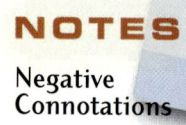

NOTES

Negative Connotations

Some words are always considered negative, while other words may or may not be considered negative, depending on their context.

Negative Words

Just as some words carry positive meanings, other words convey negative meanings. If you want your reader to feel positively toward you and to respond favorably to your communication, avoid negative, unfriendly words in your writing.

Some negative words such as *complain, disappointing, inferior,* and *unfortunately* are negative in almost any context. No matter how you use them, you'll probably convey a negative meaning to your reader. Learn to substitute words like *cooperation, service,* and *sincere.*

Another group of words are negative because of the context in which they appear. For example, the words *neglect, blame,* and *error* do not bring a

LEGAL & ETHICAL 2-1

Sales Pitch. Words are extremely important in advertising and sales promotions. Writers use positive words to produce desirable psychological effects. What are some words or phrases that are frequently used in sales promotions and advertising? Are such words used in an ethical way? Are there any potential legal problems with the use of "promotional" words?

negative response when you write, "We neglected to tell you...." or "We take full blame for the error." Yet, when used with the words *you* or *your*, these words arouse anger, as in, "You neglected to...." or "Your error caused...." or "You are to blame for...."

Negative words should be used with caution, if at all. They are likely to make readers feel you are criticizing them and to cause them to become angry with you. In these cases, your communications definitely will have a negative impact.

Checkpoint 2.2

Go to CD-ROM
Activity 2-4
To test your skills.

1. What does the use of bias-free language in a business communication suggest about the writer?
2. Which sentence is better, in your opinion, and why?
   a. *We offer special assistance for deaf and blind customers who are also old.*
   b. *We offer special assistance for senior customers who have hearing or vision impairments.*
3. If you know the gender of the person you are writing to, do you think that you should still use bias-free words?

Chapter 2 Summary

The basic writing process includes choosing words, developing phrases, and forming sentences and paragraphs to produce a coherent message. The fundamental element of the message is the word—choosing words begins the process. The ability to choose precise words to express your thoughts is essential in both written and oral communication. Your communications will be clear and effective if you choose simple, concise, appropriate, correct, positive, and specific words.

As you begin the writing process, refer to the lists and tables of words and phrases in this chapter. Using these lists and tables to choose acceptable words will assist you in developing your message.

Take some time to review the principles discussed in this chapter. Make a list of any words or phrases that you feel do not present your communication skills positively. As you progress in your studies, remove these words when you feel you have mastered their replacements. Begin to collect letters and other kinds of communication items that you get in your personal mail or on your job (with your employer's permission). You will need these items to analyze the activities you will encounter later in the course.

Choosing the Right Words

Chapter 2
Online Exercises

Objective:
These online activities will introduce you to the use of online dictionaries and online thesauri.

Go to **bcw.glencoe.com,** the address for the *Business Communication at Work* Web site, and select Chapter 2. Next, click on Online Exercises. You will see a list of Web site links that will bring you to different online dictionaries and online thesauri.

Activity 2.1

1. Select one of the online dictionary Web sites to visit.

2. Key *netiquette* in the **Search** box (some Web sites may use an **Enter Word** box).

3. Print one definition of *netiquette* by clicking on the File menu and selecting Print. Click OK.

4. Search for the definitions of the following computer terms: *flame, newbie, search engine, Internet, Internet service provider, emoticons, computer virus,* and *multimedia.* Some words will have more than one definition; select the definition that best relates to computer jargon. If a term is not listed in the dictionary site you selected, return to the *Business Communication at Work* Web site and select another. Once you've located a word, make a printout of its definition.

5. On the back of your printout of the definition for *netiquette*, write at least one sentence for each word you've looked up for this exercise. Make sure you use the correct word and eliminate any unnecessary words from your sentences.

6. Write your name on the front of the printout, and hand it in to your instructor.

Activity 2.2

1. Select one of the online thesauri Web sites to visit.

2. Key *work* in the **Search** box (some Web sites may use an **Enter Word** box).

3. Find two synonyms for the noun *work*. Make a printout.

4. Find two synonyms for each of the following words: *business* (noun), *rescind* (verb), *worthy* (adjective), and *very* (adverb).

5. On the back of your printout of the synonyms for *work*, write at least two synonyms for each word you've looked up for this exercise. For each word, which synonym provides the clearest meaning of the word?

6. Write your name on the front of the printout, and hand it in to your instructor.

CHAPTER 2 WORKSHEETS

NAME _____ DATE _____

PRACTICE 1

Synonyms

Instructions: Look up the following words in the thesaurus on your word processor (or in a hard copy). Write the words that are listed as having similar meanings. If antonyms are listed, list those also, using the notation **ANT.**

1. opportunity _____
2. evaluate _____
3. ethics _____
4. harass _____

Antonyms

Instructions: Identify and circle the antonym (the word opposite in meaning) for the word in bold at the left:

1. **construct**	assemble	fabricate	raze	rear
2. **antagonize**	alienate	appease	contradict	dispute
3. **pertinent**	applicable	appropriate	germane	irrelevant
4. **oppose**	advocate	contest	hinder	thwart
5. **encourage**	dissuade	influence	sanction	stimulate

Positive and Negative Words

Instructions: Listed are words that generally have a negative connotation. Identify a positive word that may be used in place of each negative word:

1. crisis _____   4. cagey _____
2. obstinate _____   5. trouble _____
3. criticism _____

Confusing Words

Instructions: From the list on page 34, select five sets of words that have meanings you are unsure of. Find the words in the dictionary, and write them and their exact meanings on the lines below.

1. _____
2. _____
3. _____
4. _____
5. _____

Choosing the Right Words   41

CHAPTER 2 WORKSHEETS

NAME _____ DATE _____

PRACTICE 2

Using Familiar Words

Instructions: Write sentences using the words from the previous exercise appropriately.

1. _____
2. _____
3. _____
4. _____
5. _____

Recognizing Inappropriate Words

Instructions: Follow the instructions given for each numbered item.

1. **Simple words.** Rewrite the following sentences, substituting simple words for the underlined words and phrases in the sentences.

   a. The teleconference will <u>afford us an opportunity</u> to <u>interrogate</u> the <u>numerous</u> <u>remuneration</u> proposals and <u>consummate</u> the rumors.
   _____

   b. <u>It is requested that</u> we <u>effect the destruction of</u> the <u>antiquated</u> software packages.
   _____

2. **Concise words.** Delete the extra words and rewrite these sentences.

   a. This is to inform you that we will take under consideration your recommendation to postpone until a later date our evaluation of the properties.
   _____

   b. I want to take this opportunity to thank you for providing an opportunity for me to experience success in developing my skills.
   _____

3. **Conversational words.** Substitute a conversational word or phrase for each underlined phrase in the sentence below.

   <u>As per our conversation</u>, I am <u>taking the liberty of sending you under separate cover</u> a complimentary copy of our new book.
   _____

4. **Appropriate words.** Replace the underlined words that are not appropriate.

   We are <u>anxious</u> to address the <u>principle</u> problems with the student <u>assistance</u> in the <u>personal</u> office and <u>they're</u> <u>amount</u> of absences, which have <u>effected moral</u>.
   _____
   _____

CHAPTER 2 WORKSHEETS

NAME _____   DATE _____

5. **Correct words.** Substitute correct words for the underlined words that are incorrect.

   <u>Between you and I</u> she has a <u>long ways</u> to go to become a programmer. <u>Irregardless</u> she had <u>less</u> errors than the <u>person</u> <u>which</u> we interviewed; I am <u>real pleased</u> with <u>a lot of</u> her work. <u>I don't have but</u> two days to <u>try</u> <u>and</u> notify her.

   _____
   _____
   _____

6. **Specific words.** Underline the general, vague words in each sentence and then substitute a specific word.

   a. I read several books this week.
   _____

   b. There was a poor turnout for the seminar.
   _____

   c. I'll deliver the package as soon as possible.
   _____

   d. It's a long way to the shopping mall.
   _____

   e. The department has a high turnover rate each year.
   _____

   f. The stockholder received a low rate of return on the investment.
   _____

   g. The software package isn't very expensive.
   _____

   h. The student had a high grade point average for the first semester.
   _____

7. **Positive words.** Underline the positive words and circle the negative words in each sentence.

   a. We are fortunate to have you as a customer and want to encourage you to tell us how we can better serve your needs.

   b. Unfortunately, we need to inform you that you are delinquent in the payment of your account and have ignored our previous requests and neglected to tell us of any problems you may be experiencing.

Precise Word Choices

Instructions: In the following sentences, underline the words and phrases that are vague or overly general. On the lines below each sentence, rewrite the sentence to make it more specific. NOTE: You may assume any information necessary to make the sentences specific.

1. Take the bus to our house on Saturday.
   _____
   _____

Choosing the Right Words

CHAPTER 2 WORKSHEETS

NAME _____ DATE _____

2. I would like to apply for the position advertised in the paper.

3. We will be there early for your next meeting.

4. Contact me if you need assistance with the project. I am here every day.

5. Many people have registered for your next teleconference.

PRACTICE 3

Sentence Revisions

Instructions: The following sentences contain many of the following: complex words, excess words and phrases, trite expressions, inappropriate words, vague words, incorrect words, and negative words. Underline the words and phrases that need to be improved. On the lines below, rewrite the sentences simply and concisely, substituting friendly, conversational expressions. NOTE: You may assume any information necessary to make your revisions clear and direct.

1. **Incorrect words.** Mary's announcement did irreparable damage to employe moral.

2. **Excess and incorrect words.** We need you to fill out the attached form in order that we can foreword you're password so that you can excess the computer system.

3. **Excess, vague, outdated words.** I am doing some research on word processing and was wondering if you would be so kind as to allow me to talk to you people about the aforementioned topic.

4. **Negative and excess words.** We are in receipt of your complaint regarding your health club membership and are sorry to have to inform you that it is our policy that we cannot refund your money even though you are moving from the area.

Bias-Free Language

Instructions: In small groups, discuss terms that may be considered biased or that discriminate against people on the basis of race, culture, gender, age, religion, physical or mental condition, or socioeconomic level. Make a list of the terms, and list appropriate bias-free words to use in place of the terms.

CHAPTER 2 WORKSHEETS

NAME _____ DATE _____

PRACTICE 4

Business Letter Analysis

Instructions: From your portfolio of letters that you are collecting, select a business letter. Analyze the business letter according to the principles and techniques presented in this chapter. Complete the following form, which includes principles and techniques from Chapters 1 and 2.

a. What is the purpose of the letter? _____
_____

b. Who is the intended audience of the letter? _____

c. Is the tone of the letter positive? If it is not positive, what changes should be made? _____
_____

d. Did the writer practice the seven Cs of effective correspondence?

	Yes	No	If no, explain why
Courteous	___	___	_____
Considerate	___	___	_____
Clear	___	___	_____
Concise	___	___	_____
Complete	___	___	_____
Correct	___	___	_____
Consistent	___	___	_____

e. Did the message achieve its purpose? _____ Yes _____ No

f. **WORD CHOICE:** Did the writer use the following:

	Yes	No	Examples:
Simple words	___	___	_____
Concise words	___	___	_____
Conversational words	___	___	_____
Trite expressions	___	___	_____
Clichés	___	___	_____
Appropriate words	___	___	_____
Bias-free words	___	___	_____
Correct words	___	___	_____
Specific words	___	___	_____
Positive words	___	___	_____

If used, were the following used correctly?

Homonyms	___	___
Antonyms	___	___
Synonyms	___	___

Choosing the Right Words

CHAPTER 3
Developing Sentences and Paragraphs

Objectives

After completing this chapter, you will be able to:

1. Construct sentences using the four basic structures
2. Identify the subject and verb in sentences
3. Write clear, concise, and effective sentences
4. Develop clear, concise, coherent, and effective paragraphs

WORKPLACE APPLICATIONS

Prewriting

Experienced writers know that the act of writing is a process with several stages—prewriting, drafting, and revising. **Prewriting** is the planning stage. It is the part of the writing process in which you gather and organize your thoughts. It is like preparing a room to be wallpapered. If the preparations are not done right, the wallpaper won't stick to the walls. As in wallpapering, the preparations of prewriting may seem like more work than the act of writing itself, but the effort always pays off.

Taking the First Steps

The first thing to do in prewriting is choose your topic and gather information. Use any of the following techniques to generate topics and collect information: brainstorming (see also page 133), freewriting, asking questions, reading books and articles by experts, taking notes or keeping a journal, interviewing experts or colleagues, and **visualizing** or imagining.

Once you know your topic and have gathered your information, the next step is to arrange your ideas in a way that will make sense to your readers. **Outlines** are the most efficient way to organize ideas. A balanced outline will have at least two or three main points (Roman numerals I, II, III). Here is the beginning of a sample outline.

 I. The department needs to cut costs in order to meet its new budget.
   A. Reduce purchases of office supplies
   B. Increase electronic communications
      1. Will reduce amount of paper used in printers
      2. Will reduce use of toner in printers

Your outline is like a blueprint. As you write your first draft, just flesh out the ideas in the outline with details, statistics, facts, and other pieces of information that your reader needs to know.

Thinking Critically

Situation: You are an efficiency expert who has been hired by a manufacturing company to increase its productivity. You have visited the site, walked the production lines, and talked to managers and workers. Now you must prepare a report for the company's owners.

Ask Yourself: How would you plan, or prewrite, your report? Include a partial outline of your report in your answer.

> *Effective communication requires skills, and skill development takes practice. A person cannot improve his [or her] tennis game merely by reading tennis books or watching great tennis players. He [or she] must get out on the court and practice what he [or she] has read or seen, progressing slowly through different levels of proficiency.*
>
> **Stephen R. Covey,
> Motivational Author**

In Chapter 1, you learned the basics for communicating effectively. In this chapter, you will concentrate on one part of those basics—developing your message in a clear, concise, correct, and logical manner—through the formation of sentences and paragraphs. To convey your meaning successfully in written communications or in oral conversations requires expertise in word choice. In addition, you must always be aware of the seven tests of effective communication, the seven Cs, referred to previously: courteous, considerate, clear, complete, concise, correct, and consistent. As you apply the principles you learned in the previous chapters and use your skill in choosing the right words, you will be ready to continue with the communication building process:

- Assembling the words into phrases
- Connecting the phrases to form sentences
- Grouping the sentences into paragraphs
- Organizing the paragraphs into coherent messages

Writing Sentences and Paragraphs

Just as the fundamental element of your message is the word, the **sentence** is the foundation for the effectiveness of your message. A sentence is a group of words that expresses a complete thought. Successful business communication consists of strong, well-constructed sentences and paragraphs. Simple words must be chosen carefully with the level of the audience in mind. Then the words must be put together in an acceptable order to form meaningful, effective communications. To do this, you must:

1. Construct sentences by choosing words carefully and organizing the words to express a complete thought.
2. Join sentences to form paragraphs.
3. Fit the paragraphs smoothly into a coherent communication.

How well you construct your sentences plays a very important part in determining how well you state your ideas. If you arrange and connect your sentences effectively, you can lead the reader through your ideas—your goal is to present ideas so that they flow smoothly through the reader's mind.

Sentence Structures

As you know, a **sentence** is a group of words that expresses one complete thought. In identifying sentences, we look for subjects and verbs, clauses and phrases. A good sentence must have the correct framework (see Figure 3-1).

Figure 3-1
A good sentence must have the correct framework.

Sentence Components

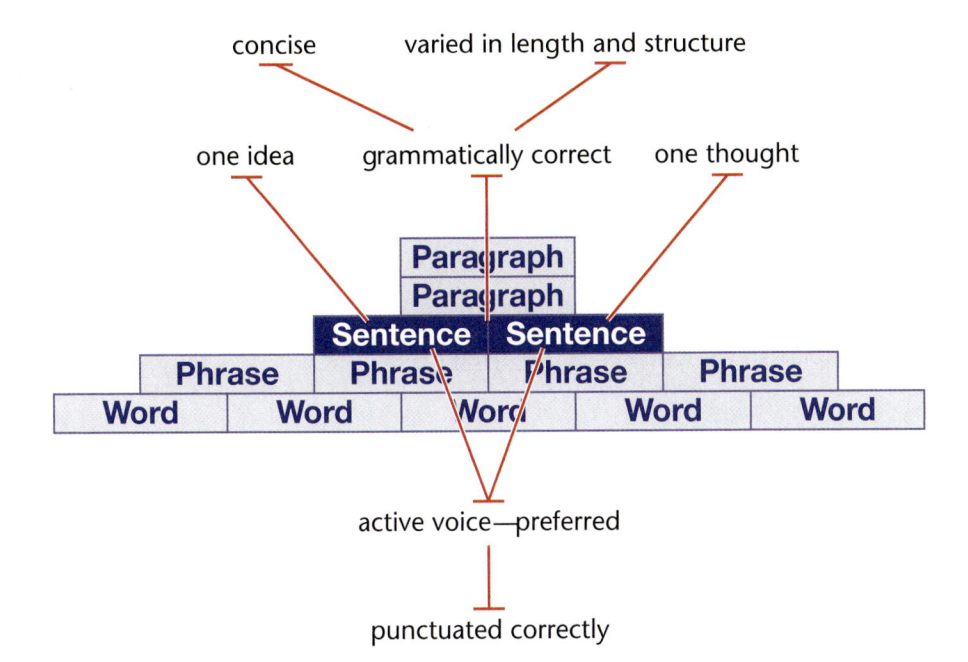

The **subject** of a sentence identifies the person, place, activity, quality, idea, or thing about which something is said; it tells who or what is being discussed. A subject may be a word, phrase, or clause. The **verb** (predicate) expresses action or a state of being. A verb may be a word or phrase.

Pat drives five miles to work each day.
> Subject: Pat (*who*)
> Verb: drives (*action*)

Pat seems anxious about the marathon.
> Subject: Pat (*who*)
> Verb: seems (*state of being*)

A **clause** is a group of related words containing a subject and a verb. The two kinds of clauses are independent and dependent.

An **independent clause,** also known as a main clause or principal clause, expresses a complete thought and can stand alone as a separate sentence. For example:

Jim called the company.

A **dependent clause,** also known as a subordinate clause, does not express a complete thought and, therefore, cannot stand alone as a sentence:

because the toy was broken

Even though a dependent clause has a subject and a verb, it still needs another clause to make it a complete thought or sentence, as in the following examples:

Jim called the company because the toy was broken.   OR

Because the toy was broken, Jim called the company.

NOTES

Stand Alone Clause

An independent clause expresses a complete thought and can stand alone as a separate sentence.

NOTES

Subordinate Clause

A dependent clause does not express a complete thought and cannot stand alone as a sentence.

Developing Sentences and Paragraphs   49

Dependent clauses are introduced by subordinate conjunctions, such as *because, before, as soon as, if, since, unless*, or relative pronouns, such as *who, whom, that, which,* and *whose.*

A **phrase** is a group of two or more words that lack a subject and a verb. Phrases can be used as nouns, adjectives, or adverbs. For example:

Before 9 a.m. is the best time to see him.

The time to play is now, not tomorrow.

Let's plan to eat lunch after the meeting.

Types of Sentences

A sentence contains a subject and a verb, and expresses a complete thought. Sentence structures can be classified according to one of the four following types:

1. A simple sentence contains a subject and a verb—one independent clause.

Jan operated the VCR in the meeting.

A simple sentence can contain two or more subjects joined by a conjunction, such as *and* or *or*, or two verbs joined by a conjunction.

Jan and Kim operated the VCR.

Jan dimmed the lights and operated the VCR.

2. A compound sentence contains two or more independent clauses.

The clauses are closely related and equally important; they are emphasized equally, as in the following example:

Jan operated the VCR, and Kim used the video camera.

3. A complex sentence contains one independent clause and at least one dependent clause.

The clauses are related but are not equal in importance or emphasis. The independent clause expresses the most important idea and is most strongly emphasized.

Since Jan operated the VCR, Kim used the video camera.

4. A compound-complex sentence contains two or more independent clauses and one or more dependent clauses.

Since Jan operated the VCR, Kim used the video camera, and Keith coordinated the slides.

Another example of the compound-complex sentence follows:

Jan used the overhead VCR because the projector was broken, and Kim used the video camera.

In the sentence above, the independent clauses are these:

Jan used the overhead projector.

Kim used the video camera.

The dependent clause that cannot stand alone is

because the computer was broken

The compound-complex sentence may have been written as follows:

Because the computer was broken, Jan used the overhead projector, and Kim used the video camera.

CONSTRUCTING SENTENCES

All your written communications must comply with commonly accepted standards of written English. Otherwise, you will distract your reader, and both you and your message will lose credibility.

Conversational Language

The specific "rules" for constructing sentences need not be complicated. The current trend in business communication is to use conversational language rather than rigid, formal writing.

FORMAL	This firm represents the interests of Philip Ingersoll in his claim for damages arising as a result of the automobile accident which occurred on January 15.
CONVERSATIONAL	I represent Philip Ingersoll who was injured in an automobile accident on January 15.

In business communication situations, use a style of writing that is closer to actual speaking than to the language of a college textbook. Remember, communication takes place more effectively when the reader is thinking about content rather than the manner in which it is expressed.

Guidelines for Writing Effective Sentences

Here are nine guidelines for writing effective sentences:

1. Sentences should contain only one idea.

Sentences that contain more than one idea weaken the message. Too many ideas expressed without a pause tend to run together in the reader's mind.

WEAK	Thank you, Ms. Johnson, for your letter of April 30 complimenting the *National Business Report* and giving us your summer address, where we will send your next three copies, beginning with the June issue.

Did you find yourself reading this sentence twice? Were you confused by the time you got to the end of the sentence?

GLOBAL DIVERSITY 3.1

Using Titles
The American use of first names in the workplace is disconcerting to Brazilians, who are accustomed to very defined social status/age and rank/position forms of address. Use the word "Seu" before the first name for men and "Dona" before the first name for women. You would call your male business associate "Seu Pedro" and your female business associate "Dona Ana." *Would you recommend that the conversational style of writing be appropriate for different cultures? What would be some of the advantages and disadvantages of using the conversational style?*

Developing Sentences and Paragraphs

In this example, the writer is trying to do two things: (1) thank the customer for her letter, and (2) tell her that her request will be handled. Neither idea stands out because the two ideas are joined in one sentence. A simple change will stress both ideas.

STRONG   Thank you, Ms. Johnson, for your letter of April 30 complimenting the *National Business Report.* Beginning with the June issue, your next three copies will be sent to your summer address.

Putting too many ideas into one sentence frequently results in a run-on sentence, which is not only confusing but also grammatically incorrect. A **run-on sentence** consists of two or more independent clauses without the proper punctuation. A run-on sentence sometimes may not have a coordinating conjunction, such as *and, but, or,* or *nor;* therefore, the sentence is composed of two independent clauses that run on.

I have completed this project I am ready for another one.

Run-on sentences can be corrected by making separate sentences from the independent clauses, by adding appropriate punctuation, or by adding an appropriate coordinating conjunction.

The following run-on sentence, taken from an actual memo, contains three ideas:

RUN-ON   Please be prepared to discuss your ideas at the meeting, they don't have to be typed, if possible, they should be written in outline form.

This sentence could be confusing even if it were correctly punctuated. (It isn't.) Notice how much clearer it is when the three ideas are separated:

CLEAR   Please be prepared to discuss your ideas at the meeting. They don't have to be typed; if possible, they should be written in outline form.

Give more emphasis to an idea by dividing it into two parts and expressing each part in a separate sentence. Even though the following weak example is not a run-on, the message is much stronger as two sentences:

WEAK   We promise you excellent service in the future, and please let us know how we can make your next flight more enjoyable.

STRONG   We promise you excellent service in the future. Please let us know how we can make your next flight more enjoyable.

2. Sentences should contain one complete thought.

A group of words that gives merely part of an idea is a **sentence fragment.** Because a sentence must express one complete thought, a sentence fragment is not a sentence. A fragment splits one thought into two parts, as in the following example:

NOTES

Keep the Focus

A sentence should convey a single thought.

Thinking Cap 3.1

Discuss: How would you improve the following run-on sentence?
I would like to sell you on one idea the value of my services as a financial counselor can benefit you and your family.

FRAGMENT   To update your records and actively reflect Hale Manufacturing's economic standing. We submit the annual report for your review.

The first part of this example is not a complete sentence. An idea is started in the first statement and completed in the sentence that follows. The two statements should be joined to express one complete thought.

SENTENCE   To update your records and actively reflect Hale Manufacturing's economic standing, we submit the annual report for your review.

The following example illustrates another sentence fragment:

FRAGMENT   The brochure describes some of the more advanced techniques of making sound investments. Including a candid analysis of the strategies and risks involved.

The part *Including a candid analysis of the strategies and risks involved* expands the idea expressed in the first sentence but is not a complete sentence in itself. For a complete sentence join the two parts.

SENTENCE   The brochure describes some of the more advanced techniques of making sound investments, including a candid analysis of the strategies and risks involved.

Sentence fragments, usually introduced by prepositions or participles, are frequently found as opening and closing ideas in business letters. Sentence fragments are problems, especially in either of these positions, because the first and last few words of a message should be the most emphatic. The following openings contain sentence fragments:

WEAK OPENINGS   Realizing that an insurance company must make fast, fair adjustments. The Scranton Insurance Agency pledges to give you the best service available in the Mt. Horeb area.

With reference to your suggestion concerning refunds. I appreciate this information and will follow up within a week.

You can make these openings grammatically acceptable by simply substituting a comma for the first period in each of them. You can make them much stronger, by effectively rewording the sentences.

STRONG OPENINGS   An insurance company must make fast, fair adjustments. The Scranton Insurance Agency knows this and pledges to give you the best service available in the Mt. Horeb area.

Your suggestion concerning our refund policy is welcome. Within a week I hope to have a solution to this problem of refunds.

Thinking Cap 3.2

Discuss: How would you correct the following sentence fragment?
No matter how well known or how prosperous your business may be. New customers must be added to your clientele constantly if the business is to survive.

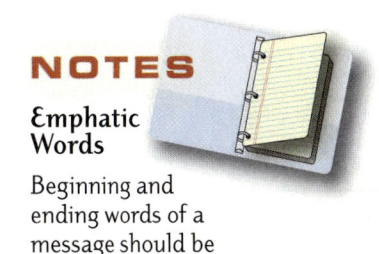

NOTES
Emphatic Words
Beginning and ending words of a message should be emphatic.

Developing Sentences and Paragraphs   53

Rewording can also turn a weak closing containing a sentence fragment into an effective, strong closing, as in the following example:

WEAK CLOSING	Thanking you for your courtesy and cooperation in this matter.
STRONG CLOSING	I will appreciate your cooperation.

Sometimes the deliberate use of a sentence fragment can be very effective, especially to establish an informal, friendly tone. A fragment can be made to express a complete thought if an exclamation point or a question mark is placed after it, as in the following examples:

That's right—*lifetime protection!* Worldwide, 24 hours a day.

Tonight! Our special Sundown-to-Sunup 40 Percent-Off Sale—*don't miss it!*

This informality may be useful in a sales letter or direct mail advertisement in which the writer must quickly establish both friendliness and trust in the reader. Such informality, however, may be inappropriate in other business communications. The receiver may interpret it as sarcasm, insincerity, or deficiency in grammar. If the receiver is angry, worried, or fearful, he or she will not appreciate a very informal writing style. For this reason, use sentence fragments sparingly—only when you have a clear purpose in mind and you are able to anticipate your reader's reaction.

3. Sentences should use the active voice.

Effective writing creates force through the use of action verbs—those used in the active voice rather than the passive voice. In Chapter 1, active and passive voices were defined this way:

ACTIVE VOICE	The subject of the sentence *performs* the action described by the verb.
PASSIVE VOICE	The subject *receives* the action described by the verb.

The active voice creates the illusion of movement while the passive voice limits movement. The passive voice may be the worst offender in dull, weak writing. Although the passive voice can be used to soften a negative statement, for example, it should be used sparingly.

Why does the passive voice hurt readability? Consider the following example in the active voice:

ACTIVE VOICE	Brian read the letter.

This simple sentence brings a picture of Brian reading to the reader's mind. Active-voice sentences emphasize the action—the "doing" that the sentences describe. Now let's put our example into the passive voice:

PASSIVE VOICE	The letter was typed by Brian.

Thinking Cap 3.3

Discuss: How would you improve the following weak opening and weak closing? **WEAK OPENING:** Although your holiday shopping may be almost done. We would like to suggest a gift that we believe is perfect for a member of your family. **WEAK CLOSING:** Looking forward to calling on you sometime soon.

In the passive version, the writer needs six words to tell what took only four words in the active voice. Notice, also, how the emphasis has shifted. The mental picture is now of a letter—no Brian, no reading, just a letter. The action is gone, and the person who did the acting is gone, too. This shift of emphasis eliminates interest and clarity in passive sentences; they become poor forms of communication. This example illustrates two major drawbacks to using passive constructions:

NOTES

Active vs Passive

The active voice is more direct, concise, personal, and vigorous than the passive voice.

1. They require more words without adding to the meaning.

2. They weaken the sentence's impact by taking away emphasis from the action and the person who performs the action.

To keep your writing flowing and lively, stress the "people element." Write in the active voice to give the reader a picture of the subject performing the action. Communicating in the active voice creates a stronger message—one that is more direct, concise, personal, and vigorous.

Checkpoint 3.1

Select the more effective sentence or sentences in each of the pairs below. Explain your choices.

1. a. *Our sales have increased for three straight quarters in a row, we should be proud of our company's performance so far this year.*

    b. *Our sales have increased for three straight quarters in a row; we should be proud of our company's performance so far this year.*

2. a. *Once we receive your payment, we will send you a receipt and an updated copy of your account.*

    b. *Once we receive your payment. We will send you a receipt and an updated copy of your account.*

3. a. *The client made a generous offer. We recommend that you take it.*

    b. *A generous offer was made by the client. We recommend that you take it.*

4. Sentences should be grammatically correct.

Basic English errors in sentences may make the receiver think the sender is ignorant or careless—or both. What is good English, and what are the rules of good English? The "rules" are actually general agreements among the users of English on how to use the language for various purposes in various circumstances. Your goal, as a successful communicator, is to use the rules followed by the majority of skilled writers and speakers in the business world. In order to keep your grammar skills at the highest level, review all grammar rules in Appendix A at the back of your textbook, or use the Student CD-ROM that is available with this textbook as a review method.

Developing Sentences and Paragraphs

> **NOTES**
>
> **Verb Agreement**
>
> A verb should agree with its subject in person and in number.

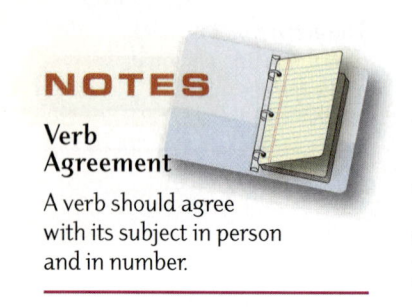

Subject and Verb Agreement. A glaring error that communicators make is neglecting to check for agreement between the subject and verb. A verb should agree with its subject in person and in number:

- A singular subject requires a singular verb.
- A plural subject requires a plural verb.

Remember to check your writing closely for subject and verb agreement. You can find specific guidelines and examples to assist you in determining subject and verb agreement in Appendix A. If you're using the Student CD-ROM, which is available with this textbook, go to Topic 9 of the *Interactive Grammar* section; then select one of the concepts on subject and verb agreement.

Parallel Construction. **Parallel construction** improves sentence clarity. Parallel construction simply means using similar grammatical structures in phrases, clauses, and lists to express similar ideas.

Using parallelism is important in all writing, especially when dealing with series, contrasts, and comparisons. Look at the following sentence, which contains a series in list format:

Effective sentences should:

- Contain only one idea
- Use the active voice
- One complete thought
- Naturally fit together

Notice that the items in the list are not parallel in construction. One way to make this sentence parallel is to have each of the elements of the series start with an appropriate verb.

Effective sentences should:

- Contain only one idea.
- Use the active voice.
- Contain one complete thought.
- Fit together naturally.

Notice, also, the parallelism in the list of objectives at the beginning of this chapter. What makes the list parallel in construction?

Carelessness is a major contributor to grammatical errors. Writing in a sloppy manner may be easier than writing carefully, but it may also become a difficult habit to break. To avoid the habit of sloppy writing, develop the habit of editing each sentence that you write to ensure that it is correct.

How do you know what is correct, or standard, English usage? Through reading, listening, writing, speaking, studying, and practicing the rules of grammar, you can develop an instinct for correct English usage. In addition, knowledge of the rules of grammar and punctuation is essential.

The ability to recite the rules of grammar and punctuation will not necessarily prevent you from making errors. However, the ability to recognize errors will aid you in creating mechanically correct messages. Once you recognize your errors, you can turn to a reliable reference manual or English grammar handbook to verify the rules, correct mistakes, and improve usage habits.

To assist you in your writing, Appendix A at the end of this book briefly summarizes rules of grammar and punctuation. Review the rules and the examples until you are confident that you can apply them correctly. In addition, an up-to-date, reliable dictionary and a comprehensive English-usage handbook or reference manual will help you in developing communications and are important resources for your personal library.

NOTES

Know Your Mistakes

The key to correct writing is recognizing your own errors.

5. Sentences should be punctuated correctly.

Commas are perhaps the most troublesome of all punctuation marks. Placing commas incorrectly or otherwise misusing them may cause the meaning of sentences to be unclear. The reader may then need to reread sentences several times to understand the intended meaning. Commas are misused in three ways:

1. They are omitted where they are needed.
2. They are inserted where they are not needed.
3. They are misplaced within the sentence.

In each case, the error usually hinders the reader's understanding.

One common mistake is to omit one of a pair of commas. For example, commas are needed to set off appositives or explanatory expressions. In the following example, *the editorial assistant* is an appositive, which should be set off by commas. By omitting one of the commas, the sentence conveys a different meaning.

INCORRECT: Rosemary Fitzgerald, the editorial assistant called while you were out of the office.

CORRECT: Rosemary Fitzgerald, the editorial assistant, called while you were out of the office.

Another common error is to use unnecessary commas. For example, a comma may be incorrectly inserted between a subject and its verb.

INCORRECT: Analyzing the data and presenting recommendations by November 4, will be difficult.

CORRECT: Analyzing the data and presenting recommendations by November 4 will be difficult.

Misplaced commas may interrupt the flow of a sentence and cause some hesitation in the reader's understanding.

INCORRECT: The most important topic, and also the most frequently discussed, was the discount rate.

Developing Sentences and Paragraphs

CORRECT: The most important topic and also the most frequently discussed was the discount rate.

Let good usage and common sense be your guides to correct punctuation. Follow accepted rules in punctuation to assure that the receiver will clearly understand your message. Be sure to review the punctuation rules in Appendix A of this textbook.

6. Sentences should be concise.

Concise communication uses as few words as possible to communicate the message in a clear, courteous manner. Whether long or short, a sentence should be concise. Concise is the opposite of *wordy*; it is not the opposite of *long*. If your sentences are concise, they contain no wasted words.

You have already learned to avoid needless repetition and to use concise words and phrases. You know it is important not to use three or four words to express an idea if one or two words express the idea as well. Now continue a step further in the communication building process—learn to write concise sentences.

Thinking Cap 3.4

Discuss: How would you improve the following wordy sentence?
I regret to inform you that the agent from whom you originally purchased your contract is no longer with the company and I am his replacement.

Eliminate Useless Words. Organize sentences to eliminate words that do not help to make the meaning clear or the tone courteous. For example, the opening words *It is, There are,* and *There were* generally add nothing to sentences except words. They also tend to lead into stiff, formal writing and passive constructions. When you have used one of these beginnings, try rearranging the sentence to eliminate the phrase.

WORDY: There are several options available to you.

CONCISE: You have several options.

Avoid Repetitiveness. Vague sentences that are limited in meaning waste time and inhibit the receiver's concentration. The only reason for restating a question or an idea that already has been stated clearly is to gain emphasis. However, overusing this technique may cause the receiver to become bored and frustrated, especially if the repetition has no purpose or is used to restate the original vague statement. The following rambling paragraph is an example that may create frustration:

WEAK: I would like to ask a question about your summer school course offerings in the computer science curriculum. The offerings at the Madison campus seem to be geared to upper-level students, and I am having difficulty finding introductory-level courses to take. It would help if you could send me schedules from your Reedsburg, Watertown, and Portage campuses, so that I can decide what I want to take this summer and reserve a dorm room early. When these schedules are available, will you please send them to me?

In the above example, the writer's question is buried in a clutter of unnecessary information. The writer is simply requesting summer school schedules; he or she can solve the other problems after receiving the schedules. Is the following example a more forceful request?

STRONG: Please send me summer school schedules for the computer science curriculum at your Reedsburg, Watertown, and Portage campuses.

Omit Obvious Statements. If you agree that concise writing helps your letter accomplish its purpose, then you will also agree that omitting facts the receiver already knows is wise. Stating the obvious wastes words and risks offending the receiver by implying that he or she is ignorant or forgetful. Further, when obvious statements are used at the beginning of business letters, the receiver may assume that the writer does not know how to begin.

Many writers begin by telling the reader that they received his or her letter, which they are now answering, or by restating what the reader said in that letter. The fact that the writer is sending an answer is evidence enough that the reader's letter has been received. Do not waste the most effective position in a letter, the opening, by telling the reader "In reply to your letter of March 23, . . ." or "In your letter of May 7 you stated that . . . ." If a reader doesn't remember all the details of the original letter, a quick glance at the file copy will refresh his or her memory. The goal of the response is to give the reader an answer, not to echo the reader's letter.

The best way to begin a business letter is usually by directly answering the reader's question. Although there are a few situations when you should not begin the letter with the main point (we'll discuss those in a later chapter), opening a letter with a direct response is usually more effective. Look at these examples:

WEAK: I am in receipt of your letter which is dated March 25. You wanted to know the current prices of our various brands and models of camcorders; so I am enclosing our latest price list, which will cover all this information.

STRONG: Here is our current price list, listed by brands and models, for our camcorders.

WEAK: I am replying to your letter of October 9. With this letter you enclosed a check for $101.23, the total amount due since August.

STRONG: Thank you for your check for $101.23, which clears your account.

As with beginnings, writers often have trouble with letter endings. After answering the reader's questions and giving information, a writer may then fall back on trite phrases. Look at this example:

TRITE: Thank you again for your interest in our product. If you need further information with regard to this matter, or if we may assist you in any way, please don't hesitate to contact us.

Thinking Cap 3.5

Discuss: How can the following sentence be improved? As we come to the end of another record-breaking year at Haeffeners Manufacturing, I want to take this opportunity to congratulate you on your outstanding sales performance as a manufacturer's representative during your first full year with the company.

Developing Sentences and Paragraphs

If thanks have been given once, that's usually enough—say thanks twice and you may appear insincere. Actually, the best expression of gratitude is to do what the reader wants. Similarly, offering further information or assistance in your ending may appear courteous or may mean that you are not sure your answer was complete. Assume that if the reader needs more information or help, he or she will let you know.

Your letter should end with a positive tone. Deleting vague endings, like avoiding obvious beginnings, improves the letter. Take this actual business letter as an example:

> Dear Mr. Anderson:
>
> Thank you for your recent request for more information about our Computer Programming program, which you noticed in our catalogue.
>
> We appreciate your interest in our Computer Programming program. Information about the program and the fall schedule are enclosed.
>
> Ruth Joyce, our academic advisor, will contact you. Ms. Joyce will be able to assist you with the application and registration processes. She will also be able to answer specific questions about the program.
>
> Again, thank you for your interest in our programs. Meanwhile, if we can be of further help to you, just call on us. We'll be glad to assist you in any way. Best wishes as you continue your education.
>
> Sincerely,

Now let's eliminate the first paragraph of this letter. Is the letter weakened? No. Next let's look at the last paragraph. Can it be rewritten to make it more concise and clear? Yes.

> Dear Mr. Anderson:
>
> We appreciate your interest in our Computer Programming program. Information about the program and the fall schedule are enclosed.
>
> Ruth Joyce, our academic advisor, will contact you. Ms. Joyce will be able to assist you with the application and registration processes. She will also be able to answer specific questions about the program.
>
> Thank you for your interest in our program. Best wishes as you continue your education.
>
> Sincerely,

> **LEGAL & ETHICAL 3-1**
>
> **Claim Confusion.** Analyze the following paragraph from an insurance policy:
>
> "In the event of an Occurrence or circumstances which could reasonably give rise to a Claim, written notice containing particulars sufficient to identify the Insured and all reasonably obtainable information with respect to the time, place, and circumstances there of, and the names and addresses of the injured and of available witnesses, shall be given by or for the Insured to the Company, or the Company's designee as stated on the first page of this policy, as soon as practicable."
>
> Is there a more concise way of stating the information while still maintaining all the legal points included?

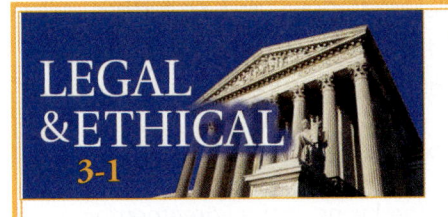

7. Sentences should be varied in length.

For quick, clear, easy reading, all sentences should be short and simple, right? Wrong! Sentences averaging around 17 words in length are considered about right for fast reading. Good sentences can be longer than 20 words or as short as 4 or 5 words for variety and emphasis. Imagine the monotony of a message in which each sentence is exactly 17 words long. The message might put the reader to sleep!

Varying sentence length can enliven writing style. A short sentence placed between two long sentences emphasizes the thought of the short sentence. A few very short sentences help to give the message "punch." Too many short sentences, one after another, can make a letter choppy. Look at the following examples:

> **NOTES**
> **Sentence Variety**
> Vary the length of sentences.

CHOPPY: We received your shipment of February 18. It contained four boxes of designer swimwear, Stock No. 1187. There was one box each in Misses sizes 8, 10, 12, and 14. But we ordered four each in Junior sizes 5, 7, 9, and 11. You can see this on the copy of the order, which is enclosed.

STRONG: Your February 18 shipment of four boxes of designer swimwear, Stock No. 1187—one each in Misses sizes 8, 10, 12, and 14—arrived today. However, the shipment should have consisted of four each in Junior sizes 5, 7, 9, and 11, as shown on the enclosed copy of the order.

Even more irritating to readers than the short, choppy sentence is the long sentence that rambles on and on. This writing fault also hinders readability. In the following example, the writer has jumbled the ideas to the point that the sentence must be reread—perhaps several times—to make any sense:

RAMBLING: In reply to your letter of March 1, we desire to enter it upon the record that, out of our six (6) percent commission to be paid to us by the Colbys for making sale of this property for them, we agree to pay you a commission of three (3) percent of the sale price, amounting to $3,000, as a service to you and as compensation for the

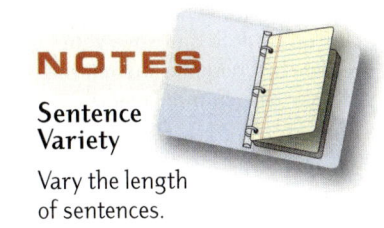

Developing Sentences and Paragraphs

work and expense of closing the sale, and we further agree that no portion of this charge shall be assessed against or paid by the purchaser.

The following example is much easier to read:

STRONG: I want to put on record the terms of the agreement you asked about in your March 1 letter. Our commission for selling this property is to be paid by the Colbys. We agree to pay you a commission of three (3) percent of the sale price, amounting to $3,000, at the closing. We further agree that no portion of this amount shall be charged to the purchaser.

Lengthy sentences result from using too many dependent clauses or from overusing the words *and, or,* and *so.* Avoid these two careless writing habits when your goal is clear, effective communication.

The *And* Habit. The *and* habit, which leads to run-on sentences, is illustrated in this excerpt from a business letter:

WEAK: We presently employ 93,466 persons at 11 sites in the greater Houston area, and this makes us the third largest private employer in the area, and we hope you will see fit to include these figures in your brochure, and we thank you for your cooperation.

You can usually correct this kind of error by eliminating some of the *ands* and breaking up the run-on structure into several sentences. Sometimes, rephrasing the ideas or putting them in the form of a clause makes the new sentences more varied and interesting. Is the following example better?

STRONG: With 93,466 employees at 11 sites in the greater Houston area, Van Buren Manufacturing is the third largest private employer in this area. We would appreciate your including these figures in your brochure.

Instead of the phrase *and so,* use transitional words such as *therefore, consequently,* and *accordingly* to connect clauses:

WEAK: Our warehouse in Seattle stocks the Z-45 gasket, and so the manager there has agreed to ship one to you.

STRONG: Our warehouse in Seattle stocks the Z-45 gasket; therefore, the manager there has agreed to ship one to you.

The Dependent-Clause Habit. Chains of dependent clauses produce confusing sentences. A series of overlapping clauses, each hanging on to the one before, introduces new ideas and expands previous ideas so fast that the

---

Thinking Cap 3.6

Discuss: How can the following confusing message be improved?
We have asked our representative, Mrs. Beth Zimmerman, to make an appointment to meet with you to discuss ways to keep your life insurance policies up to date and save you money by changing the method of your premium payments.

NOTES

Use Connectors

Use transitional words to connect clauses.

reader can barely grasp one idea before the next one arrives. Examples of this type of writing are often seen in legislation and legal documents.

Notice all the clauses introduced by the word *which* in this long sentence from a memo:

WEAK: Ms. Jamie Kerr will take Atlantic Air Flight 376 at 4:15 p.m., which should arrive in Omaha at 6:10 p.m., which means that you should plan to meet her and accompany her to the hockey awards banquet, which begins at 7:30 p.m.

Breaking the main ideas into sentences helps the reader understand the information in the message more easily, such as in the following example:

STRONG: Ms. Jamie Kerr will arrive in Omaha at 6:10 p.m. on Atlantic Air Flight 376. Please plan to meet her and accompany her to the hockey awards banquet, which begins at 7:30 p.m.

Vary your usage of short words, long words, short sentences, and long sentences. Generally, avoid using too many of any one element in your writing.

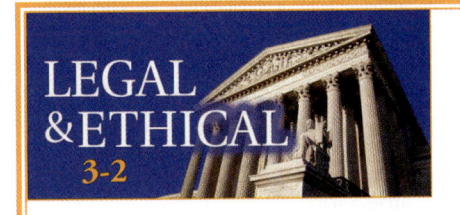

LEGAL & ETHICAL 3-2

Legal Ease. In legal writing, one sentence often consists of several phrases and clauses. Analyze the following paragraph from an actual mortgage note:

"The undersigned is given the privilege of prepayment in any amount at any time without penalty, provided that if the undersigned sells her residential property in the City of McFarland, Wisconsin, at any time during the term or the extended term of this note, the entire net proceeds of such sale shall be applied on account of the interest and principal then due on this note, which shall then be fully due and payable as to any remaining unpaid balance unless otherwise agreed by the holder hereof."

What is the paragraph actually conveying? Is there a better way to word this paragraph and still maintain the legal information required?

---

8. Sentences should be varied in structure.

We have already seen that a long string of very short sentences makes for choppy writing, that a sequence of very long sentences makes reading difficult, and that sentences all the same length make a letter boring to read. Another shortcoming that affects the reader's reaction is identically constructed sentences. A series of sentences having the same construction becomes monotonous and may seem to talk down to the reader.

Besides varying the length of your sentences, you should also vary their structure and pattern. One way to achieve variety in your writing is with different sentence beginnings. Since the way you begin a sentence usually determines the pattern for the sentence as a whole, concentrating on the beginnings is a logical way to control sentence patterns.

You can also vary the structure of your sentences by utilizing a combination of simple, compound, complex, and compound-complex formations. To review these formations, see pages 50–51.

Developing Sentences and Paragraphs

NOTES

Natural Flow

Sentences should flow naturally.

9. Sentences should fit together naturally.

Just as the words in a sentence should be arranged for smooth reading, so should the sentences in a message. Each sentence should smoothly follow the previous one and flow naturally to the next one. Similarly, one paragraph should lead naturally to the next paragraph to guide the reader from one central thought or point to the next. In writing sentences that fit together smoothly, you will find that it helps to (1) refer in some way to the preceding sentence and (2) use transitional words and phrases, or connectives.

Connectives. Some examples of transitional words and phrases include those shown in the following chart:

Transitional Words and Phrases	
also	likewise
as	moreover
as a result	neither . . . . nor
because	next
but	on the other hand
consequently	otherwise
either . . . . or	previously
first (second, etc.)	rather
for example	similarly
for instance	then
however	therefore
in addition	thus
in comparison	unlike
in contrast	while
in this way	

In the following example, the sentences are clear but are poorly connected to one another:

> Your proposal has a great deal of merit. A number of questions need to be answered. A comprehensive market research program should result in an appropriate solution.

Adding a connective ties the thoughts together:

> Your proposal has a great deal of merit. Although many questions must still be answered, we should be able to determine an appropriate solution through a comprehensive market research program.

Without connectives, you risk leaving the reader guessing about the relationship between the statements in your message.

POORLY CONNECTED SENTENCES: We agree with many of the suggestions in your report. We shall put some of them into effect immediately. We shall delay action on the remainder and get reports from other sales representatives.

Thinking Cap 3.7

Discuss: How can the following sentences be improved? You were right when you suggested that your March statement was not correct. A correction is forthcoming on your next statement. The error occurred because a payment you made on February 28 had not been credited to your account before the March statement was printed.

IMPROVED SENTENCE CONSTRUCTION: We agree with many of the suggestions in your report and will, therefore, put those into effect immediately. After we have studied reports from other sales representatives, we will decide what to do about your other suggestions. (The word *will* is more often used in modern communications than the word *shall*, and the two have slightly different meanings.)

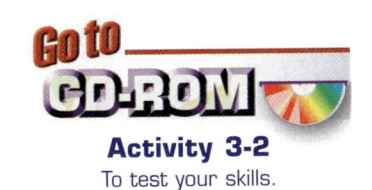

Go to CD-ROM

Activity 3-2
To test your skills.

Checkpoint 3.2

Select the more effective sentence or sentences in each of the pairs below. Explain your choices.

1. a. *The results of the survey will be released, by January 3.*
   b. *The results of the survey will be processed by January 3.*

2. a. *Before signing the contract, look at the conditions listed on page 9, which explain that the company will not reimburse you for certain expenses. These expenses include photocopying and mileage.*
   b. *Before signing the contract, look at the conditions listed on page 9, which explain that the company will not reimburse you for certain expenses, which include photocopying and mileage.*

3. a. *In your e-mail yesterday, you requested that I double-check the number of invitees to attend the luncheon tomorrow. Twenty-three people will be attending the luncheon tomorrow.*
   b. *Twenty-three people will be attending tomorrow's luncheon.*

DEVELOPING AND ARRANGING PARAGRAPHS

After choosing words and combining them into sentences, the next step in building your message is grouping the sentences into paragraphs. A **paragraph** is made up of one or more sentences that make a single point or relate to a central theme. The main function of a paragraph is to make reading easier by grouping sentences in a way that effectively conveys meaning. Organizing paragraphs deserves the same care that is given to choosing words and structuring sentences.

NOTES

The Main Idea

A paragraph is a group of sentences relating to one central idea.

Business letters usually have one major purpose or cover one major subject consisting of several items or parts, each of which is developed into a paragraph. Writing a business letter, then, is a matter of identifying the major subject or purpose and deciding on the points that make up that subject or purpose.

Determining how to organize the points—the paragraphs—in the most appropriate order is the next step. Even when a letter deals with more than one major subject, its organization need not be too difficult. Begin by identifying each of the major subjects you will discuss and the items or parts that make up each subject. Then put the ideas and sentences into the order

Developing Sentences and Paragraphs

NOTES

Paragraph Unity

Unity in a paragraph means that all sentences relate to one topic.

NOTES

Summing It Up

A topic sentence summarizes the main idea of the paragraph.

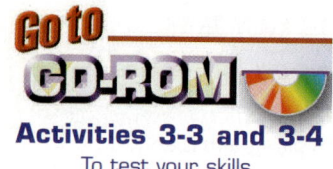

Go to CD-ROM

Activities 3-3 and 3-4
To test your skills.

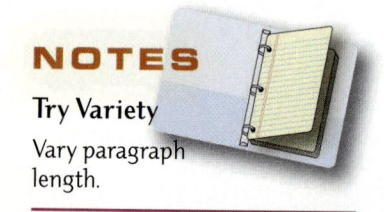

NOTES

Try Variety

Vary paragraph length.

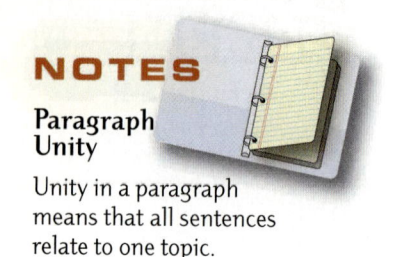

most likely to achieve your purpose. In order to develop good paragraphs, you will need to address the following concepts:

- Unity
- Length
- Emphasis
- Coherence

Paragraph Unity

Unity in a paragraph exists when all the sentences in the paragraph relate to one topic. Unity is important because a paragraph containing unrelated ideas confuses the reader. To obtain unity, include only relevant material and exclude all irrelevant material. Ask yourself, "Is this word, this sentence, this paragraph essential to the development of my main thought?" Remember, each paragraph should contain one part of the major subject.

One step in achieving unity in a paragraph is to identify the topic sentence. The **topic sentence** is the sentence that expresses the main idea of the paragraph. The topic sentence is usually found at the beginning of the paragraph, but it may appear at the end or in the body of the paragraph. The other sentences in the paragraph should develop and support the main idea found in the topic sentence.

Each paragraph should contain only one topic sentence. When you introduce a new topic, you need to start a new paragraph. By starting a new paragraph, you prepare the reader for the shift from one phase of the general subject to another. The unity of a paragraph may also be affected by the number of sentences within the paragraph. If you limit the number of sentences you use, you are likely to focus on the main idea and have a more unified paragraph.

Paragraph Length

In effective written communications, the length of paragraphs should be varied. Paragraph length is perhaps more important in business letters than in any other written communication. Because most people are so busy that they simply do not have time to wade through a series of long, rambling paragraphs, they may merely skim a line or two in each paragraph. Using short paragraphs of a few sentences in combination with longer paragraphs will give emphasis to your main ideas and keep the reader's attention. The longer the paragraphs the more likely the reader will skim the paragraphs looking for the main ideas.

Short paragraphs can, as a rule, be read faster than long paragraphs. Also, most readers like the breaks that white space provides. At times, a paragraph as short as one sentence or one line may be effective. Remember, though, that too many short paragraphs—just like too many short sentences—give a choppy effect and may make the reader feel that the page is crowded with ideas.

66   Chapter 3

You can tell that a longer paragraph is appropriate when, after editing, you decide that the last sentence of the paragraph is still on the same topic as the first sentence. In this case, breaking the paragraph into two or three paragraphs would destroy its unity.

In both short and long letters, arranging paragraphs effectively can improve a letter's appearance and readability. A short letter, for example, should be broken into two paragraphs, even when the letter is only two or three sentences long. A one-paragraph letter rarely looks attractive, and it may give your reader the impression that you did not care enough to write more than a few lines.

In contrast, in a long letter, varying the length of paragraphs is important. One-sentence and two-sentence paragraphs tend to stand out in a letter, especially if longer paragraphs precede and follow. Consequently, shorter paragraphs attract the reader's attention and signal "This is important." Use these very short paragraphs to emphasize important ideas.

At the same time, if any paragraph runs over eight lines, you should consider breaking it into two or three short paragraphs. Think of reasonably short paragraphs in a business letter as varying from two to eight lines, with an average length of four or five typewritten lines.

Opening and closing paragraphs should be shorter than the average paragraph. Brief opening and closing paragraphs give a letter a brisk, businesslike appearance.

Since a reader may hesitate to wade into a long, solid mass of words, a short opening paragraph is especially important. A two-, three-, or four-line opening paragraph invites the reader to start reading. Similarly, by using a short closing paragraph, you can often stress the one idea that you want to leave with the reader.

NOTES

Keep It Short
Keep opening and closing paragraphs short.

STRONG OPENING:	Yes, Mrs. Bloome, you are entitled to a three (3) percent discount on your first order.
STRONG CLOSING:	To get your copy of our free brochure, just fill in the enclosed postpaid card and return it.

Emphasis

Effective paragraph **emphasis** means giving the important points in your message special prominence so that your reader will know that these points are important. Paragraph emphasis can be achieved by position, proportion, repetition, balance, length of paragraphs, sentence structure, and mechanical techniques.

Position

Put an important word, phrase, or clause at the beginning or the end of a sentence, of a paragraph, or of the whole message. The beginning and ending are the strongest locations within a sentence or paragraph, with the beginning being the stronger. Likewise, as we have discussed earlier, the most important location in a letter is the opening and the second most important is the closing.

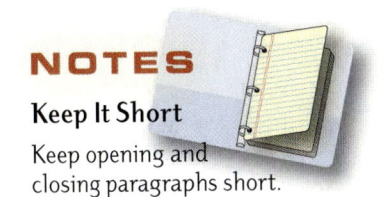

Developing Sentences and Paragraphs

Usually, the topic sentence is at the beginning of the paragraph. However, the topic sentence may be at the end of the paragraph and may be used to summarize the main point. Sometimes the topic sentence may be found within the body of the paragraph.

Proportion

The most important point in the message usually occupies the most space. Do not clutter a letter with trivial details.

Repetition

Repeating key words and phrases and using parallel sentence structure throughout a paragraph can provide emphasis. You must be cautious when using repetition since it can decrease the effectiveness of the message when it is overused. Here is an example of repetition used effectively:

> By using the new vocabulary builder, *you will discover how* to find the right word and how to avoid hackneyed words. *You will discover how* to increase your word power and how to put that power to profitable use.

Balance

Emphasis is gained by balancing words, phrases, clauses, or sentences. Do not strain for this effect or your writing will sound forced. By balance, we mean paragraphs should have a variety of words, phrases, clauses, and sentences. For example, using only one-syllable words can make your sentences unbalanced:

> The man left home and did not come back.

The following balanced sentence is effective:

> The more words you know, the better you can express your ideas.

Length of Paragraphs

Remember, paragraph length affects the emphasis—basically, shorter paragraphs have more emphasis.

Sentence Structure

When using a variety of sentence structures, remember that simple sentences are more emphatic.

Mechanical Techniques

Emphasis may be added to paragraphs by using such features as all-capital letters, boldface type, unique type fonts, underlining, highlighting, bullets, and color. Using any of these features excessively will decrease the effectiveness of the features to show emphasis. In addition, you will strengthen the emphasis in your messages if you:

- Avoid generalizations and other vague expressions.

WEAK:	As a rule, we ordinarily make an exception for such circumstances as yours.
STRONGER:	Your circumstances merit our making an exception.

- Change passive constructions to active.

  WEAK: Your check must be mailed to us immediately in order to avoid legal action.

  STRONGER: To avoid legal action, you must mail your check to us immediately.

- Eliminate general sentence openings that lack emphasis.

  WEAK: There are several new features planned for our next issue.

  STRONGER: Among the new features in our next issue will be . . . .
  OR
  Featured in our next issue will be . . . .

- Watch the placement of transitional expressions. Transitional expressions are usually more effective *after*, rather than before, an important word, phrase, or clause.

  If you have a particular problem, however, please write to me about it.

Coherence

You have learned the importance of smooth movement from one sentence to the next. When the ideas in a paragraph are linked in a logical fashion, the paragraph is coherent. **Coherence** is the result of an orderly presentation of your message. Main points should follow each other in logical order. Paragraphs should fit together to allow ideas to flow smoothly from one idea to the next.

For ease in understanding a message, the paragraphs in the letter must also fit together so that the reader will be led naturally from the opening paragraph to the closing paragraph without having to reread.

You can achieve coherence in your paragraphs by:

- Being complete and organized in your writing.
- Placing sentences in the most understandable order.
- Using appropriate connective and transitional words and phrases to link ideas together.

Two enemies of coherence in a sentence are misplaced modifiers and unclear antecedents. Remember that modifiers are phrases, clauses, or words that tell more about the meaning of another word. An antecedent is a noun or noun phrase to which a pronoun refers.

Be sure to place every modifier where it clearly modifies the word it is intended to explain or qualify. Put phrases as close as possible to the words they modify. Take special care to correctly place participial and infinitive phrases. This will avoid the dangling modifier, which may result in an unintended, possibly humorous meaning, as in the following example:

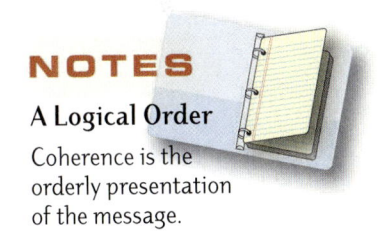

NOTES

A Logical Order
Coherence is the orderly presentation of the message.

Developing Sentences and Paragraphs

INCORRECT:	After being examined in your home, you may return the encyclopedias if not completely satisfied.
CORRECT:	After examining the encyclopedias in your home, you may return them if you are not completely satisfied.

Be sure that every pronoun has a clear antecedent. In the following example, the antecedent for the pronoun *they* is unclear.

INCORRECT:	The letters should be checked for errors, and *they* should be neatly corrected.
CORRECT:	The letters should be checked for errors and *the errors* should be neatly corrected.

The following letter is poorly organized, which results in a lack of coherence.

INEFFECTIVE PARAGRAPHING:

When the Lyons brand first appeared in our annual Brand Preference Survey five years ago, it was at the bottom of the list—in 13th position, to be exact. But, it didn't stay at the bottom for long.

Every year since, Lyons' brand preference rating has risen. And in this year's survey, it *zoomed!* Now Lyons is Number 2 in brand preference.

Lyons has passed Koch and King—and it's closing in fast on Number 1 Harker! At its present growth rate, Lyons should be Number 1 by next year.

Moving from 4.47 percent brand preference six years ago to 21.9 percent today is a growth history unmatched by any competitor in the industry! And during this period Lyons has been a major advertiser in *The American Dream*. While we won't take all the credit for Lyons' accelerated brand preference, we, too, have helped!

How would you organize the paragraphs to make this letter more effective? Use the new paragraph mark (¶) to indicate paragraph breaks that make reading easier. Now compare your version with this possible solution:

MORE EFFECTIVE PARAGRAPHING:

When the Lyons brand first appeared in our annual Brand Preference Survey five years ago, it was at the bottom of the list—in 13th position, to be exact.

But, it didn't stay at the bottom for long. Every year since, Lyons' brand preference rating has risen.

And in this year's survey, it *zoomed!*

Now Lyons is Number 2 in brand preference. Lyons has passed Koch and King—and it's closing in fast on Number 1 Harker!

At its present growth rate, Lyons should be Number 1 by next year. Moving from 4.47 percent brand preference five years ago to 21.9 percent today is a growth history unmatched by any competitor in the industry!

And during this period Lyons has been a major advertiser in *The American Dream*. While we won't take all the credit for Lyons' accelerated brand preference, we, too, have helped!

Were you successful in making the paragraph read more effectively? In the suggested solution, the letter was made more coherent by regrouping the paragraphs. Notice that the sentences are complete and placed in a more understandable order. Note also that transitional words and connectives are used to link the ideas together effectively.

Chapter 3 Summary

Effective communication is achieved when sentences and paragraphs are developed according to the principles presented in this chapter. The development of coherent messages is vital to creating effective business communication. The four basic sentence structures provide for clarity, variety, and emphasis in your writing. Concentration on paragraph unity, length, emphasis, and coherence will result in paragraphs having an organized, effective message.

Check the paragraphs you write to see that they are related to each other and to the central theme of the message. Then polish the message until the entire message flows smoothly.

Use the "Checklist for Effective Sentences" below as a handy reference. This list presents the guidelines for constructing effective sentences.

Use the "Checklist for Effective Paragraphs" as a basic guide for organizing your sentences into paragraphs. If you forget one of the elements, you may go back to the section in the chapter and review it. Then, recheck your writing.

Complete the Worksheet Exercises and the Internet Exercises now as your instructor directs.

✔ CHECKLIST FOR EFFECTIVE SENTENCES

Sentences Should:

- Contain only one idea. _____
- Contain one complete thought. _____
- Use the active voice. _____
- Be grammatically correct. _____
- Be punctuated correctly. _____
- Be concise. _____
- Be varied in length. _____
- Be varied in structure. _____
- Fit together naturally. _____

✔ CHECKLIST FOR EFFECTIVE PARAGRAPHS

Check Paragraphs for:

- One main idea only _____   emphasis _____
- unity _____   coherence _____
- length _____

Developing Sentences and Paragraphs

Communication at Work

The Longaberger® Company

Newark, Ohio

It was a wild idea—a giant basket-shaped building to serve as the home office for the Longaberger Company. Founder Dave Longaberger had always been unconventional. Since 1973, he had built a company that sold millions of dollars worth of high-quality handmade baskets directly to consumers through a network of independent sales associates. In 1997, his wild idea for his company's headquarters became reality and an icon that symbolized his unconventional business wisdom.

The seven-story building, shaped like a woven market basket, sits on a twenty-five acre campus in Newark, Ohio. Two upright handles arch above the roof. Each handle weighs seventy-five tons and is heated in winter to prevent ice from forming.

Innovation, vision, and strong leadership set Dave Longaberger apart as he built his company. But is that all it took? What about communication? What role does it play in the success of a company like Longaberger?

Two Longaberger employees talk about the importance of communication in their jobs.

> *". . . solid written communication skills are really essential to most any position in business today."*

Rachel Mackey, Senior Employee Communications Representative

Longaberger employs more than 7,000 people at several different sites. That's a large number of people who need information about benefits enrollment, employee orientations and training, technology, and other company policies. As Senior Employee Communications Representative, Rachel Mackey, 25, makes sure Longaberger employees get the correct information.

Communicating with so many employees can be challenging. "Some segments of the employee audience may be accustomed to terminology that other segments aren't," Rachel explains. "We need to make sure we use language that conveys what we mean and is received in the way we intend it."

Rachel, who has a Bachelor's degree in journalism, says, "As communications professionals, we naturally place a high priority on the basic writing communications skills of proper spelling, punctuation, and grammar, while allowing for a natural amount of stylistic differences."

She adds, "Even beyond working within communications, solid written communication skills are really essential to most any position in business today."

Once Rachel has the right words, she has to find the right method of communicating the message. Increasingly, e-mail is the method of choice. "When I need to communicate a fairly complex issue to a large group of people, I find it's best to do so in writing, and usually that's e-mail for me, and, less frequently, a written memo," says Rachel.

Communication at Work

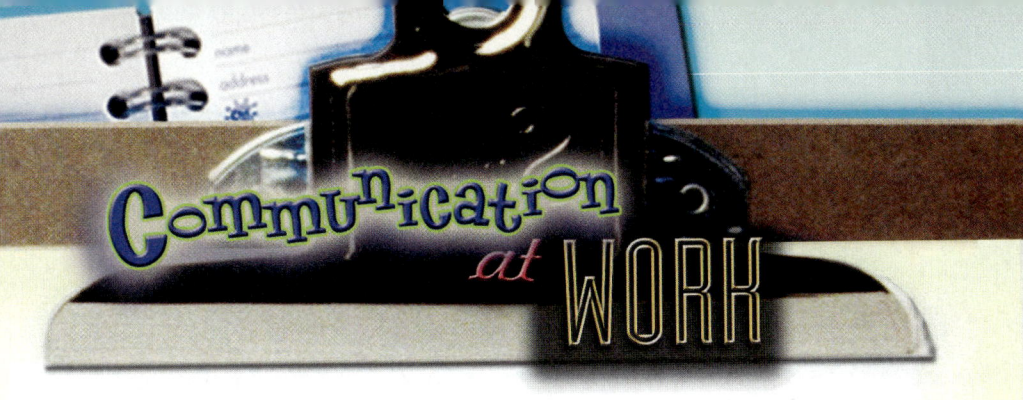

Mary Kaufmann, Director of Sales Field Relationships

Mary Kaufmann, the director of Sales Field Relationships at Longaberger, echoes Dave Longaberger's philosophy of "Listen, Learn, and Lead" when she says, "I have learned to listen a whole lot more and talk a whole lot less."

Mary, who is 36 and has an MBA, is responsible for developing ways of strengthening the relationship between the company and its sales associates and customers. She is the liaison, or link, between the company and the independent sales directors.

Mary, like Rachel Mackey, relies heavily on technology for communicating. As she sees it, modern technology saves her valuable time. "Technology has changed the way we work. We use e-mail and voice mail so much now," she says. "In the past if we had to make a decision on a program change, we would pull everyone into a room and talk it through.

"With deadlines and so much to do, we don't always have time to meet. Now, I leave a voice mail for the right people and ask them to call my assistant to give her their input. She types up everyone's input and sends it out for all to see."

With less time taken up by meetings, "we are less connected personally and have less chance to catch up on the personal relationship-side of people at work. To stay connected, I walk the floor and make a point to invite people to lunch."

"Our business runs on our ability to talk to each other in groups large and small," says Mary. "It is very important for our people to be able to communicate clearly." "And honestly," she adds, "we have found that people care more about hearing the simple truth than polished language or words."

Some people might consider that a wild idea.

> 66 . . . Our business runs on our ability to talk to each other in groups large and small, . . . 99

Discuss

1. In a large company such as Longaberger, if you wanted to send a message to an individual who may not have a computer, what would be the best way to make contact?

2. What are some of the benefits and drawbacks of sharing information over e-mail as opposed to sharing it in meetings?

The Longaberger Home Office is a registered trademark of The Longaberger® Company.

Chapter 3
Online Exercises

Objective:
These online activities will introduce you to the use of online newspapers.

Go to **bcw.glencoe.com,** the address for the *Business Communication at Work* Web site, and select Chapter 3. Next, click on Online Exercises. You will see a list of Web site links that will bring you to different online newspapers.

Activity 3.1

1. Select one of the online newspaper Web sites to visit.
2. Key *telecommunications* in the **Search** box (some Web sites may use an **Enter Word** box).
3. Select an article about *telecommunications* that interests you. Print the article by clicking on the File menu and selecting Print. Click OK.
4. Search for articles that contain the following telecommunications terms: *cellular, modem, voice mail.* Select one article for each term that interests you and best relates to telecommunications. If a term is not listed in the newspaper Web site you selected, return to the *Business Communication at Work* Web site and select another. Once you've located each word, make a printout of each article.
5. Read each printout. Look for the following items in each sentence and paragraph: active voice, subject and verb agreement, independent and dependent clauses, parallel construction, and paragraph arrangement. Note on each article any errors in sentence and paragraph structure.
6. On a piece of paper, write a paragraph discussing the different sentence and paragraph structures in each article. Make sure you use correct sentence and paragraph structure in your writing.
7. Write your name on the front of each printout and your paper. Hand it in to your instructor.

Activity 3.2

1. Select one of the online newspaper Web sites to visit that is different from the site you selected in Activity 3.1.
2. Read the different options available at the newspaper Web site. Use the article to link to an article on a major current event that interests you.
3. Print the article by clicking on the File menu and selecting Print. Click OK.
4. Working from the printout, underline two examples of each of the four types of sentences. Above each sentence, identify the type. Use the following abbreviations: *S* (simple), *CMPD* (compound), *CMPLX* (complex), *CC* (compound-complex).
5. On the back of your printout, write a paragraph discussing the use of emphasis in the article you selected. Consider the following elements: position, proportion, repetition, balance, length of paragraphs, sentence structure, and mechanical techniques.
6. Write your name on the front of the printout, and hand it in to your instructor.

CHAPTER 3 WORKSHEETS

NAME _____ DATE _____

PRACTICE 1

Using Active Voice

Instructions: Underline the simple subject once and the verb twice in each of the following sentences. In the space provided, indicate whether the sentence is written in active voice (AV) or passive voice (PV). Rewrite the passive voice sentences in the active voice.

1. The express package was delivered by the mail carrier. 1. _____

2. The supervisors recommend their staff for promotions. 2. _____

3. Donations for the community fund raiser will be collected by Jamie Sheridan. 3. _____

4. On the Friday preceding Memorial Day, only 11 members were present at the weekly staff meeting. 4. _____

Making Subjects and Verbs Agree

Instructions: Underline the simple subject and circle the correct verb choice in each of the following sentences.

1. The Senate (has, have) voted against further cuts in the education budget.
2. The majority of Warren's expenses (was, were) reimbursed through project funds.
3. Everyone except Doug and Linda (think, thinks) that we should continue the investigation.
4. Jacobson & Wright (is, are) a famous manufacturing company in our state.

Identifying Independent and Dependent Clauses

Instructions: In the following sentences, underline each independent clause with one line and each dependent clause with two lines.

1. Patients receive advice which influences their decision to have a living will.
2. Our San Francisco personnel will be asked to relocate to Los Angeles, but the closing of our Dallas and Houston offices will cause approximately 75 layoffs.
3. Be sure to ask for permission from each of your references before you prepare the final draft of your résumé.

PRACTICE 2

Using Parallel Construction

Instructions: Rewrite the following sentences to make them parallel.

1. Megan takes piano lessons, is a member of the gymnastics team and reads novels.

Developing Sentences and Paragraphs 75

CHAPTER 3 WORKSHEETS

NAME _____ DATE _____

2. Her morning schedule consisted of stops at the florist, bakery, garage, and to pick up dry cleaning.

3. Jerry applies the rules fairly and is consistent.

Improving Weak Sentences

Instructions: These examples from business letters include sentence fragments and awkward, choppy, two-idea, or wordy sentences. Rewrite them on the lines provided, adding appropriate punctuation.

1. After giving it careful consideration, the trip was approved by Ms. McDonald. (NOTE: Use active voice.)

2. In the event your choice has been sold out. Your check or money order will be cheerfully refunded. (NOTE: Eliminate wordiness, sentence fragment.)

3. I should appreciate it very much if you would restamp the endorsement on that particular check and if possible forward the check to us and of course we shall return it for your files upon verification. (NOTE: Eliminate wordiness and run-on sentence.)

Paragraphing a Letter

Instructions: Read the following letters and decide where paragraph breaks would be most effective. Use the new paragraph (¶) mark to indicate appropriate paragraph breaks.

1. Dear Mr. Blakely: Because the law stipulates that the owner of a sole proprietorship and his or her business are one, the owner is personally responsible for the obligations of the business. If you, as a sole proprietor, incur a debt, it makes no difference whether it is a business debt or a personal debt; you are fully liable in either case. A business debt will jeopardize your personal assets; a personal debt will jeopardize your business. The nature of your business creates several problems that are best solved through insurance. For example, to experience the challenge of being in business for yourself, you are paying a price in terms of sacrificed benefits. While you are aware of these problems, you need an experienced insurance agent to help you find solutions. I would like the opportunity to provide you with the type of security benefits that you would have as an employee. I will call you next week to discuss the many benefits available to you through our sole proprietorship insurance programs. Sincerely,

CHAPTER 3 WORKSHEETS

NAME _____ DATE _____

2. Dear Mr. Hanson: Your first issue of *Green America* should arrive next week. The feature article should be very helpful to you, Mr. Hanson, because it gives the results of a study on environmental hazards on vacant real estate. The study was conducted over a three-year period in major metropolitan areas of the U.S. In future issues, such noted environmental experts as Daniel Borum and Jacqueline Floyd will be interviewed extensively regarding ways landowners can appropriate funds for cleanup of hazardous waste sites and ways to communicate effectively with the Environmental Protection Agency. Each issue also contains briefs of the latest rulings by the EPA as well as cost-effective measures to limit landowner liability. A new feature is a question-and-answer column which will allow you, as a subscriber, to submit questions to a panel of experts in the industry. We know that you will enjoy reading each issue of *Green America,* and that it will be as helpful to you as it has been to other commercial real estate executives during the past fourteen years.
Sincerely,

PRACTICE 3

Writing Sentences

Instructions: Write sentences for each sentence structure: simple, compound, complex, and compound-complex.

1. Simple: _____
2. Simple: _____
3. Compound: _____
4. Compound: _____
5. Complex: _____
6. Complex: _____
7. Compound-Complex: _____
8. Compound-Complex: _____

Writing and Revising a Paragraph

Instructions: Write a rough draft of a paragraph.

1. Complete the sentence below and use it as the topic sentence of your paragraph.
   My ideal vacation is _____
2. Write three or four additional sentences to further describe or enhance your topic sentence.
   _____
   _____
   _____

3. Rewrite your draft of your paragraph. Review your paragraph by reflecting on the principles you have learned in this chapter. Make any corrections or additions. Use the checklist to evaluate your writing.
   ____ Unity _____
   ____ Length _____
   ____ Emphasis _____
   ____ Coherence _____

Developing Sentences and Paragraphs

CHAPTER 3 WORKSHEETS

Name _____ Date _____

PRACTICE 4

Business Letter Analysis

Instructions: From the portfolio of letters that you are collecting, select a business letter. Analyze the business letter according to the principles and techniques presented in this chapter. Complete the following form, which also includes principles and techniques from Chapters 1 and 2.

Did the writer follow the nine guidelines for writing effective sentences?

	Yes	No		Yes	No
Contain only one idea	___	___	Be concise	___	___
Contain one complete thought	___	___	Be varied in length	___	___
Use active voice	___	___	Be varied in structure	___	___
Use correct grammar	___	___	Fit together naturally	___	___
Use correct punctuation	___	___			

For any guideline marked "no," note the problem(s) on the letter.

Review the paragraphs in the letter. Do the paragraphs have unity, emphasis, and coherence? What about the paragraph length—are the paragraphs usually long or short?

	Yes	No		Yes	No
Unity	___	___	Coherence	___	___
Emphasis	___	___	Length	___	___

a. What is the purpose of the letter? _____

b. Who is the intended audience of the letter? _____

c. Is the tone of the letter positive? If it is not positive, what changes should be made? _____

d. Did the writer practice the seven Cs of effective correspondence?

	Yes	No		Yes	No
Courteous	___	___	Complete	___	___
Considerate	___	___	Correct	___	___
Clear	___	___	Consistent	___	___
Concise	___	___			

e. Did the message achieve its purpose? ___ Yes ___ No

f. WORD CHOICE: Did the writer use:

	Yes	No		Yes	No
Simple words	___	___	Appropriate words	___	___
Concise words	___	___	Bias-free words	___	___
Conversational words	___	___	Correct words	___	___
Trite expressions	___	___	Specific words	___	___
Clichés	___	___	Positive words	___	___

If used, were the following used correctly?

	Yes	No
Homonyms	___	___
Antonyms	___	___
Synonyms	___	___

unit 2

Basics for Communicating Effectively

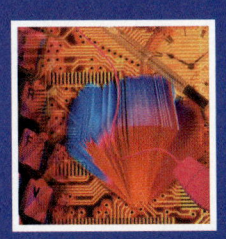

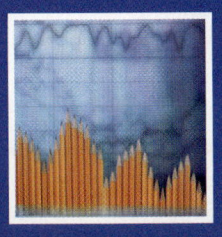

- **Chapter 4**
  Developing Listening Skills

- **Chapter 5**
  Planning and Organizing Business Messages

- **Chapter 6**
  Using Technology to Improve Communication

- **Chapter 7**
  Formatting Business Messages

CHAPTER 4
Developing Listening Skills

Objectives

After completing this chapter, you will be able to:

1. Explain the importance of listening
2. Describe the active listening process
3. Identify and interpret various nonverbal communications
4. Identify barriers to effective listening
5. Identify techniques for active listening

WORKPLACE APPLICATIONS

Cultural Diversity

Today the population of the United States is more diverse than ever before. As a result, the American workforce is more diverse as well. **Cultural diversity** refers not only to differences of culture, race, or ethnicity, but to differences in gender, age, class, education, religion, sexual orientation, physical size, or mental capabilities. In the business world, people who are different often feel excluded, isolated, or misunderstood. Bringing a culturally diverse workforce together is one of the challenges of modern business, but one that has lasting benefits.

The Rewards of Diversity

The main challenge that cultural diversity presents a business involves facing and overcoming prejudices and biases. People often fall back on **stereotypes** and assumptions that keep them from respecting their coworkers and from communicating effectively. Assumptions, such as thinking that a pregnant coworker will not be able to carry her fair share or that an older coworker will not be innovative, interfere with the flow of communication in the office. One way to break down obstacles is the deliberate use of good speaking and listening skills, no matter whom you are speaking with or listening to. Listening with respect, avoiding preconceptions, and using **inclusive language** are strategies that help foster a sense of mutual respect among coworkers.

When cultural diversity in the workplace is valued and respected, the benefits are enormous. A company that respects all of its workers creates a loyal and confident community whose members will work together to solve problems and grow the business. A culturally diverse business is attractive to potential employees with a wide range of interests, strengths, and backgrounds, which in turn helps the company gain access to new markets and form strong ties to the community in which it is based. A successful company meets the challenges that cultural diversity presents and turns them into advantages.

Thinking Critically

Situation: After a staff meeting, you have lunch with several new coworkers. During lunch, your coworkers complain of feeling that their voices are not heard during meetings, which are run by a manager who has been with the company for twenty years.

Ask Yourself: You have been with the company for five years. What advice would you offer your coworkers? What could you do to make your coworkers feel more included at meetings?

> *We were given two ears but only one mouth. Some people say that's because we should spend twice as much time listening as talking. Others claim it's because listening is twice as hard as talking.*
> —**Unknown**

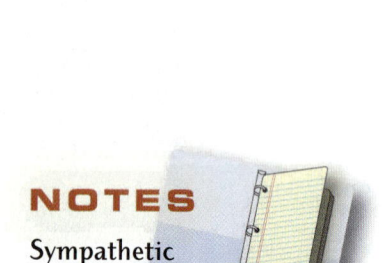

Have you noticed that you can say the same thing to three different people and have it interpreted three different ways? Have you ever found yourself saying to someone else, "I didn't hear you say that" or "I didn't know THAT is what you meant?" When you listen to someone, do you give that person your full attention or do you "fade in and fade out" while they are talking to you? How do you communicate as a listener? Indeed, many communication problems are the result of poor listening skills.

The greatest amount of time spent in communicating is devoted to listening. Communication studies reveal that you spend about 80 percent of your waking hours communicating and at least 45 percent of that time listening. Listening is the most frequently used method for gaining information. Even though the amount of time spent listening is great, little time is devoted to developing effective listening skills. Many people seem to feel that listening comes naturally; after all, they have been listening all their lives—they were born with listening skills. Also, they tend to equate listening with hearing.

Just as with written correspondence, when you read very carefully to determine exactly what the writer means, you need to listen very carefully to determine what the speaker means. You would not answer a letter after only reading the first paragraph. However, many times in listening, we start thinking about our answer or our comments before the individual who is talking to us has finished speaking.

When you listen, you take in information from the sender, and you respond by acknowledging that you are listening. Your acknowledgement encourages the speaker to continue communicating. This process needs to be done in a nonjudgmental and empathetic manner.

NOTES

Sympathetic Ear

Effective listening is nonjudgmental and empathetic.

UNDERSTANDING THE IMPORTANCE OF LISTENING

Listening is a vital skill in the business environment because it is one of the primary means of interacting with other people. Lack of communication is often cited as the reason for unnecessary problems within the business environment. These problems may include misunderstandings, misconstrued instructions, misinterpreted information, hurt feelings, damaged relationships, humiliation, embarrassment, hostility, and frustration. In contrast, effective listening can lead to a more collaborative environment, the creation of new ideas, better problem solving and decision making, improved relationships, fewer errors and conflicts, and reduced stress.

In analyzing reasons for miscommunication, it is important to note that often it is the messenger who is blamed for not communicating effectively. In reality, the problem may lie with the receiver who may not have been listening. The receiver may have *heard* the messenger, but may not have really *listened* to the messenger.

Your success in the business world is dependent on how effectively you listen to others, such as your supervisors, coworkers, employees, and customers. Much of the information needed to do your job comes to you in verbal form. Effective listening aids you in:

- Gaining new information and ideas
- Making decisions
- Understanding, clarifying, and resolving issues and problems, and
- Developing relationships, cooperation, and teamwork.

Defining Active Listening

Often when people talk to each other, they are distracted or preoccupied with other thoughts. Thus, they do not listen effectively. The key to effective listening is to become an **active listener**—focusing on the message from the speaker's point of view. In order to achieve this, let us look at what is meant by "listening" and by "focusing on the message from the speaker's point of view."

It is important to understand that there is a difference between merely "hearing the words" and "listening for the message." For example, have you ever been in a class where the instructor asked the class to turn to page 56 and within a minute or so a student asked "what page did you say"? That student heard the instructor; the student just wasn't listening. As this situation points out, listening and hearing are not the same thing. Just because your brain understands the words spoken does not mean that your mind will understand the meaning of those words.

Hearing Versus Listening

Your brain receives messages (physical sounds) through your senses—"the hearing process." Then, your intellect, or mind, must interpret and retain those messages—"the listening process." If you do not "listen," the messages are lost. In order to listen, you must focus your attention on interpreting the message. Therefore, whereas it is true that you must hear in order to listen, it is not always true that *if* you hear, you are indeed *listening*.

Thinking Cap 4.1

Discuss: What are some techniques you could use to insure that you heard and interpreted correctly the instructions for a project?

Thinking Cap 4.2

Discuss: How can you tell when someone is not really listening to what you are communicating?

LEGAL & ETHICAL 4-1

Overpayment. Due to a mix-up, a company that purchases goods from your business has to cancel a large order. The company owner has offered to reimburse you for the money your business has already spent in expectation of the order. In a phone conversation you explain that $5,000 will cover your expenses. The company owner, who seems distracted during the conversation, agrees to that amount. But when you get the signed check a week later, you realize they have instead paid you for 5,000 units, a much larger sum. What are your legal obligations in this situation? Your ethical obligations?

Developing Listening Skills

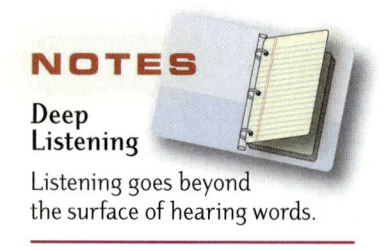

When you only hear the words, you are not really listening to understand the intended meaning of the message. You are more concerned about the words themselves, rather than their meaning or the message that the speaker is trying to convey. However, when you "listen for the message," you attempt to understand the message by going beyond the surface of hearing the words and delving into the deeper meaning of what the sender is trying to communicate.

To achieve this, the listener has to perceive the message from the sender's point of view. This is similar to the use of the "you approach" in communicating, wherein you place yourself in the other person's position and attempt to see things from that person's perspective.

In writing a letter, you try to put yourself in the "receiver's shoes" and write from the point of view of what the receiver needs and understands. Similarly, in listening, you need to put yourself in the "speaker's shoes" in order to understand the message that the speaker truly is conveying. In active listening, you, the listener, must focus your attention on the speaker.

NOTES
Deep Listening
Listening goes beyond the surface of hearing words.

THE PROCESS OF ACTIVE LISTENING

Now, let's look at how communication flows in a typical verbal conversation. Usually, the speaker begins with a statement about some problem, issue, or concern. The receiver responds to the speaker. The listener's response will serve either to encourage or discourage the speaker from continuing. If the response is perceived as favorable, the speaker will continue; however, if the response is perceived as unfavorable, the speaker may end the conversation. If the listener looks confused or puzzled, the speaker may try to clarify what was said. Or if the listener responds positively by nodding the head or by looking interested or by saying something nonjudgmental such as "uh huh," the speaker will continue the conversation.

Next, let's look at the active listening process as it relates to these types of conversations. What do you need to do to be an active listener so that you are listening rather than just hearing? As the listener, you will need to do the following:

1. Paraphrase what the speaker has said,
2. Interpret the meanings and the feelings of what you heard,
3. Analyze the nonverbal clues, and
4. Provide feedback to the speaker.

Paraphrasing the Speaker

The active listening process begins with the listener paraphrasing what the speaker has said. The listener has to perceive the message from the sender's viewpoint. Therefore, you, the listener, repeat in your own words what you think the speaker has said. You are checking with the speaker to clarify and confirm understanding; the speaker knows then whether you understand what has been said. At this stage, you may need to ask questions to clarify, such as "would you repeat . . .", "can you clarify what you mean by . . .", or "what I believe I heard you say was . . ."

When paraphrasing what has been said, you are neither judging the message nor agreeing with the speaker, you are simply stating what you think the speaker has said.

Interpreting Meanings and Feelings

The active listening process goes beyond paraphrasing the words to actively trying to grasp the meanings and the feelings of what is heard. Therefore, you need not only show understanding by paraphrasing the literal content of the message but to reflect on any underlying emotional content as well.

To help you interpret the speaker's words in terms of feelings, in addition to paraphrasing the words, you might add, "I gather that you felt confused [or frustrated or upset or saddened] when . . ." In another situation, you may respond, "I sense that you feel your integrity was questioned and that has really hurt you." Although it is critical to listen to the words that are said, it is equally important to understand the attitudes and motives behind them.

Analyzing Nonverbal Clues

Inherent in listening for meaning is the analysis of nonverbal cues, including tone of voice, gestures, and facial expressions. A good listener checks to see if the words are consistent with the body language because, although the person's verbal message may convey one thing, the gestures, facial expressions, and tone of voice may convey something else.

For example, you may say that you are extremely happy with the outcome of a project, but your facial expressions and tone of voice might indicate that you are not pleased. In another situation, an employee might tell his or her supervisor that the employee's responsibilities had not been defined and communicated. However, if the employee is shifting nervously in the chair with eyes cast downward and the body very tense while saying this, the message is undermined. The body language does not match the spoken words. It is important to remember that people's words don't always communicate what they mean, but their body language usually does. The following section on "interpreting nonverbal communication" will assist you in analyzing nonverbal clues.

Providing Feedback

Providing feedback to the speaker is an important part of the active listening process. You, as the listener, can use various verbal, nonverbal, and nonjudgmental responses to acknowledge that you understand and are interested in what the speaker is saying. Typical responses include nodding your head, smiling, and interjecting an occasional comment such as "I see," "Oh," "that's interesting," "tell me more," "uh huh," or "really," in addition to those provided in the preceding paragraphs.

Speaker:	My team failed to complete our project on time and it will cost the company big bucks. I'm afraid my supervisor will blame me.
Listener 1:	Don't worry about it. You are probably overreacting.
Listener 2:	I always get blamed for things. Why the other day . . .
Listener 3:	I wouldn't lose any sleep over it.
Listener 4:	Really (nodding head); you think your supervisor will blame you for missing the deadline?

With which of these listeners do you feel the speaker would be more inclined to continue the conversation? Which one shows the most interest in the speaker's situation? Listener 4's response would encourage the speaker to continue. When the listener is an active listener, the conversation may proceed along these lines:

Speaker:	My team failed to complete our project on time and it will cost the company big bucks. I'm afraid my supervisor will blame me.
Listener:	Really (nodding head); you think your supervisor will blame you for missing the deadline?
Speaker:	Yes, because I was the team leader. But it wasn't my fault. Jim never does his part, is always absent, and messes up everybody else on the team. I just don't know . . . [long pause]
Listener:	So Jim was a problem for the team?
Speaker:	Yes, he was. He never does what the team assigns him. That's typical on every project he is on. He's been like that for years. The supervisor never does a thing. Now it will be my fault.
Listener:	I understand that you are anxious about the situation. It is really unfair if you get blamed for Jim's negligence.

Notice how the listener gives feedback to the speaker, is nonjudgmental, paraphrases what the speaker has said, and "listens between the lines." All of these are part of active listening and result in the speaker having confidence in the listener and in continuing the conversation.

Listening Works

Active listening has several benefits—including forcing people to listen attentively to each other—that will result in fewer misunderstandings. In emotional or conflict situations, people are more likely to explain what they feel even if those feelings include fear, anger, or resentment. If people listen effectively to each other by listening for the speaker's point of view and by attempting to understand the meanings and the nonverbal communication, they will be more likely to overcome their differences and solve mutual problems.

It is much easier to listen in relaxed, friendly situations. However, when you are involved in a conflict or an emotional situation, active listening becomes crucial to solving the dispute or problem.

Checkpoint 4.1

1. Which of the following is the most difficult for you as a listener: *paraphrasing, interpreting meanings, analyzing nonverbal clues,* or *providing feedback*? Which is easiest?
2. Why is it important to interpret the meanings and feelings behind what another person is saying?
3. How are the strategies of interpreting meanings and feelings and analyzing nonverbal clues similar?

INTERPRETING NONVERBAL COMMUNICATION

Communication takes place on many levels simultaneously. **Nonverbal communication** is described as everything but words. Significant communication takes place without words. It has been estimated that between 80 and 90 percent of communication is nonverbal. Active listening involves paying attention to the nonverbal as well as the verbal messages you send to the other person.

Nonverbal communication reflects an individual's attitudes, emotions, and feelings and is demonstrated through body language, gestures, tone of voice, and facial expressions. One's body language can determine whether one makes a favorable or an unfavorable impression. You send out signals to the speaker as to whether you are effectively listening and understanding what the speaker is saying. How you use your eyes, hands, arms, and body

Developing Listening Skills

NOTES

Nonverbals

Nonverbal communication relates to body language, gestures, tone of voice, and facial expressions.

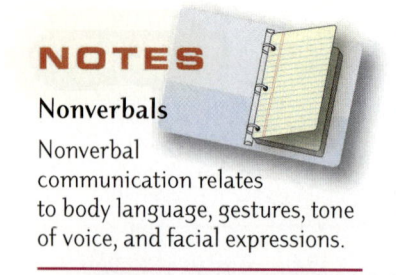

all influence how the speaker perceives your attitude. If you are looking around the room, yawning, fidgeting, or looking bored, you will be sending a negative message. However, if you maintain eye contact with the speaker, nod your head in acknowledgment, and smile when appropriate, you will be sending a positive message. The use of positive body language usually shows interest in the other person and the conversation.

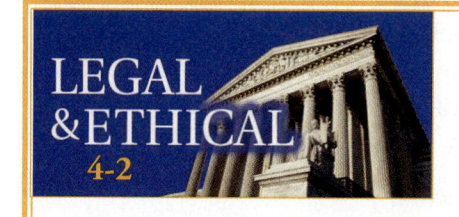

LEGAL & ETHICAL 4-2

Bargain Shopping. After much haggling, a salesperson at a local furniture store agrees to offer you a discount on a desk you are buying. The next day, when you return to pick up your purchase, it is the owner who rings up your sale. Although the owner is polite, it is clear from his tone and from the expression on his face that he is not happy with the deal and not happy with you. Is his behavior ethical? Does the owner have a legal obligation to honor the discount offered by his salesperson?

Nonverbal Messages

Problems in communicating arise when the spoken words do not match the tone of voice or the body language of the speaker. Your nonverbal cues usually reflect your true feelings more accurately. You are more likely to remember what you see rather than what you hear. Body language and facial expressions are usually more honest than spoken words. Therefore, when words and nonverbals do not match, people tend to doubt the words and believe the body language.

Thinking Cap 4.3

Discuss: Identify some situations for which the use of negative nonverbal communication may be beneficial or valuable.

You often use gestures or body movements to reinforce what you are saying. Consequently, it is important to become aware of the interpretations people give to your nonverbal communications. Table 1 lists some of the more common ways you communicate nonverbally and the meanings or interpretations that are generally associated with those actions and behaviors.

Understanding Body Language

Body language usually reflects the speaker's attitudes and emotions. When negative body language is being communicated, it is important to remember that it may have no connection to the speaker's message; it may only be the result of the person being tired or preoccupied with other matters. Therefore, it is important to note changes in body language during the communication process. If a person's body language changes during the conversation, it may be due to the conversation. Generally, positive body language is usually more reliable than negative body language.

It is also important to realize that most gestures and nonverbal communication are not universally recognized. The following list reflects the interpretations attached to the nonverbals by people in the United States. These same gestures may be interpreted quite differently in various countries and cultures. For example, the "Okay" gesture in the United States represents

88   Chapter 4

Table 1 — Interpreting Nonverbal Messages*

Nonverbal communication	Interpretation of behavior
Brisk, erect walk	Confidence; ambition
Arms relaxed	Openness
Arms folded in front of body	Resistance; defensiveness
Talking with hands	Involvement; openness
Hands behind head/leaning back	Egotism; superiority; control; power
Hands clasped behind back	Anger; frustration; apprehension
Relaxed posture	Openness; no barriers
Slouching/slumped posture	Disinterest; laziness; boredom
Negative facial expressions/frowning	Rejection; dislike
Tense body	Concern; apprehension; worry
Sitting/leaning forward	Interest; listening
Leaning on elbow/chin in hand	Boredom
Leaning away from speaker	Disinterest
Shifting in chair	Dishonesty; boredom
Good eye contact	Interest
Staring into space	Boredom
Eyes looking downward	Dishonesty
Shifting eye movement	Nervousness; untrustworthiness
Smiling	Warmth; openness; accepting
Tilted head	Interest; openness
Nodding agreement	Interest; agreement; understanding
Head down	Rejection
Shrugged shoulders	Indifference
Fidgeting	Boredom; nervousness; impatience
Yawning	Boredom; confusion
Tapping/drumming fingers	Impatience
Patting/playing with hair	Uncertainty; insecurity; anxiousness
Biting nails	Insecurity; nervousness
Doodling	Boredom
Foot swinging/tapping	Boredom
Finger pointing	Aggressiveness; anger; blame
Fists clinched	Aggressiveness; anger
Playing with an item	Boredom; nervousness

* Nonverbal communication varies by culture and country.

Go to CD-ROM
Activity 4-1
To test your skills.

Developing Listening Skills

Thinking Cap 4.4

Discuss: What are some other examples of nonverbal communication that you have observed? How may they be interpreted?

acceptance; in other countries the interpretation can be the opposite, or even obscene. Body language also varies between cultures. In spatial relationships, Americans and Europeans usually stand an arm's length apart, Asians will stand farther apart and Middle Easterners stand closer and are more touch oriented. Roger Axtell, author on international communication, recommends that when communicating with people from other cultures, one needs to be reserved in using gestures or to observe how those people use gestures, and to use gestures accordingly. [Roger Axtell, *The Do's and Taboos of International Trade*, 1993].

To convey positive messages, maintain good eye contact and posture; smile; nod and occasionally express agreement verbally to reinforce nods. Eliminate behaviors that have a negative connotation. It is important that the positive nonverbal actions be appropriate and sincere. Even positive gestures can become negative if they are exaggerated or lack sincerity.

BARRIERS TO EFFECTIVE LISTENING

Global Diversity 4.1

Body Language
Cambodians consider the head the most precious part of the body, and the feet the least sacred. Touching another person's head is considered as offensive as pointing your toes toward them during conversation or showing them the sole of your shoe or the foot. *Imagine that you are planning to travel to a foreign country on business. How would you prepare yourself to avoid behavior that might embarrass yourself or insult someone else?*

How effective are your listening skills? Do you "hear" words or do you "listen" for meaning? Do you find that you have engaged in one or more of the following activities while someone is speaking to you?

- Hearing "selectively" (hearing what you want to hear rather than what is actually said)
- Rehearsing what you are going to say next
- Failing to concentrate on what the speaker is saying
- Being distracted by the speaker's mannerisms or by outside influences
- Thinking of ways to impress the other person
- Interrupting the speaker before he/she is finished talking
- Making judgments about the speaker or about what the speaker is saying
- "Fading in and fading out" because you feel you can predict what the speaker is going to say

All of these actions inhibit your ability to be an active listener. There are many barriers that prevent us from listening effectively. These barriers can be grouped into the following: lack of concentration, assumptions, biases and prejudices, selective listening, and distractions.

Lack of Concentration

As you are listening to someone, you may find that you lose concentration and your mind starts to wander, perhaps thinking about dinner that evening, plans for the weekend, or a conversation with a friend. Your mind tends to wander as you are listening because your brain is capable of comprehending much faster than the rate at which someone speaks. In fact, it has been estimated that individuals can think four times faster than they can talk. Therefore, you can be mentally distracted by other things unrelated to the message.

You may focus on preparing your next comment rather than on listening to the speaker. You may be eager to talk and want to demonstrate your knowledge and understanding.

You may also fail to concentrate when you are preoccupied with other issues, concerns, or problems. You may be upset because of an argument that morning at home or an issue at work. Many times your emotions impede or act as barriers to your listening. You may become so consumed with an emotion that it is difficult to listen effectively.

In addition, you may just stop listening and lose concentration because of something the speaker has said that may have angered you or have led you into a different thought process.

Assumptions

Have you been in situations when you felt you knew what the speaker was going to say before he or she actually said it? Making assumptions about the communication before it begins becomes a barrier that inhibits effective listening. This is evident when a listener responds to a statement before a speaker has finished talking. The listener hears only part of what is said, assumes the rest of the message, and begins responding before the speaker has finished. Thus, the speaker's thoughts are not completed. This results in the listener forming conclusions based on partial information, and making assumptions that therefore may be incorrect.

Thinking Cap 4.5

Discuss: What types of prejudices might hinder the active listening process? How do they hinder it?

Biases and Prejudices

Judging what the other person is going to say as irrelevant, illogical, or unimportant and not valuing the speaker as a person are both barriers to listening. Prejudices and biases often interfere with what is being heard.

Prejudice toward the messenger

This barrier exists when the listener prejudges the worth or value of the person who is delivering the message. This is prejudice against the messenger, not the message. If you have a poor opinion of the speaker, you may not listen to the message. You may think, "Oh, here goes Mary again—always clueless, always talking."

Prejudice toward the message

This barrier exists when the listener perceives the message to be of low importance or a waste of time. When you, as the listener, perceive the message to be irrelevant or of no value, you will not listen effectively. You may find yourself thinking, "I have more important things to think about than this," and then allow your mind to wander off.

GLOBAL DIVERSITY 4.2

Gender Gap

In some cultures, women are considered subservient to men and have not achieved positions in the business world. *How would a female "messenger" be perceived in a business situation involving males from a culture where women are viewed as "less than" their male counterparts?*

Selective Listening

The listener who sifts through communication choosing what to consider and what to disregard is engaged in selective listening. This also happens when a listener hears only what he or she wants to hear or expects to hear, or hears only those parts that confirm his or her own opinions and views. This results in partial information, lack of understanding, and misguided perceptions.

Distractions

Interruptions, background noises, other conversations, telephones, and competing activities are just a few of the distractions that can hinder the listening process. In addition, the speaker's actions such as fidgeting, jingling coins, and clearing one's throat, also distract from listening. As the listener, you begin thinking about the *distraction* rather than the *message*.

NOTES

Listening Barriers

Lack of concentration, assumptions, biases and prejudices, selective listening, and distractions are all barriers to effective listening.

Checkpoint 4.2

Go to CD-ROM

Activity 4-2
To test your skills.

1. Suggest at least two strategies for improving one's concentration while listening.

2. From a business perspective, what are some of the benefits of overcoming biases and prejudices in the workplace?

3. What is the difference between showing prejudice against the messenger and showing prejudice against the message? Is one less fair than the other, or are both equally unfair?

ACTIVE LISTENING TECHNIQUES

Developing an active listening attitude is crucial to becoming an active listener. This attitude can assist in breaking poor listening habits and overcoming listening barriers. There are many techniques and practices that you can use to become an active listener. The following are some of these techniques and practices that will enhance your listening skills.

Prepare yourself physically by:

1. Showing alertness through your body language. Let your posture and behavior reflect your interest:

   - Face the other person directly.
   - Maintain good eye contact.
   - Lean forward slightly.
   - Be comfortable and relaxed.

2. Allowing an appropriate physical space between the speaker and you, the listener [2–3 feet is a comfortable distance for most people].

Prepare yourself mentally by:

1. Approaching the situation with an open mind and guarding against jumping to conclusions.
   - Be objective and withhold judgments and interpretations until the entire message has been presented.
   - Avoid practice of listening only for statements that support your own opinions, beliefs, or interests.
   - Avoid tuning out the speaker because you think you know what he or she is going to say next.
2. Focusing on the content of the message, not the delivery of the message or the speaker's appearance or mannerisms.
3. Listening for the meaning of the total message, both verbal and nonverbal. This includes paying special attention to the speaker's tone of voice, body language, facial expressions and other nonverbal cues as well as the spoken words, taking note of what is *not* being said as well as what is being said.
4. Keeping your emotions from influencing your responses and your interpretations of what the speaker has said.
5. Using your mental processing ability to keep you focused by concentrating on the message rather than wandering off to other topics and issues.

Prepare an environment that encourages communication by:

1. Providing appropriate feedback and responses to the speaker, both verbally and nonverbally.
2. Showing sensitivity through your choice of words in responding to the speaker. Some words automatically produce a mental barrier that impedes listening. Responding with words or phrases such as "you should . . ."; "why did you . . ."; "wrong!"; "you never . . ."; "you missed the point"; and "as usual, you . . ." may cause the speaker to stop communicating.
3. Establishing a physical environment that is void of possible distractions. This includes being aware of possible distractions and ignoring them. In addition to mentally blocking out the distractions, appropriate actions may include moving the conversation to a quieter location, turning off phones, shutting doors, or closing windows.

An active listening attitude can help tremendously in breaking your poor listening habits. When you acknowledge the other person both verbally and nonverbally, you build trust and increase rapport.

Developing Listening Skills

✔ CHECKLIST FOR LISTENING SKILLS

In Listening Situations, Are You:

	YES	NO
Alert to body language?		
Focused on the content of the message?		
Listening for what is **not** being said?		
Careful to avoid distractions?		
Providing feedback for the speaker?		
Keeping an open mind?		

Chapter 4 Summary

Often overlooked, listening plays an important role in our personal and professional lives. In business, it encourages the sharing of ideas, enhances teamwork, eliminates mistakes and misunderstandings, and reduces stress. It may impact how we connect with others more than speaking does.

Active listening requires you to understand the difference between hearing and listening and to focus on the message from the speaker's point of view. You can enhance your effectiveness as a listener by paraphrasing the speaker's words, interpreting the words for meaning, deciphering nonverbal clues, and providing feedback to the speaker. Because communication takes place on many levels, it is important to understand the influence of nonverbal communication on the communication process.

Effective listening is a skill that can be developed through practice. Although most people were born with the ability to hear, they have to develop the skill of listening.

Chapter 4

Online Exercises

Objective:
These online activities will provide you with information about cultural diversity and prejudice.

Go to **bcw.glencoe.com,** the address for the *Business Communication at Work* Web site, and select Chapter 4. Next, click on Online Exercises. You will see a list of Web site links that will bring you to different cultural diversity Web sites.

Activity 4.1

1. Select one of the cultural diversity Web sites to visit.
2. Select five articles that look interesting to you and click on them. Print each article you choose. You may need to return to the *Business Communication at Work* Web site to select your five articles.
3. Read through the articles to gain a better understanding of cultural diversity.
4. On a sheet of paper write a paragraph describing what you have learned from visiting the cultural diversity Web sites. Some questions you may consider in your paragraph include:
    a. How can listening help promote an awareness of cultural diversity in the workplace?
    b. How does an awareness of cultural diversity promote equality in the workplace?
5. Write your name on your paper and on each printout, and hand the assignment in to your instructor.

Activity 4.2

1. Select one of the cultural diversity Web sites.
2. Find the definition of *prejudice*. You may need to click on the Web site's search engine and key *prejudice* in the **Search** box.
3. Return to the *Business Communication at Work* Web site. Click on three more cultural diversity Web sites and find the definition of *prejudice.*
4. On a sheet of paper, write in your own words a definition of *prejudice* based on your readings from the various Web sites you visited.
5. Write a paragraph describing a situation in which you saw prejudice or experienced prejudice in school or your workplace.
6. Write your name on your paper, and hand it in to your instructor.

Developing Listening Skills

CHAPTER 4 WORKSHEETS

NAME _____ DATE _____

PRACTICE 1

Describe Listeners

Instructions: Respond to the following questions as directed.

1. Think of a person whom you know and whom you feel "really listens" to you and others. List things that the person does, verbally and nonverbally, that make you feel that he or she is listening to you.

   _____
   _____
   _____
   _____
   _____
   _____

2. Describe an individual whom you feel is not a good listener when involved in a conversation. List things that the person does, verbally and nonverbally, that make you feel that he or she does not listen to you or others.

   _____
   _____
   _____
   _____
   _____
   _____
   _____

PRACTICE 2

Reflect on Your Listening Skills

Instructions: Respond to the following questions as directed.

1. When in a conversation, are you an active listener? Rate yourself on the following scale: 0–5, with 0 being never and 5 being always.

   _____ I listen to the message from the speaker's point of view.

   _____ I paraphrase what the speaker has said.

   _____ I interpret the meaning and feelings in addition to the words.

   _____ I look for and analyze nonverbal clues.

   _____ I provide feedback to the speaker.

   _____ I provide positive feedback to the speaker, encouraging the speaker to continue.

CHAPTER 4 WORKSHEETS

NAME _____ DATE _____

2. Analyzing your response to the last question, list some actions you can take to improve your active listening skills.

_____
_____
_____
_____
_____
_____
_____
_____
_____
_____

3. Which of the following activities do you sometimes engage in while listening to others? Check those that apply and describe a specific situation for each.

_____ hear "selectively"

_____
_____

_____ rehearse your next comments

_____
_____

_____ fail to concentrate

_____
_____

_____ interrupt the speaker before the speaker is finished

_____
_____

_____ make judgments about the speaker before the message is communicated

_____
_____

_____ make judgments about the message before the message is communicated

_____
_____

Developing Listening Skills

CHAPTER 4 WORKSHEETS

NAME _____ DATE _____

PRACTICE 3

Observing Nonverbal Communication

Instructions: *Select a television show, such as the news, a talk show, or a drama, in which there is heavy interaction between two (or possibly among three) people. Turn off the volume of the television set. Now, watch the people and observe their nonverbal communication. Describe the nonverbal communication that takes place.*

1. Situation (interview on the news, discussion in a drama)
   _____

2. Describe the nonverbal communication given by the various participants (look for facial expressions, gestures, and body language).
   _____
   _____
   _____
   _____
   _____
   _____
   _____

3. Can you determine the tone, atmosphere, or feelings of the participants by observing only the nonverbal communication? If yes, please describe.
   _____
   _____
   _____

PRACTICE 4

Analyze Listening Skills

Instructions: *The following exercise requires three individuals. Perform the exercise three times as follows.*

1. Designate one individual to be the speaker, one individual to be the receiver, and one individual to be the observer. Because you will perform this exercise three times, each individual will be able to participate in each role.

2. The speaker for the current round selects and begins talking about one of the following topics:

   a. "Some of the greatest challenges for me in going to college are . . . because . . . ."

   b. "The most difficult things for me to cope with when working on a team or in a small group are . . . because . . . ."

   c. "The types of television shows that I find most enlightening are . . . because . . . ."

CHAPTER 4 WORKSHEETS

NAME _____ DATE _____

    d. Select a current issue either in your college, in your community, or in society in general that you feel strongly about, and provide reasons for or against it.

3. After the speaker has finished, complete the questions for your particular role in that round. The observer for the round may complete some of the questions during the role play.

4. After all of you have responded to the round in writing, discuss your observations with each other.

Speaker:

Instructions: Answer Yes or No *to the following. If* Yes, *provide an example of how the receiver achieved what is described in the statement. Then complete the rest of the questions based on your observations.*

1. Do you feel the receiver

   _____ clarified what you were saying by paraphrasing?

   _____

   _____ understood exactly what you were saying?

   _____

   _____ paid attention to the meanings and feelings you were conveying?

   _____

   _____ analyzed your nonverbal clues?

   _____

   _____ provided positive feedback?

   _____

   _____ made you feel like you wanted to continue talking?

   _____

   _____ made you feel like you wanted to end the conversation?

   _____

2. Identify some of the receiver's nonverbal communication.

   _____
   _____

3. Elaborate on any of the above answers. Then, discuss your feelings about the situation and whether you felt the receiver was actively listening.

   _____
   _____
   _____
   _____

Developing Listening Skills

CHAPTER 4 WORKSHEETS

NAME _____ DATE _____

Receiver:

Instructions: Answer Yes or No to the following. Then complete the rest of the questions based on your observations.

1. As the receiver, did you

    _____ clarify what the speaker was saying by paraphrasing?

    _____ pay attention to the meanings and feelings the speaker was conveying?

    _____ listen for total meaning; analyze the speaker's nonverbal clues?

    _____ provide positive feedback?

    _____ focus on the content of the message, not the delivery of the message?

    _____ avoid emotional involvement?

    _____ avoid being distracted by outside influences?

    _____ keep an open mind; maintain objectivity?

    _____ remain sensitive to the words used in responding to the speaker?

    _____ refrain from interrupting the speaker?

    _____ reflect interest in the speaker through your body language?

    _____ take advantage of your mental processing power?

2. What specific actions did you take to clarify the message and to reflect the speaker's point of view?
    _____
    _____

3. What specific actions did you take to provide positive feedback?
    _____
    _____

4. Identify some of the speaker's nonverbal communication.
    _____
    _____

5. Comments: Elaborate on any of the above answers. Then, discuss your feelings about the situation and whether you felt you were actively listening.
    _____
    _____

6. What would you do differently the next time, as an active listener, to improve?
    _____
    _____
    _____

Chapter 4

CHAPTER 4 WORKSHEETS

NAME _____ DATE _____

Observer:

Instructions: Based on your observations, complete the following questions.

1. Identify some of the speaker's nonverbal communication.
   _____
   _____

2. Identify some of the receiver's nonverbal communication.
   _____
   _____

3. Identify the methods used by the receiver to provide feedback. Was the feedback positive (encouraging) or negative (discouraging)?
   _____
   _____

4. Do you feel the receiver was an "active listener?" Yes _____ No _____

5. Please discuss the reasons for your answer. You may refer to the above lists in your discussion to support your position.
   _____
   _____

6. What actions could the receiver take to improve his/her active listening skills?
   _____
   _____

PRACTICE 5

Cross-Cultural Nonverbal Communication

Instructions: Write a one-page report on nonverbal communications as used in different cultures. Select an area (or areas) of nonverbal communication, and research that area to learn of differences. You may use the Internet or your library for your research, searching under the terms of *cross-cultural communication* or *cross-cultural nonverbal communication*.

_____
_____
_____
_____
_____
_____

Developing Listening Skills

CHAPTER 5

Planning and Organizing Business Messages

Objectives

After completing this chapter, you will be able to:

1. Identify the categories of communications and explain when they are used
2. Analyze situations to select the best approach when responding to communications
3. Apply the direct approach in preparing positive communications
4. Apply the indirect approach in preparing negative or bad news communications
5. Apply the persuasive approach in preparing sales letters or other persuasive communications
6. Develop planning procedures for organizing communications

WORKPLACE APPLICATIONS

Time Management

Thanks to technology, we can do many tasks faster than ever before; however, doing something faster does not always make us more satisfied. In fact, technology often makes us feel pressured to do more in less time. **Time management** is about using your hours and minutes wisely. It means taking control of your time and spending it thoughtfully.

Know Your Strengths

The key to time management is understanding yourself—your habits, strengths, goals, and tasks. To begin, ask yourself some questions. For example, do you prefer to work alone or in groups? Are you a logical thinker (who loves math) or an abstract thinker (who loves the arts)? Do you learn better by watching or listening or doing? Do you jump right into tasks or do you procrastinate? Can you stay focused for hours or are you easily distracted? Consider your long-term and short-term goals. For instance, do you want to start your own business or work for a corporation? Once you know what you are like and what you want to accomplish, you can begin managing your time.

Choose a system that favors your habits and personality. For example, if you are a person who needs to see "the big picture," then a monthly calendar may help. If you love technology, then a **personal digital assistant** might be just what you need. Writing down a schedule is not enough, though. It must be a schedule that works for you. For instance, if you are not a morning person, then schedule meetings for the afternoons and save mornings for other things. Remember, time is not tangible, although we measure it as if it were. We actually experience time differently at every moment, depending on how we use it. Try to manage your time in a way that makes you feel satisfied, productive, and successful.

Thinking Critically

Situation: You have just been promoted to a managerial position. Now, people come to you all day with questions. Although you enjoy working directly with your staff, you find that you can't finish your own work. At the end of the day, you feel as though you have not accomplished anything.

Ask Yourself: What are some time-management solutions to your problem?

103

> *The worse the news, the more effort should go into communicating it.*
> —**Andrew S. Grove, Chairman, Intel Corporation**

Whether you are communicating face-to-face, on the phone, via videoconferences, in group meetings, or through letters, faxes, memos, reports, or e-mail, you are creating an impression of yourself and of your organization. The principles and techniques presented in the previous chapters will assist you in building your communication skills effectively—both orally and in writing.

As you continue developing your communication skills, keep these basics in mind:

- Determine the purpose of the communication.
- Identify the audience.
- Consider what your audience needs to "hear" in order for your communication to be effective.
- Develop your message in a clear, concise, correct, and logical manner.
- Maintain a positive attitude throughout the communication.

You'll use these basics as you analyze specific situations and determine how you will respond to them.

ORAL AND WRITTEN COMMUNICATION

Oral communication has definite advantages over written communication. One important advantage is that it is a more personal form of communication and is quickly transmitted. Also, oral communication provides the advantage of immediate feedback. If the communication is face to face, you will be able to observe the receiver's reaction, clarify what has been said, answer additional questions, and smooth out any misunderstandings.

With written communication, your reading and comprehension skills are important because you do not have the advantage of looking at the sender of the message. You must read carefully to be sure you understand what is being requested before you respond. However, in all communication, you must be clear, concise, and complete. You must create and transmit a positive tone. You need to look at the situation from the receiver's viewpoint—using the "you attitude." Therefore, to achieve all of these in your writing, you will need to plan your message.

PLANNING FOR EFFECTIVE COMMUNICATION

An important part of your personal preparation for communicating in the workplace includes acquiring a thorough knowledge of your organization and its policies and procedures. When you are communicating as a representative of your organization, your personal views become secondary. Your responsibility is to sincerely reflect the attitudes and policies of the organization. Even if you disagree with a policy, you are bound by it. Never make a customer or client aware of your disagreement.

Never blame another person or department for an error or an unpopular decision. Remember that you are speaking for your organization as a whole—not for yourself or solely for your own department. Your job as a business communicator is to present your organization's viewpoint in terms that your receiver can accept. To do this, you need to represent your organization in a way that shows the receiver that your organization's position is a fair one.

Armed with a thorough understanding of your organization, you are ready to plan what should be included in your communication. You do this for the same reason you make a grocery list before shopping or prepare an agenda for a meeting—so you won't forget anything. Just as a good grocery list can eliminate a second trip to the store and an agenda can prevent extra meetings, a good letter plan can prevent having to send a second letter to complete the job.

LEGAL & ETHICAL 5-1

Questioning Authority. Are you acting in an ethical manner when you support your company's policy or procedure while you personally feel that the policy or procedure is wrong?

The first step in message planning is to identify the following, which we discussed in Chapter 1:

- Purpose of the communication
- Intended audience
- Content of the communication
- Organization of the message

Determining the Purpose of the Communication

A communication has one or more of the following purposes: to request, to inform, or to persuade, as well as to build goodwill. Before you can plan an effective communication, you must determine which of these purposes you are trying to achieve. Ask yourself the following questions:

- What is the specific purpose of the communication?
- What, if anything, is being requested?
- What information must the message include?
- What response would you like it to bring?
- What is the best media to use to communicate the message?

Planning and Organizing Business Messages

As you think through the background facts of the communication you are planning, the purpose of the communication should become clear. For example, the purpose of a credit manager's writing a collection letter might be "to collect $250 from Larry DeLonge without losing him as a customer." And the purpose of Larry DeLonge's reply might be "to pay $100 on my account and promise the store the $150 balance in 30 days."

> ✔ **CHECKLIST FOR COMMUNICATION**
>
> **To Check Your Reason for Communicating, Ask:**
>
> What is the purpose? _____   What response should result? _____
>
> What is requested? _____
>
> What must be included? _____   What is the best media to use? _____

> 66 *To improve communications, work not on the utterer, but the recipient.* 99
> —**Peter Drucker, Author**

Thinking Cap 5.1

Discuss: How does Drucker's quote support the need to identify the audience and to use the "you attitude"?

Identifying the Intended Audience

The most important factor to consider when you are planning a business message is the intended audience. Ask yourself the following questions about the message's receiver:

- Who is the receiver?
- What is known about the receiver's background, knowledge, interests, and experiences?
- How does the receiver feel about the situation?
- What does the receiver need or want to hear?
- What does the receiver expect from you?
- What objections might you expect from the receiver?

The answers to these questions will assist you in putting yourself in the receiver's position and seeing things from that perspective. The more you know about how your receiver thinks and feels, the better chance you have of getting your message across. Remember, a written business message is successful only if the reader (1) reads it, (2) understands it, and (3) reacts favorably to it.

To interest and influence the receiver, you must be able to look at both your side and the receiver's side of the situation. By doing so, you can learn what kind of help the receiver expects to find in your communication.

If you are answering a letter, whether orally or in writing, review and analyze the background information contained in the letter itself before you communicate with the receiver. Be sure to read the letter carefully to learn all you can from it. Then, if you need additional facts, check your files for previous correspondence, reports from sales representatives, and other pertinent records. Then use common sense, your general business knowledge, and any specialized knowledge of your organization to decide what background facts are important and how they can best be used to make your response successful.

As you prepare all your letters, consciously practice adapting to the receiver—composing with the receiver in mind—and you'll soon master the technique. Just remember to do the following:

- Think through the situation you are writing about.
- Imagine your receiver as best you can.
- Write directly to your receiver.

Developing the Content

The purpose of a communication will determine what its basic content will be. The content will then determine what approach to take in planning the communication.

In discussing the development of a message's content, we will focus on business letters. Business letters can be roughly grouped into three categories:

1. **Positive communications**—"Yes" letters (routine/informational communications)
2. **Negative communications**—"No" letters
3. **Persuasive communications**—Sales letters

As you plan a letter, you will need to determine which of these categories is appropriate for your letter. Then, depending on the answer, you will decide on the most effective approach to present the ideas in your letter.

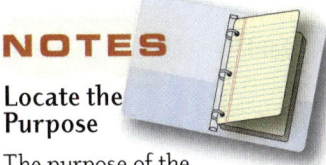

> **NOTES**
> **Locate the Purpose**
> The purpose of the communication determines the content. The content determines the approach.

> **Thinking Cap 5.2**
> **Discuss:** Do you agree with Grove's quote, "The worse the news, the more effort should go into communicating it"? Why is this statement true?

ORGANIZING THE MESSAGE

Each category of message—positive, negative, and persuasive—requires a specific approach: direct, indirect, or persuasive. As you study each approach, think of other situations in which you might write such a communication. Each approach is detailed in the table "Organization for Business Messages." (See Table 1 on page 108.)

Positive Communications

Much of the business correspondence that a communicator handles is the daily correspondence that requests or provides information. If the information to be sent is routine, simple letters are written or form letters (letters prepared for recurring situations in which only the date and the name of the receiver need to be changed) are used. Routine positive letters can be written in a straightforward manner, since they tell the reader what he or she wants to hear. This type of letter can get directly to the point; therefore, the order in which the content is arranged is called the direct approach.

> **NOTES**
> **Positive Approach**
> Positive communications require the direct approach. In the direct approach, begin with the good news.

Planning and Organizing Business Messages

Table 1 — Organization for Business Messages

The Direct Approach
(For Positive News, Including Inquiries, Requests, Good News, "Yes" Messages)

Direct Plan

Section	Description	Plan Element
Opening:	Start with what receiver wants to hear (good news) or specific information needed to make a request.	Good News or Main Idea
Middle:	Give explanation of good news or details. Ask specific questions to help receiver give answer.	Explanation or Details
Closing:	Make specific request for action tied with appreciation. Express goodwill. Resell organization and/or product or service.	Goodwill or Resale

The Indirect Approach
(For Negative News)

Indirect Plan

Section	Description	Plan Element
Opening:	Use pleasant, neutral, or relevant statement. Never start with bad news.	Buffer
Middle:	Give reasons, explanations, or facts about the negative news—tell why. Make explanation receiver-oriented and positive—tell what you can do instead of what you can't do.	Reasons and Explanations
	Give bad news after the reasons.	No—stated or implied
Closing:	Use pleasant, relevant comment to end on a positive note.	Buffer

The Persuasive Approach
(For Sales Letters and Special Requests)

Persuasive Plan

Opening:	Use relevant idea that gets the receiver's attention.	Attention
Middle:	Give explanation and description that expands opening idea and generates receiver's interest.	Interest
	State benefits that will convince receiver to take the action requested. (Mention warranties, guarantees, and enclosures. Play down cost and other possible negatives.)	Desire or Conviction
Closing:	Make courteous, specific request for action; make it easy for receiver to say "yes."	Action

The Direct Approach

The easiest and most pleasant communication task is telling your receiver *yes* or transmitting good news. In these situations, you use the **direct approach** and follow one basic rule: *Start with the good news.* Then the receiver will know immediately that your message is imparting beneficial information. The good news will put the receiver in a friendly, receptive frame of mind that will help him or her react favorably to the remainder of the message.

In the direct approach, the good-news opening is followed by a detailed explanation. This is done in a logical order with the most positive details being presented first. Be sure to provide all the information the reader needs to understand your response or take further action.

The last paragraph of the letter should build goodwill and leave the reader in a friendly frame of mind. End it with a positive statement related to the specific situation discussed in the letter. You may want to refer again to the main idea of the letter—the good news.

Examples of the routine types of correspondence that use the direct approach are the following:

- Request appointments or reservations
- Request information about products and services
- Answer *yes* to inquiries and requests
- Grant adjustments and credit
- Send goodwill messages

Whenever you can say *yes* to a receiver's request or tell your receiver something he or she will be pleased to hear, use the direct approach.

Figure 5-1 on page 110 is an example of a positive communication that shows the direct plan in action:

THE BACKGROUND	A personal banker for Hometown Bank has notified Ms. Marcia Crary that her application for a home equity loan has been approved.
THE CUSTOMER'S REQUEST	Ms. Crary had applied for a home equity loan by completing the bank's application form.
THE ORGANIZATION'S POLICY	Ms. Crary has been approved for a $10,000 home equity loan. To activate the loan, Ms. Crary needs only to write a check on the loan account. Once the check is processed, the bank will send her an acknowledgment indicating the interest rate and repayment schedule.

GLOBAL DIVERSITY 5.1

Forming Bonds

In some countries, such as Brazil, "Getting straight to the point" is considered quite distasteful. Relationships are more important than the actual communication—doing business is considered a type of social interaction. Brazilians prefer to be comfortable with each other before getting down to business. *A prospective Brazilian client is arriving in town next week to discuss a potential business arrangement with you. How do you go about planning a meeting with this client?*

Go to CD-ROM Activity 5-1
To test your skills.

Planning and Organizing Business Messages

THE LETTER'S JOB The letter should welcome Ms. Crary as a new home equity loan customer, explain how to activate the loan, give information about Hometown Bank's other services, and express pleasure in serving Ms. Crary's financial needs.

THE APPROACH Because Hometown Bank is granting Ms. Crary's request, the writer selects the direct approach.

Figure 5-1
This letter is written in the direct approach.

Hometown Bank
1234 West Bank Street, Darling, WI 53511 • Phone 608-555-8576 • Fax 608-555-8577

January 23, <YEAR>

Ms. Marcia Crary
809 S. Murray Street
Darling, WI 53511

Dear Ms. Crary:

Congratulations! Your home equity loan has been approved. You now have $10,000 available for your remodeling project, your new car, or any project for which you need additional cash.

All you need to do is write a check for the amount you need, up to $10,000, and you will activate your loan. We have enclosed a checkbook for your convenience. Once your check has been processed through our bank, we will send you an acknowledgment with the interest and repayment details.

You may be interested in the other financial services that we can provide for you. We have various types of checking and savings accounts as well as several options for retirement planning. Please call me at (608) 555-8576 for an appointment to discuss your other financial needs.

We appreciate the opportunity you have given us to serve you. We look forward to assisting you in meeting your future financial needs.

Sincerely,

Richard Swenson

Richard Swenson
Personal Banker

Enclosure

NOTES

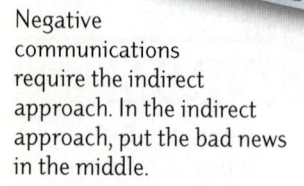

Soften the Blow

Negative communications require the indirect approach. In the indirect approach, put the bad news in the middle.

Negative Communications

The challenging or problematic communications in business are those that give the receiver bad news or refuse a receiver's request. In these situations, your goal is to help the receiver understand and accept the message. These negative communications have to be carefully prepared to avoid causing anger or loss of the reader's goodwill. An indirect approach is required when responding to these messages.

The Indirect Approach

In using the **indirect approach,** the basic rule to remember is to put the bad news in the middle. Begin a negative communication with a neutral paragraph that acts as a buffer or cushion between the reader and the bad news. If you blurt

110 Chapter 5

out the bad news in the opening of your letter, the receiver may quickly become disappointed, angry, or both. These feelings will then affect the reader's interpretation of everything else you say. If you start your letter with a refusal, for example, the reader isn't likely to accept the explanation or alternative you give next, if he or she reads it at all!

Because people would rather hear good news than bad news, a buffer paragraph helps you establish a rapport with the receiver. Beginning on neutral ground helps to prepare the receiver for a negative message and to make him or her more receptive to your explanations.

When using the indirect approach, organize your letter into the following three parts:

Opening Paragraph—Buffer. Begin your message by providing details that will help smooth the way for your unpleasant or unfavorable message. If there is anything positive in the situation or anything that you and the receiver can agree on, begin with that. For example, if nothing else, let the receiver know that he or she was right to contact you about a problem. The buffer paragraph should:

- Pertain to the subject of the message.
- Be brief and congenial.
- Maintain neutrality—not indicating either yes or no.
- Serve as the transition to the explanation.

Middle Paragraph(s)—The Reasons and the Refusal. In the middle paragraphs, present the detailed facts that will justify your negative message, beginning with your strongest reason and working down to the weakest. The negative information, or refusal, stated quickly and explicitly in clear and positive terms, should be placed immediately following this explanation.

In some instances, the refusal may be implied rather than stated explicitly. However, it is extremely important that the receiver clearly understands this part of the message. You may then follow the refusal with another reason or an alternative, if appropriate. Remember to emphasize what *can* be done rather than what *cannot* be done. Putting the refusal in the same paragraph with the reasons for de-emphasizes the refusal.

Ending Paragraph—Closing. By the end of the letter, you are past the difficult parts of stating the reasons for the negative news. You can then offer a counterproposal or alternatives to what the reader asked. Perhaps you can resell your point of view. In the ending paragraph, make sure the closing is neutral, courteous, positive, and personalized, if possible. You should *not* restate the refusal or refer again to the main idea, the negative message.

Tone is very important in all communications, but there is added emphasis on tone in negative messages. The receiver of these messages needs to feel that his or her request has been taken seriously. Therefore, these messages should be tactful and considerate and reflect a sincere interest in the receiver and respect for his or her viewpoint.

NOTES

Indirect Approach

Beginning: Give details to help smooth the way.
Middle: State negative information clearly and in positive terms.
Closing: Be courteous and positive.

Planning and Organizing Business Messages

Examples of types of messages that use the indirect approach include ones that do the following:

- Refuse appointments, claims, or reservations
- Communicate unfavorable decisions
- Turn down invitations
- Say no to inquiries and requests
- Refuse an order
- Refuse to make adjustments or give credit
- Turn down a job applicant

Because you are giving reasons for saying no in indirect approach letters, these letters are almost always longer than direct approach letters. Look at the indirect approach in action (see Figure 5-2 below).

The following example shows the indirect plan used in Figure 5-2.

THE BACKGROUND The associate dean at Bakersville College must respond to Mr. Larson, a student in the Commercial Art program who has requested receiving transfer credit from other programs.

Figure 5-2
This letter refuses the student's request. The indirect approach is required.

Bakersville College
1801 Panorama Drive • Bakersfield, CA 93305

July 18, <YEAR>

Mr. James Larson
1672 Walnut Grove Avenue
Edmund, OK 32098

Dear Mr. Larson:

You have chosen an exciting career! Your program in Commercial Art here at Bakersville College will provide you with the skills and knowledge required in this growing field. The exposure you have had through seminars to some of the areas you will be studying will be beneficial.

Our college does transfer credit from other colleges and universities that are accredited through a national organization. The courses need to have been taken for credit, and the student must have received a minimum grade of C to qualify for transfer. These standards—an accredited college and a level of individual achievement—help us to maintain the quality of our programs and courses and to treat each student equally and fairly.

Even though your experiences do not qualify for college credit, you will find they will enrich your courses and program while at Bakersville. You will have many valuable experiences to share with your fellow students.

My best wishes to you as you begin your program. If I can be of assistance to you in meeting your educational needs or concerns, please contact me directly.

Sincerely,

Jerry Butler

Jerry Butler
Associate Dean
Art Department

THE STUDENT'S REQUEST Mr. Larson has requested receiving nine credits for three of the major courses in his program. He feels that he should be able to transfer these based on seminars and noncredit courses he has attended through various career institutes and programs.

THE COLLEGE'S POLICY The college does transfer credits from other accredited colleges for courses that apply directly to the student's program and in which the student earned a minimum grade of C. The college's transfer of credit policy is applied only for credit classes. The college does not recognize noncredit courses and seminars for college credit.

THE LETTER'S JOB The letter should deny Mr. Larson's request for the conversion of his noncredit courses and seminars to college credits toward his program. The policy behind the denial should be explained: the policy treats everyone equally by providing basic guidelines for transferring credits; it requires the minimum grade of C to ensure a basic level of student competency in the subject area; it standardizes the type of institutions from which credit may be transferred (accredited colleges and universities), which helps maintain program quality; and it helps to ensure that students meet the college's program requirements and exit competencies.

THE APPROACH Since the associate dean will have to say no, an indirect approach, beginning with a buffer paragraph, is required for the response.

GLOBAL DIVERSITY 5.2

Yes Means No

In some cultures, professionals will avoid saying *no*. If a request cannot be met, they may say it is inconvenient or under consideration, or even, "Yes, but it will be difficult." These responses may mean no or probably not. Conversely, straightforwardness is an essential part of doing business in the Netherlands. Even if you find it difficult to say *no*, you will find that your Dutch counterparts will prefer and appreciate a candid reply. *How do you know when* Yes *means yes and when* Yes *means no?*

Checkpoint 5.1

1. Why is the direct approach an effective way to communicate good news?
2. What are the key similarities and differences between the direct approach used in positive communications and the indirect approach used in negative communications?
3. Do you think it is fair to the receiver to use the indirect approach in a negative letter? Why or why not?

Planning and Organizing Business Messages

Activity 5-2
To test your skills.

Persuasive Communications

The third category of business letters includes letters in which the reader must be persuaded to do as you ask, to be "sold" on an idea. Some examples of this type of letter are the following:

- Sales letters that attempt to obtain an order for a product or a service
- Sales promotion letters that try to set up a future sale without pressing directly for an order
- Persuasive request letters asking people to donate time and/or money to a charitable cause
- Job application letters

Communications of this type use the persuasive approach.

The Persuasive Approach

The **persuasive approach** is used to motivate the receiver to read or listen to your entire message and to react positively to it. Getting the receiver to do what you want, to accept what you say, or to agree with you requires the persuasive approach.

In the persuasive approach, the main rule is to *place the call for action at the end of your message*. When you use the persuasive approach, you need to provide complete information for the receiver. This way the receiver can imagine using or benefiting from the product or service you are selling or promoting before you ask for action.

Now let's look at the "AIDA plan"—attention, interest, desire, and action—for structuring effective persuasive communications. Each part of the plan may require one or more paragraphs to develop the idea fully.

Attention. The first sentence of the opening paragraph should capture the receiver's attention. In addition, the paragraph should set the tone of the communication and prepare the receiver for what follows. To accomplish this, it is important to *promise or imply some reward or advantage for the receiver*.

Various techniques for capturing attention can be used, including starting the paragraph with a question, a quote, or a statement.

- A question—*Do you need a relaxing, effortless vacation in the near future?*
- A quote—*Time is money. Our tapes can save you time and money as you record your messages.*
- A statement—*You should strive to eat five servings of fruits and vegetables each day. Our fruits and vegetables are so fresh, you'll find it easy to eat your five servings.*

Whatever opener you use must be relevant to the subject or purpose of the communication and should somehow connect the receiver with the topic. When trying to capture attention, be careful in using gimmicks that may offend or may seem silly or childish to the receiver. Remember to avoid

NOTES

The AIDA plan
- Attention
- Interest
- Desire
- Action

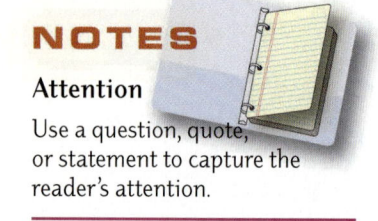

NOTES

Attention

Use a question, quote, or statement to capture the reader's attention.

trite expressions and clichés that don't contribute to the communication's meaning.

Interest. After capturing the receiver's attention, you need to arouse the receiver's interest. To accomplish this, you need to *describe how the recommendation, product, or service would benefit the receiver*. You need to make the benefit or value apparent to the receiver.

A description presented with a "you attitude" will help the reader imagine himself or herself using the product or service. For example, you may show a benefit or value to the receiver as follows:

> **After a hard day at work, imagine how great you will feel relaxing in our Relaxomatic recliner.**

Desire. To create in the receiver the desire to take the action you want, it is important to connect the benefits that you are offering to the receiver's needs. To do this, you need to *provide physical details of your product or service*, such as dimensions, materials, colors, special features, and specifics about the guarantee, maintenance, and so on. Sometimes stimulating both interest and desire may be accomplished in one paragraph. You may present proof of benefits to stir interest and follow that with specific details, which will help stimulate and support the receiver's desire for positive action.

> **Timeless and long lasting, Relaxomatic genuine leather will conform to the contours of your body.**

Action. The previous paragraphs (attention, interest, desire) should lead directly to action on the receiver's part. Now is the time to *ask the receiver to take immediate action*. You should identify the exact action desired and make it easy to act—the request for action should make the receiver's positive response as easy as possible. Courteously tell the receiver where or how the response should be made:

> **Enclosed is an addressed, stamped envelope for your prompt response to the survey.**

The AIDA plan will provide you with the foundation for creating persuasive communications. Of course, each communication situation has to be treated individually if you are to get the response you want. No two products or services are alike, nor are any two groups of receivers.

Let's look at an example of the persuasive plan in action (see Figure 5-3, on the following page).

This example shows the persuasive plan used in Figure 5-3.

THE BACKGROUND	The loan officer of the Easy Payments Mortgage Company, Susan Ripp, is writing a letter to Mr. Eric Swenson, a prospective loan applicant.
THE LETTER'S JOB	The letter should persuade Mr. Swenson to call to discuss the new EasyPayer homeowner loan. Hopefully, this request will lead Mr. Swenson to apply for a homeowner's loan.

NOTES

Interest
Arouse the reader's interest by describing some benefit or value for the receiver.

NOTES

Desire
Create desire for the receiver to take action by connecting the benefits you are offering to the receiver's needs.

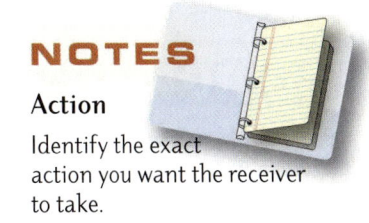

NOTES

Action
Identify the exact action you want the receiver to take.

Planning and Organizing Business Messages

Figure 5-3
This letter used the persuasive approach to get the reader to place a telephone call.

EPMC EASY PAYMENTS MORTGAGE COMPANY
1535 West Main Street, McFarland, WI 53558   Phone: 1-800-555-4800   Fax: 715-555-1292

February 16, <YEAR>

Mr. Eric Swenson
1846 Ridge View Road
McFarland, WI 53558

Dear Mr. Swenson:

Imagine how great it would feel to pay off all your bills . . . to get extra cash for those special home improvements . . . to refinance and save thousands of dollars. Now you can!

The new EasyPayer homeowner loan from Easy Payments Mortgage Company is designed to help you do this. Even if you have experienced credit problems in the past, you will find that you can refinance at a lower interest rate resulting in lower monthly payments. Now it is easier to get the money you need without all the hassles.

You can start saving money every month by consolidating your bills into one low monthly payment. The benefits of the EasyPayer homeowner loan include:

- No hassle—No waiting
- Low interest rates
- No application fees
- Low monthly payments
- Money for any purpose
- Easy qualifying terms

You can start your loan application by telephone in just 15 minutes. Please make an investment in your financial future by calling me today at 1-800-555-4800. Our offices are open to serve you between 9 a.m. and 7 p.m. daily.

Sincerely,

Susan Ripp

Susan Ripp

jos

Activity 5-3
To test your skills.

THE APPROACH   Use the persuasive approach. Get the reader's attention in the opening sentence with a statement that makes the reader stop and think and then continue to read.

If you want to write effective sales letters, for example, take this advice from an advertising copywriter: "Don't use formulas. Rely on your knowledge of *why* people buy things." When you can accomplish this, receivers will take the action that you desire. We will discuss more techniques for writing sales letters in Chapter 11. Use the checklist on the following page to help you analyze your messages.

Developing a Written Plan

Many situations will require you to write down ideas when planning the content and organization of communications. Putting your ideas in writing will help you clarify and organize them. A written plan can assist you by:

- Clarifying your thoughts.
- Ensuring inclusion of all important details.
- Making the actual writing faster and easier.

When you are first learning to prepare business communications, you will find that extensive written plans are extremely helpful. As you become more experienced, you may find that only the more complicated messages will require detailed written plans.

As you become more confident of your communication ability, your written plan should become *brief and simple.* You need to jot down only a few words to suggest each point you wish to make in your communication. You may write your notes on a separate sheet of paper or in the margins of the correspondence you are answering, or you may key them directly into the computer.

Many beginning letter writers have found the procedures outlined in "Planning Your Message" (Table 2, on page 118) helpful as they developed planning skills. Follow these steps precisely in planning your first letters. Later, as you gain experience, you may eliminate some of the steps and adapt the procedures to your own work habits.

In addition, the table "Organization for Business Messages" (Table 1, on page 108) illustrates and summarizes the direct, indirect, and persuasive approaches for communicating messages. You can use this table alone or along with the more general "Planning Your Message" as you refine your planning skills. A brief review of the approaches is shown in Table 3 on page 120. You may want to have this table handy as you begin your rough draft in the next section. (See Figure 5-4, on page 119.)

✔ CHECKLIST FOR PLANNING ORGANIZATION

Check the Structure for Persuasive Communications as You Complete Each Step:

| Attention | _____ | Desire | _____ |
| Interest | _____ | Action | _____ |

Checkpoint 5.2

1. Which element of the persuasive approach (AIDA plan) do you think is most effective?
2. Can you think of other elements to add to the AIDA plan that might persuade readers? What are they?
3. Explain why you do or do not think that persuasive communications should be honest.

Planning and Organizing Business Messages

Table 2 — Planning Your Message

Procedure	Example
Step 1 Write the main and secondary purposes of the message concisely.	**Primary Purpose:** To respond/provide information regarding stenciled golf shirts **Secondary Purpose(s):** To include additional information that creates a desire for our golf shirts To "sell" the customer on our product To "get the order"
Step 2 Jot down all points to be covered in the message that will accomplish the primary and secondary purposes. Include every detail you think of (whether important or not) as you think of it. This process (called brainstorming) will stimulate both good and bad ideas that can be sorted out later.	**Brainstorming List:** Thanks for the request Quality of golf shirts Many colors, designs, types of materials Various sizes, prices, lettering Delivery time Guarantee paint won't run Design included in cost Best quality of shirts Golf bag design Shipping costs Free delivery on $150 orders Designs Cost of stenciled name Price determined by factors: style/size/lettering Can request rush orders Seasonal designs Fax number for ordering
Step 3 Cross out any duplicate items, which often happens in brainstorming; delete any items that can be omitted without sacrificing friendliness or completeness. Group similar ideas together.	**Edit Brainstorming List:** Delete "quality of golf shirts," "types of materials"—both covered—"best quality of shirts." Delete "seasonal designs"—not relevant to "golf shirt" request. Group "delivery time," "rush order," "free delivery on $150 orders," "shipping costs" together. Eliminate "designs"—covered under "golf bag design."
Step 4 Choose the best approach. Determine receiver reaction and appropriate approach (direct, indirect, or persuasive).	**Determine Reader Reaction and Approach:** Receiver will be pleased Use direct approach
Step 5 Based on the approach you chose, number the items in the edited brainstorming list in the order in which you will cover them in your message. The result will be a plan from which you quickly compose a draft of your message.	**Arrange Items in Proper Sequence:** 1. Thank you for the request 2. Golf bag design available 3. Best quality of shirts 4. All hand stenciled 5. Paint guarantee 6. Specifics on colors, sizes, styles, lettering, prices 7. Shipping and delivery information 8. Fax and phone numbers for questions and orders

Writing a Rough Draft

You are now ready to write a first draft, or **rough draft.** You have analyzed all the facts related to your message, made notes on what you should say, and selected the best approach for saying it, including the best order of presentation. Now, you must turn the letter plan or informal outline into a letter. Keep in mind two factors that have influenced your planning: (1) the person to whom you are writing and (2) your reason for writing.

If a letter is to accomplish its purpose, the content must be correct and appropriate, the style must be clear and natural, and the tone must build goodwill.

Figure 5-4
A rough draft is written quickly to cover the basic ideas.

ROUGH DRAFT

Thank you for your interest in our hand stenciled golf shirts. Yes, we do have a design specifically for golfers—a golf bag leaning against a flag. Our shirts are 100% cotton and are the best quality brands available. All designs and lettering are hand stenciled. The paint we use is guaranteed not to run or bleed. We have two styles that we would recommend for your group—the Henley (three-button) and the classic crewneck, both are short sleeved. These are both available in white, natural and grey.

	Sizes	**Price**
The Henley	M, L, XL	$27.95
	XXL	31.95
The Classic Crewneck	S, M, L, XL	$21.95
	XXL, XXXl	23.95

Please note that the above price includes the design. If you wish names stenciled on the shirt, there is an additional cost of $3.00 for first and/or last name.

Because each shirt is individually hand-stenciled, we take pride in shipping our orders quickly. We usually need two weeks for delivery but often can accommodate rush orders. The cost of shipping is $5.00 per order. On orders of $150 or more, shipping is free. Please call us at 1-800-555-8954 or fax us at (244) 1-555-1298 if you have further questions or would like to place an order. We look forward to serving you.

Planning and Organizing Business Messages

Table 3 — Choosing the Best Approach for Reader Reaction

Anticipated Reader Reaction	Type of Message	Message Approach
Receiver will be pleased.	Good-news	Direct
Receiver will be displeased.	Bad-news	Indirect
Receiver will be neutral (neither pleased nor displeased) or will have at least some degree of interest.	Neutral or Informational	Direct
Receiver will have little or no initial interest.	Persuasive	Persuasive

Remember also that you build goodwill with every letter you write by:

- Emphasizing what the receiver wants to know.
- Avoiding or subordinating negatives and other ideas that may be unpleasant to the receiver.
- Using friendly words and reflecting a sincere desire to serve.

In composing the rough draft, *concentrate only on content.* Keep these tips in mind while writing:

- Develop your rough draft directly from your letter plan or informal outline.
- Use double spacing to allow space for marking revisions.
- As quickly as you can, write, keyboard, or dictate your rough draft.
- Don't be concerned with spelling, grammar, style, tone, or references in your text—if you stop to check on a point, you might forget what you started to say or interrupt the natural flow of the letter.
- Write the message in your own words. Imagine the receiver is across the desk from you or at the other end of the telephone to help you write as naturally as you speak.

In actual business practice, most letters are written without a detailed outline. Likewise, experienced communicators do not usually develop detailed outlines for telephone calls, e-mail, or face-to-face conversations. When you need to respond to complex and/or problem situations, however, it is helpful to jot down an informal outline, note comments on previous communications, or develop a rough draft. Remember, it is never wrong to write an outline to help you compose the best possible message.

Study the rough draft in Figure 5-4 on page 119. The draft was developed using the example in "Planning Your Message" (Table 2, on page 118).

> **NOTES**
>
> **Rough It Out**
>
> To help you compose complex messages, you may develop an outline or rough draft. When writing a rough draft, concentrate only on content.

This first draft covers the basic ideas. The draft contains abbreviations, shortcuts, and errors, which will be edited later. Also, it needs to be reviewed to check for the "you attitude," appropriate tone, and word choice. Take a few moments to react to this first draft. Quickly mark any problems or actual errors that you think the writer should revise.

After you have written the rough draft, you are ready for the next steps:

1. Edit and correct the rough draft.
2. Prepare the letter in final form.
3. Proofread the final letter.

These steps will be explained in more detail as you continue your study of business communication. Keep your receiver in mind as you begin to formulate ways to improve the rough draft.

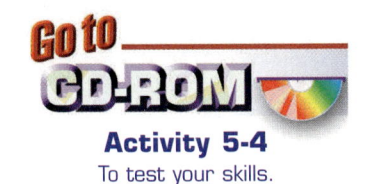

Go to CD-ROM
Activity 5-4
To test your skills.

CHAPTER 5 SUMMARY

Because it is important for every communication to follow the seven Cs of effective communication, it is necessary to plan every communication. Planning your message includes determining its purpose, identifying the audience, developing the content, and organizing the message.

Business communications can be categorized as routine/informational and "yes" letters, negative communications, and persuasive communications. Depending upon the category, the appropriate approach—direct, indirect, persuasive—is selected.

Mental planning is an important part of all successful communications; written planning is used especially for inexperienced writers and for complex and/or difficult situations.

Complete the Worksheet Exercises as assigned. The Online Exercises may be completed now if you have access to the Internet.

Planning and Organizing Business Messages

Chapter 5
Online Exercises

Objective:
These online activities will help you manage your day-to-day activities and enable you to find ways to save time as a student.

Go to **bcw.glencoe.com,** the address for the *Business Communication at Work* Web site, and select Chapter 5. Next, click on Online Exercises. You will see a list of Web site links that will bring you to different time-management Web sites and search engine links.

Activity 5.1

1. Select one of the time-management Web sites to visit.
2. Look for a link to time-management articles or time-management tips. Read about several time-management tips.
3. On a sheet of paper, list four tips that will help you manage your time more efficiently.
4. Return to the *Business Communication at Work* Web site and repeat step 3 by clicking on the other time-management Web sites. Visit at least two more Web sites.
5. Write a paragraph describing the tips you learned. Some questions you may consider in your paragraph include:
   a. How does technology help in managing your time?
   b. Are the tips you learned realistic for your daily life? Why or why not?
   c. How can you apply these tips to your daily life?
6. Write your name on your paper, and hand it in to your instructor.

Activity 5.2

1. Click on one of the search engines.
2. Key *student time management* in the **Search** box (some search engines may use an **Enter word** box).
3. Click on one of the results that seems interesting to you and that contains tips on student time management.
4. On a sheet of paper, list three tips that will help you manage your time as a student.
5. Return to your search results by clicking the **Back** button.
6. Find and print another article about managing time.
7. There are two types of errors: typographical and substantive. Typographical errors are mistakes in keying text. Substantive errors cause problems for readers trying to understand the text. Working from the printout, search for any typographical errors. Circle any of these errors that you find and write in the correction.
8. After reading the text, think of any substantive errors in the article. Write a paragraph describing how you would fix these errors. If there were no substantive errors, describe why there were no such errors.
9. Write your name on your paper and printout, and hand it in to your instructor.

CHAPTER 5 WORKSHEETS

Name _____ Date _____

PRACTICE 1

Choosing the Best Approach

Instructions: Read each of the following purposes for writing a letter, then indicate:
1) What the receiver's reaction will be (pleased, displeased, neutral, or little interest).
2) Which approach you as the writer would take in responding (direct, indirect, or persuasive).

1. To notify an applicant that he or she has been accepted into college.
   Reaction: _____ Approach: _____

2. To thank a customer for placing a large order.
   Reaction: _____ Approach: _____

3. To deny an insurance claim.
   Reaction: _____ Approach: _____

4. To ask for an appointment to discuss a new investment plan.
   Reaction: _____ Approach: _____

5. To confirm a reservation.
   Reaction: _____ Approach: _____

6. To refuse a request for credit.
   Reaction: _____ Approach: _____

7. To decline a speaking invitation.
   Reaction: _____ Approach: _____

8. To send a catalogue that a client requested.
   Reaction: _____ Approach: _____

9. To replace defective merchandise.
   Reaction: _____ Approach: _____

10. To reject a job applicant.
    Reaction: _____ Approach: _____

11. To collect an overdue account. (Note: Key word is *overdue*.)
    Reaction: _____ Approach: _____

12. To congratulate a former colleague on a promotion.
    Reaction: _____ Approach: _____

13. To notify club members of an upcoming meeting.
    Reaction: _____ Approach: _____

Planning and Organizing Business Messages

CHAPTER 5 WORKSHEETS

NAME _____ DATE _____

14. To ask for an interview for a job where there is no known vacancy.
Reaction: _____ Approach: _____

15. To thank a human resources manager for a job interview.
Reaction: _____ Approach: _____

16. To deny a request for transfer within the company.
Reaction: _____ Approach: _____

17. To ask for an appointment to demonstrate your new product line.
Reaction: _____ Approach: _____

18. To turn down an invitation to a business dinner.
Reaction: _____ Approach: _____

19. To ask for donations to a specific fundraising campaign.
Reaction: _____ Approach: _____

20. To interest a potential customer in advertising in your newspaper.
Reaction: _____ Approach: _____

21. To disapprove a request for advanced standing for a class.
Reaction: _____ Approach: _____

22. To approve a home equity loan.
Reaction: _____ Approach: _____

23. To reactivate or reestablish a business relationship. (Note: Key word is *reactivate*.)
Reaction: _____ Approach: _____

24. To notify a customer of a billing error that results in a larger amount owed by the customer.
Reaction: _____ Approach: _____

25. To compromise on an adjustment. (Note: Key word is *compromise*.)
Reaction: _____ Approach: _____

Selecting an Approach

Instructions: Which approach (direct, indirect, or persuasive) is described by the following statements about messages?

Message	**Approach**
1. Begins with a buffer statement	_____
2. Puts the main message in the first paragraph	_____
3. Puts the call for action at the end of the message	_____
4. Uses the AIDA plan	_____
5. Puts the negative in the middle	_____
6. Ends with a neutral statement	_____

CHAPTER 5 WORKSHEETS

NAME _____   DATE _____

Planning Your Message: Brainstorming and Sequencing Ideas

Instructions: After reading the description of each situation:
- Identify the primary and secondary purposes of the communication.
- Identify the receiver's reaction.
- Identify the appropriate approach.
- Brainstorm and jot down all the items that you might include in your communication.
- Select the items needed.
- Arrange the items in the correct order of inclusion in the message according to the appropriate approach. Number each item you want to include, starting with 1, which will be the first part you will include in your message.

1. *Situation:* Your business club, Business Professionals of America (BPA), has received a list of businesspeople from the local speaking bureau who have volunteered to speak to your group. As chair of the program committee, you are to contact Norma Nelson of Professional Images to speak to your club on the topic of business etiquette at next month's club meeting.

    Primary purpose of letter: _____

    Secondary purpose of letter: _____

    _____

    Receiver's reaction: _____

    Approach: _____

    Brainstorming list: **Order:**

2. *Situation:* You are an assistant to Holly Ames, President of the Hemingway Corporation. She has decided that Hemingway's conference room needs to be redecorated. Write a letter to Philip Ingwell, an interior designer with Designs Unlimited, to ask for an appointment to discuss and develop a bid on redecorating the conference room.

    Primary purpose of letter: _____

    Secondary purpose of letter: _____

Planning and Organizing Business Messages

CHAPTER 5 WORKSHEETS

NAME _____ DATE _____

Receiver's reaction: _____

Approach: _____

Brainstorming list: **Order:**

_____   _____
_____   _____
_____   _____
_____   _____
_____   _____
_____   _____
_____   _____
_____   _____
_____   _____
_____   _____

3. *Situation:* A Girl Scout troop of 20 members has requested a tour of your cereal manufacturing plant, Crunchy Cereals. Because of health and sanitation regulations, you discontinued tours five years ago. You can send product samples for each scout and lend the troop a color film or videotape showing the cereal manufacturing process.

Primary purpose of letter: _____

Secondary purpose of letter: _____

Receiver's reaction: _____

Approach: _____

Brainstorming list: **Order:**

_____   _____
_____   _____
_____   _____
_____   _____
_____   _____

4. *Situation:* You are the human resources manager of Winnetka Company. You are to write a letter to be mailed to employees' homes telling them about the company picnic. This will be the company's first picnic, and your goal is to get all employees and their families to attend. You want your letter to be so clear that no employee will call you with questions.

CHAPTER 5 WORKSHEETS

NAME _____ DATE _____

Primary purpose of letter: _____

Secondary purpose of letter: _____

Receiver's reaction: _____

Approach: _____

Brainstorming list: **Order:**

5. *Situation:* Your company, Sunshine Cruise, Inc., is planning a special New Year's cruise to the Bahamas from December 27 to January 3. You have been assigned to write a letter to previous customers to convince them to join the cruise.

Primary purpose of letter: _____

Secondary purpose of letter: _____

Receiver's reaction: _____

Approach: _____

Brainstorming list: **Order:**

Planning and Organizing Business Messages

CHAPTER 5 WORKSHEETS

NAME _____ DATE _____

_____   _____
_____   _____
_____   _____
_____   _____
_____   _____

6. *Situation:* You have received a message from Charlene Ohnstad regarding a picture she had framed at your gallery. She indicates that she does not like the color of one of the two mattings used and that it was not the one that she had selected. Therefore, she wants you to redo the framing and matting for her picture. You have checked her original order and the actual matting used. No error was made; the matting she ordered was used. You will need to inform her that she received the matting that she ordered and that you cannot redo the picture unless she pays for it (the cost of the new matting and labor, with a 20% discount on labor charges).

Primary purpose of letter: _____

Secondary purpose of letter: _____

Receiver's reaction: _____

Approach: _____

Brainstorming list: **Order:**

_____   _____
_____   _____
_____   _____
_____   _____
_____   _____
_____   _____

7. Assume that you were to respond to Ms. Ohnstad over the telephone instead of by letter.

   a. Would you use the same items in your oral response?

      Yes _____   No _____

   b. Would you reorder the brainstorming list for a phone conversation?

      Yes _____   No _____

   c. If you did reorder the list, what order would you use and why?

   _____
   _____

CHAPTER 5 WORKSHEETS

Name _____ Date _____

PRACTICE 2

Outlining and Preparing a Rough Draft

Instructions: You are the assistant sales manager for Brasel Professionals, a placement service for office temporaries. You must answer a request for "more information about Brasel's services" from Mr. Jason Byrd, Office Manager of Independent Researchers, Inc., 121 Ashlea Drive, Fort Worth, TX 76129. Your letter should have two purposes: 1) to impress upon Mr. Byrd that he should think of Brasel whenever he needs temporary office help, and 2) to smooth the way for a representative to call on him.

1. Here are the letter plan notes you have made. Number them in the sequence that you would use them in your letter.

   _____ Monica Randolph (our sales representative) will call

   _____ Established 1966

   _____ Professional help when <u>you</u> need it

   _____ Clients include Fortune 500 firms (example)

   _____ Clients include small firms (example)

   _____ Well-trained secretaries

   _____ Clerical help (filing clerks)

   _____ Others (typists, receptionists)

   _____ Also accounts receivable help

   _____ Word processing help

   _____ Telephone survey specialists

   _____ P. 4 of brochure (research services)

   _____ Wide range—help for 1 day or 1 year

   _____ Sales rep—appointment

   _____ Staff is experienced

   _____ In business for many years

   _____ Research specialists (brochure, p. 4)

   _____ Thank you

2. What will be the receiver's reaction to your letter? What approach will you use?

   Reaction: _____

   Approach: _____

3. Revise the outline notes given, crossing out unnecessary or repetitious items and joining related items. Renumber the items in the order in which you would present them in the letter. Then, in the space provided, rewrite your notes in the revised sequence.

   _____

   _____

Planning and Organizing Business Messages   129

CHAPTER 5 WORKSHEETS

NAME _____ DATE _____

_____
_____
_____
_____
_____
_____
_____
_____
_____

4. Based on your outline, prepare a draft (preferably by composing directly on the computer) of the letter to Mr. Byrd.

_____
_____

PRACTICE 3

Analyzing Letters From Your Files

Instructions: From the letters that you have been collecting, select a good-news letter, a bad-news letter, and a persuasive letter. Analyze each of the letters to determine which approach it used and if it was organized appropriately. Use the forms provided as a guide as you analyze your letters.

1. Good-News Letter

   Approach used: _____

   Opening: Was the main idea or good news presented? _____

   If not, describe the opening paragraph. _____

   Did it resemble one of the other approaches? _____

   If so, which one? _____

   Middle: Were details or explanations given? _____

   If no, describe the middle paragraph. _____

   Closing: Does the closing lead to goodwill or resale? _____

   If not, comment on closing. _____

   Overall comments on letter: _____

2. Bad-News Letter

   Approach used: _____

   Opening: Is a buffer paragraph used at the beginning? _____

   If so, describe the buffer used. _____

   If not, describe the opening paragraph. _____

CHAPTER 5   WORKSHEETS

NAME _____ DATE _____

Did it resemble one of the other approaches? _____

If so, which one? _____

Middle: Were reasons, explanations, or facts given for the negative news? _____

If not, describe the middle paragraph. _____

Was the bad news given *after* the reasons? _____

If not, when was the bad news given? _____

Did the writer tell what could be done instead of what could not be done? _____

Is the bad news stated directly or implied? _____

Closing: Does the closing end in a positive tone with pleasant, relative comment? ___

If not, comment on closing. _____

Overall comments on letter: _____

3. Persuasive Letter

   Approach Used: _____

   Opening: Did the opening get the receiver's attention? _____

   If not, describe the opening paragraph. _____

   Did it resemble one of the other approaches? _____

   If so, which one? _____

   Middle: Did the middle create interest and desire? _____

   Did the explanations expand the opening idea? _____

   Were benefits given to convince the receiver to act? _____

   If not, describe the middle paragraph. _____

   Closing: Is there a specific request for action? _____

   Is the request for action courteous? _____

   Does the writer make it easy for the reader to act? _____

   If not, comment on closing. _____

   Overall comments on letter: _____

   _____

   _____

   _____

   _____

Planning and Organizing Business Messages

CHAPTER 6

Using Technology to Improve Communication

Objectives

After completing this chapter, you will be able to:

1. Identify and use appropriate office equipment to enhance your writing skills
2. Describe how facsimile machines and other workplace technologies are used to improve communication skills
3. Create and use your e-mail address book
4. Create and send e-mail messages
5. Use proper electronic mail etiquette
6. Use word-processing software to improve your writing
7. Use the Internet to research information
8. Use spreadsheet and presentational applications

WORKPLACE APPLICATIONS

Brainstorming

Brainstorming is a prewriting strategy that helps writers identify the key content and focus of their writing. As the term suggests, brainstorming is a quick, often chaotic, list-making activity that writers use to generate ideas about a topic. Brainstorming may be done alone or in groups, on paper or out loud. The strength of brainstorming as a planning strategy is that writers can express their thoughts openly, without **censorship** or judgment, and therefore discover their strongest points.

Let the Ideas Flow

You begin brainstorming by identifying the general topic or purpose of your intended message. The next step is to record every idea you associate with your topic. Ideas may be expressed in complete sentences, phrases, or single words. The process of brainstorming will stimulate both good and bad ideas, as well as associations that are completely irrelevant. Your impulse may be to judge ideas as they are offered. Do not reject or refuse any idea that is suggested, and do not hesitate to share your own. Throw all the ideas—ingenious or ordinary—into the mix. In the end, you will have covered all the expected points and made new and creative connections as well.

Brainstorming ends only when all possible ideas have been exhausted. The result is usually a long, comprehensive, and varied list of ideas. The next step is to process the ideas—to edit out duplications, delete unrelated thoughts, and identify and clarify the strongest ideas that remain. By focusing on the strongest ideas in your list, you automatically find the core of your message. Knowing your message in turn makes it easier to express yourself effectively in writing.

Thinking Critically

Situation: You work as a sales representative for a company that makes educational software. Sales have leveled off in recent months, and your employer wants you to identify new potential customers and to write a letter that will interest them in your company's products.

Ask Yourself: With a partner, brainstorm a list of potential customers and points about your products that would appeal to them.

> *Any sufficiently advanced technology is indistinguishable from magic.*
> —**Arthur C. Clarke, Author**

In the current workplace, computers are everywhere. Today it's difficult to go into any business without noticing the presence of some type of computer performing a task. In traditional office settings, computers are used to handle and store information, as well as process information using programs such as word processors and spreadsheets. Computers are used to perform large calculative tasks, as well as to keep databases of business information ready for retrieval by employees who need access to specific sets of data.

The other significant advance in business technology has come with the advent of the Internet. Through the Internet, businesses have expanded their markets and images into the arena of the World Wide Web. This chapter will discuss various aspects of the technologies found in the workplace and describe how their functions can help you to improve your communication skills in the workplace.

Technology in the Office

Technology has always played a role in offices since the beginning of business. In ancient Egypt, merchants used bead and wire abacuses to conduct business and calculate transactions. In 1890, William Burroughs pioneered the first commercially successful mechanical adding machine in America, which advanced individuals' capacities to perform complex calculations with greater speed and accuracy than ever before.

Throughout history, technology has helped individuals perform tasks and process information. Each advancement, from the abacus to the adding machine to the personal computer, has extended employees' abilities and range of functionalities.

The following sections will discuss in detail some of the more popular technologies found in the modern business environment.

Computers

It is difficult at this point in history to envision a workplace without computers. Computers are used in a variety of business environments. From scanners that automatically log inventory into modern warehouses to the large computers that monitor and control lighting and air conditioning in urban skyscrapers, computers are everywhere in the workplace.

The History of Computers in the Workplace

It wasn't until the late 1950s and early 1960s that computers became prevalent in the workplace. This was due to the invention of the **transistor** in 1948, which replaced **vacuum tubes** that were used in first generation computers. With these second-generation computers utilizing stored **programs** and **programming languages,** a computer could perform a variety of business tasks that previously had to be done by hand. It was at this point that jobs such as programmers and analysts came about.

The Modern Computer

With the invention of the **integrated circuit** by Jack Kilbey in 1958, computers started to dramatically decrease in size while increasing in computing power. The **personal computer**, or **PC**, as it's traditionally known, was produced by IBM in 1981. After this breakthrough, IBM and IBM-type clones became prevalent in the day-to-day operations of almost any business. As the use of computers became more extensive in business, new ways of utilizing their capabilities came about. Computers could now be linked together via **Local Area Networks**, or **LANs**. In this manner, computers could share such things as memory, software, and information. With the integration of the global web, or the **Internet**, opportunities were recognized for further expanding business potential.

The Computer's Role in the Workplace

With the integration of computers into the workplace, tasks that previously would have taken longer amounts of time now can be accomplished with less manpower and with faster speeds. Computers are used in the business world to create, store, and manipulate data. For example, companies might use **spreadsheet programs** such as Lotus Notes® or Microsoft® Excel to track machine parts at a manufacturing company. Spreadsheets can tabulate, organize, and filter data, as well as keep a historical record of inventory, shipping, and receiving. These spreadsheet documents may also be stored on a central company **server** computer. This central storage option can allow different individuals to access the same document to make changes when necessary. This sharing of documents and files from a central location greatly reduces the amount of time required to store, manipulate, and retrieve data.

NOTES

Computing Options

Computers offer a variety of methods for creating, storing, and researching information. Businesses also use computers to track information about their employees and customers.

Fax Machines

Facsimile (or fax for short) is the process of encoding information and transmitting it over either telephone lines or radio broadcast, then receiving it in the form of a hard copy document. In addition to computers, fax machines have played an extensive role in the modern workplace. Even as electronic documents become the norm for most businesses, the fax machine is still an integral part of the modern workplace because many documents still need to be in paper form, for the purpose of having signatures on documents and other reasons.

With today's fax machines, integrated circuits and computers have made it possible to fax data via a radio signal that provides a clear transmission of data through the air. Because of this advancement, individuals can now send faxed paper documents with small computers and computer devices. With the advent of wireless communications in the form of personal digital assistants, or PDAs, and cellular phones, faxes can be sent and received virtually anywhere.

Thinking Cap 6.1

Discuss: What sorts of documents might you want to send over a facsimile, rather than using the postal service or e-mail?

Using Technology to Improve Communication

135

Fax Machines in the Workplace

In today's typical office, fax machines are used to send and receive documents from a variety of sources. Daily reports, contracts, and even weekly newsletters are faxed to businesses all around the globe. With the addition of the cellular telephone and wireless communications, salespersons in the field can receive documents on the road or at a client site. Fax transmission technology also allows engineers and workers who are operating in desolate regions to receive information crucial to the success of what they are working on. In such remote places as Antarctica, researchers utilize fax transmission technology to send data back and forth to be analyzed by scientists in laboratories in the furthermost corners of the world. Fax technology is utilized in many capacities in business, education, and research.

Scanners

Scanners capture an image of a document or object so that it can be stored for later use and manipulation. Scanners have allowed individuals and companies to preserve what originally were hard copy documents electronically.

The Modern Scanner

Compared to fax machines, scanners are a relatively new piece of office technology. Scanners allow people to capture an image of an object or of a hard copy document (whether it is text or pictures), and then save it to a computer for printing or further manipulation of the image. Scanners operate in the following manner. The user takes the image he or she wants to scan, say, a photo, and places it inside the scanner. The scanner then illuminates the image so that the photo device can read its small components, or pixels. Once the object is illuminated, light reflects from each pixel and is converted into electric current by an electronic component in the scanner known as the **photocell.**

Scanners in the Workplace

In the contemporary office workspace, scanners play an important role. In businesses that utilize graphics or photographic technology, scanners are a necessity. For instance, clients of graphic design firms may have existing artwork in hard copy that they wish to incorporate into new material. Graphics firms can scan those images in order to incorporate them into new documents that they are creating for their clients. The same idea also works in the world of photography. Often individuals or companies have photographs that need to be incorporated into their material. In this manner companies can use existing materials by scanning photos or negatives, and then incorporate them into new documents.

Other uses for scanning technology include copying documents. For some smaller companies, this is a worthwhile alternative to purchasing an expensive copier. Larger companies can make use of scanning technology to create document archives for business documentation such as past invoices and order requests. With the use of an auto-feeder, multiple documents can be scanned and archived, providing a secure storage alternative to hard copies stored in filing cabinets.

GLOBAL DIVERSITY 6.1

Global Computing
Computer software is available in many languages. Many U.S. companies conduct business outside the United States, which requires employees to communicate using this software. *What are the implications of this for you as you face employment with companies that do business globally?*

136

Chapter 6

Personal Digital Assistants

As our need to be independent of the physical workplace grows more and more, developers are continually looking for ways to expand the computing power of the workplace into the mobile arena. One way companies have developed this is through the creation of the **personal digital assistant**, or **PDA**. A PDA is a handheld device that incorporates many features found in personal computers, such as computing, telephone and fax features, and the ability to link them up to other computers. A PDA can combine functions so as to become a cellular phone, e-mail messaging device, and personal organizer. Whereas a laptop computer uses a keyboard, a PDA uses a stylus that recognizes handwriting.

Newer PDAs have keyboard attachment options. In this way, users can link their PDAs to their desktops, and move documents freely from their workstations to the PDA devices.

Other types of PDAs can perform various computing functions and link to a user's main workstation via a **docking station** to share files and information for use away from the office. With the addition of smaller wireless modems, PDAs can now be used in various capacities from smart digital cellular telephones to wireless Web browsers. Through the use of PDAs, businesspeople can stay connected to their offices via portable and versatile devices that offer a great alternative to laptop computers.

PDAs in the Workplace

PDAs are continuing to sprout up in all areas of business. In many business environments, workers and management alike must fill out hard copy forms to keep company records. Through the use of a PDA, workers can record information in a format that can be utilized by a personal computer. For example, in the executive air service industry, both ground crew and pilots often use PDAs to coordinate the paperwork related to getting a chartered flight to its destination. Everything from pre-flight checks to travel plans of passengers can be handled on a PDA, and accessed at a moment's notice.

Real estate agents use PDAs as well, as they are often out of the office on client calls and often do not have a continual link to the office. Real estate agents make use of PDAs to store, retrieve, and display photographs of properties to be viewed by clients. They also make use of spreadsheet applications such as Pocket Excel that can calculate the exact monthly payment a client would have to make based on the terms of their mortgage and their initial down payment.

For professionals who constantly need access to information but do not have the luxury of a desktop computer in their work environment, PDAs are a welcome addition to their work situations.

Voice Mail

Voice mail has become a standard in most offices. Before leaving a message for someone on voice mail, you should organize your ideas. You may find it helpful if you make a few notes before leaving your message. Because most

NOTES

PDA

A personal digital assistant is a handheld portable computer.

NOTES

On the Move

Laptop computers and PDAs offer flexibility and convenience in accessing information from locations outside the office.

voice mailboxes have a limited recording time, your message should be clear, complete, concise, and direct. Spell out difficult names and give numbers slowly. You should always include your phone number in your message.

Other Workplace Devices and Technologies

In addition to computers, scanners, fax machines, and PDAs, offices use a variety of "auxiliary technologies" to perform various business functions. With the advent of the **laptop computer**, workers were no longer tied to the office. The creation of a portable computer made several jobs much easier. Now salespeople could take their product and market data directly to the client site. Workers now could perform computations for various business applications in the field, as opposed to collecting data that had to be input into a computer back at the company office. Laptops allow for complete and functional business mobility.

The digital age has also spawned such devices as **digital still** and **digital video cameras**. These photographic technologies that were once exorbitant in price are now accessible by professionals from all walks of business life, from the corporate level down to the small business owner. Individuals now can capture still and video images for incorporation into training, marketing, and promotion materials, in videos and low-cost print production.

Business professionals are also now able to use low-cost **printers** to meet their needs for creating business documents from computer applications. At one point, printers were expensive, cumbersome machines that cost thousands of dollars to purchase and maintain. In today's workplace, individuals make use of low-cost laser and color printers to produce a wide variety of forms and documents. Whereas earlier printers required technical support from the manufacturer, current printers are virtually maintenance free, normally needing only regular cleanings and reloadings of ink.

Many devices that are part of the contemporary working office have greatly increased efficiency and mobility, as well as the ability to use different modes of communication. In the next section, we'll take a look at a communication medium that has revolutionized how we conduct business and interact with other people: e-mail.

Checkpoint 6.1

1. In your opinion, what is the greatest contribution computers have made in the workplace?

2. In your mind, which is the most useful computer-based tool in the office—the personal computer, fax machine, scanner, photocopier, or personal digital assistant?

3. In your experience, what are some benefits and drawbacks of wireless technology?

The Internet: Keeping the World Connected

At this point in history, it is getting difficult to remember what our world was like without the Internet. In a typical workday many of us send scores of e-mail messages in order to communicate with one another and spend hours searching for information on the **World Wide Web**. Whether transmitting weekly sales reports to your sales staff, asking for information from another company, or sending your résumé to apply for a job, people have made the Internet a common addition to existing modes of communication.

Information Services and the Internet

You may have heard the term **information highway**. This term accurately describes what is available to the writer through the computer and the Internet. The Internet is nothing more than computers around the world that are linked together to form an enormous network. Using your computer **modem**, you can access an **Internet Service Provider**—a company with a server that is connected to other computers that form a network. Then you will use a browser (software such as Netscape Navigator® or Microsoft® Internet Explorer) to help you move around on the Internet and perform searches. Or you may use commercial online services that provide access to the Internet for an hourly and/or monthly fee. You may subscribe to services such as Prodigy, America Online (AOL), or CompuServe (a subsidiary of AOL). By using any of these services, you can research information on topics such as news, sports, entertainment, airline reservations, and travel tips, to name a few.

How do you use information services and the Internet? You dial into your Internet Service Provider, such as AOL, access the Internet, and search for information around the world. Because you are connecting only to your local service provider in most locations, there are no long-distance phone charges. You do pay a nominal monthly or annual fee to your provider to connect to the Internet.

A vast amount of information is on the Internet, and it is increasing each day. For example, if you need information on a current event that has affected a financial situation, you can research the information on the Internet. If you need to know a ZIP Code, the ZIP Code directory is online. Phone books for every city in the United States are available, too, and all major and many smaller newspapers are online. With the Internet, up-to-the-minute governmental, legal, scientific, and business information is available to you with just a few keystrokes on the computer.

Thinking Cap 6.2

Discuss: How do you think businesses best use the Internet? What would be common types of information a business might need to locate?

How E-mail Works

E-mail is one of the earliest uses of the Internet. In the early days of the Internet, it was used by researchers and government agencies to send messages back and forth regarding the status and development of research and

Using Technology to Improve Communication

government projects. In the contemporary use of e-mail, applications such as Microsoft® Outlook and Lotus cc:Mail® allow you to view, organize, and store e-mail messages for viewing and use at another time. Though the form of the e-mail may have changed a bit since its inception, the basic concept of how e-mail works has changed very little.

In order to send and receive e-mail, you must use some type of **e-mail client**, as was mentioned previously. This allows you to compose and send messages either in plain text or in the form of an image file, such as HTML. You address your message just like you address a regular mail letter, but with the recipient's e-mail address, which is a combination of his or her **username** and **domain name**. The username is the part that identifies who the recipient is within the domain, whereas the domain name is the name of the site or domain that the message will be sent to. In an e-mail address, the @ symbol is used to separate the username from the domain name. Therefore, if your name is Jane Doe, and your domain name is janeswebsite.com, then your e-mail address would read perhaps something like *jdoe@janeswebsite.com*. The username configuration is the choice of the domain administrator, so other format options such as *j.doe* or *j_doe* instead of just *jdoe* may be used.

Whether your e-mail exists as part of your company infrastructure or you are linked to an Internet Service Provider, both systems make use of a **mail server**. A mail server is a computer that is responsible for routing e-mail messages from your domain to other addresses throughout the Internet.

The Rules of Etiquette

This section will take a look at some of the rules of etiquette that apply to e-mail in both a business and personal context.

For starters, unless it's agreed upon otherwise, e-mail messages in a business context should be kept somewhat short and concise. You want to get your message across, but you want to do it without rambling on unnecessarily. Make sure you get to what you're saying, and that you're clear in saying it. Other basic rules you should follow in your e-mail communication include:

- Fill in the subject line.

- Follow the rules of grammar, spelling, punctuation, and capitalization as with other written communications. Proofread as you would any written communication before you send it.

- Keep your messages on a "need to know" basis. Send a message only to those persons who should receive the information.

- Do not use e-mail for security-sensitive materials unless steps have been taken to protect messages via coding, etc. Also, remember that e-mail is not confidential.

- Remember that many companies have instituted e-mail policies that state that e-mail is to be used for business-related purposes only.

- Use the seven Cs of effective communication when writing your message.

E-mail Connection
If e-mail capabilities are available, e-mail messages to your classmates and to your instructor.

NOTES
Watch Your Language
E-mail messages are not confidential. If the message is deleted, it is still in the system.

- Try not to overuse punctuation. If you have a need for emphasis, let your words take care of it. Otherwise, your sentence will look like you are yelling (Like this!!!!!).

Using Abbreviations. Because e-mail is a rapid form of communication, abbreviations are commonly used. This being said, you should probably keep their use to a minimum. Things like FYI (for your information) and BTW (by the way) are perfectly acceptable. You may be able to get away with such usages as TTYL (talk to you later) if you assume the recipient is relatively e-mail-savvy. It probably is best to avoid lengthier abbreviations such as TNSTAAFL (there's no such thing as a free lunch), and ROTFL (rolling on the floor laughing). These might do nothing but confuse the person you're trying to impress.

The Use of E-mail Threads. E-mail works best when you send something to someone and get a reply. Often that reply will cause you to think of another thought, and so you reply as well. You wouldn't start another e-mail, because the line of thinking is within the original message. This cycle of e-mail and response is known as a thread. You traditionally don't want to break the thread of thinking within an e-mail, because it then is hard to follow the line of thinking that has been created from several e-mail exchanges. Therefore, try to keep the same line of thinking within the same thread. If it's a new thought or query, you may then go and start a new message with a new subject line.

Flaming. A **flame** is an e-mail version of a verbal attack. It is usually a reply to an e-mail that you have sent that was not received favorably. Oftentimes, flames are generated when the sender of the message did not truly intend to step out of line. If you for some reason respond with a flame of your own, then you and the recipient will be engaged in what is known as a **flame war**, which are volleys of insults and general meanness that get thrown in each other's direction. No one wants to engage in this type of verbal exchange. Therefore, use common courtesy and a sense of restraint when using e-mail to communicate; following the basic rules of written and verbal politeness should suffice.

Go to CD-ROM
Activity 6-1
To test your skills.

NOTES
Emoticons
Small symbols have been created for use in e-mail that provide indication about someone's state of mind, and are also often humorous.
- :-) smiley
- ;-) wink
- :-(frown
- :-D surprise
- :-/ bewilderment
- ;-} sneer
- :-O loud sound
- :-P cynical smile.

LEGAL & ETHICAL 6-1
Logging On. What are the legal/ethical ramifications of employees using the Internet for personal use during business hours?

Making the Most of E-mail

Most people would think that the use of e-mail is limited simply to sending and receiving messages. Whereas this may have been the case in the early days of e-mail, it is no longer that way. With newer e-mail applications, users can perform a number of tasks and make additions to messages so as to better communicate. In this section, we'll take a look at some of the features of e-mail that increase its messaging functionality.

Using Technology to Improve Communication

Thinking Cap 6.3

Discuss: Do you think e-mail will someday replace the current postal system?

Using Attachments

Though you can send e-mail messages back and forth to other people, you can also include separate documents or files along with the e-mail. This add-on file is called an **attachment**. By adding attachments, you are able to send all types of files and electronic images to the recipient of your message. Sending attachments back and forth is a great way for businesspeople who are in multiple locations to collaborate on projects and to cut down on traditional mail and shipping costs.

Utilizing the Mailbox Feature

Mailboxes are features that are unique to each e-mail client. Through the use of mailboxes (like In/Out boxes on your real desktop), you can organize your incoming and outgoing mail into different files for retrieval when you need them again. You can compose a message, then store it in your Outbox mailbox to be sent when you are ready, or perhaps the next time you connect to the Internet. Most newer e-mail applications come with default mailboxes, such as an Inbox, an Outbox, and a Deleted Items folder. In addition to these, you can create and name your own mailboxes so as to create your own system of organization.

Implementing Filters

In a business environment where several messages can come and go every day, it's often hard to keep track of it all. Through the use of a **filter,** you can automate the way that the e-mail application keeps track of your messages according to parameters that you set up yourself. For example, you can set up a filter that sends any e-mail with a particular subject line directly to the trash. You can also set up a filter that will forward a copy of every e-mail with specific words in the subject line directly to a colleague or coworker. You might also want to flag certain messages that arrive from certain people or route them directly to a particular folder. As you receive more and more mail, filters will help you organize your messages quickly and efficiently.

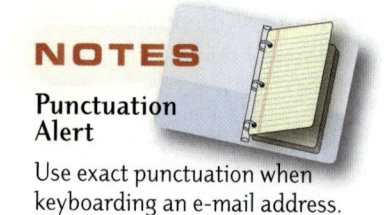

NOTES

Punctuation Alert

Use exact punctuation when keyboarding an e-mail address.

Address Books

In addition to the previously mentioned features of e-mail, most e-mail applications include a feature known as an **address book**. An address book allows you to keep a list of the e-mail addresses of your contacts, friends, and coworkers. This saves time in that you don't have to type out the address of each individual every time you want to send a message. In most programs, you can highlight the name of the person and then click a button or drop down a menu that will add that person to your address book.

If you want to address an e-mail to someone who is in your address book, you simply open a new message and click on the To: area; the address book will open, allowing you to choose the recipient from your address book. It's that simple!

Creating and Using Mail Lists

Another important component of the address book is the ability to create a mailing list. A mailing list is a group of e-mail recipients that you might need to send the same message to at once. To create a mailing list, you simply type an entry in your address book, named something like Sales Staff, for instance, add all the appropriate e-mail addresses to the Address field, and then save the list. When you want to send a message to all the people on the Sales Staff mailing list, create a new message, address it to the "Sales Staff", and press *Send*, and they will all receive it.

The idea of mailing lists also extends to the Internet. Mail lists, or **Discussion lists**, as they are sometimes called, are a mail format where you can share information, request advice, and get opinions on particular topics from a variety of individuals. These lists are organized by subject, from cooking tips to gardening to just about anything.

Checkpoint 6.2

1. Do you think e-mail etiquette is useful?
2. In your own experience, what is the best characteristic of e-mail?
3. What new communication technologies can you imagine for the future? Suggest a new type of technology that you would like to see in the workplace.

USING APPLICATION TECHNOLOGY

Though advances in business-related applications such as Microsoft® Office have been significant over the years, many individuals do not realize the power and capability that these products have. In the next section, we will look at how you can use various business-based applications and products to meet your needs in the workplace.

Word Processing

Word processing applications are some of the most popular applications that individuals use with a computer on a day-to-day basis. In the world of business, people use word processing software, or **word processors,** to create business documents, fax covers, newsletters, and even Web pages. Using word processing software such as Microsoft® Word, users can make documents that look visually appealing and professional. Word processing software has become quite sophisticated—writers can now use a spell checker, a thesaurus, and a grammar checker to help produce writing that has fewer errors. Now instead of plain black text on white sheets of paper, word processing documents are dynamic pages that can contain different types of media content.

Using Technology to Improve Communication

To begin, word processors can use a variety of fonts, text styles, and colors to make documents more understandable and visually appealing. Most word processing software now allows you to embed clip art and other types of graphical images directly into your document. This type of feature makes the production of newsletter publications, annual reports, and diverse types of documents possible with little extra cost. In addition, audio and video clips can be embedded directly into most word processing documents. Word processing has come a long way from the time when its sole purpose was to produce simple black text documentation.

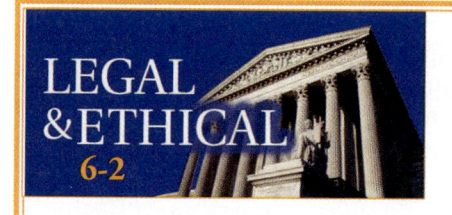

LEGAL & ETHICAL 6-2

Software Piracy. A fellow employee comments to you that he has received the latest version of Microsoft Office software for his office computer. He tells you he took the software home and put it on his home computer so he can do some of his work at home. Company policy is that employees may not violate license agreements pertaining to computer software; therefore, they may not copy software, under threat of termination. What are the legal and ethical issues involved in this situation? Should you report this incident knowing it could cost your fellow employee his job?

Spell Checker

Spell checkers help writers check their spelling. Software manufacturers have continued to improve spell checkers by increasing the size of their dictionaries, adding antonyms and synonyms, and identifying the words as nouns or verbs for the writer.

Even though you will use the spell checker when using your computer, you should strive to maintain excellent spelling skills. You can't be sure that you will never have to write something without your computer, and many times your supervisor or a coworker may ask you how to spell a word. Here are three simple suggestions that will help you maintain spelling skills when you are not using a computer:

Thinking Cap 6.4

Discuss: Because of rolling blackouts, your workplace has gone several days without electricity. How much of your job can you accomplish without power? Should a company be able to function without the lights on?

1. Check each word carefully.
2. Consult a dictionary when you are unsure of how to spell a word.
3. Keep a current list of your personal spelling demons. Memorize the correct spelling of each word on your list.

Remember, a spell checker can only check for misspellings; it cannot check for misuse of words. For example, you may wrongly use *effect* instead of *affect* in a sentence. However, the spell checker will not point out the error because the word is spelled correctly.

Thesaurus

The thesaurus assists the writer in thinking of that "right" word by offering synonyms—words that have the same or nearly the same meaning. The thesaurus also lists antonyms—words that have an opposite meaning.

Grammar Checkers

Writers have always needed references to verify spelling, grammar, punctuation, capitalization, and word usage. With the increased use of computer and word processing programs, rapid checking of spelling, grammar, and the like became necessary. Word processing manufacturers quickly saw this need and incorporated spell checkers and grammar checkers into their various programs. For example, Corel® WordPerfect contains the grammar checker Grammatik® as one of its tools. Grammatik checks for a number of writing problems, including the percentage of passive sentences, and recommends that writers use no more than 10 percent passive sentences.

Similarly, Microsoft Office contains a spell checker and a grammar checker in its word processing programs. By default, as you are keying a Word document, for instance, the program automatically checks spelling and identifies any misspelled words or words that are not in the program's dictionary, such as proper names. The program also identifies grammar errors as part of the spelling and grammar checker tools.

Outlining on the Computer

Making an outline helps you organize your writing so that your thoughts will flow easily from idea to idea. Many writers say developing an outline is the most difficult part of writing. You can create an outline quickly using brainstorming techniques and keying your outline directly on the computer. You can use the cut-and-paste feature of word processing software to make changes quickly and easily to your outline.

Most word processing software offers an outlining feature as part of the program. Other software, such as PowerPoint®, a presentation program, also offers an outlining feature. With this program, you can create slides or overhead transparencies; the program automatically creates an outline based on the transparencies. Using the outlining feature of any program helps you organize your ideas quickly into a logical sequence.

Suppose your company is short of parking space. You are asked to prepare a proposal that would identify what information is needed to solve the problem and some possible solutions. An outline is the best place to organize your ideas before you begin writing.

Here is how your proposal outline might look:

I. Information needed

    A. Parking lot measurement

    B. Number of present parking spaces

        1. Regular

        2. Physically challenged

        3. Privileged

  C. Number of employees presently using lot

  D. Number of employees who carpool

  E. Number of entrances and exits

 II. Possible solutions

  A. Restripe all of the present lot for standard-size vehicles

  B. Check other close locations to rent or purchase parking space

  C. Restripe present lot to accommodate varying sizes of vehicles

  D. Purchase land and build a new parking garage

  E. Provide incentives for carpooling

  F. Adjust work schedules to eliminate crowding

You'll notice that the ideas are arranged in a logical sequence in the outline. For example, ideas that relate to the information needed were listed under that topic, and possible solutions were listed under that topic head.

Spreadsheet Applications

Before the advent of **spreadsheet applications**, keeping records and inventories was a tedious task. Organizing ledger sheets and inventories into sections of rows and columns was a time-consuming task. With spreadsheet software, this format has been automated. In addition to storing and viewing data, spreadsheet software can be configured so that calculations are performed on the various cells within the spreadsheet. This provides a powerful tool for businesses that need to keep track of such things as inventory items, pricing, and other types of tabulated information. In addition to storing and organizing information, spreadsheets offer the user the ability to calculate data and then recalculate data if parameters have changed within the spreadsheet file. For example, a small shop owner can track his weekly inventory using a spreadsheet. At the end of each workday, he can generate a new spreadsheet that shows him what has been sold, what's left, and what will need to be ordered at the end of the week.

  In addition to storing and calculating data, spreadsheets are also good for charting data. Spreadsheet programs can take the row and column data that you have and make a visual representation in the form of line charts, column charts, and pie charts. This is a great asset for businesspeople who need to see financial and fiscal information in graphic form.

Database Applications

Before the advent of the computer, most **databases** were kept in a hard copy format, often filling many rooms within a business. A good example of a hard copy database would be the old Dewey decimal classification system that is still used in some public libraries.

A computer database is a collection of information that is stored in a way that can be accessed, retrieved, and manipulated. Within database software, information is stored as records in individual **tables**. A **field** would represent one particular aspect of any database record. For example, a large superstore might use a product database that contains all the products they purchase from other vendors. The fields in each product database record might consist of information such as the item's SKU number, description, the number of units of that item currently in the store, the wholesale price, and the retail price. If other information is required, then the database software can be reconfigured to accommodate other fields.

Data of this type can be queried, which means that the user of the database can search the database for specific information. If a superstore wants to find out how many fireplace inserts they sold in the month of January, they can configure the database for that type of query, therefore having that information on hand when it's needed. Databases are a great tool for keeping track of large numbers of items or people.

Presentational Applications

Presentational Applications, such as PowerPoint, allow you to create presentations, which can be used as graphics to illustrate information and concepts to a group. Presentation applications are the next logical step in presentational aids such as overhead projectors and slide film projectors, incorporating aspects of these earlier aids into its new format. This type of software produces a document that is typically known as a slide show. A slide show is a collection of presentation files, or "slides," that come together to form a presentation. Each slide is a stand-alone entity within the group and can display different types of text, graphics, or embedded audio or video clips.

Presentation software combines features from other software, such as word processors and spreadsheets, so that information can be shown in different formats. For example, a presentation may consist of an outline that the readers can follow while the presenter speaks. A presentation application can also incorporate statistics, either in the form of straight numbers and text or, graphically, in the form of column and pie charts.

In newer versions of presentation software, the slide show can often be saved as an HTML document, which then allows the presenter to post his presentation to a Web site so that others can come to a specific Internet address and view the contents of the presentation. Presentation software extends a businessperson's ability to communicate to large groups by integrating several different formats of information into a single production.

Personal Information Applications

Personal Information Applications incorporate various tools for communicating to other individuals in a workgroup. Software of this type usually includes note pads, address books, and calendars. Some of the more frequently used types, such as Microsoft Outlook and Lotus Notes,

Using Technology to Improve Communication

incorporate e-mail into their suites as well. This integration of typical desktop communication devices enables the workers to be organized and stay connected to their peers and workgroups.

For example, many versions of **collaboration software** come with appointment calendars. This allows employees to keep track of specific days and times for meetings and appointments. Often software of this type is stored on a central computer, so that colleagues can make appointment requests for others. The software checks the appointment calendars of those who are requested to attend a meeting, then finds an appropriate date and time based on everyone's schedule. No longer do businesspeople need to make so many attempts to arrange or check on a meeting time. This relieves the pressure of setting up the meeting, because meeting time setup is automatic.

Software of this type can often be synchronized to a PDA, which allows workers to take their contacts, note pads, and appointment books with them, so they can keep up to date on meetings and appointments while away from the office.

Using Technology to Improve Your Writing

Communicating effectively through writing means producing communications that are error-free and that meet the highest professional standards. Business professionals and support personnel, therefore, must develop the composing, editing, proofreading, and formatting skills necessary to produce such communications. Advances in office technology have placed increased emphasis on these skills, which are required for job success.

Taking Responsibility for Errors

If you do your own composing, editing, and proofreading, you are responsible for any errors in your final product. Even though a support person might proofread your writing, you are the person who will sign the document—and the impression the communication makes on the receiver reflects on you, the signer. Because the first impression can often be a lasting impression, you should always strive for error-free copy.

Edit or revise your communications while they are in rough draft form. This process involves more than correcting spelling, grammar, punctuation, and similar errors. Editing requires looking at a written communication critically to see if revising the content or the way it is organized will improve it. Proofreading requires checking the final copy to make sure it is free from any errors. Check your communication for positive tone, and use your checklists from previous chapters to be sure that you are using the seven Cs of effective correspondence.

Editing the Message

Written messages that contain incorrect facts, figures, dates, and even more serious errors are sent and received every day. Avoiding these and other errors in written communication is a matter of knowing the rules of language use and of developing editing and proofreading skills. A document should be edited carefully before a final copy is prepared.

Follow these guidelines to edit your message:

- Pay careful attention to details. For example, check spelling of names, references to dates, money amounts, room locations, and so on.
- Read the message for meaning. Consult your planning notes to check for accuracy of information.
- Check tone and style, using the writing principles you learned in Chapters 1–5.
- Use proofreaders' marks to mark corrections. Refer to the inside front cover of this text for a list of proofreaders' marks. Mark all changes using a contrasting color of ink; use a different color for each revision so that you will not get confused when making the changes.

Proofreading the Message

Many writers say they have to print a hard copy of their communication to proofread thoroughly since proofreading on the computer screen can be difficult, especially if a document is lengthy. Errors in spacing, for instance, are easy to miss on the computer screen.

To proofread a document thoroughly, use the following procedures:

1. Spell check the document.
2. Proofread the document on the screen from beginning to end.
3. Use the View, Zoom, or Print Preview feature on your computer to check placement of elements on the page.
4. Run the grammar checker if it is a separate feature in your word processing software.
5. Print the document and proofread the hard copy.
6. Check for grammar, spelling that the spell checker could miss, capitalization, number usage, and punctuation. Check for numbers such as street addresses and ZIP Codes, when appropriate.
7. Look for confusion of similar words, such as *to, too, two; quite, quiet; its, it's; your, you're; led, lead; hear, here; by, buy; there, their*. Refer to Chapter 2 and review the sections on word choice.
8. Watch for transposition of letters within a word, such as *from* for *form*.
9. Check for transposition of words in phrases, such as *it if is* for *if it is*.

Go to CD-ROM
Activity 6-2
To test your skills.

Using Technology to Improve Communication

149

10. Check for omission of words, of phrases, of spaces between words, and of one of a pair of commas, dashes, quotation marks, or parentheses. Check for broken paragraphs, especially at page breaks. Check hyphenated words to be sure that they are divided properly at the end of lines.

The best way to proofread is to scrutinize every detail of every part of your document. Remember that proofreading is not the same as reading; you must pay attention to small details. Be certain to compare a corrected printout to the original edited version to be sure all revisions have been made and no new errors have been added.

You would be surprised how many business letters are mailed without dates or signatures because of carelessness. Proofread the final copy to be sure it is free from any error before you send it to the receiver. Reading a document aloud is a good proofreading technique to detect errors and check for readability.

CHAPTER 6 SUMMARY

In this chapter we have covered various facets of computing and business technology that apply to the workplace. In the first part of the chapter, we looked at several typical and contemporary pieces of office equipment and technology. These included the computer, fax machine, scanner, and PDA.

We then moved on to the Internet and to an in-depth look at e-mail, the details of how it works, and the rules of etiquette for communicating online. Finally, we ended with an overview of various business applications. We covered the use of word processors, spreadsheets, databases, presentational applications, and personal information applications, and reviewed some tips for proofreading the documents you create when using these technologies.

Chapter 6

Online Exercises

Objective:
These online activities will help you brainstorm and review planning for effective communications.

Go to **bcw.glencoe.com**, the address for the *Business Communication at Work* Web site, and select Chapter 6. Next, click on Online Exercises. You will see a list of Web site links that will bring you to search engines and ergonomic Web sites.

Activity 6.1

1. Select one of the search engines to visit.
2. Key *project management software* in the **Search** box (some Web sites may use an **Enter Word** box).
3. Click on a link that discusses project management software. Select an article at the Web site that you think is interesting. If you cannot find an article return to your search results and select another Web site.
4. After reading the article, return to your search results. Select four additional links that discuss project management software. Read one article from each Web site you visit.
5. On a sheet of paper, write a paragraph discussing what you learned about project management software from your readings. Before writing your paragraph, brainstorm as many details as you can on your paper.
6. Write your name on your paper, and hand it in to your instructor.

Activity 6.2

1. Ergonomics is the study of the relationship between the worker and the work environment. Work-related injuries are a major focus of ergonomics. Select one of the ergonomic Web sites to visit.
2. Read an ergonomic news story that you find interesting. The story may be located on the homepage, or you may have to click on a link such as **What's New**.
3. On a sheet of paper, answer the following questions about the purpose of a communication and audience analysis:
   a. What is the purpose of the article?
   b. Who is the intended audience of the ergonomics article?
   c. Based on the article, what information, if any, is known about the receiver's background, knowledge, interests, and experiences?
4. Write a paragraph discussing the ergonomics issue you read about. You may consider the following questions in your paragraph:
   a. Do you think that resolving the ergonomics issue will improve working conditions for a person?
   b. Does the issue affect everyone in the workforce?
   c. What affects will the issue have on an employer?
5. Write your name on the front of the printout, and hand it in to your instructor.

Using Technology to Improve Communication

CHAPTER 6 WORKSHEETS

NAME _____ DATE _____

PRACTICE 1

Using Technology to Capture and Refine Ideas

Instructions: Brainstorm your ideas for the following situations. You may add any information you feel is necessary to broaden your ideas. After you have completed the brainstorming session for each exercise, develop an outline using the ideas that you have logically arranged under each major and minor topic.

1. You have been asked to write about the advantages and disadvantages of allowing employees to use their computers for personal use before work, during their lunch hour, and after work.

2. You would like your company to allow you to install legally a copy of a software program at home so you can work there. Brainstorm the advantages and disadvantages.

3. You have been asked to submit recommendations for adding voice mail to the telephones of each employee in your company. Brainstorm the advantages and disadvantages.

4. You have heard several employees who use the computer constantly complain of their wrists hurting. You know that prolonged use of a keyboard can cause carpal tunnel syndrome—serious and painful damage to the wrists. Brainstorm your ideas to formulate a request that each computer in your company be equipped with a wrist pad to help avoid injury to the wrists.

5. No e-mail message is private, even when it has been deleted; it is still retained by the system. The system administrator at your company has advised you that several employees in your department have been abusing the system by sending personal messages and visiting each other by e-mail. You must now send an e-mail message outlining the company policy about the personal use of e-mail. Brainstorm the main points you will include in the message.

PRACTICE 2

E-mail and the Internet

Instructions: Compose the following e-mail messages:

1. Your manager has a staff meeting scheduled in conference room A-11 for Friday, May 15. The air-conditioning in that room is not working, and the workmen will be installing a new system on that Friday. Compose an e-mail message advising your manager that you have moved the staff meeting to conference room B-14 on the eleventh floor and why.

2. Compose an e-mail to your manager requesting vacation time for March 15–19 to be off during your children's spring break.

3. Compose an e-mail to the Payroll Department and request a credit union payroll deduction form to be sent to you. You want to increase the amount to be deducted from your pay to be sent to your credit union savings account.

4. Research information about two Internet providers available in your area and compose a one-page report on the computer. Include each provider's name, the computer requirements to make a connection, the numbers of hours per month you may be online, and the cost the provider charges.

CHAPTER 6 WORKSHEETS

NAME _____ DATE _____

PRACTICE 3

Proofreading and Outlining Skills

Instructions: Practice the concepts you have learned in this chapter by perparing the following outlines:

1. Compose a paragraph or two on the computer explaining all you need to do to assure yourself a document you have written is correct and acceptable according to the principles of writing you have learned in Chapters 1–5. Be sure to include the checklist information in your composition.

2. Create an outline; then compose a short report from the outline about your career goals. Include your major area of study, the number of hours you have completed, and the number of hours you have remaining toward your degree. Identify the company (or industry) where you would most like to work after graduation. Include a minimum salary you expect to make as a beginning employee. Explain your long-range goal(s)—what you would like to have accomplished professionally ten years from today. Include the outline with the report for your instructor.

3. Contact a local hospital and research how their medical records are transcribed. Ask the following questions:

    a. Do you use a desktop transcribing unit or a remote system?
    b. Do you transcribe with a word processor or computer?
    c. What word processing software do you use?
    d. What version of the software do you use? What type of network is used? How is it linked to the server and the users?
    e. How do you make copies? How many typically?
    f. What two major problems do you encounter from those who dictate?
    g. How would you improve the system in use?
    h. Add any other information you think is important.

   Create an outline from your research. Compose a rough draft from your outline directly on the computer. Print a copy and then edit it using proofreaders' marks. Revise the rough draft on the computer; print and proofread the final printed copy. Turn in the outline, edited rough draft, and final copy to your instructor.

Using Technology to Improve Communication

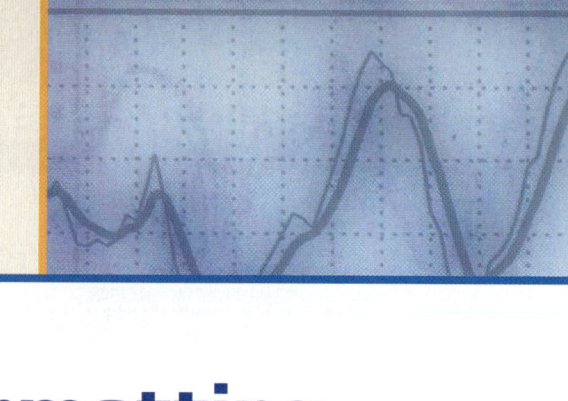

CHAPTER 7

Formatting Business Messages

Objectives

After completing this chapter, you will be able to:

1. Describe the differences between memos formatted on printed memo forms and plain paper
2. List the advantages of using a memo template on word processing software programs
3. Identify the parts of a memo
4. Identify other types of internal messages
5. Identify the four major parts of a letter
6. Describe correct formatting for each of the letter parts
7. Format the two most popular letter and punctuation styles
8. Describe the composition and format of continuation pages
9. Identify the proper format for addressing envelopes for the USPS
10. Demonstrate the correct way to fold business messages for three commonly used business envelopes

WORKPLACE APPLICATIONS

Etiquette

Etiquette is the set of recognized guidelines for behavior in social situations. It is more than the rules that explain which fork to use or when to put your white shoes back in the closet. Etiquette provides guidelines for living in a chaotic world. In the business world, etiquette is still important, despite the practice of **casual Fridays.** It reminds us to be courteous, to put our best selves forward, and to be thoughtful and respectful of our coworkers and customers.

Rules of Interaction

Business etiquette is a set of guidelines for navigating the workplace. Anyone who works comes into contact with other human beings, either in person, through writing, or over the Internet or telephone. Any situation that calls for contact with another person is one in which business etiquette can help. The rules of etiquette call for your awareness of yourself as an individual and as a representative of your company or product. You always want to make a good impression, and etiquette can help.

Etiquette guidebooks offer tips on how to manage your appearance and modify your behavior so as to make the best impression possible. They stress the importance of good grooming, thoughtful habits, and cultural customs.

Although it may be tempting to dismiss the rules of etiquette, it is important to remember that demonstrating good manners is always in style. When you show yourself to be a mannered and polite person, you make a positive impression on the people you meet and work with. They perceive your good manners and courteous behavior as a sign that you are an intelligent, decent, respectful, and, above all, trustworthy individual. And they will probably want to work with you on a regular basis. No amount of advertising can buy that kind of public relations.

Thinking Critically

Situation: You are a sales representative who has traveled to meet with a potential customer. The customer keeps you waiting and then takes a phone call during your presentation. When you finish, he tells you that he has never been impressed with your company's products.

Ask Yourself: How would business etiquette help you manage the situation? What would you say to the customer? How could the customer improve his own behavior?

155

> **The first impression is a lasting impression.**
> —Unknown

You have studied the principles and techniques of effective business communication at work in the previous chapters. Before looking at specific types of business messages, think about the first impression when the recipient opens your message. How does the message look? Does it look as if a professional prepared it?

Computers and technology have changed the way we format business messages. Many word processing software programs come with several different templates for memos and letters. In this chapter we'll look at appropriate formatting for business messages.

Formatting Memos

Written communications within a business organization are called **internal memorandums** or **memos.** In many organizations, particularly large ones, memos exchanged internally far outnumber external letter communications. In all organizations, in-house memos are vital to efficient operations. Every memo has a job to do, whether it's a simple reminder or a persuasive request.

The memo is valuable for internal communications because a memo:

- Carries a special informality (because both writer and reader are part of the same organization).
- Provides a written record (unlike a phone call).
- Can be delivered *instantly* by electronic mail or facsimile or delivered by hand.

NOTES

Time Savers

Using memos for interoffice communication saves time.

Memos save time. They use a simple format, which is designed to be efficient and productive, and they do not require the formality of an inside address, salutation, or complimentary closing. By using this simple format, the writer can concentrate on the content. Memos are not typed on letterhead stationery. Often plain paper or preprinted forms can be used rather than expensive letterhead paper.

Memo formats vary from organization to organization. A standardized format isn't necessary since memos are sent only to people within an organization. Look at the format of the memo shown in Figure 7-1.

Types of Memos

Most organizations prefer to use 8 1/2- by 11-inch paper. All correspondence will be the same size and will, therefore, be less likely to get lost in the files.

Plain Paper

Since most organizations now use computers, the trend today is to print memos on plain paper. To set up the memo the easiest and fastest way on plain paper, follow these guidelines. Refer to Figure 7-1 for an example of a memo printed on plain paper.

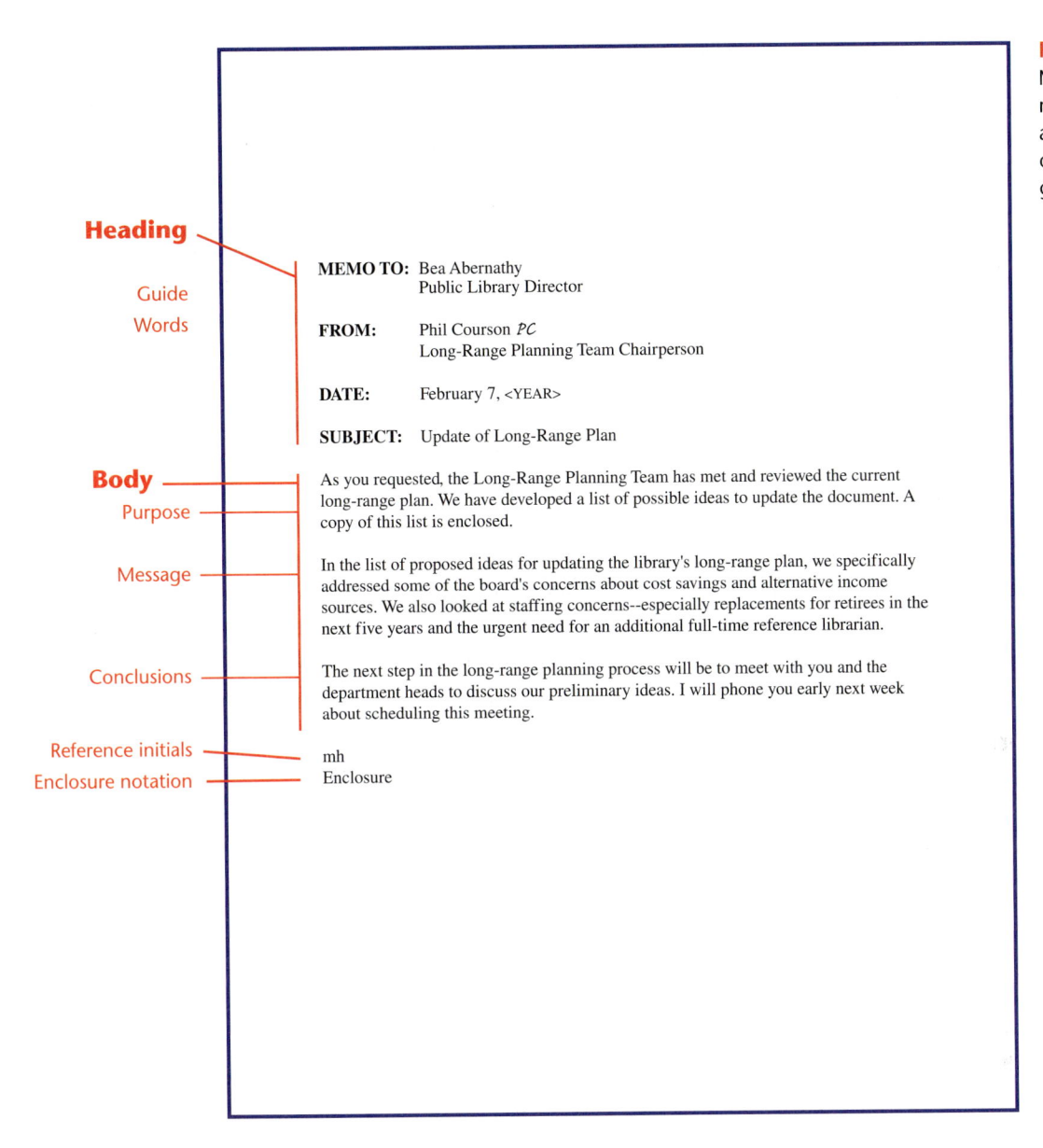

Figure 7-1
Memo formats may be set up according to an organization's guidelines.

Heading
- Guide Words

MEMO TO: Bea Abernathy
Public Library Director

FROM: Phil Courson *PC*
Long-Range Planning Team Chairperson

DATE: February 7, <YEAR>

SUBJECT: Update of Long-Range Plan

Body
- Purpose

As you requested, the Long-Range Planning Team has met and reviewed the current long-range plan. We have developed a list of possible ideas to update the document. A copy of this list is enclosed.

- Message

In the list of proposed ideas for updating the library's long-range plan, we specifically addressed some of the board's concerns about cost savings and alternative income sources. We also looked at staffing concerns--especially replacements for retirees in the next five years and the urgent need for an additional full-time reference librarian.

- Conclusions

The next step in the long-range planning process will be to meet with you and the department heads to discuss our preliminary ideas. I will phone you early next week about scheduling this meeting.

Reference initials — mh
Enclosure notation — Enclosure

- Use the default side margins. Usually the side margins are 1 inch or 1 1/4 inches (6-inch or 6 1/2-inch line).

- Position the insertion point approximately 2 inches from the top of the page. Most word processing programs have a 1-inch top margin.

- Double-space the guide words in the heading (***MEMO TO:, FROM:, DATE:, SUBJECT:***) in all-capital letters at the left margin. These guide words are in bold type to make them stand out from the other text.

- Insert a colon after each heading guide word.

- Tab once after the colon following each heading guide word.

- Using capital and lowercase letters, key the addressee's name, the sender's name, the date, and the subject on the appropriate line at the tab stop.

Formatting Business Messages

Templates

Most word processing programs offer the following:

- A choice of templates (style sheets) for memo forms
- The capability of creating and storing your own template
- A "macro" feature with which you can create an electronic memo form, including the heading text and tab stops. A macro feature provides a series of steps, which are executed in order when the feature is activated or the key is pressed.

An example of a template from a popular word processing program is shown below in Figure 7-2.

Preprinted Paper

Most organizations no longer use preprinted memo forms since keying text from a computer onto preprinted forms can be time-consuming. If a computer is being used with preprinted forms, the person keying the memo would need to create a custom template that would help with aligning the appropriate information after each printed guide word in the heading.

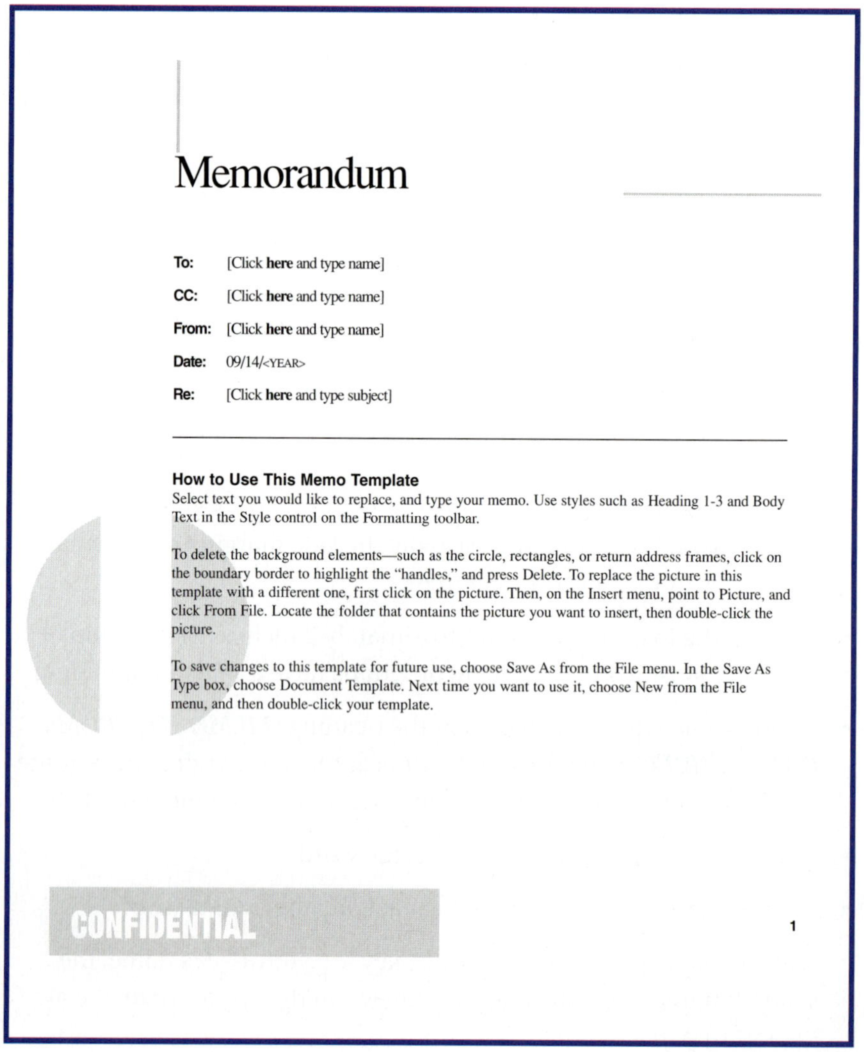

Figure 7-2
Templates from word processing software can be used for creating memos.

Memorandum

To: [Click here and type name]
CC: [Click here and type name]
From: [Click here and type name]
Date: 09/14/<YEAR>
Re: [Click here and type subject]

How to Use This Memo Template
Select text you would like to replace, and type your memo. Use styles such as Heading 1-3 and Body Text in the Style control on the Formatting toolbar.

To delete the background elements—such as the circle, rectangles, or return address frames, click on the boundary border to highlight the "handles," and press Delete. To replace the picture in this template with a different one, first click on the picture. Then, on the Insert menu, point to Picture, and click From File. Locate the folder that contains the picture you want to insert, then double-click the picture.

To save changes to this template for future use, choose Save As from the File menu. In the Save As Type box, choose Document Template. Next time you want to use it, choose New from the File menu, and then double-click your template.

CONFIDENTIAL

Side margins—equal distance from the left and right edges of the paper—should be included that would align the lines attractively with either the guide words or approximately 0.25 inch from the colon following the longest guide word.

Parts of a Memo

A memo has two main parts: the heading and the body.

Heading

Organizations often have a standard format for supplying information found in the heading. However, all memos should contain the following minimum information in the heading:

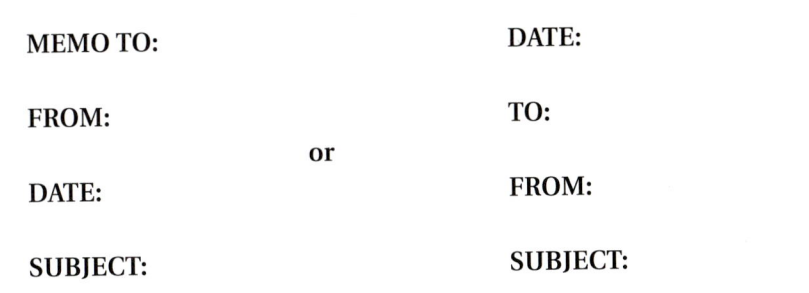

MEMO TO:	**DATE:**
FROM:	**TO:**
DATE:	**FROM:**
SUBJECT:	**SUBJECT:**

or

NOTES

First Things First
The memo heading lists the addressee, writer, date, and subject.

If your organization has several divisions or offices in more than one location, the heading may also include information such as the following:

DIVISION: OR **DEPARTMENT:**

LOCATION: OR **FLOOR:** OR **BRANCH:**

PHONE: OR **EXT:**

As we will see, the different parts of the heading may be arranged in different patterns and tailored to fit individual organizations.

MEMO TO: The name of the person or persons to whom your memo is being sent is keyed on the same line as **MEMO TO:**. By using the heading guide word **MEMO TO:**, you eliminate the need to key **Memorandum** at the top of your paper. Memos may be addressed to:

- An individual
- Several individuals
- A division or department
- All personnel

If your memo is being sent to a large group of individuals, the heading may look better if you list the recipients' names in a Distribution List at the end of the memo (the heading shouldn't take up more than half of the page). In the example in Figure 7-3a, the word **Distribution** after **MEMO TO:** is a part of the heading. To list the names in a distribution list, double-space after the reference initials, attachment notation, or copy notation (whichever comes last), then key

Formatting Business Messages

Figure 7-3a
This request memo illustrates proper format for a two-page memorandum.

Chatham Medical Center
Village Landing
Chatham, MA 02633

MEMO TO: Distribution

FROM: John R. Doran
Administration

DATE: September 15, <YEAR>

SUBJECT: Part-Time Employment and Early Retirement for Nonprofessional Staff

The number of nonprofessional employees in relation to occupancy rates in each of Chatham's three facilities is very high and costly. I need your suggestions about ways to encourage early retirement or part-time employment for approximately 600 of our full-time nonprofessional staff. Our professional staff is adequate in number, and the present ratio of professional staff to occupancy rates is acceptable.

The key points brought out in the executive staff meeting last Thursday are summarized here:

1. Chatham is experiencing declining occupancy rates in its three facilities, as are other hospitals in this area and throughout the nation.

2. Year-to-date through August, Chatham Central has a 77.1 percent occupancy rate; Chatham East, 75.7 percent; and Chatham West, 67.5 percent.

3. These rates were in the 80th percentile in years past and are projected to decrease even further by the end of the fiscal year.

4. Changes in Medicare reimbursement policies, increasing trends toward insurance co-payments, wellness programs, and outpatient clinics are some of the major factors contributing to fewer hospital admissions and shorter stays.

Thinking Cap 7.1

Discuss: What are the advantages and disadvantages of listing names in alphabetical order on a memo distribution list? In rank order?

Distribution: and double-space. List the names of the recipients in the order preferred by your organization. For example, some organizations follow the traditional style of arranging the names first by rank, and then in alphabetical order. For simplicity, many organizations list all the names in alphabetical order regardless of rank. If space is tight, arrange the names in two or more columns.

When your memo is finished and copies have been made, highlight the recipient's name or place a checkmark on each copy beside the name of the person who is to receive that copy. The memo shown in Figure 7-3b illustrates the copy of a memo intended for S. Myler.

Although courtesy titles (*Mrs., Ms., Miss,* and *Mr.*) are generally omitted in memo headings, business titles such as *Vice President* or *Sales Manager* may be used in these situations:

- The addressee has several titles, and a particular memo pertains to the responsibilities associated with only one of them

- The name of the addressee could be confused with that of another employee (for example, Paula M. Martin and Paula N. Martin)

- The writer wishes to show respect to a superior

- The writer wishes to assure prompt and *accurate* delivery of the memo

> Distribution
> Page 2
> September 15, <YEAR>
>
> With hopes of avoiding layoffs next year, Chatham is urging employees to take early retirement or go to part-time status. Currently, 11 percent of our workforce is classified as part-time employees. We have to initiate a strategy that will double that percentage. There are approximately another 200 employees who are eligible for early retirement options.
>
> To continue on the present course will jeopardize not only the existence of Chatham, but also the financial well-being of its many employees and the caliber of health care provided for this community.
>
> Please give me your immediate feedback as to how we can achieve these necessary goals through attrition instead of layoffs.
>
> df 6_staff
>
> <u>Distribution:</u>
>
> J. Bergstrom
> B. Bowles
> M. Briglow
> S. Craig
> L. Dubea
> C. Ervin
> J. Hughes
> J. Kider
> E. Myler
> S. Myler ✓
> S. Schade

Figure 7-3b
Note that the names for the distribution list are in alphabetical order. The copy for each person is checked off the list.

FROM: The writer does not use a courtesy title but may include a business title, department, location, and/or phone number for identification purposes and to facilitate a response.

DATE: The date should be written in full and not abbreviated or expressed in figures. A complete date is necessary to prevent oversights and miscommunications, and it will prove helpful for future reference. In fact, some organizations put the date line first in the heading.

SUBJECT: The subject line serves as the title of your message and as an aid in filing the memo for future reference. When writing a subject line, remember to do the following:

- Be concise—use a phrase (not a complete sentence) that tells the reader the content of the message.
- Be specific—for example, don't use *Marketing Information* on all memos written by the Marketing Department.
- Capitalize the important words.
- Omit a period at the end of the subject line.
- Leave a double space between the subject line and the body of the memo.

NOTES

The Body

The body of the memo contains the message and any reference lines.

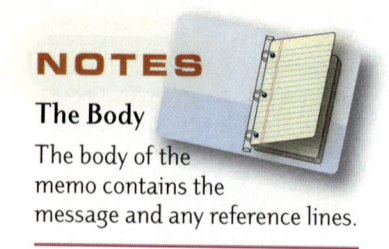

Body

The **body** of the memo contains the message. Follow these general guidelines for preparing the body:

- Leave one blank line between the heading and the body.
- Single-space the body text, leaving one blank line between paragraphs.
- Use block paragraphs (no paragraph indentions) to save time; however, indenting paragraphs is permissible.

The reference lines on a memo are each placed below the message on a separate line at the left margin in the following order:

1. Reference initials.
2. Attachment notation.
3. Copy notation (use *c:*, an abbreviation that means *copy to*). Some authorities suggest and some offices use the abbreviation *cc:* that means *courtesy copy*.

The **reference initials** are the initials of the person who keyed the document. After the person's initials, you may include the file name under which the document will be stored electronically. (See Figure 7-3b.)

An **enclosure notation** indicates that another item, such as a pamphlet, form, booklet, or other printed material, is included with the memo. An **attachment notation** is used when something is physically attached to the memo with a staple or paper clip. A **copy notation** is used when a copy of the memo is sent to a third party who has an interest in the subject of the memo. (Styles of reference initials, enclosure notations, and copy notations are illustrated later in this chapter.)

Signing the Memo

Memos, like letters, should be signed before they are sent. The easiest and quickest way for you to sign a memo is to write your initials after the keyed name in the **FROM:** line.

    FROM: Chris White

Some writers prefer to have their names and titles placed at the bottom of their memos so that they can sign them just as they would sign a letter. When this style is used, key the name four lines below the message, starting at the center.

Thinking Cap 7.2

Discuss: Why should a memo be signed at all? What are the advantages and disadvantages of the two methods of signing a memo that are described here?

. . . additional items for the September committee meeting at extension 4839.

                               Chris White
                               Chris White

Other Types of Internal Messages

In addition to the traditional memo, there are many other methods of transmitting internal written messages.

Preprinted Message Forms

Information that is regularly collected as a routine office task is often recorded on **preprinted message forms.** Two commonly used types of preprinted message forms are telephone message forms and routing forms.

Telephone Message Forms

Since every organization conducts business over the telephone, most organizations routinely use a preprinted telephone message form. When taking a telephone message, be sure to fill out the telephone message form completely and verify the following information while the caller is still on the line:

- **Phone number.** Always get the caller's phone number; verify it by repeating it to the caller.

- **Caller's name.** Ask the caller to spell his or her name (unless you know the name) and include *both* first and last names on the form.

- **Message.** Repeat the message to the caller to be sure it is accurate.

Routing Forms

Sharing publications and other written information improves the communication in organizations. Often, there is only one copy of a publication or report that should be circulated among a group of employees. In this case, develop a **routing form** to attach to the communication. A routing form lists the names of the people who should see an item. By glancing at the routing form, each receiver can tell who still needs to see it. Usually, each recipient checks off or initials the form beside his or her name before routing it to the next person.

Other Message Forms

Other examples of message forms include the following:

- **Service request forms**—forms used to request a type of service. These forms may be used to request photocopying, maintenance, or other services specific to the company. The forms may be preprinted.

- **Supply request forms**—forms used to request a specific item. These forms may request that an item be ordered either from the supply room or requisitioned from an outside supplier.

- **Attendance reporting forms**—forms used to record absences or to request a leave of absence or vacation time. Some companies use preprinted forms for employees to initial or sign every day when they report to and leave work.

Go to CD-ROM
Activities 7-1 and 7-2
To test your skills.

NOTES: Taking Messages
When taking a phone message, always repeat the phone number to the caller after you've written it on the phone message form.

Formatting Business Messages 163

When a high volume of communications warrants it, an organization can save time by developing preprinted forms to communicate information. The key for successful use is to fill them out *completely and accurately.*

Informal Notes

Brief, informal messages that should be prepared quickly are often written on small notepads. The notepads can be made of plain paper, but many organizations print notepads for their employees with a heading such as the following:

From the Desk of Jane Smith

A Note from Jane Smith

Jane Smith, Customer Service Department

Informal notes are usually handwritten, but they may be keyed. Like other communications, informal notes should be signed and dated.

An informal note to a coworker is useful when the coworker is busy or away from his or her desk temporarily. Sometimes these notes are left primarily to get immediate attention since electronic-mail messages may not be read as quickly as a note will be seen. A typical informal message might read *Judy, I need to talk with you about the Bookwalter property.*

Another kind of informal note is the Post-it® note. **Post-it notes** are very popular for writing reminders or simple instructions. Attaching a Post-it note to a form that needs a signature is much quicker than writing a cover memo.

NOTES
Leave Your Mark
An informal note should be dated and signed.

Electronic Messages

Electronic messages include fax and e-mail messages.

Fax

Written messages that must be transmitted immediately from one office to another are often sent through facsimile, or fax, machines. As you learned in Chapter 6, a **facsimile machine** is an electronic scanner connected to telephone lines that can transmit a facsimile, or copy, of a document quickly from one office to another. A fax resembles a photocopy of a document, but it is sent in a matter of minutes over telephone lines. When you fax a letter or document, always include a cover sheet carrying information about the transmission, such as the name(s) of the person(s) sending and receiving the fax, the number of pages being sent, and the telephone and fax numbers of the sender and receiver.

E-mail

Large organizations often use electronic mail for most of their internal communications. **Electronic mail,** or **e-mail,** is sent over computer networks and appears on the receiver's computer monitor on command. An e-mail message uses a memo format. Many abbreviations and acronyms (initials) are acceptable to save time. Review the specifics about e-mail in Chapter 6.

Figure 7-4
Companies often use forms like the one shown to correspond quickly.

```
INSTRUCTIONS TO SENDER:                    INSTRUCTIONS TO PERSON ADDRESSED:
A. REMOVE YELLOW COPY FOR YOUR FILE.       A. WRITE REPLY AT BOTTOM OF FORM.
B. REMOVE AND SEND BLUE COPY TO PROPER     B. REMOVE CARBON FROM FORM.
   PERSON.                                 C. RETURN PINK TO SENDER. RETAIN WHITE
C. SEND REMAINDER OF FORM INTACT WITH         FOR YOUR FILE.
   CARBONS TO PERSON ADDRESSED.

                          Anchor Insurance Company
                              860 Anchor Way
                           Greensboro, NC 27420
                              919-555-4321

Mail To (Use mail codes when applicable)    From (Show mail code, complete address)
        Charles Anderson                         G. L. Anderson
        Greensboro 210                           Memphis 048


Subject Message  Change in Coverage on Policy ACC1933

The owner of Policy ACC1933 has requested a change in coverage of this policy. The
appropriate change form, which has been signed by the policy owner, is attached.

Please process this change and return the company-endorsed change copy to me.


Signed_____  Date_____


Reply
The company-endorsed change form is enclosed, as you requested. Please attach
it securely to the policy and forward to the policy owner.




Signed_____  Date_____
```

Message-Reply Forms

The letter from Anchor Insurance Company, which is shown in Figure 7-4, and the message-reply form from Functional Business Furnishings, shown in Figure 7-5 on the next page, provide space for both the writer's message and the addressee's reply. These two-way message forms are useful for organizations with representatives in the field who do not always have support personnel available to prepare their correspondence. The top part is used to state the message; the bottom is used for the reply.

The **message-reply form** saves time and is easy to use; the snap-out form is a preassembled pack made with pressure-sensitive or carbon paper between the copies of the form. The message forms include the following:

- An original for the recipient
- A copy to be returned to the writer
- A file copy for the writer
- An extra copy for a third person, if needed. A copy of the form can then either be faxed or mailed to the recipients.

Formatting Business Messages

Figure 7-5
Messages can be sent on a form on which the receiver can send a reply message.

Functional Business Furnishings
194 Easton Way • Orem, UT 84057 • Phone 555-1126

MESSAGE	REPLY
TO	DATE
DATE	
BY	SIGNED

INSTRUCTIONS TO SENDER
1. KEEP YELLOW COPY 2. SEND WHITE AND PINK COPIES INTACT

INSTRUCTIONS TO RECEIVER
1. WRITE REPLY 2. DETACH STUB, KEEP PINK COPY, RETURN WHITE COPY TO SENDER

While these message forms were very popular at one time, the availability of laptop computers has decreased their usefulness. Today sending a message by computer is much easier and faster.

Figure 7-6
Memo-letters similar to this one can be used to transmit information between branch offices.

☐ **Commercial Division**
1777 Kirby Parkway
Seattle, WA 98028

CARY-LINKOUS Realtors

☐ **Relocation Division**
1929 National Parkway
Seattle, WA 98028

MEMO~LETTER

TO Gary Knox, Commercial Division
Elaine Donelson, Relocation Division

DATE November 11, <YEAR>
SUBJECT Teamwork Effort to Capture Relocation Business

Please meet in my office on Friday, November 15, at 2:30 p.m. to discuss a teamwork approach which I believe will translate into profitability for our company.

I believe that the timing is right for us to capture a large share of the relocation business. I have some ideas that will help our divisions work together to contact the major accounts in our area. Please be prepared to present your own ideas as well, and let's develop a plan.

Harold Ford HF

Memo-Letters

A **memo-letter** uses a preprinted form to send a message, in memo format, to a branch office or to a field representative of the sender's organization. If the representative works from a small office or an office in his or her home, or is traveling from one field location to another, faxing the message might be practical.

Notice that the Cary-Linkous memo-letter shown in Figure 7-6 lists the branch offices, making it very easy for the writer to give his or her return address and phone number by merely checking the appropriate box. Also notice that there is room in the space beside and below the heading **TO:** for several names. The extra lines could also be used to specify the addressees' locations, especially if copies are to be mailed to other branches.

Checkpoint 7.1

1. The president of your company sends every staff member a memo explaining a change in policy. Why is a memo more effective than an e-mail, a telephone call, or an announcement at a staff meeting?

2. What are the advantages of a memo over other forms of communication?

3. What are one advantage and one disadvantage of not having a standardized memo format?

PARTS OF A BUSINESS LETTER

The appearance of your letter may be the first impression that your reader has of you and of the organization that you represent. You want that first impression to be a positive one. Professional-looking letters are arranged in a standard sequence with standard parts. The four basic parts of a business letter—**heading, opening, body,** and **closing**—and the information that can be included in each part are shown in Figures 7-7 and 7-8 on the following pages.

NOTES

Looks Matter
A letter's appearance should make a positive impression on the reader.

The Heading

The heading has these parts: a letterhead or return address and a date line.

Letterhead or Return Address

Almost all organizations use letterhead stationery for their letters. The letterheads may be designed and printed by a professional printer; they may be prepared with a template that comes with a word processing program; or they may be created by an individual using different typefaces and sizes. Letterheads should include the following information:

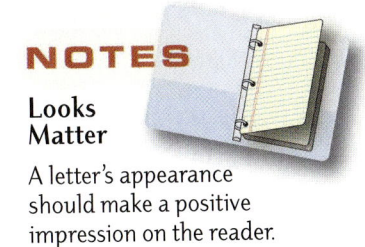

Formatting Business Messages

167

Figure 7-7
Appearance is the first part of the impression you create about yourself and your organization. This letter is shown in block style. All lines begin at the left margin.

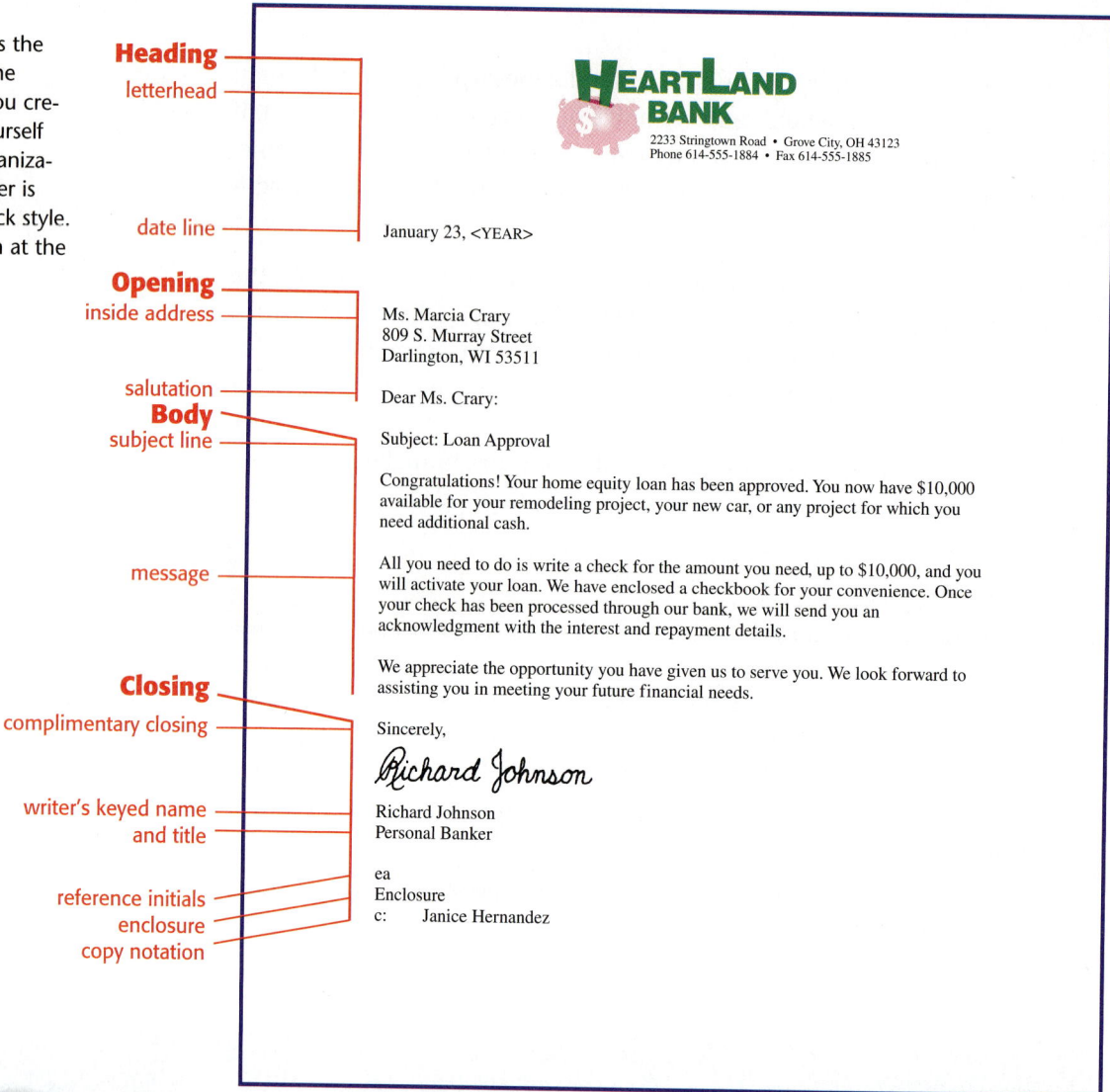

Heading
- letterhead
- date line

Opening
- inside address
- salutation

Body
- subject line
- message

Closing
- complimentary closing
- writer's keyed name and title
- reference initials
- enclosure
- copy notation

HEARTLAND BANK
2233 Stringtown Road • Grove City, OH 43123
Phone 614-555-1884 • Fax 614-555-1885

January 23, <YEAR>

Ms. Marcia Crary
809 S. Murray Street
Darlington, WI 53511

Dear Ms. Crary:

Subject: Loan Approval

Congratulations! Your home equity loan has been approved. You now have $10,000 available for your remodeling project, your new car, or any project for which you need additional cash.

All you need to do is write a check for the amount you need, up to $10,000, and you will activate your loan. We have enclosed a checkbook for your convenience. Once your check has been processed through our bank, we will send you an acknowledgment with the interest and repayment details.

We appreciate the opportunity you have given us to serve you. We look forward to assisting you in meeting your future financial needs.

Sincerely,

Richard Johnson

Richard Johnson
Personal Banker

ea
Enclosure
c: Janice Hernandez

NOTES

Return Address Options

Before the date:

1426 West 15th Street
Tifton, GA 31794
March 15, <YEAR>

After the Signature:
Sincerely,

Don Anderson

Don Anderson
1426 West 15th Street
Tifton, GA 31794

- Name of your organization
- Mailing address
- Phone and fax numbers
- Logo or graphic, if your organization uses one
- E-mail address, if available

If you are using plain paper to write a personal business letter such as a job application letter, a return address is required. The return address may be placed above the date or below the keyboarded signature.

If you are placing your return address above the date, never include your name or your organization's name. Begin with your street address on the first line and place your city, state, and ZIP Code as the second line. Key the date line beneath the return address.

Another way to include your return address is to key it below your keyed name in the closing. Keying the address after the signature keeps the name and address together; however, it looks less formal.

Figure 7-8
Letters have a heading, date, opening, body, and closing. This letter is shown in modified-block style.

PRO STYLE COMPANY
1810 Draft Street ♦ Richardson, TX 75080 ♦ Phone 972-555-1218

April 9, <YEAR>

Mrs. Heather Michaels
Berbaum Corporation
43 Brickyard Road
Fredricksburg, VA 22401

Dear Mrs. Michaels:

The modified-block style is the most frequently used letter style in business today.

The format for this letter style has the date line, complimentary closing, company name, and writer's signature and title beginning at the horizontal center. All other lines begin at the left margin (unless you wish to indent the paragraphs). Enclosed is a sample letter showing indented paragraphs.

The modified-block style usually uses standard or mixed punctuation. This means that a colon is typed after the salutation and a comma after the complimentary closing, as illustrated in this letter.

Please return the enclosed reply card if you would like to receive one of our Training Department's booklets on letter formats.

The enclosure notation below shows an acceptable style for specifying the items that are enclosed.

Sincerely yours,

PRO STYLE COMPANY

Dennis R. Hillard

Dennis R. Hillard
President

dms
Enclosures: Letter
             Reply Card

Date Line

The date line should be on one line and should contain the following:

- The name of the month, spelled in full
- The day of the month, expressed in digits
- The year, written as four digits

Always spell out the month and include all four digits for the year so that the date will not be misinterpreted. For example: The business translation of *8/3/03* is "August 3, 2003"; however, the military or European translation of *8/3/03* is "March 8, 2003." Look at how the date of February 25 appears in both business style and military or European style:

BUSINESS STYLE: February 25, 2003

(Month Day, Year [requires comma])

MILITARY STYLE: 25 February 2003   OR   25 Feb 03

(Day Month Year [no comma])

GLOBAL DIVERSITY 7.1

Dating Confusion
People in European countries write the day ahead of the month when giving dates. Example: The conference will be 26 July to 1 August. *Could this be confusing to non-Europeans?*

Formatting Business Messages

If you are using plain paper and the return address is at the top of the letter, key the date immediately below the city, state, and ZIP Code. If the return address is under the signature, key the date two inches from the top followed by three blank lines. If you are using letterhead stationery, the date line should be at least two lines below the letterhead.

The Opening

The purpose of the opening is to direct the letter to its destination and to greet the reader. The opening includes an inside address and a salutation. Sometimes an attention line is used.

Inside Address

The inside address includes the following:

- Name of the addressee
- Job title of the addressee (if applicable)
- Name of the addressee's organization (when available)
- Room number, apartment number, suite number (if applicable)
- Street address or post office box number
- City, state, and ZIP Code or country, if applicable

You can avoid errors in your letters if you use the following guidelines.

Name of the Addressee. Make every effort to identify specifically the name of the person who will be reading the letter. Letters addressed to "To Whom It May Concern" or "Current Occupant" are the most likely to be disregarded.

- Write the addressee's name exactly as he or she writes it.
- If you know the correct courtesy title (*Mr., Mrs., Miss,* or *Ms.*), use it with the name.
- If you are writing to a woman and are unsure of her preference for a courtesy title, omit the courtesy title rather than offend her.
- If you are unsure of the addressee's gender, omit the courtesy title and use the first name along with the last name.
- If you do not know the name of a specific individual, you may use a job title *(Sales Manager)* or department name *(Sales Department)* as the addressee. Repeat the title or department name in the salutation.
- When addressing a letter to a doctor, use *Dr.* for the courtesy title; avoid using double titles (*Dr.* and *M.D.* mean the same thing).

    INCORRECT: Dr. Mildred E. Griggs, M.D.

    CORRECT: Dr. Mildred E. Griggs OR Mildred E. Griggs, M.D.

Both of the correct forms use this salutation: *Dear Dr. Griggs:*

Job Title of the Addressee. Incorrectly identifying the recipient's job title will undermine your message before the first line is read. As with the name of the addressee, accuracy improves the chances of your communication being read.

- Use the addressee's job title (*Human Resources Manager, Sales Manager, Maintenance Superintendent*) when you know it.
- Key this title on a separate line under the addressee's name. If the title is long, break it into two lines but indent the second line two or three spaces.

  Mrs. Martha Ramiraz
  Office Manager and
    Personnel Administrator

Street Address. House numbers and building numbers are expressed in figures, except for the number one, and are written without a prefix. Street designations (*Street, Avenue, Road*) should be written in full rather than abbreviated. Directions used in street names (*North, South, East, West, Southeast, Northwest*) should be written out to avoid misreading.

INCORRECT:	1 Carriage Lane
CORRECT:	One Carriage Lane
INCORRECT:	#520 Dawn Street OR No. 520 Dawn Street
CORRECT:	520 Dawn Street

For street names that are numbers, spell out numbers up to and including ten; use figures for numbers over ten.

INCORRECT:	7430 7th Street
CORRECT:	7430 Seventh Street
INCORRECT:	606 Fourteenth Avenue
CORRECT:	606 14th Avenue

Omit the ordinal endings *st, d,* and *th* when a word like *North* or *South* separates two numbers:

INCORRECT:	606 South 14th Avenue
CORRECT:	606 South 14 Avenue

Some cities, such as Washington, D.C., use **section designations**—*NE, NW, SE, SW*—after some street names. Follow these formatting guidelines when using section designations:

- Place the designation on the same line as the street name.
- Separate the section from the street name with a comma.
- Key the section in all-capital letters with no periods.

GLOBAL DIVERSITY 7.2

Street Addresses
In some countries, the street name appears ahead of the house or building number. Example: Koperstraat 45
What sources can you consult in order to ensure your letters are correctly addressed?

Formatting Business Messages

171

INCORRECT:	One Carriage Lane,
	NW
	Washington, DC 20510
CORRECT:	One Carriage Lane, NW
	Washington, DC 20510

A section designation is an important part of the street address and should not be excluded.

Post Office Box Number. A post office box number may be used in place of the street address:

> Mr. Alan Ubanhower
> P.O. Box 132
> Rock Hill, SC 29730

If both a street address and a post office box number are provided, the box number should be keyed just above the city, state, and ZIP Code. The postal service will deliver to the address given on the line preceding the city, state, and ZIP Code. Sending mail to a post office box is usually faster.

Correspondence delivered by other carriers, such as Federal Express (FedEx) and United Parcel Service (UPS), requires a street address and usually the telephone number of the recipient.

City, State, and ZIP Code. The city, state, and ZIP Code should always appear on one line. Follow these guidelines:

- Do not abbreviate the name of the city unless it is customarily abbreviated. For example, *St. Louis* and *St. Paul* should be written with the word *Saint* abbreviated. *Fort Myers* and *Mount Pleasant*, on the other hand, should be written with the words *Fort* and *Mount* spelled out.

- Use the two-letter state abbreviations (both capital letters with no periods and with no space between them) recommended by the USPS, or write the name of the state in full. The two-letter abbreviations are used only with ZIP Codes in addresses; they are not considered correct abbreviations in other written material. Leave one space (use no punctuation) between the state and ZIP Code.

INCORRECT:	Cleveland, Oh. 44100-1718
	OR Cleveland, OH. 44100-1718
CORRECT:	Cleveland, OH 44100-1718

- All addresses should contain a five-digit ZIP Code. In addition, the USPS recommends the use of the nine-digit ZIP Code ("ZIP Plus Four") whenever possible. The additional four digits allow the mail to be sorted by electronic equipment according

NOTES

State Abbreviations

Two-letter state abbreviations are always two capital letters with no period and are used only with ZIP Codes in addresses.

to the delivery route. When using the nine-digit code, place a hyphen between the two parts of the ZIP Code as shown in the previous example.

- When writing to someone in another country, key the name of the country in all-capital letters on a separate line as the last line of the address. If you are sending mail from another country to someone in the United States, key UNITED STATES OF AMERICA in all caps on the line below the city, state, and ZIP Code.

Multiple Addresses. There will be instances when your letters will be addressed to more than one individual. Follow these guidelines:

- When the addressees are at the same address, list the names in alphabetical order, and then give the address. Include all names in the salutation.

> Mrs. Donna Olson
> Mr. Robert Plawyer
> Miss Angela Queen
> Hurletron Corporation
> 2856 Fairchild Avenue, SE
> Washington, DC 20017
>
> Dear Mrs. Olson, Mr. Plawyer, and Miss Queen:

- When the addressees are at different addresses, key the inside addresses one under the other with a blank line between, or key the inside addresses across from each other with the second address starting at the center point. Include all names in the salutation.

Attention Line. The attention line is an optional part of a business letter opening, but it may be used when you do not know the name of the person to whom you need to write. In this case, use an attention line and refer to the person by title (*Reservations Manager*), or use the name of a specific department (*Advertising Department*). Whenever possible, you should omit the attention line and write directly to an individual by name or by job title.

When using an attention line, follow these rules:

- Key the attention line above or below the company name in the inside address or
- Key the attention line one double space (leave one blank line) below the inside address and one double space above the salutation.
- Key in all-capital letters or use initial caps and lowercase letters:

ATTENTION: SALES DEPARTMENT or **Attention: Sales Department**

- Use a colon after the word *Attention:*
- Use one of these salutations:

LADIES AND GENTLEMEN: or **Dear "Organization Name":**

GLOBAL DIVERSITY 7.3

Destination Known
When addressing mail to another country, put the name of the country in all-capital letters as the last line of the address. *Why is this important?*

The attention line is placed on the first line of the inside address if you are using window envelopes or electronically copying the inside address to create the envelope address. Look at the following example:

**Attention: Purchasing Department
Branson, Inc.
1334 Magnolia Road
Wytheville, VA 24382**

Ladies and Gentlemen:

A letter with an attention line is considered to be addressed to the organization for the purpose of the salutation rather than to the person, title, or department named in the attention line. The correct salutation would be *Ladies and Gentlemen:* or *Gentlemen and Ladies:* Remember, it is always preferable to address your letter directly to an individual, thereby eliminating the need for an attention line.

Salutation

The salutation greets the reader and helps set the tone of the letter. When preparing salutations for business letters, follow these guidelines:

- Leave a double space (one blank line) above and below the salutation.
- Start the salutation at the left margin.
- Abbreviate the titles *Mr., Mrs., Ms.,* and *Dr.,* but spell out titles such as *Major, Professor,* and *Reverend.*
- Capitalize the first word and any noun or title in a salutation:

    **My dear Miss Marsh
    Dear Father Tedrick
    Dear Senator Taylor**

- Key a colon after the salutation, unless open punctuation is used.

Determining what salutation to use can sometimes be confusing. An important concern is avoiding sexist language. Remember, however, that the salutation must agree with the addressee named in the inside address. Here are some guidelines for each type of addressee:

Individual. The salutation for an individual, such as Mr. Jeff Winland, uses a courtesy title and last name: *Dear Mr. Winland.* If you are on a first-name basis with Mr. Winland, use *Dear Jeff.*

Individual—Title Preference or Gender Unknown. Drop the courtesy title and use the full name if you don't know the addressee's gender: *Dear Gerry Fulton.* Do the same if you don't know a woman's preference for the courtesy title: *Dear Ann Garcia.*

Organization, Department, or Box Number. Use this salutation: *Ladies and Gentlemen.* If the group is composed entirely of women, use the salutation *Ladies;* likewise, a group of men should be addressed as *Gentlemen.* Never put *Dear* in front of these salutations.

Official Greetings
Search for appropriate salutations to use when writing letters to judges, members of Congress, the President of the United States, the governor of a state, mayors, or other public officials.

Another alternative is to repeat in the salutation the organization or department name used in the inside address: *Dear General Motors* OR *Dear Consumer Relations Department.*

Job Title. A letter that gives a job title as addressee uses the same title in the salutation: *Dear Personnel Manager.*

When you are sending a form letter, it is often impossible to know the gender and the title preference of each addressee. In this situation, using a salutation such as *Dear Customer, Dear Friend,* or *Dear Parents* is a friendly alternative to using both first and last names in the salutation. (Note that the use of the salutations *Dear Sir* and *Dear Madam,* now considered sexist, is rapidly declining in business correspondence.)

Less traditional salutations that start letters in a friendly, conversational way are growing in popularity. These "dearless" salutations have been used for some time in sales promotion letters but are now being used in other informal business letters as well. Look at the following unusual salutations:

> Good morning, Steven Franklin
> Hello, Mrs. Molari
> Happy Holidays, Miss Ivoniva

A letter may also start immediately with the message. In this case, the reader's name is inserted in the first sentence.

> Miss Katherine Watts
> 10 East 53 Street
> Worcester, MA 01608
>
> Thank you, Miss Watts, for your suggestions, which will help us to serve you more efficiently.

NOTES

Dear No More

"Dearless" salutations common in sales promotions are being used in other business letters.

The Body

The body of the letter contains the writer's thoughts. The body consists of the message and an optional subject line.

Subject Line

If used, a subject line precedes the message of a letter and is used to tell the reader in one glance what the letter is about. Although it is an optional part of the letter, its use is increasing—it can prove very helpful to both reader and writer. A subject line is:

- Keyed a double space (one blank line) above the message and a double space below the salutation.
- Keyed using all-capital letters or initial capitals and lowercase.
- Keyed without the word *Subject.*
- Centered, begun at the left margin, or indented, depending on the letter style.

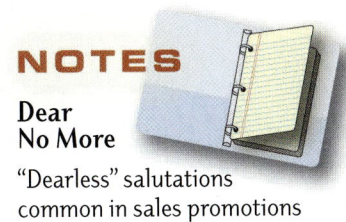

Dear Mr. Nichols:

Revision of Admissions Policy

Dear Miss Storm:

SERVICE CALLS ON WEEKENDS

Message

When keying the message, follow these rules:

- Single-space each paragraph.
- Double-space (leave one blank line) between paragraphs.
- Block all paragraphs in a block-style letter.
- Either block or indent the first line of each paragraph one-half inch in a modified-block letter.

Paragraphs that are too long are not easy or inviting to read. When writing your message, use these guidelines:

- Your first and last paragraphs should be no more than four lines (not four sentences) long.
- All other paragraphs should be no more than eight lines (not eight sentences) long.

The Closing

The closing in a business letter typically includes a complimentary closing phrase, the writer's name and title, and reference initials. The closing may also include the keyed name of the writer's organization, an enclosure notation, a copy notation, and a postscript.

Complimentary Closing

The **complimentary closing** is a parting phrase that indicates the message has ended. The complimentary closing is keyed as follows:

- A double space (one blank line) below the last line of the message.
- At the left margin in block-style letters; at the horizontal center point in modified-block style letters.
- With only the first word capitalized.
- With a comma following the closing (unless you are using open punctuation).

The tone of the complimentary closing should match that of the salutation. For example, if you have greeted your reader with *Dear Marcy,* you will probably want to close with *Sincerely.* Here are some typical closings:

FORMAL	PERSONAL
Very sincerely yours,	Sincerely yours,
Respectfully yours,	Cordially yours,
Yours very truly,	Sincerely,
Very truly yours,	Cordially,

Organization Name. In some business organizations, the name of the organization is included in the closing to indicate that the organization—not the letter writer—is legally responsible for the message. If used, the organization name should be keyed in all-capital letters on the second line below the complimentary closing phrase (see Figure 7-9a).

Writer's Name and Title. Leave three blank lines for your handwritten signature, and then key your name. Your title or department can be placed on either the same line with your name or on a separate line for a cleaner visual look, depending on which location will make your lines most nearly the same length (see Figure 7-9b).

A man does not use a courtesy title (*Mr.*) before either his handwritten or his keyed signature unless his name could also be a woman's name. A woman who wants to specify her courtesy title (*Miss, Mrs.,* or *Ms.*) should include the courtesy or professional title in either the handwritten or the keyboarded signature but not in both places. See the examples in Figures 7-9c and 7-9d.

If more than one person will sign the letter, follow the same format as that used for multiple addresses. Depending on the length of your letter, either key the signatures one under the other, allowing three blank lines for each signature, or place the signatures across from each other, starting the second signature at the center point.

Reference Initials. The initials of the person who dictated a letter and the person who transcribed it are usually keyed at the left margin, a double space (one blank line) below the last line in the signature section. The dictator's initials may be omitted in situations in which the dictator is also the signer of the letter. Some popular reference-initial styles are the following:

SME:PRG

MVL/ef

GCBrown:sn

Mls#gm_quote (assistant's initials and document file name)

owc (assistant's initials only)

jr:mj

Figure 7-9
The handwritten signature fits above the keyed name.

a

Sincerely yours,

LOVETTE CONSTRUCTION CO.

Art Troglia
Art Troglia, President

b

Cordially yours,

Deidre N. Mayfair
Deidre N. Mayfair
Reservations Manager

c

Sincerely,

Rozlynn Dolcani
Mrs. Rozlynn Dolcani

d

Sincerely,

Anne-Marie McLeod
Anne-Marie McLeod, Ph.D.

Formatting Business Messages

Enclosure Notation. An **enclosure notation** notes anything that is included in the envelope with the letter. The enclosure notation should be positioned at the left margin on the next line below the reference initials. The notation helps the writer remember to include the enclosures and tells the reader enclosures should have been sent. If there is more than one enclosure, the number of enclosures may be indicated. The following are examples of enclosure notations:

Enclosure	Enclosures 2
Check enclosed	Enclosures:
2 Enc.	1. Catalog
	2. Reply card

Copy Notation. If you want the addressee of your letter to know you are sending a copy to someone, key a copy notation one line below the enclosure notation (if used) or one line below the reference initials. Notations can be made in one of the following ways:

c: Selena Harris	pc: Selena Harris
c Selena Harris	Copy to: Selena Harris
cc: Selena Harris	Copy to Selena Harris

While *cc* formerly stood for carbon copy, now it means *courtesy copy*; likewise, *pc* stands for *photocopy,* and *c* stands for *copy to.* Key a **blind copy notation** if you do not want the addressee to know you are sending a copy of a letter to one or more other persons. Use *bc, blind copy to,* or *bcc* only on the file copy and any other copy on which the notation is desired. Do not key the blind copy notation on the original letter. The bcc notation may be placed on the upper left corner of the file copy or where you would place the cc notation.

Here are some accepted styles for reference lines, including reference initials, enclosure notations, and copy notations:

PH:dh	PCN/rl
Enclosure	Copy to Cindy Owens
c: Mrs. Frieda Lightner	
	RWP:jeh
JCR:al	Enc. 4
c: Hubbard & Smithe	cc: Jean Picard
	Kate Miligan

Postscript. A postscript or note added at the end of a letter can be used to give strong emphasis to an important idea that has been deliberately withheld from the body of the letter. Limit the use of postscripts to take advantage of their attention-getting qualities. Using a postscript to express an afterthought may be viewed by the reader as poor planning and organization.

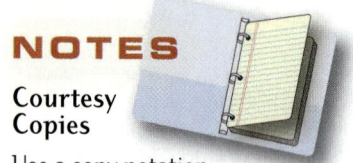

NOTES

Courtesy Copies

Use a copy notation when you send a copy of the message to another person(s).

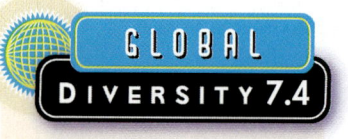

GLOBAL DIVERSITY 7.4

Irish Address

In Ireland, "Mr," Mrs," and "Miss" are considered words rather than abbreviations. Do not add a period to these courtesy titles in your correspondence with your Irish counterparts. Also, the Irish tend to refer to surgeons as "Mr" rather than "Dr."
While composing letters to potential clients in Ireland, you decide you're more comfortable punctuating according to U.S. grammar rules, because the other way just doesn't look right. What are the possible effects of your decision? What might be the recipients' reactions?

When using a postscript, key it on the second line below the last item of your letter. Key *PS.* or *PS:* and leave two spaces before the first word of the postscript or omit the abbreviation *PS*. The following are accepted postscript styles:

mls
Enclosure

PS. Mail the card today!

JCR:al
c: Hubbard & Smithe

PS: Drop by our booth at the conference for a visit!

EEB:dm

For your complimentary copy, just call collect (903) 555-4289.

> **NOTES**
>
> **Last Words**
>
> A postscript is recognized without PS. or PS: simply because of its position at the end of the letter.

LETTER STYLES

The way the letter parts are arranged is called the **style** of the business letter. Many companies have selected a particular letter style as their preferred style. If you must select a letter style, you should consider the design of your organization's letterhead as well as the image you want to convey. Two popular letter styles are the modified-block and full-block formats.

Modified-Block Style

The letter style that is used most often is known as the **modified-block style** (shown in Figure 7-10 on page 180). Follow these guidelines when formatting a modified-block-style letter:

- The date line, complimentary closing, and keyed signature start at the center point.
- Leave three blank lines after the date.
- Paragraphs may be blocked or indented.
- Single-space the body of the letter.
- Leave one blank line between paragraphs.
- Use vertical centering: For one-page letters, center the letter vertically (top to bottom) on the page. For multipage letters, position the date line two inches from the top of the paper or two blank lines below the letterhead. The second page should begin one inch from the top edge of plain stationery and should contain a heading.

Formatting Business Messages

Figure 7-10
Modified block is a popular style of letter.

PRO STYLE COMPANY
1810 Draft Street ♦ Richardson, TX 75080 ♦ Phone 972-555-1218

April 9, <YEAR>

Mrs. Heather Michaels
Berbaum Corporation
43 Brickyard Road
Fredricksburg, VA 22401

Dear Mrs. Michaels:

The modified-block style is the most frequently used letter style in business today.

The format for this letter style has the date line, complimentary closing, company name, and writer's signature and title beginning at the horizontal center. All other lines begin at the left margin (unless you wish to indent the paragraphs). Enclosed is a sample letter showing indented paragraphs.

The modified-block style usually uses standard or mixed punctuation. This means that a colon is typed after the salutation and a comma after the complimentary closing, as illustrated in this letter.

Please return the enclosed reply card if you would like to receive one of our Training Department's booklets on letter formats.

The enclosure notation below shows an acceptable style for specifying the items that are enclosed.

Sincerely yours,

PRO STYLE COMPANY

Dennis R. Hillard

Dennis R. Hillard
President

dms
Enclosures: Letter
              Reply Card

Full-Block Style

Another letter style that is appropriate for use in business is **block style**, which is illustrated in Figure 7-11 on page 181. Follow these guidelines when formatting a block-style letter:

- Start all lines of the letter at the left margin.
- Leave three blank lines after the date.
- Do not indent paragraphs.
- Single-space the body of the letter.
- Leave one blank line between paragraphs.
- Use vertical centering: For one-page letters, center the letter vertically on the page.

Figure 7-11

The block-style letter is easy to use with software programs or word processors.

KC Papers
P.O. Box 53
Kansas City, MO 64141
Phone 816-555-1200

February 15, <YEAR>

Mr. Larry Irons
102 Ray Court
Hillsboro, TX 76645

Dear Mr. Irons

Subject: Block Letter Style

All lines begin at the left margin with a block-style letter, as shown here. This style has a neat, streamlined appearance, as you can see, and looks very modern. It eliminates many extra typing strokes and motions and, therefore, helps to increase letter production rates.

This letter also illustrates the open style of punctuation, which means that punctuation is omitted after the salutation and complimentary closing.

When a subject line is used, it may be typed as shown here. The word Subject may be omitted, or the entire line may be typed in capital letters. Since the subject line is considered part of the body, it should be typed a double space above the body and a double space below the salutation.

The c notation below shows an acceptable style for indicating that copies of this letter are being sent to two persons.

Sincerely

Mary L. Carr

Mary L. Carr
Public Relations Director

lk
c: Ralph Lawrence
     Jim Barnes

- For multipage letters, position the date line two inches from the top of the paper or two blank lines below the letterhead.

- Subsequent pages should begin one inch from the top of plain stationery and should contain a heading.

Punctuation Styles

The two punctuation styles commonly used today are standard and open. **Standard punctuation** (formerly called **mixed punctuation**) calls for a colon after the salutation and a comma after the complimentary closing. Standard punctuation is the most commonly used punctuation style. **Open punctuation** requires no punctuation after the salutation and the complimentary closing. Although open punctuation requires fewer keystrokes than standard punctuation, open punctuation is used less frequently in business writing.

Formatting Business Messages

NOTES

Continue the Heading

Letters and memos of more than one page need a heading on each continuation page.

Continuation Pages

Continuation pages, or pages beyond the first page, are formatted the same way for both letters and memos. If the first page of a letter is printed on letterhead stationery, the continuation pages should be printed on plain paper that matches the letterhead in color, weight, and finish.

If a letter or memo is more than one page in length, each page after the first page must have a heading. The heading should be placed one inch from the top of the page and should include the following information:

- Name of the addressee (who the message is to)
- Page number
- Date that appears on the first page

The heading can be keyed horizontally or placed vertically on separate lines. Both styles are illustrated here:

Mrs. Nancy Holler   2   May 3, <YEAR>

Mr. Robert Pape III
Page 2
August 28, <YEAR>

Most word processing programs have a "header" that allows you to key the heading once, and the header is automatically inserted on all pages along with the correct page numbers. Another command suppresses the heading on the first page.

When keying continuation pages, leave one blank line below the last line of the heading, and use the same side margins as on the first page of the letter or memo. In addition, follow these guidelines:

- Never divide the last word on a page.
- Carry at least two lines (not two sentences) of the body of the message to the second page. Do not key only the closing of a letter or the reference lines of a memo on the second page.
- If a paragraph is divided at the end of a page, leave at least two lines at the bottom of the first page, and carry at least two lines to the top of the second page. Do not divide a paragraph containing fewer than four lines.

Thinking Cap 7.3

Discuss: You keyboard a letter and discover that only the closing lines appear on the second page. What could you do to "fix" the problem?

182   Chapter 7

A single line of text at the top or bottom of a page is referred to as a "widow" or an "orphan". Most word processing programs have a feature that will automatically prevent widow and orphan lines.

Checkpoint 7.2

1. What does the following salutation suggest about the writer of this letter? *Dear Human Resources Director*. How would you improve the salutation?
2. Why do you think it is important to list reference initials and copy notations on a letter?
3. How would you decide which letter and punctuation style to use in a letter?

ADDRESSING ENVELOPES

USPS Mail

To address mail correctly for the United States Postal Service (USPS) you should follow specific guidelines concerning envelope size, address format on envelopes, and special mailing notations.

Go to CD-ROM
Activity 7-3
To test your skills.

Envelope Size

In order for the USPS to process mail with its automated scanning and sorting equipment, the mail must meet certain size guidelines. The minimum size for envelopes is $3^{1/2}$ by 5 inches, and the maximum size is $6^{1/8}$ by $11^{1/2}$ inches (for odd-sized envelopes, you might pay a surcharge).

Numerous sizes of envelopes are available but most business letters are mailed in one of these two sizes:

- No. 10 envelopes (legal size—$4^{1/8}$ by $9^{1/2}$ inches); most common size
- No. $6^{3/4}$ envelopes (letter size—$3^{5/8}$ by $6^{1/2}$ inches)

NOTES

No. 10
Most organizations use No. 10 envelopes for mailing business letters.

Address Format

When addressing a No. 10 envelope, such as the one shown in Figure 7-12, follow these guidelines:

- Single-space the address regardless of the number of lines.
- Position the address on the lower half of the envelope (two inches from the top) and starting at the centerpoint (four inches from the left edge) of the envelope.

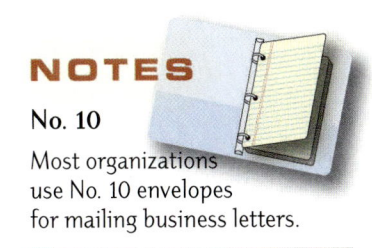

Formatting Business Messages

Figure 7-12
The USPS recommends that the placement of the letter address on the envelope follow published guidelines.

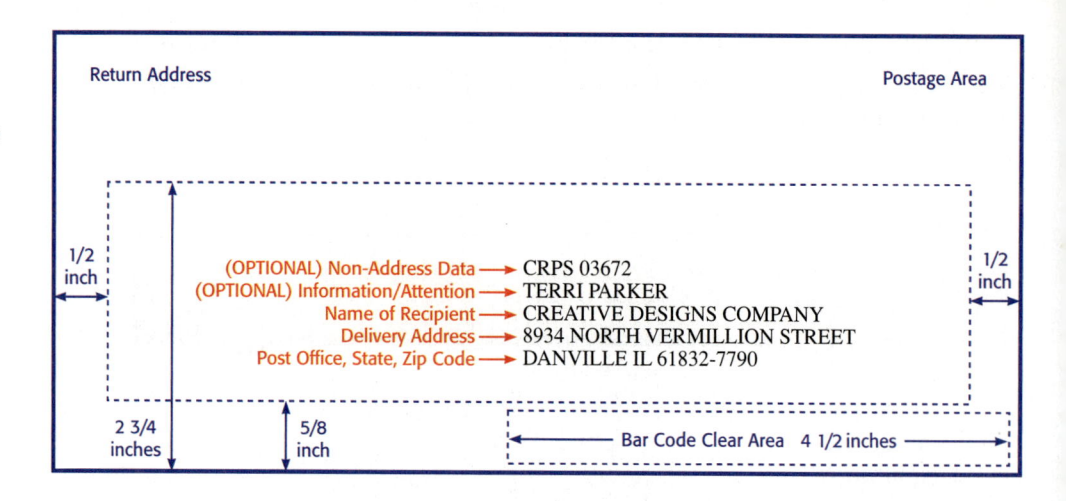

```
Return Address                                                          Postage Area

    1/2                                                                      1/2
    inch                                                                     inch
         (OPTIONAL) Non-Address Data  → CRPS 03672
         (OPTIONAL) Information/Attention → TERRI PARKER
                    Name of Recipient → CREATIVE DESIGNS COMPANY
                    Delivery Address  → 8934 NORTH VERMILLION STREET
              Post Office, State, Zip Code → DANVILLE IL 61832-7790

    2 3/4        5/8
    inches       inch         ← Bar Code Clear Area  4 1/2 inches →
```

- Key the address using capital and lowercase letters and appropriate punctuation. (Note: The mailing address may also be keyed in all-capital letters with no punctuation as shown in Figure 7-12.)

- Always place the city, state, and ZIP Code on one line and use the same rules you use for inside addresses (see pages 170–174 in this chapter).

- Never place anything below the city, state, and ZIP Code on the envelope. If possible, use the ZIP Plus Four—it allows automatic sorting of mail in the order it is delivered on the route.

- To accommodate automatic sorting equipment, allow at least 1/2-inch margins on each side of the address block and a 5/8-inch margin below the address block for the USPS to print a bar code.

Many word processing programs have an envelope feature that will automatically copy the inside address on your letter and print it in the correct location on the envelope. Another option allows you to print the bar code to match the ZIP Code, either above or below the address.

Occasionally an organization will mail letters in window envelopes. A **window envelope** allows easy letter insertion with the inside address showing through the window of the envelope. The envelope would not need to be addressed since the address shows through the window.

When formatting a letter for a window envelope, be sure to leave an extra blank line after the inside address. When the letter is folded and inserted in the envelope, check carefully to see that the complete address shows through the window.

The steps for folding a letter for a window envelope are shown in Figure 7-13 on page 186.

Special Notations. The following optional notations may also be included on the envelope:

- **Special mailing notations.** Key any special mailing notations (*AIRMAIL*, *CERTIFIED*, or *REGISTERED*) in all-capital letters below the stamp or postage meter insignia.

- **Recipient notations.** Key any recipient notations (*PERSONAL*, *HOLD FOR ARRIVAL*, or *CONFIDENTIAL*) a double space below the return address.

- **Attention lines.** Key an attention line, if used, as the first line of the mailing address.

Interoffice Envelopes

For sending internal communications, most organizations use interoffice envelopes that are reusable. These envelopes are usually made of brown or gray paper and are large enough to accommodate several 8½- by 11-inch sheets without folding. A string, snap, or adhesive tab on the back holds the envelopes closed; lines on the front (and sometimes on the back) are used for writing the names and departments of the addressees.

When using an interoffice envelope, be sure to mark through the last recipient's name. Before placing your correspondence inside the envelope, write the name of the person to receive your communication on the envelope. You are less apt to forget to put the addressee's name on the envelope if you follow this procedure.

Interoffice mail may also be mailed in a sealed No. 10 envelope. To avoid having the interoffice mail accidentally metered for postage, it is a good idea to use an envelope with a different logo or of a different color than those used for external mail.

Go to CD-ROM
Activity 7-4
To test your skills.

Folding Business Messages

The size of the envelope determines the way you fold your letter or memo. You want to fold your message in such a way that the thickness of the paper is distributed evenly throughout the envelope. This lessens the chances of your envelope becoming jammed in postal equipment.

LEGAL & ETHICAL 7-1

Junk Mail. Sara received a mailing in a window envelope. Through the window, she could read the words *Pay to the Order of* and then her name and address. The paper looked like the paper that checks are printed on. When she opened the envelope, she found a check for $20. If she cashed the check, she would be signing up for a two-year membership to a book club, and she would receive a book and an invoice for $25 each month. What is the likely effect of this sort of advertising? Is this a legal and ethical way to attract customers?

No. 10 Envelope

When folding a letter or memo for a No. 10 envelope, follow these steps shown in Figure 7-13 below:

1. Lay the letter or memo face up on the desk or table.
2. Fold the bottom third of the letter or memo up and crease neatly.
3. Fold the top third down and crease neatly.
4. Insert the last crease into the envelope first.

No. 6 3/4 Envelope

When folding a letter or memo for a No. 6 3/4 envelope, follow these steps:

1. Place the letter or memo face up on the desk or table.
2. Bring the bottom half up to within 1/2-inch of the top and crease neatly.
3. Fold the right third toward the left and crease neatly.
4. Fold the left third toward the right 1/2-inch from the right edge and crease neatly.
5. Insert the last crease into the envelope first.

Figure 7-13
Follow these simple directions to fold a letter correctly for different types of envelopes.

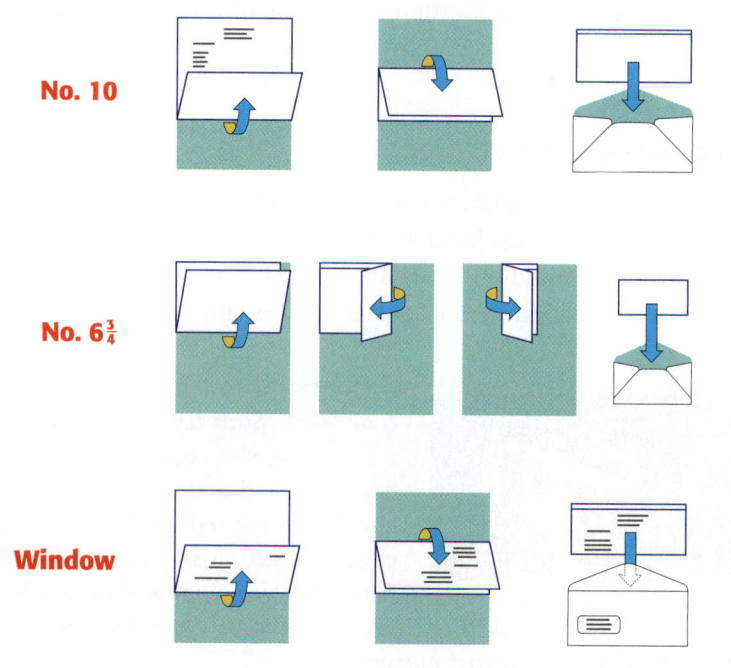

No. 10

No. 6¾

Window

Chapter 7

✓ CHECKLIST FOR FORMATTING BUSINESS CORRESPONDENCE

Did You Include the Following Parts in Your Business Message?

MEMO	YES	NO
Recipient's name?		
Your name?		
Date?		
Subject?		
LETTER		
Return address?		
Date line?		
Inside address?		
Salutation?		
Subject line? (optional)		
Complimentary closing?		
Enclosure notation? (optional)		
Postscript? (optional)		

Chapter 7 Summary

In this chapter the format for business messages was discussed and illustrated. You learned that memos can be prepared on plain paper, preprinted forms, or software templates. Other types of internal messages, including preprinted forms, informal notes, and electronic messages, and their formats were also covered.

The parts of a business letter—heading, opening, body, and closing—were covered, including the guidelines for formatting each part. The two basic letter styles, modified-block and block, were explained along with the proper way to fold letters for business envelopes. The USPS guidelines for addressing envelopes to be processed by automated sorting and scanning equipment were given.

Prepare the Worksheet Exercises as directed by your instructor. You can complete the Online Exercises now if you can access the Internet.

Formatting Business Messages

Communication at WORK

Anne Williams, Administrative Assistant

BPA International Marketing Office

Arranging for a Spanish translation of a document or sending off a news release to Hong Kong is all in a day's work for Anne Williams. Anne is the administrative assistant in the sales and marketing office of BPA International. BPA audits the circulations of magazines, business-to-business publications, and Web sites.

Emphasis on Communication Skills

"Most of my communication is directed to our sales staff and other BPA employees. I interact by phone and fax on a daily basis with my coworkers, as well as our clients, and follow up on calls to support our marketing staff," Anne explains.

Because Anne writes letters and memos on a daily basis, basic communication skills receive much of her attention. "I place great emphasis on the basic written communication skills of spelling, punctuation, and grammar, because I believe BPA is affected by my performance."

Listening is a communication skill that Anne also puts to good use in her job. "From time to time," she says, "I receive calls from individuals who are not quite sure what they need. I try to keep them calm and ask simple questions as to what exactly they are looking for."

Anne, who is 46 years old, is pursuing a Bachelor's degree in business management at Brooklyn College. She has been with BPA International for twelve years. During that time, she has come to appreciate the instant communication brought about by the Internet and e-mail.

> **"** I place great emphasis on the basic written communication skills of spelling, punctuation, and grammar, because I believe the company is affected by my performance. **"**

"E-mail and the Internet have improved communication greatly for me," says Anne. "I send e-mail to our marketing sales reps on a daily basis. In the case of a client's request, or sending a news release to Hong Kong, I can get a response in minutes."

Whether it's sending an e-mail to one of the sales reps or listening to a client's request for information, Anne is always aware of her communication skills. "It's important," she says, "to have strong written and spoken communication skills in my position because the staff and clients are depending on me."

Discuss

1. Considering that e-mail and the Internet have improved our ability to communicate quickly and clearly, how do you determine the best method of communication to use in each situation?
2. What problems might result when a company has a voice-mail line for customer complaints and inquiries?

Chapter 7
Online Exercises

Objective:
These online activities will help you gain a better understanding of business etiquette.

Go to **bcw.glencoe.com,** the address for the *Business Communication at Work* Web site, and select Chapter 7. Next, click on Online Exercises. You will see a list of Web site links that will bring you to different search engine links and business etiquette Web sites.

Activity 7.1

1. Click on one of the search engines.
2. Key *business etiquette* in the **Search** box (some search engines may use an **Enter word** box).
3. Click on one of the results that seems interesting to you. Find an article that provides suggestions for business etiquette.
4. On a sheet of paper, write a business letter to your instructor describing what you learned about business etiquette. Remember to include the following parts of the business letter:
   a. The heading
   b. The opening
   c. The body
   d. The closing
   Use the modified-block style for your letter.
5. Hand in your letter to your instructor.

Activity 7.2

1. Select one of the business etiquette Web sites to visit.
2. Click on Thailand. You may have to type *Thailand* into a **Search** box on the Web site.
3. Print out tips on business etiquette in Thailand. You may also use tips on business protocol in Thailand.
4. Write a memo to your instructor describing the tips you learned. Remember to include the parts of a memo (heading and body). Also, provide a title to your addressee.
5. Some questions you may consider in your memo include:
   a. How does business etiquette in Thailand differ from business etiquette in the United States?
   b. Why do you think it is important to have an understanding of the business etiquette of other countries?
6. Hand your memo in to your instructor.

Formatting Business Messages

CHAPTER 7 WORKSHEETS

NAME _____ DATE _____

PRACTICE 1

Writing Applications

Instructions: Complete these exercises for applications practice with memos and letters. Your instructor may assign specific exercises for you to complete for evaluation.

1. Formatting a Memo Heading. In the space provided, write the memo heading items in the correct order.

    SUBJECT: _____

    MEMO TO: _____

    DATE: _____

    FROM: _____

2. Arranging Letter Parts: The Heading. Each of the lines in the following letter parts may have format errors or errors in the order of its presentation. Arrange the lines in correct order using the blank lines provided in the answer column. Make any other corrections needed.

    Brookhaven, MS 39601 _____

    August 20, 20<YEAR> _____

    94 College Drive _____

3. Arranging Letter Parts: The Opening. Each of the lines in the following letter parts may have format errors or errors in the order of its presentation. Arrange the lines in correct order using the blank lines provided in the answer column. Make any other corrections needed.

    Burlington, NC 27215 _____

    24637 North 62 Street _____

    Miss Claudia Worden _____

    Dear Claudia: _____

4. Arranging Letter Parts: The Closing. Each of the lines in the following letter parts may have format errors or errors in the order of its presentation. Arrange the lines in correct order using the blank lines provided in the answer column. Make any other corrections needed.

    a. Sincerely yours, _____

    Director of Marketing _____

    Bruce Allen _____

    Enclosures 3 _____

    BA:ms _____

CHAPTER 7 WORKSHEETS

NAME _____ DATE _____

    b. LYRIC MUSIC CO. _____

        Cordially, _____

        TS/jw _____

        Mrs. Terry Swaim, Manager _____

    c. Mr. Dale Beyers _____

5. Addressing an Envelope. Mark the errors that appear on these envelopes:
   a.

```
┌─────────────────────────────────────────────────────────┐
│  Terri White                                            │
│  35 Elm Street                                          │
│  Rossville, IL 60963                                    │
│                                                         │
│                                                         │
│                         Mr. Bill Smith                  │
│                         Potters Woods Lane              │
│                         Danville, Il. 618325            │
│                                                         │
│                                                         │
└─────────────────────────────────────────────────────────┘
```

   b.

```
┌─────────────────────────────────────────────────────────┐
│  Ronald Johnson                                         │
│  Telluride, COL                                         │
│                                                         │
│                                                         │
│                      Middleboro Foundation              │
│                      Dr. Hadar Eiser, M.D.              │
│                        306 Fifteenth St.                │
│                        Livonia, Mi 48152                │
│                                                         │
│                                                         │
└─────────────────────────────────────────────────────────┘
```

Formatting Business Messages

CHAPTER 7 WORKSHEETS

NAME _____ DATE _____

PRACTICE 2

Proofreading Memos and Letters

Instructions: *Respond to the following business messages as directed.*

1. Read the memo carefully; use proofreaders' marks to edit and mark any errors you find. Underline the misspelled words, and then make a list in which you write or key them correctly.

   MEMO TO: Merilyn Shepherd
   Steve Downing
   Carolyn Jensen
   Richard Trower
   Jerry O'Bryan

   SUBJECT: Multicultural Team Project

   DATE: 4/6/year

   FROM: Judy Brewer, Chairperson of Multicultural Team

   The multicultural teem project this year will be a bake sale of food items from each country represented by our membership. We need you help to promote the bake sale.

   The local Gateway Mall has donated space in their center court for the bake sale. Would each of you help us advertise the event by distribute the enclosed fliers too family, friends, and acquaintances within the next weak?

   JUDY BREWER

   lp

   _____
   _____
   _____
   _____

CHAPTER 7 WORKSHEETS

NAME _____ DATE _____

2. Letter Styles and Punctuation Styles. Indicate in the space provided which letter style is illustrated and which punctuation style is illustrated.

a. Letter Style b. Letter Style c. Letter Style d. Letter Style

_____ _____ _____ _____

Punctuation Style Punctuation Style Punctuation Style Punctuation Style

_____ _____ _____ _____

3. Correcting Letter Parts: The Heading. The lines of the following letter parts are in the correct order, but they contain errors. Mark your corrections in the parts, and write them correctly on the lines provided.

   No. 735 East 7th Street   _____
   Montgomery, Ala., 36109   _____
   Dec. 6th, 19<year>   _____

4. Correcting Letter Parts: The Opening. The lines of the following letter parts are in the correct order, but they contain errors. Mark your corrections in the parts, and write them correctly on the lines provided.

   Human Resources Manager   _____
   Williams Travel Firm   _____
   Fourteen 7th Street, NW   _____
   Washington 20003 DC   _____
   Dear sir,   _____

5. Correcting Letter Parts: The Closing of a Block-Style Letter. The lines of the following letter parts are in the correct order, but they contain errors. Mark your corrections in the parts, and write them correctly on the lines provided.

   Sincerely Yours,   _____
                                        _____
   Word Processing Digest   _____
   Miss Marcy Sanders   _____
   es;MS   _____
   copy to: Mr. Shawn Young   _____
          Mr. David Sheehan   _____

Formatting Business Messages

CHAPTER 7   WORKSHEETS

NAME _____ DATE _____

PRACTICE 3

Preparing Communications

Instructions: Use the following information for the messages for Questions 1 and 2: Our international conference will be held in Rome, Italy, July 26 to August 1. Global Tours has available a package tour that includes airfare and lodging. A detailed itinerary including cost is enclosed. To reserve a place on the tour, you must make a $100 nonrefundable deposit. Spaces will be reserved on a first-come, first-served basis.

1. Using today's date, send a memo about the conference to Kris White, Temple Boyd, and Terry Roach.

2. Using today's date, send a letter about the conference to Dr. Peter Caruthers, Business Administration Building, 4789 Constitution Avenue, Northwest, Washington, DC 20017, and a copy to Jeannie Willis. Assume you are using company letterhead. Use a subject line and put your company name (Office Professionals) in the closing.

3. Address a No. 10 envelope for the letter you created in Question 2. Include your return address and put a confidential notation on the envelope. If you do not have an actual envelope, print or key the information on the envelope as outlined below.

4. Using the guidelines given in this chapter, complete the following items.

    a. Fold the letter (Question 2) for a No. 10 envelope. How many folds does the letter have? _____

    b. Fold the memo (Question 1) for a No. 6 3/4 envelope. How many folds does the memo have? _____

unit 3

Effective Messsages

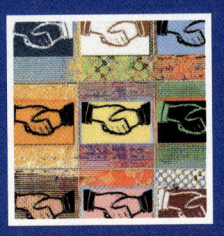

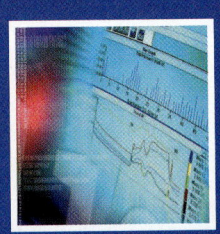

- **Chapter 8**
  Messages That Promote Goodwill

- **Chapter 9**
  Messages for Inquiries and Requests

- **Chapter 10**
  Claim and Adjustment Messages

- **Chapter 11**
  Persuasive Messages

- **Chapter 12**
  Order, Credit, and Collection Messages

CHAPTER 8

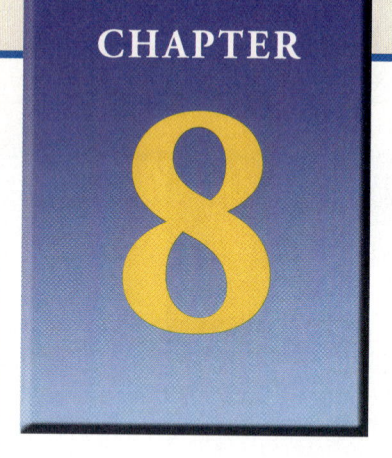

Messages That Promote Goodwill

Objectives

After completing this chapter, you will be able to:

1. Explain the importance of goodwill communications
2. Explain the importance of projecting a positive tone
3. Describe how to communicate using the "you attitude"
4. Identify and use techniques for promoting a service attitude
5. Compose a variety of goodwill letters, including thank-you messages, notes expressing welcome and congratulations, invitations, announcements, get-well messages, and sympathy messages
6. Compose letters that maintain or reactivate business

WORKPLACE APPLICATIONS

Conflict Management

When people who have different interests, goals, and experiences work together, conflict is bound to occur. Although *conflict* is a word that has negative connotations, it can actually be a productive business tool. Conflict during a planning session can inspire people to analyze their own assumptions, challenge the ideas of others, make **compromises,** and try new ideas. Conflict turns negative, however, when it gets personal—when people show disrespect for the ideas and the feelings of others. Negative conflict causes hurt feelings and disrupts the atmosphere of the workplace. When conflict interferes with people's lives and affects their productivity, it needs to be managed.

Conflict management is not about smoothing over conflict and making things nice. It is a strategy for transforming negative conflict into something positive. Conflict management takes effort and a certain amount of honesty and **diplomacy,** but it can result in a stronger, more productive workplace. If you find yourself in conflict with a coworker, try the following strategies:

- Sit down, one on one, with the person in a neutral place, such as a conference room.
- Invite the other person to explain his or her point of view of the conflict.
- Listen actively. Show respect. Don't interrupt.
- When it is your turn to speak, first ask any clarifying questions. Make sure you understand the other person's point of view.
- Share your point of view. Don't ignore emotions, but don't indulge them. Try saying "I felt (emotion) when you (whatever the person said or did)." This shows that you take responsibility for your feelings and are not blaming the other person.
- Think about a compromise. Offer a fair solution.
- If all else fails, agree to disagree, and move on.

Thinking Critically

Situation: You are a newly promoted supervisor in the department. A departmental meeting erupts into conflict when one coworker accuses another of "wasting people's time" with his "stupid and useless ideas." The two coworkers have had a longstanding feud.

Ask Yourself: Discuss how you would handle the conflict between the two coworkers.

> **Seek first to understand, then to be understood.**
> —**Stephen R. Covey, Motivational Speaker**

The favorable attitude and feeling people have toward a business is known as goodwill. Goodwill is an intangible asset—a quality that is difficult to describe and measure. This asset is very important, however, because the image people have of a business, or what people think of a business, often determines where they do business. For this reason, organizations invest huge resources in creating and developing goodwill. As an employee, you can strengthen or you can destroy that goodwill based on the manner in which you communicate.

PROMOTING GOODWILL

Goodwill messages are an important part of the good customer relations that all successful businesses constantly strive to achieve. Writing messages that promote goodwill can also help you as an individual in building a reputation as a thoughtful person. You can convey goodwill in many ways; a friendly smile, a cheerful greeting, a cooperative spirit, and a sincere compliment are easy ways to build goodwill with the people you see each day. You should also respond to the goodwill expressions of others. Return a friendly smile with a friendly smile, a cheerful greeting with a cheerful return greeting, and a compliment with a sincere thank-you.

Thinking Cap 8.1

Discuss: Think about a company or business that you like to patronize. What is the image you have of that company? How did you develop that image? How do you feel about the company? Why do you feel that way? Now, think about a company that you have decided not to patronize. What is the image you have of that company? How do you feel about the company? Why do you feel that way?

The personal touch of goodwill messages and letters helps to build good human relations both inside and outside an organization. **Internal goodwill letters**—goodwill messages to employees and other associates—enhance cooperation and make the organization's work go more smoothly. **External goodwill letters**—goodwill messages to customers—show interest, and showing interest in customers is the best way to keep them.

You can assist in building and maintaining your organization's goodwill by projecting genuine interest, fairness, courtesy, and friendliness in all your workplace communications, including your business correspondence. Consider each piece of communication an opportunity to influence a person's attitude toward your organization and possibly even an opportunity to ensure future business. Start by projecting a positive tone.

PROJECTING A POSTIVE TONE

Tone is attitude—the way the message sounds, the feeling the communication conveys to the receiver. In written communication, tone is transmitted not only by words, sentences, and paragraphs but also by the perceived spirit behind them. In spoken communication, it is transmitted by the voice, facial expressions, and body language as well as by the words used. How you say something influences your receiver just as much as what you say.

Your communications will project a positive tone that appeals to the receiver if you follow these suggestions:

- Use the "you attitude"—emphasize the receiver's viewpoint.
- Show a sincere interest in the receiver.
- Accentuate positive rather than negative ideas.

Communicating a "You Attitude"

Developing a "you attitude" may well be the single most important skill needed to establish a positive tone in your communications. You should seek first to understand your receiver, then to have your message understood. Seeking to understand your receiver means looking at a situation from the receiver's viewpoint rather than from your own.

As you begin your communication, use your imagination to visualize your reader's reaction to your letter. Picture your reader receiving and reviewing your communication—will he or she be receptive to its message?

The "you attitude" means focusing on the receiver's interests and needs rather than on your own. In order to do this, you must put yourself in the receiver's shoes and consider that individual's background, knowledge, interests, needs, and emotions.

Look at how using the words *you* and *your* makes a difference in the following two sentences:

> We have 16 business programs to meet various educational and career goals.

> You may select from 16 business programs the one most beneficial to you for your educational and career goals.

These sentences contain the same information, but which one seems more personal to you? Which one seems to focus attention on the reader's needs?

Remember that merely using the words *you* and *your* in a sentence does not create a "you attitude"; the content of the sentence must put the reader in a positive light:

YOU WORDS: Your error caused the delay, and you alone will be responsible for the charges on your bill.

YOU ATTITUDE: We are sorry about the delay and will have our shipping department look into it. We will, of course, accept responsibility if we are at fault in any way.

Which sentence gives the reader a better feeling? Although the words *you* and *your* do not appear in the second sentence, that sentence carries a "you attitude" because it expresses a positive attitude toward the reader. The first sentence, on the other hand, uses "you words" but lacks the spirit of the "you attitude." The first sentence sends a negative message as it places all the blame for a problem on the reader. Even though the second sentence

Thinking Cap 8.2

Discuss: "Seek first to understand your receiver." What are ways in which you can do this in written and oral communications?

makes use of the words *we* and *our*, it is still more reader-oriented than the first example.

Now let's look at how the "we attitude" can affect the tone of a message.

WE ATTITUDE: We have been pleased to sell fine automobiles for more than two decades. We supply the finest imports to customers from all over the United States. We are proud to be the only dealer in this area for both the Jaguar and the Alfa Romeo.

The ideas in this example are good, but they are expressed from such a self-centered viewpoint that they create a boastful, negative impression. As you can see, the words *we* and *our* contribute to this negative impression. This message certainly does not focus on the reader or emphasize the reader's viewpoint. Notice the difference when the same ideas are expressed by adding "you words" and a "you attitude":

YOU ATTITUDE: To serve you as your exclusive Jaguar and Alfa Romeo dealer is a privilege at Classic Imports. Our showroom is stocked with an array of beautiful and desirable automobiles to satisfy your discriminating taste.

By putting the reader into the picture, the writer creates a reader-centered letter, a letter with a "you attitude."

Showing Sincere Interest in the Reader

Demonstrate a genuine interest in your readers as individuals by showing respect for their intelligence, judgment, opinions, and preferences. Put distractions aside when you are communicating, and concentrate on satisfying your reader and on representing your organization. The attitude you project in the tone of your letter should show the reader that you care, that you are looking at things fairly, and that you are genuinely interested in communicating.

When we fail to take a genuine interest in our readers and their needs or when we let our emotions influence our communication, we are likely to destroy a positive tone. If you are sincere in your respect for the reader's intelligence, it will be evident by what you say and how you say it. If you make offensive statements to a reader, your communication will have the opposite effect from the one you intend. Avoid the following destroyers of a positive tone in your writing:

1. Talking down to the reader
2. Exaggerating
3. Showing doubt, irritation, or indifference
4. Criticizing, arguing, or being sarcastic
5. Showing anger

GLOBAL DIVERSITY 8.1

Card Games

Cambodians exchange business cards with both hands as a sign of respect to the other person. When someone gives you his or her business card, take a few seconds to study it. In some cultures, stuffing a card into a pocket without reviewing it first could end the business relationship. *In the United States, it is polite to shake hands during introductions. If someone refused to shake your hand when you offered it, and instead put their hands in their pockets, how would you react? Would it affect your opinion of the person?*

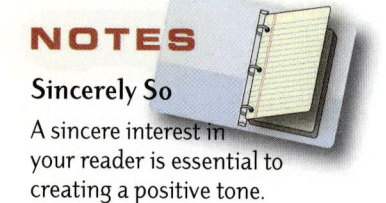

NOTES

Sincerely So

A sincere interest in your reader is essential to creating a positive tone.

1. Talking Down to the Reader

A letter has a condescending tone when the writer "talks down" or "preaches" to the receiver. This communicates that the writer lacks respect for the receiver; this tone may provoke resentment from the receiver. You will find that sharing ideas or making suggestions will generate a more receptive attitude than trying to force acceptance of your views. Most people want to be treated as equals and appreciate being asked rather than told. Look at the following letter. Would it attract you to Bormann's Back-to-School Sale?

> **CONDESCENDING TONE:** Now is the time when all smart shoppers are taking advantage of the special money-saving buys at Bormann's, while our Back-to-School sale is in progress.

The message that everyone else is doing something implies that the reader is out of step if he or she is not doing it, too. According to this letter, "all smart shoppers" are coming to Bormann's. Does this mean that the reader is not intelligent if he or she does not shop at Bormann's?

A better approach is to stimulate interest by letting the reader decide that "now is the time" to shop at Bormann's:

> **CONGENIAL TONE:** Come in today and take advantage of the special money-saving buys at Bormann's Back-to-School sale.

Keep in mind that the reader, like everyone else, prefers to think and act independently and is more likely to respond favorably if you make your appeal through sound reasoning. You can guard against talking down to the reader by putting yourself in the reader's place. After you have written a letter, read it as if you were the receiver and imagine your response.

GLOBAL DIVERSITY 8.2

Getting Personal

While people from some cultures tend to communicate in a direct, straightforward, concise manner, others tend to communicate in a more elaborate and personal way, especially in the beginning and ending of their letters. These individuals may use "flowery" language and perhaps a more formal tone. Middle Easterners and Japanese people often write in this gracious style, for example. *When would it be appropriate to adopt a more personal tone in your letters as opposed to being straightforward and direct?*

2. Exaggerating

A letter may sound insincere when it contains any of the following forms of exaggeration:

- Bragging
- Gushiness
- Flattery
- Excessive humility
- Unlikely promises

Let's look at each of these examples of exaggeration.

Bragging. Boasting creates an impression of insincerity and weakens your credibility; be prepared to back up everything you say when describing your products and services. Embellishments, inflated statements, and superlatives such as "the best," "outstandingly superior," and "incomparable" seldom sound convincing to the reader unless you give specific evidence to back up your claims.

Messages That Promote Goodwill

Gushiness. Gushy language in business letters may make the reader feel that the writer is insecure about a product or service. The use of flowery words and too many strong adjectives and adverbs may appear to the reader as a way of compensating for the writer's uncertainty about the message.

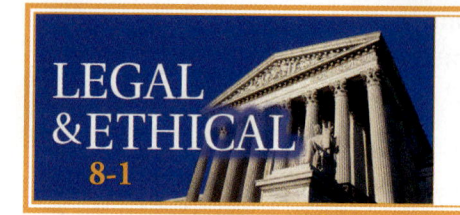

> **LEGAL & ETHICAL 8-1**
>
> **Product Hype.** Writers of sales letters and advertisements sometimes exaggerate their products and services in their communications. Is this ethical? What are the implications of the inflated words and statements they use? What could be the ramifications on the business they represent? What could be some of the legal consequences of this practice?

Excessive politeness can make a message sound insincere and inappropriate. Avoid using overlong paragraphs and excessive repetition of the reader's name. Although using the reader's name once in the body of a letter can personalize the letter, using the reader's name repeatedly sounds phony.

Flattery. Flattery can be even more damaging than gushiness. Nothing is wrong with giving a compliment that has been earned, but avoid embarrassing the reader with outright flattery.

If the flattery is too intense, the reader may feel that the writer is extremely insincere.

Excessive Humility. Excessive humility in a letter may signal to the reader that the writer has little self-respect. If, as a writer, you apologize to the point of degrading yourself and your organization, you are destroying the reader's confidence in you.

Nothing is wrong with saying you're sorry, but don't overwork the subject. Excessive apologies aren't necessary if you have taken steps to remedy the problem for which you are apologizing—solving the problem is what the reader is really interested in.

Unlikely Promises. If you make exaggerated promises such as "We will take care of each order the minute it comes into our office" or "Just a telephone call and our technician will be right there," your reader may be skeptical of everything you say. Remember, it is especially important to guard against making rash promises you may be held to legally.

To a reader, a promise appears likely to be fulfilled when it is backed up by reliable information. For example, when a businessperson can verify for a customer that certain stock is available and can promise specific shipping dates and methods, the customer is likely to believe the communication.

Go to CD-ROM — Activity 8-1: To test your skills.

> **LEGAL & ETHICAL 8-2**
>
> **Broken Promises.** As with other forms of exaggeration, making unlikely promises can result in problems for the communicator. What may be some of the results of making promises that you cannot keep? What may be some ethical and legal consequences?

3. Showing Doubt, Irritation, or Indifference

Negativism in the form of doubt, irritation, and indifference destroys the sincere tone you want your letters to have.

Doubt. Be careful not to use language that expresses doubt about your reader's integrity or reliability. Referring to "your claim" or saying "we are surprised" about something the reader said or did implies that you do not believe the reader.

Irritation. Revealing in a letter that you are irritated does not help you accomplish your purpose in writing the letter. You merely arouse the reader's resentment at your lack of respect for him or her.

When responding to a customer's complaint about a product, a letter written in an irritated tone might make the customer vow never to buy from your company again. Rather than belittling the customer, a message that maintains the customer's goodwill might instead explain the cause of the problem, outline an action taken to correct the problems, and describe how the customer can prevent a recurrence.

Indifference. A common reason retail stores lose customers is indifference—an apparent lack of interest or enthusiasm in meeting the customer's needs. Whether a store's employees actually display an attitude of indifference doesn't matter. If customers perceive indifference—even if it is only imagined—they are likely to take their business elsewhere. Consequently, a major concern of retailers should be to convince customers that the retailers really care about them.

4. Criticizing, Arguing, or Being Sarcastic

Criticizing, arguing, or making a sarcastic remark in your letters will only destroy your message and reflect negatively upon you and your organization. The reader can only read the actual words you have written, harsh as they may be. He or she cannot respond to or look for other clues to your intended meaning.

When you talk with someone face to face, you usually do your best to keep the conversation pleasant. You try to put the other person at ease, and you avoid sounding critical or saying anything he or she might resent. On the other hand, when you write a letter, the temptation is greater to ignore the reader's feelings and think only of your own. For instance, you may be tempted to "needle" the reader by using sarcasm. Sarcasm, however, will not only offend the receiver but may also sabotage the entire effect of your message. Remember that in a written message you can't soften the tone by smiling or listening to the reader's side, as you can in face-to-face conversation.

How would you feel if you were a supervisor, and you received this memo from your boss?

> Congratulations to you and your staff on developing a successful training contract with Collins and Ripp. Three must be your lucky number as this is the second contract that required three attempts

Messages That Promote Goodwill

before acceptance. Let's hope that number can change to "two" or ideally to "one" for future contracts.

Wouldn't you respond more positively to the following?

> Congratulations to you and your staff on securing a successful training contract with Collins and Ripp. Developing these contracts does present problems. However, with the challenges we have experienced, I am sure we will now be able to move ahead quickly with additional contracts in this area.

5. Showing Anger

Showing anger in a letter provokes a reader's hostility, which makes transacting business impossible. Even though your anger may be justified, never let it show in a letter.

If you do feel angry about a situation, it is better to wait until your anger has passed and you can see the situation clearly and calmly before you begin writing. Then approach the situation logically and develop a courteous, reasonable letter that will help the reader see your viewpoint. You will be much more likely to solicit a favorable response and improve relationships when you "keep your cool." How would you describe the mood of the writer of this letter, which was addressed to the president of a large organization?

> Did you really think you could get away with taking my stereo system back to "fix it" and not refund my money? This piece of junk has never worked right, and I don't want it "fixed" or replaced—I want my money back so I can buy one that works.

How would the organization president feel about this customer after reading it? Let's look at a more straightforward revision:

> On March 6, 19—, I purchased your Placemar Stereo system, Model PS4288, (Order no. C92-3324). On March 30 I returned it because it was not working properly and requested my money back. I do not want this system repaired, nor do I want a new one. Please send me a full refund.

Go to CD-ROM
Activity 8-2
To test your skills.

Focusing on Positive Ideas

In developing a positive tone in your letters, it is important to remember that the reader is more interested in what you *can* do than in what you *cannot* do. You cannot always answer *yes* to a request, but you can say *no* with a friendly tone if you stress the positive and play down the negative. Your letters should sound helpful and encouraging to the reader.

Even a few negative words in a letter can sound unpleasant; and, as we discussed in Chapter 2, several negative words can create an unpleasant overall effect on the reader. Look at the following paragraph, for example:

> We were sorry to receive your letter stating that there is something wrong with your Roger's CD player. It is too bad that you found this merchandise to be unsatisfactory. Just ship it back to us, and we will send you another one just like it.

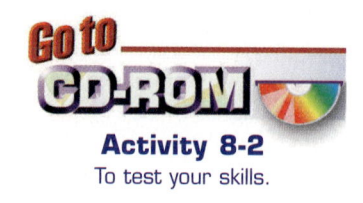

Now let's take the paragraph apart and see what gives it such a negative tone. At first glance, *We were sorry to receive your letter* sounds as if it might be saying the company is sorry to get the letter. The sentence beginning with *It is too bad* suggests that although the customer found the merchandise to be unsatisfactory, perhaps no one else has. The final sentence, *Just ship it back to us, and we will send you another one just like it*, fails to answer the customer's concerns and conveys indifference to their situation. How should the CD player be shipped? Will the customer really want another one just like the faulty CD player, or one that works properly?

Here's the way the letter might have been written if the writer had been thinking of the reader's viewpoint:

> Thank you for writing us about the Roger's CD player we sent you recently. We are sorry that it is not working properly. We have instructed our carrier to deliver a new system to you next week and to pick up the system you are returning. I'm sure your new Roger's system will give you many hours of listening pleasure.

These two letters contain the same facts—but do you sense the difference in tone?

Checkpoint 8.1

1. What are the possible benefits and drawbacks of showing sincere interest in your reader?
2. How would you characterize the tone of the excerpt from the letter below? Explain your answer.

    Because we think you are so special, Ms. Evans, we are offering you, and you alone, a once-in-a-lifetime opportunity. So call us today, Ms. Evans. You can reach us at our convenient toll-free number at any hour of the day or night. Ms. Evans, we're waiting for your call!!

3. What changes would you make to improve the excerpt in question 2?

PROMOTING A SERVICE ATTITUDE

All your written communications should create the impression that your organization is a friendly one that is interested in the people it serves. Even though you aren't trying to sell goods or services in every letter, you are trying to sell ideas and the organization you represent.

Service Attitude Checklist

In order to build goodwill for your business, you will need to find many ways to project a service attitude in your correspondence. A service attitude is made up of both a sincere interest in the customer's welfare and the willingness to do a little more, to give a little extra.

Messages That Promote Goodwill

NOTES
Service Attitude Checklist

____ Anticipate questions and provide answers

____ Include additional, relevant information

____ Make it easy to respond

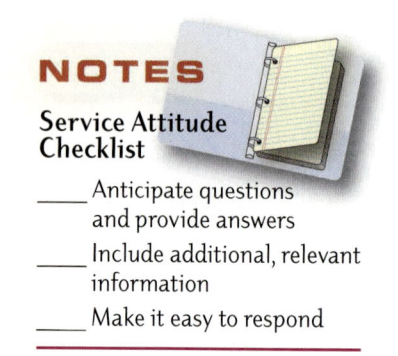

A well-expressed service attitude will pay dividends (including monetary ones) for your organization and for you. In addition, you will have the personal satisfaction of doing a job well. Your service attitude will show the reader that you desire to serve rather than just make a profit.

You can express a service attitude by anticipating a customer's questions and providing needed information before it is requested; by including information you know will be of particular interest to the reader, such as an article or a brochure; and by making it easy for the reader to respond to your letter by enclosing an addressed, postpaid reply card or envelope, if appropriate.

Gestures like these build and maintain goodwill. They convey a thoughtfulness that people will notice and appreciate.

Dealing With "Bad News" Situations

In letters that contain good news, building goodwill is fairly easy. When organizational policy or other circumstances prevent replies that customers would like to have, however, building goodwill is more challenging. This is the case in the following "bad news" situations, in which you may need to answer *no* to a customer or client's request, state that a customer or client has made an error, or state that a customer or client's criticism of the organization's products or service is unjustified.

Skillful writers, using tact and imagination, are able to build goodwill even in these problem situations. Three frequently used techniques to promote goodwill follow:

1. Beginning with a "goodwill idea"
2. Considering the customer or client's viewpoint
3. Selling the organization's viewpoint

1. Beginning With a "Goodwill Idea"

Open the letter with something the reader will be pleased to hear. This is true whether the main message of the letter is good or bad news for the reader.

In a "bad news" letter, rather than starting with an unpleasant idea that will immediately set up a barrier between you and the reader, start with an idea you know the reader will agree with. This gives you an opportunity to gain the reader's attention while you gradually introduce your point of view.

2. Considering the Customer or Client's Viewpoint

You can build and maintain goodwill for your organization by keeping the reader's point of view clearly in mind at all times. By doing this, you can build goodwill even when you must tell people *no* or that they are wrong. You would, of course, avoid saying to someone, "You are wrong."

In these situations, you should take the time to find out what the person's position is. Try to look at things from the customer's perspective by asking yourself questions such as the following: "What type of response might he

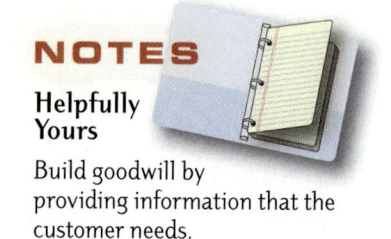

NOTES
Helpfully Yours

Build goodwill by providing information that the customer needs.

or she appreciate?" "What might the person consider a reasonable alternative if his or her request cannot be accommodated as specified?" "What explanations might the customer or client accept?"

For example, suppose you represent a camera company, and a customer wants you to replace a camera that has a two-year warranty that was purchased four years ago. In saying *no* to the replacement, consider if the customer would appreciate alternatives such as a trade-in allowance on a new camera, an estimate for repairs, a recommendation for similar cameras, or some other type of assistance that your organization is willing to provide. If the customer wants to buy a new camera, then you would want to know what the customer values most in cameras—the cost, the brand, the attachments, the ease of use, or something else. With this information, you would know how to respond and which selling points to stress.

Try to discover and point out benefits to the customer in a situation where few or none may be apparent. Above all, try to express the organization's point of view in such a way that the customer or client accepts it and is still friendly toward your firm. Your letter should make it easy for the customer to agree with you.

3. Selling Your Organization's Viewpoint

In writing business letters for problem situations, you cannot build goodwill by losing your temper or showing annoyance. Look at this example:

> You certainly are not entitled to the 2 percent discount you took, as you could clearly have seen if you had read the terms of our invoice.

This writer missed an opportunity to promote goodwill. To sell the organization's viewpoint, the writer should have explained the reasons behind the company policy, pointed out the fairness of the policy to all customers, including the reader, and described possible benefits of the policy for the customer.

By using these three steps, the writer could have replied diplomatically as shown in this revised example.

> Thank you for your check for $1,372.84 in payment of our invoice 8970K for $1400.86. We notice that you have deducted the 2 percent discount offered on payments made within ten days of the date of purchase. To be eligible for the discount, you needed to have sent your payment by August 30, ten days from our invoice of August 20. However, your check is dated September 15. We assume that this was an oversight—that you intended to send your check within ten days.
>
> As payments made within ten days of the purchase date represent a savings to us, we want to share that savings with customers who have contributed to that savings. Therefore, in fairness to all our customers, we have to maintain the ten-day discount period. May we have your check for $28.02?

In the revised letter, notice that the writer doesn't demand payment but instead immediately catches the reader's interest by drawing attention to the difference in the payment amount and the invoice amount. Then the

Thinking Cap 8.3

Discuss: You are working in a store when a customer comes in and requests a refund for a faulty hair dryer. You examine the hair dryer and find that the customer has damaged it. You cannot give the customer the requested refund. You have carefully followed the three steps for selling the organization's viewpoint, but the customer is still insisting on the refund. How will you handle the situation?

Go to CD-ROM
Activity 8-3
To test your skills.

Messages That Promote Goodwill

writer leads the customer gently to the organization's point of view. By the time the reader gets to the last paragraph of the message, he or she should be ready to answer *yes* to the question, "May we have your check for $28.02?"

Letters as Goodwill Messengers

You must care how your letters sound if you want them to build goodwill. Try to visualize each letter as a goodwill ambassador for your organization. Evaluate the effectiveness of your "letter salesperson" in the same way as you would a real salesperson—keep in mind that a salesperson may be both personable and courteous but still not be successful in making a sale.

Go to CD-ROM
Activity 8-4
To test your skills.

WRITING GOODWILL MESSAGES

> *What you do when you don't have to determines what you will be when you can no longer help it.*
> —Rudyard Kipling

Thinking Cap 8.4

Discuss: You see an acquaintance who has on a new suit and who looks especially nice. You comment, "Terri, you really look sharp today. I like your new suit." Terri gives you a funny look. How would you feel about Terri's reactions? How do you think Terri should have reacted?

Letters written only to build or maintain goodwill are unique because they are letters that do not have to be written. If such letters were not sent, no material change in the existing situation would result. When someone takes the time to send a goodwill letter, it is appreciated and remembered, resulting in valuable improvements in human relations. Conveying a thank-you or congratulations in writing rather than verbally is especially effective since the recipient of your message will have a tangible reminder of your goodwill thoughts. You should look for opportunities to send written goodwill messages to others.

Whatever their specific purpose, goodwill messages, like other successful business communications, share certain characteristics beyond their desire to generate reader approval. These characteristics include naturalness, sincerity, friendliness, and enthusiasm.

Of these characteristics, sincerity is probably the most important in a goodwill letter. Pretending to be sincere won't work—a reader can detect this and will feel as if you are trying to manipulate him or her. Remember to avoid using humor in a goodwill letter because humor may be perceived as sarcasm. You may risk losing the sincere tone of your message if you try to inject humor into it. What happened in the message that follows?

> Congratulations on your recent promotion to senior account executive. How does it feel to be part of the senior citizen crew? Now you too can be part of the problem instead of part of the solution. Ha!

All goodwill letters share one purpose: to generate goodwill by showing sincere interest in the reader.

Typical goodwill messages include the following:

- Letters of thanks and congratulations
- Letters that announce, invite, or welcome
- Letters that express get-well wishes or sympathy
- Letters that maintain or reactivate business

208   Chapter 8

As an example, look at the goodwill letter written by a vice president of Capital Communications, Inc., to one of its customers, Pantry Stores, Inc., in Figure 8-1. The letter salutes the grocery chain for its support of a community activity. Can you answer *yes* to the questions on the *"Checklist for a Goodwill Letter"* below when you read this letter?

✔ CHECKLIST FOR A GOODWILL LETTER

	YES	NO
1. If you were the receiver, would you like to receive this letter?	___	___
2. Will the receiver feel that you enjoyed writing the letter and that you mean everything you say?	___	___
3. Did you keep the spotlight on the receiver?	___	___
4. Did you avoid including specific sales material?	___	___

GLOBAL DIVERSITY 8.3

No Bias

When writing goodwill messages, be sure to use gender-neutral words. Many people are offended by sexist language. For example, referring to *he* can be offensive to a female executive, and referring to police officers as male can be offensive to a female police officer. *Can you think of other words that may be offensive? Share these with your class during discussion.*

Capital Communications, Inc.
919 Cannon Street • P.O. Box 27836 • Memphis, TN 38187-0466
email capcommun@cci.com
901-555-2400 • Fax 901-555-4377

June 2, <YEAR>

Mr. Bruce Allen, President
Pantry Stores, Inc.
316 Belgian Street
Germantown, TN 38138

Dear Mr. Allen:

A business like yours is a credit to our community. Your commitment to helping satisfy some of the community's needs makes anyone associated with you proud.

The future growth of our city will be enhanced by its ability to obtain a National Football League franchise. A sellout of the upcoming exhibition game is critical to this effort. At the Expansion Committee meeting today, I learned that Pantry Stores is supporting this drive by purchasing 200 tickets to the game.

I was even more impressed to learn that you donated those 200 tickets to the young people of The Boys and Girls Club. They will certainly appreciate the opportunity to see live at Liberty Bowl Stadium the biggest sporting event of the year.

While I am sure your generosity will not be widely publicized, we at Capital Communications, Inc., wish to compliment you.

Sincerely,

Zan Whitsett

Zan Whitsett
Vice President

sm

Figure 8-1
This goodwill letter salutes a business for supporting a community activity.

Messages That Promote Goodwill

THANK-YOU MESSAGES

You can find many occasions for writing personal thank-you messages—for example, when someone gives you a gift, does you a favor, interviews you for a job, or recommends you for a promotion. A thank-you message is an appropriate response to any act of thoughtfulness or kindness. You will also find many other opportunities for writing thank-you letters to build goodwill for you and your organization.

Organizations often send letters of appreciation to a new customer for a first order, to an established customer for a particularly large order, to an individual or an organization for completing an outstanding job, or to someone within the organization for doing something he or she is not required to do.

Occasionally (it should happen much more often!) such letters of appreciation are also sent to customers who order the company's products regularly and pay their bills on time; to employees who consistently do their work well but quietly; and, to individuals and organizations who cooperate on routine jobs but get little attention.

Other opportunities for sending thank-you messages include special occasions—such as anniversaries and holidays—and occasions when organizations or individuals provide special services or take on extra responsibilities where the only "pay" is a message of appreciation. In these latter situations, sending a thank-you message is a must.

Thinking Cap 8.5

Discuss: Why would sending a thank-you letter to a person and sending a copy to the person's supervisor be doubly appreciated?

Go to CD-ROM

Activities 8-5, 8-6, and 8-7
To test your skills.

LEGAL & ETHICAL 8-3

Anonymous Caller. A bank has set up a fund to help with medical expenses for a child in the community who has a terminal illness. A call comes from a woman in the community who donates $5000 to the fund, but the woman requests that her donation be kept anonymous. The employee taking the call has caller ID on her phone, so she knows who the donor is. When the child's family learns a large donation has been made, they ask for the name of the donor so they can thank him or her. Would it be legal or ethical for the bank employee to tell them the donor's name?

MESSAGES OF CONGRATULATIONS

A message of congratulations or commendation is much like a message of appreciation—each recognizes and expresses interest in a worthwhile achievement or important milestone. A letter of appreciation thanks someone for doing something special or going an extra mile, implying a job well done. A letter of congratulations tells a person "well done" for getting a promotion, winning an award, completing a project, and so on, and implies a thank-you for getting the job done.

When your friends celebrate special events or receive honors or special recognition, they should be congratulated. Similarly, businesspeople send congratulatory letters to customers, clients, and employees on occasions such as anniversaries, graduations, births, marriages, promotions, retirements, openings of new businesses, purchases of new homes, the winning of elections, and the receipt of awards. When you send congratulatory letters such as these, you convey a pleasant message and create a favorable image of you and your organization in the recipient's mind. The following congratulatory note was sent to an executive who recently became vice president of the company:

> Congratulations, Mrs. Santana, on your recent promotion to vice president of Mode Software Corporation. You certainly have earned the promotion. Under your capable leadership, I know that the business will continue to grow and prosper.

Remember, it is important to distinguish messages that are primarily goodwill messages from those whose main goal is sales. The emphasis is on goodwill when a leading child care service sends a beautiful baby diary to new parents and attaches the following message:

> Congratulations to the proud parents from The Cradle Club—the child care service with the most loving and reliable babysitters in town!

Although the goodwill message was used in this case as an attention-getting device for promoting the child care service, the focus is on the goodwill message.

Certainly the contractor who received the following sales message was not fooled into thinking it was a sincere, personal message simply because it began with a congratulatory statement:

> Congratulations! I just read the good news that you've been selected as the architect for the new public library in Danville. As the architect, you will be looking for materials that will be durable as well as economical. Hillard's building supplies are both durable and economical . . .

A letter like this one is pure sales promotion with a gimmick opening—it's not likely to build goodwill. A goodwill message should focus attention on the occasion that inspires it. If the writer instead seems more interested in his or her own organization than in the important events in the reader's life, the reader naturally feels tricked.

Remember that when you write a letter on your organization's stationery, you speak for your organization as well as for yourself—your organization is talking through you. Therefore, when you write a congratulatory message on letterhead stationery, whatever good (or bad) feeling is aroused in the reader will be directed to your organization as well as to you personally. Because you are using your organization's letterhead, your organization will be remembered by the receiver; don't spoil the good impression resulting from a congratulatory message with an unnecessary sales pitch.

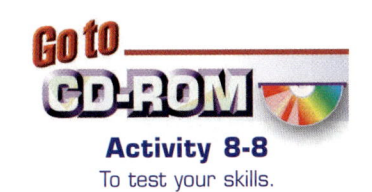

Go to CD-ROM
Activity 8-8
To test your skills.

Messages That Promote Goodwill 211

Letters That Invite, Announce, or Welcome

Special occasions and special services often present occasions for writing goodwill letters.

Invitations

Two types of invitations that you may be called upon to create are (1) formal invitations and (2) informal invitations.

1. Formal Invitations

Formal invitations are sent to invite someone to a special event such as the dedication of a new building or a dinner in honor of someone, or to invite someone to a special event such as a wedding. Formal invitations usually follow a traditional format, with each line of the invitation being centered on the card (see Figure 8-2). Before preparing a formal invitation, refer to an up-to-date etiquette book for correct wording and arrangement of information.

If you wish to receive a reply to your invitation, include an R.S.V.P. This phrase, which comes from the French "Reply, if you please," has been simplified to mean "please reply." Some invitations you send will include a reply card for the recipient to complete and return to you; others will include a phone number so the recipient can phone a reply. The degree of formality of the event usually determines which method is appropriate. In any case, a reply is expected.

Thinking Cap 8.6

Discuss: What does "Black Tie" on a formal invitation mean?

Figure 8-2
A formal invitation is printed on heavy card stock with each line of text centered.

Senator Sally Black

requests the pleasure of your company

at dinner

on Tuesday, the first of May

Nineteen hundred and ninety-nine

at seven o'clock in the evening

at the Syracuse Country Club

384 Country Club Way

R.S.V.P.   Black Tie

GLOBAL DIVERSITY 8.4

Respond, Please
R.S.V.P. is an abbreviation of the French expression repondez-vous s'il vous plait. Is this still a correct expression? Do you think all cultures respond similarly?

Chapter 8

2. Informal Invitations

In contrast to formal invitations, informal invitations are written in letter format in a more casual style. In addition to extending an invitation to an event or social gathering, they should provide the following specifics about the event, including day, date, time, type of function, reason for the function, location, who is included in the invitation, dress requirements (if any), and a request for a reply.

Look at the informal invitation shown below. Note how it includes all the necessary information while retaining a casual style.

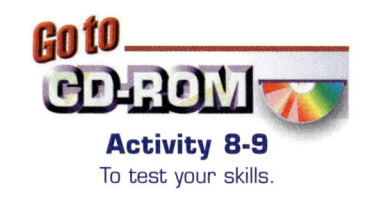

Go to CD-ROM
Activity 8-9
To test your skills.

Dear Mr. Griggs:

Mr. Cade has asked me to invite the members of the Historical Acquisitions Committee for the Ford County Museum to meet with him for lunch on Tuesday, March 14, at the Beef House Restaurant at 12 noon. He would like very much for you to come.

Mr. Cade wants the committee to discuss plans for the centennial fund-raiser to be held in July. Please call me at 555-4452 by Monday morning, March 13, to let me know whether you will be able to attend.

Sincerely yours,

Deborah Fetters

Deborah Fetters
Assistant to Mr. Cade

Figure 8-3
An informal invitation must contain all the necessary details the reader needs to know.

Replies to Invitations

When you receive an invitation, you should reply whether or not you intend to accept the invitation. When accepting an invitation, you should express pleasure at being asked, confirm all the details, and make it clear exactly who and how many will be attending.

When refusing an invitation, you should express regret at being unable to attend, repeat the details of the invitation, and thank the recipient for the invitation. Provide a general explanation of why you can't attend. Remember to always strive to keep the goodwill of the person who extended the invitation when you write. Look at the note in Figure 8-4 for an example of a refusal of an informal invitation.

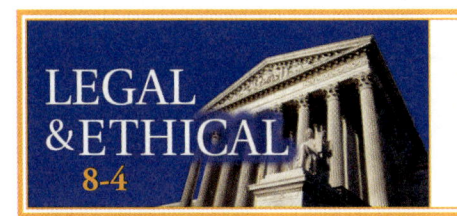

LEGAL & ETHICAL 8-4

Unable to Attend? Assume you refuse your employer's invitation to a company dinner because you just don't want to go. You tell your boss you have another commitment, but your coworker knows you don't really have any other plans. Is this ethical behavior? What are the possible ramifications?

Messages That Promote Goodwill

Figure 8-4
An informal refusal presents the refusal in a kind but clear manner.

> Dear Mr. Henry:
>
> Thank you for your kind invitation to speak at your annual broker/dealer conference in St. Louis, Missouri, on Saturday, September 10.
>
> I have another speaking engagement that same day that I committed to several months ago. Therefore, I will not be able to accept your invitation. If I could help with your conference in any other way, I would be happy to do so.
>
> Best wishes for a very successful conference.
>
> Sincerely,

Announcements

Goodwill announcements can be formal or informal. Formal announcements are printed on card stock using much the same language as that of a formal invitation. Remember to consult a reference manual or an up-to-date etiquette book for proper wording. Announcements can also follow the informal format of a flyer or a letter. Announcements can be sent for the following occasions:

- Major business changes—the opening of a new business, a new location for an existing business, or an expansion or reorganization of facilities. These announcements usually include an invitation to visit.

- Personnel changes—a promotion of an employee, the appointment of a new official, or the hiring of a new representative of a company.

- New services or policies—extended operating hours, improved credit terms, or a new line of products. These announcements often invite the receiver to try the new service being offered.

In the message shown in Figure 8-5, a credit union uses a letter to announce a new direct deposit plan.

Figure 8-5
This friendly letter points out the benefits of direct deposit.

> Dear Credit Union Member:
>
> Now you can have safety and convenience with direct deposit of your paycheck or any other check you receive regularly.
>
> The plan is confidential and very convenient because it deposits your paycheck directly into your checking account every payday--even when you're away. Of course, you'll still receive your paycheck stubs.
>
> To make your paycheck deposits automatic, simply complete and sign the enclosed authorization card, and return it in the enclosed reply envelope. That's it. We'll see that your business office gets the card.
>
> Sincerely,
>
> Larry Williams, Manager

Welcome Messages

Letters of welcome are written for many occasions. These messages may be morale builders; usually, these messages have a definite sales flavor. They might offer greetings to new members of an organization or a "welcome aboard" message to a new parts supplier.

> Welcome to Central Illinois Bank. I was pleased to learn this morning that you have opened an account, and I want you to know that all of our personnel are ready to make it easy for you to use our many services.
>
> We sincerely appreciate your confidence in us as expressed in the opening of your account, and we will do our best to make your association with us both pleasant and profitable for you.

Although these letters usually discuss an organization's services and products and invite readers to call or visit, they avoid specific sales promotion. They can be seen as benefiting both sender and receiver. For example, many retail stores and service firms regularly send letters welcoming new residents of the community in order to build goodwill and gain new customers.

In writing a letter of this type, follow these steps:

1. Begin with a statement of welcome.
2. Comment favorably on the newcomer's choice of a place to live.
3. Mention what your organization has to offer.
4. Include a special discount or incentive to encourage the newcomer's business.

GET-WELL WISHES AND SYMPATHY LETTERS

When a personal friend or a business acquaintance is ill, he or she would welcome get-well wishes from you. If the illness is not serious and recovery is expected, you can send a humorous get-well card or a cheerful, happy letter. On the other hand, if the illness is serious or the person is recovering from a major operation, then you should send a more subdued card or letter unless you're sure that person would enjoy a joke.

Remember to be optimistic when you are writing to someone who is ill. Mention once at the beginning of the letter how sorry you are that the person is ill. After that, talk about a return to normal life, as did the writer of the following letter:

> I just learned that you had some major surgery over the weekend. I certainly hope you will soon be up and about again. When you are up to visitors, please call me so I can stop by. In the meantime, please work on a speedy recovery.

Messages That Promote Goodwill

Activity 8-10 — To test your skills.

Sympathy and Condolence Messages

Messages expressing sympathy or condolence are sent to people who have experienced a death or serious illness. They are often the hardest letters to write because of their negative aspects. Consequently, many people tend to put off writing these messages until it is too late to send them. Remember, it is important to get in the habit of sending a sympathy message when the situation calls for it. In doing so, you will build goodwill with your thoughtfulness.

Sympathy messages should usually be short. Although you don't want to seem curt or unfeeling, you should still be concise. As a rule, limit your letters of sympathy to two paragraphs. The first paragraph should express sympathy, and the second paragraph should take a calm and optimistic look toward the future. Remember to be careful with your use of the word *death*. The more you use substitute words to avoid the dead person's name and the words *die* and *death*, the longer you will extend your talk of the death and dwell on the reason for the grief.

If you knew the deceased personally, use the "magic formula" for writing a condolence letter: cite a personal incident or some small thing the deceased said or did that showed him or her to be a kind, considerate, and thoughtful person. This intimate touch, something personal that you alone are able to share about the deceased, will mean more to the recipient than all the flowery phrases and fine-spun sentiments you could write. The fact that you are writing to express your sincere feeling is the important thing to the recipient.

LETTERS THAT MAINTAIN OR REACTIVATE BUSINESS

Many organizations use routine customer cooperation as an occasion to send a goodwill letter, as illustrated in the following letter to a new customer who has just made the final payment on a special 90-day account. The credit manager did not have to acknowledge the payment, but he showed interest in the customer and built goodwill by doing so.

> Special customers like you have made possible our success since the day we opened 40 years ago! Thank you for your final installment payment, which we received today. Your account has been marked "paid in full."
>
> We appreciate your promptness in paying off your account. Please visit us again.

Follow-up letters sent after a customer has purchased a product or service build goodwill because they show an organization's interest in customers' reactions and the desire to improve its products and services.

Activities 8-11 and 8-12 — To test your skills.

Letters That Reactivate Business

Letters are also often sent to customers whose accounts have been inactive for a long time. This is a way of trying to find out why formerly active customers are no longer coming around. These letters may try to persuade customers to return to the business by offering a fine gift or discount, as does the letter below:

> Here's a sale you won't want to miss! The Wardrobe's once-a-year BIG sale of merchandise from all departments starts on Tuesday, October 10. You will have to see the prices to believe them! Drastic markdowns have been taken on our finest fashions and accessories.
>
> To let you know how much we've missed you, we're sending along a welcome-back gift—a certificate good for $10.00 off any purchase of $75 or more.

Thinking Cap 8.7

Discuss: How would you feel if you were the customer in Legal/Ethical situation 8-5? Will the store get the customer back? Did the store build goodwill?

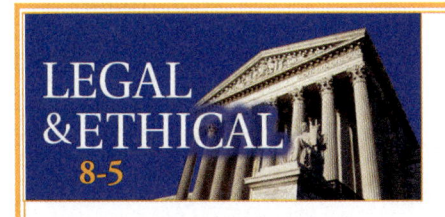

LEGAL & ETHICAL 8-5

Read the Small Print. A large department store sends a letter to a former customer trying to persuade the customer to return. A coupon worth $20 if used within 30 days is enclosed with the letter. The former customer goes to the store and selects a $25 item, but when she takes the item to the sales associate to pay the difference, the sales associate tells her that the coupon is valid only for purchases of $100 or more. Sure enough, in very small print at the bottom of the coupon is a disclaimer statement to this effect. Even if this is legal, is it ethical. What would likely be your reaction in this situation?

APPLYING PRINCIPLES FOR GOODWILL LETTERS

Here is a quick-check reminder of the principles you should emphasize in writing a goodwill letter:

1. Write sincerely.
2. Make the reader feel important.
3. Keep the message as natural and friendly as a person-to-person chat.
4. Send the letter promptly.
5. Avoid the use of humor in a goodwill letter because there is a fine line between humor and sarcasm.

Don't take any chances that may lead the reader to misinterpret your goodwill letter—it's safer to stick with a straightforward message that is sincere.

Checkpoint 8.2

1. Why is a letter an effective way to build goodwill?
2. What other ways besides letters can a business or organization use to build goodwill?
3. In your opinion, who benefits more from goodwill messages—the sender or the receiver?

✔ PRINCIPLES OF GOODWILL CHECKLIST

	YES	NO
1. Is the message written with sincerity?		
2. Will the message make the reader feel important? Is the emphasis on the reader throughout the message?		
3. Does the message sound like a person-to-person chat? Is the wording natural and friendly?		
4. Did the message avoid humor? Humor may be interpreted as sarcasm, which totally defeats the purpose of your goodwill message.		

CHAPTER 8 SUMMARY

Your workplace communications should create favorable impressions and promote goodwill as well as accomplish specific objectives. Choosing appropriate words and developing and organizing coherent messages are vital to effective communications. Equally important, however, is establishing a positive tone.

To establish and maintain goodwill, you must concentrate on creating a positive tone. A positive tone is established by projecting a "you attitude," showing sincere interest in the reader, and focusing on positive ideas. You should also avoid using any of the destroyers of the "you attitude" and positive tone. You build and maintain goodwill by promoting a service attitude and by reselling your products, services, and organization.

Building goodwill—a priceless commodity that individuals as well as businesses need to be successful—is the primary purpose of all of the messages we have discussed in this chapter. Whether a message is in the form of a note, memo, or letter, a written goodwill message will make a more positive impression on a reader than a verbal goodwill message because it is tangible evidence of the sender's thoughtfulness.

P's and Q's
Search for an etiquette or "Miss Manners" Web site to look up information dealing with goodwill messages.

Chapter 8

Online Exercises

Objective:
These online activities will introduce you to the use of e-mail search Web sites and online yellow pages.

Go to **bcw.glencoe.com**, the address for the *Business Communication at Work* Web site, and select Chapter 8. Next, click on Online Exercises. You will see a list of Web site links that will bring you to different e-mail search Web sites and online yellow pages.

Activity 8.1

1. Select several e-mail search Web sites to visit.
2. If you have an e-mail address, search for your e-mail address. If you do not have an e-mail address, search for your telephone number.
3. Search for either the e-mail address or telephone number of someone you know.
4. On a sheet of paper, compose a fictional e-mail to a friend describing how successful or unsuccessful you were in finding his or her e-mail address or telephone number. You should also discuss the differences you found in the various e-mail search Web sites. Make sure your e-mail projects a "you attitude" and shows a sincere interest in the reader.
5. Write your name on your paper and hand it in to your instructor.

Activity 8.2

1. Select one of the online Yellow Pages to visit.
2. Choose a business whose address you would like to search. Enter the business's name, city, state, or a ZIP code to locate the business. Follow the instructions to obtain a map to the business. Some online Yellow Pages may require you to click on a Yellow Pages link before entering the address information.
3. Print the map of the business.
4. On the back of your printout, write a paragraph that provides instructions on obtaining a map through an online Yellow Pages service, or you may write a paragraph about your experience in obtaining the map. Some questions you may want to consider in your paragraph include:
    a. What information should you have prior to entering the Web site?
    b. How difficult did you find the process of obtaining a map?
    c. Do you prefer online Yellow Pages or standard Yellow Pages? What are the advantages and disadvantages of each?
5. Write your name on the front of the printout, and hand it in to your instructor.

Messages That Promote Goodwill

CHAPTER 8 WORKSHEETS

NAME _____ DATE _____

PRACTICE 1

Projecting a Positive Tone

Instructions: *Each of the following communications projects a poor tone. On the lines provided, rewrite each passage to project a positive tone to the reader. Supply any necessary details to make the paragraphs or sentences more logical.* ***Hint:*** *After rewriting a sentence, check by reading it from the reader's point of view.*

1. Revise sentences 1a–1b to project a "you attitude."

   a. Our seminar will introduce strategies that we feel will be beneficial in planning for a financially secure retirement.

   _____
   _____

   b. We cannot guarantee course availability in your program area if you do not register within 10 days of the date of this letter.

   _____
   _____

2. Revise sentences 2a–2b to eliminate negative words and negative ideas.

   a. Rest assured that your complaint about not receiving the Wallace bread maker is being thoroughly investigated.

   _____
   _____

   b. If you will accept our deepest apologies, we will never again be caught making such an error.

   _____
   _____

3. Revise sentences 3a–3b to eliminate exaggeration.

   a. We are recognized by the top stitchers in the Midwest as the only store in the Midwest region offering top quality merchandise and a complete line of the very best designs and materials used for stitchery projects.

   _____
   _____

   b. Considering your great expertise in quality management and your vast experience in team building training, you are the perfect individual to work with our CIS group to assist them in developing team skills.

   _____
   _____
   _____

CHAPTER 8 WORKSHEETS

NAME _____ DATE _____

4. Revise this opening paragraph to eliminate the negative attitude and focus on positive ideas.

   We are sorry to inform you that the Travel-Lite suitcase, Model X4457, you asked about is temporarily out of stock in our warehouse, just as Ms. Cummings of our Hilldale store informed you. We anticipate getting some in by next month and having them available at the Hilldale store, if you can wait that long. Just check back with them in six weeks or so.

   _____
   _____
   _____
   _____

5. Revise this opening paragraph to eliminate the "me attitude" and the condescending tone.

   I know that you have anxiously been awaiting my fall appearance schedule. I am excited to announce that I will be visiting numerous fine stores throughout the country this holiday season. It is my wish that each and every one of you is able to visit with me when I am appearing at a location convenient to you.

   _____
   _____
   _____
   _____
   _____

6. Revise this opening paragraph to eliminate the negative tone and attitude of impatience with the customer.

   As we have discussed at least twice on the phone with you, we cannot fix your camera free of charge nor will the manufacturer. As we pointed out, you bought your camera in July 1999. As a special promotion, we provided a two-year extended warranty to the normal one-year warranty which came with the camera. That means that your warranty expired in July 2002. As it is long past that date, you will need to pay for any repairs you want us to make.

   _____
   _____
   _____
   _____
   _____
   _____
   _____
   _____

Messages That Promote Goodwill

NAME _____   DATE _____

7. Revise this opening paragraph to eliminate the "we attitude" and incorporate the more friendly "you attitude."

We are happy that you chose to purchase your new car from our dealership. We want you to know that you can depend on our service department for all your needs. To facilitate any services you may need, we are assigning Jessie Kramer, our Customer Relations Manager, as your contact person. His phone number is enclosed for your convenience.

_____
_____
_____
_____

PRACTICE 2

Problem Situations

Instructions: Study the brief analyses of the following problems. Then describe your objective in solving each problem. Write an effective opening paragraph for a letter to the customer or client involved.

1. In December, Mrs. Julie Schultz returns her leaf blower to Andersons' Equipment, where you are employed as a customer service representative. You must reply to the angry letter in which she insists that the leaf blower was delivered after the first snowfall in late November, too late for use in her yard. You have obtained from your shipping department a delivery slip, which was signed by Mrs. Schultz on October 15, the delivery date agreed upon at the time of purchase. You also note that the leaf blower has been used extensively.

   The customer's request: Mrs. Schultz demands that the store accept the leaf blower and provide her with a full refund.

   The organization's policy: The full refund cannot be approved on this seasonal merchandise. The refund policy states that merchandise must be returned within 30 days to qualify for a full refund. Also, the merchandise must not have been used.

   a. **Your objective when you write to Mrs. Schultz:**
   _____
   _____

   b. **Goodwill opening paragraph:**
   _____
   _____
   _____
   _____
   _____
   _____

CHAPTER 8 WORKSHEETS

NAME _____ DATE _____

2. You work for Midwest Technical College. The Animal Technician program has a waiting list of potential students. Jenny Holcutt was accepted from the waiting list and notified to contact the school by July 20 if she wanted to enter the program and register for classes. Your school received no response from Jenny and on July 25 accepted another individual into the program from the waiting list. On July 26, a letter arrives from Jenny (dated July 17) indicating she wants to enter the program and register for fall classes, but there is no opening for Jenny in the program at this time.

The client's request: Jenny Holcutt says she responded in a timely manner to the school, but her response was delayed in the mail. She feels she has a right to enter the program in the fall.

The organization's policy: The school's position is that they have a commitment with the student accepted on July 25 and cannot remove that student to allow Jenny to enter the program. They waited an additional five days after the July 20 deadline before accepting the next student on the waiting list. The program has many limitations, including the number of students allowed each semester, the laboratory stations required by each student, and professional certification requirements, all of which prevent the school from taking in more students.

a. **Your objective when you write to Jenny:**

_____
_____
_____
_____
_____
_____

b. **Goodwill opening paragraph:**

_____
_____
_____
_____

Instructions: Rewrite the following letters using positive language and showing a service attitude. Your goals are (1) to build goodwill, and (2) to resell your products or services and your organization.

3. We are sorry that you received a damaged video in your order of *Comedy Classics* sent to you recently. We do not know what caused the problem, but these things do happen. Therefore, we are sending you another copy of video #3, which will complete your set. We hope that the *Comedy Classics* will provide many hours of entertainment for you and your family.

_____
_____
_____
_____
_____
_____
_____

Messages That Promote Goodwill

NAME _____ DATE _____

4. We regret to inform you that we no longer carry the Betty Beautiful Dolls collection. The last three years we carried them our sales were very low. In fact, we had to discount them 50% in order to sell them. I have heard that some stores in town may still have a large supply of these dolls.

_____
_____
_____
_____

5. We are very sorry that we failed to send the data/fax modem with your new computer system. We are sending it today. Thank you for your order, and we look forward to serving you in the future.

_____
_____
_____
_____

6. Letter Analysis: From your portfolio of letters that you are collecting, select a business letter. Analyze the business letter according to the principles presented in this chapter. Use the "Business Letter Analysis" Worksheet in Chapter 3.

7. From your portfolio of collected letters, select one that illustrates principles related to goodwill presented in this chapter.
Evaluate it.

PRACTICE 3

Writing Applications

Instructions: For each writing application, prepare a message that will build goodwill. Make a plan, write a rough draft, edit the rough draft, and prepare (keyboard) each letter on a separate sheet. Supply details to make your letters cordial and interesting. Proofread your final draft; correct any errors. Print your letter for your instructor as directed. Writing assignments are presented in order of increasing difficulty.

Thank-You and Appreciation Letters

1. Write a thank-you note to your friend Kyle Samson, 101 White Way, Tifton, GA 31794, who found your lost book bag containing your books, homework, and computer disks and delivered it yesterday to your home or apartment.

2. Write a thank-you note to a friend who gave you for graduation a nice desk pen set with your name engraved on it.

3. Write a thank-you letter to Miss Gina Alford (Office Manager, Tektronics Inc., 389 Conron Street, your city and state), for coming to your business communication class today to speak on the importance of communication in the workplace. Her talk was excellent, and she shared some current statistics to back up her belief that the ability to communicate effectively is the most important skill you can have in today's business world.

CHAPTER 8 WORKSHEETS

NAME _____ DATE _____

4. You belong to a group called Business Partners, which is made up of about 15 students and 15 businesspeople. This group shares and discusses ideas about important workplace skills. You usually meet at 7:30 a.m. every other Tuesday for about an hour in one of the conference rooms at the local mall. The mall has notified your group that effective next week, there will be a $30 room charge for each meeting, but Business Partners has no money. Tom Whitsell, president of the First National Bank, 2 East Main Street, your city and state, has volunteered to let your group meet in the Community Room at the bank. You've been selected by the group to write a letter thanking him for the free meeting room.

5. You are general manager of WKLL, the public broadcasting television station in your area. Thank a viewer (Mr. John C. Henderson, 1611 Cedar Court, your city and state), who has donated an Oriental rug for an auction that will be held as part of the station's semiannual fund drive.

6. You are president of your college's Student Advisory Council. Write a letter to a nationally known tennis personality (Mr. Andre Agassi, 137 Volley Court, Alameda, CA 94501), to express appreciation for the inspiring statements he made at your college convocation concerning drugs and alcohol. Substitute a more original approach for the usual "thank you for" opening.

Letters of Congratulations

1. Write to a classmate who was recently named the recipient of a $500 scholarship from your local Rotary Club. The classmate was chosen to receive the scholarship based on scholastic achievement.

2. One of your coworkers has been named Employee of the Month. This person always seems to be in a good mood and has a smile and a friendly greeting for everyone—customers and coworkers alike. This coworker consistently demonstrates excellent customer service skills.

3. Write to one of your former teachers who has received recognition or an award for public service or volunteer work (for example, "Citizen of the Year") in your hometown.

4. You read in the newspaper that one of your high school teachers is retiring. He taught at your high school for 35 years, and you were a student in one of his classes. You know he loves to fish and to travel. You considered this teacher one of the best. Write a letter of congratulations to him.

5. As president of your town's Economic Development Corporation, write to Mary Mervis, owner of Mervis Industries (1950 East Fairchild Street, Meadville, PA 16335), to congratulate her on the recently completed addition to the plant and the new production line, which will provide 60 new jobs.

6. Write a letter of congratulations to an acquaintance who has just been promoted to assistant vice president of operations at your local Fidelity Bank. This person has always been extremely helpful to you and very courteous whenever you needed anything at the bank. You learned about the promotion through an article in your local *News Gazette.* Enclose a copy of the picture and article from the paper.

Invitations, Announcements, Welcome Letters

1. Write an informal invitation letter for your supervisor, Mr. Freemont Ireland, marketing director, Lakeview Medical Center, to welcome Donald L. Glines, a new member of the board of Lakeview Medical Center. Mr. Glines is president of Fresh Alternative Food, Inc., 7856 Commercial Boulevard, Berea, OH 44017. Invite Mr. Glines to a lunch meeting at noon next Wednesday at the Rivercrest Country Club. The purpose of the meeting is to discuss matters concerning the medical center. Ask Mr. Glines to notify you by telephone whether he can accept the invitation.

Messages That Promote Goodwill

NAME _____ DATE _____

2. Write the copy for a formal invitation to Lakeview Medical Center Foundation members. The copy should invite them to the Annual Recognition Program, which will be held on Friday, May 23, at 7 p.m. at Berea Country Club, 45 Country Club Drive, Berea, OH, and it will be a black-tie affair. Include in the invitation a request for a reply.

3. You are the administrative assistant to Mary Mervis, who is president of Mervis Industries. Write a letter announcing an open house at Mervis Industries, to be held the first Sunday of next month from 1 p.m. to 6 p.m., to show off the new addition. At the open house, plant tours showing how Mervis operates will be offered. You will also give door prizes and serve refreshments.

4. As president of Soundesign Corporation, welcome Miss Gail Timmons, owner of The Now Sound, as a new dealer. Now Sound's address is 823 Sonic Avenue, Nashville, TN 37207. Miss Timmons has just agreed to distribute Soundesign products in her area. The representative in her area is Gary Cole.

5. You are a communications officer at a state college. Write a form letter to go along with the brochure your college is sending to guidance counselors in the high schools throughout your state. The brochure *Choosing a College* is not slanted in favor of any college or type of college, but your letter may include some low-pressure selling of your school.

6. As mayor of your town, welcome Jim Street, director of the new minimum-security prison (now under construction), and his wife to your town. Their address is 1316 Confinement Avenue, Anderson, IN 46011.

Get-Well and Sympathy Letters

1. Write a sympathy note to a coworker whose 83-year-old mother passed away recently. You did not know the mother.

2. Write a get-well message to a classmate or coworker who has been home with a bad case of the flu. You expect the person to make a complete recovery in another week or so.

3. Write a get-well letter to Susan Strum, a good friend and coworker, who is home recuperating from surgery. Susan's address is 3589 Maple Drive, your city and state.

4. Write a get-well message to a coworker who suffered a heart attack a couple of days ago but is expected to make a full recovery and return to work in a couple of months.

5. You are an assistant to Tom Anderson, president of Futio Corporation. Mr. Anderson asks you to write a sympathy letter for his signature to Greg Livingston, president of Techcom, Inc., 3900 Willow Lake Boulevard, Stamford, CT 06904. Mr. Robert Gaines, executive vice president of Techcom, with whom Mr. Anderson had done business for years, died recently. Mr. Gaines and Mr. Livingston had worked together at Techcom for more than 20 years.

6. Write a condolence letter to the president of your company, Bruce Weinard, whose father passed away recently after suffering a stroke. You have a lot of respect for Mr. Weinard, and you know he was very proud of his father—he often referred to him in a positive way in his speeches. You met his father once at a company picnic and had a short conversation with him.

Letters Maintaining or Reactivating Business

1. Assume you are a sales associate working in The Shoe Emporium. A customer, Tiffany Clay (214B Pine Street, Paxton, MA 01612) bought two pairs of expensive Naturalizer shoes today. You want to keep her as a customer. Write a note to help maintain her business; enclose your business card.

CHAPTER 8   WORKSHEETS

NAME _____   DATE _____

2. Write a short note to go along with a coupon for a free holiday gift. This note will be sent to customers who have made a purchase in the past year at the boutique where you work as a sales associate. Your boutique is open from 10 a.m. to 7 p.m., Monday through Saturday.

3. As advertising manager for Copy Cats (see business card), write a letter to Mr. Fred Griffin expressing appreciation for his business. Griffin's firm, The Mitchell Company (see business card), recently moved to a new location, and you delivered a very large order of printed materials there.

CopyCats

- Legal Briefs
- Binding
- Manuals
- Newsletters
- Business Cards
- Letterhead
- Envelopes
- Padding

22 N. Second Street, Suite 306
Jackson, MS 39236
(205) 555-2300   (205) 555-2369

THE MITCHELL COMPANY

FRED GRIFFIN
Vice President and
Development Manager

P.O. Box 12690
Jackson, MS 38238

(205) 555-1200
FAX (205) 555-1264

4. David Collins (1812 Military Drive, Batesville, AR 72501) purchased a $1000 GT refrigerator from your Appliance World Store. He has been making agreed upon payments regularly for two years. Today he paid off his account with Check 356 for $310. Write him a letter to acknowledge the payment. Be sure to build goodwill.

5. As general manager of Goldsmith's Department Store, write a letter to Mrs. Marjorie Rutherford (83 Chateau Drive, Ashland, OH 44805), a former charge customer whose account has been inactive for several months. Your goal is to regain her as a regular customer.

6. As manager of Deno's Desktop Publishing Services, write a letter to Mr. Jim Marble (1919 Lynch Road, Azusa, CA 91702), a former customer who has not done business with you for six months. Your goal is to get him back as a customer.

Messages That Promote Goodwill

CHAPTER 9

Messages for Inquiries and Requests

Objectives

After completing this chapter, you will be able to:

1. Explain the importance of handling routine correspondence
2. Write and sign a letter for your supervisor
3. Explain the steps for handling correspondence responsibilities
4. Write routine communications
5. Write effective inquiries and requests
6. Practice techniques for answering yes to an inquiry or request
7. Practice techniques for answering no to an inquiry or request
8. Write an effective form letter to reply to an inquiry
9. Write an effective cover letter

WORKPLACE APPLICATIONS

Customer Service

The expression "the customer is always right" may not be entirely true, but it does convey the right attitude. After all, no business can survive without customers, especially repeat customers. Repeat customers purchase your products or services again and again. They think well of your business and tell others about it. The way to generate such loyalty is not just to provide an excellent product or service, but to make sure that employees who interact with customers know what they are doing. **Customer service** is a business's public face, and it is the key to getting and keeping customers.

Connecting With Customers

Customer service is essentially any contact between a business and its customers. Whether the contact is over the telephone, through writing, or in person, how you respond to customers will affect your entire relationship with them. Sales representatives should offer support and honest advice to customers. If your business can't meet customers' needs, help them anyway. If customers have complaints, respond by listening carefully and acting promptly. By doing so, you generate **goodwill** among customers, which brings them back to you later.

Successful business owners know that they never get a second chance to make a first impression. They also know that bad impressions have a deeper impact than do good ones. Businesses that place a priority on customer service and have a highly visible commitment to quality, hire employees who are enthusiastic, polite, and knowledgeable. The customers may not always be right, but they do have a right to expect prompt, courteous, and competent service. When they know they will receive it, they will return for more.

Thinking Critically

Situation: You return a defective appliance to a department store. The customer service representative tells you he can't do anything without a receipt. When you show the receipt, the representative rolls his eyes and slowly prepares a store credit. When you ask for cash instead, the representative tells you "It is not store policy to give cash."

Ask Yourself: Prepare a critique of the representative's performance. What advice would you offer on how he can improve his skills with customers?

> **"Diplomacy is the art of knowing what not to say."**
> —**Matthew Trump, Writer, Mother Earth News**

The ability to handle routine communication situations effectively on a daily basis will make you a productive, valued employee. In this chapter we'll look at techniques for preparing the routine correspondence that you will be writing. We'll also look at how to write form letters and how to decide when they are appropriate. Being able to ask for information—sending inquiry and request messages—is important to help you and your organization make good business decisions. Knowing how to give information—answering inquiry and request messages—is an equally important part of doing business and maintaining customer goodwill.

Handling Routine Correspondence

All organizations need customer-focused employees who can handle routine questions from people inside and outside the organization. You should take the initiative to learn as much as you can, as quickly as you can, about your organization so that you can handle routine inquiries yourself. Some inquiries can be handled with a quick response by phone. (In this case, you should mail or fax a written follow-up communication so that a written record will be available to you and the receiver.) Other routine inquiries will require you to send a written response. In this chapter, we'll concentrate on routine written messages, although many of the same principles apply when handling inquiries by phone or face-to-face.

If your job responsibilities include handling the mail for your supervisor(s), you should follow these steps when a letter arrives:

1. Open the letter. Attach the envelope to the letter for verification of the date it was mailed and the return address.
2. Review the message.
3. Underline or highlight the main points.
4. Determine whether a reply is necessary.
5. If a reply is needed, make notes for a reply and determine if the reply should be made in writing, by phone, or by some other method. If a written reply is needed, write so that documentation of the message is established.

Signing a Letter

When writing a routine letter or memo, you must decide whether to sign your own name or your employer's name. Generally, this decision is made by your supervisor and is based on company procedures.

Correspondence You Sign

Letters and memos that you sign should reflect your writing style and be written from your perspective. For instance, you should refer to your employer in the third person—"Mrs. Dudley suggested" or "Mr. Downing requested." In memos, your name appears in the FROM line. In letters, your name and title should be keyed below the complimentary closing, as illustrated here:

> Sincerely,
>
> *Malynda Moore*
>
> Malynda Moore
> Assistant to Viv Dudley

Thinking Cap 9.1

Discuss: When you sign your employer's name to a document, why should you add your own initials just under the handwritten name? Why is it important to always secure permission before signing someone else's name to any document?

Correspondence You Sign for Your Employer

When you write a message and sign your employer's name, try to adopt your employer's writing style, making the message sound like one he or she would have written. Write from your employer's perspective—use the first person (*I* or *we*) instead of *Mrs. Dudley* or *Mr. Downing*. When you sign your employer's name, add your own initials unless instructed otherwise.

Accepting Correspondence Responsibilities

You will find many ways to improve your correspondence skills. You can strengthen your abilities by accepting the following five basic responsibilities:

1. Check incoming messages for factual discrepancies.

Errors in dates and figures are especially common. Suppose you receive a letter that gives the date of a monthly meeting as Thursday, June 8. You should automatically check the calendar to verify that Thursday is June 8. Should you find that Thursday is June 9, you need to write or call the sender for clarification. In your request for clarification you then might tactfully write or ask, "Am I correct in putting this meeting on the calendar for Wednesday, June 8?"

2. Record all promises you make for further communication.

For example, when you write or tell someone that your employer will contact him or her in a few weeks to arrange a meeting, immediately enter a follow-up reminder on your desk calendar or in your tickler file. (A **tickler file** is an electronic filing system used as a memory aid to keep track of deadlines and due dates.) At the appropriate time, call your employer's attention to the need to confirm arrangements for the desired meeting.

3. Confirm in writing any appointments arranged orally.

Never trust your memory. Embarrassing and costly mix-ups often occur when the time, location, or other appointment details arranged in telephone and face-to-face conversations are not confirmed in writing.

GLOBAL DIVERSITY 9.1

Idioms
In England someone checking his or her calendar about an appointment might say, "I'll check my diary." Instead of picking you up for an appointment at two-thirty, an English person might say, "I'll fetch you at half past two." *Can you name some idiomatic expressions you use in your daily life?*

Messages for Inquiries and Requests

4. Recognize the importance of sending goodwill messages promptly.

Regularly check newspapers and trade journals for items that suggest occasions for sending letters of appreciation, congratulations, and other goodwill messages from your employer.

5. Proofread all correspondence you write, sign, and mail for your employer.

Use the spelling and grammar tools that are available on most word processing software programs. Errors in keyboarding, spelling, and word usage that you fail to detect reflect unfavorably on you, your employer, and the organization you both represent. A misspelled word in a transmitted letter or memo says to the receiver, "You're not important" or "I'm too busy or too careless to check for errors."

PREPARING ROUTINE COMMUNICATIONS

You may write several types of routine communications on your own initiative or at your employer's request. They include the following:

- Information letters
- Acknowledgments
- Referral letters
- Transmittal letters
- Follow-up correspondence
- Internal communications

Information Letters

You may often find it appropriate to prepare letters giving routine information. The exchange between office support personnel of Galaxy Satellite Systems, Macon, Georgia, and the Kansas City, Missouri, Chamber of Commerce illustrates such correspondence. See Figure 9-1a on the next page for Ms. Marble's letter requesting information, then look at the reply sent to Ms. Marble from Marion Merkle, Administrative Assistant at the Kansas City Chamber of Commerce in Figure 9-1b.

Acknowledgments

A communication received while your employer is away from the office requires an acknowledgment. Some typical letters you will write for your employer are those acknowledging receipt of letters, information or material, gifts and favors, and remittances.

Figure 9-1a
The writer of this letter requests routine information about an event.

> Dear Kansas City Chamber of Commerce:
>
> Please send me the opening and closing dates of your Festival of Lights this year. A group of Galaxy Satellite Systems managers would like to include a day at your famous festival during a conference trip to Kansas City.
>
> Sincerely yours,
>
> *Diane Marble*
>
> Diane Marble
> Assistant to Bradley Pontecore

Figure 9-1b
Letters are sent in response to requests for information.

> Dear Ms. Marble:
>
> Our Festival of Lights this year opens on Thursday, November 20, and ends on Saturday, December 30.
>
> We have added your name to our mailing list to receive all special announcements concerning the daily tours, parades, concerts, and other attractions. We believe your managers will find our Festival of Lights an enjoyable part of their trip.
>
> Best wishes for a successful conference in Kansas City.
>
> Sincerely yours,
>
> *Marion Merkle*
>
> Marion Merkle
> Assistant to Tom Szott

Letters

When you receive a letter that must be held for your employer's attention, business courtesy requires that you send a stopgap letter. A **stopgap letter** is a short, direct acknowledgment that explains why an answer will be delayed, and when it may be expected.

When writing a stopgap letter, be careful not to obligate your employer or to give out confidential information about why he or she is absent.

Another example of a stopgap letter is one written to explain that more time is needed to prepare a complete answer. Often a person writing for information does not realize that it might take several days and communication with several departments to get the facts together for a reply. When this is the case, send a short note—usually over your employer's signature—to explain the delay. See Figures 9-2 and 9-3 on the next page.

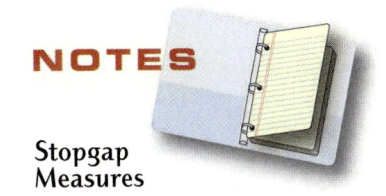

NOTES

Stopgap Measures

A stopgap letter is sent when there will be a delay in answering a message.

Messages for Inquiries and Requests   233

Figure 9-2
In this stopgap letter, the writer explains that an answer will be delayed.

Dear Mr. Weinard:

Thank you for your August 14 letter asking Senator Myers to speak at your Soil Conservation meeting at 7 P.M. on September 10.

Senator Myers is out of the office this week. As soon as she returns, I shall bring your invitation to her attention.

Sincerely yours,

Jeanene Lowery

Jeanene Lowery
Assistant to Senator Myers

Figure 9-3
In this stopgap letter, the writer explains why a delay is necessary.

Dear Mr. Kukla:

You can expect the information you asked for in your April 12 letter in a few days. In order for my report to be helpful to you, I must get data from both the sales and the advertising departments.

I am glad to cooperate with you on this project and expect to send a complete answer by the end of the week.

Cordially yours,

Carol Willis

Carol Willis
District Manager

When a delayed reply is a common occurrence in a business, a form letter or postal card may be sent for acknowledgment. If you are employed in an office that processes property loss claims, for example, you could build goodwill by acknowledging each claim on the day it was received with a brief message such as the one shown in Figure 9-4. Even though this letter is a form letter, notice how it appears to be individually written—word processing software programs make it easy to personalize a form letter.

Information or Material

You should always write acknowledgments when packages, requested information, and other messages or materials are received. These acknowledgments should be direct, concise, and courteous. They should include a thank-you to the sender as well as the details needed to identify the material received, which

Go to CD-ROM
Activity 9-1
To test your skills.

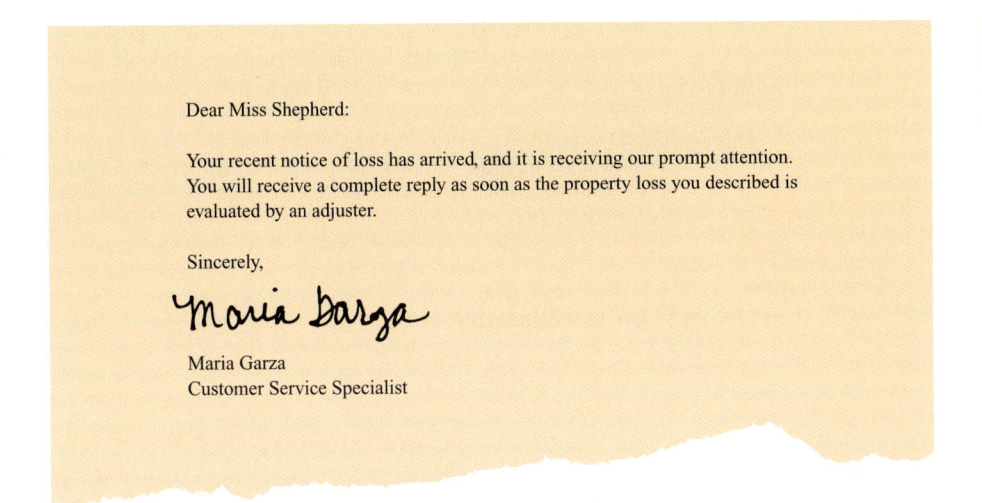

Figure 9-4
In this form letter, the writer acknowledges that correspondence has been received.

> Dear Miss Shepherd:
>
> Your recent notice of loss has arrived, and it is receiving our prompt attention. You will receive a complete reply as soon as the property loss you described is evaluated by an adjuster.
>
> Sincerely,
>
> *Maria Garza*
>
> Maria Garza
> Customer Service Specialist

Figure 9-5
The acknowledgment form is a record for the files.

> Dear Mrs. Lowery:
>
> The signed contracts relating to the Mitchell case arrived this morning. Thank you for sending them so promptly.
>
> Sincerely,
>
> *George Byron*
>
> George Byron
> Assistant to Michelle Hicks

is important because the acknowledgment becomes a record for the files. You may want to use a form message when you need to send many similar acknowledgments. The principles of good writing are illustrated in the routine acknowledgment of signed contracts shown above in Figure 9-5.

Gifts and Favors

Simple and sincere thank-you acknowledgments should be written for gifts (such as flowers to mark an open house or the dedication of a new building) and favors (speaking to a professional group in response to a request) as well as for congratulatory and other goodwill letters received from clients and friends. Look at the example shown in Figure 9-6 on the following page.

Remittances

Remittances (payments) by check are seldom acknowledged. They simply show up as a credit on the customer's next statement—the customer's canceled check serves as notice that the payment was received. Some

Messages for Inquiries and Requests

Figure 9-6
A simple thank-you letter acknowledges a gift.

> Dear Miss Gotardo:
>
> You were most generous to send copies of your interesting booklet, *E-Mail Etiquette*, for all the members of our office staff. Your commonsense discussion of using e-mail to save time—with checklists and clever illustrations—will certainly help our employees be more productive.
>
> Sincerely yours,
>
> *Carolyn Sennhenn*
>
> Carolyn Sennhenn
> Assistant to Mrs. Henderson

managers believe, however, that the goodwill gained by a written acknowledgment outweighs the time and expense of writing the letter. A letter acknowledging a remittance should: be brief, express appreciation, give the amount and form of the remittance, tell what the remittance is for, and build goodwill through a warm, friendly tone.

See how the letter in Figure 9-7, acknowledging a payment by Mr. Hensley on his account, follows these five guidelines.

Figure 9-7
This acknowledgment follows the five guidelines.

> Dear Mr. Hensley:
>
> Your Check 534 for $300 arrived today and has been credited to your account. We do appreciate your prompt payment, which reduces your account balance to $150.
>
> Cordially,
>
> *Tom Mellon*
>
> Tom Mellon
> Credit Manager

You should always send a letter acknowledging a remittance in the following situations:

- When a customer pays his or her first invoice
- When a customer makes the final payment on an installment loan
- When the remittance is an unusually large one
- When a monetary gift (solicited or unsolicited) has been received

Referral Letters

Sometimes a letter received by you or your employer can be answered better by someone else in your organization. You should, of course, refer the letter to this person for a reply. If the person you refer the letter to is not in the same office as you, or for any other reason cannot reply immediately, you should send a referral letter to the writer of the original letter, as shown in Figure 9-8. Then send a copy of the referral letter, along with a request to reply, to the person who will be answering the original letter.

Thinking Cap 9.2

Discuss: Why should you send a copy of a referral letter to the person to whom you are referring your reader?

Figure 9-8
A referral letter is sent to the writer of the original letter and a copy of the referral is sent to the person who will respond.

Dear Terry Swanson:

Thank you for your January 18 letter about service on your telephone answering machine. Our distributor would be the best person to answer your questions.

I am therefore referring your letter to Mr. Mark Winters, manager of the service department at Clifton Private Telephone Inc., 389 Technology Avenue, El Reno, OK 73036.

Cordially yours,

Mr. Lynn Cole

Lynn Cole

mx
c Mark Winters

Transmittal Letters

Transmittal letters are cover letters sent to accompany information or other materials you are sending. The transmittal letters you write may be as simple as the following:

> Here are the advertising mats you requested. Your interest in promoting the X-R-size bicycle in Detroit's newspapers is appreciated.

Follow-Up Correspondence

At times, you may need to follow up on information or articles that were requested by you or your organization or promised to you but have not been received promptly. You may also need to follow up on enclosures that were omitted from correspondence. When you write follow-up messages such as the one in Figure 9-9, observe these guidelines:

- Remind rather than criticize.
- Be brief, but recall the earlier communication or discussion.
- Identify the promised item(s).
- Explain what you want the recipient to do.

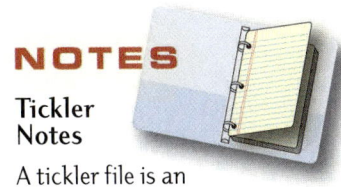

NOTES

Tickler Notes
A tickler file is an important tool to help you keep track of items that may need follow-up.

Messages for Inquiries and Requests

Figure 9-9
This follow-up letter reminds the recipient that action is needed.

> Dear Mr. Natho:
>
> We have not received the committee report on proposed changes in insurance coverage, which was promised for last Friday, May 3. Mrs. Avondale must have it by May 10. She needs this information to prepare for a meeting with the insurance company on May 13.
>
> Please forward the committee report to Mrs. Avondale by May 8.
>
> Sincerely yours,
>
> *Frances Sutton*
>
> Frances Sutton
> Assistant to Mrs. Avondale

Compare the follow-up correspondence in Figure 9-9 with the example that follows. Which letter would you rather receive?

> Your letter of April 5 indicated that a copy of the proposed company logo for the American Chemical Corporation was enclosed. However, the logo was not in the envelope when the letter reached us. Will you please send us another copy today?

Internal Communications

Sometimes when you write internal communications, you use your own signature. At other times, you may write messages that your supervisor will sign. Regardless of who signs these communications, tone and accuracy are

Figure 9-10
This memo is a concise internal communication.

> **Bremer Enterprizes**
> 47 Skyway Drive • Indianapolis, IN 46290
>
> **MEMO TO:** All Employees
>
> **FROM:** Carol Craig *CC*
>
> **DATE:** November 2, <YEAR>
>
> **SUBJECT:** Reception for Retirees
>
> The reception for our retirees is next Friday, April 27, from 3 to 5 P.M. in the Bremer Conference Room.
>
> With your generous contributions, a pen-and-ink drawing of the historic library building will be presented to each retiree as a thank-you for many years of contributions to our organization.

Chapter 9

important. **Internal communications,** or communications people within an organization send to each other, include the following:

- Brief, informal messages (often handwritten) on notepaper or self-stick notes
- Electronic messages (e-mail)
- Memos
- Memo-reply forms with pressure-sensitive paper for copies
- Preprinted message forms used for telephone messages, photocopy requests, complaints, routing, authorization, and so on

Regardless of who signs these communications, tone and accuracy are important. The memo from Carol Craig, shown in Figure 9-10, is an example of a concise internal communication. Other internal communications, including memos, are detailed and illustrated in Chapter 7.

INQUIRIES AND REQUESTS

People write **inquiry letters**—letters that ask for information—when they want to know more about a product or service. People write **request letters** when they want a specific action to be taken. Inquiry and request letters can be grouped into these three types:

- Appointment and reservation requests
- Buying inquiries
- General requests

All three types of inquiry and request letters use the direct approach, but each type calls for special techniques. Notice the difference in techniques used in letters that will benefit the reader from the ones that will benefit the writer.

Appointment and Reservation Requests

A writer sends an **appointment request** to set up a meeting and a **reservation request** to reserve lodging or dining accommodations. To prevent misunderstandings, these letters must include exact dates and all other details pertinent to the appointment or reservation. If you are making an appointment or reservation request in another country, you must also check on business etiquette and customs appropriate for that culture. For example, in the United States people are expected to be prompt for appointments; in other cultures, people may be considered rude if they show up at the appointed time.

Requests for Appointments

When requesting appointments, you should include the purpose of the appointment or meeting, day and date, time, and place.

GLOBAL DIVERSITY 9.2

24-Hour Clock
In many European countries, times are expressed according to the 24-hour clock. For example, a 2 p.m. appointment would be at 1400 hours. *You're scheduled for a meeting at 1200 hours. What type of meeting will it likely turn out to be?*

Messages for Inquiries and Requests

Notice that the letter shown below in Figure 9-11 gives these details and then asks for confirmation.

Figure 9-11
This request for an appointment gives the details of the appointment.

Dear Mr. Poulson:

I would like to demonstrate our new Tek-Segno 1650 Color Scanner/Copier to you in our office showroom on Monday, June 3, at 2 P.M. You will be able to judge for yourself the increased capabilities of the 1650 as described in the enclosed color brochure.

I'll call you next week to make sure this date and time fit your schedule.

Sincerely,

Thinking Cap 9.3

Discuss: If you find you are going to be late for an appointment or unable to make an appointment, what should you do and why?

Go to CD-ROM
Activity 9-2
To test your skills.

Additional correspondence may be saved if you offer some alternate dates and times in your initial request for an appointment. If you must change the time or date of a scheduled appointment, do so as soon as possible as a courtesy to the person you are meeting.

The letter to Mr. Poulson (Figure 9-12) requests that an appointment be rescheduled. The letter does the following:

- Asks for a change in the date of an appointment
- States the reason for the change
- Gives the receiver the opportunity to set the date for the next appointment

Figure 9-12
This request gives the receiver an opportunity to reschedule an appointment.

Dear Mr. Poulson:

Will it be convenient for me to demonstrate our new Tek-Segno 1650 Color Scanner/Copier to you next Thursday instead of next Monday? Can we reschedule our meeting for June 6 at 2 P.M.?

We are exhibiting at a business and office products show in Chicago on June 3, 4, and 5, and I have just been assigned to work that exhibit.

If Thursday, June 6, is not convenient for you, would you suggest a later date? I'm looking forward to meeting with you.

Sincerely,

LEGAL & ETHICAL 9-1

Cancellation Policy? Carlos calls a local restaurant and makes a dinner reservation for two for the next night at 7 p.m. Carlos and his girlfriend, Maria, decide at the last minute that they would rather order pizza in. Maria asks Carlos if he should call the restaurant and cancel the dinner reservation. Carlos says that it's not necessary. Is this legal? Is this ethical? What are the pros and cons of keeping appointments and reservations? What if Carlos had not shown for a dentist appointment? An appointment with his attorney? An appearance in court?

Requests for Reservations

Requests for reservations for overnight accommodations at hotels and motels should include the following details:

- Number of adults and number of children who will be staying
- Number of rooms needed
- Number and size of beds needed per room
- Smoking or nonsmoking room preference
- Number of nights you will be staying
- Arrival and departure days, dates, and times
- Name of the convention or group meeting you will be attending (if applicable)

If you are planning to arrive after 6 P.M., you should guarantee your reservation by sending a deposit or giving your credit card number and expiration date. Be sure to ask the hotel or motel to send you a written confirmation of the reservation details, including the rate and the confirmation number. This will enable you to verify the details and to present the confirmation upon your arrival, if necessary. Also, you may wish to request a corporate rate when you make the reservation if your travel is business-related. The reservation letter, shown below, could be mailed or faxed.

Reservations Department
Hyatt Hotels
3789 Constitution Avenue
Washington, DC 20016

Dear Reservations Department:

Please reserve a nonsmoking room with one double bed for one adult for six nights Sunday, March 14, through Friday, March 19 at the corporate rate. I will be attending the National Distance Learning Convention.

I would appreciate receiving a written confirmation before March 1.

Sincerely,

NOTES

Get It in Writing

A written confirmation allows you to check details of your reservation and to have a written record of the reservation.

GLOBAL DIVERSITY 9.3

Punctuality

Be on time for any meetings in Indonesia. The meetings traditionally start late, and your Indonesian business associates will likely arrive late. However, you are expected on time, and should never make any comment about the meeting starting late or any person arriving late. *How does this compare to the way meetings are run in the United States?*

Figure 9-13
This reservation request includes pertinent details.

Messages for Inquiries and Requests

Today, telephone and/or e-mail/Internet reservation requests are common. Letters are rarely written to make lodging requests.

LEGAL & ETHICAL 9-2

Five-Finger Discount? Mike has made a reservation for overnight accommodations in the Mayflower Hotel. When Mike is ready to leave his hotel room, he packs a set of the hotel's towels in his suitcase because he needs some in his apartment. He feels the towels are just like the little bottles of shampoo and body lotion that are provided in the bathroom. Are Mike's actions legal? Are they ethical? If every guest took towels, who would absorb the cost?

Guidelines for Requesting Appointments and Reservations

When writing appointment and reservation requests, use the direct approach (see Chapter 5, page 109) and follow these four guidelines:

1. **Make sure the facts are accurate.** Think of the problems one error in a date could cause for the receiver and for you. You can help to prevent such errors by always giving the day of the week along with the date. Develop the habit of checking the day and date with your calendar every time—don't trust your memory!

2. **Give all the pertinent details.** Remember, simple requests should be concise and specific. For example, state exactly what you are requesting, such as, "Please send a free copy of your pamphlet *Going to Court* to the address above."

3. **Keep the tone courteous and friendly.** Use a customer-service attitude —keep your tone one of asking rather than demanding.

4. **Keep the closing simple.** Expressing appreciation, indicating future action, or saying that you look forward to your future meeting or trip are appropriate ways to end an appointment or reservation request.

Buying Inquiries and General Requests

A **buying inquiry** asks for information about products or services the writer is interested in purchasing. In a **general request,** the writer seeks information without any intention of buying or selling. This type of request asks for details and facts that the recipient can give with a minimum amount of time, effort, and expense.

Guidelines for Buying Inquiries and General Requests

When you write a buying inquiry or a general request, use the direct approach discussed in Chapter 5, page 109, and follow these six guidelines:

1. **Begin with your questions.** Get to the point immediately (use the direct approach) and tell the reader exactly what you need to know.

NOTES

Need Information?

A buying inquiry asks for information about products and services the writer is interested in purchasing. A general request asks for information without the writer's having any intention to buy or sell.

---

242   Chapter 9

2. **Word each question carefully.** Ask for specific information—vague or ambiguous questions are easily misunderstood. First, use questions rather than statements. Notice that the question in the following example is shorter than the statement. Also, the question mark immediately tells the reader that an answer is expected.

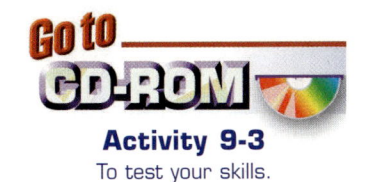

POOR: I would like to know the colors in which the Corian countertop is available.

IMPROVED: What colors are available in the Corian countertop?

Second, make your questions specific, not general. A general question usually brings a general answer, which often repeats what you already know instead of giving you the details you want. Wouldn't the specific question in the following example bring you more information than the vague question?

VAGUE: What can you tell me about your cellular phone?

SPECIFIC: How does your cellular phone compare with the Gallaxy cellular phone in price, memory size, and range?

Third, avoid questions that can be answered *yes* or *no*. Some questions can be specific, but they still may not tell you what you really want to know. For example, a *yes* answer would be satisfactory for a question such as "Do you have it in stock?" However, a *yes* answer to the question, "Is it available in any other color?" would not bring the information you want to know.

POOR: Is the guarantee on the magnolia tree a good one?

IMPROVED: What is the length of the guarantee on the magnolia tree, and what does it cover?

3. **Briefly explain why you are asking.** Include all the facts that will help the recipient answer you, including the use you plan to make of the information you are requesting. This is especially important if you are requesting general information with no intention of buying products or services. For example, you need information for a research report. You may add that fact to your request so that the receiver knows why you need the information.

If you are writing in response to an advertisement, you should include the following information:

- Name of the publication where the advertisement appeared
- Date of the publication
- Page number

You may wish to enclose a copy of the advertisement with your letter.

4. **Omit details that are not helpful to the reader.** Incidental comments lengthen a letter unnecessarily and make it harder for the reader to determine

Messages for Inquiries and Requests

the exact information you want. For example, mentioning that you are interested in a franchise when your real purpose is to ask for information on corporate housing would be confusing to the recipient.

5. **Put each question in a separate paragraph or a numbered list.** A letter that groups several questions in a single paragraph is hard to answer. In a letter like this, the reader must make a special effort to identify each question and may easily overlook one.

By contrast, you can make your questions stand out by numbering them and putting them in a list, as in the inquiry shown in Figure 9-14. You may include explanations of your need to know the answers at the beginning, at the end, or in the paragraph with the questions, whichever is most appropriate. See the explanation with question 3 in Figure 9-14 for an example.

Figure 9-14
This letter numerically lists questions to be answered.

> Ladies and Gentlemen:
>
> Please send me answers to the following questions about the Cozy Camcorder advertised on page 27 of your October *Multimedia Catalog*.
>
> 1. Will the image stabilization feature work while videotaping from a moving car or truck?
>
> 2. How should I clean the 3.5" color LCD screen?
>
> 3. Can the automatic preset date and time feature be turned off after I start to videotape? I would like for the date and time to show briefly at the beginning of the event I am videotaping, but I do not want it to display throughout the entire event.
>
> 4. Is there a guarantee on this camcorder; if so, what does the guarantee cover?
>
> I will appreciate receiving this information within two weeks, since I plan to purchase a camcorder soon.
>
> Sincerely,

6. **Close with motivation for action.** Stop when you are finished—too many beginning writers tend to repeat in the closing sentences things they have already said, just because they do not know how to stop. A good way to close an inquiry is to motivate the individual for action such as (1) giving the date by which you need the information or results, or (2) saying you are looking forward to or will certainly appreciate receiving the information.

Checkpoint 9.1

1. What is the difference between an acknowledgment letter and a follow-up letter?
2. Explain why you agree or disagree that letters of inquiries are more effective than telephone calls.
3. Explain the problems in the following excerpt from a request letter. What improvements would you make?

   I am interested in your hair care products. Please send me some information about your most popular products. Also, are your products tested on animals? Can you send me samples?

REPLIES TO INQUIRIES AND REQUESTS

When you receive an inquiry or a request letter about your organization's products or services, consider the writer a prospective customer. Answer the inquiry the very day you receive it, if possible, while the sender's interest is highest. Remember, it takes no more time to answer the letter today than to answer it next week, and the results will be better.

If you are unable to answer the inquiry immediately, write to the sender to explain the reason for the delay and to give a time when you can send an answer. Many organizations spend thousands of dollars on advertising to attract inquiries and then throw away the results by the haphazard way they handle the inquiries. Remember that it is more costly to attract a new inquiry than it is to follow up promptly on the inquiry you have.

NOTES

Quick Response

Reply to inquiries and requests promptly—ideally within one business day—while your reader is still interested.

Letters Answering *Yes* to Inquiries and Requests

Use the direct approach (see Chapter 5, page 109) when you say *yes* to an inquiry or request, and be sure to follow these four guidelines:

1. Give the exact information requested.

In the first sentence of your letter, write that you are granting the request or answering the inquiry; then go on to answer each question asked. A common error made in answering inquiries is failure to answer all of the questions. You can prevent this error by highlighting or underlining on the letter of inquiry the points or questions you need to address. Then, before you send your reply, double-check with the original letter to see that you have adequately covered each point or question.

When answering *yes* to a request for an appointment or reservation, remember to repeat in your letter all the pertinent details. An answer to a request for a reservation is shown in Figure 9-15 on the following page.

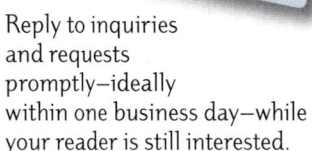

Figure 9-15
This answer to a reservation request covers all the pertinent details.

> Dear Mrs. Wear:
>
> Thank you for your registration form and deposit for the First Financial Planners Annual Broker Dealer Conference to be held September 8-11 in St. Louis, Missouri. We're happy you will be attending the conference.
>
> The Sheraton-Westport Hotel has set aside a block of rooms at a special discounted rate for conference attendees. The rate is $110 for a single, $120 for a double. To make reservations, call 800-555-2000 before September 1.
>
> American Airlines is offering conference attendees up to 45 percent off the regular fares. To make flight reservations, call 800-555-1155, and refer to identification number F9906.
>
> When you arrive at the conference, be sure to register before noon on Wednesday, September 8, so that you can attend the 1 p.m. special roundtable discussion on the impact of market timing.
>
> Sincerely,

NOTES

Highlighting

To be sure you will answer all the questions in an inquiry, mark (underline or highlight) the points or questions to be addressed in the letter.

2. Express appreciation for the inquiry.

Tell the writer of the inquiry, either directly or by implication, that you are glad he or she has written to you about one of your organization's products or services. In your reply, write in the spirit of service and goodwill—the tone should express your appreciation.

3. Sell your organization or product.

An inquiry tells you that the writer was interested in your organization or product when he or she wrote, but what guarantee do you have that the interest is still "hot"? In your reply, capitalize on the prospective customer's interest by showing the potential benefits. Give examples that will let the customer visualize receiving the benefit of this item.

4. End with a positive closing.

If appropriate, offer to give further assistance, and end with a goodwill closing.

When inquiries are clear, concise, and specific, they are easy to answer. Look at the letter of inquiry shown in Figure 9-16. Immediately after this request for information was received, the reply shown in Figure 9-17 was written. Because all the customer's questions could be answered positively, the writer used the direct approach.

When you reply to a letter containing several questions, be sure to *answer every question completely* using one of these formats:

- Put each answer in a separate paragraph.
- Number each answer.

If you have a positive answer for every question, simply answer the questions in the order they were asked. If you don't have a positive answer for

Figure 9-16
A clear, specific inquiry is easy to answer.

Alpine Van Lines
2478 North Clark Street
Chicago, IL 60600

May 4, <YEAR>

Hammermill Papers Group
Division of Hammermill Paper Co.
19 Treeline Way
Erie, PA 16512

Ladies and Gentlemen:

Please send me some information about the paper you make that is suitable for letterhead stationery.

I've been asked to do some research and write a proposal to recommend the paper and layout for new letterhead stationery for my organization. Specifically, I'd like to know:

1. What weight of paper you would recommend for letterhead.
2. What percent of cotton fiber content the paper should have.
3. Whether it is proper to use colored paper for letterhead.
4. What information should be included in the letterhead.

Could you please reply by July 7, since my proposal is due a few days after that?

Sincerely,

Terri White

Terri White, Co-Director
Marketing and Public Relations

---

every question, start with your most positive answer and work your way down to your least positive answer. This sequence will prevent you from starting your letter with a negative answer.

Letters Answering *No* to Inquiries and Requests

Remember, never start your letter with bad news. When you must say *no*, use the indirect approach (see Chapter 5, page 110), and deliver the bad news gently and tactfully. Strive to let courtesy and thoughtfulness shine through your letter. Be sure to give the reasons or explanation for your refusal before you actually say *no*. A gracious refusal is much like a persuasive request—you are asking your reader to accept your decision as the only fair answer under the circumstances.

NOTES

Positive Start

Never start your letter with bad news.

Messages for Inquiries and Requests

Figure 9-17
A reply to an inquiry should address every question.

Hammermill Papers Group
19 Treeline Way
Erie, PA 16512
Phone 814-555-1761 • Fax 814-555-1762

May 6, <YEAR>

Terri White, Co-Director
Marketing and Public Relations
Alpine Van Lines
2478 North Clark Street
Chicago, IL 60600

Dear Ms. White:

Enclosed are samples of the paper we recommend for letterhead stationery. We are happy to answer the questions in your May 4 letter because the content and design of your organization's letterhead create a first and lasting impression of your organization.

1. Most letterhead is printed on 16-, 20-, or 24-pound paper. The weight is figured as the weight of four reams of 8½-by-11-inch paper.
2. Paper for letterheads should have a minimum of 25 percent cotton fiber content. Paper to be used for documents that need to be kept more than 10 years should contain 100 percent cotton fiber content. The heavier the weight and the higher the cotton fiber content, the higher the quality (and the price) of the paper.
3. Although white is the predominant color of paper used for letterheads, colors like beige, ivory, gray, pale blue, and pale green are gaining in popularity.
4. A good letterhead should answer the questions "Who?" (name of your organization), "What?" (the nature of your business), and "Where?" (mailing address). Be sure to include your phone number and fax number in addition to your address.

I have enclosed the booklet, *The Letterhead Analyzer,* which gives an analysis of the psychological effect of different colors used for letterheads. The booklet also contains several sample letterheads that won awards for outstanding design and layout last year.

I suggest that you consider hiring a professional graphic artist to help design your letterhead. If you have additional questions, please write again or call me at (814) 555-3312.

Sincerely,

Marilyn Hunter

Marilyn Hunter

ms
Enclosure

Keep in mind that a negative communication has three purposes:

- To say *no*
- To provide reasons or an explanation
- To keep the goodwill of the reader

To accomplish these purposes effectively, use the following guidelines:

1. View the letter as an opportunity to "talk it over."

Give your reader whatever encouragement you can—not just a plain no. If you think, "I must decline this invitation or this order or refuse this request," you will probably write negatively. On the other hand, you will probably write constructively if you think, "What can I do to encourage this person even though I have to say no?"

2. Start with a friendly buffer paragraph.

What do you expect when you receive a letter with one of these beginnings?

> It is my unpleasant duty to inform you that . . . .
>
> I'm sorry to tell you that we cannot grant your request . . . .

Do you immediately close your mind to whatever else the writer may say? You may think that the writer is not interested in helping you, in building goodwill, or in keeping your friendship. The writer seems concerned only with saying *no* and getting an unpleasant task completed. But suppose a letter begins this way:

> Your proposal for a joint meeting of Phi Beta Lambda (PBL) and Future Business Leaders of America (FBLA) is exciting, Emily.

Aren't you more likely to read the rest of the message with an open mind?

3. Tell the reader why you cannot say *yes*.

In your explanation, imply that you would rather say *yes* than *no*. Also, try to compliment the reader in some way. Although her request to book a video was denied, the PBL president who received the following explanation certainly felt that she had chosen a worthwhile film:

> Many PBL groups throughout the nation have enjoyed *Preparing Your Portfolio for the Job Interview.* In fact, Emily, it is our most popular video. Last April we had three additional copies made so that it would be available to more clubs, but even these are booked well in advance.

4. Avoid a negative refusal.

Explain before you refuse; a blunt no should be avoided. If your letter does a good job of explaining, the reader will realize that you cannot do what he or she has asked—the *no* is inferred. If you must directly state your refusal (to be sure it is clear to your reader that you are not granting the request), avoid emphasizing it or putting it in negative terms. Notice how the business letter shown in Figure 9-18 on the following page dwells on the negative and almost obscures the positive points. In contrast, the revision shown in Figure 9-19 expresses interest in the reader and tries to keep his business while refusing the request.

5. Give encouragement and, when you can, give help.

Sometimes you can take the sting out of a *no* with a helpful suggestion. For example, a department store representative, in declining an order for an article not carried by the store, may tell the customer where he or she can make the purchase. The reservations manager of a Chicago hotel, not able to make the reservations requested, made this suggestion:

> If you can conveniently rearrange your travel plans to arrive in Chicago on June 10, we shall be glad to reserve a double room for you and your wife. If you must be here on June 5, you might write for help to the Greater Chicago Hotel Association at 105 Michigan Avenue, Chicago, IL 60600.

NOTES

Soft Landing
When you have to say *no*, soften it by offering a helpful suggestion if at all possible.

Figure 9-18
A letter that dwells on the negative conceals positive points.

> Dear Mr. Bargaree:
>
> We are sorry that your portrait has been damaged. This rarely happens to Supreme photos.
>
> I regret to advise you that we cannot hold negatives for a long period of time because we lack sufficient storage space; therefore, we will not be able to reprint your portrait. I am, however, processing a refund in the amount of $19.95, which you should receive within the next six weeks. I am also returning the damaged 5 by 7 portrait to you with a free coupon.
>
> Please accept our apologies for this problem, as we greatly value your patronage.
>
> With kindest personal regards,

Figure 9-19
The revision of the bad-news letter expresses interest in the customer while refusing a request.

> Dear Mr. Bargaree:
>
> We were happy to hear that your family was so pleased with your portraits. We are sorry that one was damaged. Because our storage space is limited, however, all negatives are destroyed ten days after an order has been filled.
>
> Your 5 by 7 portrait is being returned, along with a refund of $19.95. You should receive both in about two weeks.
>
> Please use the enclosed coupon for a complimentary 5 by 7 color portrait when Supreme Photos returns to Alton on November 7.

In the following response to a student's request for help with a research study, the public relations manager at Covenant Hospital made the student aware of another possible avenue of assistance:

> While Covenant Hospital has no funds available to help with your worthwhile project, state money has been appropriated to fund research projects that will benefit the inner-city areas. I suggest you present your proposal to the State Health Agency at 1800 Peachtree Boulevard, Atlanta, GA 30303.

6. Close pleasantly with a look toward the future.

In your last paragraph, don't stress or repeat the negatives. For example, closing with "We hope our inability to grant your request does not inconvenience you too much" would leave the reader thinking how dissatisfied he or she is about your refusal. Also, do not include an apology in your last paragraph. Saying "We are sorry that we couldn't send the information you requested" accents what you *cannot* do. Instead, emphasize what you *can* do (see Figure 9-20). Some possibilities include the following:

- Offer an alternate solution.
- Express your desire to cooperate further.
- Offer a wish for the reader's success.
- Make a pleasant off-the-subject remark.

Go to CD-ROM

Activity 9-4
To test your skills.

Figure 9-20
This bad-news letter ends on a positive note.

Dear Mrs. Jordan:

Thank you for applying for a position at Multimedia Entertainment Inc. I certainly enjoyed meeting you this week and having the opportunity to discuss career opportunities with you at our company.

Because of its position as a leader in the industry, Multimedia Entertainment Inc. offers unique public relations challenges and opportunities. I think you would find the entertainment industry an exciting one to work in, and being associated with a Fortune 500 company would be an especially nice bonus.

Although we currently have no openings in public relations, I will keep your résumé in our active file for 90 days. I'll be sure to give you a call if a job opening develops that fits your skills and abilities.

We sincerely appreciate your interest in Multimedia Entertainment Inc.

Cordially,

FORM REPLIES TO INQUIRIES

To save time, form letters and cards are often used in business to reply to inquiries. They are sometimes prepared in connection with advertising campaigns to make responding to the anticipated number of inquiries more efficient. Look at the form letter shown on the following page in Figure 9-21, which was prepared to answer inquiries about lodging and tours at Yellowstone National Park.

In today's electronic offices, a form letter can be prepared on the computer by merging a database of names and addresses with a form letter. A letter produced in this way looks like an individually keyed letter, which always leaves a more positive impression with the recipient than a photocopied or printed form letter.

NOTES

Time Savers
Form letters are used to save time and to get a quick reply to people who have sent letters of inquiry.

Cover Letters

Printed advertising brochures, price lists, catalogs, checks, reports, and business forms are often sent to customers, dealers, and others. Sending one of these items without comment would probably seem a bit abrupt to the recipient—perhaps like someone walking into a room without knocking. Instead, you will find that writing a short, friendly **cover letter** is both courteous and helpful. Usually the cover letter accompanies the item being sent. Therefore, the cover letter serves as a *transmittal letter*. If the item is bulky, however, the cover letter may be attached to the outside of the package or mailed separately, as is the letter shown in Figure 9-22 on the following page.

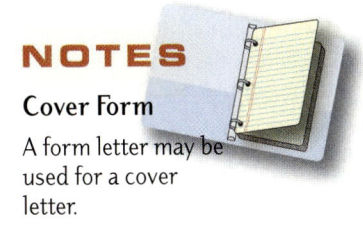

NOTES

Cover Form
A form letter may be used for a cover letter.

Messages for Inquiries and Requests

Figure 9-21
A form letter can be especially useful if you receive many inquiries.

> **Yellowstone National Park**
> P.O. Box 168, Yellowstone National Park, WY 82190
>
> <DATE>
>
> Dear Prospective Visitor:
>
> We are pleased to answer your request for information about Mammoth Hot Springs. The enclosed material should answer many of your questions about the area.
>
> We appreciate your interest in Yellowstone National Park and look forward to having you visit the park soon.
>
> Sincerely,
>
> *Brian Weston*
>
> Brian Weston
> Superintendent
>
> Enclosures 2

As we have seen, an already-prepared letter can be especially useful if you receive a flood of inquiries or orders. A form letter can also serve as a cover letter, such as the one shown in Figure 9-23 on the next page, which accompanies a book from the Illinois Audubon Society.

A cover letter should tell the purpose of and point out pertinent details about the item being sent. In the letter, the sender can stress how the receiver may use the item and can thereby stimulate interest and prompt action on the receiver's part. A cover letter also becomes a file record of the date and the reason something is sent or received.

Figure 9-22
This cover letter could be attached to the outside of a customer's package.

> Dear Customer:
>
> The drapery samples you requested are being mailed to you today in a separate package.
>
> If you need help in making your selection or placing your order, just call 800-555-8000 and ask for one of our decorators. Your order will be filled within two weeks.
>
> Sincerely,

Figure 9-23

A form letter can serve as a cover letter. (Courtesy of the Illinois Audubon Society.)

The Illinois Audubon Society
Established 1897

Marilyn F. Campbell
Executive Director

January 14, <YEAR>

Mrs. Bruce Renwick
1508 West Acres Road
Joliet, IL 60435

Dear Mrs. Renwick:

I am pleased to send a copy of the *Illinois Wildlife and Nature Viewing Guide*, which you recently requested.

I appreciate your order and hope that you will enjoy and use the guide frequently. Please note that the Society was a primary sponsor of this statewide publication, which includes information on 94 sites in Illinois that your family can visit to observe and enjoy our state's unique natural areas and wildlife.

Due to your purchase, and that of many others, the Society has been able to add another 120 acres to the beautiful War Bluff Valley Sanctuary in the heart of the Shawnee National Forest. Perhaps you can visit it sometime this year. (You will find directions for getting there on page 113 of your new guide!)

Thank you for supporting our sanctuary program and helping preserve habitat for birds and other wildlife.

Sincerely,

Marilyn F. Campbell

Marilyn F. Campbell
Executive Director

425B N. Gilbert   P.O. Box 2418   Danville, Illinois 61834-2418   217-446-5085   Fax 217-446-6375

A cover letter that accompanies a shipment of merchandise can create personal contact with customers and can lay the foundation for future sales. Sending only the merchandise that was ordered is all a company has to do, but sending a cover letter adds the "something extra" that can strengthen the goodwill between the company and its customers.

For example, mail-order houses often receive requests for their catalogs, which are usually offered free in advertisements. When people ask for a catalog, a sales opportunity is created. A cover letter sent with the catalog may make the most of this opportunity by generating interest in specific products or in categories of products.

Follow these four guidelines for writing a cover letter:

1. Start by identifying the item.

Introduce the item pleasantly by identifying it and giving your reason for sending it. (You may be sending it in response to the reader's request.)

Messages for Inquiries and Requests

2. Stress the reader's use of the item.

The fact that you are sending something isn't as important as the fact that your reader can use or enjoy it. Avoid the selfish-sounding *I am enclosing* and the obvious *You will find enclosed, Enclosed please find,* and *Enclosed with this letter is (are).* Use the more concise *Enclosed is (are)* or *Here is (are).*

3. Be specific, but choose details carefully.

Arouse the reader's interest in the item you are sending by referring to specific advantages he or she may gain from it. For example, mentioning page numbers and marked excerpts in a booklet can stimulate reading and encourage buying. Remember that the cover letter is only one part of the message and should never overshadow the enclosure.

4. Close with a forward look.

Write a closing designed to promote goodwill and future business. Even when there seems to be no immediate possibility of a sale, try some sales promotion—but don't forget to stress the service attitude.

Go to CD-ROM
Activity 9-5
To test your skills.

Checkpoint 9.2

1. Can anything positive come from writing a negative letter? If so, what?
2. Why is beginning a negative refusal with a buffer paragraph an effective strategy?
3. Which of the following closings is more effective? Explain your answer.
    a. We sincerely appreciate your interest in Natural Harvest hair care products.
    b. We are sorry that we are unable to send you samples, but we have enclosed coupons for our newest line of Natural Harvest hair care products.

EVALUATING YOUR WRITING

Business messages, no matter how simple and informal, or complex and formal, require careful planning, preparation, and review. Use the checklist shown on the next page to evaluate a communication before you send it. If you can answer *yes* to the questions, you've written an effective business message. If you answer *no* to any of the questions, make some revisions before you send the message.

✔ CHECKLIST FOR EVALUATING YOUR WRITING

	YES	NO
1. Does your communication look attractive?		
2. Is your communication accurate with respect to language, grammar, punctuation, spelling, and keyboarding?		
3. Did you use the correct approach? (Direct approach for positive communications; indirect approach for negative communications)		
4. Is your communication concise while including enough information to make the message clear?		
5. Will the reader know exactly what to do and when to do it, without further communication?		
6. Is the tone positive? Will the communication build goodwill?		
7. Have you used the "you attitude" by showing genuine concern for your reader rather than for yourself or your organization?		
8. Does the message present a favorable image of you, your employer, and your organization?		

CHAPTER 9 SUMMARY

Routine correspondence will be a daily occurrence for any employee, and the ability to handle this type of correspondence will make any employee more productive. Inquiries and requests, such as appointment and reservation requests, buying inquiries, and general requests, are commonplace in today's business world. They help keep information flowing. These letters are very straightforward because they use the direct approach.

Replying to inquiries and requests completes the exchange of information, whether it be orally or in writing. Answering *yes* to inquiries is easy because you simply use the direct approach; start right out with the information requested or the good news. Answering *no* to inquiries takes more planning because you should use the indirect approach; never start a message with bad news. When you must say *no*, it is important to keep the recipient's goodwill. Whenever possible, offer a helpful suggestion along with the *no*.

Messages for Inquiries and Requests

…

Chapter 9

Online Exercises

Objective:
These online activities will allow you to explore customer service on the Internet.

Go to **bcw.glencoe.com,** the address for the *Business Communication at Work* Web site, and select Chapter 9. Next, click on Online Exercises. You will see a list of Web site links that will bring you to airline Web sites and online retail stores.

Activity 9.1

1. Select one of the airline Web sites to visit.
2. Search for a flight from an airport near your home to a city that you would like to visit in the United States.
3. Search the same trip that you selected in Step 2 on the remaining airline Web sites.
4. On a sheet of paper, write a paragraph describing the airline with the best online customer service. Some topics you may consider for your paragraph include:
   a. visual appeal of the Web site.
   b. variety and ease of finding a flight on the Web site.
   c. organization of the Web site.
5. Write your name on your paper and hand it in to your instructor.

Activity 9.2

1. Select one of the online retail stores to visit.
2. While exploring the Web site, answer the following questions on a sheet of paper:
   a. Can you order items online? If so, is there any information about having a secure Web site?
   b. Does the company have an e-mail address and/or contact information? If so, what is the address and/or information?
   c. Does the company provide a telephone number?
   d. What features make this Web site interesting?
3. Search the other Web sites listed for this activity.
4. Repeat Step 2 for each of the other Web sites.
5. Write a paragraph discussing your experience with exploring retail Web sites. Some questions you may consider in your paragraph include:
   a. Which Web site was the most user friendly?
   b. How could you improve the customer service on any of the Web sites?
6. Write your name on the front of the printout, and hand it in to your instructor.

CHAPTER 9 WORKSHEETS

NAME _____ DATE _____

PRACTICE 1

Routine Correspondence

Instructions: Read the situations below and indicate which type of routine correspondence should be sent by writing the appropriate letter in the blank.

- A. Informational letter
- B. Acknowledgment letter
- C. Referral letter
- D. Transmittal letter
- E. Follow-up correspondence
- F. Internal communications

1. You received an invitation for your supervisor (who is on vacation) to speak at the Small Business Awards Banquet. _____

2. You received a request for information about the Covered Bridge Festival. _____

3. You received a request for pricing information on digital cameras that Doug Six, Marketing Manager, would be better qualified to handle. _____

4. You have not received the travel expense report from Frank Halstead that you needed a week ago. _____

5. You received a $500 check as full payment on Mr. Ramaro's first order for luggage. _____

Writing Requests

Instructions: The following letters make requests. On the lines below each question, indicate what information is missing or incorrect.

1.
> Dear Mr. Hinkle:
>
> I would like to schedule an appointment to talk to you.
> Will Friday be OK?
>
> Sincerely,

_____
_____
_____

Messages for Inquiries and Requests

NAME _____ **DATE** _____

2.

> Dear Reservations Department:
>
> Please reserve one room for two nights, June 3 through June 5. I'll be checking out on June 6 by noon. I need one bed at the corporate rate since I will be attending the Instrument Society of America's national convention.
>
> Oh yes, I'd like a nonsmoking room too. Please guarantee the room for late arrival.
> Sincerely,

_____
_____
_____
_____

General Inquiries

Instructions: *Analyze these questions and indicate how they can be improved.*

1. What can you tell me about the vacation package you advertised in the paper the other day?
   _____

2. How much should I expect to pay for dinner in New York?
   _____

3. What would it cost to personalize the oil painting in your catalog?
   _____

4. Explain the difference between these two sentences:
   a. I would like to know the colors the oven is available in.
   b. What colors does the oven come in?

_____
_____
_____
_____

NAME _____ DATE _____

5. Compare these two questions and determine which one is better and why.

   a. Is the radar detector a good one?

   b. What is the range of the radar detector, and what does the warranty cover?

   _____

   _____

   _____

   _____

Analyzing an Inquiry

Instructions: In preparation for replying to the following inquiry letter, highlight or underline the points that will need to be covered in the answer.

February 15, 1998

Mr. Bob Montgomery
Marketing Director
Ace Bakeries
900 West Washington Boulevard
Coraopolis, PA 15108

Dear Mr. Montgomery:

I am planning a cake and punch reception for our company's 50th anniversary celebration on Sunday, April 26. We expect about 500 people to attend. I want some chocolate cake and some white cake. How much chocolate and how much white cake will I need to order? I know some people don't like chocolate cake.

Do you deliver and set up the cake? Can you provide people to cut and serve the cake and punch?

How much punch will we need? What will all this cost?

Please send me a written quote by March 1.

Sincerely,

Jeanne Moore

Jeanne Moore

Messages for Inquiries and Requests

259

CHAPTER 9 WORKSHEETS

NAME _____   DATE _____

PRACTICE 2

Writing Inquiries and Requests

Instructions: Respond to the following situations as directed.

1. **Information Letter.** Your employer, Mr. Ralph Castle, receives a letter from Mrs. Cindy Nolting (Community Services Director, Kettering Inc., 4930 North Prairie Avenue, Cleveland, OH 44100), asking the dates of the Summerfest Celebration that your company cosponsors each year. Reply to her letter; sign your own name. Information needed for your reply: Celebration begins with a 5 p.m. parade on July 2 and ends with fireworks at dusk on July 4. Homemade ice cream and carnival rides are available throughout the celebration. Proceeds from the event go to sponsor local children who participate in the Special Olympics.

2. **Acknowledgment Letter.** Your supervisor, Jane Ann Foltz, left yesterday (March 10) and will be traveling on business in Europe until April 1. In today's mail, she receives a letter from Sally Freed, mayor of her hometown, Aberdine, North Carolina, asking her to be the main speaker at the dedication of the new city hall in Aberdine on July 6 at 2 p.m. Mayor Freed's address is 9967 Meadowlawn, Aberdine, NC 28315.

3. **Referral Letter.** You are an assistant to John Spezia, Athletic Director at Jewell College. Among today's mail is a letter from Deborah Habben, a prospective student, expressing interest in attending Jewell College and being a member of your swim team. Deborah (1505 Sherman Street, Danville, IL 61832) was an outstanding swimmer throughout her high school years and won numerous awards. Deborah asks about available financial aid and scholarships to attend Jewell College. You and Mr. Spezia decide to refer Deborah to Mr. Jim Heeren, Director of Financial Aid and Scholarships. You feel he would be better able to answer her questions. Sign Mr. Spezia's name to the letter.

4. **Transmittal Letter.** Send a copy of the article, "Business Card Etiquette," from the July issue of *International Business* to Christie Jahn. Christie Jahn recently started work as a trainer for Progressive Learning Systems, 8657 Broadway Boulevard, Newberne, WV 26409. Christie expressed an interest in doing some research on business card etiquette at a recent conference you both attended.

5. **Follow-Up Correspondence.** You are preparing the programs and the certificates for the annual Service Awards Recognition Program for your supervisor, Mrs. Diane Marble. You have asked each department in your company to send you the names of their service award winners by October 1. Today is October 7 and you have all of the information you need except the winner's name from the Purchasing Department (Anna Lou Wiggins is the supervisor of that department). The information for the programs is due at the printer's October 10. Write the appropriate correspondence.

6. **Appointment Letter.** Write a letter to Mr. Alroma Moffitt to set up an appointment for the second Tuesday of next month to work on the advertising campaign for the Vermilion County Fair and Exposition. You work for the farm manager at Second National Bank; Mr. Moffitt works for Dan Pipkin Advertising Agency, Inc., 429 Walnut, Dixon, IL 61021.

7. **Reservation Letter.** Write a letter to the Four Seasons Hotel, 98 San Jacinto Boulevard, Austin, TX 78712, asking for a reservation for yourself for one night—you will be attending a two-day desktop publishing seminar on Monday and Tuesday, September 4 and 5. Request a nonsmoking room with a queen-size bed. Guarantee the room with your American Express Card account number 223-5555-50, which expires November of next year.

CHAPTER 9 WORKSHEETS

NAME _____ DATE _____

8. **General Request Letter.** In today's edition of your local newspaper, you read an interesting article on page B-2 about weekend vacation spots in your area. The article mentions a free pamphlet entitled *Weekend Wonders* that you can get by writing to Weekend Vacations in care of your local newspaper. Enclose a preaddressed, stamped No. 10 business envelope with your request.

9. **Letter Answering *Yes* to an Inquiry.** Here is an answer to a prospective customer's inquiry about your new deodorant bar soap called FRESH SCENT. Rewrite it following the principles presented in Chapter 9.

> Dear Customer:
>
> We received your October 14 letter. As requested, we are sending a sample of our new deodorant bar soap called FRESH SCENT.
>
> Sincerely,

10. **Letter Answering *Yes* to a Request.** Answer the following request by sending the booklet and wishing the writer good luck on his garage sale.

> Ladies and Gentlemen:
>
> Please send me a copy of the Garage Sale Kit that you advertised in the March issue of *Antiques and Treasures* magazine. We're planning our first garage sale this summer and will appreciate receiving this information.
>
> Sincerely
>
> *John Jestis*
>
> John Jestis
> 378 Timberland Road
> Millersburg, KY 40348

11. **Letter Answering *No* to an Inquiry.** Answer the letter in Question 10, but this time say *no* to the request because your entire supply of Garage Sale Kits is gone. There are no plans at the present time to reprint them. Send a photocopy of the page from the kit that contains tips for successful garage sales.

12. **Form Reply to an Inquiry.** You are receiving numerous requests for information about your Browning yo-yo exhibit and demonstrations. Write a form letter that will give the following information: Dates—May 17–18; Location—Palmer Civic Center; Admission—$2; Hours—exhibit from 9 a.m. to 9 p.m., demonstrations at 2, 5, and 7 p.m. both days.

13. **Cover Letter.** You are an assistant in the Sleep Clinic at St. Vincent Hospital in Indianapolis, Indiana. A prospective patient, Bill George, 507 West Woodlawn, Danville, IL 61832, has called and asked for some information on sleep apnea and snoring. Send a copy of the free booklet, *Sleep Apnea and Snoring*, which is prepared by the American Sleep Disorders Association. Write a short cover letter to go with the booklet.

Messages for Inquiries and Requests

CHAPTER 9 WORKSHEETS

NAME _____ DATE _____

PRACTICE 3

Writing Applications

Instructions: Respond to the following situations as directed.

1. **Reservation Letter.** You and a colleague are planning to attend the annual convention of the National Business Professionals. The convention is being held on April 5, 6, 7, and 8 at the New York Marriott Marquis in New York City. The address is 1535 Broadway, New York, NY 10036. You and your colleague will share a room, desire two queen-size beds, and will arrive about 8 p.m. on April 5. You plan to check out at noon on April 8. Draft the letter plan to make the hotel reservations and then write the letter. (Be sure to check a calendar.)

2. **Reservation Letter for Major Event.** You are employed by Mrs. Betsy Porter-Peck, a partner at Porter and Peck law firm, 85 Walden Street, Concord, MA 01742. As president of her high school graduating class, she is responsible for planning the upcoming ten-year class reunion of Messick High. Compose an inquiry letter for Mrs. Porter-Peck to Ms. Trudy Noyes, Banquet and Convention Manager of the Four Seasons Hotel, 1919 Union Avenue, Omaha, NE 68056, asking her to quote rates for the following:

    a. A banquet room to seat 125 to 150 people for the last Saturday night in May
    b. A dance floor and stage for a six-piece band to provide after-dinner dancing
    c. A dinner menu of shrimp cocktail, grilled chicken breast, baked potato, mixed vegetables, apple or cherry pie à la mode, iced tea, and coffee
    d. A two-night room package (with a discounted rate) for the last Friday and Saturday nights in May for class members who want to spend the weekend

    You will also need a podium and microphone for the welcoming remarks at 6:30 p.m.; dinner should be served at 7 p.m.; dancing will begin at 8:30 p.m.; and you will need the room until 12 midnight. You prefer round tables seating eight to ten people each. Twelve people will be seated at the head table. Your decorating committee will handle table decorations and a floral centerpiece for the head table. Ask the hotel to confirm all details by January 15 so that you will have time to finalize the plans and arrangements and send the invitation letters out.

    Write a letter plan on the lines below and then write the letter.

    _____
    _____
    _____

3. **Buying Inquiry Letter.** Your doctor tells you to keep a chart of your daily blood pressure for three months. A friend of yours tells you he purchased a SunMark Blood Pressure Monitor that he likes. You decide you might like to purchase one also rather than make a daily trip to the drugstore to use the blood pressure machine there. Write a buying inquiry letter to Omron Healthcare, Inc., 300 Lakeview Parkway, Vernon Hills, IL 60061. Since you travel occasionally, you are wondering if the blood pressure monitor is portable. You also wonder if it comes with automatic inflation as well as manual inflation, and how many and what size batteries it requires. Ask about the cost, warranty, ease of use, and accuracy of the blood pressure readings. Tell the company you are considering purchasing one of the monitors, but you need answers to these questions to help you make your decision.

4. **Reply to an Inquiry.** You are employed as an administrative assistant at Del's Paper Corporation. Reply to the following inquiry, and enclose an order form and a preaddressed post-paid envelope. The information you need is listed at right:

CHAPTER 9   WORKSHEETS

NAME _____   DATE _____

28-lb. paper:	8.5 x 11 inches	
	100 sheets per box	
Prices:	1-4 boxes	$21.95 ea.
	5-9 boxes	$19.95 ea.
	10-25 boxes	$17.95 ea.
Colors:	Blue Carrara	#DT1351
	Almond Creme	#DT1431
	Green Marble	#DT1341
	Sapphire	#DT0076

Shipping and handling are included in the price.
  (New Jersey residents add 5.75% sales tax.)
To order by mail, complete and mail the order form.
Add $10.95 for next-day delivery.
Payment options: credit card, personal checks, company checks, and money orders.
Sorry, no CODs.

The following inquiry, from Mr. Dave Pearson, asks for information on designer paper from your catalog. Write Mr. Pearson and tell him that the paper he wants is on page 26 of the catalog. Enclose an order form and a preaddressed postage-paid envelope.

April 16, <YEAR>

Del Paper Corporation
936 Wisconsin Avenue
Secaucus, New Jersey 07094

Ladies and Gentlemen:

Please send me information about your designer paper. Specifically, I am interested in the following:

1. What colors of paper are available?
2. What weight is the paper?
3. How many sheets are in each box of paper?
4. What is the cost of the paper?
5. How long does it take to get the paper delivered?

We are interested in printing some of our own fliers and notices, and we want them to be eye-catching.

I look forward to hearing from you.

Sincerely,

THE BRICK WALL

Dave Pearson

Dave Pearson
2478 Michigan Avenue
Chicago, IL 60042

Messages for Inquiries and Requests

CHAPTER 10
Claim and Adjustment Messages

Objectives

After completing this chapter, you will be able to:

1. Explain the value of complaints
2. Write routine claim letters
3. Write persuasive claim letters
4. Write letters granting adjustments
5. Write letters denying adjustments
6. Write letters compromising on adjustments
7. Write form letters for adjustments

WORKPLACE APPLICATIONS

Decision Making

Making decisions is an essential part of running a business. Of course, everyone makes decisions every day, but business decisions often have a lot at stake. Employees' jobs, customers' satisfaction, and the company's growth may be affected by a decision. Experienced decision makers do not form decisions based on instinct or emotion. They have the patience and foresight to work through the process of making a solid decision.

- **Identify goals.** By setting a goal, decision makers must consider how every decision they make will help reach that goal. For example, a company's goal may be to cut costs. What decisions need to be made in order to reach that goal?

- **Get the facts.** Before making a final decision, decision makers need hard data—facts, figures, and statistics—and input from knowledgeable people in order to guide them. An informed decision is usually a good one.

- **Evaluate risk.** Every decision involves risk. That is what makes decision making so difficult. Decision makers have to figure out what is at stake—who will benefit and who may be hurt—by the decision. They must ask, "Is reaching my goal worth the risk?" For example, a decision to cut jobs may save a company money in the short term, but will it cost goodwill in the community in the long term? Is that outcome compatible with the goal?

- **Make the decision and stand by it.** Decision makers should take responsibility for their decisions. Of course, even experienced decision makers make mistakes, and they take responsibility for those, too. They know that even good decisions may have unexpected consequences, and they should acknowledge when a decision is wrong. Experienced decision makers learn something every time they prepare a decision.

Thinking Critically

Situation: The advertising firm you work for has sent a major project to the printer. While your supervisor is away on a business trip, the printer calls about a serious problem with the project. The printer needs a decision before the end of the day, or the project will be delayed many months.

Ask Yourself: What steps would you take to make a decision?

> *Let the buyer beware.*
> —Unknown,
> Roman maxim

Customer service and quality are popular "buzzwords" in the operation of both large and small organizations today. In order for an organization to stay in business, its customers and clients must be satisfied with the way they are treated and with the quality of the products and the services they receive.

Ideally, everything runs smoothly in the operation of an organization—there are no mistakes, no problems, no defects, and no misunderstandings. Even in the best-managed organizations, however, problems will occur. For example, you may purchase a clock that doesn't keep accurate time, or receive a credit card statement with an error on it, or get home from the fast food restaurant without one of the sandwiches you ordered. When a product or service does not meet your expectations, you become disappointed and you usually feel like complaining.

Whether you complain verbally or in writing, you should use the principles presented in this chapter to get the best results. In some situations, you must put your claim in writing to protect your rights. This chapter will also present principles for responding to claim letters.

CLAIM LETTERS

Written complaints should not be called *complaint letters* because *complaint* implies irritation, unpleasantness, negativism, and even anger. Using a word with such negative connotations could lead to a bad attitude toward customers or clients. Instead, letters expressing dissatisfaction should be called **claim letters.** A claim letter asks for an adjustment to correct the problem in a courteous, direct manner.

NOTES

Making a Claim

Written complaints should be called claim letters and should courteously ask for an adjustment to correct the problem.

Value of Complaints

When errors and problems are reported to an organization, everyone benefits. Put yourself in the place of the owner or manager of an organization and consider these questions:

- Would you rather have satisfied customers and clients spreading good reports about your organization or unhappy customers and clients complaining about your products or services?
- Can you satisfy unhappy customers if you don't know why they are dissatisfied?

Unless someone tells you that something is wrong, you may never know about the problem, and the error will simply be repeated again and again.

Researchers estimate that every time a customer is dissatisfied or feels wronged, 125 people will hear about it—either directly or indirectly. With this potential negative publicity, reputable organizations are eager to discover, analyze, and correct defects in their products and services as well as problems with how customers are treated.

An organization's primary source of information about such defects is requests for adjustments from its customers. Many organizations also actively seek information about potential problems by providing questionnaires at the place of business or by sending a checklist-type questionnaire to customers with a postpaid, preaddressed envelope. Look at the questionnaire Sandburg Appliances sent to customers to obtain feedback on their service (see Figure 10-1).

General Guidelines for Claim Letters

Follow these six guidelines for writing a claim letter:

1. Send the letter promptly.

Many organizations have a policy that exchanges, returns, refunds, and adjustments must be made within a specified time period, such as 30, 60, or 90 days from the date of purchase. In addition, the warranty on a product may run out or the guarantee may expire if you delay too long. Psychologically, a prompt letter seems more valid to the recipient than a letter about a problem that occurred some time ago.

Sandburg
Appliances

Dear Valued Customer:

Thank you for your recent purchase from Sandburg Appliances, which was delivered by our shipping department.

Please fill out and mail the attached card to let us know how our service rates. We are always looking for ways to serve you better.

We appreciate your business and want to do everything we can to make sure that you enjoy shopping at our store and that you are satisfied with your purchases.

Sincerely,

Bruce Meachum
Customer Service Manager

	YES	NO
Was your visit to our store pleasant?	☐	☐
Was the sales associate helpful?	☐	☐
Did the delivery truck arrive on schedule?	☐	☐
Were delivery persons careful?	☐	☐
Did they place or install your appliance as you requested?	☐	☐

If you have any suggestions for ways we can improve our service, please write them below.

____
____
____

Figure 10-1
The company shows its service attitude by asking for customer feedback.

Thinking Cap 10.1

Discuss: How would you feel if you made an innocent mistake in filling a customer's order and the customer wrote a letter to your supervisor's boss? How do you think the customer should have handled the situation?

2. Write to the responsible person or to the customer relations (customer service) department.

Some consumer advocate groups recommend that you send your claim letter to the owner or president of the organization. This tactic may work, but it won't earn any goodwill for you and may in fact cause you problems in future dealings with the organization. First, you should send your letter to the person responsible for correcting the error or problem to allow him or her an opportunity to resolve the problem. Sometimes you may not know who is responsible and will need to send your letter to the customer relations or customer service department. Then, if you get no satisfaction from this first claim letter, write to the top person in the organization.

3. Ask for the adjustment you think you deserve.

You don't want your letter to be just a complaint letter. Instead, tell the recipient what you think should be done to solve your problem. Ask for a specific adjustment—the recipient will either grant it, refuse it, or make another offer. If you are not sure what adjustment to request, ask the recipient to study the circumstances and suggest a fair solution.

4. Assume that the problem was unintentional.

Reputable organizations will want to keep your goodwill and do the fair thing. Whenever you write a claim letter, follow these guidelines:

- Don't show anger or disgust.
- Don't argue or threaten.
- Don't use profanity.
- Don't question your reader's integrity.

Tell your story calmly and clearly, with confidence that you will be treated fairly.

5. Present all facts and details clearly and honestly.

Give your reader a complete and unbiased picture on which to base a decision about the adjustment you requested. To do this, give a description of the original transaction with all the pertinent facts, including:

- Date and place of purchase, agreement, or services
- Company representative's name or number, if available
- Terms of payment
- Copy of the sales slip or receipt
- Account number
- Invoice number (or a copy of the invoice)
- Copy of the warranty or guarantee

Then present a clear, concise explanation of your problem. To determine whether your explanation is clear, reread it as though you were unfamiliar with the situation. Look at the example shown in Figure 10-2.

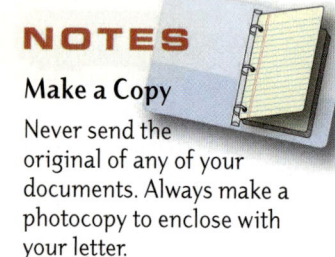

NOTES

Make a Copy
Never send the original of any of your documents. Always make a photocopy to enclose with your letter.

Figure 10-2
A claim letter should present all facts clearly.

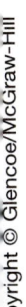

Alan Mason Detective Agency
7442 West LaSalle Street – Suite 204
Chicago, IL 60602

312-555-5227

Civil and Criminal Investigations

July 20, <YEAR>

General Electronics Company
8956 West Fourteenth Avenue
El Paso, TX 79900

Ladies and Gentlemen:

Please repair or replace the Model 290 Alphanumeric Caller ID Display Unit we purchased for our office.

After only three weeks of use, the LCD display no longer lights up.

Enclosed is the Caller ID unit, a copy of the sales receipt showing the date of purchase, and a copy of your warranty, which guarantees material and workmanship for one year.

Sincerely,

Mary Bailey

Mary Bailey
Office Manager

ec 34-callID
Enclosures

Never make untrue statements or exaggerate in your claim letter. Doing so is unethical, and your credibility might be questioned.

LEGAL & ETHICAL 10-1

Return Policy? Last July, Chad purchased a "Mr. Cup" coffeemaker with a three-month warranty. He had been using the coffeemaker about seven months when it stopped working on February 2. Chad wrote a claim letter to the manufacturer saying that he had received the coffeemaker as a Christmas gift and that he would like a replacement since it was still under warranty. Is this legal? Is it ethical? What are the possible ramifications of Chad's action?

---

6. Keep a copy of the letter and all enclosures.

Usually a claim letter will be handled promptly; but in case you do need to follow up, you want proof that you have already attempted to get an adjustment. If you handle a claim in person or by phone, make written notes of your conversation, including:

- Name of the person you spoke with
- Date and time of the conversation
- Details of the conversation's content

Claim and Adjustment Messages

Routine Claim Letters

When you have a legitimate claim and anticipate the granting of the adjustment you're asking for, use the direct approach. If you feel you will need to convince your reader to make the adjustment you are asking for, you may need to use the persuasive approach, which we will discuss later in the chapter.

A letter making a routine claim and requesting an adjustment will be easy to write if you think of it as a three-step process and follow these three steps:

Routine Claim Letter

Direct Approach

Paragraph 1: Ask for a specific adjustment.

Paragraph 2: Explain what's wrong.

Paragraph 3: Give identifying information.

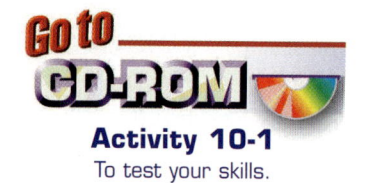

Go to CD-ROM
Activity 10-1
To test your skills.

Figure 10-3 illustrates an effective routine claim letter that follows this plan. Notice that the writer used the direct approach in asking for an adjustment.

Checklist for Routine Claim Letters

Use the "Routine Claim Letter Checklist" on the next page as a guide when you write claim letters. Your instructor may ask you to turn to the Worksheet exercises at the end of the chapter and use the checklist as you complete the exercises for claim letters.

Figure 10-3
An effective routine claim letter uses the direct approach.

> Dear Customer Services Manager:
>
> Please send us a replacement or a refund for the damaged fine art copy of a Monet watercolor painting that we are returning to you today by Federal Express.
>
> When the painting arrived on April 2, the glass was broken and one corner of the painting was torn.
>
> On February 15, we ordered a framed fine art copy of a Monet watercolor painting, Catalog No. 54399, for our newly remodeled reception area. We sent our Purchase Order 3367 with our Check 3436 for $325, which included shipping and handling.
>
> Sincerely,

✓ ROUTINE CLAIM LETTER CHECKLIST

	YES	NO
Is the letter sent promptly?		
Is the letter addressed to the person or department that made the error?		
Does the first paragraph ask for a specific adjustment?		
Does the letter assume that the mistake was unintentional?		
Are the facts presented objectively?		
Does the second paragraph explain the problem in a clear, concise manner?		
Does the third paragraph give identifying information?		
Is the letter courteous?		

Persuasive Claim Letters

You may need to use the persuasive approach when writing a claim letter if you feel there might be some reluctance on the part of the receiver to grant the adjustment you are requesting. When you are presenting a routine claim that is backed by a guarantee or product warranty, you can be reasonably sure the adjustment will be granted without persuasion. If you think your claim may have to be approved by a claims adjuster or a manager, however, you should use the persuasive or indirect approach. You may need to gently point out the benefits to the reader of granting the adjustment.

Never display your anger in a persuasive claim letter—you do not want to make the one person who can help you angry. If you threaten to involve attorneys, for example, your reader will probably not respond because he or she will assume that either you are not a reasonable person or that you will use anything in writing against him or her in court.

When writing persuasive claim requests, use the indirect approach by following these three steps:

Persuasive Claim Letter

Indirect Approach

Paragraph 1: Give identifying information.

Paragraph 2: Explain what's wrong.

Paragraph 3: Ask for a specific adjustment.

Look at the letter in Figure 10-4 on the following page, which uses these three steps to make a persuasive request for an adjustment.

If the writer of this letter had used the direct approach instead and had asked for the reduction of the bill in the beginning, the reader would have been less apt to consider the adjustment.

Go to CD-ROM

Activity 10-2
To test your skills.

Claim and Adjustment Messages

Figure 10-4
The writer uses three steps to make a persuasive request for an adjustment.

> Dear Mr. Brady:
>
> When I spoke with you on May 6 about cleaning and repairing the 1899 Regina music box that I inherited from my mother, you told me you would look at it and call me the next day with an estimate to put it back in good working order. On May 13 you called and quoted me a price of approximately $500 for the repair and said you would need it about six weeks.
>
> On July 6 I called you to see if my music box was ready. I had hoped to have it in time for a family reunion at our home on July 24, but you indicated you still needed more time to work on it.
>
> On August 16 you called to tell me the music box was ready and you would mail me the bill. When the invoice arrived this morning, I was shocked to see that it was for $1100. This is more than double the estimate you gave me on May 6. I feel you should have called me for approval before exceeding your original estimate by $600. Frankly, had I known it would cost this much I don't believe I would have had the music box repaired. You said yourself that even in good working condition it is only worth about $3000.
>
> Because the work took twice as long as estimated and the price is more than double the original quote, please reduce the invoice to your original estimate of $500.
>
> Sincerely,

Checklist for Persuasive Claim Letters

Use the "Persuasive Claim Letter Checklist" below as you write persuasive claim letters. Your instructor may ask you to go to the Worksheets at the end of the chapter and complete the exercises for writing persuasive claim letters. Be sure to use the checklist to help you compose your letters.

✔ PERSUASIVE CLAIM LETTER CHECKLIST

	YES	NO
Is the letter sent promptly?		
Is the letter addressed to the person who made the error?		
Does the first paragraph include identifying information?		
Does the second paragraph explain the problem clearly?		
Does the last paragraph ask for a specific adjustment?		
Does the letter assume that the mistake was unintentional?		
Are the facts presented objectively?		
Is the letter courteous?		

Checkpoint 10.1

1. In your opinion, is it fair to call letters from customers "claim letters" instead of "complaint letters"?

2. Do you agree or disagree with the idea that claim letters have value for a company or business?

3. What are the similarities and differences between a routine claim letter and a persuasive claim letter?

Adjustment Letters

An **adjustment letter** is a response to a claim. When a business determines that a claim is justified, some adjustment is made. Even if an adjustment doesn't appear to be justified, an organization may decide it is in its best interest to make the adjustment in order to maintain or build goodwill.

Customer satisfaction and goodwill are such important assets that some progressive organizations have established specific departments to respond to customer claims promptly and graciously. These departments may be known in different industries as departments of customer service, consumer affairs, student services, patient services, customer relations, or guest services. Adjustment personnel should strive to resolve customer claims fairly, quickly, and tactfully, since success depends on customer satisfaction. Whether a claim is granted or refused, the adjustment letter, like other forms of business communication, should strive to build and maintain goodwill.

If you are asked to respond to claim letters, you have three choices:

1. Grant the adjustment requested.

2. Refuse the adjustment.

3. Offer a compromise.

Let's look at how to approach each one of these responses.

> *Always do right. This will gratify some people—and astonish the rest.*
> —**Mark Twain**

NOTES

Customer Resources

Many organizations handle customer questions and claims through a specific employee or department.

Letters Granting Adjustments

When you write a letter granting a request for an adjustment, use the direct approach and follow these steps:

Letter Granting an Adjustment
Direct Approach
Paragraph 1: Give the good news.
Paragraph 2: Give an explanation and a thank-you.
Paragraph 3: Resell the product or the service, and/or resell your organization.

These three steps are used effectively in granting an adjustment to a customer who has returned a patio umbrella (see Figure 10-5 on the following page).

Note the organization of the letter to the customer, Mr. Bregenzer:

1. First comes the news the customer wants to hear most—a new patio umbrella is on its way.

Claim and Adjustment Messages

Figure 10-5 Notice the steps used for granting an adjustment for a customer.

<DATE>

Dear Mr. Bregenzer:

Your new patio umbrella is being mailed prepaid today. It should arrive in a few days.

Thank you for returning the torn one. Because a mended umbrella might not be water-resistant, we are sending you a new one so that you can keep your patio table protected. You will notice that the new umbrella is made of vinyl-coated nylon, which has proved superior to the polyester and cotton one you bought last year.

When you need patio furniture and accessories, you will find everything from small tables to fountains in our latest catalog. You can rely on our guarantee of high quality and satisfaction or your money back.

Sincerely,

Figure 10-6 Notice the inappropriate tone and wording of this letter.

CAR CARE CO.
3788 North Belmont Avenue
Midland, MI 48640
Complete Auto Service   1-800-555-7834

January 17, <YEAR>

Jeri Gleisner
P.O. Box 376
Midland, MI 48640

Dear Jeri:

As you can see your window is repaired--<u>at no cost to you</u>.

The problem did not start the day (Dec. 19) your car was in our service department for a thermostat. The problem was that the regulator-to-glass attaching screws were loose, which happens as the door and window are used over a period of time (usually a couple of years or more). So, your blaming us <u>for breaking</u> your window <u>was unfounded</u> and, I might add, not the truth. First the window starts to not close tightly then becomes worse. At the time your car was here, the window was down approximately 1", so the problem had to start sometime before that, and we were being held responsible.

We have enjoyed many years of auto service to all kinds of people and with many different makes and models of cars and are not in the habit of breaking customers' cars or being accused of the same.

Respectfully,

CAR CARE CO.

Sam Grundy

Sam Grundy
Service Manager

2. Next comes the writer's appreciation for the customer's calling attention to the defect in his umbrella.

3. Then the writer explains the change in materials—this is an explanation owed to the reader, and in this case it is one that makes the organization look progressive and concerned.

4. A final appeal for another sale is made—the appeal is appropriate in this case because the requested adjustment has been granted and the customer will be satisfied.

Follow these four guidelines for writing a letter granting an adjustment:

1. Tell the reader that full adjustment is gladly granted.

Give the good news in the first sentence. Don't let the reader feel you are doing him or her a favor, even if you feel that you are making a special concession. Instead, convince the reader that goodwill and friendship are more important to you than any money involved and that your organization always wants to take good care of its customers. Notice the difference in the tone of the two letters from Car Care Co. shown in Figures 10-6 and 10-7. Which letter would you rather receive?

Thinking Cap 10.2

Discuss: What is the difference between the two Car Care Co. letters shown in Figures 10-6 and 10-7? Which letter would you rather receive and why?

Figure 10-7
Notice the appropriate wording and tone of this letter.

CAR CARE CO.
3788 North Belmont Avenue
Midland, MI 48640
Complete Auto Service   1-800-555-7834

January 17, <YEAR>

Jeri Gleisner
P.O. Box 376
Midland, MI 48640

Dear Jeri:

Your car window now works like new.

The window would not close completely because the screws attaching the regulator to the glass were loose. This happens from the normal use of the door and window. It usually takes a couple of years or more before the screws can loosen sufficiently to prevent the window from closing tightly.

Once this starts, the window gradually gets worse until it won't close properly. The loosening car window develops over a period of time and not in one day. This is apparently what had happened the day your car was in our shop to replace the thermostat. You, of course, would have no way of knowing this, but we were glad to investigate and repair the window at no expense to you.

We look forward to handling your repair needs in the future.

Respectfully,

CAR CARE CO.

Sam Grundy

Sam Grundy
Service Manager

rt

2. Express sincere appreciation for the reader's adjustment request.

Acknowledge your reader's inconvenience in writing the letter and waiting for an adjustment, but be careful not to use negative wording. Emphasize that you welcome this opportunity to set things right. Let the customer know how his or her letter has helped the organization improve its products or service.

3. Stress your organization's effort to prevent further dissatisfaction.

Accept the blame and apologize if your organization is at fault for a problem. If appropriate, explain what caused the problem, but don't assign blame, such as saying the problem was due to a computer error. Also, don't make the mistake of telling your reader, "This will *never* happen again." No one can promise a mistake or problem won't be repeated. Notice that it may be appropriate, however, to explain what your organization is doing to prevent this problem from happening again, as shown in Figure 10-8.

4. End the letter positively.

Don't end with a negative phrase, such as "We hope you do not have any more trouble with your Valic Vaporizer." The best ending for a letter granting an adjustment makes no reference to the original problem. End on a positive note that implies future dealings, and don't overlook the possibility of promoting sales of related products or services or at least reselling your organization.

Thinking Cap 10.3

Discuss: Why should you not promise your reader that "this will never happen again?"

Figure 10-8
Welcome the opportunity to solve the problem. Show how you plan to keep the problem from reappearing.

> Dear Ms. Jones
>
> Thank you for bringing to our attention the lack of performance of your new radio. Your taking time to write us gives us an opportunity to work with you on a solution to this situation.
>
> We welcome the opportunity to replace this radio, but need to have the item sent to us before we can replace it. Just as soon as you return it for inspection and verification of the problem, we will have another radio shipped to you by overnight courier. By doing this, you will help us determine the problem so that we can take steps in our production process to eliminate the cause.
>
> Enclosed is a label addressed to our attention for you to use in returning the radio.
>
> Sincerely
>
> Mark Mendoza

Go to CD-ROM
Activity 10-3
To test your skills.

Letters Denying Adjustments

Granting an adjustment is not always the appropriate response to a claim. Sometimes after considering a customer's claim, you may determine that an adjustment cannot be granted. In that case, you must send a letter denying the adjustment—the message that organizations least like to send and customers least like to receive. Saying *no* is not the only purpose of letters denying adjustments. They are also used to rebuild customer goodwill, although this may be a difficult task.

Use the indirect approach when writing letters denying adjustments:

Letter Denying an Adjustment

Indirect Approach

Paragraph 1: Start with a buffer (never start with bad news).

Paragraph 2: Give an explanation.

Paragraph 3: Say *no* to the adjustment.

Paragraph 4: Close with a buffer.

You may wish to review the summary of the indirect approach in Chapter 5, and the Chapter 9 section "Letters Answering *No* to Inquiries and Requests," page 247, for other techniques to help you write effective bad-news messages.

Look at the letter answering a customer's request for repair or replacement of the transmitter for her automatic garage door opener (see Figure 10-9). The writer of the letter realizes that the customer, Mrs. Fulk, must be convinced of the organization's position and be kept as a customer (after all, she did buy an expensive item).

The following five guidelines will help you when you write a letter denying an adjustment:

1. Support the reader's point of view in your opening buffer paragraph.

Never start your letter with the bad news; use a friendly opening buffer. Since the customer probably thinks he or she is right, try to coax—not force—him or her to accept what you consider a reasonable solution to the problem. Be sure the customer realizes that you understand the problem and that you will be fair.

Dear Mrs. Fulk:

You are right to expect high-quality merchandise from The Danley Overhead Door Company, Mrs. Fulk. We try to give you the best for your money and to stand behind our products when they fail as a result of defects in material and workmanship, as our warranty states.

We appreciate your sending the door opener to us for analysis. It appears that the opener has gotten wet. Excess moisture over a period of time causes corrosion to form on the integrated circuit board. After corrosion buildup reaches a certain level, the transmitter will not work. Our service manager estimates that cleaning and repairing your door opener would cost $54.

Since your door opener is several years old, you may want to consider replacing it with a new one. We have made many improvements to our door openers since yours was manufactured, including a sealed circuit board that would prevent the possibility of damage from moisture. A new door opener, which costs $74.99 postpaid, should give you even longer service than your old one did.

Please let us know whether you want to repair or replace your opener.

Sincerely,

Figure 10-9
When writing bad-news messages, care must be taken to avoid offending the customer.

Claim and Adjustment Messages

2. Assure the customer that the request is appreciated and has received individual consideration.

The requested adjustment is important to the reader. In your letter, make sure you show that the reader's point of view is also important to your organization.

3. Present the explanation before the decision.

Stress what *can* be done and emphasize your purpose—to be fair to all customers. Don't blame and don't argue. Avoid unfriendly, negative expressions, such as *your complaint, your error, you misinterpreted, you neglected, you claim, you are mistaken, our records show,* and *your ignorance.*

With a truthful and tactful explanation, lead the customer or client to accept your solution as the only reasonable one.

4. Be courteous even when answering an angry or a distorted claim.

If you answer an angry letter sarcastically, you may lose both your self-respect and your customer. Instead, completely ignore any insults; and concentrate on writing an answer that is friendly, rational, and professional. Doing this usually costs less in terms of money and time to keep the customer you already have than to find a new one.

5. Try to leave the reader in a pleasant frame of mind.

A friendly but concise closing is especially important when a requested adjustment is not granted.

Letters Compromising on Adjustments

When either directly granting or denying an adjustment is inappropriate, you may decide to offer a compromise. This would be a reasonable response when both the seller and the buyer share responsibility for problem situations or when responsibility is uncertain. Remember that, regardless of responsibility, businesses want to correct problems in order to keep customers' goodwill.

As we have discussed earlier, if any part of your message contains bad news, you should use the indirect approach. Follow these steps when writing letters compromising on adjustments:

GLOBAL DIVERSITY 10.1

When Yes Means No
The native language of Indonesia, Bahasa Indonesia, has 12 words that imply *yes* but really mean *no*. Even with a correct translation, the literal translation for these 12 words would be *yes* because the culture requires a polite, agreeable response. Because saying *no* to someone is considered impolite, you should not assume that a positive response means you have agreement. *How can you be certain that yes means yes?*

Go to CD-ROM
Activity 10-4
To test your skills.

Letter Compromising on an Adjustment
Indirect Approach
Paragraph 1: Start with a buffer (never start with bad news).
Paragraph 2: Give an explanation.
Paragraph 3: Say *no* to the adjustment.
Paragraph 4: Offer a counterproposal or compromise.
Paragraph 5: Close with a buffer.

See how the writer of the letter shown in Figure 10-10 uses these five steps in offering a compromise on an adjustment. In the letter, the writer tries to retain the customer's goodwill by repairing a broken product with no labor charge, even though the warranty has expired.

The following five guidelines will help you when you write letters presenting a compromise adjustment:

- **Reflect pleasant cooperation in the buffer opening.** Start your letter with a pleasant, cooperative statement, but don't imply that you are granting the request. If the customer thinks you are granting the request in the first sentence, he or she may not read the rest of the letter, thinking the matter is settled.

- **Explain why you are denying the requested adjustment.** State the facts and reasons behind your decision thoroughly and courteously. By giving a logical explanation before you say *no* to an adjustment, you may be able to prevent a negative reaction from the customer.

- **State or imply the refusal.** Make the refusal clear, but deemphasize it.

- **Offer a counterproposal or compromise.** A counterproposal or compromise should be given willingly and graciously or not at all. Remember to let your service attitude show.

- **Use a buffer closing.** In the closing suggest what action the customer should take, but leave the decision to him or her.

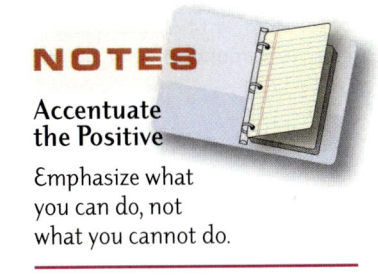

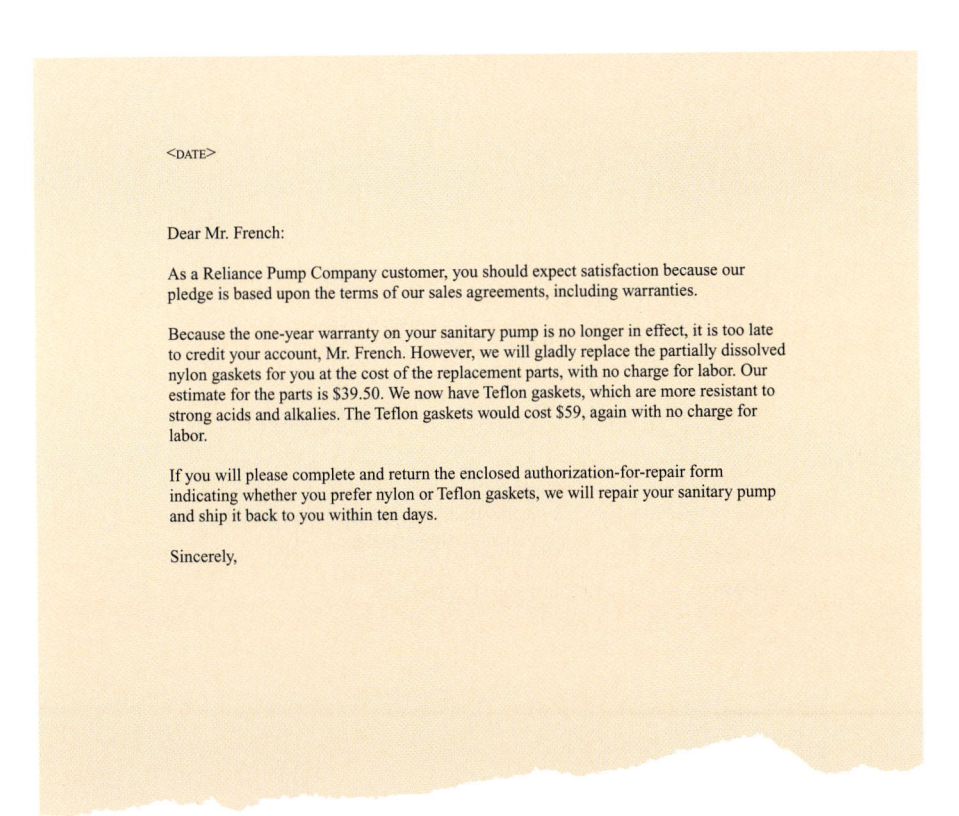

NOTES

Accentuate the Positive
Emphasize what you can do, not what you cannot do.

Go to CD-ROM
Activity 10-5
To test your skills.

Figure 10-10
Messages should strive to retain the customer's goodwill.

<DATE>

Dear Mr. French:

As a Reliance Pump Company customer, you should expect satisfaction because our pledge is based upon the terms of our sales agreements, including warranties.

Because the one-year warranty on your sanitary pump is no longer in effect, it is too late to credit your account, Mr. French. However, we will gladly replace the partially dissolved nylon gaskets for you at the cost of the replacement parts, with no charge for labor. Our estimate for the parts is $39.50. We now have Teflon gaskets, which are more resistant to strong acids and alkalies. The Teflon gaskets would cost $59, again with no charge for labor.

If you will please complete and return the enclosed authorization-for-repair form indicating whether you prefer nylon or Teflon gaskets, we will repair your sanitary pump and ship it back to you within ten days.

Sincerely,

Claim and Adjustment Messages

Thinking Cap 10.4

Discuss: Why would an organization use a form letter rather than write an individual letter to respond to each claim?

Form Letters for Adjustments

Form letters are commonly used in adjustment correspondence. They can be a problem because their tone and style sometimes suggest "mass production" or insincerity; but even a form letter, carefully written, can stress personalized service and genuine concern for the reader. A form letter should sound like an individually written letter.

Read the two form letters shown in Figure 10-11 and Figure 10-12. They are routine adjustment letters responding to a problem with a magazine subscription. Both are concise, clear, correct, and complete, but which letter would you prefer to receive?

Even though both letters are form letters, the second one has been personalized, making it friendlier and less brusque than the first one. A form letter saves the writer time if the form letter does its job effectively. For further illustration of this point, reread the discussion, "Showing Sincere Interest in the Reader," in Chapter 8.

Figure 10-11
A routine adjustment letter should be clear, correct, concise, and complete. Is this one?

> Dear Sir or Madam:
>
> This letter is to acknowledge receipt of your recent communication relative to your subscription.
>
> It is necessary that you fill out in detail the enclosed form and return it immediately.
>
> We will get back to you when we have located and corrected the problem with your subscription.
>
> Very truly yours,

Figure 10-12
A routine adjustment letter should take care of an adjustment clearly, concisely, correctly, and completely. Does this one do that?

> Dear Mrs. Jensen:
>
> Thank you for letting us know that you have not been receiving your copies of *Ancient Antiques*.
>
> We are checking with our Circulation Department to see what has happened. Unless we need additional information from you, you can expect to start receiving your copies of *Ancient Antiques* within ten days.
>
> Your interest in our biweekly magazine is appreciated.
>
> Sincerely,

Checkpoint 10.2

1. What is the most important outcome of an adjustment letter for a business?
2. Why is it important to maintain a courteous tone when responding to an angry claim letter?
3. What is the most challenging part of writing a letter of adjustment?

Chapter 10 Summary

One of the best ways to resolve problems or errors that you encounter in business dealings is to write a claim letter requesting an adjustment. Writing a routine claim letter using the direct approach is appropriate if you can reasonably expect the adjustment to be granted. If your claim is not as clear-cut, you should write a persuasive claim letter using the indirect approach.

When you are responding to a claim letter, you have three choices. If you grant the adjustment, use the direct approach and give the good news in the opening sentence. If you deny the adjustment or compromise on the adjustment, use the indirect approach—never start a letter with bad news.

To save time, you can prepare a form reply for an adjustment when you receive numerous requests about the same problem. A form reply should still sound and look like a personal letter.

The problems in the Worksheet give you a chance to demonstrate your understanding of adjustment correspondence. Prepare the exercises your instructor assigns, and submit them as directed.

Chapter 10

Online Exercises

Objective:
These online activities will allow you to practice writing claim letters, as well as help you search for a job.

Go to **bcw.glencoe.com,** the address for the *Business Communication at Work* Web site, and select Chapter 10. Next, click on Online Exercises. You will see a list of Web site links that will bring you to online retail stores and career Web sites.

Activity 10.1

1. Select one of the online retail Web sites to visit.
2. Search for the store's return policy. You may have to click on several links to find the policy. Make note of stores you have selected that do not have a return policy on their Web site, and find one that does have a policy.
3. Repeat Step 2 for three other online retail stores.
4. On a sheet of paper, answer the following questions:
   a. Did you come across any stores that did not have a return policy on their Web site? If yes, which ones?
   b. Which Web sites allow you to return products through the mail?
   c. Which Web sites require you to return the merchandise to a physical store?
5. Write a routine claim letter trying to return merchandise that you could purchase from one of the retail Web sites. Remember to use the "Routine Claim Letter Checklist" provided in Chapter 10.
6. Write your name on your paper, and hand it in to your instructor.

Activity 10.2

1. Select one of the career Web sites to visit.
2. Search for an article that relates to careers or working life. If the Web site you have chosen does not provide an article that interests you, visit another career Web site by returning to the *Business Communication at Work* Web site and visit another career Web site.
3. On a sheet of paper, write a paragraph describing new information you discovered in the article. You may want to consider the following questions in your paragraph:
   a. Have your views changed about the career you researched? Why or why not?
   b. Does your educational experience match up with the career you have chosen? What additional classes are necessary for this career? Does this influence your decision about your career?
   c. Aside from education, what requirements are necessary for this career?
4. Write your name on each printout, and hand it in to your instructor.

CHAPTER 10 WORKSHEETS

NAME _____ DATE _____

PRACTICE 1

Concept Review

Instructions: In the spaces provided, respond to the following questions.

1. What is wrong with the following claim letter?

   > Dear Sir:
   >
   > I have had it with companies like yours! You sold cheap, defective merchandise to me. It makes me really mad that you think you can get away with treating me like this.
   >
   > Your Ruttle Sandwich Maker that I ordered is absolutely worthless it smells awful when I use it like burnt electrical wiring when I turn it on and one side does not heat at all.
   >
   > I expect some satisfaction or you'll really be sorry!
   >
   > Angrily,

   _____
   _____
   _____
   _____

2. On August 1 you ordered a dozen VCR tapes, Catalog No. 7873, for $29.99, from a mail-order company: Spector Products, 413 Speltor Avenue, Williamstown, VT 05679. You charged the order to your Spector account 9978 4447 3498 4683, which expires next year in August. The first three tapes you recorded turned out to be defective—there's a lot of static on the tapes. What would you do?

   _____
   _____
   _____
   _____

3. You rented for $40 a video camera to videotape your cousin's graduation exercises. At the exercises, the battery in the camera lasted exactly 5 minutes. You became extremely angry because you rented the camera in good faith that it would work during the graduation exercises. No backup battery was provided when you rented the camera, and there was no opportunity to exchange the camera for one with a fully charged battery. What would you do?

   _____
   _____
   _____
   _____

Claim and Adjustment Messages

CHAPTER 10 WORKSHEETS

NAME _____ DATE _____

4. You ordered 500 No. 10 business envelopes with your return address printed in the upper left-hand corner. When the envelopes and Invoice 33367 for $25.99 arrived from Stine's Stationery Supplies, 310 South Seymour Street, St. Louis, MO 63100, you discovered your Zip Code was printed incorrectly. You check your order form immediately and find that you filled in the correct Zip Code. What would you do?

_____
_____
_____
_____

5. This letter was written in reply to a claim letter. Please evaluate it, pointing out its strengths and weaknesses.

> Dear John:
>
> You have a lot of nerve asking us to replace a leather chair that you have obviously damaged with a sharp object. You should know that you can't use sharp objects on leather. We are going to replace your chair, but if you damage this one, you are on your own.
>
> Sincerely,

a. What is the purpose of this letter? _____
_____

b. Will it keep the reader's goodwill? Why or why not? _____
_____

c. What approach should have been used by the writer of this letter? _____
_____

d. What are the strengths of this letter? _____
_____

e. What are the weaknesses of this letter? _____
_____

CHAPTER 10 WORKSHEETS

NAME _____   DATE _____

6. This letter was written in reply to a claim letter. Please evaluate it, pointing out its strengths and weaknesses.

> Dear Mr. Jefferson:
>
> I regret to inform you that we cannot refund your money for the balled and burlap silver maple tree with a 1½-inch diameter trunk you bought from us two years ago. Our guarantee is only for one year from the date of purchase, and the copy of the sales slip you sent with your letter clearly shows you bought the tree two years ago.
>
> You probably didn't water the tree as directed on the printed instructions that came with the tree. Thank you for your interest in our trees. I've enclosed a coupon for 25 percent off your next tree.
>
> Sincerely,

a. What is the purpose of this letter? _____
_____

b. Will it keep the reader's goodwill? Why or why not? _____
_____

c. What approach should have been used by the writer of this letter? ___
_____

d. What are the strengths of this letter? _____
_____

e. What are the weaknesses of this letter? _____
_____

Claim and Adjustment Messages

CHAPTER 10 WORKSHEETS

Name _____ Date _____

PRACTICE 2

Routine Claim and Adjustment Messages

Instructions: Practice your skills at writing claim and adjustment letters by responding to the following situations.

1. On December 29 you order one pair of binoculars, Stock No. BN0374, for $24.80 (including shipping and handling) from Stevens Merchandise Center, P.O. Box 94800, Houston, TX 77290. You charge your order to your Bonus Credit Card, account 5580-466-823-009, which expires 9/<YEAR>. You note that the mail-order form advertises a 15-day free trial on all merchandise. The binoculars arrive on January 27. You had intended to use the binoculars for birdwatching, but when you try them, you discover that they are not high-powered enough for birdwatching. You decide not to keep them. On January 29 you return the binoculars in the original shipping package by first-class mail, along with a letter asking Stevens to credit your account for $24.80. Write (preferably keyboard) the January 29 letter to mail to Stevens with the binoculars.

2. Your February and March statements from Bonus Credit Card Company do not reflect a credit from Stevens (see Practice 2, Question 1). Write (preferably keyboard) a letter to the attention of the Customer Relations Department at Bonus Credit Card Company, 7739 Cronkhite Avenue, Baton Rouge, LA 70800, asking for its help in obtaining the credit.

Figure 10-13

WATCHDOG INTRUDER ALARM

Protect your office with this alarm system that looks like a wall plaque.

Free engraving on cover plate (maximum of 3 letters). Please specify letters desired when ordering and allow 3-4 weeks extra for engraving.

Catalog No. K1403 ……………………… $36.00

Shipping and handling included in all prices. Merchandise shipped in ten days from receipt of order.

SECURITY & SAFETY CO.
38 Chandler Street
Mahwah, NJ 07430

Figure 10-14

SECURITY & SAFETY CO.
38 Chandler Street
Mahwah, NJ 07430

INVOICE

INVOICE NO: D1438
DATE: October 28, <YEAR>

To:
Butch Walsh
705 North Scott Street
Clarkston, GA 30021

Ship To:

SALESPERSON	P.O. NUMBER	DATE SHIPPED	SHIPPED VIA	F.O.B. POINT	TERMS

QUANTITY	DESCRIPTION	UNIT PRICE	AMOUNT
1	Catalog No. K1403, Watchdog Intruder Alarm, Engraving LDH	63.00	63.00
	SUBTOTAL		63.00
	SALES TAX		
	SHIPPING & HANDLING		
	TOTAL DUE		63.00

Make all checks payable to: Security & Safety Co.
If you have any questions concerning this invoice, call 609-555-4381

THANK YOU FOR YOUR BUSINESS!

CHAPTER 10 WORKSHEETS

NAME _____   DATE _____

3. On September 20, Butch Walsh, 705 N. Scott Street, Clarkston, GA 30021, orders a Watchdog Intruder Alarm from Security & Safety Co., 38 Chandler Street, Mahwah, NJ 07430 (see the catalog ad shown in Figure 10-13). The alarm was intended as a gift for his supervisor's birthday on October 15. The alarm and the invoice, shown in Figure 10-14, arrived on October 30. Butch is steaming and writes the poor claim letter shown in Figure 10-15 below. Rewrite the claim letter.

4. As customer relations manager at Security & Safety Co., answer Butch Walsh's angry letter (see Practice 2, Question 3) and grant the half-price adjustment he has asked for.

5. As customer relations manager at Security & Safety Co., answer Butch Walsh's angry letter in Figure 10-15 and deny the adjustment because the item has been engraved.

6. Rewrite the poor letter in Practice 1, Question 1. You bought the Ruttle Sandwich Maker Model 99Z2 on November 6 and paid $39.99 for it with your Check 429. You have your original Invoice 99753. The address of the manufacturer is Ruttle Appliance Corporation, 2313 Swing Road, Vincennes, IN 47591.

7. You purchase a Snappy calculator watch, Model C863, which has a musical alarm that you really like. The watch comes with a warranty that guarantees material and workmanship for one year. After six months of use, the musical alarm quits working. You have your original sales receipt and the warranty. Write a claim letter to mail with the watch requesting that it be repaired or replaced. The manufacturer of the watch is WatchWorks, 111 East Oak Street, Wayne, PA 19087.

Figure 10-15

> 705 N. Scott St.
> Clarkston, Georgia 30021
> 11/1/<YEAR>
>
>
> Security & Safety Co.
> 38 Chandler Street
> Mahwah NJ
>
> Dear Stupid Security & Safety Co.
>
> You idiets sure took you sweet time about sending my order and you also goofed it up royally!!!!
>
> First I don't appreciate being charged $63 for a Watchdog Intruder Alarm that's listed in your catalogeu at $36.00. Did you think you could make a few extra bucks that way and I'd never notiec3? Well----you can't cheat me cause I won't stand for it.
>
> At least you got hte engraved initeals on the cover write. I wanted this for my supreviseor's birthday but it is passed now and I had to buy something else. Your catalogeu promised 10 day delivery and I ordered this over a month ago.
>
> I think to be fare you should give it to me for $18 which is halfprice. I'm still
>
>   Boiling Mad!
>
>
>   Butch Walsh

Claim and Adjustment Messages

CHAPTER 10 WORKSHEETS

NAME _____ DATE _____

PRACTICE 3

Writing Applications—Claim and Adjustment Letters

Instructions: Respond to the following situations as directed.

1. Assume you are V. Wayne Brown, owner of Target Construction Company, Inc., and you receive the following claim letter (Figure 10-16) from Patricia Mills. Compose a compromise adjustment letter. Explain that your cabinetmaker was unable to provide cherry wood because of a nationwide shortage and that it was necessary to use oak to complete the building on schedule. You will invoice the customer for the cabinets as agreed, but you will pay for and install mulch in the customer's flower beds.

Figure 10-16

M&M Travel Center Inc.
289 Germantown Bend Cove
Cordova, TN 38018

July 3, <YEAR>

Mr. V. Wayne Brown
Target Construction Co., Inc.
2174 Fremont Road
Memphis, TN 38114

Dear Mr. Brown:

Your contract for the construction of our office building provided for installation of cabinets in our break room. Where as the cabinets have been carefully crafted and installed as expected, they are not made of cherry, as originally specified.

Although we do not feel that replacing the cabinets at this point would warrant the inconvenience and interruptions to work it would involve, we feel that we should not be charged for them. I am requesting that the cost of the cabinets be deducted from your final bill.

Also, we were disturbed to learn that the flower beds were not mulched after the landscaping was installed. While this was not specified in our contract, we feel that mulch should be provided by Target.

Otherwise, we are very satisfied with our building and are especially pleased that you finished it a week ahead of schedule. We will be happy to recommend Target in the future.

Sincerely,

Patricia Mills

PAM/dm

CHAPTER 10 WORKSHEETS

NAME _____   DATE _____

2. You purchase an Aqua Deluxe Aquarium, Model D978, from Fish Emporium, 899 Wilson Lane, Forest River, ND 58233, for $325 in cash at a July clearance sale. A sign by the cash register says that all sales are final and no returns or exchanges will be made. Mark, the sales associate, assures you that there is nothing wrong with the aquarium. Mark states that the aquarium is on sale because the manufacturer is discontinuing that model and introducing a new one. You take the aquarium home and set it up according to the instructions, but the aquarium leaks and there appears to be no way to stop the leak.

   Write a persuasive claim letter to the manager of the Fish Emporium asking for your money back. You have the original copy of your sales receipt, which is marked paid in full.

3. Your company, Enersystem Industries, 1975 Oak Street, Oklahoma City, OK 73127, ships all merchandise FOB shipping point. The invoices clearly state the shipping policy, and a separate amount for shipping is shown on each invoice. In the past month several customers have deducted the shipping charges from their invoice before sending their payment. You've had to write an individual letter to each of these customers asking them to pay the shipping charges.

   Write a form letter to be sent to any future customers who deduct the shipping charges before paying their invoices. The letter will be prepared on a computer so it can be individualized and the actual amount of the shipping and invoice can be inserted in the letter. Avoid negative phrases such as "You are not entitled to . . ." or "You mistakenly deducted . . .," which are likely to offend customers. In your letter, assume the mistake is an honest one. Explain to customers what FOB shipping point means and point out that shipping this way allows you to sell merchandise at a lower price. Make it clear that even though you would like to allow the deduction, it would be unfair to your other customers. Ask customers to send you a check for the shipping charges.

Claim and Adjustment Messages

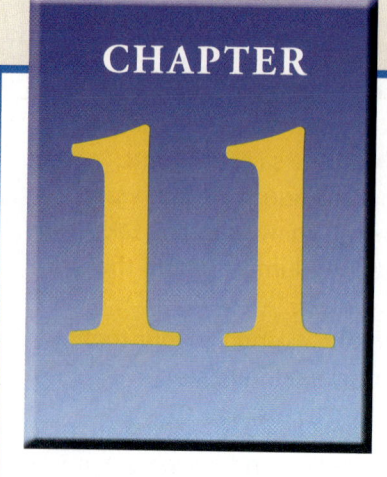

CHAPTER 11
Persuasive Messages

Objectives

After completing this chapter, you will be able to:

1. Discuss the importance of writing letters to lawmakers
2. Write a legislative letter to a lawmaker
3. Write a service letter to a lawmaker
4. Write a letter to the editor
5. Write a persuasive request letter
6. Write a sales letter

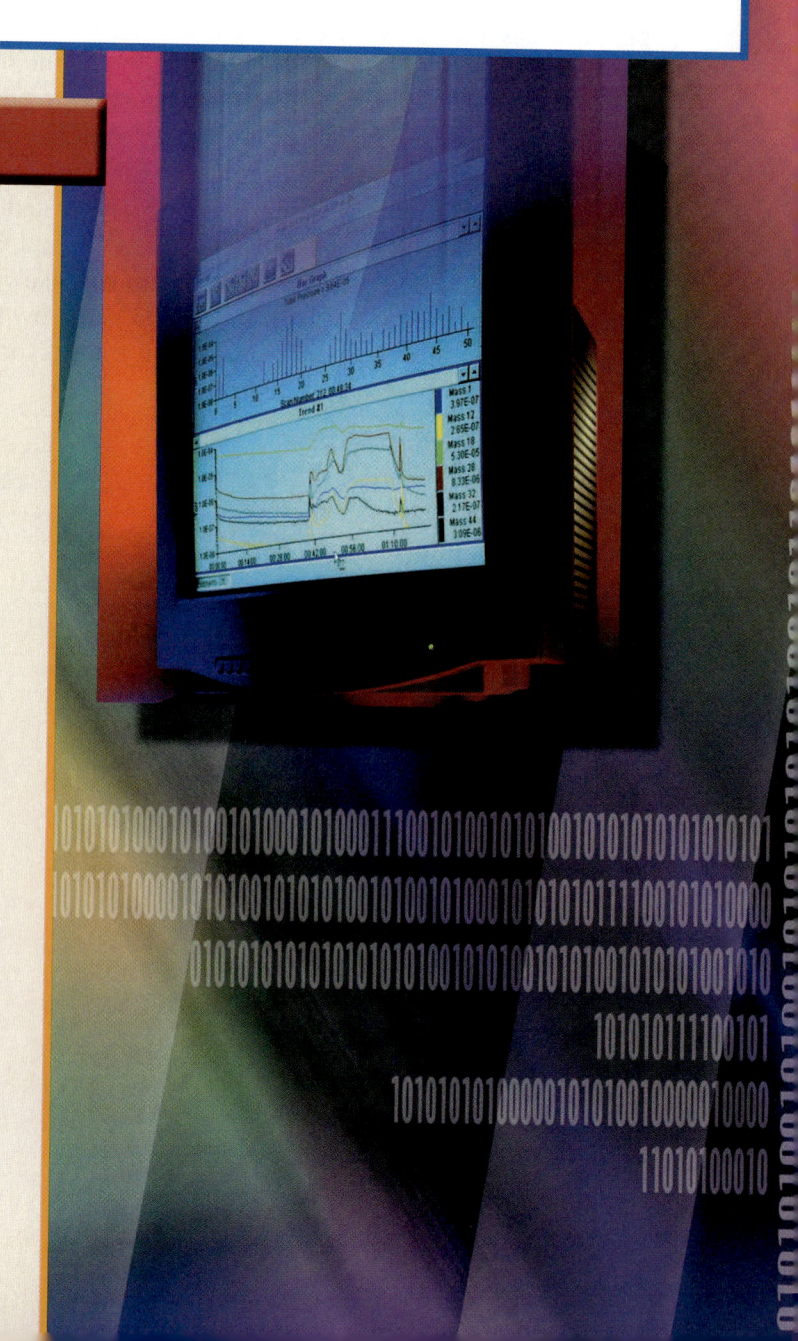

WORKPLACE APPLICATIONS

Problem Solving

"Houston, we have a problem." Those words were spoken by the commander of the space capsule Apollo 13 after an explosion on board. Few problems in the business world will be as dire, but every problem needs to be taken as seriously. **Problem solving,** like decision making, takes practice, can be done alone or in groups, and requires sufficient information and creativity. Problems are best solved through the process described below.

The first step is to define the problem. Try to state it in a sentence or two. Here is an example: "Our department has repeatedly missed the 5 p.m. Friday deadline for submitting weekly schedules."

Identifying Solutions

The next step is to **brainstorm,** or list, possible solutions. This step is best done in a group. The point of brainstorming is to generate a large pool of ideas. (For more on brainstorming, see page 133.)

After brainstorming, you should evaluate the possibilities and narrow them down to one good choice. Solutions that are not feasible can be discarded. Identify the advantages and disadvantages of the remaining solutions. The questions to ask are, "Is this a good solution?" and "Why or why not?"

Next, you should create a plan for putting the solution to work. Ask "How can we make this solution work? To whom do we talk? How long will it take?", and so on.

The final step is to implement the solution. Give it a trial run. For example, the solution to the problem of missed deadlines may be to change the day of the deadline. Try the change for a month and see if it helps. If the solution doesn't work, repeat the process until you get the results you want.

Thinking Critically

Situation: Your travel agency has only two telephone lines, which makes it difficult to check the Internet, make telephone calls, and process credit card numbers at the same time. Customers and good bookings have been lost because of delays. As the office manager, you want a solution that will not cost too much.

Ask Yourself: How would you solve the problem?

> *Everyone lives by selling something.*
>
> —R. L. Stevenson

To be successful in your career and in your personal life, you must develop the ability to persuade—both orally and in writing. To some extent, any type of communication—oral or written—requires the ability to persuade or "sell" your listener or reader on your ideas and on yourself as a person with whom others will want to be associated. In every business communication, you are also "selling" your organization's image and goodwill. In this chapter, we will discuss letters whose main purpose is to persuade others to accept your ideas and/or buy your products or services.

Maybe you question why or even how you would use your persuasive skills in writing letters or in oral communication. Let's begin our study of persuasive communication by looking at some types of communication in which your very best persuasiveness must come into play, along with your ability to use the seven Cs of communication effectively.

Writing to Public Officials and the Media

Have you ever thought about writing a letter to a public official? What about writing a letter to the editor of a newspaper or magazine? Writing these kinds of letters is one way you can participate in our political system and be sure your voice is heard.

Organizations, too, often take an interest in the larger world—local, national, and even international events can affect the future of an organization as well as the careers and livelihoods of the employees.

NOTES
Dear Mr. President
Do you know the name(s) of your lawmakers? Your letter to a lawmaker, just like your vote, does count.

Letters to Lawmakers

Lawmakers represent the citizens who live in their legislative areas, who are called their **constituents.** Lawmakers are very interested in knowing how their constituents feel on the issues being considered by their legislative bodies. One way many lawmakers seek their constituents' opinions on current issues is to send regular newsletters that frequently contain questionnaires.

The best and most convincing way to express your opinion to a lawmaker is through a written letter. You may wonder, "Will my letter really make a difference?" With rare exceptions, lawmakers not only read their mail but are very interested in the contents. Letters that aren't personally read by the lawmaker—many lawmakers receive more than 6000 pieces of mail each week—are handled by key staff personnel who then relay the contents to the lawmaker.

Your letter, just like your vote, does count. Although your letter alone may not change an existing law or add a new one, your opinion, combined with the opinions of many other constituents, can result in change. In fact, there have been several instances over the years in which Congress has repealed a law because of the avalanche of mail opposing it.

When you want to express your opinion or solve a problem, to which lawmaker or public official do you write? First, you should determine which level of government—federal, state, county, or city—has jurisdiction over the issue in which you are interested. For example, if you have a public aid question, you should write to an official at the state level. If you have a question about Social Security or the IRS, you should write to someone at the federal level. If you want to rezone property in order to open a business, you should write to a local (city or county) lawmaker. You can usually find phone numbers and addresses for government officials in your local phone book. The library or the Internet is also a good source for this information.

Characteristics of a Good Letter to a Lawmaker

Using the following guidelines will help you write an effective letter to a lawmaker at any level.

Give Complete Information About How You Can Be Contacted. Be sure to include your address and a phone number where you can be reached during normal office hours. Use your organization's stationery only if you are representing the views of your organization. Otherwise, use your personal stationery or plain paper with a complete heading, including your phone number.

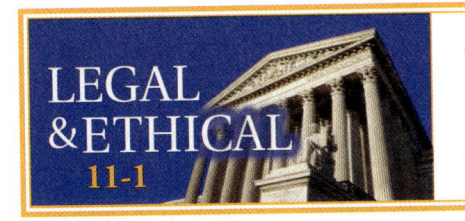

LEGAL & ETHICAL 11-1

Organizational Support? You write a letter to one of your federal lawmakers expressing your personal opinion about an environmental issue. You work for a chemical company. Would it be legal and/or ethical to use your company letterhead stationery for the letter?

Address Your Lawmaker Properly. Consult a reference manual such as *The Gregg Reference Manual*, Glencoe/McGraw-Hill, by William A. Sabin, or *The Irwin Office Reference Manual*, Glencoe/McGraw-Hill, by Jo Ann Lee and Marilyn L. Satterwhite, for correct titles and salutations to use when addressing public officials.

Use a Subject Line. Identify the topic you're writing about in a subject line. If the topic is a legislative bill, include the bill's name and number, if you can, or at least give the bill's popular title. Remember, hundreds of legislative bills are introduced each year; therefore, this identification is important.

Limit Your Letter to One Topic. Discuss only one issue in each letter, and make your discussion brief. If you wish to write about more than one issue, write a separate letter for each topic. Organize the letter using the direct approach or the persuasive approach (whichever is appropriate), and present your points concisely in a clear, logical order. You will learn more about these approaches as you study various types of persuasive messages in this chapter.

Persuasive Messages

Use Your Own Words. Petitions with dozens of signatures carry little or no weight with lawmakers because they know many of these signatures are from disinterested people who have signed the petition because they were asked, not because they felt strongly about an issue. Even form letters and postcards have less impact on the recipient than a carefully thought-out individual letter.

LEGAL & ETHICAL 11-2

Personal Endorsement. A friend asks you to sign a petition to condemn a historical building so that an investor can build a shopping mall. Is it ethical for you to sign the petition even though you do not approve of tearing down the historical building?

Tell Why and How. When expressing your opinion about a bill under consideration, tell *why* you feel the legislation is good or bad and *how* the legislation affects you, your coworkers, your profession, your community, or other people in your area of representation. Give personal examples and observations to strengthen your case. Back up your opinions with facts and figures, and include copies of pertinent articles and editorials from newspapers and magazines.

Be Courteous and Rational. Avoid starting your letter with the cliché "As a citizen and a taxpayer . . . ." Your lawmaker will likely view this kind of opening in a negative way. Don't be rude to your lawmaker or threaten him or her with a statement such as, "If you don't vote for this bill, I won't vote for you in the next election!" This makes you appear emotional, perhaps irrational. If you are perceived in this way, then you will have little or no credibility. When you are trying to persuade, logical reasons work much better than threats.

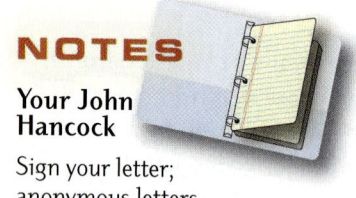

Sign Your Letter. Anonymous letters are disposed of, unread. Also, don't send photocopies of one letter to different lawmakers who represent you. Courtesy dictates that you write each one individually—an easy task with word processing.

Watch Your Timing. When you are writing about a legislative bill, it is important to express your views early in the legislative process—before a bill comes to a vote of the full legislative body. After a bill has been introduced, write to the appropriate committee members when the hearings on the bill begin. Also write to your own representatives before the bill comes to the floor for debate and vote. Your lawmakers are glad to hear from you any time, but your letter will be more effective if it arrives while they are still deciding how to vote.

Most lawmakers have a fax machine so that you can transmit your letter instantly to them. Also, members of Congress and many state legislatures have telephone "hotlines" that interested citizens can use to find out the current status of bills.

NOTES

Your John Hancock

Sign your letter; anonymous letters are disposed of, unread.

Thinking Cap 11.1

Discuss: Why is it not a good idea to write a letter to one lawmaker and then send photocopies to other lawmakers who represent you? What is an easy way to send an original letter to each lawmaker?

Make Your Letter Professional in Appearance. Use your computer to keyboard and then print your letter, if possible, because a printed letter looks more businesslike and more professional than a handwritten letter. If you must write in longhand, be sure that your writing is legible and that your name, address, and phone number are included. Remember, you must include your address to receive a reply.

Send a Follow-Up Letter, if Necessary. Almost all lawmakers answer their mail. If the reply you receive is just a brief acknowledgment, however, write again to ask for more specific information. Ask your lawmaker the following, for example:

- How do you stand on the issue?
- Do you support or oppose the bill?
- How do you think this bill will affect the people you represent?

Types of Letters Written to Lawmakers

Letters written to lawmakers fall into three general categories: (1) legislative letters, (2) service letters, and (3) follow-up letters.

Legislative Letters. Legislative letters deal with legislation, or laws, that affect everyone. Use the direct approach in most of these letters. A typical outline for a legislative letter is given in Figure 11-1 below.

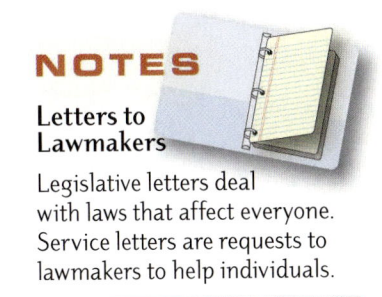

NOTES

Letters to Lawmakers

Legislative letters deal with laws that affect everyone. Service letters are requests to lawmakers to help individuals.

Figure 11-1
Legislative letters deal with laws that affect many people.

```
                                    000 Your Street Name
                                    City, State, and ZIP Code
                                    Month 00, <YEAR>


    The Honorable _____
    House of Representatives
    Room Number and Building Name
    City, State, and ZIP Code

    Dear Representative _____:

    Subject: (Identify the bill or issue here.)

    1. State your support of (or opposition to) the issue about which you're writing. Include
       the bill number, if known, and the popular title.

    2. Tell why you support (or oppose) the issue, giving local and/or personal examples,
       experiences, and observations. Quote statistics (and their source), if available, to back
       up your view. Explain the consequences of the bill's success or failure to you and to
       other constituents.

    3. Ask the lawmaker to sponsor or support (or oppose) the legislation discussed above.

    4. Express appreciation for the lawmaker's having considered your views, and ask for a
       reply that gives the lawmaker's view.

                                    Sincerely,


                                    Your Name
```

Paragraph — (bracketing items 1–4)

Your Signature — (bracketing the signature line)

Persuasive Messages 295

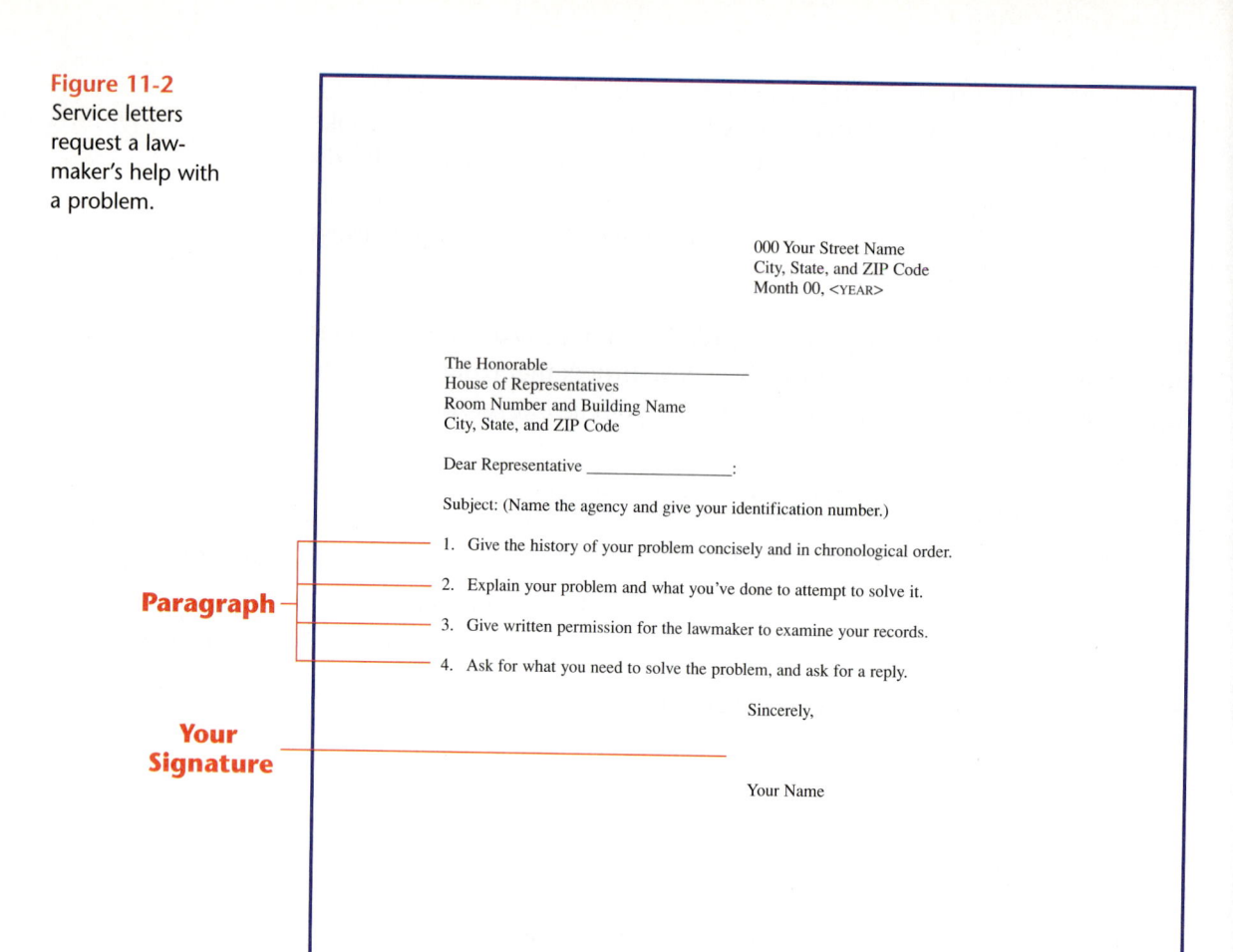

Figure 11-2
Service letters request a lawmaker's help with a problem.

```
                                              000 Your Street Name
                                              City, State, and ZIP Code
                                              Month 00, <YEAR>


        The Honorable _____
        House of Representatives
        Room Number and Building Name
        City, State, and ZIP Code

        Dear Representative _____:

        Subject: (Name the agency and give your identification number.)

        1. Give the history of your problem concisely and in chronological order.
        2. Explain your problem and what you've done to attempt to solve it.
        3. Give written permission for the lawmaker to examine your records.
        4. Ask for what you need to solve the problem, and ask for a reply.

                                              Sincerely,


                                              Your Name
```

(Items 1–4 labeled **Paragraph**; signature line labeled **Your Signature**)

Service Letters. Service letters involve requests to help individuals cut through the procedures and paperwork, or "red tape," of government programs. For example, in a service letter an individual may need help with a social security or veterans' benefits problem, with an immigration problem, or with some other program of a state or federal government agency. These letters also generally use the direct approach. See Figure 11-2 above, for a typical outline for a service letter.

Service letters should be sent to the lawmaker's local or district office in his or her home state because these offices handle most service work. In today's "Freedom of Information" age, you may need to provide a signed privacy release authorizing your lawmaker to contact the appropriate agency for help.

Follow-Up Letters. Even though your lawmakers are paid to represent you and to help you, common courtesy requires that you write a thank-you letter when they have voted the way you want on legislation and/or helped you as a result of a service letter. Review "Thank-You Messages" in Chapter 8.

Go to CD-ROM
Activity 11-1
To test your skills.

Letters to Editors

Nearly all groups in the media—from newspapers and magazines to radio and TV—encourage their readers, listeners, or viewers to send written responses regarding their publications and programs. People who write these letters of response are eager to share their convictions, knowledge, and concern with others.

Concerned citizens and conscientious organizations write letters to the media to share a view, to express a concern, to ask for help when an error has been made, to suggest an improvement, or to give information.

Because people tend to accept as fact anything that is printed or broadcast, you should feel an obligation to write a letter to the media when you see or hear a report that is erroneous or misleading. Voicing your concerns will bring other readers' or listeners' attention to the issue or report.

Characteristics of a Good Letter to the Editor

The following guidelines will help you write an effective letter to the editor. Although the focus here is on letters to be printed in newspapers or magazines, these guidelines also apply to preparing messages for radio or television broadcasts or teleconferences.

Get Right to the Point. Say outright why you're writing the letter. Give enough details so that your letter is meaningful to all readers, even those who know nothing about the topic you're discussing. Answer the obvious questions that will be in readers' minds.

Be Brief. Although short words and sentences will make your letter more readable, be sure to include all the points you think are important. Remember to limit the subject of your letter to one topic.

Be Rational. Even though you may be responding to something that angers you, skip the temptation to write a sarcastic rebuttal. Although an emotionally charged letter may help increase a newspaper or magazine's readership, it may do so at your expense. You'll feel embarrassed if you see your angry letter in print. Instead, make your letter polite and professional.

Use Good Taste. Always avoid insulting a race, ethnic group, political faction, or minority. Letters that are libelous or contain personal attacks are not published by reputable editors. A letter to the editor in which you label someone as a "stupid idiot" or a "crook" or "liar" could actually be considered libelous unless those labels are based on proven facts.

Be Fair. There are two sides to every story—your argument won't be weakened by showing that you are aware of another viewpoint. Also, be certain all your data and facts are accurate.

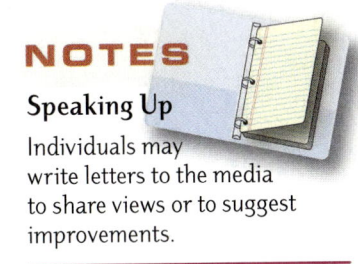

NOTES

Speaking Up
Individuals may write letters to the media to share views or to suggest improvements.

Thinking Cap 11.2

Discuss: What technique(s) could a writer use to avoid writing an emotionally charged letter?

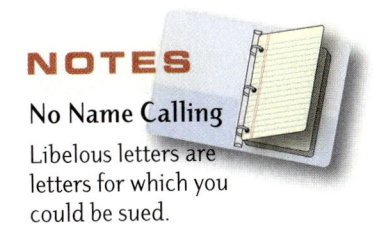

NOTES

No Name Calling
Libelous letters are letters for which you could be sued.

Persuasive Messages

Writing a Letter to the Editor

The following guidelines will help you format a letter to the editor:

Follow the Rules. Most publications have an editorial page where letters to the editor are printed along with some guidelines for these letters. Space is limited on these pages, so pay particular attention to letter length specifications. If none are given, limit your letter to 200 to 300 words. (Messages to be broadcast should often be even shorter—contact the radio or television station for guidelines.) The staff of a publication may edit letters to the editor for length, accuracy, and good taste.

Keyboard Your Letter, if Possible. Your letter should be properly formatted and have a neat, professional appearance.

Meet the "Deadline." If your letter is triggered by a recent news story or editorial, write your letter the same day the item appears, while the topic is still "news." If you wait too long, your letter may not be considered for publication.

Identify Yourself. Always sign your letter with your full name, title (if it is pertinent to the topic), and address. Also include a telephone number where you can be reached in the daytime. Your name and address (city and, if relevant, state) will probably be published with your letter. A few newspapers will withhold signatures if the editor feels the circumstances warrant it, but most will not. Magazine editors are more likely to withhold from print a name or location if the writer requests this and the topic is sensitive, but a letter still must be signed—letters sent anonymously lack credibility and are seldom published. Figure 11-3 shows a typical format for a letter to the editor.

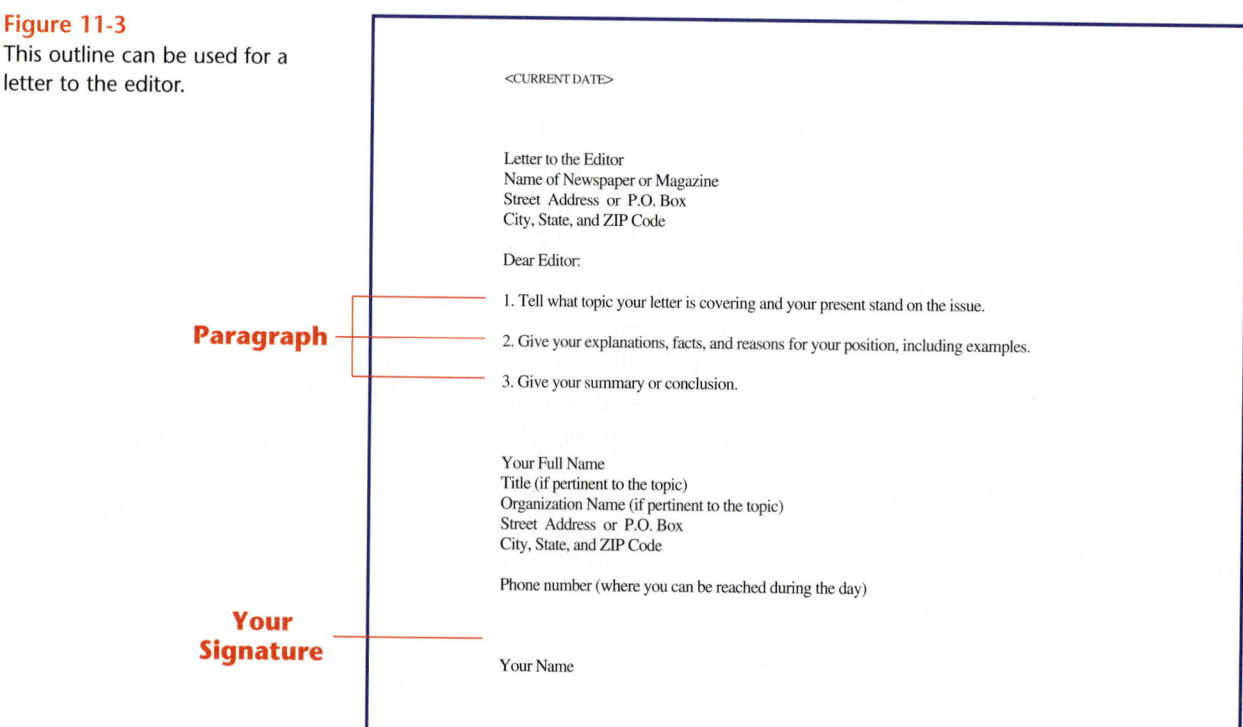

Go to CD-ROM
Activity 11-2
To test your skills.

Figure 11-3
This outline can be used for a letter to the editor.

<CURRENT DATE>

Letter to the Editor
Name of Newspaper or Magazine
Street Address or P.O. Box
City, State, and ZIP Code

Dear Editor:

1. Tell what topic your letter is covering and your present stand on the issue.

2. Give your explanations, facts, and reasons for your position, including examples.

3. Give your summary or conclusion.

Your Full Name
Title (if pertinent to the topic)
Organization Name (if pertinent to the topic)
Street Address or P.O. Box
City, State, and ZIP Code

Phone number (where you can be reached during the day)

Your Name

Paragraph

Your Signature

PERSUASIVE REQUESTS

A request for donations, cooperation, gifts, or favors (without any intention on the writer's part to buy or sell) is a **persuasive request.** This type of letter attempts to persuade the reader to spend time or money or to go to some trouble to help the writer—usually without benefit to the reader.

The letter shown in Figure 11-4 is from the Professional Business Leaders Association. The letter shows how a persuasive letter can effectively capture the interest and secure the cooperation of the reader with its approach and its use of the "you attitude."

Guidelines for Persuasive Requests

When you write a persuasive request, use the persuasive approach discussed in Chapter 5 and follow these five suggestions:

Begin With an Appeal That Will Interest the Reader

You already know a great deal about the opening paragraphs of persuasive letters from the discussion in Chapter 5. As we have seen, the approach for

Figure 11-4
This persuasive letter persuades its reader to respond to a request.

PBLA
Professional Business Leaders Association

Southeastern State College
Office of the Dean
Business Division
State University, AK 72467
Telephone 501-555-3035

October 8, <YEAR>

Dear Member

Our Professional Business Leaders Association is conducting a survey of our members to gather program information to assist the College in improving the quality of academic programs. This would in turn benefit current and future students.

The information gathered from the survey will aid us in identifying the kinds of activities in which our graduates are involved and the progress they have made in their professions, including salary attainment.

The Academic Program Review Committee can benefit from information from former students regarding the strengths and weaknesses of the programs as indicated in the survey results.

Any information gathered will be held in confidence and released only in the form of college and department summary statistics. My staff and I eagerly await your reply. Please return your completed survey in the enclosed envelope by November 20.

Sincerely

Francesca Pena

Francesca Pena, President

mas
Enclosures

Persuasive Messages

GLOBAL DIVERSITY 11.1

Gift Giving
Avoid giving white flowers as a business gift in El Salvador. They are associated with funerals and considered bad luck. *When is it appropriate to send a business gift? How do you determine what kind of gift you should send?*

---

persuasive requests is entirely different from the approach for direct inquiries. When you are asking someone about a product or service he or she is trying to sell, the reader becomes interested immediately because the inquiry presents an opportunity to sell. When you are asking for a gift or favor, however, you must point out the advantage to the reader to stimulate his or her interest. Since you want a favorable response, avoid starting with your request—get the reader interested in your story before asking for a response, otherwise the reader's reaction might be, "Why bother?"

Successful persuasive openings often use the following appeals: humanitarian, reader-benefit, individual responsibility, or personal experience.

Humanitarian or Altruistic Appeal. *Altruism* is unselfish regard for or devotion to the welfare of others; a *humanitarian* is a person promoting human welfare and social reform. The humanitarian or altruistic appeal puts its emphasis on *benefit to others,* as illustrated in this opening paragraph of a letter from the Organ Transplant Fund:

> You can have a powerful impact on another human being. The power to preserve another person's life depends upon your decision. Your generosity and caring can extend life for another person.

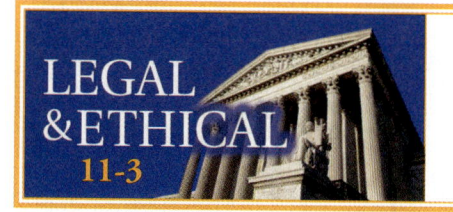

LEGAL & ETHICAL 11-3

Charitable Benefit. A persuasive letter asks readers to buy a stuffed animal and indicates that the profits will go to the victims of child abuse. Actually, less than one percent of the profits go to the charity. Is this legal? Is this ethical?

Reader-Benefit Appeal. The reader-benefit appeal emphasizes the *benefit to the reader* of responding to a request. The following excerpt from a sales manager's plea to salespersons to improve their personal appearance illustrates the reader-benefit appeal:

> How often do you take time for a second look at your appearance? Your customers do every day.
>
> Your appearance is a preview of the way you might handle your customers' business.
>
> When you take pride in yourself, your customers feel that you also take pride in what you do for them.

Individual Responsibility Appeal. A lawmaker used the individual responsibility appeal in this request for information from educational administrators:

> You are part of a carefully selected sample of educational administrators receiving this letter. Over the past five years, your experience and leadership have played a major role in increasing educational funding in the national budget.
>
> Your answers to the enclosed questionnaire are vital to lawmakers who are negotiating to preserve educational funding. . . .

Personal Experience Appeal. Recalling a pleasant childhood memory is an example of a personal experience appeal. This excerpt, from a letter trying to persuade the reader to donate money to help underprivileged children attend summer camp, illustrates this appeal:

> Remember the contrast of the cool water to the sweltering outdoor temperature when you jumped into the swimming pool as a kid at summer camp? Leaving the inner city and the asphalt jungle for a week of camping in the great outdoors is an experience youngsters never forget. The thrill of cabins, sleeping bags, and campfire cooking lives on in their memories, and the experience of closeness and sharing with role models shapes their adult lives. A donation of only $50 will enable us to send a child to Camp Kokomo for one week this summer.

> **NOTES**
> **Swing Sets and Basketballs**
> A pleasant childhood memory can be used to appeal to a reader to help with a particular charity. Remember to use the "you attitude" in explaining the reason for your request

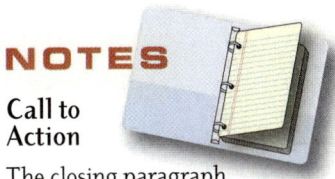

Follow Through With the Reason for the Request

After you select the theme for your opening, you should follow through with an explanation of your request. Remember to use the "you attitude" in explaining the reasons for your request. In your explanation, it is important to emphasize an advantage to someone other than yourself, the writer.

Stress to the reader or the reader's organization the advantage of responding to your request, as did the writer of this paragraph from a letter asking wholesale clothing buyers to complete a questionnaire for a fashion merchandising organization.

> Your cooperation in this project will definitely help the garment industry. Your cooperation will be of even more benefit to you as buyers, because the results of the survey will be used by our members to develop better merchandising methods and to give better service to individual buyers.

In addition, compliment the reader. This can be an effective technique in persuasive requests. The following sentence, from a letter asking a member of the local Marketing Executives Club to speak to the students in the Phi Beta Lambda Chapter, gives a compliment to the reader:

> We know that any pointers you can give us on sales and marketing techniques will be stimulating and helpful to our students.

State the Request in Definite and Specific Terms

After catching your reader's interest and giving your explanation, make your request. Be sure the reader knows:

- Exactly what you want.
- How and when he or she is to respond.

Notice how explicitly this writer requests the help of an organization member:

> Specifically, Jennifer, these are the things I am asking you to do:
> 1. Attend the monthly meetings.
> 2. Chair the Fundraising Committee. You are to form the committee and send a list of the members to the secretary by March 1.

> **NOTES**
> **Call to Action**
> The closing paragraph should stimulate action by making it easy and satisfying to respond.

PERSUASIVE MESSAGES

Submit a plan for this year's events to the secretary by April 15. Your annual committee report will be due on July 30.

3. Serve as adviser to the Budget Committee. Your experience should be especially valuable to this committee, and I have asked its chairperson, Vikki Edwards, to contact you directly.

4. Write a cover letter for the attached questionnaire, which will be sent to all members.

Stimulate Action With Closing Remarks

Closing remarks should stimulate action by suggesting that compliance will be easy and satisfying. Doesn't this closing paragraph make viewers feel that supplying the information requested by a TV station will be simple yet worthwhile?

> Our questions are easy to answer. We will not use your name. No one will try to sell you anything. We have stamped the ballot; no postage is necessary. But we do need your vote, so please fill in the few blanks on the enclosed ballot, fold it, seal it, and drop it in the mail.

Reflect an Optimistic Outlook

Effective persuasive letters show an appreciation of and confidence in the reader's favorable response. A sincere belief in people and an optimistic outlook shine through every paragraph of most successful persuasive letters. Notice the positive tone in the following excerpt from a persuasive request:

> This will be the most important vote you will cast between now and November 2. And this vote will count more because you are one of 1500 AMS members—not just one of 50 million voters in the presidential election.

Here is another excerpt using a positive tone:

> For many of us, our Phi Mu Foundation experience has been a spark that has helped light our lives. Your financial support of the Foundation today can create a living endowment to light many more lives yet to come.

Go to CD-ROM
Activities 11-3 and 11-4
To test your skills.

Checkpoint 11.1

1. Why is it a good idea to sign the persuasive letters you send?

2. Why do you think it is important to stress the "you attitude" in a persuasive request?

3. Consider the parts of a request letter—appeal, reasons, request, and closing. Rank them in the order of their importance in the letter. Explain your choices.

SALES LETTERS

Sales letters are an effective selling tool for several reasons. One of the most important reasons is **cost**—the cost of writing, producing, and mailing a large quantity of sales letters is less than the cost of reaching the same number of prospects by producing and buying time for a radio or television commercial or producing and buying space for a newspaper or magazine ad.

In addition, sales letters allow a seller to be **selective** in targeting his or her audience. The seller may select a mailing list according to prospects' professions, geographic areas, ages, incomes, interests, and so on. By selecting a mailing list carefully, the seller is virtually assured of reaching a certain number of "qualified" prospects. These lists are available from companies that collect and compile them for a fee. Sales letters can be **adapted** to a variety of purposes and target audiences making them an effective selling tool.

Computer software enables the sender to **customize** each letter for a specific customer as if he or she were the only person receiving an offer, when, in fact, these sales letters are produced quickly and inexpensively in large quantities.

> **NOTES**
>
> **Letter Sales**
>
> Sales letters are effective selling tools for these reasons: cost, selectivity, customization, adaptability.

Direct Sales Letters

Direct mail (usually sales letters) is sent to potential buyers with the hope that a sale will be forthcoming. Direct mail promotions often use some device (gimmick or attention grabber) to get the customer to open the envelope and read the message. "Free Gift Inside!" or "Urgent—Open Immediately!" or a similar message may be printed on the envelope. Inside, the consumer may find a letter, a brochure, or a coupon, plus other items trying to grab his or her attention. Much of this mail is considered "junk mail" by most of us—people have become so used to it in their mailboxes that even organizations with products or services of real value sometimes feel they have to "shout" for attention.

In contrast, sales letters to businesspeople may use all the devices of direct mail, but they are usually able to get to the point without resorting to gimmicks. In our discussion we will focus on sales letters as they are used in business.

Direct-mail sales letters do, however, have certain drawbacks. Because many people consider all direct-mail advertising junk mail, a sales letter may be discarded before it is read even though it is well written and makes a spectacular offer. In addition, even a "successful" sales letter will usually draw a positive response from no more than 5 percent of the total number of people receiving the mailing.

Indirect Sales Letters

Letters written specifically for direct-mail selling are not the only sales letters. Examples of situations that result in indirect sales include the following:

- A writer acknowledges receipt of a large order with a thank-you letter that also resells the customer on the organization's product or service.

Persuasive Messages

- A writer introduces a new sales representative to a customer, which paves the way for that representative to call for an order.
- A writer tries to persuade a superior to approve a project or an expense by selling that person on the reasons the project or expense should be approved.
- A writer sends an application letter for a job that sells his or her qualifications to a prospective employer.

Principles of Writing Sales Letters

To write successful sales letters, every business writer must keep in mind the following principles:

- **Know your products and services.** Be aware of the advantages and disadvantages of your products and services—why they appeal or should appeal to people. In fact, know as much as you can about them.
- **Know your potential customers.** Learn everything you can about your customers—who they are, where they are, what their needs are, and how to get through to them.
- **Know how sales are made.** Concentrate on what motivates people to buy, what appeals are likely to prove successful, and how to get people to act.
- **Remember the basics of effective writing.** Apply the good writing principles you have learned, especially those that pertain to persuasive messages. Be sure to practice the techniques of clear communication that you learned in Units 1 and 2 of this book.

Thinking Cap 11.3

Discuss: Without additional knowledge and training, would you be able to write an effective sales letter about selling a combine or corn planter to farmers? Why or why not?

Planning Sales Letters to Individuals

Before you begin drafting a sales letter, you should take five important steps. Until this initial planning is completed, it is virtually impossible to write an effective sales letter.

Analyze the Prospects in Terms of the Product

First, from research or experience build a composite prospect—identify the characteristics that describe the most likely prospect or customer for your products or services. The sex, age, occupation, geographic location, financial situation, and other characteristics of the "average" prospect will determine what appeals you will use in your letter. Defining your targeted customers' characteristics will help you discover the needs and desires of these prospective buyers. For example, you wouldn't try to sell a "Sixty-Five Plus" insurance plan to college students. Nor would you try to sell homeowners' insurance to apartment dwellers; however, you may try to sell renters' insurance to them.

Prepare a List of Prospects

Thinking Cap 11.4

Discuss: Would you try to sell snowblowers to residents of southern Florida or southern California? Why or why not?

Next, you need a good mailing list. The obvious place to start is your organization's own list of customers. As previously mentioned, you can also buy lists from companies that specialize in compiling and selling them. To be effective, a mailing list must contain correct names and addresses, and the people and organizations listed must have characteristics in common that make them likely prospects for your products or services.

Analyze the Product in Terms of the Prospects

What specific features of your product or service make it attractive or useful or appealing? What features should be emphasized? What features should be played down? (This analysis is usually made along with your analysis in the first step.) Letters that present a product or service in terms of what prospective buyers think of it and how they can use it do more than make sales—they win satisfied customers.

Determine the Central Selling Point

The **central selling point (CSP)** should be the item of information most likely to persuade the prospect to buy a product or service. The CSP might be appearance, durability, comfort, convenience, price, or any other positive feature that is likely to have the greatest influence on your reader's purchasing decision. After analyzing the prospects and the product, build your letter around this central selling point.

NOTES

What Sells It?
The central selling point (CSP) of a letter is the information most likely to persuade the prospect to buy a product or service.

Make a Plan for the Letter

One formula for a sales presentation is the **AIDA approach—attention, interest, desire, action.** Review "The Persuasive Approach" in Chapter 5. Using this formula, you first get the prospect's attention—that means getting him or her to read your letter—by promising a benefit. Then, you arouse your prospect's interest by helping him or her imagine using your product or service. Next, you try to convince your prospect of the desirability of buying. Finally, you attempt to get your prospect to act—to send in an order or to subscribe to your service. You want the reader to take the desired action you are suggesting.

Many effective sales letters will not fit such a set pattern. Be creative—rather than let a formula dictate your letter, link your product or service with the prospect's desires and needs by giving sufficient factual information to be convincing.

NOTES

AIDA
An effective formula for a sales letter is AIDA (attention, interest, desire, action).

Writing Sales Letters to Individuals

The purpose of your sales letter is to give the reader the incentive to buy and use your product or service. After you have planned the letter, follow these guidelines when you actually write your sales letter.

Capture Reader Attention and Interest in the Opening

The opening sentences of a sales letter are critical. If the prospect doesn't read the letter, then no sale will result no matter how good the offer is. To get the letter off to a fast start and to get the prospect reading, the central selling point and the promise of a benefit to the buyer should be woven together at the beginning.

The possibilities for different forms, styles, attention-getting opening ideas, gimmicks, and devices are limited only by your imagination. Often you can capture the reader's attention in one of the following ways:

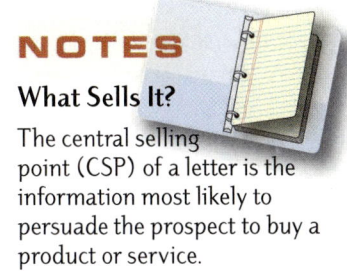

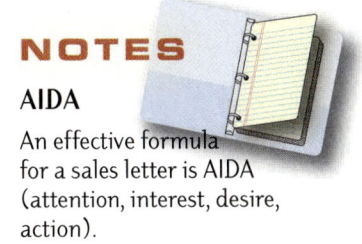

Persuasive Messages

- Arrange the first sentence as a headline—perhaps in all capitals or in color—or as a faked address block.
- Present a humorous cartoon or a striking color display such as a page banner in color or a color item.
- Attach a simple gadget such as a coin, stamp, or coupon.

You should be aware, however, that some tricky openings are like the bang of a door—the noise gets attention, but the attention doesn't last unless the person who hears it is interested in finding out why the door was banged.

If you use an attention-getting device, be sure it leads right into the heart of your message. For instance, you might use a cartoon that is a pictorial presentation of the CSP of your letter, or you might attach a stamp identified as "the postage needed to send for a Passport to Adventure." Remember, any unusual opening should point toward the reader benefits you stress in your letter.

The following are some popular sales-letter openings with sufficient "you attitude" to capture the reader's *interest*—not merely attract momentary attention.

Special Feature or Discount. The effective sales letter shown in Figure 11-5 captures the reader's attention by maintaining the facilities for various types of meetings and those for persons with special needs.

GLOBAL DIVERSITY 11.2

Word Meanings

When selling products in another country, a literal translation may not send the right message. One famous goof was made with Pepsi Cola's "Come Alive with Pepsi" slogan. In Taiwan the literal translation of that slogan was, "Pepsi brings your ancestors back from the grave." *How can you avoid errors like this when advertising in other countries?*

Figure 11-5

The opening of a sales letter should attract the reader's attention.

OUR PLACE

112 Garnet Place • Los Angeles, CA 90024 • Phone 213-555-9292 • FAX 213-555-1129

June 2, <YEAR>

Make Our Place "**your place!**"

Our Place offers the finest accommodations for your business associates who need overnight accommodations. Our guest suites are equipped with comfortable furnishings including a sitting area and a desk. All of our rooms are designed to be accessible to persons with special needs. In addition, our staff is committed to making your guests feel at home while they are living at Our Place.

We also offer facilities and services for all-day meetings as well as conferences that last for several days. Our Place can provide meeting rooms for groups as small as 10 or as large as 100. We will consult with you to determine your needs. Further, we promise to work with you to ensure that your participants are comfortable during their time with us.

For your convenience, a brochure that describes our services as well as an information request card is enclosed. Our Place is ready to greet your business associates and host your next conference. We look forward to hearing from you.

Sincerely,

Julio Cortez

Julio Cortez
Guest Coordinator

mj
Enclosures

Answer to the Reader's Problem. Almost all successful sales-letter openings are variations of this opening—answering a reader's problem. This natural type of opening is usually a winner, because all of us are interested in finding answers to our problems. In this case, the answer is always the use of the product or service advertised.

A sales letter introducing a vacuum cleaner uses this kind of opening.

> You can double your cleaning power *free* for 15 days with America's most advanced vacuum cleaner! We'll include a year's supply of bags *plus a valuable free mystery gift!* Want to revolutionize your cleaning methods? It's easy—with the amazing new Speedo Vacuum cleaner.

Unusual Headline, News Item, or Statement of Fact. An obvious statement, like "Spring is just around the corner" or "School will be starting again in a few weeks," lacks imagination and attracts no attention or interest. On the other hand, an unusual headline, news item, or statement of fact usually leads the prospect to read further.

The following three openings are excerpts from successful sales letters:

> Every issue in government and politics has three sides—the *pro* side, the *con* side, and the *inside.* GOVERNMENT JOURNAL gives you *all* sides.
>
> ATTENTION: PEOPLE WHO HAVE SUBSTANTIAL MONIES IN SAVINGS ACCOUNTS, CERTIFICATES OF DEPOSIT, ETC.
>
> URGENT REMINDER: The deadline is 12:01 a.m.

The sales letter shown in Figure 11-6 on the following page taps the reader's imagination in the opening sentence.

Thought-Provoking Question. A question with an obvious *yes* or *no* answer, such as "Could you use more income?" or "Do you like people to laugh at you behind your back?" is usually boring. In contrast, a question that challenges the reader to do some thinking is an excellent way to arouse interest in a message. Often, a question is better than a statement because it gives the reader a share in the idea of your message—while thinking of an answer to your question, the reader may sell himself or herself on your idea. Naturally, the idea, the answer to the question, involves the use of the product or service you are selling. Look at this example:

> MORE INFLATION AHEAD . . .
>
> WHAT CAN <u>YOU</u> DO ABOUT IT?

Notice the opening question of the letter shown in Figure 11-7 (page 309). This letter is general enough to be set up on a computer and mailed to an entire list of mortgagees (people who have borrowed money).

Witty Comment or an Adaptation of a Familiar Saying. A clever phrase, a play on words, or the adaptation of a familiar saying usually gets attention. If the interpretation suggests disagreement with an accepted idea, it may have particular appeal. Such openings must be closely related to the central selling

Figure 11-6
This sales letter captures the reader's imagination immediately. (Courtesy of First Financial Planners, Inc.)

First Financial Planners, Inc.
FINANCIAL PLANNING

FIRST FINANCIAL PLANNERS BUILDING / 15455 CONWAY ROAD / CHESTERFIELD, MISSOURI 63017 / (314) 537-1040

ROY M. HENRY
President – First Financial Planners, Inc.
Registered Principal – FFP Securities, Inc.
President – FFP Advisory Services, Inc.

November 24, 1997

John Q. Smith
3210 Any Street
Some Town, ST 00000-0000

Dear Mr. Smith:

What if there existed a MAGIC BOX that, if money were placed in it, the funds would:

Accumulate free of State and Federal income tax!

Allow you to borrow from the box as though it were a...

"TAX FREE BANK"

Be contractually guaranteed at little or no cost.

At your death, all of the untaxed assets in the box, minus any loans or withdrawals which will reduce the death benefit, would pass to your heirs totally free of State and Federal income tax!

Guess what?

This Magic Box exists! It is called life insurance--specifically variable universal life insurance.

I'll call you in a few days to show you some ways the Magic Box could work for you or a loved one.

Sincerely,

Roy M. Henry
Registered Principal

* There may be tax implications associated with early surrenders and overfunding of the life insurance.

NOTES

Raising Interest

Remember that if the letter presents a challenging question and involves the use of the product or service, the interest of the reader may be raised.

---

point. Here's an illustration from a Hart Drug Corporation letter about cold medicines:

A HART TO HEART TALK ABOUT A COLD PROPOSITION

Another example is on a letterhead in which the organization name—Dartnell—appears as skywriting:

Skywriting soon disappears . . . but withholding tax is here to stay.

An Anecdote, Fable, or Parable. A story opening—if the story is a good one—usually arouses interest. A good story can be effective as a sales letter opening if it relates to the central selling point of the letter and doesn't overshadow the message itself. Read the following opening from a writer who has placed a bid to win a project:

As a youngster, did you ever toss a stone over a cliff or down a very deep well—then wait and wait to hear it land?

Figure 11-7
Asking a thought-provoking question challenges the reader.

SUNBURST MORTGAGE COMPANY
4000 Parkway Drive • P.O. Box 3412 • Raleigh, NC 10755 • 409-555-3231

November 14, <YEAR>

Mr. Dwayne R. Shelby
2954 Dunedin Cove
Greensboro, NC 27410

Dear Dwayne:

Taking care of yourself and your property is an important responsibility for anyone.

Would you be interested in some help?

You can be protected by an insurance policy as you protect your valued real estate with a mortgage policy that pays whether you live or die. Athough most policies will pay off a remaining balance if you die, Sunburst has gone one step further. Our plan works both ways—if you die, it's insurance; and if you live, it's savings.

This unusual policy may enable you to have the funds you need to pay your mortgage off early, or it could be used to build a cash reserve fund to make your payments in case of financial distress. You can think of several other ways you would like to use these funds, we're sure.

Please take time now to complete and return the enclosed postage-free card. Information will be on its way to you as soon as we receive the card from you. You'll be glad you took the time to make this investment in your future.

Sincerely,

Frank T. Timer

Frank T. Timer, CLU

Enclosure

We tossed a stone down your well, in the form of a price quotation on March 14, and it hasn't landed yet.

Keep the Message Interesting and Informative

Skillfully build the interest aroused by your opening sentences—a sales letter in which even one paragraph drags usually means one more letter in the wastebasket. Your letter about your product or service succeeds when it leads the reader to say, "I didn't know this product or service would do that for me. I want or need it." The letter from Dorothy J. Robinson shown in Figure 11-8 on the following page is a good example of a sales letter that keeps the message interesting and informative.

Build the Message Around the Reader

The benefits the reader thinks a product or service offers will influence his or her decision about buying. Often a prospective customer knows little or nothing about the product or service you are offering and has no interest in learning about your product or service when starting to read your letter.

Figure 11-8
In this sales letter, the message is interesting and informative. (Courtesy of Dorothy J. Robinson.)

DOROTHY J. ROBINSON & ASSOCIATES

446 Oak Street • Danville, Illinois 61832 • (217) 442-5565 • Fax: (217) 442-5589 • **800-373-3019**

November 25, 20___

John Q. Smith
3210 Any Street
Some Town, ST 00000-0000

Dear Mr. Smith:

When you go to a deli to buy some sliced meat, you don't carry it home loose in your hand—you ask them to wrap it. If you plan to freeze some of it to use later—you double wrap it.

What about your money?

Unwrapped money is money in a CD or Passbook account where the gain (usually low) is currently taxed (a 1099 form in the mail each year).

Single wrapped money is money in an annuity, IRA, 401K, etc. where the gain is tax deferred but eventually taxed when you take it out, plus, if you are under age 59 ½, a 10 percent penalty is added.

Double wrapped money is money inside a life insurance contract where the gain is tax deferred and can be accessed on a tax advantaged basis during your lifetime. At death it passes TAX FREE to your beneficiaries, minus any loans or withdrawals, which will reduce the death benefit.

I will call in a few days to set a time when I can show you how double wrapping your money can be a significant advantage to you.

Sincerely,

Dorothy J. Robinson
Registered Representative

Stocks • Bonds • Options • Mutual Funds • Business and Personal Financial Planning • Life, Health, and Disability Insurance
Securities offered through FFP Securities, Inc., Member NASD & SIPC

Bring your reader into the picture by showing how he or she can enjoy your product or service in a special way or how it can save time, energy, or money.

Your sales letter will hold the reader's interest when it gives information on how to live more comfortably or how to do a better job. Specifically, your message may appeal to one or more of these basic desires:

- To be comfortable, healthy, and attractive to others
- To have attention, praise, material possessions, relaxation, and enjoyment
- To avoid pain, trouble, and criticism, or
- To protect personal reputations and families

In your message, you may stress an appeal to desire—an **emotional appeal**—or an appeal to reason—a **rational appeal.** In most cases, however, you will want to touch on both appeals since buying usually depends on both reason and desire.

With the exception of impulse purchases, people seldom buy something just because they have a logical reason for buying it or just because they want it. For example, a rational reason to buy a car is that you *need* it for transportation, but you make decisions about style, color, and other features based on what you *like*.

One benefit of your product or service usually appeals most forcefully to a targeted group of prospects. Make this benefit the central selling point of a letter to that group. As you develop this leading appeal, back it up with a discussion of other benefits that may also appeal to these prospects.

Suppose you are selling shoes, for example. Although your CSP may be your product's durability, you would also certainly want to mention such features as good fit and comfort. In another letter your CSP may be style. In that letter, while stressing that the shoes are stylish, you might also point out that they fit well, are comfortable, and keep their fine appearance with continued wear. In every sales letter, develop the appeal from the reader's viewpoint.

> **NOTES**
>
> **A Varied Approach**
>
> Most successful sales messages combine rational appeals (appeals to reason) and emotional appeals (appeals to desire).

Use Accurate Information and Show Sincere Interest in the Reader

Concentrate on facts, not on opinions or exaggeration. Misinformation in a sales letter is unethical and can endanger the success of your message. Your reader may be fooled by misrepresentation and may believe you once—but certainly not twice. Remember that most organizations depend on *repeat sales* for their profits.

Being sincere in selling includes having confidence that the service you offer will be useful, practical, and economical for the buyer. Your sales message will not reflect sincere interest in the reader unless you believe that when you make a sale, you make a friend. Remember that making friends—developing trust—is the key to making repeat sales.

Convince Your Reader That the Time to Respond Is Now

Imagine yourself talking with, instead of writing to, your prospective buyer. Think of the reasons the prospect might give for not buying or for waiting until later to decide to buy. Then answer those objections in your letter before the reader has a chance to think of them.

At times the reader may object or hesitate because he or she cannot accept all the claims you have made for your product. You must therefore present *evidence* to back up your statements. The following are three kinds of evidence often used to back up sales claims effectively.

> **NOTES**
>
> **One Move Ahead**
>
> Anticipate the prospective buyer's reasons for not buying and answer those objections before the buyer refers to them.

Vivid Description of the Product's or Service's Use. Why does the reader *need* your product or service? To answer this question, take a problem-solving approach. First, you must identify a problem that the reader has. Then, in your letter, present your product or service as a solution to that problem.

> **LEGAL & ETHICAL 11-4**
>
> **Refund Tactic.** A classmate buys a laptop computer with a money-back guarantee. This person uses the computer to write two term papers for his classes and then returns the computer to the store to get a refund. Is this legal? Is this ethical?

Sample, Trial Use, or Money-Back Guarantee. Sometimes you can provide tangible evidence—a free sample or a trial use of your product or service—so that your reader can personally test your claims. Another way to convince the reader that all you say about your product is true is to offer a money-back guarantee. Or you may suggest that no payment is necessary unless or until the customer is satisfied that your product lives up to the sales promises. Notice how well the writer of the following excerpt from a sales letter understands the importance of evidence:

> Perhaps you are skeptical. It's natural for you to want proof about a sales claim. I want to prove mine by having you try the SAFEGUARD system in your own home without me around to put on any pressure. In short, you be the judge. Either the SAFEGUARD system is good—and will work well—or you return it at no cost to you.
>
> You don't need to make up your mind now. Just mail the enclosed postpaid card. In a few days the SAFEGUARD system will be there for you to try.

Performance Facts and Endorsements by Users. Facts based on actual experiences with a product or service or testimonials from current customers offer strong sales support. Both performance facts and testimonials, including authentic endorsements, are sometimes included in sales letters. More often, though, survey and test results, as well as authentic endorsements, are used in brochures or other literature enclosed with a sales letter.

If your reader puts off a decision to buy until later, his or her enthusiasm for your product may cool. To avoid this and encourage an early decision, sales offers may present incentives such as a reduced price or added product or service features. For example, suppose you are trying to persuade a reader to buy an air conditioner in January. The prospective customer may ask,

> Why should I buy now—why not wait until summer?
>
> I just don't have that much money to spend right now.

Your sales letter wouldn't mention these objections, of course, but it could anticipate them. You might want to offer incentives such as the following:

- A reduced January sale price, which will go back to the regular price in February

- A storage plan, by which you keep the air conditioner until the customer requests delivery and installation

- Extended credit arrangements, with the first payment delayed until April 1

Avoid High-Pressure Selling

Never try to force the reader to buy—most people resent being ordered around. Don't even tell the reader he or she needs what you are selling. Instead, you will usually get better results by telling what your product or service can do and then leaving the decision to buy to the reader. Be sure to avoid exaggerated comparisons between your product or service and your competition's product or service.

NOTES

No Bullying
Never try to force the reader to buy.

Introduce the Reader to the Enclosure

If you send a brochure or other enclosure with your sales letter—and you will usually want to do this—you can make the enclosure an integral part of your sales message if you keep two ideas in mind:

- First, refer to any enclosures only after you have provided enough information to interest the reader. Make the reader want to finish reading your letter before making a decision about buying.

- Second, refer to an enclosure by suggesting that the reader observe something interesting about it or by offering the reader a specific course of action. The sentence "I have attached a reply card" sparks no interest and prompts no action on the reader's part. In contrast, the reader is drawn to action by these directions: "All you have to do is check your choices on the enclosed postpaid reservation certificate, fold, seal, and drop it in the mail."

Talk About Price at the Best Psychological Moment

Naturally, somewhere in your letter you must talk about the cost of the item you are selling. Few people will decide to buy a product before they know its cost. If you think the reader will consider your product a bargain at its price, then stress the price—as good news—by mentioning it near the beginning of your letter. In this case, price may even be the central selling point headlined in your opening sentences. On the other hand, if you think your price may seem high to the reader, present it toward the end of your letter—make the reader want your product before he or she knows the cost. Also, make the cost seem less by showing how much the reader will be getting for the money. Notice how cost is linked to benefits in this excerpt from the next-to-last paragraph of a sales letter:

> Teachers and parents have discovered the tremendous value of *Nature Magazine* in educating youngsters through the mystery and fun found only in this fantastic nature-oriented magazine. It's filled with great pictures and true stories about children around the world, science and adventure, games and puzzles—everything a child loves. A gift subscription for a full year (12 issues) of *Nature Magazine* is only $18.

Here's another excerpt showing the same technique:

> Cook with this 21-piece set for 15 days. Fry with it . . . braise with it . . . boil with it. Try your old favorites and take a stab at something new. You're under no obligation. But if you're as delighted as I'm sure you will be . . . keep it—for just $12.95 a month for the next 12 months.

Persuasive Messages

NOTES

Closing Call

The closing paragraph of your sales letter is often the key to getting the reader to act.

Close With a Request for Action

The closing paragraph of your letter is often the key to getting the reader to act. The closing paragraph should tell him or her exactly what to do—without specific, easy-to-follow directions, the reader may only *think* about buying your product or service. Be positive when you request action—assume the reader wants to do as you ask. The following are examples of positive, specific requests for action:

- Ask the reader to fill out and send in the enclosed order form.
- Ask the reader to come into the store for a demonstration session—tell *where* and *when* the session will take place and *what* it will include.
- Ask the reader to invite a representative to call, and give the representative's name, phone number, and office hours.

Whenever you can, point out a reason for acting at once. Remember that the longer the reader waits before acting on your suggestion, the less likely he or she will be to act at all. Even when the reader is interested in your product and wants to buy, a little push for action from you is usually needed. Your closing paragraph can provide this push with a *three-way call for action*—in closing, tell the reader all of the following:

- What to do
- How to do it (make it easy)
- Why it should be done promptly

Notice how the italicized words in these closing paragraphs from an effective sales promotion letter demonstrate the three-way call for action.

> Take just a moment to *jot your name on the enclosed postpaid order card, drop it into a convenient mailbox,* and we'll see that your E-Z Go pullcart is on the way in less than a week.
>
> If you send a check or money order, we'll pay all express charges. Or, if you prefer, we'll send the pullcart COD. Just *check the appropriate box on the order card.*
>
> With an E-Z Go pullcart, *your next round of golf will be the easiest and most enjoyable you have ever played!*

Short closing paragraphs often combine the three elements of a call for action in one or two sentences:

> There's no need to bother with a check at this time—I'll be glad to bill you later—but do *avoid missing a single exciting issue* of LEISURE TRAVEL by *returning the postpaid card today.*

Look at the Superior Mobile Communications sales letter shown in Figure 11-9. This letter doesn't use a high-pressure sales approach, but it does ask for action in its last paragraph.

Go to CD-ROM
Activity 11-5
To test your skills.

Figure 11-9
Closing with a request for action prompts the reader to respond.

SUPERIOR MOBILE COMMUNICATIONS
10 Schrock Road • Westerville, OH 43081 • 614-555-5536

October 8, <YEAR>

Mr. Charles H. Gold
936 Lane Road
Columbus, OH 43230

Dear Mr. Gold:

Since business demands a great deal of you--making your time very limited and your decisions critical--when you need answers, you need them NOW.

Superior Mobile Communications understands your need for fast responses. We can help you put the resources you need within fingertip reach anywhere you travel. How? Through car telephone service you can maintain constant contact with your office and important clients. You can make those necessary decisions and meet those crucial deadlines from the convenience of your own car.

Literally thousands of busy executives, just like you, are using car telephone service every day to improve their business by converting wasted travel time into productive travel time.

Give me a call at 614-555-5536, or complete and return the enclosed reply card. I'll be happy to answer any questions you may have and to provide you with a personal demonstration on the cost savings of a car telephone.

Don't let another day go by. Call today and stay in touch tomorrow.

Sincerely,

SUPERIOR MOBILE COMMUNICATIONS

Paula R. Martin

Paula R. Martin
Personal Communications Representative
Mobile Telephone Sales

dms
Enclosure

Checkpoint 11.2

1. Identify one advantage and one disadvantage of sending indirect sales letters.

2. For you, what would be the most challenging and the easiest part of writing a sales letter?

3. In your opinion, why is high-pressure selling usually not effective?

Writing Sales Letters to Dealers

Before you prepare a sales promotion letter for a prospective customer, ask yourself, "How will this customer benefit from the product or service I'm selling?" Then plan your letter around the answer: your product will help

Persuasive Messages

your reader have more fun, do a better job and do it more quickly and easily, or to save money.

When the prospective customer is a dealer (an authorized sales agent), you should ask the same question. The answers—the benefit to the reader—will be different, however. Dealers are interested in products and services that will help them play their own role (to sell the products to consumers) better and will increase their profits and decrease their expenses. You will, therefore, need to use a somewhat different sales approach in your letters to dealers.

You can stress two important benefits in your sales letters to dealers: turnover and markup.

Emphasize a Quick Turnover

Naturally, a retailer is more interested in how much product can be sold in a short time than in any other fact about the product. No matter how much potential profit can be made on an item, as long as it sits on the shelf, it earns no profit for the dealer. Letters to dealers should therefore stress how fast a product will sell—how fast it will "turn over"—and give facts to prove its popularity with the dealer's customers.

Stress a Profitable Dealer Markup

After salability, the dealer's next interest is **markup,** the difference between the price the dealer pays for the product and the price at which it is sold. (This difference is not the profit; other selling expenses must be deducted before the dealer makes any profit. Turnover and markup, however, are important factors in determining the profit.) Your sales letter should convince the dealer that the difference between buying price and selling price is large enough to ensure a worthwhile profit.

The opening paragraph in letters to dealers usually captures attention and arouses interest if it tells what a product or service can do for the reader. A successful opening may be a direct comment about the salability of a product and the markup on the product, as is the following:

A quick sale and a 60 percent markup are yours

When a customer spots

EASY-BOY DELUXE RECLINERS

On your showroom floor!

When you are writing a sales letter to a dealer, make sure to adapt your whole letter to the dealer. Talk about customers' use of your product and the features they will like. Talk about prices and the advantages of buying in quantity. Also, stress the ways in which you (the manufacturer and/or distributor) can help the dealer increase the sale of your products. The following are examples of aids you might offer to the dealer for this purpose:

- National advertising, which will bring customers into the dealer's store asking for the advertised product or service
- Copy for the dealer's newspaper advertising

Figure 11-10
This promotional letter informs the receiver of a promotional package.

Promotions Unlimited
1192 South College Street
Ann Arbor, MI 48104
313-555-4831

February 25, <YEAR>

Mr. Anthony DeLourdes
102 Vaughn Street
Ann Arbor, MI 48104

Dear Mr. DeLourdes:

How do your customers react to the words "FREE" and "WIN"? The TREASURE CHEST (shown in detail in the enclosed brochure) will appeal to passersby because you offer them the opportunity to WIN it! All the prospective customer has to do is complete an entry form with name and address and drop the form into a box!

In one package, you get everything you need for a successful promotion: the TREASURE CHEST containing prizes for the whole family, a giant colorful window poster, 1000 entry forms, and an entry box.

The cost? Only $49.95 each! The result? The TREASURE CHEST will bring shoppers inside your doors!

Take a moment to fill in the postpaid order card and drop it into the mail. Your TREASURE CHEST will be shipped the day after we receive your order. If you're not completely satisfied, just return the package within 10 days, and you will owe nothing.

If you enclose your check with your order, we'll prepay all freight charges.

Sincerely,

Andre Perkins

Andre Perkins
Senior Marketing Manager

Enclosures

- Store display materials and suggestions
- Envelope stuffers (flyers), posters, catalogs, and other publicity items

A variation of the dealer sales letter is seen in the letter about a promotional package offered by Promotions Unlimited (Figure 11-10).

Replies to Inquiries as Sales Letters

Every inquiry you receive about your products or services is important because it opens a door for your sales message. Sales promotion letters written to answer these requests for information are often called **invited,** or **solicited, sales letters.**

The big difference between invited sales letters and other sales promotion letters is that you start invited sales letters with a direct answer to a question asked in an inquiry. You do not need the attention-getting openers used in sales promotion letters because you already have your reader's interest—the reader is interested in the answers to his or her questions. You can best hold that interest by answering all questions—direct and implied—completely and promptly.

NOTES

Sales Invited
Sales promotion letters written to answer requests for information are called invited, or solicited, sales letters.

PERSUASIVE MESSAGES

Figure 11-11
This sales cover letter invites the reader to make an appointment.

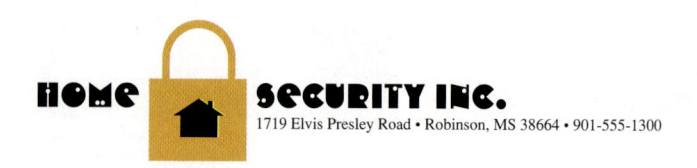

HOME SECURITY INC.
1719 Elvis Presley Road • Robinson, MS 38664 • 901-555-1300

June 19, <YEAR>

Mr. David Hearst
3801 Priscilla Road
Memphis, TN 38119-7229

Dear Mr. Hearst:

The FBI Uniform Crime Report states that 85 percent of home burglaries are performed by amateurs. These unskilled amateurs are in the home an average of 4 to 7 minutes because they know it takes the police an average of 13 minutes to respond to an alarm.

They literally run through your home looking for anything of value, anything that can be sold easily. They know they don't have the time to spend looking for things that are not readily accessible to them because the police are going to be there in a few minutes. Let me emphasize that this all takes place whether there is an existing alarm system or not.

No one can do anything to completely stop the professional. But Home Security, Inc. has come up with a way to cost him or her a lot of time and trouble and to virtually eliminate the theft of your valuables by the amateur.

As illustrated in the enclosed brochure, the product you need is a safe—custom-built to specifications, completely fireproof and completely hidden somewhere in the home, office, or car. The safe includes a specially designed double-entry system and is placed in a location easy for the owner to get to but completely hidden from anyone else. We have just eliminated 85 percent of the burglars.

Our concept is quite simple: "If they can't find it, they can't steal it." We can proudly say that for more than ten years in business, not one of our safes has ever been found.

We look forward to talking with you about incorporating this convenient system in your home. I will call you next week to set up an appointment.

Sincerely,

Ronald E. Anderson

Ronald E. Anderson
Account Manager

lac
Enclosure

In invited sales letters you should, of course, stress the advantages to the reader of using your product or service. You should also close with the three-way call for action, which tells your reader (1) what to do, (2) how to do it (make it easy), and (3) why it should be done promptly.

For help in writing a sales letter in reply to an inquiry, refer to Chapter 9, "Messages for Inquiries and Requests."

Cover Letters as Sales Letters

Cover letters often succeed as sales messages and may be as effective for that purpose as answers to inquiries or as uninvited cold-turkey sales letters. Look at the Home Security letter shown in Figure 11-11, which illustrates this type of letter. For a review of cover letters, reread "Cover Letters" in Chapter 9.

Writing a Sales Letter Series

A series of sales promotion letters may be sent to prospective buyers when the seller feels that one letter won't accomplish the job of selling the product or service. The two most common kinds of sales letter series are the wear-out series and the campaign series.

Wear-Out Series

In the wear-out series, a number of sales letters are prepared. *Each is complete in itself and independent of any other letters or advertising plans.* The first letter is sent to a selected list of prospects. Then other letters are sent at intervals to each prospect. The series continues for as long as the seller believes the prospect may still be in the market. Every letter in the series tries to get an order. This type of letter series is used chiefly for selling inexpensive merchandise. An example might be a series of letters to sell scale model antique cars.

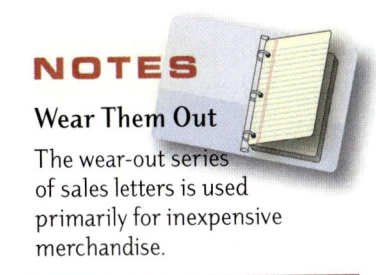

> **NOTES**
>
> **Wear Them Out**
> The wear-out series of sales letters is used primarily for inexpensive merchandise.

Campaign Series

In the campaign sales series, a number of sales letters are prepared. *Each one builds on the preceding one.* As you plan these letters, decide on the number of letters to be sent and the intervals—often 10 to 15 days—at which they will be sent. Plan to send a complete series of letters to each prospect; ordinarily, you would not expect an order from your prospect until all the letters had been received. Frequently, this direct mail advertising is coordinated with newspaper, magazine, radio, and TV publicity. This type of letter series is used primarily for selling expensive merchandise. An example might be a very expensive luxury car.

Chapter 11 Summary

In persuasive messages you are selling your ideas as well as your organization's image and goodwill. The four types of persuasive messages discussed in this chapter are letters to public officials, letters to the media, persuasive requests, and sales messages. Either the direct approach or the persuasive approach (depending on your topic) may be used in the letters to public officials and letters to the media. Remember, in the direct approach, start with your request and follow with your reasons, explanations, and selling points; in the persuasive approach, wait until the end of your message to ask for the action you want. The persuasive approach is also used for persuasive requests asking for donations, cooperation, gifts, or favors, and for sales letters written to sell a product or service. The persuasive approach usually uses the AIDA formula—attention, interest, desire, and action.

Take a moment to review the chapter before you complete the exercises in the following Worksheets. You may also want to complete the following Online Exercises if you have access to the Internet.

Online Exercises

Chapter 11

Objective:
These online activities will allow you to practice writing persuasive messages.

Go to **bcw.glencoe.com,** the address for the *Business Communication at Work* Web site, and select Chapter 11. Next, click on Online Exercises. You will see a list of Web site links that will bring you to government related Web sites and online newspapers.

Activity 11.1

1. Select one of the government related Web sites to visit. You may also select an online newspaper to visit.
2. Click on information about a government official (senator, representative, governor, etc.) where you live. You may have to click on several links to find the information. If you chose an online newspaper, enter the name of one of your government officials in the **Search** box.
3. On a sheet of paper, write a letter to your government official about an issue that concerns you. Remember to include the following information:
    a. Give complete information about how you can be contacted.
    b. Address your lawmaker properly.
    c. Use a subject line.
    d. Limit your letter to one topic.
4. Write your name on your letter, and hand it in to your instructor.

Activity 11.2

1. Select one of the online newspapers to visit.
2. Click on the editorial/opinion link. On some Web sites, you may have to click on the print edition link first.
3. Find an editorial/opinion article that you find interesting and read it. If you do not find an article that interests you, return to the *Business Communication at Work* Web site and select another online newspaper to visit.
4. On a sheet of paper, write a letter to the editor expressing your opinion about the article you read. Remember to follow these guidelines when writing your letter:
    a. Get right to the point.
    b. Be brief.
    c. Be rational.
    d. Use good taste.
    e. Be fair.
5. Write your name on your letter, and hand it in to your instructor.

CHAPTER 11 WORKSHEETS

NAME _____ DATE _____

PRACTICE 1

Persuasive Messages

Instructions: Respond to the following situations concerning persuasive messages as directed.

1. If you were to write to a lawmaker about the following issues, indicate the most appropriate level of lawmaker you would write to—federal, state, county, or local. If you have difficulty with these, you may study about the different branches of government before you continue. Your instructor will probably have some excellent resources to suggest. You may want to research these topics on the Internet.

   a. Social Security _____
   b. One six-year term for the President _____
   c. Selective service system _____
   d. The court system _____
   e. Public aid _____
   f. Aid to families with dependent children _____
   g. Mail service _____
   h. State lottery _____
   i. Illegal aliens _____
   j. Violence and sex on television _____
   k. The prison system _____
   l. The death penalty _____
   m. Financing for our public and private schools _____
   n. Drugs and drug abuse _____
   o. Drunk driving _____
   p. Gun control _____
   q. Missing and/or abused children _____
   r. Changing the national speed limit _____
   s. Nuclear weapons and nuclear war _____
   t. Military spending and military strength _____
   u. The space program _____
   v. The economy _____
   w. Medical care and/or Medicare _____
   x. Government spending _____
   y. Any other topic that relates to problems or issues in your state, city, or county _____

CHAPTER 11 WORKSHEETS

NAME _____ DATE _____

2. Indicate whether the following letters to lawmakers would be service letters or legislative letters by writing **S** for service or **L** for legislative in each blank.

   _____ a. A letter to request that people over 65 be exempt from paying capital gains tax.

   _____ b. A letter to get disability payments for your father, who has health problems and is no longer able to work.

   _____ c. A letter requesting graduated drivers' licenses for people under 18.

   _____ d. A letter requesting a decrease in the penalty for underestimating state income tax.

   _____ e. A letter requesting mandatory car insurance for drivers.

   _____ f. A letter requesting help to get your aunt's social security checks corrected.

3. The following letter was written to persuade a company to replace a lawnmower that would not start. Analyze the letter and indicate improvements that should be made in the organization and content.

   > March 15, <YEAR>
   >
   > Ladies and Gentlemen:
   >
   > You sold me a piece of junk! At Christmastime I bought a factory-rebuilt lawnmower with a 30-day warranty. With all the cold weather and rain we've had the last 2 months, I had no occasion to use the lawnmower until today. When I tried to start it--nothing! The motor ground a few times but it never started. I want you to live up to your advertisements that say, "Satisfaction Guaranteed." It's not my fault the weather has been so bad. The 30 days should start from the first day I used the mower.
   >
   > Angrily,

4. Write the closing paragraph of a persuasive request to ask Jewel Martin to be a guest speaker in one of your classes. You want her to share her experiences of starting a new job after graduating from college last year.

   _____
   _____
   _____
   _____
   _____

CHAPTER 11 WORKSHEETS

NAME _____ DATE _____

PRACTICE 2

Sales Letters

Instructions: Develop your skills at writing sales letters by responding to the following situations.

1. Use each of the following ideas to write the opening sentence for a sales letter that will capture the reader's attention and interest (you pick the product or service):

   a. Special price or discount

   _____

   b. Answer to the reader's problem

   _____

   c. Unusual headline, news item, or statement of fact

   _____

   d. Thought-provoking question

   _____

   e. Witty comment or an adaptation of a familiar saying

   _____

   f. Anecdote, fable, or parable

   _____

2. Collect three pieces of direct mail advertising, and identify the AIDA parts of each letter (attention, interest, desire, action).

3. On a separate sheet of paper, list the appeals (both emotional and rational) used in each of the three letters you collected for Question 2 of Practice 2.

4. If you were writing a letter to sell clothes, list several appeals that you would use to get the prospective buyer to purchase the clothes. Indicate which one would be your central selling point.

_____

PRACTICE 3

Letters That Persuade

Instructions: Make a letter plan before writing these letters.

1. **Lawmaker letter.** Look up the names and addresses of the lawmakers who represent you. Pick an issue that is of interest to you, and write (preferably keyboard) a letter to the appropriate lawmaker. Remember to write to your state lawmakers about state issues and to your federal lawmakers about national laws and issues. Before you write, research your topic by reading articles in newspapers and periodicals. (In addition to looking at current subjects in the news for a topic, review the list of ideas in Practice 1, Question 1.) Make your letter plan when you feel comfortable with the issues presented.

Persuasive Messages 323

CHAPTER 11 WORKSHEETS

NAME _____ DATE _____

2. **Persuasive request letter.** You are the president of your local high school's Band Boosters, and you are organizing a fund-raiser to send the band to perform at Disney World. Write a letter to a local restaurant to ask them to donate a gift certificate for a free meal to use in a silent auction. Make your letter plan before you start writing.

3. **Persuasive request letter.** As president of the Student Advisory Council of your school, write a persuasive request to Don Newcombe, a noted lecturer, whose office address is 104 Harvey, Philippi, WV 26416. Ask Mr. Newcombe to address an assembly on the topic "Drugs and Alcohol." The assembly will be the first Friday of next month at 2 p.m. in the Conference Center. You will pay travel, meal, and hotel expenses but no fee. Make your letter plan before you start writing.

Check your letter plan by the following:

_____ 1. Get the reader's attention.
_____ 2. Appeal to the reader's interest in the topic.
_____ 3. Give the topic and day, date, time, and place of the event.
_____ 4. Discuss financial arrangements.
_____ 5. Ask for a reply by (date).
_____ What changes did you make in your plan? Why?

4. **Persuasive request letter.** As November approaches, the general manager of the FM radio station Rock 103—The Eagle—asks you to assist in preparing for the "Coats for Kids" charity project. Following the general manager's instructions, write a persuasive request in the form of a script to be read on the air. Read the note from Sharon Anderson and use the following letter plan:
   1. Get the listeners' attention.
   2. Announce the name of the project.
   3. Explain to listeners what you want them to do.
   4. Give them some ideas on where to get coats (used, old, or outgrown coats, and so on).
   5. Tell them what Rock 103 will do with coats they donate (remember to plug Swift Cleaners).
   6. Remind them how good they will feel about helping the homeless.
   7. Make it easy to respond by asking them to use your drop box on their way to work.

**FROM THE DESK OF
SHARON ANDERSON**

Debbie,

Please write the script for our public service announcement for the annual "Coats for Kids" Christmas project. Ask our listeners to donate their used coats to be cleaned, compliments of Swift Cleaners at 1400 Poplar Avenue. The coats will be sorted by size, cleaned, and given to the homeless.

Be sure to mention the convenient drop box on our parking lot at Fourth and Front and that we need the coats by November 15 to allow time for cleaning.

CHAPTER 11 WORKSHEETS

Name _____ Date _____

PRACTICE 4

Promotion Letters

Instructions: Plan and prepare (preferably keyboard) sales promotion letters that present the products described in the following exercises. Write to prospective buyers in terms of the buyers' needs and desires. Supply sufficient specific details to make each letter an effective sales message.

1. **Sales letter.** Your product is a subscription to a newspaper or magazine. Select a newspaper or magazine that you read regularly. Compose a sales letter to persuade your readers that they will find it as enjoyable and as worthwhile as you do.

2. **Sales letter.** Write a letter to convince the readers of your monthly magazine that they should buy a special publication featuring ten great mystery stories. If readers order the book, they will receive a free bonus gift; they may return the book within seven days if not satisfied. The hardbound volume consists of 931 pages and has sixty-one full color illustrations. The book costs $19.98, payable in three monthly installments of $6.66 with no charge for interest, postage, or handling.

3. **Sales letter.** As a representative of a large mail-order house, write a letter to consumers to promote insulated boots made of water-resistant leather. The boots are ideal for work or sport. They are available in men's sizes 7-12, widths B-E, and sell for $72.99 (5 inches high) or $82.99 (7 inches high). They also have a one-year warranty: If a leak occurs because of defects in material or manufacture, the boots will be replaced. You are enclosing an order form. Payment may be made by check, charge card, or COD.

4. **Sales letter to dealers.** Plan and write a letter in which you try to sell at least 100 leather pocket appointment books (for the coming year) to a retailer for Christmas stock. They make good-looking gifts at a price that the dealer's customers will appreciate—and at a markup the dealer will like. Be sure to describe the books' features and uses as the customers will see them. (Add details as you prefer.) You are enclosing an order form and postpaid envelope. The retail price for a book is $3.97; the dealer's cost is $1.99 each, or $1.79 each for an order of 100 or more.

Persuasive Messages

CHAPTER 12

Order, Credit, and Collection Messages

Objectives

After completing this chapter, you will be able to:

1. Describe the process of ordering merchandise
2. Write effective order letters
3. Discuss ordering by phone, fax, and the Internet
4. Describe the different formats for replying to orders
5. Discuss the situations in which sending an order acknowledgment is required
6. Compose routine and special acknowledgments
7. Write an acknowledgment refusing an order
8. Request credit
9. Discuss the steps to perform a credit reference check
10. Write messages that extend or refuse credit
11. Design a collection letter series and list the techniques used

WORKPLACE APPLICATIONS

Constructive Criticism

When you make a mistake and don't realize it, you probably want someone to set you straight. You may not enjoy having your efforts criticized, but, at the same time, you can't learn from your mistakes if you are not aware of them. Criticism, then, is an unpleasant but sometimes necessary tool. **Constructive criticism** is the *only* kind of criticism that is acceptable in the workplace. It focuses solely on the error, not on the person who made it. The point of constructive criticism is to offer suggestions that a worker can use to improve his or her performance.

Critical Guidelines

If you offer constructive criticism to a coworker, the following steps can help:

- Meet with the person in private, and then point out the person's error. Focus only on the error. *Example:* "Nina, I noticed that you have not been signing out when you leave the office."

- Explain your concern about the error. If you mention your feelings, be sure to focus on the error as the cause, not the person. "The staff and I are often frustrated because we waste time hunting for you."

- Suggest a specific change or correction. "Why don't you make sure you walk by the sign-out board on your way out?"

- Assure the person of his or her value before ending the conversation. "Your input is important. That's why we need to know where you are throughout the day."

Always be polite and professional when giving criticism. Also, be prompt. Don't wait until your coworker's error becomes a chronic habit. If you are on the receiving end of constructive criticism, stay calm, be positive, and, if necessary, apologize. Try to see the problem from your coworker's point of view.

Thinking Critically

Situation: A coworker has volunteered to key in and distribute notes from the weekly meeting. Twice this month he has not delivered the notes before the next meeting. Without the notes, time is wasted as people discuss items that have already been resolved in previous meetings.

Ask Yourself: How would you offer constructive criticism to your coworker? What suggestion would you make?

> **The first order of business is an order; without an order, there is no business.**
>
> —Unknown

Orders are the lifeblood of any organization. Without orders for its products and/or services, a business organization cannot survive, but getting the orders is only half the battle. Receiving payment is just as important in keeping an organization in business. In this chapter we will discuss messages that deal with placing orders (by both traditional and electronic methods), writing order letters, acknowledging orders, buying on credit, and collecting payments.

SENDING ORDER MESSAGES

With today's technology, there are many convenient ways (both oral and written) for customers to order products and services. These include completing and mailing or faxing purchase order forms, placing orders by phone or fax, and ordering via the Internet.

Mail-Order Forms

Some organizations sell their merchandise only through mail-order catalogs. Many other companies also market their products through catalogs. Mail-order companies include **order forms** with their catalogs for the following reasons:

- They help the buyer give complete order information.
- They are faster and easier to read than order letters.
- They are convenient for both the buyer and the seller.

Thinking Cap 12.1

Discuss: Why can't private shipping companies or carriers such as Airborne, UPS, etc., deliver to a post office box?

When you are completing an order form, remember that only the United States Postal Service can deliver to a post office box number—all other shipping companies (FedEx, Airborne, UPS, etc.) require a street address. Mail orders usually include an additional charge for shipping and handling, which is paid by the buyer. In addition, some organizations are required to charge sales tax. Sales tax rates vary from state to state.

Sometimes you may want to send an order by mail, but no order form is available, or you need to include explanations that will not fit on the order form. In this case, you will need to write an **order letter.**

Order Letters

Order letters are easy to write because (1) capturing the attention and interest of your reader is no problem (your letter is bringing business), and (2) no convincing or persuading the reader is necessary. All you have to do is write a letter that can be read quickly and that makes it easy for the reader to fill your order. If you write clearly enough to let the recipient know exactly what you want and make satisfactory plans to pay for it, you'll get a response.

When you write an order letter, you should use the direct approach. For clarity, an order letter should contain the same information that an order form does. You should give every order letter the **who, what, where, when, why,** and **how** test to be certain it will accomplish its intended purpose. The following are five guidelines for writing effective order letters.

Write Orders, Not Just Hints

Legally, an order letter is the "offer" portion of a contract. The "acceptance" portion of the contract is completed when the seller sends an acknowledgment or sends the merchandise. When writing orders, be sure to use specific and direct openings such as "Please send me . . ." or "Please ship . . ." rather than vague phrases such as "I've been thinking about . . . ," "I'm interested in . . . ," or "I'd like to . . . ."

Give a Complete Description of Each Item

Include the following information in your order letter:

- Name of product
- Catalog (or model or stock) number
- Description of product, including the following, if appropriate:
    1. color
    2. size
    3. material
    4. grade or quality
    5. pattern
    6. finish, and
    7. any other details available
- Unit price
- Quantity
- Total price for desired quantity
- Any other related information that would help identify the exact product you are ordering, such as where the product was advertised

Give the Order Information in a Clear Format

To make your letter easy to read, do either of the following:

- Write one, single-spaced paragraph for each item you are ordering, and separate the paragraphs with double spacing.
- Arrange your order in a table format similar to that of an order blank.

When you are giving several sets of items, quantities, and prices, you will find that using a table format makes your message clearer than writing the information in sentences.

> **NOTES**
>
> **Writing Orders**
>
> An order letter should include the same information that you find on an order form. Apply the *who, what, where, when, why,* and *how* test to order letters.

Tell How You Will Pay for the Order

Indicate which of the following forms of payment you will use:

- Personal or company check
- Cash on delivery (c.o.d.)
- Money order
- Credit card

If you want your order to be charged to a credit card, give the name of the credit card, the credit card number, and the expiration date printed on the card. Also, if the printed name on the credit card differs from the signature and keyed name on the order letter, be sure to include the exact name of the cardholder. Remember to add any applicable shipping charges and sales tax to the total cost of your order. (See Figure 12-1.)

Tell Where and When You Want the Merchandise Shipped

In your order letter, specify a shipping address, or ask to have the merchandise sent to your return address found at the top of the letter or below your keyed name. Also, if you need the order by a certain date, be sure to include that date in your order letter. If you have a preference regarding the method of shipment, you will need to specify that. Otherwise, the seller will choose the shipping

Figure 12-1
This is a well-written letter that follows the five guidelines for order letters.

ACCURATE CPAs

- 132 Voorhees Street
- Harrogate, TN 37752
- 1-800-555-9756
- Fax 1-800-555-9756
- e-mail: accurate_CPA@acc.com

February 25, <YEAR>

Compudata Corp.
1557 S. Grove Highway
LaPlume, PA 18440

Ladies and Gentlemen:

Please send me the following, as advertised in your Fall/Winter catalog on page 39.

Quantity	Item No.	Description	Price	Amount
2	143-A	TaxFax Software	$69.95	$139.90
1	189-B	Protec Software	$23.75	$23.75
			Subtotal	$163.65
		Add shipping and handling charges		$7.00
			TOTAL	$170.65

Enclosed is my Check 1226 for $170.65. Please ship the software to the address in the letterhead. We would appreciate receiving the software by March 7.

Sincerely,

Carol Willis

Carol Willis
Office Manager

bs
Enclosure

Chapter 12

method and will send the merchandise when it is convenient. This may be a problem for you if, for example, you need the merchandise in a hurry. In that case, you may be willing to pay the extra cost for overnight delivery.

Merchandise is shipped either **FOB destination** or **FOB shipping point**. (FOB stands for "free on board.") If merchandise is shipped FOB shipping point, the buyer pays shipping charges over and above the cost of the merchandise. If merchandise is shipped FOB destination, the seller pays the shipping charges, and those charges are included in the price of the merchandise. For example, if merchandise is shipped FOB Chicago, the seller pays the shipping charges to Chicago, and the buyer pays the shipping charges from Chicago to the destination.

> **NOTES**
>
> **Free on Board**
> Merchandise is shipped FOB destination (seller pays shipping charges) or FOB shipping point (buyer pays shipping charges).

Phone and Fax Orders

Radio, television, newspapers, magazines, and newsletters all carry ads to sell products and services. These advertisements often give a phone or fax number (usually toll-free) you can use for ordering. One advantage of ordering this way is that it enables you to find out immediately if the product you want is in stock or if it can be back-ordered. You can also get the approximate date of delivery.

When ordering by telephone or fax, you should give the same information you give in a written order letter. Be cautious, however, when giving your credit card number over the phone for payment—make sure that someone does not overhear you and later use your credit card for unauthorized expenditures. A good rule of thumb is this—if you initiate the call, it is usually safe to give your credit card number for payment. If someone calls you (a telemarketer) to sell a product or service, then you should be more cautious about giving out your credit card number.

Make notes about your phone order, including the date and time you called as well as the name of the person with whom you spoke. In other words, you can create your own written record of the order.

> **Go to CD-ROM**
> **Activity 12-1**
> To test your skills.

Internet Orders

Online shopping is in its infancy, but it is growing fast. Many products and services can now be purchased from Web sites on the Internet. You can click through products on a shopping Web site just as you would flip through the pages of a catalog. Select the product(s) you wish to order, key in your credit card number and shipping information, and click to send your order to the company offering the item for sale.

The main concern consumers have about online shopping is the fear of sending credit card information over the Internet. Because of this concern, many shopping sites on the Web automatically encrypt all of the personal information of the buyer as well as the buyer's credit card information. **Encrypting** the information means it is scrambled and can't be read as it travels over the Internet. Once the buyer's order and payment information arrives at its destination, it is locked into a computer that has no connection to the Internet.

> **Internet**
>
> **Virtual Bookshelves**
> Go to amazon.com and look at the information on some of the millions of book titles listed. Verify the ordering instructions.

Order, Credit, and Collection Messages

To counteract consumers' fear, credit card companies are using a system called Secure Electronic Transactions (SET). This system was jointly developed by MasterCard and Visa for transmitting credit information over public networks. SET assures consumers that the seller's payment procedure has been tested for security. This is usually indicated by the appearance of a lock symbol on the bottom of the screen.

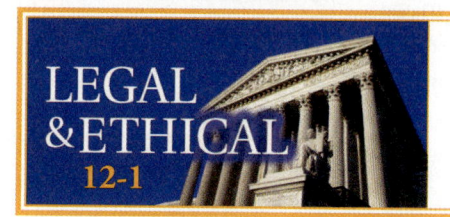

LEGAL & ETHICAL 12-1

Hidden Charges. An ad offers antique coins for sale for $59 each. Nothing is said about any other costs. You order a coin, and when the invoice arrives, it includes a shipping fee of $10 and a handling fee of $15. The postage on the small box is $3. Even if this is legal, is it ethical? What would your response be?

Acknowledging Order Messages

NOTES

Prompt Response

Acknowledging an order is an opportunity to resell your product and your organization as well as encourage future orders. Acknowledgments should be sent promptly.

Legally, an acknowledgment message completes the contract of a sale; but for the seller, its major purpose is to encourage future orders. Although some organizations take orders for granted and think acknowledgments are unnecessary, you should remember that orders may not be routine for the buyer. A letter acknowledging an order can actually be an excellent opportunity to resell your product and your organization. The acknowledgment should be sent promptly to take advantage of the opportunity to resell your organization and its products.

Form Replies to Orders

Types of order acknowledgment used by businesses include the following: postal cards, acknowledgment forms, duplicate invoices, or form letters.

Postal Cards

Postal cards with "filled-in" or "merged" information are particularly favored by large organizations doing business with customers by mail, such as catalog houses and large department stores. Some of these firms send cards printed with general acknowledgments, but most firms use preprinted cards that provide space for filling in details about a specific order and the expected date of shipment. (See Figure 12-2.) Sending these acknowledgment cards is especially important when the merchandise is being shipped to someone other than the buyer.

Acknowledgment Forms

Acknowledgment forms are usually set up like a form letter with several different items and a box in front of each. The sender simply puts a check mark in front of the items that apply to the particular order.

Deutsch Brothers

Dear Customer:

Thank you for your order for:

    10 Tallman White Dress Shirts
    Size 16 x 34, Style A

Your order is scheduled to be shipped on:

    Tuesday, September 23, <YEAR>

Figure 12-2
Many businesses use acknowledgment cards that can be filled in and mailed quickly.

Thinking Cap 12.2

Discuss: If you order a gift box of cheese and jelly to be sent to a friend as a gift, why is it important for the seller to send you an acknowledgment card?

Duplicate Invoices

When an order is processed, the seller must prepare an invoice or a bill. At that time, an extra copy of the invoice can be made and marked as an "Acknowledgment—This Is Not an Invoice," or something similar. The acknowledgment copy can then be sent to the customer immediately. When the customer receives it, he or she will know that the seller is processing the order. The customer also knows the final cost and the payment terms. Often the shipping date is shown, too. Remember that a duplicate invoice is the least effective method of acknowledgment because many customers resent receiving a copy of the bill before receiving the merchandise they ordered.

Form Letters

Individual letters do the best job of building goodwill. With the technology available today and the ease of personalizing letters, individual acknowledgment letters are becoming economically feasible. We will discuss the content and outline for letters like these later in this chapter.

    Form replies to acknowledge orders should reflect the same care in preparation that your organization gives to filling an order. Sending an unprofessional-looking card or letter may give a customer the impression that you will also be sloppy in processing his or her order. Or a cold, formal acknowledgment may make a customer see your organization as cold, formal, and uncaring.

    You can use form acknowledgments successfully if you remember that no matter how many orders you get each day, each order is important to the customer who sent it. The form letters you use to acknowledge orders should be revised and updated periodically so your frequent customers will not feel as if they are being taken for granted.

Thinking Cap 12.3

Discuss: What is the advantage of sending an acknowledgment form with the appropriate items checked over an individually written acknowledgment letter?

Order, Credit, and Collection Messages

Situations Requiring Acknowledgments

An acknowledgment is a must in the following situations:

Customers' First Orders

Never miss the opportunity to make your first impression on a customer a positive one. You want to welcome the customer and encourage him or her to buy from you again.

Incomplete or Unclear Orders

When information is missing in an order, it is important to get the missing information so that you can fill the order. When asking for this information do not criticize your customer. Don't tell them they forgot something—just *ask* for the information you need, and encourage a quick response by enclosing a reply envelope.

Unusually Large Orders

When you receive a large order, you can build goodwill for future business by letting your customer know that you noticed and appreciated it.

Orders for Discontinued Items

When you receive an order for a discontinued item, you have a real opportunity for selling when you suggest an alternate product. You may do this by sending a form message to the customer with printed information about the substitute item. Look at the form acknowledgment shown in Figure 12-3. The form is part of the wraparound (printed material that is folded and fastened around an enclosure) used to hold the enclosed information about the substitute item. The back page of this form is the order blank.

Orders Requiring a Delay in Shipment

Occasionally an item will be out of stock; therefore, it must be back-ordered and shipped later. You can help keep the customer's goodwill by informing him or her when shipment can be expected.

Figure 12-3
This message form gives important information to customers.

Deutsch Brothers

THANK YOU FOR YOUR ORDER...

We have something similar to what you ordered—a flyer with a picture and description of it are enclosed.

For your convenience, an order form and postpaid return envelope are enclosed.

Remember Deutsch Brothers' money-back guarantee ensures your complete satisfaction.

Orders for Products Sold Only Through Dealers

Although it may be your policy to sell your products only through dealers, it is never a good idea to use the phrase *it is our policy*—a customer may expect you to change your policy. Instead, explain what your policy is. If you must, say "it is our practice"—that phrase isn't quite as strong.

Orders From Customers With Poor Credit

Sometimes an order must be refused because of the unsatisfactory condition of the account of a customer buying on credit. Discussing the details of the customer's credit history will only make the customer defensive. In these cases, try to find an alternative payment method for the customer. For example, you might offer to send the order COD or ask the customer to send 50 percent of the payment before you ship the merchandise.

Thinking Cap 12.4

Discuss: Why would some organizations sell their products only through dealers? Can you name an organization that does this?

ORDER ACKNOWLEDGMENT LETTERS

Each situation in the previous section will require either a routine acknowledgment letter, a special acknowledgment letter, or an acknowledgment refusing an order. These types of acknowledgments are discussed next.

Routine Acknowledgments

A **routine** acknowledgment should be sent when a complete and accurate shipment can be made. When you write a routine acknowledgment, use the **direct** or **good-news** approach, and follow the guidelines as you reply to:

- A customer's first order
- An unusually large order

1. **Start With the Good News.** Tell when and how the merchandise will be shipped. Assure the customer that you are handling the order promptly and efficiently, but be careful not to promise that the goods will be delivered on a specific date. Usually it is safer to tell the customer when the merchandise was shipped.

2. **Repeat the Essential Details of the Order.** In your acknowledgment, repeat the essential details of the order including the date of the order, order number, product name(s), quantity, size (if applicable), cost, and any other applicable information. Remember that it is much easier to read information in a list form than in paragraph form.

3. **Build Goodwill.** To build goodwill, thank your customer for the order. Emphasize your service attitude by stressing how your product or service can help him or her and by using a sincere and friendly tone. To be sure your letter projects the best image of you and your organization, make it look professional.

Thinking Cap 12.5

Discuss: Why should you avoid promising that the goods will be delivered on a specific date?

Order, Credit, and Collection Messages

Go to CD-ROM
Activity 12-2
To test your skills.

Thinking Cap 12.6

Discuss: Indicate which is a better opening: "Thank you for your order for . . . ." or "We have received your order for . . . ." Why?

NOTES

Keep It Positive

In a bad-news message, keep the emphasis on what you can do rather than on what you can't do.

4. **Resell Your Product and Your Organization.** Reassure the reader about the quality of your merchandise (including any guarantee or warranty) and the reliability of your organization. Show genuine interest in the customer and a desire to serve. Avoid using self-centered phrases such as "Our product . . .," "We also make . . .," and "We'd also like to sell you . . . ." Instead, use the "you attitude," and be specific about the advantages of your merchandise and your service. Also, tell the customer that you are looking forward to future orders.

Special Acknowledgments

A special acknowledgment should be sent when you cannot fill an order in a timely manner. An acknowledgment letter for **bad-news** situations like these should use an **indirect plan** and should be sent in reply to the following:

- An incomplete or unclear order
- Orders for discontinued items
- Orders requiring a delay in shipment

In these messages, place the emphasis on what you *can do* rather than what you *can't do.* Whether you are speaking or writing, avoid negative words such as *can't, delay, unable, won't, failed, forgot, error,* and *mistake.* Use the following plan for writing special acknowledgments:

1. **Thank the customer for the order.** Indicate your appreciation for the order, or, if appropriate, say something favorable about the merchandise.

2. **Repeat the essential details of the order.** List the essential details of the item(s) ordered. (See the list under "Routine Acknowledgments" on page 335.)

3. **Address the problem.** Specify what information you need to complete the order (remember to avoid emphasizing the customer's error), state the reason for a delayed shipment, or suggest an alternate product if a requested one is unavailable. If you ask for a response from the customer, include a reply card or a return envelope to help you get a prompt, complete answer.

4. **Give shipping information.** If you will be shipping an order, state when and how the shipment will be made.

5. **Resell your product and your organization.** You can effectively use resale techniques here by pointing out the quality of your products and the reliability of your organization. By reselling your merchandise, you remind the customer that delivery is worth waiting for.

6. **Promote goodwill in the closing.** A goodwill closing should indicate your desire for the reader to be satisfied with the merchandise or your desire to give good service to your customer, or both. The letter shown in Figure 12-4 acknowledges an incomplete order.

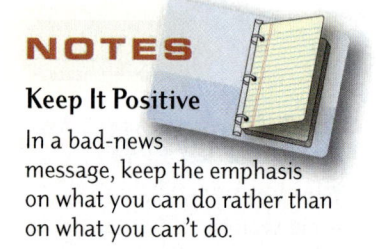

Electronic Things, Inc.
4102 Lightening Blvd.
Weed, CA 96094
1-800-555-8890

April 2, <YEAR>

Mrs. Pat West
1416 Walnut Street
Smithfield, NC 27577

Dear Mrs. West:

Thank you for your order for a caller ID unit, to be charged to your credit account.

Please sign the credit charge line on the enclosed order form and return it to me in the enclosed postpaid envelope. Your signature is only a formality but a necessary one. Your caller ID will be mailed as soon as I receive this order form.

This caller ID unit has been very popular, and I'm sure you will be pleased with your selection.

Sincerely,

Susan Weir

Susan Weir, Manager

ws
Enclosures

Figure 12-4
If the order is incomplete, tell the customer what you will do as soon as the missing information is received.

Go to CD-ROM
Activity 12-3
To test your skills.

NOTES
Bad-News Approach
An acknowledgment refusing an order is a bad-news message and should use the indirect approach.

Acknowledgments Refusing an Order

Some orders must be refused. For example, it may be the policy of your organization not to sell directly to customers but only through dealers. Or a customer's account may be in unsatisfactory condition, which prevents you from shipping the merchandise on credit. Letters refusing orders call for the **indirect plan,** or the "sandwich approach," with the **bad news** in the middle. Use the following outline for these letters:

1. **Start with a "buffer."** Thank the customer for the order, and repeat the details of the order. Do not start with the bad news.

2. **Give an explanation.** In a positive way, tell *why* you cannot complete the order, and stress what you can do, along with the advantages of this to the reader. Offer to help the reader in any way you can—give the name of the nearest dealer, explain credit terms, or offer an alternative to sending the requested merchandise.

3. **Say *no* clearly and tactfully.** Many times your explanation will imply the *no* that is coming. Be sure, however, that the refusal is clear.

Thinking Cap 12.7

Discuss: When you reply to an order, is the following appropriate to tell the buyer: "You forgot to include the size with your order." Why or why not? Can you suggest a better way to convey this information?

Order, Credit, and Collection Messages

Figure 12-5
This letter acknowledges a customer's order while refusing to complete the transaction.

Custom Fit Ski Corporation
1562 Eastgate Spur
Minneapolis, MN 55400
612-555-7748
Fax 612-555-9234

August 3, <YEAR>

Mr. Paul Rouse
2490 Lahr Street
Spokane, WA 99202

Dear Mr. Rouse:

Thank you for your order for one pair of CustomFit snow skis, Model G31, size 11C.

The CustomFit snow ski is well made and has been the best-selling snow ski in America for many years. It is made by craftspeople who take pride in their work. Only the finest materials are used in manufacturing CustomFits.

CustomFit snow skis are sold nationwide through a very fine network of distributors. These outlets carry a complete inventory of the models available.

Because we want you to be perfectly happy with your new skis, we are returning your money order for $219 and requesting that you contact Jim Sewell at:

SnoQuip Company
512 Swallow Avenue
Spokane, WA 99202

Jim is one of our leading dealers, and he will see that your skis are perfectly fitted for comfort. We are sending you a flyer showing our latest models, along with a coupon worth $10 on your new CustomFits.

Remember, Mr. Rouse, CustomFit skis are known as "The Skis That Love to Touch Snow."

Sincerely,

Abe Sunderman

Abe Sunderman

mc
Enclosures
c: Jim Sewell

---

4. **End with a "buffer."** Resell your organization and your products. Notice how this outline for an acknowledgment refusing an order is used in the letter to Mr. Rouse shown in Figure 12-5. This letter will make Mr. Rouse feel the refusal is advantageous to him. When you explain the reasons for saying *no* in a positive way, a reasonable customer will understand. Acknowledgment letters can provide an opportunity to build goodwill and encourage future orders.

Checkpoint 12.1

1. Why is it important to use specific and direct openings in an order letter?

2. What are the advantages of the four ways to place an order—letter, telephone, fax, and the Internet? What are the disadvantages?

3. In your opinion, why are acknowledgment letters effective in building customer goodwill and limiting mistakes in transactions?

CREDIT LETTERS

Buying and selling on credit have pretty much become the standard for doing business today. By extending credit, the seller is able to simplify and speed up the process of purchasing. In fact, most organizations are eager to sell on credit because it increases their profits. Sales volume goes up because credit customers buy more merchandise of better quality on a regular basis.

Customers are also eager to buy on credit because of the convenience of a "cashless" process that allows them to buy merchandise and services by phone, or fax, or on the Internet. Buying on credit also allows customers to take advantage of volume and discounts or sale pricing. For example, a customer might not have the cash until next week to purchase merchandise that is on sale today. By next week, the merchandise will be back to its regular price. Using a credit card enables the customer to take advantage of the sale price without having the cash to pay for the merchandise.

The major reason customers wish to establish credit is convenience. With credit, consumers can:

- Buy now and pay later.
- Avoid carrying cash or writing checks.
- Exchange products and buy on approval more easily.
- Receive advance notice about sales, product promotions, and other special events.

Requesting credit and checking credit references usually do not require a letter. Instead, forms and form letters are used.

LEGAL & ETHICAL 12-2

Markdowns. A customer buys a toy for a child's birthday and uses a credit card to pay for it. Two weeks later the same toy is on sale at the same store for 20 percent off. Would it be legal for the customer to buy another toy on sale and the next day return the original unopened toy with the original receipt for a credit refund? Is this ethical? How else could the customer approach this situation?

Requesting Credit

A buyer wanting to purchase on credit will have to complete a credit application from a business organization or a major credit card company. All credit applications request both personal and business information such as the following:

- **Personal**—Name, address, Social Security number, telephone number, and date of birth
- **Employment**—Name and address of present employer, position, length of employment, and monthly compensation

Order, Credit, and Collection Messages

- **Credit References**—Bank and other credit references
- **Financial Obligations**—Rental or mortgage payment, auto payment, and other installment loan and revolving account information

When completing the credit application, remember that honesty is a critical element because the information you provide will be checked. When a customer applies for credit, his or her credit will likewise be verified.

Checking Credit References

After receiving a signed application for credit, the credit department of an organization will verify the information on the application by sending a form letter or questionnaire, such as the one shown in Figure 12-6, to the banks and credit references listed. The credit department will usually contact a local credit bureau for a report of the credit history of the applicant. When checking credit references, an organization must follow the laws governing this process—credit information must be kept confidential.

Evaluating Credit Information

Once the replies to these credit reference inquiry letters are received, the credit department will decide, based on its credit guidelines, whether to

Figure 12-6
A credit inquiry is sent to verify references supplied by the applicant.

<DATE>

Ladies and Gentlemen:

SUBJECT: Credit Inquiry

Your name has been given by the following applicant as a credit reference:

Mr. John Sleevar
Lake City Village
Suite 364
4802 East Jefferson Street
Port Huron, MI 48060

In order to accurately evaluate this credit application, we would appreciate your giving us the confidential information requested below:

1. Date the account was opened
2. Terms of the account
3. Credit limit
4. Current balance
5. Past due amount
6. Date of last activity
7. Payment history
8. Remarks

Feel free to add additional comments on the back of this letter. For your convenience, a postpaid return envelope is enclosed. Your help will certainly be appreciated, and all information will be kept confidential. Please call on us when we can reciprocate.

Sincerely,

Credit Department

Enclosure

extend or refuse credit. The applicant's credit standing or credit rating will be considered in this decision. A prospective customer's **credit standing** is his or her overall financial reputation or history of financial responsibility. The customer's **credit rating** is a credit agency's appraisal—based on reports from creditors—of the credit standing at any one time.

> **NOTES**
>
> **Credit Checks**
>
> Credit standing means the overall financial reputation or history of financial responsibility. Credit rating is a credit agency's appraisal (based on reports from creditors) of an applicant's credit standing at any one time.

The following **four Cs of credit** normally form the basis for extending credit privileges:

1. **Character** refers to an individual's sense of honesty and ethical dealings with others. This quality is demonstrated by a *willingness* to meet financial obligations and pay debts.

2. **Capacity** is the *ability to pay*. Capacity is evidenced by an individual's income or potential income.

3. **Capital** refers to an individual's tangible assets in relation to debts. (Capital is also used to determine a debtor's *ability to pay* if the debtor does not pay willingly.)

4. **Conditions** refers to the general business trends, local business influences, or current demand for particular products and is frequently considered in evaluating an applicant for credit.

Once a credit application has been evaluated by an organization, a letter is sent to the customer granting or refusing credit.

Letters Extending Credit

Few letters are more welcome to a customer than one extending credit. Writing one is a pleasant task—you are telling someone who has gone through the process of applying for credit and whose credit standing has been investigated that he or she rates high enough to be given credit privileges. That's good news to anyone!

When writing a letter extending credit, use the **direct approach** and follow this outline:

- Welcome the new charge customer, and express the wish for a pleasant association.

- Outline special privileges that are available to charge customers, such as advanced notice of sales.

- Explain the terms of payment.

- Encourage the customer to use the new charge account, and enclose promotional material.

- Build goodwill by indicating your eagerness to serve the new customer well.

The letter from Shepherd's, shown in Figure 12-7, uses the good-news approach and covers each of these five points. The writer begins with a welcome and the good news that the customer's credit account is ready for use.

Order, Credit, and Collection Messages

Figure 12-7
This letter uses the good-news approach.

Shepherd's Shopping Mart
86 Halsted Avenue
Kansas City, MO 64119
1-800-555-0937

July 20, <YEAR>

Mrs. Linda Gilmore
419 Oak Street
Lee's Summit, MO 64081

Dear Mrs. Gilmore:

Welcome to Shepherd's family of many satisfied customers who say "Charge it, please." Your account is ready for use when you next visit our store. Our staff will do everything possible to make your shopping here pleasant and satisfying.

The enclosed credit card is your key to happy shopping. Shepherd's offers a wide selection of practically everything for you, your family, and your home—at reasonable prices.

You will receive a monthly statement of purchases shortly after our closing date, the 25th of each month. Then you may have until the 15th of the next month to pay your bill. From the fine way that you have handled charge accounts at other stores, we know that you will make prompt payments.

Mrs. Gilmore, we invite you to enjoy the convenience of your charge account to the fullest by taking advantage of Shepherd's many special services, such as telephone shopping with the help of our personal shoppers, free parking at the back of the store, prompt and efficient delivery throughout the city and suburbs, and even a nursery for the preschool set.

Come in often to shop or just to browse around. You are always welcome at Shepherd's.

Sincerely,

Jane Browne

Jane Browne, Credit Manager

jb/ei
Enclosure

GLOBAL DIVERSITY 12.1

Smart Shoppers

While traveling in many other countries, you can charge purchases to a major credit card in the local currency, and the amount will appear on your credit card statement in both U.S. currency and the currency of the country you were visiting. The exchange rate is usually better than you can get on your own at a bank or a business in another country. *What is the benefit of being able to charge items on your credit card?*

The second paragraph calls attention to the significance of the enclosed credit card. The writer might have noted other privileges that charge customers receive, such as advance notice of sales. Details about payment terms, which must be explained to new charge customers, are placed in the middle of the letter, after the good news and before the light sales promotion appeal and pleasant closing.

Rather than send a personalized letter like the one from Shepherd's, many businesses notify credit applicants of acceptance by sending a form message that includes an explanation of monthly statements and payment procedures. A personalized credit acceptance letter, however, goes much further in strengthening a credit relationship, building goodwill, minimizing collection problems, and increasing sales. The major reason organizations sell on credit is *to increase profits.* Sales figures go up because credit customers buy more merchandise of better quality on a regular basis.

Letters Refusing Credit

An organization cannot afford to extend credit to every customer who asks for it. After you have gathered and evaluated an applicant's credit information, your organization must then decide whether the account would be more likely to (1) increase sales and profits, or (2) become an uncollectible account.

If the information indicates that the applicant is a poor credit risk, then you must send a **credit-refusal letter.** Every credit-refusal letter has two objectives:

1. To say *no* tactfully
2. To keep the goodwill of the customer

The credit-refusal letter is a difficult letter to write since it is a *bad-news* letter—you are telling the applicant that credit cannot be approved. Use the *indirect approach* when writing this letter and follow this outline:

- Start with a buffer (something neutral)
- Give reasons for the refusal
- Give the refusal (stated or implied)
- End with a buffer (express interest in reevaluating credit status later)

In a credit-refusal letter, you will need to identify the reason for refusing credit to the applicant. The following are the main reasons for refusing credit:

- Applicant's lack of established credit
- Applicant's overextension of credit, which may result in an inability to pay bills on time
- Applicant's unwillingness to pay debts according to credit reporting agencies

Regardless of the reason(s) for refusing credit, your letter must be clear about why credit is not extended. On the other hand, it should be tactful. Remember that you want to convince the applicant that buying on a cash basis now will be to his or her advantage. A harsh credit refusal can discourage the customer from paying cash or reapplying for credit later.

Consider the credit-refusal letter written to a college student who applied for credit from an oil company (see Figure 12-8 on the following page). How could you rewrite this credit refusal, de-emphasizing as much as possible the reason for the refusal? Doesn't the letter shown in Figure 12-9 do a better job?

The opening statement serves as a cushion because it is positive in tone. The reason for refusal is indicated in the second and third paragraphs—although it is not stated directly, it is clear enough. The key here is the interest shown in reevaluating the applicant's credit status later. And, of course, there is a cordial invitation to "pay as you go" in the closing.

> **NOTES**
>
> **Saving Grace**
>
> Every credit-refusal letter has two objectives: (1) to say *no* tactfully, and (2) to keep the goodwill of the customer by using the bad-news, indirect approach.

> **Thinking Cap 12.8**
>
> **Discuss:** How would you react to the curt turndown to a request for a gasoline credit card in Figure 12-8?

Order, Credit, and Collection Messages

Figure 12-8
This credit-refusal letter lacks goodwill.

> Dear Miss MacIntyre:
>
> Regretfully, we do not issue credit to college students. Please reapply after you are employed full-time. Until then, we want to encourage you to remain a cash customer. We will do all we possibly can to make your purchases of our gasoline and related products worthwhile.
>
> Yours very truly,

Figure 12-9
This credit-refusal letter politely says no.

> Dear Miss MacIntyre:
>
> Your credit application is a clear indication that you are satisfied with our efforts to serve your automobile needs. Thank you for sending it to us.
>
> Because college students have a difficult time building a credit rating while they are getting an education, we would like to make a suggestion to you.
>
> Once you are employed full-time, please send us another credit application. We'll be happy at that time to welcome you as a new addition to our growing family of charge customers.
>
> In the meantime, Miss MacIntyre, let us continue to serve you on a cash basis. Our gasoline and related automotive products are designed to extend the problem-free life of your car.
>
> Sincerely,

Go to CD-ROM
Activity 12-4
To test your skills.

Checkpoint 12.2

1. Why do you think it is fair, or unfair, to base a person's credit standing on his or her character?

2. Why do you think it is, or is not, important for a business to review each customer's credit standing?

3. Do you think it is better to be known as a business that is strict about the people it extends credit to or as a company that extends credit to every customer?

COLLECTION MESSAGES

> *Creditors have better memories than debtors.*
> —**Benjamin Franklin,** *Poor Richards Almanac,* **1736**

A natural result of credit is customers buying more and buying better quality merchandise; therefore, it's not surprising that a certain number of "buy now and pay later" customers either fail to or are unable to "pay later." This creates what is referred to in business as "bad debt" and causes the seller to start the collection process in order to minimize losses.

An important part of being competitive in business is the ability of an organization to deal effectively with customers who do not pay their bills. It is certainly not a pleasant task to remind or urge customers to pay what they owe, but it is a critical function of business. When a payment is not received on time, correspondence is sent to remind the customer that payment is past due. Messages that attempt to collect payment are referred to as **collection letters;** they are written because of the need to persuade customers to pay.

Collection letters have two objectives:

1. To get the money owed by the customer
2. To keep the customer's goodwill and future business

Collection-Letter Series

Most organizations use a series of collection notices and letters that are sent at predetermined intervals. This series begins with friendly reminders such as a routine statement of account and ends with a last call for payment. Every communication in the collection series should include: (1) the amount owed and (2) the due date.

Statement of Account

Most organizations send statements each month to their credit customers. These statements provide the customers with a record of charges, the total amount due, and the date due.

If the payment is not received on time, a duplicate copy of the statement is sent as the first stage in the collection series. A friendly reminder, such as "If you haven't sent us your payment, please do so today!" may be added to this statement.

NOTES
Accounts Past Due
Collection letters attempt to persuade customers to pay. Every communication in the collection series should include the amount owed and the due date.

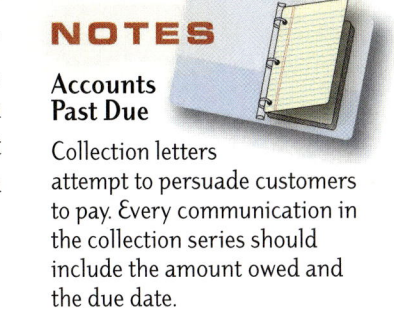

Go to CD-ROM
Activity 12-5
To test your skills.

Figure 12-10
This credit reminder has a somewhat impersonal tone.

Remember us . . .

As you relax in your Relaxasizer Chair,

We would be as comfortable as you are if we had your payment.

Please send us your check for $449.50 so you can rest with a clear conscience.

Good Furniture Company
821 Harrigan Drive • St. Paul, MN 55101 • 612-555-2005

Impersonal Reminder

If payment is still not received, a form letter is sent—it may be either one that is not personalized or one in which you can fill in the date and customer's name, address, and account information. In these messages, it is important to maintain the position that the customer is trustworthy and intends to pay. The tone of the message should be friendly. The Good Furniture Co. reminder shown in Figure 12-10 on the previous page has an impersonal tone. The letter shown in Figure 12-11 has a more personal touch.

Figure 12-11
Notice the personal tone of this reminder letter.

Shepherd's Shopping Mart
86 Halsted Avenue
Kansas City, MO 64119
1-800-555-0937

February 11, <YEAR>

Mr. Adam Reynolds
356 Oceanway Drive
St. Louis, MO 63147

Dear Mr. Reynolds:

RE: Your account, number 933-87723-9

We value having you as one of our charge customers.

It is important, though, that payments be made promptly each month. Your good credit reputation is very important to you. The amount due of $302.78 on your account should be paid before your next billing date.

If your check and this letter passed in the mail, please disregard this letter and accept our thanks.

Sincerely,

John Hollingsworth

John Hollingsworth
Collection Department

Personal Reminder

In the next stage, a personal letter, usually no more than a couple of paragraphs in length, is sent. In writing one of these letters, you should take care to ensure that the customer will consider it a reminder—not a demand for payment. The message should attempt to persuade the recipient to pay and should not intimidate. The message shown in Figure 12-12 on the next page illustrates the tone you should use in such a reminder.

> Dear Mr. Kerans:
>
> A duplicate statement of your credit charges from December 19 is enclosed.
>
> This note is sent to you as a friendly reminder that the balance on your account is past due. Please take a few minutes today to send us your check for $277.24.
>
> For your convenience, a postpaid, addressed envelope is enclosed.
>
> Sincerely,

Figure 12-12
A personal reminder will likely encourage a response.

Request for an Explanation

When a credit customer does not respond to a personal reminder message, you can assume that something is preventing the customer from paying. The reason may be that the customer is unhappy with the purchased merchandise or is facing financial difficulty. Whatever the reason for holding up payment, you want the customer to (1) explain why the payment hasn't been made or (2) settle the account.

Review the letter shown in Figure 12-13, which illustrates the approach generally used in requesting an explanation. Note that the writer of this message did not threaten. Instead the tone reflects the assumption that the customer is basically honest. Remember, the object of the message is to get the money owed and to keep the customer's future business.

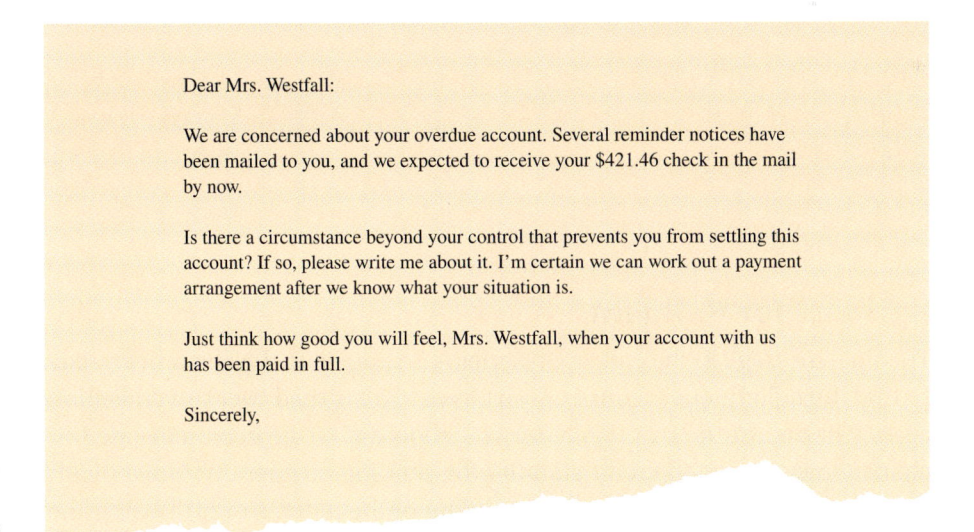

> Dear Mrs. Westfall:
>
> We are concerned about your overdue account. Several reminder notices have been mailed to you, and we expected to receive your $421.46 check in the mail by now.
>
> Is there a circumstance beyond your control that prevents you from settling this account? If so, please write me about it. I'm certain we can work out a payment arrangement after we know what your situation is.
>
> Just think how good you will feel, Mrs. Westfall, when your account with us has been paid in full.
>
> Sincerely,

Figure 12-13
A request for an explanation assumes the customer is honest.

If the customer does write or call you to explain why a bill hasn't been paid, it is important for you to maintain a service attitude. Is the customer short on cash? Ask for a smaller or minimum payment. Is the customer dissatisfied with the product or service in some way? Decide on a mutually agreeable resolution to the problem. Your service attitude will help you keep the customer's goodwill.

Order, Credit, and Collection Messages

NOTES

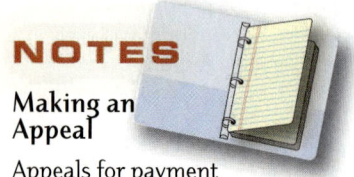

Making an Appeal

Appeals for payment are typically made to the customer's pride or sense of fair play.

Appeal(s) for Payment

If there is no response to the request for an explanation, you would send the next letter in the collection series—a direct appeal to the credit customer to pay. This is a stern letter, but it should be calmly written. In this kind of letter, typical appeals are to the customer's pride or sense of fair play.

Your appeal for payment should not threaten to take the debtor to court unless you actually plan to do so. Give the customer another chance to save a good credit standing by sending payment before the deadline—usually 10 to 12 days from the date of the letter. Look at the appeal for payment shown in Figure 12-14—this letter is an example of a courteous request for payment, which appeals to both the customer's pride and the customer's sense of fair play.

Figure 12-14
This request for payment is courteous yet insistent.

> Dear Mr. Binkley:
>
> Because of your good credit reputation, you were able to purchase a $259.83 cashmere coat from us more than three months ago. We were glad to place your name on our credit list at that time, and we made it clear that accounts are due on the 15th of the month following the purchase. When you bought the coat, Mr. Binkley, you accepted those terms.
>
> Your credit reputation is a valuable asset. We want you to keep it that way because of the advantages it gives you. You have enjoyed a liberal extension of time; but to be fair to our other customers, you must pay the amount that is past due by February 10.
>
> Won't you please send us your check for $259.83 today?
>
> Sincerely,

NOTES

Last Call

In a last call for payment, never threaten the customer; state the consequences simply and regretfully.

Last Call for Payment

The final message in the collection series is an appeal to the customer to pay so that the delinquent account doesn't have to be turned over to a collection agency or an attorney. In this letter you should give the customer one last chance to save a good credit standing by sending payment before a deadline—usually five to ten days from the date of the letter. Never threaten the customer; state the consequences simply and regretfully. Notice how the letter shown in Figure 12-15 tries to keep the friendship of the customer by stressing interest in playing fair.

Finally, if you discover that the customer does not intend to pay, you should consult a collection agency or lawyer about a merchandise-return or repossession strategy. You must observe the laws in your state governing collection procedures.

Figure 12-15
This last call for payment tries to keep the customer as a customer.

> Dear Mrs. Barker:
>
> Your credit reputation is important to you, Mrs. Barker.
>
> For some time now, we have been writing to you in an effort to clear up your balance of $512, explained in the attached statement. So far you have not sent us a check or an explanation, although six messages have called the debt to your attention.
>
> Can't we still settle this account in a friendly way? If you send your check for $512 now, you can continue to buy computer equipment and accessories on our regular credit terms. The agreement with our collection agency, however, does not allow further delay. We must turn your account over to the Adkins Collection Agency unless it is taken care of within ten days.
>
> The choice is yours. If your check reaches us by November 16, your credit standing with us will still be good and our friendly business relations will continue.
>
> Please mail your check for $512 today. Protect your credit reputation.
>
> Sincerely,

Payment Acknowledgment

When a customer writes you about a past-due account, answer with a personal letter. Don't send the remaining letters from the collection series. If the customer responds to a collection letter with payment in full, you should send a special thank-you message, as shown in Figure 12-16.

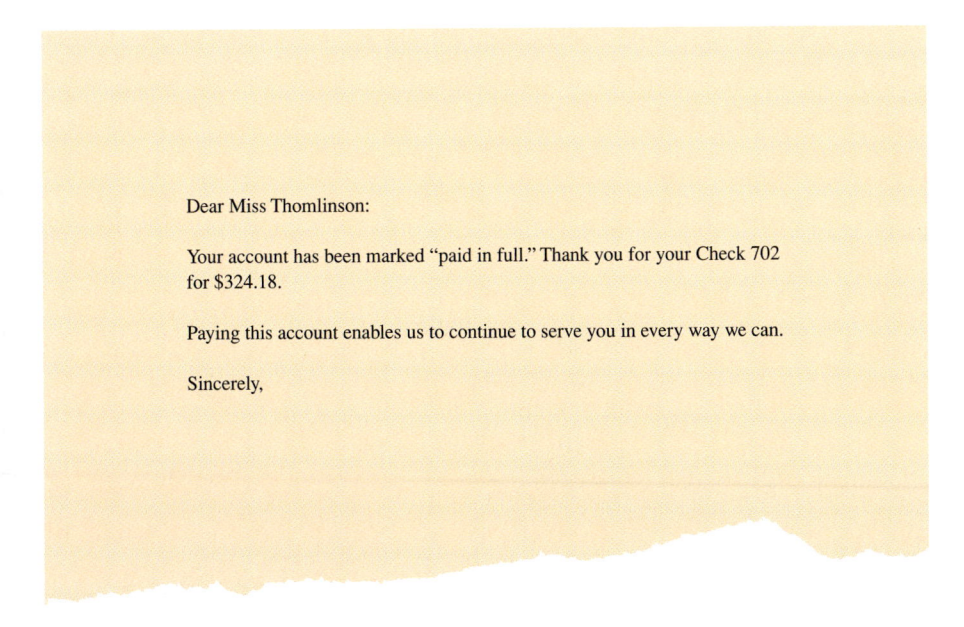

Figure 12-16
This thank-you promotes goodwill.

> Dear Miss Thomlinson:
>
> Your account has been marked "paid in full." Thank you for your Check 702 for $324.18.
>
> Paying this account enables us to continue to serve you in every way we can.
>
> Sincerely,

Chapter 12 Summary

All of the messages discussed in this chapter deal with the functions of business that keep our economy going. Products and services may be ordered by one of several effective methods: order forms, letters, telephone, fax, and the Internet.

When an organization receives an order, an acknowledgment is always appropriate and offers an opportunity to build goodwill. Several circumstances in particular require acknowledgments. Depending on the circumstances, this may be a routine acknowledgment, a special acknowledgment, or an acknowledgment refusing an order.

Credit allows buyers to buy more and better quality merchandise. Customers complete forms to apply for credit, and organizations send forms to investigate the credit references. Messages granting credit are good-news messages and can get the credit relationship off to a positive start. Messages refusing credit should be courteous and keep the door open for the future.

Credit means "buy now, pay later"—if a buyer doesn't pay on time, then a series of collection letters should be sent. The tone of these messages is important—their goal is to persuade the customer to pay. Current laws must be observed when writing credit and collection messages.

Your instructor may assign various Worksheet Exercises for you to complete. The exercises on the CD-ROM are available for practice as needed.

Communication at Work

Allisun Kale Marshall
Freelance Sign Language Interpreter

There are all sorts of obstacles to overcome in the pursuit of clear, effective communication. Allisun Kale Marshall knows all about communication obstacles. She's a freelance sign-language interpreter. One day she may interpret for a deaf person who's receiving job training in the aerospace industry; the next may find her with a client at a business meeting.

As the interpreter, Allisun is usually the only one in the situation who understands both the hearing and deaf communication systems—and the rules that go with each. As she describes it, "I make sure the rules are clear."

Rules of Interaction

For example, a hearing person may speak indirectly to a deaf person by instructing Allisun to "tell him or her" something. That's insulting to a deaf person, so Allisun reminds the hearing person to speak directly to the deaf person. Turn-taking rules in conversation also can cause problems. When hearing people want to say something in a conversation, they can just interrupt one another. However, sign language is visual, explains Allisun. So she must have the deaf person's attention first before she can "interrupt" to interpret what's being spoken.

> *The clearer the communication, the better every point of view is served.*

"In order for the deaf person to get the floor, I must use a volume as well as a tone that gets attention and provides the opportunity for the deaf person to express himself. So I have to monitor my output to make sure I'm matching the client's register, level of formality, and intended message," she explains.

Experience has taught Allisun to avoid certain communications problems that might make her deaf client look bad or cause confusion. She's careful about using verbal fillers, such as *uh* and *um*, as she searches her mind for the correct words for the interpretation. An interpretation filled with *uh*s and *um*s could make her client seem unprepared or inarticulate. She's also careful when she interprets statements that might be misunderstood as being hers rather than her deaf client's. Instead of literally translating "I have a comment," Allisun might insert the client's name and say, "Bob has a comment." That way there is no confusion about who is speaking.

"In the end, the rules are the same as in any communication. The clearer the communication, the better every point of view is served."

Discuss

1. Allisun Kale Marshall describes turn-taking in conversation as a problem. Is it sometimes acceptable to interrupt a speaker in a conversation?

2. How do you feel when you are interrupted in a conversation?

Chapter 12

Online Exercises

Objective:
These online activities will allow you to learn about writing order letters and comparing credit policies.

Go to **bcw.glencoe.com,** the address for the *Business Communication at Work* Web site, and select Chapter 12. Next, click on Online Exercises. You will see a list of Web site links that will bring you to online electronic mall Web sites and online retail stores.

Activity 12.1

1. Select one of the online electronic mall Web sites to visit.
2. Choose an electronic product to research. Some examples of electronic products are computers, digital cameras, or personal digital assistants (PDAs). Note the price of the product you choose, as well as the features offered with it.
3. On a sheet of paper, write an order letter to the electronic store you are visiting. Remember to follow these guidelines:
   a. Write orders, not just hints.
   b. Give a complete description of each item.
   c. Give the order information in a clear format.
   d. Tell how you will pay for the order.
   e. Tell where, when, and how you want the merchandise shipped.
4. Write your name on your letter, and hand it in to your instructor.

Activity 12.2

1. Select one of the online retail stores to visit.
2. Click on information about the store's credit policy. Make a printout of the credit information.
3. Return to the *Business Communication at Work* Web site and select another online retail store to visit.
4. Click on information about the store's credit policy. Make a printout of the credit information.
5. On a sheet of paper, write a paragraph describing the similarities or differences in the credit policies of the two online retail stores you visited. Some questions you may want to consider in your paragraph include:
   a. What are the differences in requirements for obtaining credit at the retail stores?
   b. How do the online stores encourage customers to obtain credit at their stores (i.e. offering a free gift)?
   c. What information is required to obtain credit at the retail stores?
6. Write your name on your paper, and hand it in to your instructor.

CHAPTER 12 WORKSHEETS

NAME _____ DATE _____

PRACTICE 1

Concept Review

Instructions: Complete the problems below as directed.

1. **Orders.** Read the following opening sentences in order messages. If the opening sentence is effective, write *OK* in the blank; if it is ineffective, write *No* in the blank.

    _____ a. This morning while eating breakfast I was thinking about some of the items in your catalog.

    _____ b. Please send me one copy of your book, *The Internet Map*, by Robert Roads.

    _____ c. I am interested in a new watercolor painting for my summer home.

    _____ d. I'm thinking about one of your European Adventures this summer.

    _____ e. Please ship the following order to my office address as shown in the letterhead.

2. **Acknowledging an Order.** Read the following sentences from order acknowledgment messages. If a sentence is effective, write *OK* in the blank; if it is ineffective, write *No* in the blank.

    _____ a. You failed to give us the sleeve length of the shirts you ordered.

    _____ b. We will need a lot more information than you gave us before we can fill your order.

    _____ c. We regret to advise you that the merchandise you ordered is temporarily out of stock.

    _____ d. Your order for a truck bed liner, Stock No. 3589, was shipped this morning by UPS.

    _____ e. We would like to take this opportunity to acknowledge your recent order.

3. **Acknowledging an Order.** Review each of these situations that would require acknowledging an order. Indicate whether you should use the direct approach *(Dir)* or the indirect approach *(Ind)* when writing the letter.

    _____ a. You receive an order for four theater tickets that does not include the date of the performance the sender wants to see.

    _____ b. You must refuse a credit order because of the customer's poor credit rating.

    _____ c. You receive an order for three times the merchandise the customer usually orders.

    _____ d. You receive an order from a new customer.

    _____ e. You receive an order for a garden tractor that is sold exclusively through local dealers.

Order, Credit, and Collection Messages

CHAPTER 12   WORKSHEETS

NAME _____   DATE _____

4. **Granting Credit Messages.** Analyze these opening sentences from letters granting credit. Write **OK** in the blank if the sentence follows the principles of effective business writing; write **No** if the opening sentence should be revised.

   _____ a. Your credit application has been duly investigated and we have decided to grant you credit.

   _____ b. Welcome to Gilmore's family of satisfied customers who enjoy the convenience of shopping with credit.

   _____ c. We will send your credit card in a few days.

   _____ d. Your credit application is approved and your new credit card is enclosed.

   _____ e. We are in receipt of your application for credit with Gerry's.

5. **Messages Refusing Credit.** Analyze these opening sentences from letters refusing credit. Write **OK** in the blank if the sentence follows the principles of effective business writing; write **No** if the opening sentence should be revised.

   _____ a. We are sorry that we cannot grant you credit because of your poor credit history.

   _____ b. We appreciate your interest in opening a credit account at Gilmore's.

   _____ c. This letter is to inform you that your application for credit must be denied.

   _____ d. Your interest in establishing credit at Gerry's is truly appreciated.

   _____ e. Unfortunately, you do not qualify for a credit account with us at this time.

6. **Collection Letters.** Analyze these sentences from collection letters. Write **OK** in the blank if the sentence follows the principles of effective business writing; write **No** if the sentence should be revised.

   _____ a. We demand your payment of $89 immediately.

   _____ b. If you don't pay the balance of your account by May 2, we will be forced to contact your employer and let him know you are delinquent on your account.

   _____ c. This message is a friendly reminder of the balance of $352 on your account that was due June 4.

   _____ d. We hope you will send your check soon.

   _____ e. Won't you please send me your check for $789 or give me a call at 1-800-555-8745 so we can set up a payment plan for this amount.

CHAPTER 12 WORKSHEETS

NAME _____ DATE _____

PRACTICE 2

Order, Credit, and Collection Messages

Instructions: For each situation below, respond as directed.

1. **Order Letter.** On the lines below, analyze this letter for its effectiveness.

   > Dear Sir:
   >
   > I'm interested in a pair of ice skates. I've enclosed my Check 754 for $68.99, which includes shipping and handling.
   >
   > Sincerely,

   _____
   _____
   _____
   _____

2. **Order Letter.** Write a letter ordering the guidebook described in the following advertisement from the April 3 *USA Today* newspaper. Have the guidebook mailed to you at your home address. Enclose your Check 387 to pay for it.

   TODAY'S READING

   Visit the caves in this country and see the beautiful underground rock formations. Request a 96-page guidebook to 40 of America's best caves, which includes four-color photos, schedules, admission prices, and detailed descriptions of each cave. Send $7.50 to Cave Enthusiasts of America, 3987 59th Street, NW, Washington, DC 20009

   _____
   _____
   _____
   _____
   _____
   _____
   _____
   _____
   _____
   _____
   _____

NAME _____   DATE _____

3. **Acknowledging an Order.** As marketing manager for Compudata Corp, you receive the order letter from Accurate CPAs, Inc. (See Figure 12-1 on page 330.) Resell the software by emphasizing that it has been ranked as the number one seller by *Software Specialist* magazine every month for the last three years. This is the first order you've received from Accurate CPAs and you want to encourage future orders.

4. **Acknowledging an Order.** As a sales assistant for WalkFit Treadmills (3367 Industrial Park, Oregan City, OR 97045), acknowledge the first order from Body Works, a fitness club at 938 North Vermillion Street, LaPlata, MD 20646. The order is for a T445 Programmable Treadmill for $2599. Resell this top-of-the-line model by emphasizing its technological superiority and special safety features, which are described in the owner's manual. Enclose a coupon for a free instructional videotape of training strategies.

5. **Letter Extending Credit.** You are the credit manager for Progressive Builders. Kim Vallery has applied for credit at a local business. The business has verified with the credit bureau that she has an excellent credit history. The following letter is written to grant her credit. Please evaluate the letter.

<CURRENT DATE>

Kim Vallery
119 Section Street
Cedarville, OH 45314

Dear Kim Vallery:

We would like to thank you for your credit application. We appreciate the confidence you have shown in us and our service by desiring to establish credit with us. We require that you come by our office to sign for your credit card.

Yours very truly,

Joe Sanderson
Credit Manager

CHAPTER 12 WORKSHEETS

NAME _____ DATE _____

6. **Collection Message.** Mr. Tom Bennett, 1610 Leaf Drive, Randolph, NJ 07081, has a balance on his account of $123.53. The account is 30 days overdue. Up until now, his credit history with your company has been excellent. As credit manager, ask your assistant to write the first collection notice to Mr. Bennett about his account. Your assistant brings you the following letter for approval. Please evaluate the letter.

> <CURRENT DATE>
>
> Mr. Tom Bennett
> 1610 Leaf Drive
> Randolph, NJ 07081
>
> Dear Mr. Bennett:
>
> You owe us $123.53! Your payment is 30 days overdue.
>
> We know how to deal with deadbeat customers like you. If we do not receive payment in five days, we will sue you and destroy your credit rating.
>
> Very truly yours,
>
> <ASSISTANT'S NAME>

7. **Collection Letter.** Rewrite the bad collection letter shown in Practice 2, Exercise 6.

PRACTICE 3

Writing Applications

Instructions: Develop your skills at writing order, credit, and collections messages by responding to the following situations.

1. **Order Letter.** You have a mail order catalog from Unique Gifts Company, 9847 Krapht Street, Prestonsburg, KY 41653. On page 63 of the spring/summer catalog is advertised a business-card holder (Stock No. B-354) that looks like a miniature briefcase. Each of these business-card holders costs $9.95 including tax, plus $1.99 for shipping and handling. Name imprinting is available at $3 per holder (limited to ten letters). You want to order imprinted business-card holders for two of your friends (Gary and Brenda). When you check the catalog, you discover the order blank is missing. Write a letter to order the two business-card holders; enclose a check and have the merchandise shipped to you.

2. **Letter Extending Credit.** You are the credit manager at Chaney's Interiors, 443 Shelby Drive East, Grand Junction, CO 81501. In January, Mrs. Linda Stafford, 146 North Front Street, Grand Junction, CO 81501, applied for a credit account at Chaney's. She wants to buy on credit two Tiffany-style lamps costing a total of $364. After checking her credit rating and finding it highly satisfactory, you decide to open an installment account for her. Mrs. Stafford agrees to pay $44 down and $44 (including finance charges) on the 15th of each of the next eight months. Write the credit approval letter to welcome Mrs. Stafford as a new credit customer. The letter should be brief and appreciative with a hint of reselling and sales promotion. The approach should be direct, the confirmation of terms exact, and the closing specific and forward-looking.

Order, Credit, and Collection Messages

NAME _____ DATE _____

> 2301 Lynch Road
> West Barnstable, MA 02668
> September 25, <YEAR>
>
> Eaton's Electronic City
> 5661 Western Avenue
> Charleston, SC 29411
>
> Dear Eaton's Electronic City:
>
> Please ship one of the videocassette recorders you have on sale this month for $200.
>
> Ship the recorder to me at my address in the heading. Please charge my account for the amount of my order.
>
> Sincerely,
>
>
> Harriett Whiteman

3. **Acknowledging an Order.** You are the order entry associate for Eaton's Electronic City, and you receive the order letter shown above from Ms. Harriett Whiteman.

   You have two videocassette recorders (VCRs) on sale this month for $200 each. The Model 6450 is a 3-Head VHS VCR, and the Model 6350 is a 2-Head VHS VCR with on-screen programming. In her letter Ms. Whiteman failed to indicate which model she wants. Write Ms. Whiteman a tactful letter asking which model she prefers. Make it easy for her to reply, and use this opportunity to build goodwill and resell your product. This month you are also sending two free blank videotapes with each recorder purchased. You looked up her file and noted that her account number is 906-281-3290.

4. **Collection Messages.** You work in the credit department at Karney's. Mr. Martin Reed, 29994 N East Road, Covington, IN 47932, opened an account at Karney's six months ago. He paid each month as agreed until the June 1 payment was due—it did not arrive. You billed him on July 1 for the overdue balance of $181.69 ($179 plus interest of $2.69) and included an impersonal reminder.

   a. On July 15, you still have not heard from Mr. Reed. Write a personal reminder message for $181.69.

   b. By August 1, you have had no response to the letter you sent in Part a. Now write a letter requesting an explanation. The amount due is $184.41 (including additional interest).

   c. It's August 15, and Mr. Reed has not responded to your letter in Part b. Now write a letter using a firm appeal. The amount due is $184.41 plus interest for a total of $187.13.

   d. September 1 arrives and you still have not received a response to any of the letters you've written to Mr. Reed. Write the last call for payment of $189.85.

unit 4

Reports and Media Communications

- **Chapter 13**
  Developing Memos and Memo Reports

- **Chapter 14**
  Creating Press Releases and Newsletters

- **Chapter 15**
  Constructing and Presenting Reports

- **Chapter 16**
  Preparing Meeting Communications

CHAPTER 13
Developing Memos and Memo Reports

Objectives

After completing this chapter, you will be able to:

1. Identify the most common forms and purposes of internal communication
2. Organize memos
3. Apply the correct approach to various memo-writing situations
4. Write effective memos
5. Explain the steps in preparing a memo report
6. Describe the different types of memo reports
7. Write effective memo reports

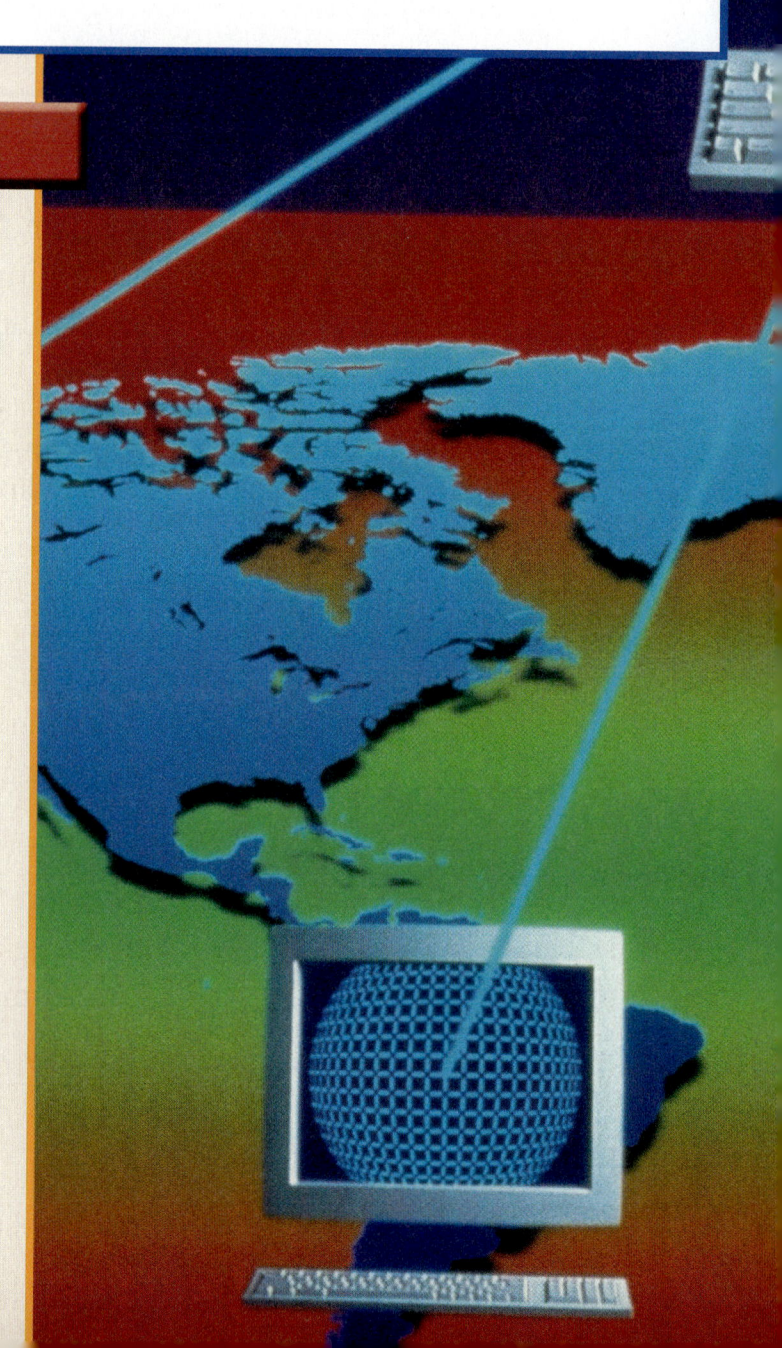

WORKPLACE APPLICATIONS

Team Building

If two heads are better than one, then imagine what three or more might be. More heads are better because when you work in a group, you have access to more ideas, perspectives, and experience. Whether you are **problem solving** or planning a project, you are more likely to succeed if you have a team working with you. Building an effective team is not easy—just ask any professional sports coach. It takes practice, patience, and constant fine-tuning.

Finding the Right People

The key to **team building** is knowing your own strengths and weaknesses. When forming a team, you may be tempted to select people who get along with you. An effective team, however, is one whose members have different strengths and abilities. For example, if you are great at giving presentations but not so good at planning or writing progress reports, then you need people on the team who can do those key tasks.

The next challenge is for the team members to learn how to work together. Team members can build trust and strong lines of communication by holding regular meetings that focus not only on work, but on the group itself.

At the first meeting, team members should invite each other to explain their own strengths and weaknesses and to outline their goals. At later meetings, the group should check in and discuss any problems, and publicly recognize each member's contributions.

Sometimes group members need to remind themselves that everyone is working toward the same goal. Each team member should continually evaluate his or her own contributions to the group as well. If it seems as though two or more heads are *not* better than one, then the team member probably has a problem that is best addressed by the whole group.

Thinking Critically

Situation: You work for a mail-order clothing company, and your manager has taken an emergency leave of absence. Now, you must plan, develop, and launch the latest catalog. You may form a team of three people to help.

Ask Yourself: What are your strengths and weaknesses in the workplace? On a piece of paper, outline your own capabilities, then write a list of the abilities you would seek in your teammates.

> *This report, by its very length, defends itself against the risk of being read.*
>
> —**Winston Churchill, Statesman and British Prime Minister**

With advances in technology, the speed and volume of communication within business organizations continue to increase rapidly. In today's businesses, the flow of accurate, reliable information and ideas through effective internal communication is essential to efficient operations. This information is used as the basis for effective decision making. Routine memos sent within organizations are perhaps the most frequently used form of written communication. In addition, most business reports are prepared in memo form. These range from brief memos to longer, more detailed reports based on research. In Chapter 7 you learned to format memos; in this chapter you will learn to write routine memos and memo reports.

INTERNAL COMMUNICATIONS

Individuals at all levels within an organization rely heavily on information they receive through memorandums (memos) and memo reports to provide them with the basis for sound decision making. Each individual in an organization plays a role in this internal communication process.

Routine memos and memo reports are written to communicate facts, ideas, statistics, and trends within an organization.

The purpose of these internal communications is to inform or to persuade the receiver through explanation, justification, recommendation, or evaluation. As in all communications, the basics for communicating effectively in memos and memo reports include:

- Determining the purpose of the communication,
- Identifying the audience,
- Considering what the audience needs to "hear," and
- Developing the memo or memo report in a clear, logical manner.

In addition, when preparing these internal communications, it is important to remember to do the following:

- Use a positive approach.
- Develop the "you attitude."
- Use the active voice.
- Apply the seven Cs of communication.
- Choose simple, familiar, conversational, appropriate words.
- Vary the length and structure of sentences and paragraphs.
- Use an appropriate tone.

If we compare memos and letters, we find that the major differences include their formats and audiences. Both, however, can be long or short, formal or informal.

Thinking Cap 13.1

Discuss: Internal communications are usually informal. What are some of the problems individuals may have writing memos and memo reports? Why might they encounter these problems?

ROUTINE MEMOS

Internal **memorandums**, or **memos**, are written communications used to communicate information to individuals within a business organization. In many organizations, particularly large ones, the number of internal memos sent is far greater than the number of letters used for external communications. In all organizations, in-house memos are vital to efficient operations—every memo has a specific purpose, whether it is a simple reminder or a persuasive request.

The memo format is valuable for internal communication because a memo does the following

- Carries a special informality and gets a friendly reception (because both writer and reader are part of the same organization).
- Provides a written record of a message.
- Allows several individuals to receive the same message.
- Communicates in all directions: Upward to supervisors, managers, and executives; downward to subordinates; and, laterally among people of equal rank, teams, and departments.
- Conveys information between departments, teams, etc.
- Reduces the time required to prepare a communication.
- Uses a variety of delivery systems including electronic mail and fax.

With today's technology and the need for instant information, memos are being delivered via fax and e-mail as well as by interoffice mail. Although the use of e-mail encourages immediate, informal responses, the planning of a memo, including the tone and organization, is still important for effectively communicating the message and generating a positive reaction.

> **NOTES**
>
> **Say It With Memos**
>
> Memos are the most frequently used form of communications within businesses. Memos clarify responsibility and provide written documentation.

Purposes of Memos

The main reason for using memos as interoffice correspondence is to *save time*. Memos are not keyed on letterhead stationery, and they do not require the formality of an inside address, salutation, or complimentary closing. This simple format permits the writer to concentrate on the content.

Although the format of routine memos is much simpler than that of letters, memos serve the same purposes *within* an organization that *letters* serve *outside* the organization. Routine memos serve to:

- Share information
- Request
- Congratulate
- Recommend
- Direct people
- Announce
- Confirm
- Inform
- Instruct
- Reply
- Express appreciation
- Persuade

Developing Memos and Memo Reports

Many organizations direct their employees to *put in writing all important information* that they communicate to others within the organization. This is done so that there will be a written record of who is responsible for the information and to whom it was sent. Even a file copy of a transmittal memo is valuable in case the original memo is lost, because the copy would list the attached documents and tell when they were sent.

Memo Planning

As you prepare to write your memo, you should review the purpose of the memo and identify its audience. In most cases, you are writing to give information. Specifically, you need to consider the following:

- Why you are writing the memo
- What situation or problem you are addressing
- Who will receive the memo
- What kind of information the receiver(s) needs
- Why the receiver(s) need(s) this information
- What questions or concerns the receiver(s) may have

Memo Organization

Good organization of a memo's message appeals to the reader because a *logical order* allows quick and easy review. On the other hand, a poorly organized memo will confuse the reader and may require a second or even a third reading. In *Never Confuse a Memo With Reality*, Richard A. Moran expresses the importance of memo organization this way: "Always have a beginning, middle, and end, whether it be a presentation, a meeting, a memo, or a letter." In the next sections you will learn how to develop these three important parts—the beginning, the middle, and the end.

Beginning: Introduction/Purpose

The opening paragraph of a memo states the purpose of the memo, identifies the specific problem or project, provides background information, and gives an overview of the information contained in the memo.

Because the first sentence of a memo determines whether the memo is read or is ignored, make your opening reader-oriented. The opening should:

- Use the "you attitude."
- Capture the reader's attention.
- Use a convincing, positive tone.
- Contain the main point if it is a positive message.

You can help make the purpose of your memo clear by referring the reader to a previous communication (another memo, a phone conversation, a fax, an e-mail, or a voice-mail message), a meeting or teleconference,

NOTES

Building Memos

The three parts of memos are introduction (purpose), discussion, and conclusions. Beginning: State the purpose—the reason for the memo. Middle: Present the discussion of your message. Ending: Present conclusions and recommendations.

or a topic of mutual interest. Study the following openings for memos to learn how this may be accomplished:

> Here is the information you requested explaining the details of the conference registration package fee I submitted on my October 15 Meeting and Conference Expense Report.

> At the April meeting, the District Board asked me to recommend a method for planning for capital expenditures. I am submitting the following methods for your consideration at our next meeting on May 28.

The information that follows your opening must relate to and support the reason you have identified for writing the memo.

Middle: Message/Discussion

The middle section of your memo presents the discussion of your message. In this section you answer questions, provide supporting data and information, and give explanations relevant to the purpose of your memo.

In the middle paragraph(s) of a memo, *cover all relevant points,* such as:

- Answering question(s) asked
- Presenting information requested
- Providing supporting data
- Giving realistic and logical explanations
- Giving the *causes* if you bring up a problem
- Stating the *reasons* for your suggested solution
- Telling *why* as well as *how* when writing a directive
- Providing enough information that the reader can *understand* new procedures and *follow directions*
- Giving reader benefits if using a persuasive strategy

Review the first example of a memo shown in Figure 13-1 on page 367. An appropriate middle paragraph for that memo might look like this:

> The registration fee of $175 included the seminar materials and notebook, as well as two lunches and one dinner. If purchased separately,
> - the registration fee was $75,
> - the materials and notebook were $75,
> - the two luncheons were $40, and
> - the dinner was $30.
>
> Therefore, the total for the individual registration for all the above is $220, while the special convention registration package cost is $175.

If, like this example, the middle section of your memo contains several related items, consider listing them and setting them off with numbers,

Developing Memos and Memo Reports 365

dashes, or bullets to make reading easier. Remember that the key to writing an effective discussion section is to cover all relevant points. Memos that offer insufficient information not only cause confusion for the reader but also cast doubt on the abilities of the writer.

In reviewing the message/discussion section of your memo, make sure you have achieved the following:

- The information meets the needs of the receiver.
- The information answers the question(s) or solves the problem(s) identified.
- The information is clear, considerate, courteous, concise, consistent, complete, and correct.

Ending: Conclusions/Recommendations

The ending of your memo should be a separate paragraph that does one or more of the following:

- Restates the memo's purpose
- Highlights key information
- Summarizes the main points of the message
- Interprets the material presented
- Makes recommendations
- Suggests future action
- Expresses a goodwill thought

Conclusions or recommendations that you make in the ending of your memo must be tied directly to the statement of purpose you made in the opening. They should also be supported by the facts you presented in the middle of your memo.

Read the last paragraph of the conference expense memo that follows. Is the conclusion it presents tied directly to the memo opening and supported by the facts in the middle paragraph?

> Although this registration fee was higher than the amount recommended by our company guidelines, the total package included approved individual functions and activities within our expenditure guidelines. By registering for the package, I was able to save the company $45 for this conference. Therefore, I feel that this expenditure meets the guidelines, and I request approval of the expense.

Now study the following closing, which clearly presents a conclusion and a suggestion:

> The statistics presented above demonstrate the need for us to upgrade our computer system. I suggest that we authorize Joe Huber to solicit proposals and bids for a new computer system.

NOTES

Tying It Together

Conclusions and recommendations must be tied to the purpose and supported by the facts presented in the middle paragraphs.

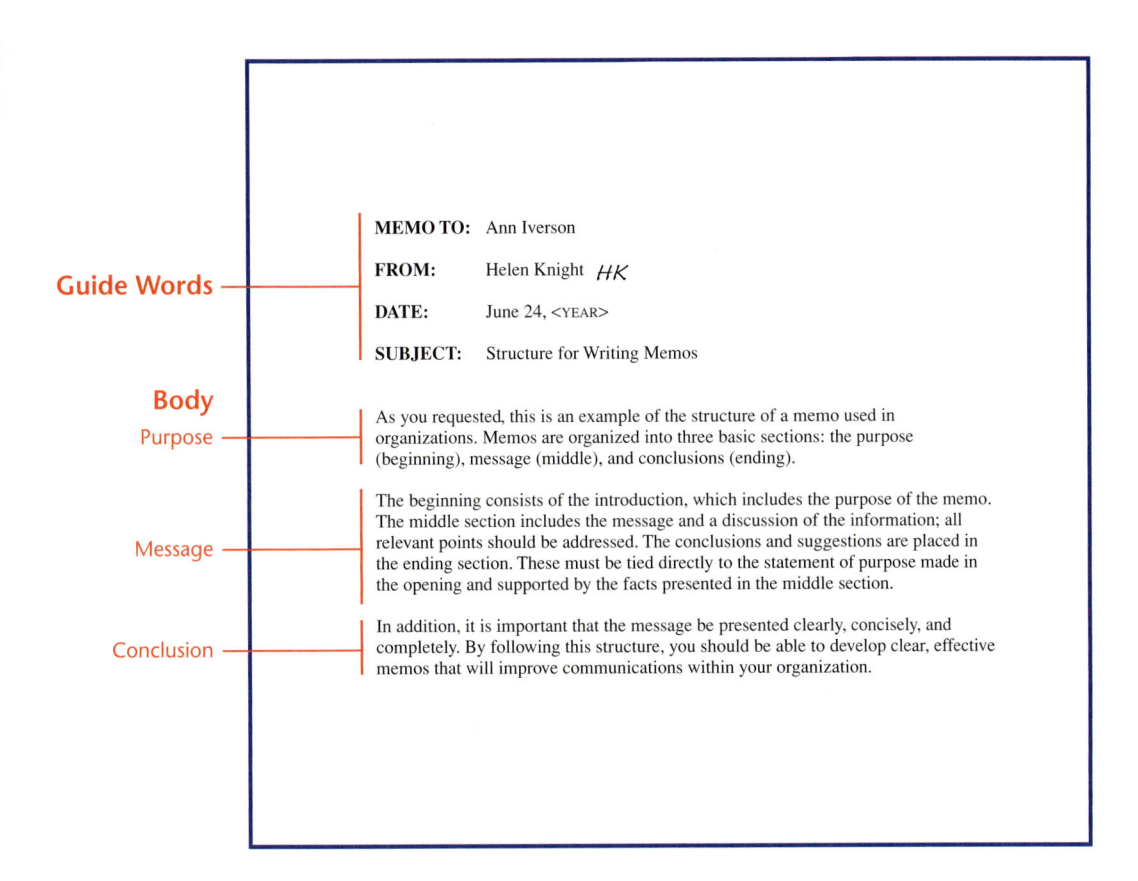

Figure 13-1
The three-part structure of a memo allows for ease of organization.

Guide Words

MEMO TO: Ann Iverson
FROM: Helen Knight *HK*
DATE: June 24, <YEAR>
SUBJECT: Structure for Writing Memos

Body

Purpose

As you requested, this is an example of the structure of a memo used in organizations. Memos are organized into three basic sections: the purpose (beginning), message (middle), and conclusions (ending).

Message

The beginning consists of the introduction, which includes the purpose of the memo. The middle section includes the message and a discussion of the information; all relevant points should be addressed. The conclusions and suggestions are placed in the ending section. These must be tied directly to the statement of purpose made in the opening and supported by the facts presented in the middle section.

Conclusion

In addition, it is important that the message be presented clearly, concisely, and completely. By following this structure, you should be able to develop clear, effective memos that will improve communications within your organization.

Approaches for Writing Memos

In addition to using the three-part structure (beginning, middle, and ending) to organize your memo, you should follow one of the three approaches for writing effective business messages. (For a review, see Chapter 5.)

Direct Approach

Most writers follow the *direct approach* in writing their memos. The direct approach is straightforward and easy for the reader to follow. When writing a routine memo using the direct approach, you should:

1. Open with the main idea/purpose.
2. Cover all the relevant points, including supporting information.
3. End with conclusions, recommendations, or requests for action.

Indirect Approach

Occasionally, you may decide that the *indirect approach* (used primarily for bad news) is a better plan for your memo. For instance, if you are presenting conclusions and recommendations that you know the receiver will oppose, you may be wise to present details and facts first before leading up to your conclusions and recommendations. Do not waste words, but do lead the reader to come to your conclusion by first explaining your point of view and building a strong case. The indirect approach would follow this plan:

Go to CD-ROM
Activities 13-1 and 13-2
To test your skills.

Developing Memos and Memo Reports

1. Give background details, facts, or explanations.
2. Present your conclusions and/or recommendations.

Although you may find the indirect approach helpful in bad-news situations, many communicators feel you should start internal messages by identifying the subject and purpose, regardless of the type of message.

Persuasive Approach

A memo requesting a special favor or approval of an idea should follow the *persuasive approach:*

1. Capture the reader's attention.
2. Create interest by showing a benefit to the reader, if possible.
3. Encourage the reader to say *yes* by logically presenting information supporting your request.
4. End your request courteously with an appropriate call to action.

Persuasive messages may also use the indirect approach.

Tone of a Memo

The tone of a memo may differ from the tone of a letter or a report written to someone outside an organization because the memo writer is often more interested in *presenting facts* than in persuading the reader. In fact, the writer is usually willing to let the reader form his or her own opinions. Although the memo writer should not forget about tact, courtesy, and friendliness, the writer assumes that the reader—a coworker—will work with him or her to serve the needs of the organization. For this reason, memos are usually written in a direct, no-nonsense style and are organized in a straightforward pattern.

Appropriate tone is still important to an effective message. Too often, writers allow a dictatorial tone to creep into their memos. *Will you please . . .* is a better beginning than *You will . . . .*

In most organizations today, the trend is toward *informality* in the tone of memos. The tone that is used, however, may be influenced by the rank of the writer in relation to the rank of the receiver. Generally, memos addressed to people above the writer's rank are more formal in tone than memos addressed to people at the same level as the writer or below the writer's rank.

Other factors that influence the formality of a memo include the purpose of the memo, the memo's subject matter, the reader's background knowledge of the subject, and the personalities of the receiver and the writer.

For instance, a memo announcing a holiday party would obviously differ in tone from a memo justifying budget cuts. A memo recognizing individuals for dedicated years of service might have a more informal tone, while a memo indicating reorganization of staff would have a more formal tone. If the receiver of a memo is knowledgeable about the subject matter, the tone of the memo might be less formal than if the receiver were not knowledgeable. Also, personalities of individuals will influence the tone of memos.

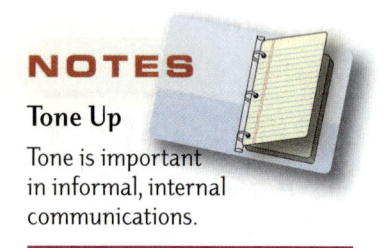

NOTES

Tone Up
Tone is important in informal, internal communications.

Some individuals have a less formal style in working with people while others have a more formal approach.

Most routine memos will do their job effectively if you:

1. Plan and organize your memo effectively using an appropriate approach and tone.
2. Edit each memo for clarity, logic, and psychological effect.
3. Proofread very carefully.

After following these three steps in preparing your memo, you should give the message a final reading from the reader's viewpoint. Evaluate your memo by using the following checklist to determine missing or partial items that you need to include or expand.

✔ CHECKLIST FOR MEMOS

Check Your Memo for:
- ____ Purpose stated
- ____ Problem/project identified
- ____ Background information provided
- ____ Needs of receiver met
- ____ Question(s) answered/problem(s) solved
- ____ Seven Cs applied
- ____ Conclusion(s)/suggestion(s)/recommendation(s) given
- ____ Appropriate approach used

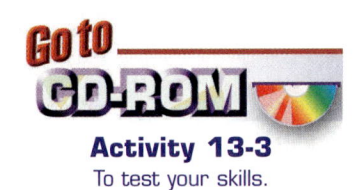

Go to CD-ROM
Activity 13-3
To test your skills.

Checkpoint 13.1

1. Why would you send, or not send, a memo that had the following beginning?

    Finally, the stats that everybody has been waiting for—the quarterly earnings figures. This has been a rough one, and I know that you all are dying to find out how we did.

2. Explain why the following conclusion is or is not effective.

    As you can see, a time management seminar is clearly worth the expense. I recommend that we hire Time Manager, Inc., to hold seminars on a bimonthly basis, and make attendance mandatory.

3. You are writing a memo to your manager. Which excerpt below is more appropriate?

    a. *Unfortunately, it appears that the organizational changes that were implemented in May have not had the positive impact we all hoped for. In fact, absenteeism is up, and we have lost six of our best employees.*

    b. *You must draw the obvious conclusion that the organizational changes you pushed on us in May have totally backfired. Our best people are bailing or not showing up.*

Memo Reports

Employees at all levels within an organization have a need for information in order to function in their respective roles. The reports you write not only serve as a basis for business decisions, but also help to evaluate your contributions to the organization and your ability to communicate your ideas in writing. Report-writing skills, in addition to your other communication skills, are thus very important to your success in business.

Types of Business Reports

The two types of business reports are the formal report and the informal report. The **formal report** is appropriate for reports that are sent outside the organization. For internal communications within the organization, the **informal report,** or **memo report,** is used more frequently. However, the formal report may also be used internally when the importance of the subject or length of the report makes the more informal memo report inappropriate.

A formal business report demands *thoroughly documented, objective,* and *detailed preparation.* The formal report is longer than a memo report and usually includes the following parts:

- Title page
- Letter or memo of transmittal
- Table of contents
- Summary or synopsis
- Introduction
- Body or text of several pages
- Tables and/or figures
- Summary
- Conclusions
- Recommendations
- Appendix
- Bibliography

The formal report will be discussed in detail in Chapter 15.

In the business world, the **memo report** is the most popular form for routine reports within an organization. While it resembles a memo because it uses the same format and structure, it is still considered a report.

A memo report is a cross between an *interoffice memo* and a *formal report.* The memo report follows the same format as a memo and uses a

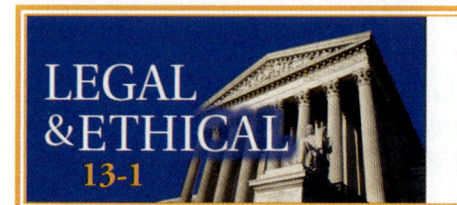

LEGAL & ETHICAL 13-1

Quoting Authorities. You are preparing an internal, informal report comparing computers. In a trade magazine, you find a complete analysis of the computers you are reviewing. You use this analysis for your report. Is this unethical? Is it illegal?

memo heading (**MEMO TO, FROM, DATE, SUBJECT**); but the body, which is usually two to five pages long, is organized like the body of a formal report and may have side headings.

Even though the memo report does not contain all the parts of a formal report, it may incorporate some of the special features found in formal reports, such as headings and graphics. The memo report is usually considerably shorter in length than a formal report and is written in an informal style using conversational language. Facts and opinions are frequently stated in the first person *(I suggest)* rather than using a stiff, formal writing style.

Similar to memos, memo reports flow upward, downward, and laterally within organizations. Timely flow of internal communication is essential, since employees at all levels within the organization rely heavily on information that is reported to them in making decisions.

Functions of Memo Reports

Memo reports communicate information or ideas, state facts, provide relevant data, and make recommendations to the receiver. Frequently, they are created to answer requests for information or to report progress on projects. In addition, they are used to justify and evaluate alternatives in the decision-making process.

Memo reports may be informational or analytical. **Informational reports** present only facts and information. **Analytical reports** present an interpretation of the facts and may include recommendations and conclusions based on the facts.

Determining the Purpose of the Report

When you begin to prepare a memo report, you need to consider two basic questions to ensure that your report will be functional and adapted to the reader: (1) Who will read the report? and (2) How will the report be used? After you have determined who will read the report and how it will be used, you should answer the following questions:

- Why is the report being requested?
- What do I, the writer, need to find out before writing the report?
- What kind of information does the reader need to understand?
- How, where, and when will the reader use the information?
- Where can the information be obtained?
- When is the information needed?

Once you have answers to these questions, you should be able to write a descriptive statement about the problem or the purpose of the report.

LEGAL & ETHICAL 13-2

Glossing Over Details. What is your ethical obligation in presenting factual, reliable, and objective information? What is meant by the "sin of omission"?

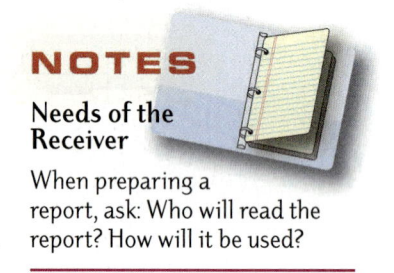

NOTES

Needs of the Receiver

When preparing a report, ask: Who will read the report? How will it be used?

Once the purpose has been defined, you are now ready to investigate the situation and gather information. Be certain that the information is factual, reliable, and objective. Present the information in an organized manner using clear, easy-to-understand language. As you analyze and interpret the information, you will develop your conclusions and recommendations for your report. After writing a draft of your report, you will need to edit and rewrite the report before distributing it to the readers.

Look at the memo report shown in Figure 13-2. This figure presents a typical format and arrangement for the memo report.

Figure 13-2
Note the logical arrangement of information in a memo report.

MEMO TO: Barbara Swalheim

FROM: Linda Bahr *LB*

DATE: July 3, <YEAR>

SUBJECT: Format for Memo Reports

Memo reports are short, informal reports used within an organization. They are considered to be a cross between a memo and a formal report because they follow the same format as a memo while they are organized like the body of a report. Used most frequently to communicate facts, ideas, and statistics, they begin with an introductory paragraph such as this.

Summary or Recommendation. This section includes either a concise summary of the content of the report or recommendations based on the results of the findings.

Background. Facts and background information necessary to fully understand the report are placed in this section.

Findings. This section reports the results of any investigation, experiment, research, survey, study, or analysis. It may include tables, charts, or graphs to assist the reader in understanding the results.

Conclusions. The final section of the memo report interprets the results of the findings.

By following this format for memo reports, you will be able to create reports to enhance the decision-making process within your organization.

lb

Types of Memo Reports

Memo reports may be classified according to the frequency with which they are generated. Typical memo reports include the following:

- **Progress/status reports:** generated at specific intervals
- **Periodic reports:** generated on a regular schedule
- **Informational reports:** generated on an "as needed" basis

Progress Reports

Progress or **status reports** are used to inform readers about the status of a specific project or activity. They usually indicate what has been done on a project, what is being done, and what still needs to be done. They are useful in monitoring and decision making.

Some simple progress or status reports are written on **fill-in forms** and are sent as needed or required by those monitoring a project or activity. Others are written as **brief narrative reports**—these may respond to requests for complex information or present ideas, explanations, or simple recommendations. Longer, more involved status reports may also contain recommendations supported by financial data or operating results.

Periodic Reports

Periodic reports, one of the most common types of reports used by businesses, are routinely prepared at regular time intervals—daily, weekly, monthly, quarterly, or annually. Two of the most common types of periodic reports are sales reports and financial reports. A monthly report on training contracts is illustrated in Figure 13-3.

NOTES

Three Choices
Types of memo reports: progress, periodic, and informational.

Go to CD-ROM

Activity 13-4
To test your skills.

MEMO TO: John Lightle

FROM: Lee Thomas *LT*

DATE: April 4, <YEAR>

SUBJECT: Computer Training Contracts

Our computer training contracts in March showed an increase of 46 percent over last year's figures. We completed 108 training contracts in March compared to 74 contracts last March.

The March contracts continued the upward trend we have seen in January and February. This trend is the result of increased advertising efforts and expansion of our computer lab facilities.

A final report is being prepared and will be distributed next week.

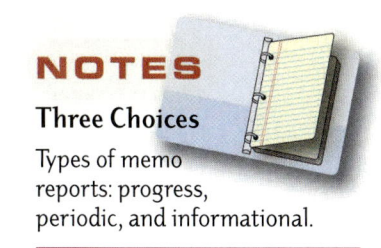

Figure 13-3
This periodic report provides a monthly update.

Developing Memos and Memo Reports

Periodic reports are often prepared on **preprinted forms,** which provide blank spaces in which to record information. The forms may also be computer files into which you insert the needed information. Using a form to prepare a periodic report reduces the likelihood that you will omit essential information. It also reduces the time required to prepare the report.

Periodic reports may also be prepared according to **standardized outlines** that ensure report uniformity. Sales reports, credit reports, audit reports, and many legal reports are prepared using a standardized format.

Informational Reports

Informational reports are simple, straightforward, factual presentations. Most reports written in business are informational reports. Their purpose is to communicate information—facts, ideas, statistics, or trends—in a direct manner. For an informational report, you will gather facts, figures, and data, organize the information, interpret and present the organized information objectively, and make recommendations, if requested.

Data retrieved from a computer file can help you prepare informational reports quickly. Although the computer may provide the data, you must interpret the data. In preparing your report, it is your responsibility to evaluate results, reach conclusions, and recommend possible solutions to a problem.

When you are using computer data to prepare a report, you may be able to save rekeying of the data by printing statistical information directly from the computer file. You may then attach a simple memo transmittal form to the printed data. Or you may electronically copy the data to create a new document, then build the memo report around the data.

Gathering Information for a Memo Report

Because a memo report often must be produced quickly, the information gathering is frequently done more casually and less rigorously than for a longer, formal report that is sent outside the organization. Still, if you are asked to collect data for an informal memo report, be as thorough and factual as your limited time allows.

Organizing the Information for a Memo Report

After you have gathered the information, you need to determine the best way to present your findings. Remember that reports should be factual and reliable. To accomplish this, you need to do the following:

- Present the facts with absolute fairness and accuracy.
- Be careful not to mix your opinions with the facts you report.
- Reserve your comments for your conclusions and recommendations, but tie them directly to the information presented and facts reported.

GLOBAL DIVERSITY 13.1

Word Meanings

As workplaces become more diverse, the challenge of communication will increase. Different backgrounds of workers mean that many more meanings can be assigned to the same topic. A sales representative who used the phrase "climate study" to refer to morale and corporate culture confused the receiver who did not relate to this meaning. *Can you think of another example of a word or phrase used in business that might be interpreted differently by employees from diverse backgrounds?*

---

374 Chapter 13

One of the most common and effective techniques of memo organization you can use is to *itemize the information*. A report that contains complex facts and ideas will be easier to read if items are (1) separated into paragraphs, (2) numbered, or (3) preceded by side headings. Using this technique will also help you write concisely and organize carefully.

Two challenges in presenting information are to communicate statistical data effectively and to process an accumulation of material. Statistical data can be communicated most easily through tables, charts, and graphs. Remember, when you use these features, introduce them with an appropriate reference in the text. All tables and graphs should also have adequate captions and labels—check yours by asking the *who, what, where, when, why,* and *how* questions.

When communicating statistical data, a table allows you to display the statistical material in logically arranged rows (horizontally) and columns (vertically) for quick, easy reading. You should use a title, a subtitle, and column headings to identify the material in a table. You can also add rules (lines) above and below the column headings and at the bottom of the table to give it a more professional look. Note how the tabular form used in Figure 13-4 makes the statistical information easy to read and interpret.

Thinking Cap 13.2

Discuss: What are some ways you can ensure that you will present facts fairly and accurately and will not mix them with your own opinions?

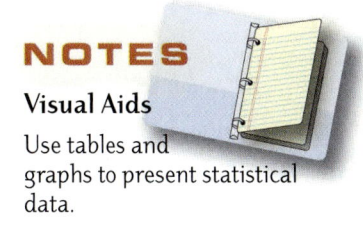

NOTES

Visual Aids

Use tables and graphs to present statistical data.

Figure 13-4
A table is an ideal way to present statistical information.

MEMO TO: John Lightle

FROM: Lee Thomas   *LT*

DATE: April 8, <YEAR>

SUBJECT: First Quarter Computer Training Contracts

Computer training contracts for the first quarter of <year> increased 40.7 percent over the first quarter of last year. This is a tremendous increase and will help cover some of the expenses incurred by our expansion of facilities and equipment.

Following are the computer training contracts for the first quarter, reported monthly, for both years:

COMPUTER TRAINING CONTRACTS
Comparison of First Quarter, Year 1 and Year 2

Months	Year 1	Year 2	Increase	Increase
January	80	60	20	33.3%
February	92	65	27	41.5%
March	108	74	34	46.0%
TOTALS	280	199	81	40.7%

The expansion of our facilities in December allowed us to increase the number of training sessions as well as expand the types of software packages offered. This has resulted in the addition of several new clients. In addition, many of our former clients have returned for training in the upgraded versions of their software.

Our goal is to maintain this increase throughout the following quarters. We plan to continue to expand our offerings for the next quarter.

It is through your efforts that we were able to have the new facilities and courses ready for classes in January. Our growth is a result of your contributions.

gm

With today's software, data can easily be converted into graph form. You can use a **line graph** or **bar graph** to show changes over a period of time and a **pie graph** to show the parts or percentages of a whole.

If you must communicate a large amount of reference material—data or statistics—that you feel is important for the receiver to have, consider putting most or all of it in a supplement (an appendix or an attachment) to your memo report. This allows the reader to scan the supplement for evidence or documentation supporting your report. The supplement also allows you to focus on the most essential facts in the body of your report.

Although your memo report should contain enough facts to inform your reader fully, too much documentation in the report body can detract from your main point. Do not overwhelm the reader by putting all data or statistics within the body. By definition, a memo report is usually a shorter report than a formal report. Remember to be as concise as possible while still being complete—a report that is too long will not be read.

Making Recommendations in a Memo Report

If you have been asked to make a recommendation, make it the **main point** of your memo. Be sure to find out whether you should describe specifically how to carry out your recommendation. Also, consider whether you should mention alternatives to your recommendation.

Including your recommendation and possible alternatives will make your memo report complete—you will be telling the reader what he or she has asked for as well as offering your own ideas.

Checklist for Memo Reports

As you develop each memo report, evaluate your message by using the following checklist to determine that your information is complete. If a coworker or another student is available, proofread together. If not, proofread the material using one or more of the proofreading methods you learned earlier.

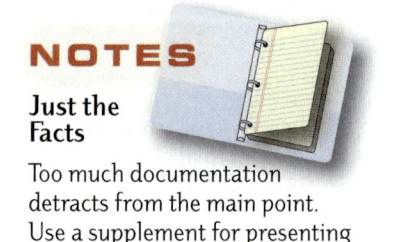

NOTES
Just the Facts

Too much documentation detracts from the main point. Use a supplement for presenting reference materials.

✔ **CHECKLIST FOR MEMO REPORTS**

Check Your Memo Report for:
____ Problem/purpose identified
____ Information gathered
____ Information organized logically
____ Clear, easy-to-understand language used
____ Information presented factually and objectively
____ Data/information analyzed and interpreted (if appropriate)
____ Conclusions given
____ Recommendations given (if appropriate)

Preparing a Sample Memo Report

Suppose you received from your employer the memo shown in Figure 13-5 below. How would you go about gathering data for the requested report? Follow these steps for preparing a memo report on an office space rental study:

1. First, read the request carefully to make sure you know exactly what information Ms. Schmitz needs. (Since her memo is clearly written and you understand what you are to do, you need not telephone her for further explanation.)

2. Review client addresses to determine their proximity to different office locations.

3. Check various business directories to find out what office space is available within the city.

Figure 13-5
Note the details outlined in this request for a report on expanding office space.

> **MEMO TO:** Marie Dimpfl
>
> **FROM:** Debra Schmitz *DS*
>
> **DATE:** September 12, <YEAR>
>
> **SUBJECT:** Office Space Rental Study
>
> As our business has continued to expand, I think we need to consider increasing our office space. Our current office does not allow for expansion; therefore, I feel we need to investigate setting up a branch office at another location in Madison.
>
> Will you please investigate the various possibilities for renting office space? We probably should concentrate on an office location that has at least 2500 square feet available.
>
> Please research such things as location, square footage available, rental cost per square foot, and the management company. Also, as you find viable locations, visit them and inspect the property itself and talk with other tenants to see if they are satisfied with the location and management services.
>
> After researching locations, please present four locations on the west side which you would recommend for our branch office—also include a couple of east-side locations in case some staff members would prefer that area. However, I would like your specific recommendation on whether you feel we should locate on the west or east side of Madison. I would appreciate this information by September 30 for our staff meeting.
>
> rbs

Developing Memos and Memo Reports 377

4. Next, look in the Yellow Pages and begin phoning management firms dealing in office space rentals. Obtain general information about their rental locations, the amount of space available at each location, an estimate of the cost per square foot, and amenities included with that cost.

5. Check the various locations for the overall quality of the exterior of buildings, accessibility to main streets and highways, and parking availability. Also, check to see if there are other types of businesses within the area and if future business and residential development is planned.

6. Study this information and narrow the choices to six to eight locations that you feel would be acceptable.

7. Set up appointments with representatives from the management firms for the locations you desire. Meet with them to discuss details of a contract and to see the interior of the spaces.

8. Visit the office spaces at the various locations and use the visits to view firsthand and judge the condition of the buildings and grounds and the interior of the offices. During your visits, talk with some of the tenants to determine whether they are pleased with the space, location, and management.

9. Analyze and compare the data you have collected for each location.

10. Select the four locations on the west side that you feel would best meet your company's needs. Also, identify two additional locations on the east side.

11. Draw conclusions and determine what recommendations you will make to Ms. Schmitz based on your research and the comparisons you have made.

12. Organize the information you have gathered, your recommendations, and your conclusions into a memo report to Ms. Schmitz.

Remember that Ms. Schmitz expects your report to be factual and reliable. To accomplish this, you will need to do the following:

- Present the facts with absolute fairness and accuracy.
- Be careful not to mix your opinions with the facts you report.
- Reserve your comments for your conclusions and recommendations.

Now read the report shown in Figure 13-6a and Figure 13-6b, which Ms. Dimpfl wrote in response to Ms. Schmitz's request. As you review this report, note that it is effective in two ways:

1. The information is presented in an orderly, easy-to-read fashion (note the side headings, for example); and

Figure 13-6a
This first page of a memo report presents recommendations and findings.

MEMO TO: Debra Schmitz

FROM: Marie Dimpfl *MD*

DATE: September 28, <YEAR>

SUBJECT: Office Space Rental Study

As you requested, I have investigated various locations on the east and west sides of Madison for opening a branch office.

RECOMMENDATIONS

In selecting a branch office location, I recommend the west side of Madison and the following locations:

- High Point Office Park
- Old Sauk Trails Park
- Seminole Center
- Enterprise Building

If the east side is the preferred location, I recommend the following locations:

- International Properties
- Virchow Krause Building

FINDINGS
1. The annual dollar rate per square foot of office space averages between $11.50 and $16.50, with a few companies at $17 and $18.
2. Except for Seminole Center, heat, light, real estate taxes, and common area charges are included in the cost per square foot.
3. Each location is in an office-park-type setting. The west side locations are all near new development areas, basically corporate headquarters. They are all within one-half mile of residential areas.
4. The buildings are all less than ten years old.
5. A survey of the properties showed them to be in excellent interior and exterior condition and to have generally satisfied tenants.

---

2. The report represents something extra because the writer not only makes the recommendations Ms. Schmitz has asked for, but she has also taken the time to present the facts clearly and has given a concise but complete comparison.

In writing memo reports, as in other phases of a job, remember to do a little more than is required. You and those with whom you work will benefit from the extra effort you make to produce a comprehensive report.

Since you are writing for coworkers when you are preparing internal communications, there are several factors to remember:

- Time factor—be concise; people do not have time to read everything they receive.
- People factor—be courteous; do not take your colleagues for granted.

Developing Memos and Memo Reports

Figure 13-6b
The table offers a quick way to compare recommended office locations.

Debra Schmitz
Page 2
September 28, <YEAR>

6. Each of the management companies was found to provide excellent services to renters and to be in sound financial condition. All companies have multiple rental properties within the city.
7. Each of the properties requires a three-year lease with the renter having the option to extend the lease for another three-year period.
8. Each of the properties would allow for minimum remodeling within the rental space. However, it would be at the renter's expense.
9. All locations have easy access to major highways.
10. All locations have large parking lots for client parking.
11. A review of our client list indicates that the majority are from either the west side of Madison or from areas west of Madison. In addition, the vast number of new developments in the area provides for a large potential client base.

DETAILS OF RECOMMENDED OFFICE RENTAL LOCATIONS

The following is a listing of the recommended locations for a branch office:

Office Location	Sq. Ft. Available	$/Sq. Ft.	Company
West Side:			
High Point Office Park 555 D'Onofrio Drive	5,500	$14.00	Welton Enterprises
Old Sauk Trails Park 1210 Fourier Drive	2,650	$15.00	Blettner Group
Seminole Center 594 Seminole Court	4,000	*$12.50	Blettner Group
Enterprise Building 6400 Enterprise Lane	3,000	$13.75	Oakbrook Corporation
East Side:			
International Properties 2702 International Lane	4,000	$14.25	Executive Management
Virchow Krause Building 4130 Lien Road	17,000	$12.75	Michelson Corporation

*Does not include heat.

CONCLUSIONS

1. These properties are similar in cost, amenities, and convenience of location. They are of the quality that our company requires.
2. Tours of each of the properties can be arranged for your review.

jos

- Information factor—be complete, give people the information they need for making decisions.

- Content factor—provide factual, reliable, and objective information.

- Organization factor—be logical, clear, complete, and concise.

One-Page Reports

In today's business world, there is an increased emphasis on keeping the length of reports and internal communications to one page. The format for one-page reports consists of:

- Statement of purpose/problem

- Recommendation

- Rationale for recommendation (listed in priority order)

One-page memo reports or summaries may be referred to as **executive summaries.** They summarize the recommendations of a report and the rationale for the recommendations. Consequently, reading the summary may eliminate the need for people to read a longer document if they are interested only in a report's findings and recommendations.

> *In the world of business, everyone needs to learn to write a one-page summary.*
> —Nancy M. Johnson, American Family Insurance

Checkpoint 13.2

1. Why is it important not to mix opinion and facts in a memo report?
2. Why do you think graphics, such as bullets and charts, make a report easy to read?
3. How would you decide if you have included too much information in a memo report?

CHAPTER 13 SUMMARY

The volume of internal communications in business is steadily increasing. Two forms of communications, the memo and the memo report, are designed for internal communications. Both are written to communicate facts, ideas, statistics, and trends.

The basic principles and techniques for effective communication can be applied to internal communications. When you plan internal communication, you must identify the purpose of the communication, the audience, and the information that is needed by the audience.

The memo report functions to present facts and information and to aid the receivers in making decisions or directing courses of action. Therefore, it is important to present all information factually and objectively.

Whether you are writing a memo or a memo report, it is important to review your communication to make sure the information presented meets the needs of the receiver, answers the questions or solves the problem, and is presented clearly, concisely, completely, and correctly.

Communication at Work

Danny Izumi, President and Director

Business Learning Center

In some ways, you might say that 34-year-old Danny Izumi is old-fashioned. Never mind that he operates a high-tech business that trains people on computer applications, Web design, and computer repair. Or that like most business people these days, he's lost without his cell phone.

Because for all the high-tech wizardry he surrounds himself with every day, Danny still believes in the basics when it comes to communication—basics such as thank-you notes to clients and strong writing and verbal skills for his employees.

As Danny sees it, strong communication equals more business. Potential employees are evaluated not only on their background and technical skills, but on their communication skills as well.

"Our job is to train people in computer skills. If my representative cannot speak or communicate with confidence, there will be no clients," says Danny. "Writing skills are critical in documenting, creating reports, and writing letters to the clients. Strong communication skills win the confidence of the client."

As for the thank-you notes to clients: "Simple, but very effective," he says, "because it's personal."

"... if my representative cannot speak or communicate with confidence, there will be no clients ..."

Open Lines of Communication

Danny and his partner have owned and operated Business Learning Center (BLC) for more than six years. BLC specializes in training for Microsoft Office applications, graphic design, Web site design, computer repair, and network administration programs.

BLC's clients include workers who are being retrained for new careers, corporate employees who need computer skills, high school students, even suburban moms who want to be able to monitor their children's online activities.

Efficient, effective communication is necessary to keep things running smoothly as a small business like Danny's grows. Much of the in-house communication at BLC is done through e-mail rather than through paper memos. Danny also uses e-mail to communicate with potential clients, to do marketing research, and to obtain product evaluations. Using e-mail also means that important memos and requests are documented.

For all the benefits of e-mail—access, faster communication, documentation—it is not always the best method of communication. "At the time it's

Communication at Work

presented, e-mail is one-way communication," says Danny. "It may not be the appropriate choice for delivering a negative or sensitive message." So he doesn't use e-mail to discuss problems or delicate issues; instead, he prefers to communicate in person.

Delivering Clear Messages

"I have experienced where some part of the [e-mail] message or memo was not interpreted as I intended. If there is an issue, I communicate face to face," he says. "Human beings communicate through the senses. I read the gestures, the body language; I sense the nervousness and apprehension." These nonverbal cues help Danny tailor his words and his delivery to make sure his message gets across.

Similarly, Danny expects that his employees will speak to him in person about their personal needs rather than firing off an e-mail requesting the afternoon off. "My employees know what kind of issues are appropriate for e-mail and what needs to be discussed in person. When they cross the line, I make sure they understand I don't appreciate the choice of method."

His ancestry and upbringing may influence the emphasis Danny places on communication etiquette. Danny was born in the United States, but as a child, he lived in Japan, a country with a strong tradition of social convention. Asked why he places such importance on strong writing skills, for example, Danny replies, "In my culture, if you can't write well, people question your education and your upbringing, which brings shame on your parents."

Danny Izumi's parents have nothing to worry about. He has learned his lessons well. After all, he still writes thank-you notes.

Discuss

1. What are some issues that would be inappropriate to bring up with your employer in an e-mail message?

2. If an issue is inappropriate for an e-mail, and you are uncomfortable discussing it face to face—perhaps because it is of a personal nature—what are your other options?

3. Why is it important for a company to be able to keep records of e-mail messages, memos, and other office documents?

Chapter 13

Online Exercises

Objective:
These online activities will allow you to practice writing memos.

Go to **bcw.glencoe.com,** the address for the *Business Communication at Work* Web site, and select Chapter 13. Next, click on Online Exercises. You will see a list of Web site links that will bring you to communication Web sites and search engines.

Activity 13.1

1. Select one of the communication Web sites to visit.
2. Search for an article that relates to electronic communication. You may have to enter *electronic communication* in the Web site's **Search** box. If the Web site you have chosen does not have an article about electronic communication, return to the *Business Communication at Work* Web site and visit another communication Web site.
3. On a sheet of paper, write a short informational report (no more than one page). You should take the following steps in writing your report:
   a. Gather facts, figures, and data.
   b. Organize the information.
   c. Interpret and present the organized information objectively.

   Remember, your report should be simple, straightforward, factual presentations.
4. Write your name on your report, and hand it in to your instructor.

Activity 13.2

1. Select one of the search engines to visit.
2. Key *photocopier machine* in the **Search** box (some Web sites may use an **Enter Word** box).
3. From your results, select five links to information about photocopier machines. At each Web site you visit, notice the differences in the features offered with the product.
4. On a sheet of paper, write a memo to your instructor, discussing which photocopier machine you think is the best. Your decision should be based on price, quality, and features offered with the product. Remember to organize your memo using the following:
   a. Beginning: Introduction/Purpose
   b. Middle: Message/Discussion. Cover all relevant points, including supporting data and explanations.
   c. Ending: Conclusions/Recommendations

   Your memo should be no more than a page in length and should use the direct approach.
5. Write your name on your memo, and hand it in to your instructor.

CHAPTER 13 WORKSHEETS

NAME _____ DATE _____

PRACTICE 1

Planning Memos

Instructions: As you prepare to write a memo, you need to review the purpose of the memo and identify the audience. For the following writing situations, identify the purpose, the audience, and the audience needs by answering the questions.

1. Ms. Kneer, the Vice President of Human Resources, has asked you to send a memo to all personnel announcing the appointment of Charles Gomez to the newly created position of training director and welcoming him to the organization. She wants you to provide some background information on Mr. Gomez: You are to select information from his résumé that reflects the qualifications and experiences that make him a good choice for this position.
   a. Why are you writing the memo?
   b. What is the situation/problem you are addressing?
   c. Who is your audience for the memo?
   d. What kind of information does the audience need?
   e. Why does the audience need this information?
   f. What are the questions/concerns the audience may have?

2. Your supervisor, Mr. Cyrus, has asked you to notify all department heads that their budgets will be due March 15 instead of February 15 and that they need to attend a training session on February 2 to learn about new procedures for preparing the budget.
   a. Why are you writing the memo?
   b. What is the situation/problem you are addressing?
   c. Who is your audience for the memo?
   d. What kind of information does the audience need?
   e. Why does the audience need this information?
   f. What are the questions/concerns the audience may have?

3. The college president's assistant has called and informed you that two members of the District Board have requested an update on international activities at the college for use in reviewing strategic initiatives. She is requesting that you, as chairperson of the student international committee, prepare a brief memo to the board indicating the current activities of the committee. (*Note:* This information could easily be presented in a memo report, but the assistant says, "They do not want a report, only a brief memo.")
   a. Why are you writing the memo?
   b. What is the situation/problem you are addressing?
   c. Who is your audience for the memo?
   d. What kind of information does the audience need?
   e. Why does the audience need this information?
   f. What are the questions/concerns the audience may have?

Developing Memos and Memo Reports 385

CHAPTER 13 WORKSHEETS

Name _____ Date _____

Planning a Memo Report

Instructions: *Just as in preparing to write a memo, you need to answer specific questions when you begin preparing a memo report. In the following memo report situation, identify the purpose, the audience, and the audience needs by answering the questions.*

1. Your company's CEO feels that the organization is in a position to have a presence on the World Wide Web. On June 10, he asks you to investigate whether it "makes sense" to have a Web site: What would be the process needed to develop the site? What would be the costs? Are there consultants who could be hired and, if so, what would be their fees? Are there people within the organization who would be of assistance either in the creative or technical development of the site? He asks you to "educate" him in this area since he has no understanding of it. He would like the information so that he will be in a position to discuss it with the Board of Directors on August 20. He will need the information for review a couple of weeks prior to the meeting.

    a. Why is the report being requested?
    b. What does the writer need to find out?
    c. What kind of information does the reader need to understand?
    d. How, where, and when will the reader use the information?
    e. How can the information be obtained?
    f. When is the information needed?

Writing Effective Openings for Memos

Instructions: *Write openings for the memo situations described in Questions 1–3 of Practice 1.*

1. Memo introducing a new employee, Charles Gomez: _____
2. Memo regarding budgets: _____
3. Memo regarding international initiatives: _____

PRACTICE 2

Writing Routine Memos

Instructions: *On separate sheets of paper, plan and prepare (using your computer) clear, concise memos for the following situations. Organize the information given, plus any other information you desire, into effective interoffice memos.*

1. Prepare a congratulatory memo for your boss, Jerome Steffens, to send to all employees within the research division. He has just been informed by human resources that the research division was the largest contributor within your organization to the United Way fund drive. Employees in the research division donated a total of $2000, which was 20 percent of the organization's total donations. Your message, though short, should project excitement.

2. Prepare a memo to Carol Bayer in the human resources department inquiring whether you are eligible to enroll in a tax-deferred annuity program. Ask for information about the procedures you would need to follow in order to enroll. Also inquire about the plans that have been approved through your company.

3. As personnel officer, write a memo dated November 15 to tell all employees of changes in their dental insurance premiums. The insurance carrier has just notified you that, effective January 1, the dental premium will go up $2 a month for each employee. The current premium is $22 a month. The additional $2 will be deducted automatically from employee paychecks starting on January 1.

CHAPTER 13 WORKSHEETS

NAME _____ DATE _____

PRACTICE 3

Preparing Information in a Readable Format

Instructions: The way information is presented affects the reader's understanding. Statistical information presented in narrative form is usually the most confusing. In the following exercises, prepare the information in table format so that it will be clearer and easier to understand at a glance. Use the table feature of a word processing program and include an appropriate title and subtitle. Prepare a first draft of your tables before keying them on the computer.

1. Arrange the following narrative information in a table format:

    The average utility costs per month for the last two years are as follows: Gas average was $150 a month last year and $160 a month this year. Electricity average was $82 a month this year and $84 a month last year, while water was $23 a month last year and $24 a month this year.

    Make a table that will show total utilities for last year and for this year as well as total electricity for both years, total gas for both years, total water for both years, and the grand total of all utilities for both years.

    Write a draft of your table in the space below before keying the final copy.

    _____
    _____
    _____
    _____
    _____

2. Your manager, Marilyn Satterwhite, has requested a brief memo report indicating the insurance sales for the branch offices for December.

    First, prepare a table with the following information: The December sales for three insurance products for three branch offices of the Great Stuff Insurance Company are as follows: The first type of insurance, whole life policies, sold $2.25 million in the Vermilion branch, $3.1 million in the Illini branch, and $1.8 million in the Rock Valley branch. The second type of insurance, universal life, sold $4.1 million in the Vermilion branch, $5 million in the Illini branch, and $350,000 in the Rock Valley branch. The third type of insurance, term insurance, sold $1.6 million in the Vermilion branch, $2.24 million in the Illini branch, and $3 million in the Rock Valley branch.

    Hint: The table should show total sales at each branch, total sales of each type of insurance, and the total of all branches and all types of insurance. Include the table in a brief memo to your manager.

    _____
    _____
    _____
    _____
    _____

Developing Memos and Memo Reports

CHAPTER 14

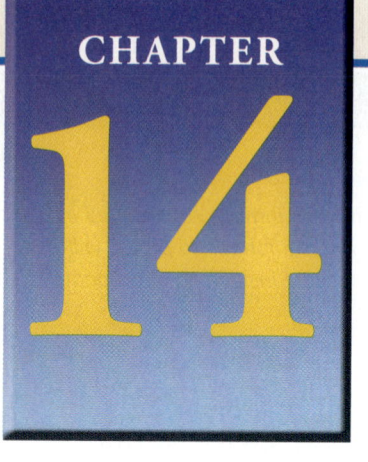

Creating Press Releases and Newsletters

Objectives

After completing this chapter, you will be able to:

1. Describe and explain the guidelines for writing a press release
2. Prepare a simple press release
3. Describe and explain the guidelines for writing a newsletter
4. Prepare a simple newsletter

WORKPLACE APPLICATIONS

Ethical Behavior

Ethics are the principles of right and wrong that guide all our decisions. We make ethical decisions every day. Some are minor—should you check the Internet on company time, or not? Some are significant—should you report a crime? Most businesses have clear guidelines about the **ethical behavior** that is expected from every employee. Unfortunately, ethical dilemmas still crop up, and an employee may have to make tough choices.

Ethical Infractions

Some ethical situations are the result of employees choosing to do wrong because they feel justified. For example, because they did not get a raise, they feel that it is okay to make personal phone calls from work, pad the expense account, or pass along confidential information. Employees who cheat on their time sheets, lie on reports, or steal office supplies are not doing anybody a favor, least of all themselves. Their actions are usually discovered, and their reputations and the company's morale are always damaged.

Some ethical dilemmas are the result of a superior asking an employee to do something wrong. For example, a supervisor might ask an employee to lie on his or her behalf or to ignore information. An employee may be forced to choose between compromising his or her principles and keeping his or her job. Of course, this situation happens rarely in businesses that have a clear ethical framework. A good company leader knows that workers want to comply with the rules of good conduct and to practice ethical behavior. Businesses that establish clear rules and hire managers who clearly respect and follow those rules offer the best support for their employees.

Thinking Critically

Situation: Although your team leader does not know it, one of your teammates is using company time to prepare and send out her résumé, and she has been to job interviews during her extended lunch hours.

Ask Yourself: What, if anything, would you do? Explain your decision.

389

> *News is what a chap who doesn't care much about anything wants to read. And it's only news until he's read it. After that it's dead.*
>
> —Evelyn Waugh, Author

When a press release is well written and designed effectively, it can build goodwill by promoting your organization. The media exposure it brings will place your company's name before readers, which can enhance your company or product image. A *press release*, also called a *news release*, announces some news that has happened or that will happen and is the accepted and standard form of communicating information to the media.

Large organizations may have a public relations department whose job is to handle the publicity designed to promote the organization. In this case, press releases are written by someone in that department. Not all companies have public relations departments, so anyone in the organization may be asked to prepare a press release. You may, therefore, be responsible at some time for writing the final copy of a press release for your company or for preparing a draft to be edited and polished by the public relations department. You may also be asked to write a press release for a service or professional organization to which you belong.

PRESS RELEASES

If you are responsible for writing press releases, you are on the "cutting edge" of what is happening in your company. You should establish good relations with your media contacts. Keep their names, company addresses, phone numbers, and e-mail addresses handy for quick reference. Remember that time is important when releasing information to the media, and a quick contact may often be necessary.

LEGAL & ETHICAL 14-1

Newsworthiness. Should you believe everything you hear or read in the news media? Are certain media biased in their views? Why or why not? Give examples of questionable news sources.

NOTES

Team Effort

All employees have a responsibility to contribute to good public relations and to their organization's positive public image.

Planning a Press Release

Making a writing plan before you begin writing is just as important for a press release as it is for other types of communication. Planning a press release involves determining its goals. You should determine the major goal of each press release. Read all the information you have gathered, then formulate an outline to save time and to be assured that your ideas flow in a clear, logical manner.

State the Purpose of the Press Release

Identify what you want to accomplish by writing the press release. For example, the purpose of a press release might be one of these:

- To announce an individual's promotion or appointment to a position
- To inform readers of a new or improved product or service

- To report financial activities
- To announce awards earned or community services donated by employees or the organization
- To advise readers of new or expanded facilities

Thinking Cap 14.1

Discuss: What types of publicity are generated by press releases?

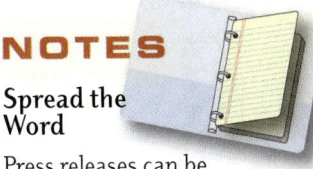

Your overall purpose in writing a press release is to entice the media into reporting, in their own words, about your company or product in order to increase your company's visibility. The media will not take the information from your press release and simply reprint it or broadcast it. You must make your press release describe something new, different, exciting, and interesting about your organization—something that the media will find newsworthy.

Identify the Target Media

Your **target media** is the person or persons to whom you are writing. You should identify what kind of media coverage you want to generate when using a press release. This coverage can take several forms—a feature news article, a radio or television interview, or a printed product review such as in a newspaper or magazine. A feature news article can be a detailed article devoted solely to the subject in your press release. On a radio or television program, the subject of your press release might be discussed, or you or someone from your organization might be interviewed. In addition, newspapers and magazines often print columns that highlight new and interesting products they think readers would enjoy or find beneficial. The Internet is becoming a favorite place to post news releases.

Guidelines for Writing Press Releases

Editors welcome concise press releases, but it is better to give them too much information than too little. Too little information may require them to make time-consuming telephone calls for additional information or clarification, or it could result in the release being tossed into the wastebasket.

Follow these guidelines when writing press releases:

NOTES

Spread the Word

Press releases can be distributed not only to media but also to associations, trade shows, audiences at speaking engagements, or any potential customers.

Set Realistic Goals

Having a clear understanding of your goals will help you focus your writing on the purpose of the press release to ensure that it will meet your expectations. Use the following checklist:

- Have I chosen the appropriate media?
- Have I identified my audience correctly?
- Have I included all the necessary information?
- Is the press release clear and to the point?

Identify an Interest Angle—Your "Hook"

Most press releases will be printed or broadcast only if the editor considers the information newsworthy; therefore, the information in the opening must grab the reader's attention. Here are some examples of how a press release might emphasize local news, human interest, or public service angles.

Creating Press Releases and Newsletters

A local news angle about the appointment of a new company president might catch the reader's interest because the reader is interested in the company's key personnel, is an investor, or has previously worked for the company.

LOCAL NEWS: Columbus native Jacob Andrews yesterday was named President of . . . .

Readers are always interested in heroic efforts by others. An example of a human interest story follows:

HUMAN INTEREST: Robert Zhang, the volunteer firefighter who last week rescued a 5-year-old boy from the icy Truckee River, will be honored this evening at 8 p.m. at the Rhineman Community Center. Robert, a manager at Henderson & Associates . . . .

The readers' interests are often piqued when they read about some free service such as in the following public service announcement:

PUBLIC SERVICE: Angus & Martin, a local investment firm, is again offering our community a free estate planning seminar entitled "Estate Planning: Investing in Future Generations."

A press release detailing a new travel discount, Fly-Away Travel, is not news because discount travel is nothing new. However, a press release describing Fly-Away Travel as a travel service that finds exclusive discount fares for families who travel with children is news. This information is news because consumers may be interested in this service.

Determine Who Should Receive Your Press Release

Ask yourself who would realistically be most interested in the information you are presenting in your press release. For example, many kinds of media outlets—newspapers, magazines, and television and radio stations—would be interested in information about Fly-Away Travel. You should create a mailing list of the media outlets that should receive your press release.

Avoid Highly Technical Language and Detail

Even if you intend your press release to go to a department at a magazine or newspaper whose staff would understand technical language, you cannot be sure that the person who initially reads the press release will have the same background. Also, even if an editor understands the technical language, he or she might pass the press release to someone who does not understand it. You should avoid highly technical language and detail except when necessary.

Press Release Format

A standard format should be followed if your press release is to be accepted and read by the media. Seven basic elements should be included in a press release. With examples of each of these elements, we will build a press release based on the public service example introduced above.

Thinking Cap 14.2

Discuss: What are the pros of issuing error-free press releases in order to maintain the organization's good public image?

- Use 20-pound white or off-white bond paper.

- Use single spacing, 1.5-inch spacing, or double spacing.

- Indent five spaces for each new paragraph, or skip two lines between each paragraph, and make paragraphs flush left.

- Use italics or bold type to emphasize key words.

- Use only one side of the paper.

- Number all pages except the first.

- Key the word **-more-** centered at the bottom of the page to indicate there is another page to follow.

- Print three number symbols (**###**) or (**END**) a double space below the end of the text to indicate the end of the press release.

- Staple, do not paperclip, the press release.

Study the completed press release shown in Figure 14-1. Notice that single spacing is used in the body, and that bold type is used to emphasize important information. The rudimentary information is given in the first three paragraphs, but what the writer really wants the reader to remember

Figure 14-1
A well-written press release can promote goodwill for your organization.

ANGUS & MARTIN INVESTMENTS, INC.
2112 Academy Boulevard
Colorado Springs, CO 80914

FOR IMMEDIATE RELEASE:

CONTACT: Mr. Jason Angus, President

Days: 719/555-0789, ext. 2070

Evenings: 719/555-0904

Fax: 719/555-3899

E-mail: jangus@juno.com

**ANGUS & MARTIN OFFERS FREE
ESTATE PLANNING SEMINAR**

Colorado Springs, CO, February 15, <YEAR>.--Angus & Martin will again offer its free estate planning seminar entitled "Estate Planning: Investing in Future Generations" on Saturday, February 28, from 7-9 p.m. at the Reisnor Community Center. If you want your estate protected for your heirs, attending this seminar is a must.

More than 200 people attended last year's seminar. Many people indicated that they plan to attend again. Some of the topics to be discussed are preparing wills, avoiding estate taxes, and setting up trust funds.

Because of the many phone calls requesting this seminar, attendance is expected to be double last year's, so come early. Angus & Martin is providing refreshments for those who attend.

"Estate Planning: Investing in the Future" is a free seminar conducted by Angus & Martin, Reisnor Community Center, February 28, 7-9 p.m.

Brochures about writing wills, avoiding estate taxes, and setting up trusts will be available. Call Jason Angus at 719/555-0789 for more information.

###

Go to CD-ROM

Activity 14-1
To test your skills.

is repeated in the next-to-the-last paragraph with the title of the seminar in bold type. An additional statement is made to emphasize that anyone attending the seminar will receive free information.

Distributing a Press Release

You may already know that you want to send your press release only to your local newspapers; if so, you'll have no problem determining where to distribute it. But what if you want the information distributed more widely throughout the entire industry or beyond? In that case, you should create a mailing list of sources that would be interested in your information. Ask yourself the following questions to help you develop your list:

- Which media outlets should receive my press release?
- How many media outlets should be included on my list?
- What resources are available to help me create a media mailing list?
- Should the press release be mailed or faxed?

Figure 14-2
This Microsoft Word press release template serves as a model for press releases.

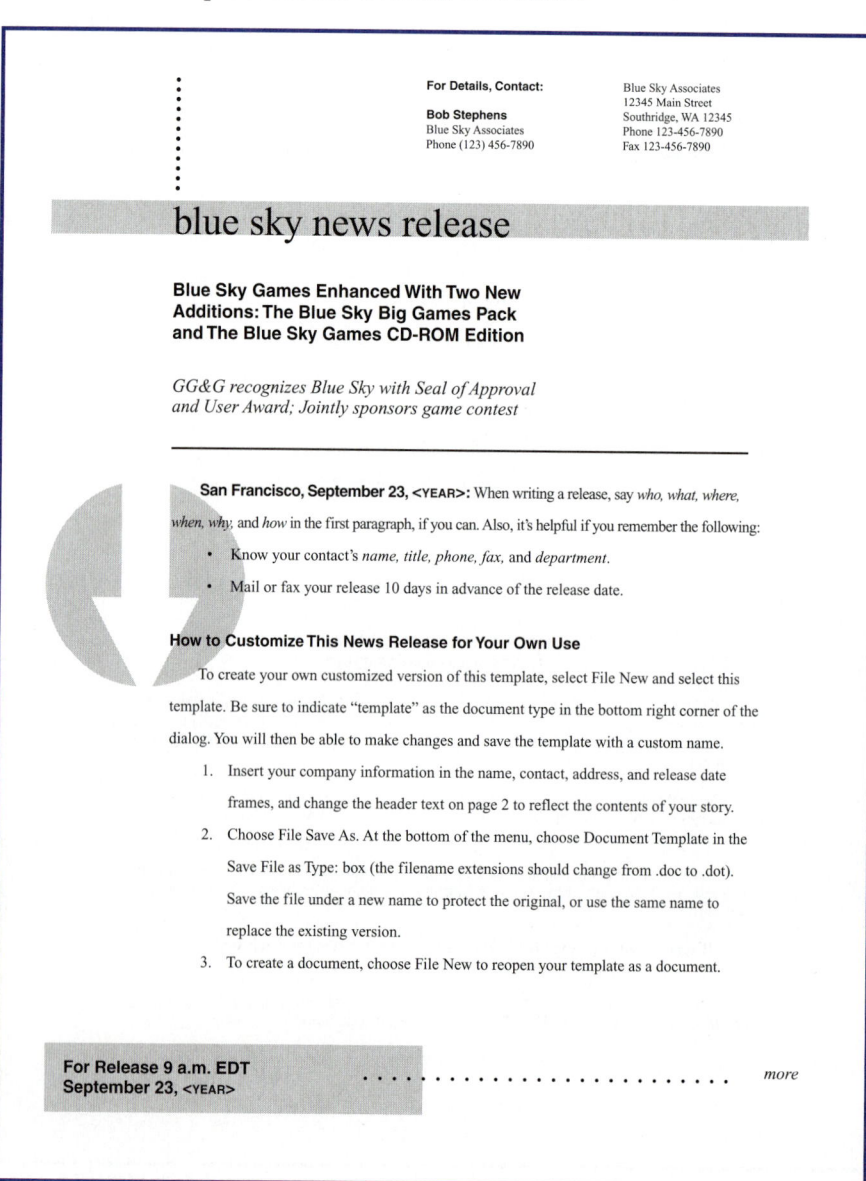

For Details, Contact:
Bob Stephens
Blue Sky Associates
Phone (123) 456-7890

Blue Sky Associates
12345 Main Street
Southridge, WA 12345
Phone 123-456-7890
Fax 123-456-7890

blue sky news release

Blue Sky Games Enhanced With Two New Additions: The Blue Sky Big Games Pack and The Blue Sky Games CD-ROM Edition

GG&G recognizes Blue Sky with Seal of Approval and User Award; Jointly sponsors game contest

San Francisco, September 23, <YEAR>: When writing a release, say *who, what, where, when, why,* and *how* in the first paragraph, if you can. Also, it's helpful if you remember the following:

- Know your contact's *name, title, phone, fax,* and *department.*
- Mail or fax your release 10 days in advance of the release date.

How to Customize This News Release for Your Own Use

To create your own customized version of this template, select File New and select this template. Be sure to indicate "template" as the document type in the bottom right corner of the dialog. You will then be able to make changes and save the template with a custom name.

1. Insert your company information in the name, contact, address, and release date frames, and change the header text on page 2 to reflect the contents of your story.
2. Choose File Save As. At the bottom of the menu, choose Document Template in the Save File as Type: box (the filename extensions should change from .doc to .dot). Save the file under a new name to protect the original, or use the same name to replace the existing version.
3. To create a document, choose File New to reopen your template as a document.

For Release 9 a.m. EDT
September 23, <YEAR>

more

396

Chapter 14

Figure 14-3
A press release template includes options for customizing text.

```
JEAN-PAUL, DELORIA & DELORIA            12345 Main Street
                                        Any City, ST 12345
                                        Phone 123-456-7890
                                        Fax 123-456-7890

Press Release


    Contact: John Stephens      FOR IMMEDIATE RELEASE
    Phone: (123) 456-7890       9 AM EDT, September 23, <YEAR>


             HOW TO CUSTOMIZE THIS PRESS RELEASE

    TO OPTIMIZE THE GRAY SHADING for your printer, click
    on the text area, and choose Borders and Shading from
    the Format menu. Select a new shade or pattern, and
    choose OK.

    TO CUSTOMIZE THIS TEMPLATE, select File New and
    select this template. Be sure to indicate template
    as the document type in the bottom right corner of
    the dialog. You can then insert your company
    information in place of the sample text and change
    the header on page 2 (for multi-page stories). Next,
    choose File Save As. Choose Document Template in the
    Save File as Type box. Save the file under a new name
    to protect the original, or use the same name to
    overwrite the original.

    To create a new document, choose File New to reopen
    your customized template as a document.

    TO DELETE A TEXT FRAME, click on the frame border
    (the frame handles should become highlighted), and
    press Delete.

                         -End-
```

Press Release Templates

Most word processing software offers press release templates to help you create a press release. These **templates** are word processing files that serve as models for creating a press release. Using a template enables you to create a press release quickly without worrying about formatting it. Review Figure 14-2 on page 396 and Figure 14-3, above, which show two Microsoft Word templates for press releases. Notice that the formatting of the releases is slightly different in style from the one introduced in this chapter, but all of the same basic information is included. Notice, also, how the instructions within each press release help you customize the release to suit your needs.

Checkpoint 14.1

1. What are the benefits of writing a concise press release?
2. Why do you agree or disagree with the statement that it is better to give too much information than too little?
3. Why is it effective to restate the specifics in the last paragraph?

Creating Press Releases and Newsletters

Newsletters

A **newsletter** is one of the best ways to keep company employees, customers or potential customers, investors, vendors, or association members, among others, informed about what is happening in your organization. The purpose of a newsletter is to educate, inform, or sell.

Often newsletters have a longer shelf life than ads or brochures. When readers find the information in them helpful, they may keep files of newsletters for reference. Or they may pass them on to coworkers or friends or even post them on bulletin boards at work. Internet users often print copies of online newsletters to circulate.

Written well and presented attractively, a newsletter can be an excellent investment for your company or organization. Whether you're using a newsletter to provide employee recognition, increase sales or referrals, educate workers or customers, or simply boost employee morale, the company should expect to gain more than it cost to produce the newsletter.

Guidelines for Writing Effective Newsletters

When writing newsletters, you must follow accepted guidelines to ensure that your newsletter will be acceptable to its target audience. Based on the target audience, newsletters fall into two categories: **external**, written to customers or potential customers, and **internal**, written to employees.

External newsletters, which target customers or potential customers, should do the following:

- Present a professional, winning image
- Introduce new services, products, or staff; company goals
- Recognize employee accomplishments
- Restate the benefits your customers receive by doing business with your organization
- Illustrate your organization's strengths with testimonials
- Demonstrate your organization's permanence, and reliability
- Provide useful information that may also lead to sales
- Indicate how the reader is to respond, if appropriate

When writing articles for an internal newsletter, you should encourage employees to submit ideas for articles that recognize achievement or explain current industry developments and other topics of interest.

Internal newsletters, which target employees, should do the following:

- Explain your organization's goals and plans for the future

- Introduce new staff, services, and products
- Educate your employees in a nonthreatening way
- Improve relations within your company
- Motivate your employees by recognizing them for achievements
- Highlight your company's community involvement

All newsletters, regardless of the intended audience, should:

- Be written by writers who can convey information persuasively
- Use proven graphic design techniques that will appeal to the reader

Now study the sample of a newsletter shown in Figure 14-4 on the following page, published by Jeff Rubin, President, PUT-IT-IN-WRITING, Pinole, California.

Newsletter "Don'ts"

The success of any newsletter comes from knowing what to do and what not to do. You should become familiar with certain "Don'ts." Watch out for the following "Don'ts" when writing newsletters:

Don't Waste Space Writing Articles That Are "Fun"

Make certain that every article has an objective that will ultimately benefit the company. Avoid including personal information that does little more than entertain (unless company philosophy allows it). Study the following examples:

POOR: Anne Reed has assumed the position of office manager in the Sales Department. Anne has worked for RECO, Inc., for 12 years; she has two children—Robert, 6 years old, and Bryan, 4 years old. She is very active in a volunteer group at Mercy Hospital. Congratulations on your promotion, Anne!

BETTER: Anne Reed has assumed the position of office manager in the Sales Department. Anne has worked for RECO, Inc., for 12 years, and has more than 10 years experience as an office manager. Anne has been very innovative in updating computer software and equipment for RECO and has helped implement the new computer security system. Congratulations on your promotion, Anne!

In the second example, you learned about Anne's expertise with computers and that she was instrumental in implementing the new security system. In the first example, you learned only about her personal life.

Figure 14-4
A sample newsletter published by Jeff Rubin. (Courtesy of Jeff Rubin, PUT-IT-IN-WRITING, put-it-in-writing.com.)

Don't Use Generic Filler Material

A newsletter should generate a return on your company's investment in producing the newsletter. Generic fillers such as recipes, famous quotations, and historical facts may be interesting, but usually the reader cannot apply this information to his or her job.

Don't Use an Unreadable Typeface

A fancy font might look attractive when you are viewing one sentence. When you are reading an entire article, however, it can become difficult to read. Keep the type simple enough and large enough to make sure your message is read.

POOR: *This Garamond Bold Italic typeface is difficult to read when used in columns of information.*

BETTER: This Arial typeface is easier to read in columns of information, as is this example of Times New Roman.

NOTES

Avoid Filler

Even though you see filler information in newspapers, do not use this type of information in newsletters.

Don't Be Wordy

Keep your writing simple and to the point. Readers are inundated with information and most have busy work environments. Keep your writing simple to understand so that the reader will immediately grasp the benefits of the information you are presenting.

Don't Forget to Document Your Facts

Readers want to know that facts and statistics support your statements. Do your research and, above all, make no factual errors!

Newsletter "Do's"

Here are some "Do's" to follow when you are writing newsletters:

Write to Express, Not to Impress

Your purpose is to communicate, not to impress your readers with your enormous vocabulary. Don't use big words when smaller words will do. Keep your writing casual, nontechnical, and conversational. Remember to identify the meaning of any acronyms you think your readers will not understand.

Avoid Clichés

A *cliché* is a trite or overused expression. If it is *needless to say*, why say it? Here are some other examples: Don't say *in the near future* or *at the present time*. Instead use *soon* and *now*, respectively.

Proofread, Proofread, Proofread

Remember that the newsletter is a reflection of your company or organization. The reader will immediately form an opinion of the organization based on the newsletter, and that can result in a negative opinion if the newsletter is full of typos and grammatical errors. To make sure your newsletter represents your company's professionalism, thoroughly proofread it—don't forget to use the spell checker, grammar checker, and thesaurus. Rewriting and revising may seem tedious, but they are necessary to produce a well-written, professional newsletter.

Make the Title of Your Newsletter an Attention-Grabber

All too often, writers focus the title of their newsletter on a company's name or an organization's name. If a reader is not already familiar with your company or organization, however, the name tells them nothing. Take a look at the following examples of titles for a newsletter whose purpose is to promote more travel by passenger train. Notice how much more interesting the second example is—it implies that traveling by train is so fast the train rails actually sing!

POOR: Amtrak Newsletter

BETTER: Amtrak's Singing Rails

Creating Press Releases and Newsletters

NOTES

Dress It Up

Graphics, white space, color, and visuals contribute to a top-quality newsletter.

Newsletter Format

Just as the writing of a newsletter must be top-quality, the formatting also must be top-quality. You don't want a well-written newsletter tossed into the wastebasket because it looks busy and difficult to read. You can improve the appearance of your newsletter by following these formatting guidelines.

Use at Least One Graphic Per Page

Graphics include photos, artwork, charts, quotes, even a colored or shaded box. Graphics attract the reader because they are usually the first things on a page to catch the reader's eye. They also provide visual breaks from solid blocks of text—row after row of text is boring and difficult to read.

Use Ample White Space

When text, graphics, and borders consume the page margin to margin, a newsletter becomes busy and hard to read. Balance the white space in your margins between articles and around graphics to keep the overall look visually pleasing. Bullets (•) help to draw attention to lists. Shaded or colored text boxes make it easy to identify important quotes or information. Most newsletters are formatted in two columns.

Use Complementary Colors, Shading, and Tints

Printing in black and white is fine, but if your budget allows, use at least one complementary color. Remember that your newsletter will be competing for the reader's attention with magazines, newspapers, or brochures—many of which have large budgets and can produce colorful, exciting images.

Use Quality Photographs

Often company newsletters contain photos that were printed using old techniques, giving them the appearance of being washed out and blurry. To avoid this problem, don't use photos taken with Polaroid or Instamatic cameras. Also, photos can be scanned using image-editing software to sharpen the photos. These programs allow you to adjust the contrast, color, and brightness levels of a scanned photo. Scanners used with desktop publishing make including photos quite easy. Digital cameras can also be used to obtain quality photographs.

Use Cartoons

Cartoons can catch the reader's interest and provide humor. These cartoons can be freehand drawings or purchased from a published source and reprinted with permission.

Check on Your Readers

From time to time send short surveys to your readers to obtain feedback about what they like and don't like in your newsletter. If the newsletter is being distributed in the office, check to see if the newsletters are read or tossed aside. This can be done by simply asking about the information in the newsletter.

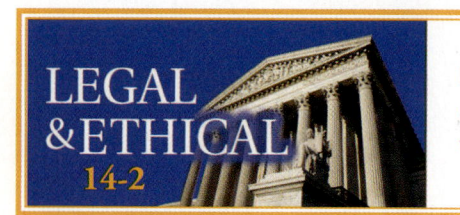

LEGAL & ETHICAL 14-2

Logo Laws. If you used someone's company logo in an article in a newsletter you were writing without obtaining permission to do so, would you be violating any copyright laws?

Newsletter Templates

The office has changed since writers began using personal computers to prepare copy for print. *Desktop publishing*—using word processing software to produce high-quality printed output or camera-ready output—has become commonplace. With this software, features such as graphics, color, rules (lines), borders, columns, and a wide array of fonts and type sizes are available with just a few keystrokes.

Study the newsletter template shown in Figure 14-5. To use a template such as this one, you simply key the text, select the area in the template where you want text to appear, and copy the created text to that position in the newsletter. In some templates, you can key text directly in the template. Every aspect of the template can be changed to suit your preferences, including the title and any graphics you want to include.

Figure 14-5
Newsletter templates can be changed to suit your preferences.

Creating Press Releases and Newsletters

Checkpoint 14.2

1. Summarize the key differences between internal and external newsletters.
2. Do you agree that it is a good idea to leave "fun" articles out of a newsletter?
3. How does a company benefit from circulating a perfectly proofread newsletter?

Chapter 14 Summary

Writing effective press releases is an important way a company can become better known to its customers or potential customers. If you are responsible for preparing press releases, you should familiarize yourself with press release guidelines and the accepted formatting rules. Remember that your overall purpose is to entice the media into reporting about your company or organization to increase its visibility. Make your press releases new, different, exciting, and interesting to entice an editor to consider them newsworthy.

Producing a newsletter is another way to advertise your company or organization. When a reader reads that first newsletter, he or she will decide if your newsletter is worth reading again. Your newsletter is competing for the reader's time; therefore, you must offer the reader information he or she believes will be beneficial.

Follow the guidelines given for writing and designing effective newsletters to ensure that your newsletter will be read, kept, and used. Make certain you print correct information. Always emphasize how your reader will benefit by reading your newsletter.

Communication at Work

Ray Durazo, President and CEO
Durazo Communications, Inc.

Successful public relations go beyond a well-written press release or newsletter. It begins before a word is written, according to Ray Durazo. He is an industry veteran and authority on Hispanic public relations.

"The essence of effective communications is understanding the audience," Durazo says. "The most important communication skill is taking the time to find out about the people with whom you are communicating, what they think, how they feel, and how they are likely to react to your messages."

Selling the Message

A case in point: Durazo's company has been part of California's antismoking campaign for ten years. The company did research to find out what messages would work better among Hispanics.

"In the mainstream, an effective tactic is to educate children about the perils of tobacco. The idea is that they will go home and lecture their parents about quitting. However, in Hispanic culture, children do not lecture parents. That would be disrespectful," explains Durazo.

"One of the strongest themes aimed at Hispanics is the concept of doing what's best for your family. Most Hispanics understand that they should avoid exposing children and pregnant women to second-hand smoke. Setting a good example for children by not smoking is also readily accepted."

Durazo disagrees with people who say "multicultural communications" isolates racial and ethnic groups.

"We live in a multicultural society in which being able to communicate with others is important," he says. "Professional communicators can serve as a filter, through which communications pass, making them more understandable and more persuasive. We can be the bridge for encouraging more positive relations among people of different cultures."

> ❝ The most important communication skill is taking the time to find out about the people with whom you are communicating, what they think, how they feel, and how they are likely to react to your messages. ❞

Discuss

1. What are examples of products sold to a specific audience?
2. How do the products' advertisements make their appeal to that particular audience?
3. What message do the advertisements give you about that audience?

Chapter 14

Online Exercises

Objective:
These online activities will provide you the opportunity to explore code of ethics Web sites.

Go to **bcw.glencoe.com**, the online address for the *Business Communication at Work* Web site, and select Chapter 14. Next, click on Online Exercises. You will see a list of Web site links that will bring you to business and professional association codes of ethics Web sites.

Activity 14.1

1. Select one of the business code of ethics Web sites to visit.
2. Explore several of the codes of ethics, searching for one that is new information to you. You may want to visit more than one code of ethics Web site to find new information.
3. Write a paragraph describing the new information you learned from the code of ethics. You may want to consider the following questions in your paragraph:
    a. How does the code help improve business ethics?
    b. Do you see any possible problems with the code of ethics?
    c. Could the business code of ethics be applied to other areas of ethics? If so, how?
4. Write your name on your paper, and hand it in to your instructor.

Activity 14.2

1. Select one of the professional association code of ethics Web sites to visit.
2. Search for a code of ethics you find interesting and print it out.
3. Return to the *Business Communication at Work* Web site and select other code of ethics Web sites to visit. Print out two more codes of ethics you find interesting and print them out.
4. From the printouts, make a list of what you think are the six most important codes of ethics.
5. On a sheet of paper write a fictional internal newsletter to a professional association regarding the six codes of ethics. Be sure to follow the guidelines for writing effective newsletters. Also keep in mind the "Newsletter Don'ts" while writing your letter.
6. Write your name on your paper, and hand it in to your instructor.

CHAPTER 14 WORKSHEETS

NAME _____ DATE _____

PRACTICE 1

Concept Review

Instructions: Write a headline for a press release for the following situations:

1. Jerri Benson is the new word processing supervisor in your Office Technology division.
2. Your company has developed a new lotion called Insta-Fleck. Insta-Fleck will instantly and permanently remove freckles when rubbed on the skin.
3. Texas Instruments in Dallas has developed a microchip that will allow computers to run at 1,000 MHz speed.
4. Tao Deng is this year's Employee of the Year for your company.
5. Your company has developed equipment that allows you to place and receive phone calls while surfing the Internet. This equipment eliminates the need for a second phone line to the Internet.

PRACTICE 2

Press Releases and Newsletters

Instructions: Respond to each of the following questions as directed.

1. Using the five headlines you created in Practice 1, indicate who your target media would be for each one—newspaper, radio, and/or television.
2. Using the situations in Practice 1, identify the purpose of each press release or article for a newsletter.
3. Write a press release or an article for a newsletter about an event in your school or community. Assume you are the event's sponsor.
4. Using the information in Practice 1, Question 4, create a press release to announce this honor.
5. Using the information in Practice 1, Question 5, create a press release to announce the development of this new equipment.

PRACTICE 3

Writing Applications

Instructions: Respond to each of the following situations as directed.

1. Locate a copy of a current newsletter from a business organization such as American Management Association, Business and Professional Women's Club, Optimist Club, Rotary Club, or from any other business-related organization. Evaluate the newsletter using the "Guidelines for Writing Effective Newsletters" on pages 398–401, and write a one-page report.
2. You are the program director for a charitable organization (select one you are familiar with or do research on an organization). The organization has received an unexpected gift of $100,000 from an anonymous donor to be used as needed. Write the press release.
3. Using the template in Microsoft Word or WordPerfect, create a one-page newsletter about your college. Use the college catalog as your source of information.

Creating Press Releases and Newsletters

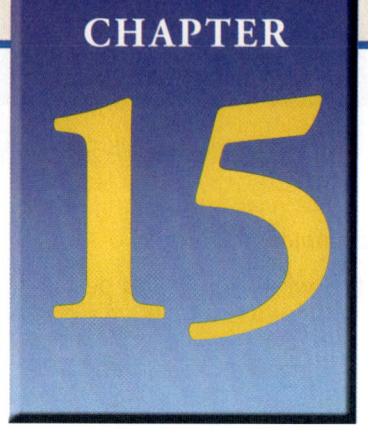

CHAPTER 15
Constructing and Presenting Reports

Objectives

After completing this chapter, you will be able to:

1. Apply the persuasive, direct, and indirect approaches to writing reports
2. Explain the various organizational patterns that can be used in writing reports
3. Prepare an informal letter report
4. Prepare a formal research report
5. Prepare a proposal
6. Use visuals in a report

WORKPLACE APPLICATIONS

Plagiarism

Plagiarism is the act of presenting another person's words or ideas as your own in writing. It is a serious offense in the business world. You would not openly steal another company's products; another person's words or ideas are no different. They are a product of the person's imagination and hard work. It is important to respect them. When writing, if you borrow even a phrase or an idea that is not accepted as common knowledge, you should credit its source, using one of the formats explained in this chapter.

Acknowledge Your Sources

Plagiarism often occurs unconsciously on the part of a writer. A writer who is researching a topic becomes deeply immersed in the words and ideas of others. It is entirely possible for a writer to forget the source of a good idea or a turn of phrase, or to forget that the idea or words even came from an outside source. He or she may forget that the idea is not common knowledge. The only way to avoid this mistake is to take notes carefully and to give credit where it is due.

When you take notes, label them with the name of each source and its author. If you wish to use the author's exact words, place them in quotation marks and include the page where you found them. Double-check that you have copied the quotation exactly.

If you use the quotation, or even a **paraphrase** of it, you must credit the original writer. Also, it is always a good idea to review your writing before submitting it. Check every phrase and quotation against your notes to make sure they are either in your own words or are credited.

Thinking Critically

Situation: You must prepare a report about the effects on productivity of playing music in the office. Several sources give the same basic information. You want to include the information in your report, but you are not sure if you should give credit, or who to credit.

Ask Yourself: How would you handle this problem with your report?

409

> *I have yet to see any problem, however complicated, which, when looked at in the right way, did not become still more complicated.*
>
> —Poul Anderson, Author

Reports are an essential part of the communication process in business. Thus, they are critical to management decision-making. Good reports do their job quickly and effectively. They communicate facts and ideas clearly and logically using straightforward language so that readers can effortlessly understand what is written. On the other hand, poor reports are vague, wordy, full of jargon, and difficult to understand; and they are often ignored because they contain unconvincing information. Developing effective report writing skills is very important to your success in business.

Approaches to Writing Reports

The flow of correct and usable information within an organization is vital to effective decision making. Reports are written to help clarify this information so that it can be clearly understood by the reader. To achieve this, it is important to use the appropriate approach when you are writing a report, just as it is when you are writing a letter or a memo. For reports you should use the persuasive, direct, or indirect approach.

Persuasive Approach

Quite often a writer must prepare a report that must convince the reader to do something about which the reader may feel positive, negative, or indifferent. Just as you learned in Chapter 5, this is called the persuasive approach to writing. You can use the persuasive approach to writing just as effectively when writing reports as when writing other types of communication. Remember to follow the persuasive approach guidelines (see page 114). You must grasp the reader's attention and hold it, tempt him or her with possible benefits, and make it easy to comply. Using the persuasive approach effectively can prove extremely useful to the skilled writer.

Direct Approach

When you present the purpose of your report at the beginning, you are using the direct approach. This approach is used when you think the reader will receive the information positively. You should begin with an introduction, usually stating the main point in the first sentence. Follow the statement of purpose with an explanation of the facts and end with a summary. This approach offers the advantage of allowing the reader to see the results of the report at a glance. Because of the volume of reading a busy executive must do, the *direct* approach is the approach most often used.

Indirect Approach

As you learned earlier, when you suspect the reader might be indifferent, or even negative, to the information you are presenting, you must lay groundwork first. In a report, this groundwork includes details that create a "hook" to stimulate interest so the reader will continue reading. When you present your conclusions and recommendations at the end of your report, after giving the reader the reasons for them, you are following the *indirect* approach.

NOTES

Audience Awareness

Always keep your audience in mind when writing a report. Ask yourself, "Are the style and organization appropriate for my audience?"

Organizational Patterns for Reports

You may choose from several organizational patterns to help you present your information in a logical manner. When you use one of these patterns, your reader will be able to follow the reasoning that leads to your conclusion. Study the following three commonly used patterns for presenting information in a report:

Compare-and-Contrast Pattern

In this pattern, which uses the indirect approach, two or more elements are compared for similarities or contrasted for differences.

Two Items Compared	Two workshops are available for training—"Better Grammar Skills" by Skillpath and "Developing Your Grammar Skills" by the American Management Association.
Item 1	"Better Grammar Skills" is a one-day workshop that reviews grammar rules identified as those most often used. A short session on writing principles is also included. The cost is $99 per person.
Item 2	"Developing Your Grammar Skills" by the American Management Association is a one-day workshop that provides one-half day on grammar and one-half day on writing principles. The cost is $79 per employee.
Recommendation	Although the workshop by the American Management Association is less expensive, the greatest problem our employees are having is with grammar. My recommendation is that our employees attend the "Better Grammar Skills" workshop by Skillpath because it offers a more comprehensive review of grammatical skills.

Journalistic Pattern

This pattern, which uses the direct approach, condenses into short paragraphs that answer the six most common questions: *who, what, where, when, how,* and *why.*

Constructing and Presenting Reports

NOTES

Just the Facts

Keep in mind that you must report accurate, valid facts rather than personal opinions when writing a report.

Main idea	An important recommendation of the Second Hoover Commission was that a style board be created to standardize style practices in government correspondence.
Who **What**	To comply with this recommendation, the General Services Administration, in cooperation with the Bureau of the Budget, coordinated the development of a government-wide correspondence manual.
When **Where**	The entire project was begun in 1958 and was completed in late 1960 in Washington, D.C.
How	A working committee representing 21 agencies was responsible for drafting the manual. The committee served under the direction of an advisory board drawn from the large departments and agencies.
Why	In developing the manual, the advisory board and the working committee sought to achieve the following objectives: 1. Provide a uniform correspondence style manual for the government. 2. Eliminate time and cost expended in preparing individual agency manuals. 3. Minimize training time for clerical personnel.
Conclusion	As a result of the cooperative effort, the standards described in the manual are a composite of good practices used in many agencies. Most agencies can adopt these practices with only minor changes in their present methods.

Cause-and-Effect Pattern

In this pattern, which also uses the direct approach, the writer presents the reasons that support his or her view or opinion.

Point of View	Should the computers in the Accounting Department be updated to Pentium II model computers? Yes, I recommend the computers be updated to Pentium IIs.
Reason 1	At present we have 486 computers with 66 MHz speed. We are still using the MS DOS operating system. Because of the size of our accounting computer software programs, it often takes several minutes for commands to be completed, files to be printed or saved, or the system to respond in other ways.

412   Chapter 15

Reason 2   The company will be upgrading to the latest release of Windows. Our present system will not support this latest release nor the newest version of our accounting software. Management has granted approval to update to these new versions.

Reason 3   The Computer Services Department will no longer support a DOS-based system.

Conclusion   Since we will not be able to continue our accounting function at its present level, the computer equipment in the Accounting Department should be upgraded to Pentium II models.

Thinking Cap 15.1

Discuss: What are the effects of freezing temperatures in Florida on the price of orange juice? Using the cause-and-effect organizational approach, identify the primary and contributing causes and effects.

Other Organizational Patterns

Study the following additional organizational patterns, which will help you write logical, clearly presented reports:

PATTERN	EXPLANATION
Time	Arrange details with respect to time: from past to the present, from the present to the past, or from the present to the future. Present your main idea first, follow it with the events as they happened or will happen, and end with a conclusion. (Indirect approach)
Enumeration	List separate details to support or explain a generalization. Begin with the main idea followed by any necessary details. (Direct approach)
Specific Instance	This pattern illustrates the main idea by telling an anecdote or describing an incident or event. Begin with the main idea, follow it with the anecdote or description of an incident or event, and end with a conclusion. (Indirect approach)
Negative Detail	This pattern eliminates all but one of several possible solutions to a problem by showing how the others do not apply. Present the main idea, follow it with the solutions that have been eliminated (leaving the recommended solution), and end with a conclusion. (Indirect approach)

Using any one of these patterns will help you write a logical, clearly presented report.

Guidelines for Writing Reports

NOTES

Need a Refresher?

Review the guidelines for writing reports just before you begin writing a report so that they are fresh in your memory.

When writing reports, you should follow all the principles of effective writing we have discussed. In addition, here are some specific guidelines:

- Know your specific purpose before you begin writing.
- Take detailed, well-organized, clearly written notes.
- Plan ahead: have all your information gathered before you begin; have a thorough understanding of the information.
- Write an outline and stick to it.
- Focus on accurate, valid facts.
- Be consistent in the format selected.
- Keep the audience in mind: be empathetic; anticipate the reader's response.
- Adapt your writing style to fit the particular situation.
- Be complete: include everything your reader needs to know, but avoid unnecessary, minute details.
- Develop coherence; ideas should follow a logical sequence.
- Write in a positive tone.
- Vary sentence length and keep sentences uncomplicated.
- Include only one main idea per paragraph.
- Keep subjects and verbs close together.
- Make use of transitional (connecting) devices and topic sentences.
- Observe proper mechanics such as spelling, punctuation, and capitalization.

Letter Reports

Go to CD-ROM
Activity 15-1
To test your skills.

Writers often find that short letter reports are a quick and easy way to send reports both inside and outside the company. The letter report style is chosen because most writers are familiar with various letter formats. This style is similar to a typical letter in that it is usually single spaced on organizational letterhead and contains standard headings for second and succeeding pages. The letter report differs somewhat from a typical letter in that it generally is longer—perhaps up to ten pages. In addition, because it is longer, side and paragraph headings may be used to help introduce

414 Chapter 15

topics quickly and specifically. Although some writers may choose to omit certain headings, the following may be included in a letter report:

- Date
- Inside address
- Salutation
- Side headings (optional)
- Paragraph headings (optional)
- Second- and succeeding-page headings
- Complimentary closing

Review the letter report shown below.

Figure 15-1
Note the headings used in this letter report.

GENERAL INSURANCE COMPANY
1675 East Summit Avenue
Suite 115
Dallas, TX 75882

January 15, <YEAR>

Mr. Adam Wright, Production Manager
Nortex Air Corporation
4850 Regal Rowe
Dallas, TX 75880

Dear Mr. Wright:

On December 10, I visited your plant to measure carbon monoxide (CO) and nitrogen dioxide (NO_2) levels associated with the smoke evolving from heated Antistat processing operations in Coex and Antistat Converting.

RESULTS OF INVESTIGATION

Both locations have local exhaust ventilation, but cross drafts in Coex may defeat the exhaust hood system. The Coex machine had no detectable CO or NO_2 in the most concentrated smoke production areas. Detection limits were less than 2 parts per million for CO, and less than 0.5 ppm for NO_2. The converting machine making bags with Antistat material showed about 5 ppm for CO, and there was no detectable NO_2. The PEL for NO_2 is 3 ppm, and for CO is 35 ppm. The worst case exposures are acceptable.

RECOMMENDATION

The Coex and converting ventilation can be improved by preventing cross drafts with permanent side baffles extending down from the canopy hood. Also, flexible vinyl strips sealing the area as much as possible but allowing easy access for maintenance or adjustment could be used.

Let me know if you need further information.

Sincerely,

Mitchel Barrows

Mitchel Barrows, CIH
Senior Loss Control Consultant

cns

Constructing and Presenting Reports

FORMAL REPORTS

The formal report is appropriate for both external and internal use. The report should be used externally when you are reporting to someone outside your organization. It may be used internally when the importance or the length of your report makes the more informal memo report or the letter report inappropriate. Formal reports are used for several purposes, including the following:

- Presenting data on a specialized subject
- Attempting to find the causes underlying a problem
- Attempting to find whether or not a problem really exists
- Analyzing possible solutions to a particular problem

Formal reports usually deal with more complex problems or problems that require investigation, analysis, research, and documentation. Examples of some complex problems might be to analyze customer purchasing habits, to study the feasibility of introducing a new product line, or to investigate whether to expand present facilities or construct a new one.

Several months of extensive research, experiments, surveys, analysis, or even interviewing might be required to complete a report. You could have a few pages or even a hundred or more when you are finished. The important point is that the formal report must be well written and well documented.

NOTES

Formal Examination

Formal reports are written to investigate or analyze problems more thoroughly than most other reports.

LEGAL & ETHICAL 15-1

E-Commerce? What are the ethics involved in going online on the Internet and purchasing term papers? Is this legal? Is it ethical?

Preparing an Outline

To provide direction for your report and the steps that take you to the finished product, you should begin with a working outline that will be refined at various stages of your report writing. Keep the primary purpose of the report in mind from the beginning, and build your outline by including the information that will help you accomplish that purpose. For example, if your purpose is to determine the local business trends regarding the use of computers and software to support your school's purchasing decisions and course design, your working outline might look something like this:

    I. COMPANIES TO CONTACT
       A. Type by product
       B. Size
       C. Number

    II. KINDS OF COMPUTERS USED
        A. Mainframe
        B. Personal computers
            1. IBM
            2. IBM-compatible
            3. Macintosh
            4. Portable
            5. PDA
    III. TYPES OF COMPUTER APPLICATIONS USED
        A. Word processing
        B. Database
        C. Spreadsheet
        D. Presentation
        E. Graphics
        F. Web page development
        G. Desktop publishing
    IV. SKILLS REQUIRED
        A. Keyboarding
        B. Programming
        C. Accounting
        D. Writing
        E. Other

> **NOTES**
>
> **Map Your Plan**
>
> An outline serves as your plan or "road map" for logical research and effective organization for writing your report.

In the final outline and table of contents, principles to apply include keeping levels of topics consistent based on importance, using parallel structure, and avoiding having only one subtopic under a main topic.

Gathering Information for Research Reports

A common type of formal report is the research report. A *research report* presents facts and findings that result from the writer's research, the writer's evaluation of these facts and findings, and the writer's recommendations or conclusions based on the findings.

Before actually writing a research report, you may need to do some extensive research to collect data. You will get the information you need for support of your chosen or assigned topic through either secondary or primary sources—or both. The purpose of your report and your working outline will help you determine the type of sources to use.

Secondary Research

First, you need to know what others have written about your topic—in other words, you should research **secondary sources** of information. These sources might be books, articles in periodicals and newspapers, speeches by experts, government documents, and electronic resources from your college or university library or on the Internet.

When gathering secondary sources, consider the reliability of the information. Is the author an authority and are the author's opinions and facts

> **NOTES**
>
> **Consulting Sources**
>
> A secondary source of information is what others have written about your topic.

Constructing and Presenting Reports 417

distinguishable? Is the information current? Using outdated sources, unless they are classics, sends your reader a negative message about your report. To save time later, make certain you set up a permanent record of the information as you start taking notes.

One method of note taking and record maintenance involves using 3- by 5-inch index cards. Write down the complete information for each source you use. Include the author's first and last names, the complete title of the work, the volume number, publisher, date of publication, and page number(s). Then, use a separate card for each quote or idea taken from that source, labeling each card with enough information to tie it to the main source card (i.e., author's name, title, or other necessary information), the quote or idea, and the page number(s) to reference. Having each quote or idea on a separate card will allow you to arrange the note cards in proper sequence for your outline.

If you are taking the information from the Internet or World Wide Web, you should also include the Web address, the date the information was last updated, and the date you accessed the information. Since electronic information changes much more frequently than printed sources, downloading and printing the information from the Internet would give you a more permanent record in case later verification of details is needed.

Primary Research

Even though you will start by researching the secondary data, your report may depend heavily on information from **primary sources,** or firsthand information. Primary source information may be gathered through the use of surveys, personal or telephone interviews, firsthand observations, or experiments. The quality of the data collected through primary sources is determined by several factors: a representative sample made up of a sufficient number of people who are qualified to give you unbiased information about your topic, a well-constructed questionnaire or other instrument for recording the information, and the care taken in tabulating and analyzing the results.

The types of questions you ask—whether in a written questionnaire, in a telephone survey, or in a personal interview—should be asked in such a way that you do not lead the respondent toward one answer or another. The responses should be easy to tabulate in order to help in your analysis. Businesses frequently contract with research firms to construct the actual questions based on the purpose and size of the survey. These research firms provide a thorough report of the results.

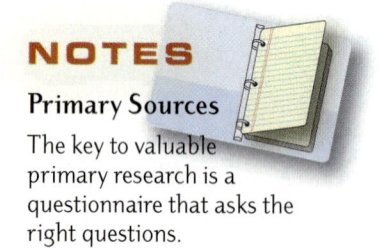

NOTES

Primary Sources

The key to valuable primary research is a questionnaire that asks the right questions.

Checkpoint 15.1

1. In your experience, what are the benefits of writing an outline for a report?
2. Which sources are better—primary sources or secondary sources?
3. Do you agree with the idea that using outdated sources sends a negative message to your reader? If so, what is that message?

Documenting Information

Remember, whenever you use another writer's material in your report—either quoted directly or paraphrased—you must give the source of the information. There are three acceptable options for listing your sources:

- **Citations**—shown with the excerpted material
- **Endnotes**—compiled in a list at the end of the report
- **Footnotes**—listed at the bottom of the page containing the excerpt

To ensure the proper format for each of these options, check *The Gregg Reference Manual* by William A. Sabin, Glencoe/McGraw-Hill, or style manuals used on your campus. Three popular documentation styles are the Modern Language Association (MLA) style, the American Psychological Association (APA) style, and *The Chicago Manual of Style* (Chicago) style.

MLA Style

In the MLA documentation style, you show in parentheses brief information about the source immediately following the citation in your report. You then show the complete information about the source at the end of your paper in the *Works Cited* list. For example, the citation within your report might say:

> "As the number of wireless phone users has boomed to 51 million in the U.S., so, too, have the types of models." (Elstrom 120).

This citation tells the reader that this quotation was taken from page 120 of a work by an author named Elstrom. To get the full information about the source from which the quotation was taken, the reader would go to the *Works Cited* page at the end of your report, find Elstrom, and see the following:

> Elstrom, Peter. "Lost in the Phone Zone?" BusinessWeek, 24 November 2002: 120–121.

If your *Works Cited* list included more than one work by Peter Elstrom, the citation within your report would need to give additional information—a shortened version of the title: *Lost*—so that the reader would know from which work by Elstrom the quotation came.

A *Works Cited* entry for this book would look like this:

> Satterwhite, Marilyn, and Judith Olson-Sutton. Business Communication at Work. Woodland Hills: Glencoe/McGraw-Hill, 2003.

To get complete information about the MLA style, see Joseph Gibaldi's *MLA Handbook for Writers of Research Papers*, 5th edition, published by The Modern Language Association of America (1999). If you have Internet access, go to the MLA Web site at www.mla.org for up-to-date information about the MLA style.

APA Style

The APA style is similar to the MLA style for citing sources. Show the author's last name and the page number from which the quotation came. If

Constructing and Presenting Reports

your report contains ideas or other materials to be cited that are spread over several pages, you would, of course, give the inclusive pages where the material is covered. If the author's name is included within the body of your report, you simply put the year in parentheses right after the author's name:

Elstrom (2002) states, "As the number of wireless phone users . . ."

If shown as a complete quote, the listing would look like this:

"As the number of wireless phone users has boomed to 51 million . . . have the types of models." (Elstrom, 2002, p. 120).

The APA style report contains a *References* list at the end of the report. As with the MLA style report, the APA *References* list should contain only sources actually cited within the report. The reference listing for the Elstrom article would look like this:

Elstrom, P. (2002, November 24). Lost in the phone zone? BusinessWeek, 120–121.

A reference listing for a book would look like this in APA style:

Satterwhite, M, & Sutton, JO. (2004). Business Communication at Work. Woodland Hills, CA: Glencoe/McGraw-Hill.

You may find more detail about the APA style in *Publication Manual of the American Psychological Association*, 5th edition, published by the American Psychological Association (2001), or by visiting the Web site www.apa.org.

Chicago Style

The Chicago style differs from the MLA and APA styles in that it makes use of footnotes or endnotes rather than including information about the source in the report narrative. If you use this style, identify other authors' works with consecutive raised numbers (superscripts). Give complete information for each number either in a footnote at the bottom of that page or in an endnote, usually called *Notes*, at the end of the report. The Elstrom citation would appear as follows:

"As the number of wireless . . . have the types of models."[3]

The footnote would appear at the bottom of the page as

[3]Peter Elstrom, "Lost in the Phone Zone?" BusinessWeek (November 24, 2002): 120.

If you were showing the same information as an endnote at the end of the report, the style would be the same except that you would place the number followed by a period on the line with the author's name and the author's last name would be shown first.

You may find more detailed information about the Chicago style in Chapter 15 of *The Chicago Manual of Style,* 14th Edition, published by the University of Chicago Press (1993).

Electronic Citations

This electronic age of CD-ROMs, Web sites, and the Internet has created new style issues. Citing sources from the Internet poses a new problem for most writers, and style manuals do not always agree on how citations should be shown. You might be including information from sites such as FTP (file transfer protocol)—used when downloading a file that you have researched, WWW (World Wide Web)—Web sites used to research information, or e-mail—used to send messages electronically from person to person(s).

While it is beyond the scope of this text to provide information on how to use each of these services, an electronic reference citation should include the following:

- Author's last name
- Author's first name
- Title of the complete work
- Version or file number if available
- Date the document was created
- Internet address
- Date you accessed the information

Net Explorations
Go to Web sites given in this section and research the MLA and APA documentation styles.

The following citation is an example of a World Wide Web reference:

Purdue University Online Writing Lab. <u>Using Modern Language Association (MLA) Format.</u> Online posting. 2002. Purdue University. <http://owl.english.purdue.edu/handouts/research/r_mla.html>. Accessed July 31, 2002.

Keep in mind also that information on the Internet is constantly changing, and your citations may need to be revised from time to time. In fact, most authorities recommend that you print the article from the Internet at the time you access it to have it for future reference.

A reference to material on a CD-ROM would look like this in the MLA style:

"U.S. Population by Age: Urban and Urbanized Areas." <u>2000 U.S. Census of Population and Housing</u>. CD-ROM. U.S. Bureau of the Census. 2000.

Thinking Cap 15.2

Discuss: Identify in what order of importance (a–f) you would conduct research for the following statements if you were to write a report on causes of poor health in the homes of the elderly living in low-income neighborhoods.
a. Inadequately staffed libraries
b. Absence of medical care
c. Causes of poor health
d. Inadequate diet
e. Unsanitary living conditions
f. Prevalence of small neighborhood stores

PARTS OF A FORMAL REPORT

Formal reports include more detailed information and generally include a number of parts. They may vary in style and form. Some may require tables, charts, or graphs to represent statistical data, while others may be created from an extensive study of what other people have written on a topic.

Constructing and Presenting Reports

Despite variations in style and form, most formal reports include the following parts placed in order in the report:

- Title Page
- Table of Contents
- Letter or Memo of Authorization or Transmittal
- Executive Summary
- Body
    - Introduction
    - Findings
    - Conclusions and Recommendations
- Appendix, if applicable (may also be placed after the Bibliography)
- Works Cited or References
- Bibliography

Body of the Report

After you prepare the working outline and do the research, you should refine the outline to reflect any reorganization required based upon the information gathered. The next step is to write the body of the report. The body of the report includes the introduction, findings, and conclusions and recommendations. The writer tells the reader what research was done, how it was done, and what the results of the investigation are. Once the body of the report is written, the remaining parts of the report can be added. Let's begin with learning about the introduction.

The Introduction

The first thing a writer should do before beginning to write a formal report is to define the purpose and scope of the report. Next, he or she should determine the procedures or methods that will be used to collect the data.

Defining the Purpose. Begin by asking yourself, "Why am I writing the report?" The answer to this question should be included in the *Introduction* of the report. For example, what if the office technology department of Truett County Community College wanted to gain current information about computer equipment, software, and skill levels used in business and industry in their local area?

Here are some statements that identify the purposes of this report and how they might be stated:

Statement of Purpose

1. To determine what computer hardware configurations local companies use.

2. To determine what software local companies currently use.

3. To determine what computer skills local companies require for entry-level positions.

NOTES

The Set-Up

The introduction defines the problem, purpose, scope, limitations, and procedures used in the report.

4. To enable the faculty to make decisions for purchasing computer equipment and software.
5. To enable the faculty to design courses around the needs of employers in Truett County.

Defining the Scope and Limitations. You can quickly see that it could take many weeks just to gather the information for a report of this magnitude. You must be careful to avoid selecting a topic that is too large in scope to be handled efficiently. You must define the scope and set boundaries that keep your research within reasonable, achievable limits. When stating the scope, you should indicate how the report is limited. Without limitations, the report might never be completed. For instance, study the following limitation concerning the computer information for the college.

Scope or Limitations

This investigation is limited to companies that employ 100 or more employees in Truett County.

Explaining the Procedures. The *Introduction* should also describe the methods that you used to gather the data and analyze it. Here is an example using the college report:

Procedures

The names and addresses of companies that employed 100 or more employees were purchased from the Chamber of Commerce of Truett and the Chamber of Commerce of Bennington, the two cities that the college serves. The list also provided the current names of the CEOs or the Human Resources Directors.

Figure 15-2 shows a portion of the completed introduction. Notice the word *Introduction* is capitalized and begins at the left margin.

When keying the body of the report, use one-inch top and bottom margins, except on pages with titles. Pages with titles should have a 1 1/2- to

INTRODUCTION

This report represents the findings of a survey conducted for the Office Technology Department of Truett County Community College. The purpose of this quantitative survey was to gain current information about computer equipment, software, and skill levels used in business and industry in Truett County. The report is limited to all companies in the cities of Truett and Bennington that employ 100 employees or more. This information will enable the Office Technology Department to make strategic decisions. Based on the information in this survey, faculty will be able to design courses concerning software currently being used in business, recommend the purchase of equipment with appropriate configurations, and integrate the computer skills required of prospective employees for entry-level positions.

Figure 15-2
The *Introduction* outlines the purpose, scope, and limitations of the report.

NOTES

Name Your Sources

Explain thoroughly and accurately the method you used to gather the data.

2-inch top margin. Usually the pages are numbered, with the numbers centered at the bottom of every page, often beginning with the Table of Contents page.

Methodology. The report should provide the reader with a detailed description of the procedures used—how the data was collected, by what means it was collected (interviews, surveys, questionnaires, experiments, etc.)—along with an analysis of the data. Notice in Figure 15-3 that the writer explains how the methodology is limited by using a paragraph heading.

Writing the parts of the report will be less difficult if you follow a carefully prepared outline and use detailed notes. You should make certain you present the facts in a clear, concise, understandable manner, always adhering to accurate, verifiable facts.

Findings

Following the methodology in the report is an explanation of the detailed findings. In the case of the college, tables were used to show the results of the

Figure 15-3
The methodology section explains how data was collected for a report.

> **Methodology.** Upon receiving support for conducting the survey from the Curriculum Development and Evaluation Department, a list of employers was obtained. A database consisting of the names of the Human Resources Directors along with their company names and addresses was established. The database was created from the <u>Major Employers: Truett Metropolitan Area</u> booklet from the Truett Chamber of Commerce, Economic Development Division, and the <u>Chamber Directory</u> from the Bennington Chamber of Commerce.
>
> The database was made up of major employers in Truett County. Manufacturers and other businesses that employed 100 or more persons were considered to be major employers and were included in the database.
>
> A questionnaire and a cover letter to the 640 employers were developed from the Chamber of Commerce lists. The questionnaire and cover letter (see Appendix) were sent October 1, <year>, asking for a response to be returned by December 15, <year>. As a follow-up procedure, 96 businesses that had not responded were called December 1–7 to encourage the return of the questionnaire. Of the 640 questionnaires mailed, 146 responses were received—a 20 percent return.
>
> **Scope and Limitations.** Although the survey is quantitative, the results do not represent the entire population of businesses in the county. Six hundred forty surveys were sent. The results are obviously limited to those businesses that were willing to take the time to complete the survey.
>
> 4

424   Chapter 15

questionnaire. Each result should be explained. For an example, see the sample *Findings* section in Figure 15-4 for the college report.

Conclusions and Recommendations

Usually this section is considered to be the most important part of the report. In the *Conclusions and Recommendations,* the results of the report will appear. The conclusions tell the reader what the results mean based upon the data collected and analyzed.

Figure 15-4
The findings section presents the results of the study.

FINDINGS

The following tables show the results of the questionnaire. Each result is shown as a percent of responses made to that particular question since not all questions were answered. The number of total questionnaires returned was 146. If the sample size (n) is less than 145, this means that a particular question was not answered by some respondents. At the bottom of each table is shown the number of responses (indicated by "n") and the percent of the 146 that number represents.

Table 1 – What Personal Computers (PCs) Do You Use?

IBM (only)	8.2%
IBM compatible	52.7%
Macintosh (only)	2.1%
IBM/IBM compatible	12.0%
IBM/IBM compatible /Macintosh	11.0%
IBM/IBM compatible /Macintosh/Other	2.1%
IBM compatible /Macintosh	7.5%
IBM/IBM compatible/Other	1.4%
IBM/Macintosh	1.4%
IBM/Other	1.4%
IBM/Macintosh/Other	.1%
Macintosh/Other	.1%
	100.0%

Sample Size = n   n = 146 or 100% responded

Source: <year> Microcomputer/Software Survey at Truett County Community College.

NOTES

Setting the Tables

You should double-space tables that have three or fewer items and single-space tables with four or more lines for easier reading.

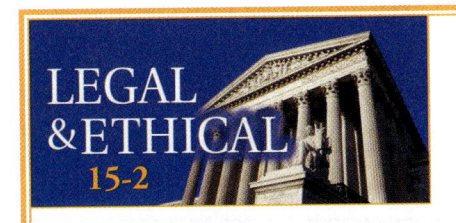

LEGAL & ETHICAL 15-2

Mission Control. You work for a company that provides space shuttles for the space program. You and your committee have received reports indicating it would be unsafe for the shuttle to lift off at temperatures below 38 degrees. The booster could fail, resulting in a breakup of the shuttle. Temperatures have ranged from 32-40 degrees in the past week. You and your committee are being pushed by company management to slant the facts in your final report to favor a liftoff of the shuttle and obscure information about the danger at lower temperatures. What is your responsibility to fairly present the facts in the final report? Would a report that slanted information in one direction be unethical? What might be some of the consequences?

Constructing and Presenting Reports

You should avoid personal observations because the validity of the report depends on conclusions and recommendations that are based upon the analysis of the data. Refer to the purpose of the report. You should list at least one recommendation for each purpose you stated. Study Figure 15-5 to examine the recommendations and conclusions of the college report.

Now that you have finished the body of the report, you can add the remaining parts of the report—*Title Page, Table of Contents, Letter* or *Memo of Authorization* or *Transmittal, Executive Summary,* and *Appendix.*

Figure 15-5
The conclusions and recommendations section presents an unbiased analysis of the data.

> **CONCLUSIONS AND RECOMMENDATIONS**
>
> Based on the information from the survey, the following is a summary of the recommendations and conclusions:
>
> - Companies are not concerned with brand names of computers. This is based upon the high number of IBM-compatible computers purchased. IBM and compatibles still lead the market in brands purchased.
> - Recommendation: Continue to purchase IBM-compatible computers.

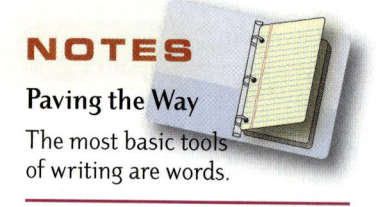

NOTES

Paving the Way
The most basic tools of writing are words.

Title Page

The *Title Page* includes the complete title of the report, the name and title of the author, the name and title of the person for whom the report is prepared, and the date the report is submitted. Study the title page for the college computer report in Figure 15-6 on page 427.

Here are some guidelines to follow when keying the *Title Page:*

- Center the page vertically and key all copy in bold.
- Change to 14-point font, and center the title in all-capital letters with a blank line between each line.
- Change to 12-point font and press Enter 2 times; then center and key the word *at.*
- Press Enter 2 times and center and key the company name and address single-spaced. Press Enter 4 times and center the words *Prepared by.*
- Press Enter 2 times, center, and key single-spaced the name and title of the person who prepared the report.
- Press Enter 4 times and center the words *Submitted to.*
- Press Enter 2 times, center, and key single-spaced the name and title of the person to whom the report is submitted.
- Press Enter 12 times, and center the date the report was submitted.

Table of Contents

You should prepare the *Table of Contents* after the report is completed so you will know how many pages are in the report and what part of the report is on what page. The *Table of Contents* is double-spaced and is on a page by itself. Use a 1 1/2- to 2-inch top margin and center the words TABLE OF CONTENTS in boldface and in all-capital letters. Preliminary information such as the *Letter of Transmittal* and the *Executive Summary* should be numbered with roman numerals. The *Table of Contents* should list all side headings and the pages where they occur. Each main section should be keyed in all-capital letters with side headings indented under the main heading. Use dot leaders to align the headings with their page numbers as in Figure 15-7 below.

Letter or Memo of Authorization or Transmittal

The *Letter* or *Memo of Authorization* or *Transmittal* introduces a formal report and gives the reader an overview of the report. You should use the direct approach when writing the letter or memo. Here are a few guidelines for you to follow:

- Use your organization's letterhead stationery.
- Use a less formal writing style—with contractions and personal pronouns.
- Announce the topic of the report.

> **NOTES**
>
> **Check Your Contents**
>
> Double check the page numbers with the report before you print it to assure that no item has moved to another page when it was edited.

A QUANTITATIVE REPORT: MICROCOMPUTER/SOFTWARE
APPLICATIONS SURVEY

at

Truett County Community College
(Address)

Prepared by

Dr. Bob Neeley
Office Technology Department

Submitted to

Dr. Ralph Kelley
Division of Business Chairperson

January 15, <YEAR>

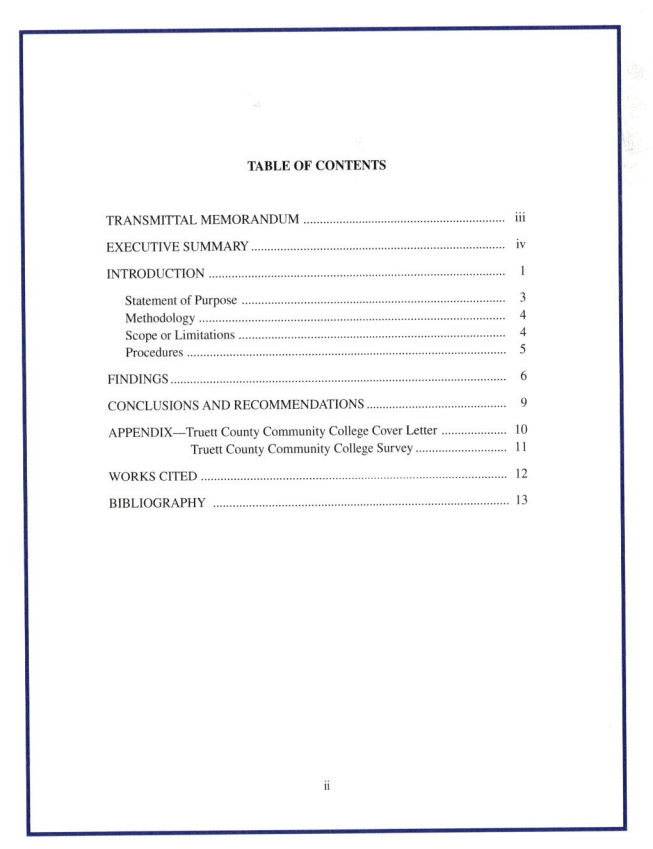

Figure 15-6 Title Page

TABLE OF CONTENTS

TRANSMITTAL MEMORANDUM	iii
EXECUTIVE SUMMARY	iv
INTRODUCTION	1
Statement of Purpose	3
Methodology	4
Scope or Limitations	4
Procedures	5
FINDINGS	6
CONCLUSIONS AND RECOMMENDATIONS	9
APPENDIX—Truett County Community College Cover Letter	10
Truett County Community College Survey	11
WORKS CITED	12
BIBLIOGRAPHY	13

ii

Figure 15-7 Table of Contents

Constructing and Presenting Reports

- Identify the person or group that authorized the report.
- Give a brief description of the report, its findings, conclusions, and recommendations.
- Close by expressing appreciation, identifying desired action, and offering assistance if needed.

Study the *Memo of Transmittal* for the college report in Figure 15-8 below.

Executive Summary

The *Executive Summary,* sometimes called an **abstract,** is a brief summary of the entire report. Executives often do not have time to read an entire report. They appreciate a summary highlighting the important information—the findings, conclusions, and recommendations. The summary may be one or two pages depending on the length of the entire report. Use side headings to help the reader quickly understand the information. Study Figure 15-9, which shows an *Executive Summary* for the college report.

Appendix

Examples of supporting materials are placed in the *Appendix.* You might include surveys, forms, tables of data, computer printouts, other reports, or

Go to CD-ROM Activity 15-2 To test your skills.

Figure 15-8 Memo of Transmittal

Figure 15-9 Executive Summary

428 Chapter 15

any correspondence related to the report. For instance, in the example of the college report, a copy of the cover letter sent to the employers is included in the *Appendix*, as shown in Figure 15-10. The cover letter is followed by the questionnaire that was sent, as shown in Figure 15-11. Some authorities place the *Appendix* after the *Works Cited* and the *Bibliography*.

Works Cited or References

If you are using the MLA style and have used material written by other people, you should include a *Works Cited* section at the end of your report. If you have used the APA style, you would include the works actually cited at the end of your report in a section called *References*. For the Chicago style, the section of works actually cited in your report would be called *Notes* or *Endnotes*. A brief *Works Cited* example is shown in Figure 15-12 on page 430.

Bibliography

A *Bibliography* placed at the very end of a report typically lists all the works consulted in the preparation of the material as well as all the works cited in your *Notes* or *References* lists. The entries are shown in alphabetical order by author or, if the author is not known, by title. A brief *Bibliography* is shown in Figure 15-13 on page 430.

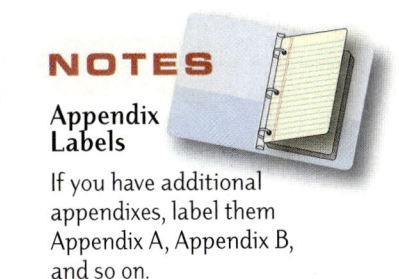

> **NOTES**
> **Appendix Labels**
> If you have additional appendixes, label them Appendix A, Appendix B, and so on.

Figure 15-10 Cover Letter

Figure 15-11 Questionnaire

Constructing and Presenting Reports

429

Figure 15-12 Works Cited

WORKS CITED

Candisky, Catherine. "Labor Force Has 'Skills Gap'." <u>The Columbus Dispatch</u> 12 June 1998, B4.

Elstrom, Peter. "Lost in the Phone Zone?" <u>BusinessWeek</u> 24 November 2002: 120.

Gibaldi, Joseph. <u>MLA Handbook for Writers of Research Papers</u>. 5th ed. New York: The Modern Language Association of America, 1999.

<u>Publication Manual of the American Psychological Association</u>. 5th ed. Washington, DC: American Psychological Association, 2001.

Purdue University Online Writing Lab. <u>Using Modern Language Association (MLA) Format</u>. Online posting. 2002. Purdue University. <http://owl.english.purdue.edu/Files/33.html> (25 September 1998).

12

Figure 15-13 Bibliography

BIBLIOGRAPHY

Candisky, Catherine. "Labor Force Has 'Skills Gap'." <u>The Columbus Dispatch</u> 12 June 1998: B4.

<u>Chamber Directory</u>. Bennington Chamber of Commerce. 1998.

Elstrom, Peter. "Lost in the Phone Zone?" <u>BusinessWeek</u> 24 November 2002: 120-121.

Gibaldi, Joseph. <u>MLA Handbook for Writers of Research Papers</u>. 5th ed. New York: The Modern Language Association of America, 1999.

<u>Major Employers: Truett Metropolitan Area</u>. Truett Chamber of Commerce, Economic Development Division, 1998.

Plesser, Andrew. "Home Sweet Home Page." <u>Working Woman</u>. November 1997, 76.

<u>Publication Manual of the American Psychological Association</u>. 5th ed. Washington, DC: American Psychological Association, 2001.

Sabin, William A. <u>The Gregg Reference Manual</u>. 9th ed. Westerville, OH: Glencoe/McGraw-Hill, 2000.

Purdue University Online Writing Lab. <u>Using Modern Language Association (MLA) Format</u>. Online posting. 2002. Purdue University. <http://owl.english.purdue.edu/Files/33.htl> (25 September 1998).

13

Checkpoint 15.2

1. What are the benefits of identifying the methods you used to collect information for a report?

2. Do you think it is effective to identify the sections of a report with headings (such as *Introduction, Methodology,* and so on)? What other ways could a writer use to show the sections of a report?

3. What is the difference between a *Works Cited* page and a *Bibliography,* and why does a reader want to see both?

PROPOSALS

Often when you make a request for something in business, such as new equipment, additional personnel, a change in procedures, or a solution to a problem, you will be asked to submit a **proposal.** The persuasive approach should be used. Proposals are persuasive documents because you are attempting to convince someone to do something. Your goal is to cause the reader to believe he or she needs to do what you are proposing. You can do this by giving your most convincing evidence first and ending with the least important. If you think your reader may object to any point in your proposal, make sure you answer those objections. In your proposal, you should include an introduction, background information, your proposed plan, associated staffing and budget needs, and a request for authorization or approval.

Sometimes a company will request a proposal to solve a problem. This request for proposal (RFP) details, in a set of instructions, exactly what the company wants done and when they want it done. Those who believe they can fulfill the RFP will then submit a proposal in response to the RFP.

> **NOTES**
>
> **Overview Proposals**
>
> Proposals that succeed are based on logical organization of facts and figures. In a proposal, be sure to include all the necessary information in an understandable way that supports your conclusion and convinces your readers.

Introduction

You should begin by briefly explaining what your request is and why you are writing the proposal. You must establish that a problem exists for which you need a solution—the problem will act as the hook to gain the reader's interest. Short internal reports are usually written in memo format. Here is an example of an introduction for an internal proposal:

> In recent months, production in our manufacturing plant has been decreasing. By the end of the first quarter, we will no longer be able to keep the promise to our retailers that they will receive goods no later than one week after placing an order. As a result, I am proposing that we add an additional evening shift to the assembly line.

The introduction tells the reader the scope and limitations of the topic and introduces the reader to what will follow.

Background Information

The background information brings the reader up to date. This part states what problem your proposal addresses and outlines the goal you intend to accomplish. When presenting background information, you should include all the details that surround the problem so that the reader will understand how and why there is a problem and why it should become a priority. Study this example of background information:

> Manufacturing has decreased in production 4 percent over the last quarter. If this decline continues, profits will also see a decline.

Proposed Plan

The proposed plan is an explanation of how you intend to solve the problem. Tell the reader what you intend to do and stress how the reader will benefit from your solution. Study this example of a proposed plan:

> To provide better levels of inventory, I am proposing that we add a shift to our assembly line. The shift would run from 3 p.m. to 11 p.m.

Staffing and Budget Needs

You must outline how the staff of your organization will be affected by your proposal. Be sure to indicate if any additional staff will be needed and

Constructing and Presenting Reports

describe ways the present staff will be involved in your proposal. For example, what staff experience and ability will be needed? Also mention additional expenses that will be incurred as a result of your proposal, including costs resulting from any change in staff. See how staff and budgeting needs are detailed in the following example:

> The following solution to the decline in production in manufacturing is proposed:
>
> - Add ten new line personnel—cost: $200,000 annually
> - Add one new supervisor—cost: $32,000 annually
> - Additional expenses—overhead: $40,000
> - Increase in production—50 percent
> - Approximate total revenue realized—$350,000
> - Approximate increase in profit—$78,000

Request for Approval or Authorization

You should close your proposal with a request for approval or authorization. Remind the reader of the benefits to him or her if your proposal is approved. Usually, it is a good idea to include a suggested deadline as well. Read the following example of a request for approval:

> I am convinced that with this additional shift, we will be able to increase profits as well as maintain our quick response to our retailers' orders. With your approval, this shift could begin by July 1.

Now study the completed internal proposal shown in Figure 15-14 on page 433, which puts together the various examples we have just seen. Pay particular attention to its format—a successful proposal should be formatted so that it looks professional and is easy to read. Notice how side headings offer the reader a clear understanding of the information in the proposal. Also notice that bullets, boldface type, and underscoring may be used to highlight key points. Should your proposal continue to a second page, you should include a second-page heading.

USING VISUALS IN A REPORT

NOTES

Point Out Visuals
You should always make a reference in the report text to any visual you use.

You have heard the saying "A picture is worth a thousand words." In formal and informal reports, as in any other writing, when you have numerical data to present to the reader, "A picture *is* worth a thousand words." A **visual** is a picture or graph, often referred to as a graphic. Word processing software offers features that make tabulating numerical data quite simple.

See Chapter 6, page 146, for more information on spreadsheet applications and their uses.

Figure 15-14
A sample proposal.

BAYBERRY MANUFACTURING
1311 Marsh Lane
Houston, TX 77602

MEMO TO: Scott Landenberger, Plant Manager

FROM: Dana Steinberg, Production Manager

DATE: April 10, <YEAR>

SUBJECT: Proposed Addition of Second Shift

In recent months, production in our manufacturing plant has been decreasing. By the end of the first quarter, we will no longer be able to keep the promise to our retailers that they will receive goods no later than one week after placing an order. As a result, I am proposing that we add an additional evening shift to the assembly line.

BACKGROUND INFORMATION

Manufacturing has decreased in production 4 percent over the last quarter of last year. If this decline continues, profits will also see a decline.

PROPOSED PLAN

To provide better levels of inventory, I am proposing that we add an evening shift to our assembly line. The shift would run from 3 p.m. to 11 p.m.

STAFFING AND BUDGET

The following solution to the decline in production in manufacturing is proposed:

- Add ten new line personnel--cost: $200,000 annually
- Add one new supervisor--cost: $32,000 annually
- Additional expenses--overhead: $40,000
- Increase in production--50 percent
- Approximate total revenue realized--$350,000
- Approximate increase in profit--$78,000

AUTHORIZATION

I am convinced that with this additional shift, we will be able to increase profits as well as maintain our quick response to our retailers' orders. With your approval, this shift could begin by July 1.

cns

Tables

One of the most basic ways to present numerical information is by showing it in a table—figures are easier to read when shown in columns. If you have only two or three lines in your table, double-space it; but, if you have more than three lines, the table will look better single-spaced. If your table is lengthy, create sets of three or four single-spaced lines, then double-space between those sets to make it easier to read. Notice the table in the memo shown in Figure 15-15 on page 434. The numerical information is much easier to read in the table than it would be in a paragraph.

Charts

Charts are a commonly used way to help readers understand data visually. Spreadsheet software offers features that create a variety of charts, including pie, bar, stacked-bar, line, and area charts. A good way to make certain that

---

NOTES

Visual Strength

For visual learners, showing percentages in a table is better than paragraph form. Showing figures in a graph makes them even clearer.

Figure 15-15
Tables make statistical material easier to read.

Season ticket sales for 2002 increased 13.7 percent over 2001. This year we sold 20,960 season tickets, compared with last year's total of 18,366. This represents a healthy increase of 2,594, which will certainly boost our operating budget as we begin the season.

The following table illustrates the season ticket sales results as they were reported monthly for the past two years.

| SEASON TICKET SALES |||||
| Comparison of 2001 and 2002 |||||
Month	2001	2002	Increase	% Increase
July	1,134	1,845	711	62.6
August	2,456	3,255	799	32.5
September	6,110	6,751	641	10.5
October	8,666	9,109	443	5.1
TOTALS	18,366	20,960	2,594	13.7

GLOBAL DIVERSITY 15.1

Diversity Report
Discuss how photographs and illustrations in a report or presentation can appear to be ethnically biased. *How can you avoid this?*

your chart will be correctly understood by the reader is to let someone else look at it and interpret what it says. Study the example of a spreadsheet that was created using Microsoft Excel™ and the pie chart created from the spreadsheet (see Figure 15-16).

Photographs and Illustrations

Photographs offer the reader a realistic view of information while illustrations provide visual descriptions such as pencil, pen, or computer-aided drawings. Other visuals you might want to use are maps, such as a map of the United States, organizational charts showing lines of authority, and flow charts that show the direction or flow of information.

Figure 15-16
Note the visual impact of the pie chart.

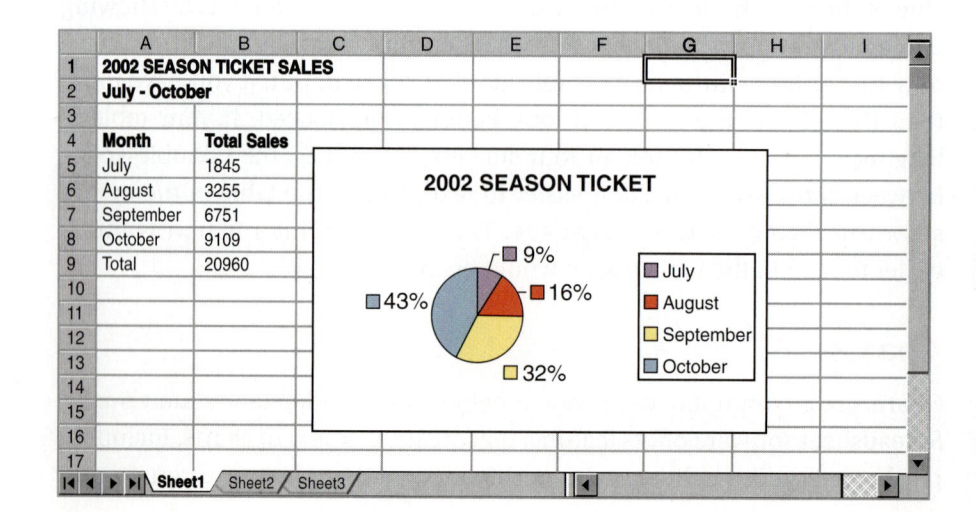

434

Chapter 15

✔ CHECKLIST FOR WRITING REPORTS

Check each item only when you are satisfied that you have completed each detail under that item. Did I:

_____ Have a specific purpose before I began writing?
_____ Take detailed, well-organized, clearly written notes?
_____ Plan ahead; have all my information gathered before I began; have a thorough understanding of the information?
_____ Write an outline and stick to it?
_____ Focus on accurate, valid facts?
_____ Maintain consistency in the format selected?
_____ Keep the audience always in mind; show empathy; anticipate the reader's response?
_____ Adapt my writing style to fit the particular situation?
_____ Include everything the reader needs to know, yet avoid unnecessary minute details?
_____ Develop coherence and follow a logical sequence?
_____ Write in a positive manner?
_____ Vary sentence length and keep sentences uncomplicated?
_____ Include only one main idea per paragraph?
_____ Keep subjects and verbs close together?
_____ Make use of transitional (connecting) devices and topic sentences?
_____ Observe proper mechanics such as spelling, punctuation, and capitalization?

Chapter 15 Summary

Reports are an essential part of the communication process in business and have become critical to the professional when making business decisions. All reports should be easy to read and understand and do their job quickly and effectively. Report writers should communicate their ideas clearly and logically, using straightforward language, correct format, and correct grammar, spelling, and punctuation.

The formal research report plays an important role in business. The report can present data on a specialized subject, attempt to find the causes underlying a problem, find whether or not a problem exists, or analyze possible solutions to a particular problem. You should develop your skills to be ready to meet the challenges of report writing in today's workplace.

Proposals are used to make requests for business needs such as new equipment, additional personnel, or changes in procedures. The goal of a proposal is to cause the reader to believe he or she needs to do what you are proposing.

Visuals can be effectively used in both formal research reports and in proposals. Remember a picture is often easier to understand than columns of information.

Chapter 15

Online Exercises

Objective:
These online activities will allow you to use search engines for conducting research.

Go to **bcw.glencoe.com**, the address for the *Business Communication at Work* Web site, and select Chapter 15. Next, click on Online Exercises. You will see a list of Web site links that will bring you to search engine Web sites.

Activity 15.1

1. Select one of the search engine Web sites to visit.

2. Key *informal letter report* into the **Search** box (some Web sites use an **Enter Word** box). Click on three search results and explore the various informal letter report Web sites.

3. Use the other search engines listed for this activity on the *Business Communication at Work* Web site to search *informal letter report.* For each of the Web sites you search, click on three results and explore the various informal letter report Web sites.

4. Repeat Steps 2 and 3 for the following terms: *formal research report, report organization,* and *writing business proposals.*

5. Write a paragraph describing your research using search engines. You may want to consider the following questions in your paragraph:

    a. How relevant was the information you found as it relates to business communications?

    b. Did you have any problems using one of the search engines?

    c. Were you able to locate all of the terms? Which ones presented problems?

    d. Which search engine did you prefer? Why?

6. Write your name on your paper, and hand it in to your instructor.

Activity 15.2

1. Select one of the popular Web site search engines to visit.

2. Click on one of the categories such as Health, Family and Culture, or Travel and Transport. Click on a link to a popular Web site that interests you in the category you have chosen. Print out the Web site's homepage.

3. Return to your search results by clicking on the **Back** button at the top of your screen. Click on two more links of popular Web sites and print them out.

4. On the back of one printout, make an outline of new information that you learned from your research.

5. On a sheet of paper write a paragraph discussing what you learned from your research. You should use your outline as the basis of your paragraph.

6. Write your name on your paper and printouts, and hand them in to your instructor.

CHAPTER 15 WORKSHEETS

NAME _____ DATE _____

PRACTICE 1

Organizing Information

Instructions: Review and organize the following steps in an information-gathering process. Number the steps in the order you would complete them, using the blanks provided.

1. a. _____ Interviewing for a job
   b. _____ Accepting a job
   c. _____ Studying the help-wanted ads
   d. _____ Weighing the retirement benefits offered
   e. _____ Sending a résumé with a cover letter
   f. _____ Looking for a job
   g. _____ Checking with a job information center

2. a. _____ Proofreading the rough draft
   b. _____ Gathering the necessary information
   c. _____ Signing the final copy
   d. _____ Organizing the information
   e. _____ Writing the letter report
   f. _____ Creating an outline

Choosing an Approach

Instructions: Indicate which approach you would use for writing an informal report in the following situations. Write **P** for persuasive approach, **D** for direct approach, and **I** for indirect approach.

1. a. _____ The carpet needs to be replaced in the Miami branch office. Funds are available, and you believe the request for new carpet will be granted.

   b. _____ You need to hire two additional staff members to be able to maintain adequately the output required by your department. Funds for the additional staff are available, but you will have to justify the need for those funds before they will be approved.

   c. _____ You have devised a new plan for routing mail in your company that will cut costs, increase efficiency, and offer more services to company staff.

   d. _____ A workshop that you want your staff to attend is available. You believe that attending the workshop will improve your staff's efficiency, but the workshop is expensive.

   e. _____ Your company has grown, adding several new offices as well as new personnel, and it experienced an increase in calls from customers. The company phone system is outdated. Consequently, you are recommending that an expensive new phone system be installed.

Constructing and Presenting Reports

CHAPTER 15 WORKSHEETS

NAME _____ DATE _____

PRACTICE 2

Constructing Letter Reports

Instructions: You are an outside insurance investigator. Combine the following ideas into a letter report for your office manager. (Note: *Not all information is important.*)

1. a. The office manager (use your instructor's name) wants you to inspect the damage done to the Atlanta Securities & Investment Company's office.
   b. The manager wrote it in a memo to you.
   c. The memo was dated January 15, <year>.
   d. You went to Atlanta.
   e. You went last week.
   f. You went on business.
   g. The Atlanta office is located at 3211 Country Lane, Atlanta, Georgia.
   h. It was raining in Atlanta when damage occurred.
   i. The area was menaced by mud slides when damage occurred.
   j. Much damage has been caused to two offices by the mudslides--the Accounting Department and the Securities Department in Building 213.
   k. It was pleasant when you left Nashville.
   l. The computer equipment and files were removed and were undamaged.
   m. You met the manager at the Atlanta office.
   n. The manager's name was Bryan Vasquez.
   o. He was formerly employed at the United States Treasury Department.
   p. You and Vasquez have a mutual interest in golf.
   q. Vasquez talked about his budget.
   r. He talked about his budget at the staff meeting you attended.
   s. He said he did not have enough money to cover the damage done by the mud slides.
   t. Vasquez has been cooperative and diligent in past assignments.
   u. Vasquez should be allowed extra funds to repair the damage.
   v. Extra funds are available.
   w. Vasquez had the damages assessed by Hillman Construction Company, and repairs will cost $150,000. A copy of the estimate is available.

CHAPTER 15 WORKSHEETS

NAME _____ DATE _____

PRACTICE 3

Presenting Reports

Instructions: Review the statements (below and on the next page) that relate to a report on VISTA volunteers and their training. Then follow these steps:

1. a. Identify the topic or central idea statement by placing its number in the blank provided.
   b. Identify the statements you would include in an introduction by placing the numbers in the blank provided.
   c. Identify the statements you would include under the three topics discussed—training, assignments, and language—by placing the numbers in each blank provided.
   d. Write a report according to your instructor's directions.

VISTA VOLUNTEERS AND THEIR TRAINING

1. You do not have to know a foreign language to join VISTA.
2. Assignments of VISTA volunteers offer outlets for virtually every talent and skill.
3. The major aim of the training is to prepare the volunteer with confidence for the assignment that lies ahead.
4. New language courses are constantly being held.
5. Criteria for joining VISTA are few.
6. Language instruction is not generally part of the VISTA program.
7. An assignment may involve aiding the physically challenged or acting as a recreation leader.
8. Another training objective is to test the abilities of volunteers in conditions of poverty.
9. Volunteers work in tenements and shacks.
10. VISTA (Volunteers in Service to America) is one of the major antipoverty programs in America today.
11. You must have no dependents under 18 years of age to join VISTA.
12. Training is a year-round operation.
13. Volunteers work among the sick and disabled, the young and old.

Constructing and Presenting Reports

CHAPTER 15 WORKSHEETS

NAME _____ DATE _____

14. Training is conducted by universities and colleges and some nonprofit private groups familiar with the problems of the poor.

15. VISTA training includes workshops, discussions, and fieldwork.

16. VISTA offers an opportunity for men and women from all economic, geographic, social, and age groups to offer their skills and services wherever poverty exists.

17. Volunteers work on Native American reservations and in migrant worker camps.

18. Training groups consist of 30 to 50 volunteers each.

19. Training programs are conducted throughout the country.

20. The Economic Opportunity Act of 1964 established VISTA.

21. The training program is designed to assist volunteers to adapt their skills to the jobs they will have.

22. You must be a United States citizen or a permanent resident of this country or one of its territories to volunteer.

23. One aim of the training program is to assist volunteers to learn techniques useful in carrying out their assignments.

24. You must be at least 18 years old to join VISTA.

25. The training program lasts from four to six weeks.

26. Volunteers work in cities, small towns, and rural areas.

Source: "Report Writing," U.S. Office of Personnel Management, Communications and Office Skills Training Institute, Dallas, Tex.

Topic sentence or main idea: _____

Introduction: _____

Training: _____

Assignments: _____

Language: _____

CHAPTER 15 WORKSHEETS

NAME _____ DATE _____

PRACTICE 4

Writing Applications

Instructions: *Prepare a letter report, formal report, or proposal according to your instructor's directions. Choose from the following topics. Use the "Checklist for Writing Reports" on page 435 to guide you in your preparation of the report.*

1. a. Recycling programs at work, home, or school
   b. Flexible work hours
   c. Writing a code of conduct
   d. Carpooling for work
   e. Investment opportunities
   f. New business venture
   g. Cottage work arrangement
   h. Upgrading equipment or software
   i. Remodeling for an exercise room
   j. Daycare center at work

CHAPTER 16

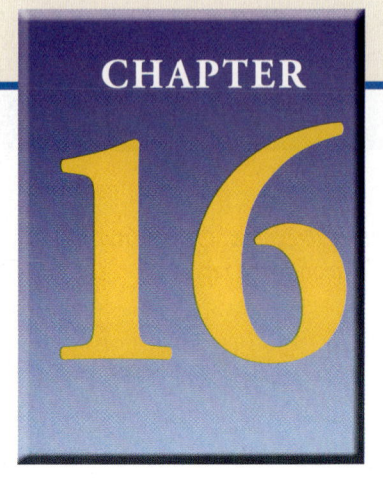

Preparing Meeting Communications

Objectives

After completing this chapter, you will be able to:

1. Compose a meeting notice
2. Compose and format an agenda
3. Prepare the minutes for a meeting

WORKPLACE APPLICATIONS

Telecommuting and Teleconferencing

Technology, such as computers and cell phones, has revolutionized the business world. Since the 1990s, telecommuting and teleconferencing have allowed people to work together despite being miles apart. Both telecommuting and teleconferencing have advantages and disadvantages, but both are now staples of modern business.

So Close, So Far Away

Telecommuting means using technology to communicate with the office while working from home or on the road. In the 1990s, experts believed that telecommuting would permanently alter the American way of business. It seemed an equation for endless productivity. Some disadvantages did appear, however. Many telecommuters felt isolated from their on-site coworkers. Some worried that they were missing out on important meetings. Managers wondered how to evaluate telecommuters' work, as they saw only the end product and not the process of accomplishing the task. Many telecommuters now make an effort to visit the office more frequently.

Like telecommuting, **teleconferencing** promised to save businesses money and increase productivity. Companies would no longer have to pay the expense of sending employees to meetings in far away places. Communication around the globe could happen with the click of a button. Yet the technology has not yet matched its potential. Teleconferencing equipment is still expensive and often finicky. In addition, many of the same objections to telecommuting affect teleconferencing. It seems that a sale is still best made and a problem is still best solved when the people involved are seated in the same room. Technology offers businesses tools with great promise, but for the moment, the best tools—human employees—still seem to perform best when they work together in the same office.

Thinking Critically

Situation: You work for a large computer software company that offers employees the option to telecommute between one and four days a week. You have been with the company for about six months and hope to be promoted. You also have a new baby at home.

Ask Yourself: Would you telecommute, and, if so, for how many days a week? Discuss the reasons for your decision.

" Time is money. "
—**Benjamin Franklin**
*philosopher,
author, inventor*

With changing organizational structures and the advent of cross-functional teams, the American business environment may be considered a nation of "meeters." Our system of business uses the meeting format for many purposes, including selling, informing, instructing, and planning. During your professional life, you will attend many meetings and may be responsible for conducting a meeting, creating an agenda, or reporting the results of meetings. Even if you are a small business owner with few employees, you will hold staff meetings.

Successful meetings result from effective planning, which includes the preparation of the following:

- **Meeting notices**—prepared and distributed before the meeting
- **Agendas**—prepared and distributed before the meeting
- **Minutes**—prepared and distributed after the meeting

Types of Meetings

Face-to-face oral communication among groups of people is essential to certain phases of business. Meetings represent an important segment of business communication because meetings can often achieve results that would be difficult to accomplish by phone, letter, or electronic mail. Meetings can range from the formal to the informal; in today's business world, both types of meetings can be held electronically.

Formal Meetings

In many organizations, formal meetings are planned, structured meetings, usually conducted by elected officers. Formal meetings follow strict **parliamentary procedure,** which means they follow a set of rules for conducting meetings. An excellent reference book for parliamentary procedure is *Robert's Rules of Order, Newly Revised* (by H. M. Robert; published by Perseus Press; on the Internet, access www.robertsrules.com).

Examples of formal meetings include these:

- Annual or quarterly corporate meetings of directors, executives, or shareholders
- Monthly board meetings of executive management groups, service organizations, and educational institutions
- Conventions for professional organizations

Informal Meetings

Informal meetings, such as staff meetings, management meetings, and project team meetings, are held as they are needed. These meetings may follow a discussion format, with one person serving as a facilitator or coordinator and another person serving as a note taker.

Electronic Meetings

Electronic meetings are becoming more and more a part of doing business. An early example of an electronic meeting was an August 1979 hour-long simulcast by Ciba-Geigy to transmit the "World Soybean Report" via satellite from the American Soybean Association meeting in an Atlanta hotel. Hundreds of people watched the U.S. segment of the four-way transmission, the first ever attempted among four countries.

By using audio, video, and/or computer equipment, including an *electronic writing board,* several groups of people at various locations can participate in a meeting. An electronic writing board allows a meeting facilitator to write, draw, or tape and print the information in a clean copy. With the push of a button, the participants or facilitator can print multiple copies. Electronic writing boards allow faxing, e-mailing, or adding graphics. An electronic board keeps crucial information from being misunderstood, misinterpreted, or just plain missed. From the recorded transmission, a record of the meeting can be prepared and distributed electronically.

Videoconferencing brings people in different locations together without their being in the same location. With a videoconference setup, groups can quickly hold an impromptu meeting with individuals from different sites. **Audioconferencing** allows an operator to dial all participants in the teleconference group, bringing each participant into the meeting as he or she is reached. Optional features, such as questions and answers and group polling, are provided at no charge through a teleconference operator. Another type of audioconference occurs when each participant dials an 800 telephone number to reach the teleconference operator. This service is ideal for participants who are traveling or are difficult to reach.

Document managers on the World Wide Web provide interfaces for creating and presenting agendas and minutes for use during meetings. These programs also provide other mechanisms for managing document-related meeting issues, such as faxing or e-mailing information.

> **GLOBAL DIVERSITY 16.1**
>
> **Language Barriers**
> Electronic meetings may remove distance barriers, but language barriers may exist among participants at different locations around the globe. *How could such potential problems be identified and dealt with in preparation for an electronic meeting?*

PREPARING MEETING NOTICES

Meetings may be called on short notice, depending on the urgency of the topic and the number of participants and their accessibility, or they may be scheduled well in advance to stimulate attendance and to allow time for preparation. A notice announces information about an upcoming meeting. The notice is usually sent ten days to two weeks prior to a board of directors' meeting. For a less formal meeting, a notice may be sent one to three days (or sometimes a few hours or less) prior to a meeting. Notifying people by telephone is time-consuming and provides no guarantee that everyone receives identical information, even if each person is reached; therefore, it is recommended that the meeting organizer send a written meeting notice.

> **Thinking Cap 16.1**
>
> **Discuss:** What are the purposes of a meeting notice?

Components of a Meeting Notice

The meeting notice and reminder should include the following:

- Name of the committee or meeting group
- Day and date of the meeting
- Time of the meeting
- Location
- Purpose of the meeting
- Agenda (a written plan for a meeting)
- Any other applicable information, such as what materials to bring

Common errors made in writing meeting notices include inconsistencies in listing the day and date and forgetting to include the meeting location or time. Be sure that each component is included in the meeting notice.

In organizations that use an electronic calendaring system, the software can be used to quickly list times when participants are available. Participants may then be notified in advance of the meeting by a written notice or through their e-mail system. Depending on the distribution of the original notice and the importance of the meeting, a notice may be followed by a reminder sent a few hours or days before the meeting.

Format of Meeting Notices

Meeting notices and reminders may take the following forms:

- Announcements
- Letters
- Memos
- Postal cards
- Meeting requests on an e-mail and calendaring system.

A reply card or a reservation slip may be enclosed or attached to the meeting notice. Participants may respond electronically or via the telephone. Study the meeting notice shown in Figure 16-1, page 447, which includes a reply card. See also the notice for a board of directors' meeting shown in Figure 16-2.

PREPARING MEETING AGENDAS

An **agenda** is a plan for a meeting. The agenda is a valuable tool for keeping the participants focused in order to achieve the meeting's desired objective—it should help those involved understand what is expected of them.

Go to CD-ROM
Activity 16-1
To test your skills.

NOTES
Make a Backup Copy
File a copy of the meeting notice including the date it was sent. Proof of the date the notice was sent may become important at a later date.

Thinking Cap 16.2
Discuss: What are some ways to avoid the most common mistakes made by those preparing meeting notices?

Figure 16-1
A meeting notice may contain a reply card for participants to complete and return.

MEMO TO: Relocation and Commercial-Investment Divisions

FROM: Josephine Landau *JL*

DATE: September 16, <YEAR>

SUBJECT: Team Effort to Capture Relocation Business

A joint meeting of the Relocation and Commercial-Investment Divisions will be held on Thursday, September 19, at 2:30 p.m., in Conference Room C on the third floor.

Mark your calendar; there will be **NO** phone or e-mail follow-up.

The purpose of the meeting is to discuss a team approach to our organization's goal of capturing a sizable share of the relocation business in the Dallas area.

Please review the attached list of major corporate accounts to be contacted following this meeting. Be prepared to share your ideas for meeting our goal.

- -

Please return your response:

Name: _____

☐   I will attend the September 19 Relocation Business meeting.

☐   I will not attend the September 19 Relocation Business meeting.

sb
Attachment

Figure 16-2
A notice of a board meeting may include a reservation slip or reply card.

NOTICE OF QUARTERLY MEETING

OF BOARD OF DIRECTORS OF

SULLIVAN INVESTMENTS INTERNATIONAL

A regular meeting of the Board of Directors will be held on Thursday, June 15, <year>, at 9 a.m. in the Seville Executive Room at the Hyatt Hotel, Interstate 35, Dallas, Texas.

An agenda is attached.

_____   _____
Signature   Date

Preparing Meeting Communications   447

Thinking Cap 16.3

Discuss: Identify at least three purposes served by an agenda.

An agenda

- Identifies the objectives for the meeting
- Prepares participants for the meeting
- Defines the time allotted to each topic, if appropriate, and the order of discussion

Every meeting should have an agenda; for most meetings the agenda should be written and distributed before the meeting. While the circumstances of some meetings preclude working from a written agenda, discarding a written agenda should be the exception rather than the rule.

Components of an Agenda

An agenda lists the items of business in the order they are to be discussed at a meeting. Successful agendas also include the approximate amount of time to be spent discussing each item. They also define each participant's specific responsibilities. An agenda sends a message that the facilitator or chair is prepared, that the meeting is planned and will be conducted in an organized fashion, and that the meeting will end when the agenda items have been covered. Preparation of the agenda for a *regularly* scheduled meeting should begin almost immediately after the last meeting. Preparing an agenda allows the facilitator to prepare any follow-up comments on previous items or to give participants an opportunity to add topics.

In addition to the list of items to be discussed at a meeting, an agenda should also include the following:

- Day and date of meeting
- Meeting objective or purpose
- Time (beginning and ending)
- Location
- Responsibilities for the listed topics, including allotted times
- Call to order
- Approval of minutes
- Old and new business
- Order in which topics will be discussed

Correspondence, reports, and other documents may be attached to the agenda as reference materials for the topics to be covered at the meeting.

Format of Agendas

The format of an agenda will vary with the circumstances of the meeting. For instance, the agenda for an informal staff meeting, such as the one shown in Figure 16-3, may be a simple list of topics in an e-mail addressed to the

NOTES

What is the Agenda?

An agenda should indicate when and where the meeting will take place, who should attend, and why they should attend, as well as the list of items for discussion.

MARKETING MANAGERS

Meeting Agenda

July 27, <YEAR>, 2:30 p.m., Conference Room C-1

1. Welcome and introductions
    New region Southwest
2. Launch for new products
    Budget
    Date, time, location
    Exhibits
    Refreshments
    Entertainment
    Responsibilities
    Printed materials
3. Quarterly reports
4. Next planning meeting

Figure 16-3
This agenda for an informal meeting includes a simple list of topics.

participants. In contrast, the agenda for a formal meeting will be written as a more structured list of topics, as shown in Figure 16-4.

When writing an agenda, make sure that the items are listed in the same, or parallel, form (see Chapter 3 for a discussion of parallelism). Write every agenda item as a noun phrase. Verbs are used for the decisions made during a meeting. For example, do not use *Giving the Treasurer's Report* as an agenda item; instead use *Treasurer's Report.* Additional examples of agenda items include the following:

NOT PARALLEL	PARALLEL
Calling to order	Call to order
Report of Budget Committee	Budget Committee Report
Reviewing Management Survey	Management Survey Review

ADVANCED TECHNOLOGIES BOARD OF DIRECTORS

Meeting Agenda

November 10, <YEAR>, 7 p.m.

Harlingen House, Enright Room
Sacramento, California

1. Call to order
2. Information items   Executive Director's report
3. Action items   Minutes, Board of Directors Meeting, June 12, <YEAR>
    Financial report, Steven Stegall, Treasurer (attached)
    Committee report, Shirley Brooks, Chairperson (attached)
    Publications
4. Old business   Management survey, Jodie Kreswell (attached)
5. New business
6. Adjournment

Figure 16-4
This agenda for a formal meeting includes a structured list of topics.

Preparing Meeting Communications

449

You may want to create an agenda using the templates provided in word processing software. Using this software, you can select either a short, informal agenda format or a longer version, which lists each topic and gives blank space for making comments about discussions, conclusions, and action items.

Agenda Distribution

Distribution of the agenda should follow your organization's policy, usual practice, or board bylaws. For example, if your organization is a corporation, there are rules and regulations that must be followed in reporting and distributing board of directors' minutes and maintaining corporate records. Once prepared, the agenda should be distributed far enough in advance of the meeting to allow review by the participants. As a rule, an agenda may be sent with the meeting notice or sent at least three to five days prior to the meeting. On the meeting day, a final agenda that includes new items may be distributed to participants. Review the agenda shown in Figure 16-5. Even though the agenda was sent in advance of the meeting, it looks like a shopping list and lacks the detail and clarity needed in an agenda. Now look at Figure 16-6, which shows an improved version of the same agenda. You can readily see how the second example follows the rules of agenda preparation.

Figure 16-5
This agenda lacks detail, violating the principles necessary for agenda preparation.

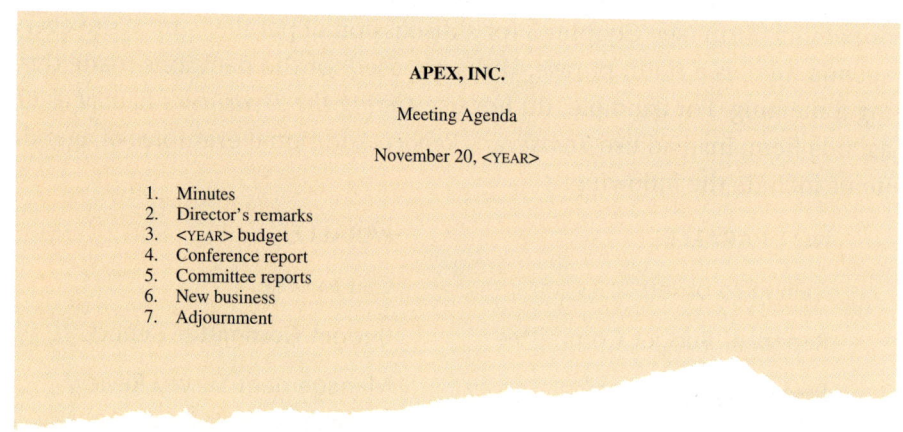

> **APEX, INC.**
>
> Meeting Agenda
>
> November 20, <YEAR>
>
> 1. Minutes
> 2. Director's remarks
> 3. <YEAR> budget
> 4. Conference report
> 5. Committee reports
> 6. New business
> 7. Adjournment

Figure 16-6
This agenda provides sufficient detail for each item. Compare this agenda with the one in Figure 16-5.

> **APEX, INC.**
>
> Meeting Agenda
>
> November 20, <YEAR>, 9 a.m. – 10:30 a.m.
>
> Paulson Hotel, Marsden Room
> Wausau, Wisconsin
>
> 1. Minutes — Approval of minutes of meeting held October 12, <YEAR>. Minutes are attached.
> 2. Director's remarks — Report attached.
> 3. Budget for <YEAR> — Budget attached. The <year> budget was approved by the Finance Committee at the September meeting.
> 4. Report on conferences — At its October meeting, staff reported on the various conferences to which representatives are invited. The report is attached. The Director intends to recommend action at the November meeting.
> 5. Committee reports — Long-Range Planning Committee drafted the report, which is attached.
> 6. New business — Management survey, Jodie Kreswell (attached)
> 7. Adjournment

Checkpoint 16.1

1. What are the benefits and drawbacks of setting an agenda?
2. If you were a new employee, what would you think of a manager who sets and keeps to an agenda? What would you think of a manager who holds meetings without agendas?
3. From a business perspective, why is it important to distribute agendas in advance of a meeting?

PREPARING MINUTES

Minutes, a report prepared after a meeting, are the official written record of the business that was conducted. (See Chapter 15 for a detailed discussion of report writing.) Minutes can be compared to a report; they have an introduction, body, and conclusion. The introduction includes the specifics about the meeting, such as day, date, time, and location. The body includes what actually happened during the meeting, and the conclusion describes actions, decisions, and information about the next meeting. Minutes can be brief or lengthy, depending on the length of the meeting's agenda—they may range from a one-page *summary* of the meeting to a book-length report of a convention or annual board of directors' meeting. Regardless of the length or format, minutes should reflect the substance of the meeting. They are used for the following purposes:

- To prevent any misunderstanding of meeting actions
- To keep absentees and other interested parties informed of decisions
- To provide a basis of discussion for the next meeting
- To provide an official written record of the meeting results

Meeting minutes, therefore, are very important.

Minutes of board and committee meetings contain the records of the actions that were taken. These minutes are critical to the decision-making process for companies and must be maintained according to the accepted style for these minutes. The American Society of Corporate Secretaries (ASCS), a professional association whose members are *corporate* secretaries, publishes various guidebooks and monographs devoted to current practices related to corporate meetings. One such guide focuses on the style and content of board and committee meeting minutes. Included in this monograph are guidelines for the corporate secretary who takes the minutes and information on the filing, retaining, and indexing of minutes. You can access the Web site for the ASCS at www.ascs.org to learn more about the work of the ASCS.

Drafting minutes should be done as soon as possible after a meeting. The more time that lapses, the more difficult it will be to recollect discussions and

NOTES

Second Look

If you are responsible for preparing the minutes, review your notes within 24 hours of attending the meeting.

Preparing Meeting Communications 451

action plans. Although participants may make notes during the meeting, they depend on the official minutes for a complete and accurate record of conclusions reached and actions required as a result of the meeting.

Agendas created using word processing software offer blank spaces to record discussion points, conclusions, and action items, which can be used for preparing minutes after a meeting.

The language style used in minutes should reflect the type of meeting. The more formal the meeting is, the more formal the wording and tone of the minutes. For example, formal minutes would reflect an impersonal and objective tone while informal minutes would typically use an informal tone and format, which may be written in summary form. In writing informal minutes, the writer may use informal phrases such as "Charlotte Whitmore adjourned the meeting."

Organization of Minutes

Minutes should be written objectively and concisely, and they should be written in the **past tense.** The first page should give the identifying information *who, what, when, where, why,* and *how.* Follow the identifying information with a summary of agenda items in **chronological order,** the order in which the business was conducted. Participants may fail to follow an agenda exactly in informal meetings; however, the minutes should reflect the agenda items as they were actually discussed.

Minutes need not be keyed verbatim (word for word) except for those formal meetings where there were motions, changes or amendments to bylaws or company policy, or majority or minority opinions. It is important that the minutes emphasize discussions resulting in an action—make sure the minutes clearly indicate what was done or agreed upon, who agreed, and when the action is required.

Remember that minutes represent a permanent record of a meeting. Consequently, minutes should be specific, complete, and accurate so that they can be referred to at some future time if necessary. For instance, a department manager may be considering increasing specific budget items based on the discussions and conclusions of a meeting held last week. The minutes should provide a written record of the results of that meeting that will assist the manager in making the decision.

When writing minutes, use a separate paragraph for each item of business covered in a meeting. To help readers locate items quickly in minutes, it is good to use some sort of headings to separate discussion points.

Format of Informal Minutes

For informal meetings, minutes may have a memo format or a minutes summary, which is a form that allows the participants to make notes. These notes serve as the minutes of the informal meeting. These two formats are discussed in the following paragraphs.

In a memo format, you would include the following:

- Memo heading

- Subject line: For example, *Minutes of the Management Review of April 20, <YEAR>, 10:30 a.m., Room 6*

- Attendance list: List the names of those who were present at the meeting, those who were absent, and those who attended as guests. The name of the person who facilitated the meeting is usually listed first.

- Agenda topics: List each topic in chronological order. You may use boldface or italic type or underscoring to highlight each topic.

- Concluding comments: Mention the time, date, and location of the next meeting, if applicable.

A **minutes summary** provides readers with discussion highlights, including what action was taken at the meeting or will be taken by an individual or group of individuals after the meeting. The summary includes many of the basic components common to formal minutes: day, date, time, and location of the meeting, those present and absent, and the agenda topics. Compare the minutes summary shown in Figure 16-7, with the memo minutes shown in Figure 16-8 on the next page.

Figure 16-7
A minutes summary of a meeting highlights actions taken at the meeting.

PRODUCT DIVISION

Minutes of the Meeting

March 14, <YEAR>

1:30 p.m. to 2:30 p.m., Room 14

PURPOSE	Seek ways to reduce production costs.
ATTENDANCE	Joe, Thomas, Mary, Rico, Juan, Marta, and Bill attended the meeting. Fred was absent.
OLD BUSINESS	Financial situation: Joe reported the last quarter's losses at 12 percent.
	Report on production levels: Joe reported that although production levels were up during the second shift, they were down in the first and third shifts. Overall the production level was down 6 percent.
NEW BUSINESS	Developed cost reduction approaches: Brainstormed to develop approaches to be considered (seek new vendors, cross-train, review procedures, retrain, review corrective actions); finalize in next meeting.
	Prioritized and assigned feasibility studies: Rank-ordered studies; Tom will bring these to the next meeting. Prepare to work on budget items in next meeting.
ADJOURNMENT	The meeting was adjourned at 2:30 p.m. The next meeting is scheduled for April 11 in Room 14.

Respectfully submitted,

Marta Ricarti

Marta Ricarti, Secretary

Figure 16-8
This example of memo minutes summarizes the topics discussed at the meeting.

MEMO TO: Production Managers Committee

FROM: Sherie Burnett (for Marilyn Sullivan) **SB**

DATE: February 21, <YEAR>

SUBJECT: Minutes of the Production Managers' Meeting, February 20, <YEAR>, 1:30 p.m., Room 14

ATTENDANCE Marilyn Sullivan (facilitator), George Harris, Farrell Schuller, Shirley Kelly, Bill Williams, Charlie Cason, Tom Bullock were present. Ray Addison was absent.

BUSINESS New product line production through January: Each new product in the 189-A line is behind production schedule for the last quarter. According to the Production report, the company is 6.7 percent behind production and 4.2 percent behind last quarter's production schedules.

Production costs for each product: George Harris reported that on the basis of last month's report, production costs were up 4.5 percent. Farrell Schuller will analyze these costs with George and prepare suggestions to ensure stabilization of production costs.

ADJOURNMENT The next Production Managers' meeting will be held at 1:30 p.m., March 20, in Room 14. The meeting was adjourned at 3:30 p.m.

sb

Distribution:

Ray Addison
Tom Bullock
Charlie Cason
George Harris
Shirley Kelly
Farrell Schuller
Marilyn Sullivan
Bill Williams

Format of Formal Minutes

The information contained in formal minutes includes the following:

- Name of the group
- Day, date, time, and location of the meeting
- Time the meeting was called to order
- Time the meeting was adjourned
- Names of those present (and, if applicable, names of persons absent and names of guests and speakers), name of the presiding person, and name of the recorder
- Announcements
- Disposition of previous minutes

- Record of the meeting, including a summary of topics covered in chronological order
- Motions presented in exact wording; name of person who made the motion and seconded it, and actions taken on motions
- Conclusions of discussions
- Name and signature of person preparing minutes

The way the minutes are presented in keyboarded form is important. Be sure to follow these guidelines:

- The heading should include the name of the group and the day, date, time, and location of the meeting. The name of the group should be in all-capital letters and boldface; all other information in initial capital letters; all lines should be centered.
- Side margins should be one inch, top margin should be approximately two inches.
- The opening paragraph should indicate the time the meeting began and who called it to order.
- The body of the minutes should note what business was conducted at the meeting and what actions were taken.
- The last paragraph should indicate the date and time of the next meeting, if applicable, and the time of adjournment.

LEGAL & ETHICAL 16-1

Corporate Oversight. According to company bylaws, the board of directors of the company where you work is required to submit to stockholders a complete written record of the annual board meeting. What might be the legal consequences if the written record contains inaccuracies? What might be the ethical consequences?

In formal and some informal meetings, a participant presents a proposal by making a **motion,** which is a component of parliamentary procedure. The person introduces the idea by saying, "I move that President Wills appoint a program budget committee to study a dues increase or other revenue enhancements." Another participant then **seconds,** or endorses, the motion. Discussion follows to allow individuals who so desire to express their views on the motion, and then voting may take place. Sometimes, however, the vote on a motion may be postponed until a specific future date to allow time for further study. Postponing a motion indefinitely is a polite way of "killing" the motion. When reporting motions in minutes, include the following information:

- The specifics of each motion made, including any amendments
- The names of both the person who made the motion and the person who seconded it (if appropriate)
- The action taken (motion passed, motion failed, or was postponed)

Distribution of Minutes

E-mail may be used to distribute the minutes of an informal meeting. However, the minutes of a formal meeting also should be mailed prior to the next meeting or distributed at the next meeting. Minutes are distributed prior to the next meeting to allow participants to

1. Verify the minutes.
2. Review decisions and responsibilities assigned.
3. Note actions taken or to be taken.

Minutes of formal meetings are not part of any permanent record until submitted for approval at the next meeting. Follow your company's rules, regulations, and/or usual practice when distributing minutes of an informal or formal meeting.

Correction of Minutes

Accuracy in the recording and transcription of minutes is absolutely essential. Careful proofreading of the minutes is a necessity so that errors are corrected before the minutes are distributed.

When it is necessary to correct minutes that have already been distributed or read, draw a line through the error using a contrasting ink color, and write the correction above it. If several lines must be corrected, draw a line through each incorrect line, make the note *See page . . .*, and key the corrections on a separate sheet with the appropriate page number. Place the date when you made the change in the margin near the correction. Do not rekey the entire set of minutes because of the danger of making additional errors. At the next meeting, the group should be informed of the corrected minutes.

✔ CHECKLIST FOR PREPARING MINUTES

	YES	NO
Meeting objective or purpose included		
Names of attendees and absentees recorded		
Name of the presiding person or facilitator indicated		
All agenda items accounted for		
Agenda topics (with appropriate comments on action taken or to be taken, identifying persons responsible) indicated		
Concluding comments (date, time, and location of the next meeting) provided		
Accuracy of information verified		
Concise wording used		
Past tense used		

If you are using word processing software, you can use the strikethrough option to show text that should be deleted from a document. Strikethrough prints text with a line of hyphens running through it, indicating that the text has been deleted. Strikethrough text looks like this:

Mr. Jackson, Treasurer, presented the financial report for the period ending ~~June 30,~~ 1999.

Checkpoint 16.2

1. Do you think having a permanent record of meeting minutes is essential for a business?
2. Why is it important to identify a meeting's participants in the minutes?
3. Do you agree or disagree that accuracy in the recording and transcription of minutes is absolutely essential?

Chapter 16 Summary

Successful meetings result from effective planning, which includes the preparation of meeting notices, agendas, and minutes.

Meetings may be formal or informal, and they may be held electronically. In many organizations, formal meetings are planned, structured meetings, usually conducted by elected officers. Informal meetings, such as staff meetings, are scheduled as they are needed.

To announce a meeting, the facilitator sends a meeting notice by mail, telephone, or e-mail and usually includes an agenda. An agenda, the plan for a meeting, identifies the objectives, prepares participants for the meeting, and defines the topics and time allotted to each topic.

Minutes, a type of report prepared after a meeting, become the official written record of the business that was conducted. Minutes of informal meetings may follow a memo format or a meeting summary format. In contrast, minutes of formal meetings should follow the format specified by the organization.

Following the techniques described in this chapter will help you prepare the documentation connected with meetings.

Communication at Work

Michael Gunn, Director of Sales

Birmingham Convention and Visitors Bureau

"Having strong communications skills is the single most important factor in our business," says Michael Gunn, 48, the director of sales for the Birmingham Convention and Visitors Bureau. Michael's job is to book conventions, meetings, and other events for the Alabama city. A convention and visitor bureau, or CVB, recruits potential clients by providing information about a city's meeting facilities, hotels, and attractions.

"Our communication is directed at potential clients looking for a place to hold their meetings, conventions, and events. We have a product that is not tangible. Therefore, we have to sell a service that only can be perceived by what we project in our communication with the customer," he explains.

Communication Sells

Michael and his staff sell their "product"—the city of Birmingham—in face-to-face meetings with clients, and through telephone calls and direct mail. E-mail also plays an important role in the communications process at the CVB. Michael and his staff use e-mail, for example, to solicit new clients as well as to communicate in-house. The sales staff can also respond to a client's request more rapidly by using e-mail. In fact, e-mail and fax machines have helped save the day for the CVB. For one convention, the attendance was underestimated. "The number of attendees grew dramatically," recounts Michael. "We were able to contact additional hotels using e-mail and faxes to get the client additional hotel rooms before the attendees were left out in the cold."

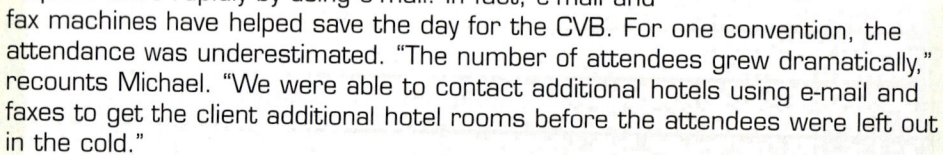

Good written and spoken communication skills are essential for Michael and his staff regardless of the medium they use to communicate with clients.

"If we cannot make good use of the English language and do not project a strong professional image, our city will be perceived in the same way," Michael says.

"We usually have one shot to make an impression, and it better be good or we are out of the race."

> "... we have to sell a service that only can be perceived by what we project in our communication with the customer..."

Discuss

1. How do good communication skills affect the success of Michael's company?
2. What different communication skills do Michael and his staff use to sell their product to potential clients?

Chapter 16

Online Exercises

Objective:
These online activities will allow you to learn more about teleconferencing and telecommuting.

Go to **bcw.glencoe.com**, the address for the *Business Communication at Work* Web site, and select Chapter 16. Next, click on Online Exercises. You will see a list of Web site links that will bring you to Web sites devoted to telecommunications.

Activity 16.1

1. Select one of the Web sites devoted to telecommunications to visit.
2. Find an article that interests you about teleconferencing. You may have to enter *teleconference* into a **Search** box on the Web site. If you do not find an article that interests you, return to the *Business Communication at Work* Web site and explore another Web site devoted to teleconferencing.
3. On a sheet of paper, write a paragraph describing what you learned about teleconferencing. You may want to consider the following questions in your paragraph:
    a. What are the advantages to teleconferencing?
    b. What are the disadvantages to teleconferencing?
    c. What additional planning is necessary for a successful meeting using teleconferencing?
4. Write your name on your paper, and hand it in to your instructor.

Activity 16.2

1. Select one of the Web sites devoted to telecommunications to visit. Make sure you visit a different Web site from the one in Activity 16.1.
2. Find an article that interests you about telecommuting. You may have to enter *telecommuting* into a **Search** box on the Web site. If you do not find an article that interests you, return to the *Business Communication at Work* Web site and explore another Web site devoted to telecommuting.
3. On a sheet of paper, write a paragraph describing what you learned about telecommuting. You may want to consider the following questions in your paragraph:
    a. Would you enjoy a career that requires you to telecommute? Use your readings to support your decision.
    b. What are the advantages to telecommuting?
    c. What are the disadvantages to telecommuting?
4. Write your name on your paper, and hand it in to your instructor.

Preparing Meeting Communications

CHAPTER 16 WORKSHEETS

NAME _____ DATE _____

PRACTICE 1

Meeting Notices

Instructions: *Respond to the following situations as indicated.*

1. **Analyze a Meeting Notice**
   As a project team member, you received the following meeting notice:
   We will meet September 15 at 2 p.m. Prepare a briefing on the status of the equipment requisitions.

   Is this notice complete? Why or why not?
   _____
   _____

2. **Prepare a Meeting Notice**
   As employee benefits coordinator for your company, prepare a meeting notice in a memo format to the Management Bargaining Team, scheduling a meeting two weeks from today at 4 p.m. in the East Conference Room. Representatives from three insurance companies will present proposals. Ask each member of the team to bring the completed salary and fringe benefit surveys distributed at the last meeting.

   _____
   _____
   _____
   _____
   _____
   _____
   _____
   _____

3. **Prepare a Meeting Notice**
   Using the information presented in Practice 2 on the following page, prepare a meeting notice as an announcement.

   _____
   _____
   _____
   _____
   _____
   _____
   _____

CHAPTER 16 WORKSHEETS

NAME _____ DATE _____

PRACTICE 2

Prepare an Agenda

Instructions: Using the information provided, write an agenda for each of the following situations:

1. A meeting of the Board of Directors of Life Underwriters has been scheduled for Wednesday, May 16, <YEAR> at 7 a.m. The president is Andy Brasfield, the secretary is Sheila Roberts, and the treasurer is Toni Stewart. Attendance will be recorded because members are dropped from the board if they have more than two unexcused absences per year. The meeting will take place in the Cavalier Room at the Essex Inn, 8912 Gilbrand Avenue, Grand Prairie, TX 75050. Attendees will discuss the following items (arrange them in the proper order for the agenda):

   - Membership committee report (John Milton is chairperson).
   - The president will appoint a nominations committee to determine a slate of officers for next year.
   - Public service committee report (Jay Wilburn is chairperson).
   - A proposal to have a booth at the Mature Expo was discussed last month but no decision was made. The proposal should be discussed again.
   - Public relations committee report (Suzie Smoot is chairperson).
   - At the last meeting the president read a letter from the United Way asking for volunteers to help with the campaign. The president must recruit more volunteers.
   - Program committee report (Ted Dodson is chairperson).
   - Sue Lawson, Director of Prestonwood Fitness Center, will speak on "Staying Fit."
   - Legislation committee report (Janet Snyder is chairperson).
   - Secretary's report.
   - Treasurer's report.

   _____
   _____
   _____
   _____
   _____
   _____
   _____

2. Refer to the meeting described in Practice 3 on the following page. Develop an agenda to be distributed to the participants prior to the meeting.

   _____
   _____
   _____
   _____
   _____
   _____
   _____
   _____

Preparing Meeting Communications

CHAPTER 16 WORKSHEETS

NAME _____ DATE _____

PRACTICE 3

Meeting Minutes

Instructions: Organize the following notes, and write the minutes of the meeting described in the notes.

Background: You are the secretary of the Administrative Board for the local Boy Scout Council. The purpose of this board is to oversee the council's programs, make recommendations for activities and equipment purchases, and serve as a public relations group for the council. There are nine members on the board, which meets four times a year. You made the following notes during the January 8 meeting.

Notes: Minutes from last meeting (October 9) approved as read. Chairperson Andrew Juliano called the meeting to order at 12:30 p.m. in boardroom at council office with the following members present: Michael Truax, Don Norenburg, Gary Thor, Phil Smith, Angela Garcia, Rose DeMayo, Van Burnett, Ed Brock (and you). Meeting adjourned 1:30 p.m.

Phil Smith suggested awarding perfect attendance certificates to Scouts at end of each quarter rather than once a year. Several members felt this was a good idea and would be an excellent motivational technique to help scouts develop the habit of being dependable.

Van Burnett gave an update on the annual Scout-O-Rama. Since the last meeting, he has received survey cards from twenty-five Cub and Boy Scout units expressing an interest in participating. Angela Garcia suggested the date be changed from the last Wednesday in February to the last Wednesday in March because of past problems with bad weather in February, which reduced attendance. A vote was taken and the motion passed. After a lengthy discussion of pros and cons, Ed Brock presented the changes as a motion, and Gary Thor seconded it.

Next meeting will be April 3 at 1 p.m.

Gary Thor, chairperson of the Advancement Committee, reported that he felt the council should recruit more volunteer specialists to assist units with advancement in the more difficult areas. Gary distributed a list of areas needing advancement assistance and some statistics showing the need. After the discussion, Michael Truax made a motion and Rose DeMayo seconded the motion to adopt this recommendation and forward it to the executive council for implementation. The members voted and the motion passed. Rose DeMayo placed the Treasurer's report on file for audit. She indicated there is $2,770 cash currently on hand.

_____
_____
_____
_____
_____
_____
_____
_____
_____

unit 5

Employment Communication

- **Chapter 17**
  Conducting the Job Search

- **Chapter 18**
  Selling Yourself to Employers

CHAPTER 17

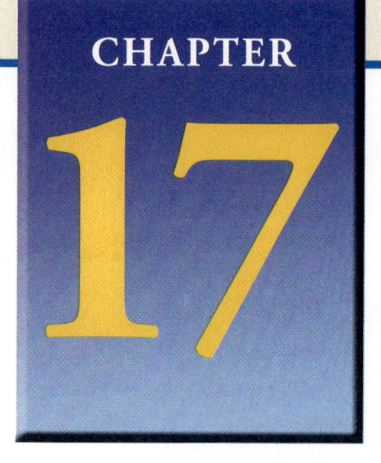

Conducting the Job Search

Objectives

After completing this chapter, you will be able to:

1. Develop a self-appraisal inventory
2. Select an appropriate résumé style
3. Prepare a résumé
4. Complete an employment application
5. Develop a portfolio

WORKPLACE APPLICATIONS

Stress Management

Stress is the result of trying to do too much in too little time. Too much stress can lead to a worker's burn-out, bad health, and lowered **productivity.** As a result, many businesses provide stress-management classes to help employees deal with stress.

The best way to handle stress is to prevent it. Experts recommend the following tips:

- **Have realistic expectations.** You know better than anyone how much you can handle. If you are taking night classes or just had a baby, then you know you can't take the big project, even though you really want it. Learn to say "no" to work you cannot finish.

- **Set your priorities.** Lack of organization is a major cause of stress. Get organized and focus only on what is important. (For more on time management, see page 103).

- **Take care of yourself.** Burn-out happens because your brain can't work nonstop. You need time for fun. Get some exercise. Eat right. If your body is relaxed and healthy, you will be less prone to stress.

If you are under stress, try these tips:

- **Ask for help.** It's actually a sign of strength to know when you need help. It is better to ask for help in order to make a deadline than to let everyone down by missing it.

- **Take breaks.** Refusing to stop does not get the job done faster. It helps to take regular breaks during the day and on the weekends. Your brain needs time to rest.

- **Never take stress out on others.** If stress makes you cranky or emotional, you mustn't vent your feelings on others. Venting is not fair, and it can hurt your reputation. Don't keep stress bottled up either. Take a break when you feel stressed. Confide your worries to a trusted friend.

Thinking Critically

Situation: Think of a time that you experienced stress at work or at school.

Ask Yourself: What were the causes of your stress? How did you handle the stress? If you had to relive that stressful time, what would you do differently? (If you do not experience stress or handle it well, think of some advice for a coworker or friend.)

> *You've got to be very careful if you don't know where you are going, because you might not get there.*
> —**Attributed to Yogi Berra, Athlete**

The employment process involves finding out where you want to go in terms of a job and a career. This process involves research—about you, your career interests, and your ideal job. Included also is marketing yourself—your education, skills, and experience—in a way that persuades an employer to hire you. In earlier chapters, you developed the ability to persuade. You will continue to use the persuasive approach in this chapter and in Chapter 18. Whether you are ready to start your career or looking for a new position, the techniques presented in this chapter will assist you.

STARTING THE EMPLOYMENT PROCESS

To prepare yourself for employment, you need to know your interests and capabilities. Equipped with this information, you can then identify a job that suits your talents and training. Begin the employment process by conducting a self-appraisal inventory.

Preparing a Self-Appraisal Inventory

As the first step in marketing your talents, prepare a detailed self-appraisal (personal) inventory of your background and experience—your qualifications. This inventory will help you assess exactly what assets you have that may appeal to an employer.

A self-appraisal inventory will help you answer questions such as:

- What work can I do?
- What work do I want to do?
- What kind of work do I do best?

In addition, your self-appraisal inventory will:

- Provide facts, dates, and other information to give to an employer
- Assist you when filling out application forms
- Provide the foundation from which to build your résumé
- Help you organize your qualifications for presentation at an interview

To prepare your inventory carefully, completely, and critically, you should examine your interests, talents, and aptitudes; skills and abilities; experience; education; career goal; and the type of position you want.

Identify Your Interests, Talents, and Aptitudes

To identify your interests and areas in which you excel, ask yourself:

- What do I enjoy doing?
- What do I dislike doing?

- What types of activities give me the most personal satisfaction?
- What are my hobbies and/or volunteer activities?
- What are my special talents or aptitudes? For example, do I speak another language? Am I skilled at working with computers?
- What do I learn most easily?
- Do I like to solve problems?
- Do I like to work in a team environment?

In listing your interests, talents, and aptitudes, focus on those that are most likely to appeal to a potential employer.

Identify Your Skills and Abilities

To identify your skills and abilities, ask yourself the following questions:

- What personal skills, qualities, and abilities do I have that would be beneficial in any type of job?
- What personal qualities do I have that make me good in a certain type of work? Think about your work experience, schooling, and activities such as volunteer work, and honestly assess your strengths.
- Are my strong points ones that employers are seeking? Can I demonstrate initiative, leadership, an ability to organize, a willingness to follow orders, an attention to detail, or an ability to work as part of a team?
- What did I learn on the job that I can use in other positions? Some examples may include learning how to use a computer spreadsheet program or developing guidelines for working with difficult customers. Focus on qualities that will demonstrate to potential employers why you should be hired.

Thinking Cap 17.1

Discuss: If you are having a difficult time completing the self-appraisal inventory, what are some steps you can take for jogging your memory?

Assess Your Experience

List all of your jobs, including part-time, summer, and freelance work, with your most recent experience listed first. Focus on the most recent and/or relevant jobs. For each position, list the name and address of your employer, your job title, significant responsibilities, achievements, and results, and the months and years you were employed. Include military experience in this section. As you describe your work experiences, ask yourself:

- What did I like and dislike about each job? Why?
- What skills were required in each job?
- How well have I learned new things?
- Why did I leave a job?
- What type of work environment do I prefer?
- Do I enjoy teamwork, and do I help resolve conflict?
- How good are my written and oral communication skills?

Conducting the Job Search

NOTES

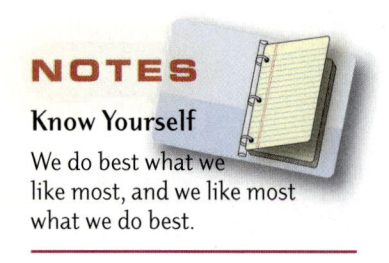

Know Yourself

We do best what we like most, and we like most what we do best.

By describing your work experience, you gain valuable insight into the type of work that best suits you.

Evaluate Your Education

List the schools and colleges you have attended or are attending and the certificates or degrees you have received, with the most recent education listed first. You may also include your degree major and any awards and special recognitions received. If you are just starting college, you may include information about your high school education. Consider including on-the-job training and special courses taken, listing the dates attended and any certificates or professional certifications you have received.

Many interviewers recommend that you not include any details about college except your degree, major, and awards, unless you are still in college or recently graduated. Include your grade point average if over 3.4 on a 4.0 scale. List four to eight specific courses that highlight specific areas necessary for the targeted job. For example, identify computer software applications, such as Microsoft Office and WordPerfect Suite, or programming languages, such as C++, that would apply to a particular position. If you are working on a degree, list the degree and in parentheses the expected date of completion (for example, *expected 2006*). Also list any scholarships or special recognitions you received. You may add another section to include achievements that are not education-related, such as an employee of the month award.

Identify Your Career Goal

With the trend toward switching jobs and careers several times in today's economy, your career goal is likely to change over time. For some, a career goal may involve moving into a management position. For others, a career goal may involve switching from a creative field to a more technical field or vice versa.

To identify your career goal, ask yourself:

- What are my career goals? What kind of work do I want to be doing three, five, or ten years from now?

- What sort of positions should I seek now in order to prepare for my career goal? For example, you might write:

   > An entry-level position in the hospitality industry where a background in public relations would be an asset.

As you identify your career goal, you will want to review various job descriptions within your career field. You will find these job descriptions beneficial in understanding the qualifications and skills needed for positions in your field. Also, the review will help you determine keywords and buzzwords used in positions; these words will be beneficial in your job search and your résumé development.

You may use various sources to find job descriptions, including the Occupational Outlook Handbook (www.bls.gov/oco/), newpaper ads,

468   Chapter 17

government job service agencies, online job postings, and company Web sites. Make a list of keywords and buzzwords to use when you develop your résumé. These will become important for creating scannable and electronic résumés, which will be discussed later.

Understanding the qualifications required will help you determine if you have the necessary skills and will show you those skills you will need to develop or enhance. As you compare those qualifications with your skills, you will know what you will need to highlight on your résumé.

Describe the Position Wanted

Consider all the information in your self-appraisal inventory, and match your skills and experience with jobs in your chosen career field. Describe the types of positions you feel you are best qualified for and prefer. List the positions in order of your preference. Ask yourself:

- What training or experience is required in order to qualify for the position I want?
- Do I enjoy the challenges involved in the positions being considered?—for example, selling a product or service or technical work that involves computers?
- What aspects of my experience, education, and skills will be most beneficial to a potential employer in this particular field?

Understanding what you can do, what you want to do, and what you do best will make it easier to explain your strengths to an interviewer. After completing your self-appraisal inventory, check it for accuracy. Be sure to use accurate descriptions, consistent dates, and correct spelling.

Once you have completed your self-appraisal inventory and analyzed job descriptions, your next step is to conduct a search for your ideal job.

CONDUCTING A JOB SEARCH

Looking for a job can be an exercise in frustration or an exciting challenge, depending on how you approach the task. Efficient planning helps you to achieve the right balance among research, preparation, and action. You may find out about potential jobs by networking with friends, relatives, and business acquaintances; reviewing classified advertisements; consulting career centers or employment agencies; and searching the Internet.

Networking

Some of your best sources for job leads are people who know you personally or professionally—friends, relatives, coworkers, classmates, instructors, and business acquaintances. Maintaining contact with employers with whom you completed internships or summer jobs is another possible

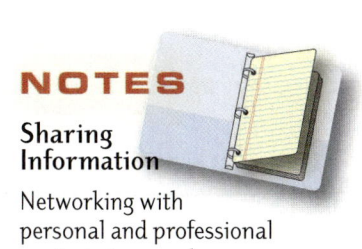

NOTES

Sharing Information

Networking with personal and professional contacts is a good source of job leads.

source of job leads. In addition, don't overlook the opportunity to join a civic or professional association—many such organizations have student affiliates on campuses.

Classified Advertisements

Classified advertisements in local and metropolitan newspapers give you a snapshot look at the businesses and industries in the area and provide information on the skills and qualifications desired by employers.

Career Centers and Employment Agencies

Career centers on college and university campuses provide students and alumni with access to job postings from local and national employers as well as opportunities to participate in on-campus job fairs involving prospective employers. *Employment agencies* contract with businesses or job seekers to fill job vacancies. These agencies charge a fee for their services; either the applicant or the employer pays this fee depending upon the agreement with the agency.

World Wide Web

The World Wide Web is an increasingly important source of information for job seekers. Using the Web allows you to access job banks and view job postings in the United States and in other countries. As a result, you greatly increase your chances of finding a job that matches your experience and skills.

Some effective job-search resources on the Web include the following:

- **Business, Industry, and Government Sites.** Numerous businesses have Web sites that include background information in a particular industry, list job opportunities, and provide contact information. In addition, state governments usually have job sites listing employment opportunities.

- **Career Centers and Job-Search Sites.** Career centers and job-search sites list job postings and offer advice on job-search topics such as choosing a career, interviewing, changing jobs, and telecommuting. Some popular job-search sites include the following:
  America's Job Bank (www.ajb.dni.us),
  Head Hunter (www.headhunter.net),
  and The Monster Board (www.monster.com).

- **College and University Sites.** Many career and placement offices located on college and university campuses have their own Web sites that provide information on job opportunities, résumés, and interviews as well as access to online searches for jobs.

Now that you have completed your self-appraisal inventory and started your job search, you are ready to prepare your résumé—a summary of your background.

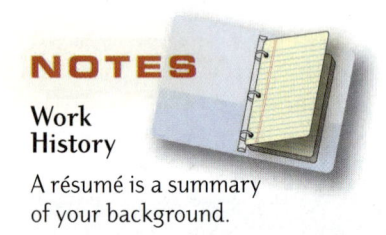

NOTES
Work History
A résumé is a summary of your background.

Preparing a Résumé

Your **résumé** should summarize your background and provide enough details to give an employer the information needed to assess your qualifications. At the same time, it should be concise. The suggestions in this section will help you prepare an effective résumé that will make a favorable impression on prospective employers. You have only one chance to make a great first impression, so your best effort is required!

An effective résumé "gets your foot in the door." It has one purpose—to get you an interview. Currently, most employers require résumés. Even if not requested or required, a résumé certainly can make a favorable impression on an employer when included with a completed employment application. On the average, only ten to twenty seconds are spent on reviewing a résumé. Therefore, the better your résumé looks, the more likely a potential employer is to read it.

Your first task in preparing a résumé is to *select* appropriate, relevant information from your self-appraisal inventory. To do this, ask yourself the following questions:

- Which parts of my training and experience relate to my job goal?
- Which parts, if any, are unrelated?

Give all pertinent details about the positions you have held that relate to your goal. Be brief in listing the details because an employer has limited time to read through numerous résumés.

Next, you must *organize* the information you have selected. To catch an employer's attention, list your strongest qualifications early in your résumé. Ask yourself the following questions:

- Is my work experience the most important part of my résumé?
- Will an interviewer be more interested in my education and training?

You will want to arrange your information in a way that grabs the employer's attention and makes your résumé stand out from a stack of résumés. Begin this process by organizing the information into parts, as described in the next section.

Thinking Cap 17.2

Discuss: Some people develop one résumé and send it to hundreds of companies. Why is this mass marketing technique not a good idea?

NOTES

Window of Opportunity

Your résumé may have less than 20 seconds to attract favorable attention.

Résumé Parts

Most résumés contain the following parts: a heading, a career objective or summary, experience, and education.

Heading

The heading appears at the top of your résumé and includes the following contact information:

- Your full name
- Your complete mailing address
- Your telephone number (including area code), fax number, and e-mail address (if applicable). Be sure the telephone number is one at which messages will be taken during business hours, or indicate when you can be reached by phone (for example, after 5 p.m.).

Career Objective or Summary

Interviewers differ on whether you should begin your résumé with an objective or a summary. An **objective** is a concise statement indicating the type of position you are seeking. The objective statement may reflect your goals for the next three to five years. A **summary** is a concise statement that sums up your experience and abilities and will assist the interviewer in assessing your qualifications. If you have written the objective or summary in a compelling way, it will catch the interviewer's attention and get your résumé to the top of the "qualified" pile.

Avoid writing an objective that is too general, such as the following:

> An interesting job with a challenging opportunity.
>
> An interesting position where I may utilize my skills and training.
>
> A job working with people.
>
> To be hired as a management trainee in a large company and eventually rise through the ranks into general management.

The first three objectives are too general—everyone wants a challenging opportunity, and almost every job requires working with people. The fourth objective would not appeal to interviewers because all too often applicants mention a desire to rise to the top of management. Remember—if you want to grab the reader's attention, make your main points early. To be effective you should change the objective on your résumé to fit the particular position for which you are applying. For example:

> To obtain an administrative support position with Hunter Oil International that involves report preparation and the use of database and spreadsheet applications.

Here are two examples of well-written summaries:

> Management trainee with A.A.S. in mid-management and 24 credits toward a bachelor's degree in business administration. Four years of experience in sales with increasing responsibility gained through full-time, part-time, and summer positions while attending college.
>
> Two years' full-time experience as a trained and competent medical secretary in a medium-sized office. Managed administrative/secretarial and clinical duties. Worked full time while pursuing an Associate's degree.

Experience

Experience is usually the key part of a résumé. This section tells the employer what you have done on the job. Begin with your present or most

---

NOTES

Define Your Objective

Omit an objective or summary unless you can focus on its purpose and write it concisely.

recent position, and work backwards to previous positions. List your duties and responsibilities, but be sure to emphasize what you have accomplished and what results were obtained. Include any volunteer work you have done. In addition to the experience you received from these activities, volunteerism also reflects initiative, ambition, and commitment. Refer to your inventory when you write this section.

NOTES

Be Revealing
In the Experience section, reveal what you have accomplished.

Education

If you are strong in experience, list experience in a section immediately following the heading. If you have recently graduated from school and do not have a year or two of work experience, list your education first. If education is your main selling point, include skills (keyboarding speed, ability to operate special equipment), knowledge (such as software programs and programming languages), and specialized training. List these items in the order of importance to the prospective employer.

If you have not completed a college degree, list the courses you have completed, such as a one-year certificate in accounting or 18 semester hours in business. If you have years of experience, then briefly mention educational credentials, *without* mentioning the dates that degrees or certificates were received, as the last item on the page. For example, the following is sufficient:

> Bachelor of Science, Business, Amber University, Dallas, Texas
>
> Associate of Applied Science, Accounting, Houston Community College, Houston, Texas

Include in this section any special training or workshops that you have attended that have enhanced your skills. Also, list any certificates or professional certifications you have obtained.

Résumé Styles

You can use one of three styles for your résumé—chronological, functional (or skills), or combination. The résumé style you choose will be determined by a number of factors, as described on the following pages. Review the sample résumés in Figures 17-1, 17-2, and 17-3 on the following pages. Study the advantages and disadvantages of each style, then select the one that will work best for you.

Chronological Résumé

The most traditional résumé style is the chronological résumé (see Figure 17-1), which presents your experience and education with the most recent information first. Information is arranged in categories using standard headings such as "Experience," "Education," and "Special Skills." This résumé style is especially effective for entry-level job seekers or for professionals who want to highlight their industry-specific job progression. Experts recommend including an objective or summary on a chronological résumé to focus the interviewer's attention.

Conducting the Job Search

Figure 17-1
A chronological résumé organizes information with the most recent experience listed first.

DARREL BOWEN

3040 Glenview Drive, Dallas, TX 75244
972-555-6052
dbowen@ispmm.net

Efficient Office Manager with 10 years' experience. Proven ability to manage office of small manufacturing or service firm. Personable, well-groomed, and accomplished as a one-person office staff and as coordinator of activities of various departments or employees within a department.

EXPERIENCE

Office Manager, 1999 - Present
North Dallas Metals, Inc., Dallas, Texas
Manages staff of eight employees. Schedules work of 40 plant employees. Prepares payroll. Supervises bookkeeping, requisition of supplies, and other clerical services. Assists in interviewing job applicants and in conducting orientation of new employees.

Office Manager, 1994 - 1999
Texas Printing Company, Dallas, Texas
One-person office force for this small printing company. Administered payroll, benefits, and recordkeeping for 35 employees. Billed customers, made bank deposits, ordered office supplies, prepared all correspondence, received customers, answered phone, filed, and maintained records for tax purposes.

Part-Time Office Assistant, 1992 - 1994
Walton Stamping Company, Dallas, Texas
Established uniform correspondence procedures. Formulated procedures for systematic retention, protection, retrieval, transfer, and disposal of records. Prepared activities reports for management.

EDUCATION

University of North Texas, Denton, Texas, B.S. in Business Administration.

SPECIAL SKILLS

Bilingual–Spanish, competency level in speaking, reading, and writing.

Computer experience with MS Word, Excel, Access, and PowerPoint.

Advantages of the chronological résumé includes its ability to:

- Appeal to more traditional interviewers.
- Fit best in conservative fields, such as law, banking, and academia.
- Emphasize a steady employment record and career growth.
- Be written easily—employment dates are usually listed first, from present to past.

Disadvantages of the chronological résumé include the fact that it:

- Makes it difficult to highlight the applicant's best experiences.
- May be an inappropriate style for someone making a career change.
- Can reveal obvious employment gaps.

Figure 17-2
A functional or skills résumé highlights skills and abilities.

Gail R. Rugario
2056 Martin Road
Indianapolis, IN 46206
Voice: 307-555-9896
Fax: 307-555-9897

OBJECTIVE	To obtain an entry-level public relations position that uses my problem-solving, leadership, and organizational skills.

EXPERIENCE	Conducted customer surveys to help improve service and increase business; resulted in increased business of 10 percent.

Directed telemarketing campaign for college capital improvements fund; raised over $175,000.

Directed special marketing campaign for local technical college; resulted in increased enrollment of 8 percent.

Wrote and edited press releases; directed mass-mailings.

Planned promotion campaigns for three retail stores.

Sold advertising spots for two leading city newspapers and a local radio station.

Coordinated advertising and edited layout for college yearbook.

COMPUTER SKILLS	Microsoft Word (Macintosh and Windows), Excel, PowerPoint, and Aldus PageMaker.

EDUCATION	B.S., Marketing; Eastern Michigan University, Ypsilanti, Michigan.

- May put undesired emphasis on job areas the applicant wants to minimize.
- May show the applicant's lack of experience.

Functional or Skills Résumé

The functional or skills résumé (see Figure 17-2), focuses more on the skills you have acquired and achievements you have attained than on the actual positions you have held. Again, information is presented in categories, some of which may include specific abilities, education, or positions held. With this style the employer quickly sees what you can do for the company, rather than having to read through the job descriptions.

Use the functional or skills style if you have extensive experience and are seeking a position outside your industry or have gaps in your employment history. For students or returning homemakers who have gaps in their employment history or who have held numerous part-time jobs, the functional or skills style may be beneficial in highlighting specific categories of abilities and skills.

Advantages of the functional or skills résumé include its ability to:

- Emphasize selected skill areas that are marketable or in demand, rather than the "when and where" of companies worked.
- De-emphasize a "spotty" employment record.
- Allow the applicant to emphasize professional growth.
- Play down positions not related to current career goals.
- Organize information by descending order of importance.

Disadvantages of the functional or skills résumé include the fact that it:

- Omits work history, which can make employers suspicious.
- Doesn't allow the applicant to highlight "prestigious" companies or organizations.
- Is perceived as too general, not specifically tied to jobs or to positions where the applicant achieved results.

Combination Résumé

The combination résumé, shown in Figure 17-3, includes parts of both the chronological and functional or skills styles, making this an appropriate style for those changing positions or careers. This style can be most effective when both skills and work experience need to be emphasized.

The combination résumé maximizes the following advantages:

- Combines the concise, targeted approach of the functional résumé with the logical progression of the chronological résumé.
- Emphasizes the applicant's relevant skills and abilities in relation to the job objective.
- Is good for career-changers.
- De-emphasizes gaps in employment.

Two disadvantages of the combination résumé:

- May end up with a longer résumé.
- Presents a challenge in determining how to organize the information.

Once you have decided which résumé style to use, your next step is to write your résumé.

What to Do in a Résumé

In addition to selecting, organizing, and formatting the information in your résumé, you should consider words carefully, maximize readability, use a checklist to evaluate your résumé, and review the résumé from an employer's perspective.

Figure 17-3
A combination résumé includes the best features of the chronological and functional or skills résumé.

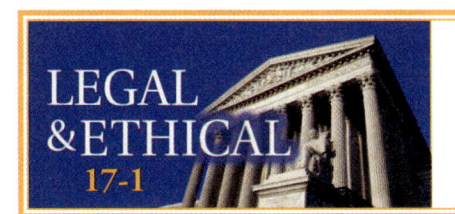

SHIRLEY A. KESTER

407 Sheridan Street
Danville, IL 61832
Voice: 217-555-8213
Fax: 217-555-8214
E-mail: sakester@compisp.com

OBJECTIVE   To obtain a medical secretarial position with a goal to become an Accredited Records Technician, using ten years' experience in service-related positions. Extensive interaction with public and responsibility for service-related records.

EDUCATION   Danville Area Community College, Danville, Illinois
Expected graduation: May 2006
Associate of Applied Science, Medical Secretary Major, and a Certificate in Computer Software Specialist

Courses include:
Medical Terminology	Physiology/Anatomy
Medical Transcription	Payroll Accounting
Records Management	Word Processing
Business Communication	Programming I, II, and III

COMPUTER SKILLS   Microsoft Office, WordPerfect Suite, Lotus SmartSuite, and PageMaker

EXPERIENCE   **Administrative Manager**
Central Illinois Telephone Company, Danville, Illinois
Supervised telephone surveyors, planned areas to be surveyed, and plotted maps of survey area.

Administrative Assistant
Lincoln Insurance Agency, Danville, Illinois
Set up file systems for potential clients, filed reference information, keyboarded correspondence, ordered and controlled supplies, made customers' appointments, answered phones, and greeted customers.

Retail Sales
Speedway Automotive Sales, Westville, Illinois
Kept sales records, took inventory, priced and sold merchandise, and operated several types of cash registers.

Go to CD-ROM
Activity 17-1
To test your skills.

LEGAL & ETHICAL 17-1

Self-Promotion. John Peterson did not graduate from a technical college but indicated on his résumé that he had an associate's degree. What are the ethical issues in misleading a prospective employer about his educational status? What are the legal consequences of misrepresenting information on a résumé?

Consider Words Carefully

Observe the following guidelines for concise, straightforward wording.

- Omit the personal pronoun *I*.
- Use phrases or short statements; do not use sentences.

Conducting the Job Search

- Begin statements with strong action words that best describe your skills and experience. Avoid verbs such as *helped* and *participated* that do not say precisely what you did and what your contribution was. Instead, use effective action words such as the following:

    Accomplished, Achieved, Adapted, Administered

    Changed, Coordinated, Compiled, Controlled, Created

    Demonstrated, Developed, Devised, Doubled, Designed

    Initiated, Installed, Interpreted, Managed

    Processed, Produced, Recommended

    Simplified, Solved, Streamlined, Standardized, Supervised

    Trained, Translated, Upgraded, Verified

A prospective employer likes to know about results you've achieved and not just your responsibilities. Therefore, describe your experience using words that establish your credibility and level of expertise. Note the following examples:

"Supervised market research projects . . ."

"Created word processing templates for Sales Department . . ."

"Able to listen effectively to dissatisfied customers . . ."

"Flexible in handling multiple tasks . . ."

Maximize Readability

Refer to the following guidelines to make your résumé presentable.

- Use a simple, clean structure and attractive format.
- Be clear and concise.
- Use bullets and listings.
- Leave as much white space between sections as possible.
- Use parallel structure for similar items. For example, if a period ends an item, place a period at the end of all items; if a heading is boldface, use boldface for all headings.
- Use simple, professional looking fonts. Keep your résumé to one page when possible. If you have several years of experience, you may need to use two pages. The heading on the second and subsequent pages should include your name and the page number.
- Keep the number of fonts to a minimum—two at the most.
- Keep capitalization, bold type, italics, and underlining to a minimum.
- Print your résumé on white or cream nontextured paper using a high-quality printer. Photocopies and dot matrix printers are unprofessional.
- Print on one side of the paper only.
- Proofread several times to eliminate spelling, factual, grammatical, and punctuation errors. Have others proofread it also.

Use a Checklist to Evaluate Your Résumé

Make sure you double-check your résumé for the items shown in the "Résumé Evaluation Checklist." The first impression your résumé creates is critical. Your résumé should be appealing to the reader. Remember—your résumé is an advertisement for you!

Thinking Cap 17.3

Discuss: Generally, résumés should be prepared on white or cream paper using a conservative format. When might departure from this recommended procedure be acceptable?

Résumé Evaluation Checklist

Check for Misspellings.

- ____ Perform a spell check.
- ____ Carefully proofread every word.
- ____ Ask a friend or relative to proofread your résumé.

Check for Punctuation Mistakes.

- ____ Be consistent in your use of punctuation.
- ____ Check ends of lines of text.

Check for Grammar and Mechanical Mistakes.

- ____ Use the present tense to describe duties you currently perform and the past tense for ones you performed in the past.
- ____ Be consistent in your use of date formats (i.e., 5/12/03 or May 12, 2003).
- ____ Check abbreviations of state names. (All state abbreviations are two letters without periods—for example, Oklahoma is OK, Texas is TX, and New Mexico is NM.)

Review Your Résumé From the Potential Employer's Perspective

Practice the "you approach" in reviewing your résumé. Put yourself in the reader's shoes. Glancing over your résumé, the potential employer will reflect on the following:

- What has this person actually accomplished on the job?
- Is there a match between this person's skills and experiences and the skills that I require for this position?
- What can this person do for our company?
- Does this person seem to care about the quality of his or her work? How does the résumé look? How organized is it? Is it error free?
- How well has this person communicated to me?
- Do I want to take the time to meet with this person? Should I call this person in for an interview?

Now, ask yourself, "Did my advertisement do its job?"

Conducting the Job Search

What Not to Do in a Résumé

Interviewers and professional résumé writers recommend that you not include the following items in a résumé:

- The word *résumé* at the top of the résumé
- The word *I*
- Sentences
- Salary information
- Reasons for leaving jobs
- A "Personal" section that includes references to age, gender, religion, race, height, weight, health condition, and marital status
- References

The preceding guidelines apply to résumés that are prepared in the traditional way. If you are preparing an electronic résumé, you need to take special considerations into account, as discussed in the next section.

Remember that it is important not to embellish your education and experience or to lie on your résumé. Your education and experience usually will be checked. If you lie on your résumé, you will be disqualified as a candidate for the current position as well as for future positions within the company.

Scannable and Electronic Résumés

Technology has had a great impact on the employment process. Previously, résumés were created on a word processing software package and mailed to potential employers. Employers would manually go through the résumés and select candidates for interviews.

Now, résumés are frequently sent to employers electronically. Employers scan résumés that were sent via postal mail and file résumés that were sent electronically, placing them together in data banks for future use in matching candidates to positions.

Scannable Résumés

To help manage the volume of résumés submitted for job openings, many employers are using electronic applicant tracking systems. Paper résumés are scanned by optical scanners that transform the hard copy data into electronic data that is used in an automated tracking system. Scannable résumés are word-focused documents with very simple layouts that are designed to be easy to scan. Therefore, they are very plain and are considered unattractive compared to the traditional résumé. A résumé that is not scannable may not be entered into the tracking system or be clearly accessed by it.

For a specific job opening, the tracking system goes through a procedure of comparing a list of desired qualifications for the job with each résumé. Keywords are at the heart of this search. The computer searches for keywords that it has been programmed to find.

As most electronic résumé searches are based on keywords, your résumé must contain keywords if it is to be considered. Keywords are words or short phrases in noun form that define the requirements of a particular job. They may include buzzwords, which are specific to the particular industry, as well as those words frequently referred to or reflected in positions such as manager, lead worker, supervisor, and trainer, and in business processes, such as continuous improvement and quality assurance. Use the list of keywords and buzzwords from your inventory and incorporate them into your résumé.

Fortunately, it is not difficult to create an electronic or scannable résumé like the one shown in Figure 17-4. You do, however, need to follow some basic guidelines, which are summarized in the following list.

- Use keywords to describe your education, experience, skills, and abilities. Avoid using action verbs such as *created, developed,* and *maintained.* Instead, use descriptive nouns such as *coordinator, manager, supervisor, administrative assistant, accountant, customer service representative, word processor,* and *sales* that relate to specific job postings.

NOTES

Improve Your Odds

If you submit your résumé electronically but fail to follow accepted guidelines for scannable résumés, you may never be considered for the position.

Figure 17-4
An electronic or scannable résumé requires special formatting in order to be read by computer programs.

DARREL BOWEN
3040 Glenview Drive
Dallas, TX 75244
972-555-6052
dbowen@ispmm.net

KEYWORD SUMMARY
*10 years' experience—Office Manager—Office Assistant
*Internal Support—Staff Training—Bookkeeping
*Payroll—Recordkeeping—Records Management
*Computer Expertise—MSWord, Excel, Access
*Bilingual—Spanish

Efficient Office Manager with 10 years' experience. Proven ability to manage office of small manufacturing or service firm. Personable, well-groomed, and accomplished as a one-person office staff and as coordinator of activities of various departments or employees within a department.

EXPERIENCE

Office Manager, 1995 - Present
North Dallas Metals, Inc., Dallas, Texas
Manages staff of eight employees. Schedules work of 40 plant employees. Prepares payroll. Supervises bookkeeping, requisition of supplies, and other clerical services. Assists in interviewing job applicants and in conducting orientation of new employees.

Office Manager, 1990 - 1995
Texas Printing Company, Dallas, Texas
One-person office force for this small printing company. Administered payroll, benefits, and recordkeeping for 35 employees. Billed customers, made bank deposits, ordered office supplies, prepared all correspondence, received customers, answered phone, filed, and maintained records for tax purposes.

Part-Time Office Assistant, 1988 - 1990
Walton Stamping Company, Dallas, Texas
Established uniform correspondence procedures. Formulated procedures for systematic retention, protection, retrieval, transfer, and disposal of records. Prepared activities reports for management.

EDUCATION
University of North Texas, Denton, Texas, B.S. in Business Administration.

SPECIAL SKILLS
Bilingual–Spanish, competency level in speaking, reading, and writing.
Computer experience with MS Word, Excel, Access, and PowerPoint for IBM systems.

Conducting the Job Search

The more keywords you use, the more likely your résumé will be recognized by an electronic résumé database and matched to job openings.

- Use commonly used fonts, such as **Arial**, Times New Roman, **Helvetica**, and Universe. Keep the size of your font between 10 and 14 points.

- Keep the design simple. If the text or design of the résumé is difficult for the computer to read, much of the information in the résumé will not be saved in the database.

- Avoid graphics and shading. The computer programs are set to read text, not graphics. Do not underline—it may make the type unreadable. Avoid using italics, vertical or horizontal lines, brackets, parentheses, columns, tabs, graphics, and boxes. However, boldface type and all-capital letters are acceptable.

- Print your résumé on white or cream paper. Avoid dot matrix printouts and low-quality photocopies. Paper size should be standard U.S. 8.5 by 11 inches.

- Place your name at the top of the page on a separate line, and list your phone number, fax number, and e-mail address each on a separate line.

- Use wide margins around the text.

- Begin all lines at the left margin.

- Do not fold your résumé, as words in the creases may not be readable by the computer.

- Mail your résumé in a 9- by 12-inch envelope.

- Do not staple your résumé as the computer may read the holes as letters.

- Do not center lines or justify text.

If you are sending a résumé that is formatted for scanning, you may want to include a traditional résumé as well. Attach a note to the scannable résumé indicating "this résumé is for scanning."

Numerous resources are available to guide you in formatting a scannable résumé, such as Joyce Lain Kennedy's *Electronic Résumé Revolution*. *Adams Job Bank* offers *Fastrésumé, a CD-ROM* that allows you to create a résumé using a specified format. For additional current information, search the Internet using various job-related keywords, such as *résumé, scannable résumé, employment,* and *careers*.

By using the latest in document-imaging technology, your résumé can be scanned into a computer database system and kept "active" for months or even years. As a result, you could be considered for positions you had never anticipated.

Electronic Résumés

Electronic résumés frequently are described as résumés that are sent in a specific text format via e-mail or the Internet. Electronic résumés are basically plain text résumés that lack the typical formatting enhancements associated with traditional résumés.

Job Posting
Access the Internet and search for information on how to post your résumé on the Internet. Prepare a brief report explaining how to post your résumé.

When résumés are sent electronically, it is important that the receivers be able to read the résumé regardless of the type of computer or software they have. To ensure readability if you are sending your résumé via e-mail, you may want to format your résumé in ASCII. ASCII is plain, unformatted text. You will need to follow the same guidelines as you would in creating a scannable résumé.

You can convert your word processing file to an ASCII file by using your word processing program's "save as" option. As with scannable résumés, many resources are available for creating electronic résumés, specifically ASCII résumés. For more information, you can search *electronic résumés* on the Internet using your favorite search engine.

List of References

In addition to your résumé, you should prepare a list of references—names and addresses of people who will verify your education and experience and can comment favorably on your qualifications. Ask instructors and former employers to serve as your references. List your references on a separate sheet of paper—do not list them on your résumé.

- List three to five references on a separate sheet to take with you to the interview to be given to the interviewer if requested. Include the position, title, address, and phone number for each person.

- References may be required on an employment application. The business value of *personal* references is often *questionable*. The preferred references should be from individuals who have firsthand knowledge of your work and can validate your qualifications as an employee.

Also, consider individuals with whom you have worked in an organization or on a committee. Colleagues are also a source for references.

When selecting references, contact the individual to see if she or he is willing to give you a positive recommendation. Inform him or her about the types of jobs you are applying for and, if necessary, briefly review some of your responsibilities and accomplishments. As you will have several references, try to select individuals who can comment on different qualities and skills. At the end of the hiring process, call or write your references thanking them and sharing the outcome of the process.

GLOBAL DIVERSITY 17.1

Global Presence
Many companies that have international operations have Web site addresses. *What cultural differences do you think will be evident in the job requirements and the qualifications requested of the applicants for positions in these international companies?*

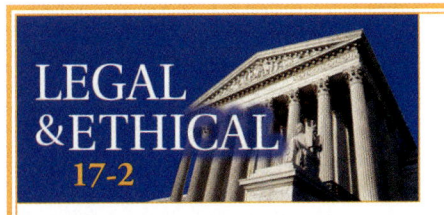

LEGAL & ETHICAL 17-2

Secrets Revealed. As previously mentioned, John Peterson misrepresented his educational status on his résumé. John sent his résumé to a company and was asked to come in for an interview. Before the interview, John completed an employment application form and again misrepresented his educational status. During the interview, the interviewer asked John about his educational background. John confirmed that he had received an associate's degree. John was offered employment on a Friday afternoon and was asked to begin work Monday morning. Because of the backlog of reference checks, the employer did not discover the discrepancy on John's application until the end of his first week of employment. What are the rights of the employer and the employee?

Conducting the Job Search

Checkpoint 17.1

1. Which of the résumé styles—chronological, functional or skills-related, and combination—works best for you? Explain your choice.
2. Why do you think that it is inappropriate to use the pronoun "I" in a résumé?
3. What are the advantages and disadvantages of preparing an electronic or scannable résumé?

COMPLETING AN EMPLOYMENT APPLICATION

Many companies have become cautious about the use of résumés as tools for providing verifiable information. Unlike employment applications, a résumé generally is not signed and does not contain a statement verifying the truthfulness of the information. Therefore, many companies require interviewees to complete a company employment application *before* the interview.

The manner in which you complete the employment application tells the interviewer the following about your ability to:

- Follow written directions
- Complete a task
- Handle details
- Exercise care and neatness in your work

Employment applications can be one page or several pages long, but all such forms ask for these basic categories of information: personal, education, experience, and references. (See Figure 17-5.)

- **Personal**—your name, mailing address, phone numbers (both home and work), and e-mail address.
- **Education**—levels of education you have completed and schools' names and addresses and dates or years attended. The longer you are out of high school, the less important it becomes to list, especially if you have attended a community or technical college or university. However, if the form asks for high school information, list it.
- **Experience**—names of companies, position titles, and dates of previous employment. A category for volunteer experience now appears on many applications.
- **References**—refer to your self-appraisal inventory for the names, titles, company names, addresses, and telephone numbers.

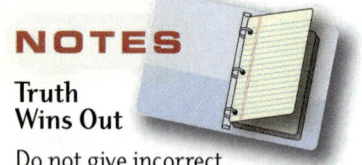

NOTES

Truth Wins Out

Do not give incorrect schooling information on an employment application. Most companies will check education references before you are hired.

Go to CD-ROM

Activity 17-2
To test your skills.

484   Chapter 17

Figure 17-5 When completing an employment application, be complete, truthful, and neat.

According to interviewers, education is the most lied about item on résumés and employment applications. Your credibility and trustworthiness will be questioned if you provide false information on your résumé. An employment application is a legal document—if you falsify information and are found out, you won't be hired by that company. If you are already employed, you can be terminated.

Occasionally an employment application will contain illegal questions, such as questions about age or marital status. You can choose to answer the questions, fill in the blank with the letters *NA* for *not applicable,* or draw a dash across the response blank.

Guidelines for Completing Employment Applications

The best suggestion you can receive from anyone on how to complete an employment application is this: Be prepared.

Thinking Cap 17.4

Discuss: Human resources personnel often insist that you complete the employment application in the office when you pick it up or just before your interview. What are the reasons for this practice?

Conducting the Job Search 485

- Take your completed self-appraisal inventory with you. Your inventory has all the information you will need. You make a poor impression if you can't remember a phone number, date, or ZIP Code.

- Never write "See résumé" across the application for any section.

- Read completely through the employment application *before* you start to fill it out. This will help you answer the questions correctly. Once you have completed the application, reread the directions, and recheck all information for accuracy.

- Take two working pens (preferably with black ink) and an ink eraser. Do not use pencil as it smudges and fades in time.

- Follow directions. If the instructions say "print," don't write in cursive style. Print legibly—most employers won't consider an application they can't read. If the directions ask you to key the information, do so. If you do not keyboard, ask someone to key the information for you.

- Carry a pocket dictionary. A spelling error could mean an automatic rejection when you apply for a position.

- Answer all questions. If the information does not apply to you, put *NA* (not applicable). If there is a place to include "other business skills" or "comments," put *something* there to sell yourself.

- Avoid listing the salary you expect. If this question is asked, answer with "open." This question can best be answered later in the hiring process. You might eliminate your chance for an interview if your amount is out of line with current salary guidelines.

- Give positive reasons for leaving previous jobs. When this information is requested, give reasons such as "better job opportunity," "career change," "career advancement," or "return to school."

NOTES

Permanent Record

An employment application becomes part of your permanent employment record if you are hired.

Remember that you start applying for the job the minute you walk in the door. Therefore, it is just as important to make a favorable impression on the office staff as on the interviewer. Follow these suggestions while in the employment office:

- Use your waiting time to find out about the company or to review your answers to possible interview questions (interview questions will be addressed in Chapter 18). If any brochures, annual reports, or advertising pieces on company products or services are in the waiting area, look at them for additional information. You will have an advantage if you have asked for copies of brochures and/or annual reports before the interview.

- Do not ask for more than one copy of the employment application.

- Have adequate supplies and information with you to complete the employment application.

- Avoid asking unnecessary or obvious questions. If you must ask questions, compile your questions as you complete the employment application, then ask all your questions at one time, thus interrupting the office staff only once.

In addition to a résumé, a list of references, and a completed employment application, you can use another form of documentation to present your credentials to an employer—a portfolio.

DEVELOPING A PORTFOLIO

One of the best ways to showcase your qualifications and talents is to develop a portfolio. A **portfolio** is a collection of your work that serves as evidence that you possess skills that are relevant to the world of work. For instance, your portfolio might include several examples of your writing, a copy of your résumé, and examples of special projects you have done, such as a report or a sales presentation. If you are applying for your first job, your portfolio might contain samples of the work you've completed in your communication and software-application courses.

An employment portfolio provides prospective employers with tangible evidence of your achievements and abilities. While your résumé provides a written summary of your past accomplishments and is normally included in your portfolio, the portfolio can assist with marketing your talents and serving as evidence of your abilities.

The contents of a portfolio can vary depending on what you discovered through your self-appraisal. The portfolio's contents and presentation may also vary based upon the kind of position you are seeking. Here are just some of the possible contents:

- Your official college transcript(s)
- A statement of your personal philosophy that relates to the career field
- A list of all your skills
- A description of experiences and accomplishments that do not fit into your résumé
- Certificates and awards you have received
- Letters of commendation and recommendation
- Newspaper articles that recognize achievements or promotions
- Programs from events you planned or participated in
- Samples of documents you wrote and prepared, including letters, memos, reports, brochures, newsletters, or proposals

Thinking Cap 17.5

Discuss: In addition to the list of portfolio contents suggested, what other items would you consider putting into a portfolio for your chosen career?

Your portfolio should be contained in a professional-looking, loose-leaf portfolio binder—perhaps with a zippered enclosure. Each page should be inserted into a nonglare plastic page cover for protection and professional appearance. Include an attractive title page and a table of contents at the beginning of the portfolio.

Even after you begin your career, you should keep your résumé up to date and continue building your portfolio.

Conducting the Job Search

By preparing your self-appraisal inventory, résumé, list of references, portfolio, and by completing the employment application you will be ready for the employment interview, which will be discussed in Chapter 18.

Checkpoint 17.2

1. Why do you think companies use employment applications to test an applicant's ability to read and follow directions?

2. In your opinion, why should a company care if a job applicant has been truthful about his or her education?

3. Why is it important to give only positive reasons for leaving past employment? What should a job applicant do if he or she has been fired from a previous job?

Chapter 17 Summary

The employment process begins with an assessment of your qualifications—a self-appraisal inventory, which serves as the basis for preparing your résumé.

A résumé is a door opener—a sales promotion tool for you. A well-written résumé presents your education and work experience in a way that gives the employer a strong message about your suitability for a particular position. Your résumé should give an employer a review of what you have done and an indicator of what you are capable of doing on the job. In short, your résumé is an advertisement about your competence. Along with your résumé, you should prepare a list of references—individuals who can attest to your competency.

Regardless of the media you use to send your résumé, it is important to have a well-written résumé with short descriptions using keywords—action words for traditional résumés and nouns for scannable résumés. Your résumé must be customized to the particular job. Your objective is to communicate your skills, knowledge, experiences, and education to the potential employer in a way that matches your abilities with the employer's needs.

Companies usually require job applicants to complete an employment application. This is a legal document upon which a company will base its reasons for hiring you. The application creates a picture of your background in a legal sense because you are required to verify the truthfulness of the information by signing the application.

Developing a portfolio that showcases examples of your best work provides an employer with tangible evidence of your skills and accomplishments as they relate to the world of work.

Chapter 17

Online Exercises

Objective:
These online activities will allow you to learn about stress and coping, as well as searching for a job.

Go to **bcw-glencoe.com,** the address for the *Business Communication at Work* Web site, and select Chapter 17. Next, click on Online Exercises. You will see a list of Web site links that will bring you to online stress questionnaires and career Web sites.

Activity 17.1

1. Select one of the Web sites that offers stress questionnaires to visit.
2. Complete the personality questionnaire offered on the Web site you have chosen. You may have to click on several links within the Web site to arrive at the stress questionnaire.
3. On a sheet of paper, write a paragraph describing the results of your stress questionnaire. You may want to consider the following questions in your paragraph:
    a. Were you surprised about your stress level? Why or why not?
    b. Do you find that answer choices to the questions limit your ability to represent your personality?
    c. What questions may have represented your stress levels better?
4. Write your name on your paper, and hand it in to your instructor.

Activity 17.2

1. Select one of the career Web sites to visit.
2. Search for an article on developing a résumé. You may need to enter the word *résumé* in the Web site's **Search** box.
3. On a sheet of paper, write a paragraph describing what you learned from your readings of developing a résumé.
4. Based on what you learned in the article and in Chapter 17, write your résumé. Your résumé should not be handwritten. Include the résumé parts discussed in the chapter (heading, career objective or summary, experience, and education), as well as the tips on what to do and what not to do in a résumé.
5. Write your name on your paper, and turn in your paper and résumé to your instructor.

Conducting the Job Search

CHAPTER 17 WORKSHEETS

Name _____ Date _____

PRACTICE 1

Self-Appraisal Inventory

Instructions: *Complete the following self-appraisal inventory by referring to the directions that precede each section.*

1. Interests/Talents/Aptitudes:

   a. What are my hobbies or volunteer activities?

   _____
   _____
   _____
   _____
   _____
   _____

   b. What are my special talents or aptitudes?

   _____
   _____
   _____
   _____
   _____
   _____

   c. What do I learn most easily?

   _____
   _____
   _____
   _____
   _____
   _____

   d. How can I relate my talents and interests to a position or career?

   _____
   _____
   _____
   _____
   _____
   _____

CHAPTER 17 WORKSHEETS

NAME _____ DATE _____

2. Skills/Abilities:

   a. What personal qualities do I have that make me good at a certain type of work?

   _____
   _____
   _____
   _____
   _____

   b. What have I learned at my current job that I can use in another position?

   _____
   _____
   _____
   _____
   _____

   c. Identify the qualities that employers care about most.

   _____
   _____
   _____
   _____
   _____

   d. Describe why you should be hired for a position.

   _____
   _____
   _____
   _____
   _____

3. Experience:

Job Title	Significant Responsibilities/Results	Company Name/Address	Months/Years

Conducting the Job Search

CHAPTER 17 WORKSHEETS

NAME _____ DATE _____

4. Education: (Begin the list with the most recent school attended.)

   School　　　　　　　Address　　　　　　　Dates　　　　　　　Diploma/Certificate/Degree
   _____
   _____
   _____
   _____
   _____

5. Career Goal:

   a. What kind of work do I want to be doing three to five years from now?
   _____
   _____
   _____
   _____
   _____

   b. What sort of position should I seek now in order to prepare for my career goal?
   _____
   _____
   _____
   _____
   _____

6. Positions Wanted:

   a. List the types of positions you feel you are best qualified for and want.
   _____
   _____
   _____
   _____
   _____

   b. What aspects of your experience, education, or skills will be most beneficial to an employer?
   _____
   _____
   _____
   _____
   _____

CHAPTER 17 WORKSHEETS

NAME _____ DATE _____

7. In the left column, list your personal traits that could help you in carrying out the duties of a position for which you want to apply. Use concrete adjectives such as *dependable, neat,* and *tactful.* In the right column, opposite each trait listed, record any evidence that shows that you possess the trait. An example of a trait is "punctual." Evidence of this trait is "arriving for class on time" and "paying bills on time."

Trait	Evidence/Proof
_____	_____
_____	_____
_____	_____
_____	_____
_____	_____
_____	_____
_____	_____

8. In the left column, list your abilities (things you can do well) that could help you in carrying out the job duties. In the right column, opposite each ability listed, jot down any evidence you can think of to show that you have that ability. Be specific. An ability could be "composing effective business letters" and the evidence of this ability might be "have written request letters asking for product information."

Ability	Evidence/Proof
_____	_____
_____	_____
_____	_____
_____	_____
_____	_____
_____	_____
_____	_____

9. References:

Name	Position/Title	Company	Address/Telephone
_____	_____	_____	_____
_____	_____	_____	_____
_____	_____	_____	_____
_____	_____	_____	_____
_____	_____	_____	_____

Conducting the Job Search

CHAPTER 17 WORKSHEETS

NAME _____ DATE _____

PRACTICE 2

Selecting Appropriate Résumé Styles

Instructions: Respond to the following situations as indicated.

Situation 1: Gayle graduated from high school within the past two years; she has worked in the insurance industry since graduation but has been employed by two different organizations. Gayle is applying for a position with a medium-sized business in the same industry. This particular business requires all résumés to be scanned. She wants to present her credentials in the best scannable format. Which résumé format should Gayle use? Explain why.

_____
_____
_____

Situation 2: Joshua is in his second year at a community college. He has worked as an intern for a computer support company since the eleventh grade. Joshua is applying for a position at another technical company. He wants to highlight important qualities and achievements. His biggest challenge is moving into a field where degrees and credentials are important. Joshua's greatest asset is his consistent experience in the same field. Joshua has been asked to submit his résumé electronically. Which résumé format should Joshua use? Describe your reasoning.

_____
_____
_____
_____

Situation 3: Harriet, an older student with prior work experience, is applying for a position in a government agency. She has gaps in her employment history but has consistent experience in her field. Harriet would like to emphasize her strong skills rather than her short-term employment record in her field. She would like to show her volunteer experience. Which résumé style should Harriet use? Explain your answer.

_____
_____
_____
_____

CHAPTER 17 WORKSHEETS

NAME _____ DATE _____

PRACTICE 3

Preparing a Chronological Résumé

Instructions: Prepare your résumé for the job you want using the chronological style. Make your résumé an attractive, easy-reference summary of your qualifications. Ask several people to give you feedback on your résumé by asking the following questions:

- Have I included an appropriate objective or summary?
- Have I presented each of my accomplishments effectively?
- Have I listed my experience in the right order?
- Have I included the key functions of the jobs I've held?
- Have I given the key functions the proper priority?
- Is it clear what kind of position I am seeking?
- Does the job title match the content of my résumé?
- Do the contents give the reader a detailed summary of my skills and abilities?
- Have I used verbs to describe my accomplishments?

Review the feedback you receive and revise your résumé if appropriate.

Preparing a Functional or Skills Résumé

Instructions: Prepare your résumé using the functional or skills style for the job you identified in Practice 3, Question 1. Ask several people to give you feedback. Review the feedback and revise if appropriate.

1. Compare the differences between your chronological résumé and your functional or skills résumé. Which style best presents your experience, skills, education, and abilities? Ask several people to give you feedback. Write a brief summary that describes the style that best represents your experience, skills, education, and abilities.

2. Present both résumés and the written summary to your instructor.

Developing a Portfolio

Instructions: Based on your instructor's directions, add a final copy of your self-appraisal inventory, résumé, and a completed employment application form to your portfolio. You may complete the form in Figure 17-5, or ask a local company for an application form to use.

Conducting the Job Search

CHAPTER 18
Selling Yourself to Employers

Objectives

After completing this chapter, you will be able to:

1. Prepare a persuasive cover letter
2. Prepare for an interview
3. Interview effectively for a job
4. Prepare effective follow-up letters
5. Prepare an effective resignation letter

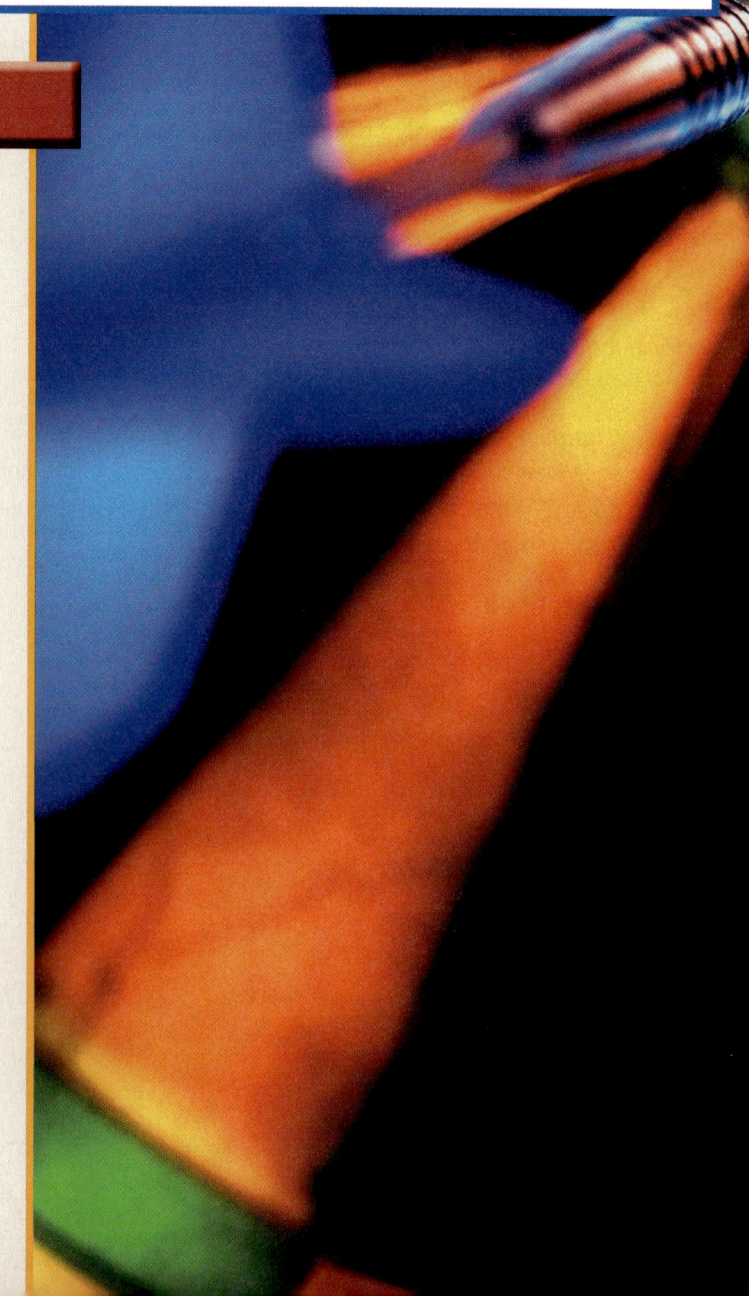

WORKPLACE APPLICATIONS

Styles of Leadership

"Captains of industry" used to be a term that described the world's most powerful business owners. The term *captain* was apt, as these leaders asserted hands-on-the-helm kind of control in their companies, rarely delegating tasks, and always pursuing their vision, forcing others to follow. While many corporate leaders still favor the model of the captain, many others have turned to the model of the coach as team leader. A team leader also must have vision and intelligence, but he or she also understands the value of treating employees as teammates. Team leaders know how to communicate their ideas, motivate their fellow workers, plan reachable goals, and assess workers' and their own performance.

Not every team leader is the head of a company. Any employee can become a team leader if he or she develops the following skills.

- **Communicating**: A good leader sets goals and communicates them in clear terms. A good leader also actively listens to feedback.

- **Planning**: In order to reach a goal, each step must be planned, and each step must be reachable. Good team leaders don't doom their coworkers to failure by withholding resources, such as time, money, or information.

- **Delegating**: A good team leader trusts his or her coworkers and gives them as much responsibility as they can handle. Delegating is one of the best ways to motivate workers because it shows that their leader trusts them to do a good job.

- **Assessing**: A good leader constantly evaluates how well a project is going. If a problem comes up, a leader must decide what steps must be taken to correct it.

- **Setting an example**: Good leaders always demonstrate the qualities they expect in others, including honesty, flexibility, patience, good humor, dedication, and a sense of personal responsibility.

Thinking Critically

Situation: Think of leaders you have admired. (They can be national leaders, teachers, or supervisors you have worked with.)

Ask Yourself: What qualities did they have? What did you learn from them? How would you use what you learned from them in the workplace? Write a journal entry that answers these questions.

> *The secret of success is doing what you ought to do, when you ought to do it, whether you want to or not. No debate.*
> —**Walter Hailey, Jr., University of Texas founder**

In Chapter 17, you learned effective techniques for writing a résumé and completing an employment application. In this chapter, we will discuss additional job-search activities. You will learn how to write an effective cover letter, prepare for an interview, participate in an interview, and write a thank-you letter to the interviewer. You will also learn how to prepare a satisfactory resignation letter.

PREPARING A COVER LETTER

Go to CD-ROM
Activity 18-1
To test your skills.

In many fields of work, writing a cover letter is the customary way to ask for an interview. This is particularly true in the following situations:

- When the employer you wish to contact lives in another city or state
- When you mail your résumé
- When you e-mail your résumé
- When you are answering an advertisement

Purposes of a Cover Letter

NOTES
Cover the Bases
A cover letter should not repeat the information on the résumé. A cover letter is more than a "cover"—it is a tool for marketing your qualifications for the job.

If your résumé is a general advertisement of yourself, what purposes does a cover letter serve? The cover letter allows you to focus attention on your strengths related to the specific job for which you are applying. The cover letter should stimulate interest in you and your résumé as well as reflect your interest in the position and the organization. An effective **cover letter** highlights the particular aspects of your skills and accomplishments that best suit a prospective employer's needs. Thus, it bridges the gap between your experience, skills, and abilities and the qualifications of the position. A cover letter, along with your résumé, helps to get you an interview.

Some authorities use the term *application letter* interchangeably with *cover letter*. The cover letter (or application letter) goes along with your résumé and introduces you to the receiver.

Preparation for Writing a Cover Letter

Before you begin writing your cover letter, be sure you have answered the following questions:

- What does the organization do, make, or sell?
- What is your central selling point?
- To whom should you address the letter?
- What type of cover letter should you write?

What Does the Organization Do, Make, or Sell?

You must understand both the organization and the position for which you are applying before you can tell an employer how your personality, training, and experience make you a good choice—ideally *the* choice—for that position. Obtain any information you can about what products or services the organization offers, how many employees it has, whether it is publicly or privately owned, and so on. The more you know about the organization and the position requirements, the more interesting and convincing you can make your cover letter. If you send a cover letter to a company that has advertised with a blind ad, you won't know or be able to learn the answers to these questions. A **blind advertisement** lists an available position without indicating the name of the company. Blind advertisements are used when:

- A company does not want their current employees to know about a position they want to fill.
- A company may not want its competitors to know of a position it is attempting to fill.
- A company wants to discourage mass mailings from all applicant sources.

What is Your Central Selling Point?

In your cover letter you can gain the reader's attention by highlighting one or two accomplishments or abilities that show you are a viable candidate for a position. Ask yourself: Of all my qualifications, which one would be the most important to the position for which I am applying? Which one will appeal most to this employer? The answer may be your experience in similar work, your ability to get along with difficult customers, your training, or a special skill, such as the ability to speak Spanish. Focusing on only one or two unique attributes will increase your chances of being remembered by the reader and of getting an interview during which you can elaborate on your other accomplishments. Your most important attributes become your *central selling point*, around which you build your letter.

How Should You Address Your Letter?

Do not address a cover letter "To Whom It May Concern." You can usually obtain the correct name, title, and address of the specific person by calling the organization to which you are applying. When answering a blind ad, use the simplified letter style that substitutes a subject for the salutation.

What Type of Cover Letter Should You Write?

Cover letters are either *solicited* or *unsolicited*. If you want to send a cover letter to several organizations where you are interested in working, then you would write an **unsolicited cover letter.** The purpose of an unsolicited letter is to create interest so that employers will contact you for an interview. In contrast, a **solicited cover letter** is sent to a prospective employer for a position which you know is open and for which you are qualified. You can readily learn about such job openings through the following sources:

- Job-hunting links on the Internet
- Help-wanted advertisements in newspapers, magazines, and trade journals
- College placement centers

NOTES

Sell Yourself

Remember that you are competing with other people who are also trying to sell their services. If your cover letter is to stand out from the others, it must highlight the specific qualifications that would make you a valuable employee.

Thinking Cap 18.1

Discuss: What is the main difference between a cover letter and a résumé? Do you think you could use a cover letter in place of a résumé?

Selling Yourself to Employers

499

- Public or private employment agencies
- Relatives, friends, or acquaintances who tell you about vacancies
- Networking through your professional organizations and individual support groups

GUIDELINES FOR WRITING AN EFFECTIVE COVER LETTER

Before you begin reading this section, refer to the persuasive approach concepts presented in Chapter 11. The cover letter is a formal business letter that accompanies the résumé whenever it is sent to a potential employer. Your cover letter is like a sales letter; it introduces you by highlighting relevant qualifications as they apply to a particular position. A cover letter usually includes a minimum of three paragraphs. Each paragraph has a different goal. An effective cover letter includes the following:

- An interesting opening that will get the interviewer's attention
- A convincing presentation of your qualifications
- A strong closing with a request for action—an interview

The following excerpts of openings, presentations of qualifications, and closings illustrate appropriate cover letter content. The letters in Figures 18-1, 18-2, and 18-3 on pages 501, 503 and 504 respectively, bring examples of these cover letter paragraphs together into effective documents.

Attract the Reader's Attention

Your opening paragraph must attract favorable attention and get the interviewer interested enough to read on. Use one of the following four ways to gain attention:

Identify the type of position you are applying for and tell how you learned about the opening

(Use this approach when you write a solicited cover letter for an advertised position.) Here is an opening written by an applicant who learned of a job opportunity from a college career office:

> Dianna Wyatt, Washington State Career Office counselor, told me that you are seeking a top-flight salesperson who can also give outstanding field demonstrations for Capri cellular phones.

This opening was written by an applicant who learned of a position from a professor:

> Mrs. Merilu Berkovitz, Director of the School of Medical Records Administration at the University of Maryland, told me you are looking for an Assistant Administrator in your Medical Records Department. Mrs. Berkovitz is confident that my college preparation and my

Figure 18-1

This cover letter relates the applicant's qualifications to the job requirements.

P.O. Box 37
Neon, KY 41840
September 6, <YEAR>

Mr. Tom Sullivan
Human Resources Manager
Consolidated Freightways
1942 Parkway Avenue
Detroit, MI 48236

Dear Mr. Sullivan:

With a recent college degree in accounting and several years of work experience, I am confident that I would be an excellent junior accountant to fill the position that Consolidated Freightways advertised in Sunday's *Detroit Herald*.

The past three years' experience in the trucking industry has increased my knowledge of the transportation field. Working in an office has increased my awareness of operations, finance, and budgeting. In addition, through my reading I have also become familiar with many of the Interstate Commerce Commission's regulations.

Since your company leases over 90 percent of its equipment, proper accounting methods for leases are vital to Consolidated Freightways' accurate financial reports. The attention to detail and accuracy, a skill that I have developed, can reduce costly accounting errors for you.

The enclosed résumé will provide you with a description of my qualifications. Please call me at 606-555-3327 to arrange a time when I may come in and talk with you.

Sincerely yours,

Rickey Lee Santiago

Rickey Lee Santiago

Enclosure

---

experience in the Medical Records Department at Giles County Hospital qualify me for this position.

Summarize your qualifications for a specific kind of position

(Use this approach in an unsolicited letter for an unadvertised position.) Specify as much as possible the kind of work you would like to do for the organization. For example:

> You will find my accounting and computer skills and inventory experiences beneficial to your company's purchasing department. I would enjoy working with your clients and promoting goodwill with other organizations both personally and by phone.

Here is another example of an opening that summarizes the applicant's qualifications:

> With my college background in marketing, along with my selling experience, I believe that I could successfully sell Peterson's products.

Selling Yourself to Employers

Refer to the organization's reputation, progress, or policies

(Use this approach in an unsolicited letter for an unadvertised position.) Because employers receive so many formula-like letters, your letter will stand out if it indicates you have researched the organization.

> The recent expansion of Northern Telecom, as reported in the *Dallas Morning News,* suggests possible openings for administrative assistants.

Here is another example of this type of opening:

> Congratulations on your No. 1 rating by *City Magazine* as a school district that seeks to motivate faculty and students to achieve high standards. As a recent University of Texas at Dallas graduate, I would like to contribute to the continued growth and success of the Allen Independent School System.

Express support for the kind of work the organization performs

(Use this approach in an unsolicited letter for an unadvertised position.) This type of opening shows the organization that you are aware of the needs of the industry.

> Retailing provides the challenge of meeting people and selling them on a product, an idea, a principle, or a goal. Your retail opening is the challenge I have been looking for and feel qualified to fill.

Here is another example of this type of opening:

> Millions of people now have access to the Internet and the World Wide Web, and the number is increasing every day. My training and experience in Web-based design would assist Design It in meeting the demands of a Web-based marketing initiative.

Present Your Qualifications Convincingly

To be convincing, the qualifications you present must be related to the work you are applying for and must be backed by evidence. Avoid statements such as "I am dependable," or "I am interested in working with people."

Notice how the following applicant uses previous work experience to tell the prospective employer he is a hard worker.

> After working as a help desk technician in the evenings and during rush periods, I learned that I enjoyed the fast pace as well as the work itself. In addition, my three summers as an intern at a computer retail store gave me valuable experience in dealing with customers.

Remember to interpret your training in terms of the work for which you are applying. The courses you have taken and the school activities you have participated in are important because of the lessons learned and the experiences you had in those courses. In your letter, instead of simply listing courses and extracurricular activities, emphasize ways in which you can perform for the

---

NOTES

Highlight Accomplishments

Stress what you have learned from your courses and school activities.

November 19, <YEAR>

Ms. Mary Caraletti
Human Resources Manager
Veterans Affairs Medical Center
1000 Locust Street
Reno, NV 89502

Dear Ms. Caraletti:

The Veterans Affairs Medical Center has been an outstanding medical facility in this area for many years, and I would like to be considered for a position on your administrative staff. Several friends of mine are employed at the Medical Center, and they are quite pleased with the excellent working conditions and the advancement opportunities.

You will find that my communication and writing skills are excellent and that I can be an asset to your hospital in both of these areas. Good grammar, neatness, accurate spelling, and precise writing have always come naturally to me. My business courses have given me a strong background, and I adapt easily to people and methods of operations.

My enclosed résumé details my education, job experience, and other information that may be of interest to you.

I would like to meet with you, Ms. Caraletti, to discuss my qualifications and possible employment at the VAMC. You may reach me at 702-555-3314 after 12:30 p.m.

Sincerely yours,

Lida Carlton

Lida Carlton
214 Loretta Avenue
Reno, NV 89502

Enclosure

Figure 18-2
This cover letter highlights the applicant's suitability for the job.

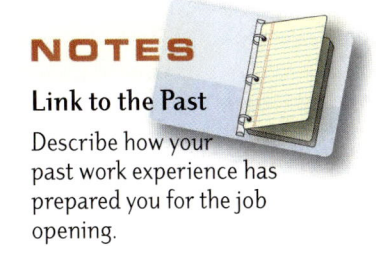

organization because of something you have learned in school or on the job. Notice how the successful cover letters in Figures 18-1, 18-2, and 18-3, and the following excerpts relate qualifications and work experience to the position.

An applicant for a job as field representative for National Clothes Company writes this description:

> My college courses in clothing construction have given me a broad knowledge of the makeup of men's and women's fashions. My sales training and marketing courses have given me many techniques about selling that I could put to good use for National Clothes Company. In my core college courses, such as psychology, humanities, social science, and public speaking, I gained a broader understanding of human behavior and learned to make fast decisions. These experiences have helped me win people to my point of view.

An applicant for a job in retailing uses this approach:

> While talking with the merchants of Lewisville as a member of the college newspaper advertising staff, I learned about business challenges and gained insight into what customers expect of a retail store. Holding several part-time positions in sales and participating in various extracurricular activities while in college taught me the value of

NOTES
Link to the Past
Describe how your past work experience has prepared you for the job opening.

Selling Yourself to Employers 503

managing my time and setting priorities, skills I would be able to put to use in your busy office.

In your cover letter, you should also adapt your work experience to the job requirements—specifically *what* you have learned from your work experience and *how* that experience will benefit a prospective employer, as shown in Figure 18-1. A prospective employer is interested in how your past work has prepared you to do the work required. Review the following example written by an applicant for the job of assistant in the purchasing department of a major manufacturer:

> I strengthened my understanding of the overall structure of a manufacturing plant and became familiar with purchasing terminology while working as an assistant in the Purchasing Department of Gateway Aluminum Corporation. This experience also provided me with a strong background in buying procedures and policies, which I can put to good use in your organization.

Figure 18-3
Note how the writer ties skills to the position sought.

June 18, <YEAR>

Mr. Donald Hickerson
Human Resources Manager
RKJ Inc.
343 Oak Street
Omaha, NE 68108

Dear Mr. Hickerson:

College training in office administration and work experience make me the ideal SUPERSECRETARY for whom you advertised in yesterday's *Omaha Star*.

I completed, with honors, the thorough and practical two-year office administration program at DeSoto County Junior College.

My keyboarding speed is now 75 words a minute, and I am proficient in word processing, spreadsheets, and databases. Besides specific skills, the business courses I took at DCJC have given me an understanding of the business world and its functions.

Employment in the Marketing Department at First National Bank of Middleton provided an opportunity to apply my training in a fast-paced office setting. I believe that my work background will enable me to adapt quickly to your office routine.

I find office work challenging and I enjoy new responsibilities. I would like to put my abilities and skills to work for RKJ Inc.

When you have reviewed the enclosed résumé, please call me at 515-555-2098 and suggest a time for an interview.

Sincerely,

Joyce Benson

Joyce Benson
405 Churchill Street
Blencoe, IA 15234

Enclosure

Close With a Request for Action

The closing paragraph provides a smooth transition from a description of your qualifications to a request for an interview. Close your cover letter with a specific request for an interview. In your closing also refer the interviewer to your résumé, and give a telephone number where you can be reached.

> My résumé, enclosed with this letter, describes my qualifications, which I believe, could be assets to American Vast Signs. I would like to meet with you to discuss the position of administrative secretary. Please call me at 801-555-8652 to let me know a time when we may meet to discuss other ways I might be of value to American Vast Signs.

Notice how the writer of the letter in Figure 18-2 (page 503) presents her qualifications. Figure 18-3 (page 504) illustrates an effective way to highlight skills in relation to the employer's needs.

A Final Check

When you complete your cover letter, ask yourself the questions in the following "Checklist for an Effective Cover Letter" to decide whether your letter is effective. Proofread your cover letter several times to ensure that it contains no spelling, grammar, or other errors. Then *mail your letter.*

✔ CHECKLIST FOR AN EFFECTIVE COVER LETTER

Check the Following Items to be Sure You Have:

	YES	NO
Written to an individual. Call the company to obtain the name of a contact person. If the name is not available, then use the person's title, such as Human Resources Director.		
Made each letter an original—not a photocopy.		
Addressed each letter and included the title of the contact person.		
Used the correct spelling of all names and the proper company name. Call the company to check the spelling if you're not certain.		
Have not overused the personal pronoun *I*.		
Directed the letter to the anticipated needs of the prospective employer.		
Made sure the letter is free of grammar, spelling, and punctuation errors.		
Edited and proofread carefully.		
Used good quality bond paper that matches the résumé.		
Used quality laser printing.		
Used proper business letter format.		
Written concisely; not exceeding one page.		

Selling Yourself to Employers

Checkpoint 18.1

1. Read the openings from two cover letters below. Identify the more effective opening and explain your choice.

    a. *I spent a year in Mexico as an exchange student. At the university, I took classes that focused on Spanish and Mexican literature, culture, and history. I lived with a host family at the time. I thought the experience would help me in the job market.*

    b. *As an exchange student in Mexico three years ago, I lived with a host family and took university courses. As a result, I speak Spanish fluently and have a good understanding of modern and traditional Mexican cultures, which I could put to good use as an assistant at the Hispanic Culture Museum.*

2. In your opinion, what is the benefit of limiting a cover letter to one page in length?

3. What errors do you find in the following conclusion of a cover letter? What suggestions would you make to improve it?

    My résumé is enclosed. Thank you for your time. I hope to hear from you.

INTERVIEWING

Once you obtain an interview, your next objective will be to use the interview to create an impression that will lead to an employment offer. The purpose of an interview is to allow the interviewer to assess your qualifications and skills beyond what is presented on your résumé. The interview also allows you to assess the organization and the available or desired position.

Preparing for the Interview

What makes an interview successful? Most interviewers agree that the key factor is *preparation*. Dedicating time, energy, and thought to preparing for the interview will help the applicant answer the following questions:

- Why did you leave your last position?
- Give me an example of one of your significant accomplishments. *Why* was it significant and *how* did you accomplish it?
- What did you like and dislike about your last job?

In a recent interview situation at a major manufacturer of paper products, the interviewer who asked these questions did not offer employment to the applicant. Why? The applicant was not prepared with effective answers and did not give the interviewer a positive impression of his qualifications.

NOTES

Aiming High
The purpose of the cover letter is to get an interview. The purpose of the interview is to get a job offer.

506   Chapter 18

Beyond preparation, interviewers have identified the following common mistakes made by applicants during their interviews:

- Late arrival
- Inappropriate dress
- Lack of confidence
- Poor attitude

How do you prepare for an interview? Appropriate preparation includes the following items:

NOTES

Making Impressions

The first impression you make on a prospective employer is with your résumé and letter or employment application form. The second is during the interview and is based on appearance.

Analyze Your Strengths and Weaknesses

Refer to the self-assessment you conducted at the end of Chapter 17 to identify your strengths and determine areas for improvement. Prior to your interview, identify two or three of your most valuable strengths, along with an example of how you have demonstrated each. Analyze areas for improvement and prepare your responses in positive terms. Suppose you did not make effective use of your time on a project in a previous situation. Prepare a response to give the interviewer a concise, articulate description of the situation and the way you will apply what you learned from that situation to the position for which you are applying. This will help you discuss how you could help to achieve the objectives and expectations of the desired position.

Research the Organization

Obtain information about the organization's product or service, its competitors, and its financial picture. Corporations publish various types of literature, such as annual reports, company overviews, and newsletters. Request and review this literature. You may also complete a search about an organization by accessing the Internet or by checking out materials from the library.

Go to CD-ROM

Activity 18-2
To test your skills.

Consider Your Responses to Questions

Common interview questions—some of which are presented as statements—and possible responses include the following:

- **Why do you want to work here?** Be prepared to answer this question based on the results of your research of the organization. You may want to mention something about the organization's product or service, its team concept, or a challenge the organization will face in the future. Relate your skills or interests directly to the company features that you selected.

- **What did you like/dislike about your last position?** When asking this question, the interviewer is looking for a response that will or will not support the position for which you are applying. In answering this question, avoid being critical of your former company (or the current one if you're still employed).

- **Why do you think you are the best candidate for this position?**
Relate your qualifications directly to the requirements of the position.

Selling Yourself to Employers

- **What have you done to show initiative and willingness to work?** Have some instances in mind to illustrate your initiative and work ethic. These instances may be from school or work or both.

- **What do you know about our organization?** You can really be impressive with your answer to this question if you have done your research carefully. Pick out major achievements of the company to illustrate your knowledge of its products, community involvements, size, successes, or other factors.

- **In performing your last job, what major problem did you encounter and how did you deal with it?** This question is usually asked to determine your problem-solving strengths. You can relate how you brought a project back online or how you facilitated the team that developed a new product or service.

- **What two or three accomplishments have given you the most satisfaction? Why?** For the answer to this question, you should have a solid two or three major accomplishments to discuss. They may be school- or work-related accomplishments.

- **How do you feel about assisting with the training of others in your department?** If you have assisted others in learning a skill, you should relate these abilities in answering this question. Helping a new employee learn procedures may be just one such example.

- **What do you consider the difference between your current or past position and the position for which you are applying?** The answer will depend on your knowledge of the new position and the comparisons you have made between it and your former or present position.

- **What is the most useful job-related criticism you have ever received?** Perhaps someone suggested that you take a course or take advantage of a training opportunity to learn a new skill to make up for a weakness.

- **Tell me about a particularly difficult problem you were able to solve.** Have a positive attitude as you answer this question based on your experiences.

- **If I had three of your coworkers here, how would they describe you?** Be positive in your answer to this question. You may want to say they would describe you as a team player, a person who sticks to the job at hand, or a person eager to learn.

- **In what type of work environment do you feel the most productive?** This answer should relate to the type of environment the job you're interviewing for offers—inside, outside, production, sales, or other characteristics you consider satisfactory.

- **How has your experience helped to prepare you for this position?** Relate your courses, your work experience, and your skills to the job.

- **Tell me about a situation in which you were criticized and how you handled the criticism.** Be very enthusiastic as you illustrate how you handled a criticism and how you learned from it. Use a positive tone as you discuss the benefits received from the criticism.

Prepare Questions to Ask the Interviewer

Most interviewers expect you to ask questions. In fact, sometimes you will be judged on your ability to ask a question that is effective in getting the information that you desire. Because you will be evaluated on your understanding of the position for which you are applying, ask questions specific to that position, such as the following:

- What are the opportunities for growth and advancement in the position?
- What type of training is required?
- What skills will the successful candidate for this position need?

NOTES

Hold Your Horses

Asking questions about salary and benefits on the first interview is inappropriate and could cause you to be eliminated from consideration.

Review Your Résumé Before Your Interview

You may have updated your résumé since you sent it to the company. If so, be sure you have an extra copy of the updated résumé to give to the interviewer. In any interview situation, have extra copies available in case you interview with other people in the company. Sometimes the interviewer may not have a copy of your résumé, especially if it went to another division or department.

Dress Appropriately

To the interviewer, inappropriate dress results from lack of planning or knowledge on the applicant's part. Remember, you want to dress to convince your interviewer that you fit into the organization. Guidelines for dressing appropriately include the following:

- Your clothes should be clean, well pressed, and conservative.
- Your hair should be clean, neat, and conservatively cut.
- Your nails should be neatly trimmed.
- Your shoes should be simple and should match or complement your clothes.
- Your jewelry should be kept to a minimum; avoid flashy and trendy jewelry on interviews.

Arrive Promptly

Interviewers consider late arrival as lack of planning. If you do not know the location of the interview, call to ask for details. Allow ample travel time—leave early if you are traveling by train, plane, or bus or if the weather or traffic may delay you. If you are driving to the interview, it's always a good idea to find the interview location a day or two in advance. You can find such things as parking, the entrance to the building, and security requirements (such as a pass needed from a security guard) ahead of time.

Selling Yourself to Employers

Types of Interviews

Interviews may be held by phone, on-site at the work location, or at a career/placement center.

- **Phone interviews** are arranged by the interviewer when a face-to-face interview is not possible or when the interviewer wants to screen applicants.
- **On-site interviews** allow the applicant an opportunity to tour a company and visit with employment personnel and hiring managers.
- **Preliminary interviews** are held at career/placement centers where employers have been invited to interview students on campus. Preliminary interviews are sometimes held at job fairs with follow-up interviews scheduled for a later date.

Interviews have different purposes, and the type of interview conducted can vary according to the purpose of the interview. For example, the following types of interviews have specific purposes in the interview process:

- **Screening interviews** are usually held when a large number of applicants have applied. These interviews eliminate those who may not be qualified for the particular position being advertised. The screening interview is also a way of selecting the best candidates when a large number are qualified. These interviews are usually highly structured and are based on a question-and-answer format to get information quickly and thus to make a selection decision.
- Another type of screening interview is the **group interview.** This type of interview is often done either to screen those who are not specifically qualified or to evaluate how people work together in a group. When a team effort is needed for a particular job, this is a good method to use to select applicants.
- A **one-on-one interview** is the usual method of most interviews. A one-on-one interview consists of the applicant and the interviewer. The interviewer may use a question-and-answer format, the stress interview, the behavioral interview, or a combination of these types to obtain the required information.
- A **stress interview** is usually held to assess an applicant's ability to respond under stress. Stress interviews are usually conducted for positions in which a person's ability to act under stress or pressure is necessary. The questions asked during such an interview are usually direct and challenging, such as asking a person to defend an opinion or a belief about a particular issue.
- **Behavioral interviews** focus on experiences, knowledge, skills, abilities, and behavioral traits, those skills or characteristics that the applicant applies consciously or unconsciously to accomplish objectives. Questions may focus either on past behavior and experiences or on situations that might happen on the job. Such questions might begin, "What did you do when . . ." or "When a customer rejects your product, how do you respond?"

The Interview Process

If you have had limited experience as a participant in interviews, it will help you to understand some of the techniques a typical interviewer may use and the reasons he or she may ask certain questions.

Building Rapport

Usually the interviewer will begin with some general questions or comments to help you overcome your initial nervousness. This is the time for you to relax—be friendly but professional. Remember that anything you hear during this initial conversation could be a clue to how the interviewer thinks, what he or she is looking for, or how you could help the organization.

Opening Statements

After a few minutes of general comments, the interviewer will usually explain in a businesslike way that the purpose of the interview is to determine if there is a match between you and the available position. The employer may provide you with a brief overview of the organization and describe the position and its requirements. At this point, the interviewer is probably observing the following:

- Your appearance and dress
- Any signs of nervousness expressed through body language
- Your willingness to interact and react appropriately

> **LEGAL & ETHICAL 18-1**
>
> **Professional Conduct.** An interviewer cannot ask discriminatory questions relating to race, age, sex, marital status, or number of children as these factors have no bearing on whether the applicant can or cannot perform the job duties. An interviewer cannot ask questions that are not job related. What questions do you consider illegal? How should the applicant respond to such questions?

The Heart of the Interview

At this point, the interviewer will begin asking two basic types of questions: (1) open-ended questions and (2) closed questions.

- The **open-ended (nondirected) questions** are general inquiries designed to get you to provide the interviewer with comprehensive information. These questions often begin with "Tell me . . .," "Describe . . .," and "When . . . ." They are used to discover how well you organize and express your thoughts, how well you communicate orally, and how consistent your views are with the image of the organization. For example, an interviewer may say to an applicant, "Tell me about your education and its help in preparing you for this position."

Thinking Cap 18.2

Discuss: The interviewer asks if you expect to start a family soon. How will you respond?

Selling Yourself to Employers

GLOBAL DIVERSITY 18.1

Job Search Customs
Interview customs differ from country to country. Interview someone from another country to get an idea how customs may differ and what interviewers may expect from applicants in another country. *What are some of the differences?*

By making this open-ended statement, the interviewer is giving the applicant an opportunity to highlight educational areas that relate to current job needs and problems. The interviewer wants to see how well the applicant is able to summarize and relate pertinent skills, point by point, to the requirements of the job. If an applicant fails to respond effectively to this type of question, employment may not be offered.

An interviewer may ask an open-ended behavior-based question which may begin *Why, What, What if, How would you,* and so forth. For example, "What if a customer needed information the next day, but your immediate supervisor (the person who would normally supply that information) was on vacation for a week. How would you handle the situation?" These questions are used to reveal rationale for decisions you have made, to determine your level of motivation, or to determine behavior in certain problem-solving situations.

- In contrast to open-ended questions, **closed questions (directed interview)** require a yes-or-no answer or are fill-in-the-blank type of inquiries. This type of interview is highly structured. This type of interview is often used as a screening interview to verify or confirm information. For example, the interviewer may ask, "You have three years' experience as a bank teller; is that correct?"

Be aware of a question that appears to be closed but actually requires an open-ended answer. For instance, "Can you work under pressure?" may appear to call for a simple answer of *yes* or *no*. In reality, an interviewer asking this question is looking for a comprehensive response that gives you an opportunity to sell your skills.

The Interview Closing

As the interview ends, the interviewer will usually present a plan of action. A specific plan is a positive sign that you are being considered. For instance, the interviewer would ask, "Because the department manager is out of the city, would it be convenient for you to return Thursday for a second interview?"

Wait and watch for the "Anything else?" question. This is a technique the interviewer uses to give the applicant another opportunity to sell himself or herself. Some applicants who are not paying attention will be eager to gather up their things and will miss this opportunity. Others won't be expecting the question and will not know how to answer. Instead, be prepared to make a very strong closing statement, such as "It would be very beneficial for you to have me in this position because of my customer service skills and three years experience."

When the interview is concluded, stand, smile, and give a firm handshake and a thank-you for the interviewer's time.

Traits That Influence Interviewers

The traits you exhibit, both unfavorable and favorable, make a lasting impression on an interviewer.

Unfavorable Traits

Traits that make an unfavorable impression on an interviewer include:

- Wandering—the inability to focus on relevant information. The interviewer's time is valuable. Your ability to focus demonstrates that you will use your time effectively if you become an employee. To avoid wandering, concentrate on the question or subject being discussed and provide informative, relevant, and concise answers.

- Compulsive talking—rambling rather than listening. Compulsive talking is "instant death" in an interview.

- Nervousness—wringing hands, touching the face, jingling coins, fidgeting, toe tapping, and so on.

- Boredom—yawning, looking out the window; mind obviously not on the interviewer.

- Being noncommunicative—quiet to the point of being unable or unwilling to communicate or interact with the interviewer. This trait is just as deadly as compulsive talking.

- Negative criticism—of an applicant's current or previous employer.

Favorable Traits

Favorable traits that interviewers welcome include:

- Friendliness—being pleasant to be around, showing sense of humor, obviously enjoying people, smiles.

- Preparedness—having taken the time to learn about the organization's products or service, its size based on volume or market area, the number of employees, and other details.

- Sincerity—genuine interest in the organization, the position, teamwork, and results.

- Work ethic—arriving early, using time productively, completing tasks.

- Pride in quality of work—doing the job right the first time and making sure the customers are satisfied.

Few people are hired at the first interview. The interviewer may have completed a summary, rating you on the following categories: appearance, effective communication, job knowledge, motivation, team player mentality, and work ethic. The interviewer usually narrows the field to a few applicants. Either a decision is made or a second interview is scheduled. The interviewer may call the top two or three applicants for a second interview to meet with the manager who has requested the position to be filled. Based on the results of the second interview, the manager may make the final selection.

Self-Evaluation

Complete a self-evaluation after each interview. Evaluate your interview preparation, responses, and skill development needed for the position to help you immediately identify any areas for improvement. Develop a written plan or checklist to help you reinforce your positive behaviors and eliminate any negative behaviors you identified. The following checklist is a good starting point for your self-evaluation.

✔ INTERVIEW SELF-EVALUATION CHECKLIST

	YES	NO
Before the Interview		
Assessed skills, abilities, and experience		
Listed and was prepared to discuss three or four important points an interviewer should know about me		
Researched information about organization		
Gathered materials needed for interview (copy of résumé, list of references, copy of cover letter, portfolio or sample of work)		
Prepared answers to possible questions asked by interviewers		
Knew location of interview (had address, telephone number)		
During the Interview		
Was pleasant to receptionist or administrative assistant who greeted me		
Had professional appearance		
Used persuasive attitude		
Was energetic and enthusiastic		
Showed positive attitude		
Used good listening skills		
Responded effectively to questions		
Observed messages sent through body language (eye contact, showed interest as a listener, favorable traits)		
Was poised and self-confident		
Tailored answers to organization's needs and position as determined by research		
The Interview Closing		
Thanked interviewer		
Smiled		
Gave one last statement about how my skills, abilities, and experience would be an asset to organization		
Gave a firm handshake		
After the Interview		
Wrote a thank-you letter to interviewer		
Wrote other thank-you letters		

GUIDELINES FOR FOLLOW-UP LETTERS

Follow-up letters include (1) thank-you letters to interviewers, (2) thank-you letters to those who assisted with your job search, and (3) other follow-up letters.

Thank-You Letter to the Interviewer

Now that you have written your résumé, created your cover letter, completed an employment application form, and interviewed for the position, one more important piece of correspondence needs to be written: the thank-you letter. Employers like conscientious employees; and by sending a thank-you letter to an interviewer, you are demonstrating that you know proper business etiquette. You are also keeping your name and your qualifications on the interviewer's mind.

> **NOTES**
>
> **Quick Response**
> A thank-you letter should be sent immediately after the interview.

What should you include in a thank-you letter? Here are some tips:

- Thank the interviewer for his or her time during the interview.

- Reemphasize one of your strong "selling points."

- If you thought of something after the interview that you failed to cover during the interview, include it, if it is a significant point.

- Invite the interviewer to contact you for additional information if necessary.

- Close the letter with a positive statement about your interest in the position. Mention that you are looking forward to the interviewer's favorable decision.

Sending this letter after the interview will give you an advantage over the other applicants—few of whom actually send thank-you letters after interviews. Since your purpose is to keep the interviewer from forgetting you, be sure to mail the letter no later than the day after the interview.

Paul Henry sent the thank-you letter in Figure 18-4 (page 516) after his interview. A similar thank-you letter is appropriate if you have been told that your application will be kept on file for consideration when a job opening fits your qualifications.

Other Thank-You Letters

Remember, writing thank-you letters to people who have helped you in your job search is important. Send thank-you letters to friends who have given you leads; to people who have been willing to give you suggestions for your job hunt; and to anyone who has been especially helpful when you were preparing your résumé or your cover letter.

If you do get the job, be sure to keep in mind those people who gave a favorable report of your qualifications or in any other way helped you to

Selling Yourself to Employers

Figure 18-4
A thank-you letter to an interviewer.

Paul Henry

1800 E. Hollywood Ave.
Salt Lake City, UT 84108

801-555-5652
phenry@compisp.net

September 14, <YEAR>

Ms. Angela Smart
Program Specialists
24135 West Del Monte
Valencia, CA 91355

Dear Ms. Smart:

Thank you for considering me for your opening as a software specialist. I have a very positive feeling about your organization and my ability to work effectively with you. My three years' experience, skills, and college background exactly fit the kind of service you want to provide to your customers.

You said that the decision on those who would be interviewed further would be made by October 1. I look forward to hearing from you. Please telephone me at 801-555-5652.

Sincerely,

Paul Henry

Paul Henry

---

achieve your goal. A letter giving them the good news of your employment is always welcome. In addition, respond to anyone who wrote you a note congratulating you and wishing you success on the new job. The thank-you letters should be short, simple, and sincere, mentioning what each recipient did for you.

Other Follow-Up Letters

If you hear nothing within a week or two after writing your interview thank-you letter, you may write a follow-up letter. Often you can make this follow-up more effective by providing additional information, such as an announcement of your graduation from college, completion of a special certificate, or completion of a temporary position.

In a follow-up letter you should mention the following items:

- The date of your previous application form or letter
- The position for which you applied and interviewed
- Your continued interest in the opening

You may also summarize and give additional information about your major qualifications, but you do not need to enclose a second copy of your résumé. Sometimes a follow-up letter will spark a response when you have had no reply to a résumé sent several weeks earlier.

After you have completed an application and interviewed for a position, it is the interviewing company's decision to offer you or someone else the position. If you are offered the position, you can accept or decline the offer. To accept the offer, you would either accept in person or by phone or fax. What type of approach would you use for this message? The good news (direct) approach, of course!

In composing your **acceptance** message, you should:

1. Begin with the acceptance—the good news.
2. Present some thoughts about your enthusiasm for the opportunity being given to you.
3. Close courteously with a commitment for a starting date.

To decline the offer means that you have decided not to work for the company that has extended the offer to you. Keep in mind that the company has taken the time to interview you and has selected you over all the other applicants based on your qualifications. You want to maintain the goodwill and friendship that you have established during the interview period. How will you do that?

In composing your **refusal** message, you should:

1. Follow the indirect approach and begin with a buffer in which you thank the company for the interview and the offer.
2. Lead into the refusal with your explanation that will ultimately state or imply your decline of the offer. A reasonable explanation should be provided that will keep the goodwill and leave the door open in case you want to reapply at some future date. Should you decline because you are returning to school, you should state that in your explanation. If you are accepting a position with another company, state the reasons why you are accepting another position, but keep the goodwill and relationship you have established in mind as you do so.
3. Close cordially with a look toward the future to end your letter on a positive tone.

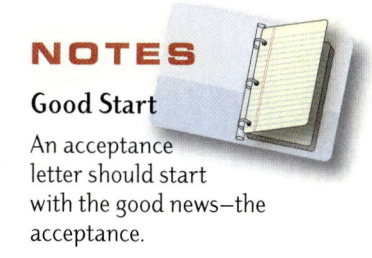

NOTES

Good Start
An acceptance letter should start with the good news—the acceptance.

Thinking Cap 18.3

Discuss: You have received offers from two companies where you recently interviewed for assistant director of communication positions. You must decline one. What will you say in your refusal? The offers are similar except for a higher salary for the one you are accepting.

NOTES

Bad News
A refusal letter must begin with a buffer.

Selling Yourself to Employers

Checkpoint 18.2

1. Why do you think it is important to be able to discuss your weaknesses, or areas for improvement, during a job interview?

2. In which type of job interview—*screening, group, one-on-one, stress,* or *behavioral*—do you think you would perform your best and your worst? Explain your answers.

3. Do you think it is fair for a job applicant to be judged on his or her appearance during an interview?

RESIGNATION LETTERS

When you decide to change jobs, you should prepare a letter of resignation. You should always notify your supervisor or employer of the changes in writing, even if you communicate your decision orally. You should give at least two weeks' notice. Whether the company wants you to complete the two weeks or not will be up to the individual company and its policy on resignations.

Although you may be angry or dissatisfied when you resign, avoid the temptation to write an emotionally charged letter. Remember that this letter will become a part of your permanent personnel file. If you need a reference from this employer in the future, the people who knew you best may be gone. The person contacted for a reference may have only your personnel file as a source of information; therefore, the reason you give for leaving should be one you can live with for the rest of your career. Remember, too, that a past supervisor or colleague may later be employed at your current place of employment.

A typical plan for a resignation letter is this:

1. Tell your plans for the position you have accepted (assuming you took another job).

2. State in a positive way that you are resigning, and indicate the effective date.

3. Offer to retrain a replacement, if appropriate.

4. State your reason for leaving, unless it is obvious or negative.

5. Tell how you've benefited from the job you are leaving.

6. Use a goodwill closing.

The resignation letter in Figure 18-5 can be adapted to fit many situations. Ending your resignation letter on a positive note will leave a favorable image of you in your personnel file.

Figure 18-5
A resignation letter should be tactful.

December 29, <YEAR>

Mr. Ivan Ludwig
Southern Telecommunications Corporation
2403 Sunset Blvd.
Arlington, TX 76015-3148

Dear Mr. Ludwig:

As I told you yesterday, I have accepted a position with Baldwin Communications, Inc. I plan to leave Arlington on January 27 to begin my new position. Please accept my resignation from Southern Telecommunications Corporation effective January 13. For the next two weeks, I will be available to train a replacement.

During the three years I have worked at Southern Telecommunications, I have appreciated the help you have given me and the professional relationship we have been able to cultivate. Working with you and the staff has been a pleasure.

Sincerely,

Thomas Cain

Thomas Cain
P.O. Box 3789A
Arlington, TX 76011

Chapter 18 Summary

During your job search, you will write cover letters for your résumés, follow-up letters, and thank-you letters. An effective cover letter highlights the particular aspects of your skills and accomplishments that best satisfy a prospective employer's needs. Thus, it bridges the gap between your experience, skills and abilities, and the qualifications of the position.

The objective of the résumé and the cover letter is to persuade a prospective employer to interview you. The purpose of an interview is to allow the interviewer to assess the applicant's qualifications and skills on the basis of information beyond that which is presented on his or her résumé. The interview also allows the applicant to assess the organization and the desired position.

During your job search, you may experience various types of interviews. After each interview, evaluate your performance and make plans to improve any weakness that you identify. Be sure to send thank-you letters to the interviewer as well as to others who helped you secure the interview.

When you decide to change jobs, you should prepare a letter of resignation. Doing so will leave a positive feeling about your resignation, not only with you, but also with those with whom you worked. A letter of resignation is necessary even if you resign in person.

Selling Yourself to Employers

Communication at Work

Jane Kappler, President

AAA Employment, Inc.

Every week in Ft. Myers, Florida, dozens of job candidates are eliminated from consideration, according to Jane Kappler, president of AAA Employment, Inc. They are not eliminated because they lack job skills, but because they lack good communication skills.

"The ability to communicate is number 1," Kappler says about looking for a job. "If you can't communicate, your experience isn't that important."

Kappler's agency recruits candidates for all sorts of jobs—from entry-level clerks to chief executive officers.

Landing the Interview

A candidate's résumé is the first step in the process. A winning résumé is professional looking and provides enough detail to convince Kappler that the candidate has appropriate experience and skills.

"Your résumé must sell you," says Kappler, who frowns on résumés that contain spelling, grammatical, punctuation, or word usage errors. "If a candidate isn't bright enough to use spellchecker [on her résumé] or relies on it solely, then you have a problem." If the résumé passes muster, then Kappler will call the potential candidate.

> **"** The ability to communicate is number 1. If you can't communicate, your experience isn't that important. **"**

The next step is a personal interview with Kappler, which will last about forty-five minutes. What does she look for when she meets a job candidate?

"I'm looking for someone who is friendly and outgoing, who looks you in the eye and has some energy. If a person looks as if they're glad to see you, then immediately you have a good feeling about that person." Overly shy or talkative candidates don't fare as well as articulate interviewees who listen for an opportunity to offer appropriate information about their experience and background.

She is also looking for someone who is well groomed. That doesn't mean expensive clothes; it does mean that a candidate's wardrobe is appropriate.

Job seekers should come to the interview prepared with letters of reference, school transcripts, and copies of other documents that may be pertinent. Arriving with these documents saves time and communicates that an individual is responsible and organized.

"It all gets to the bottom line—communication," says Kappler.

Discuss

1. During an interview, you are asked about the problems that led to your decision to leave your last job. How much detail do you provide?
2. If you know you are not the most articulate interviewee, how can you improve your chances of making a good impression at your interview?

Chapter 18
Online Exercises

Objective:
This online activity will require you to visit a personality profile Web site and complete a personality questionnaire.

Go to **bcw.glencoe.com**, the address for the *Business Communication at Work* Web site, and select Chapter 18. Next, click on Online Exercises. You will see a list of Web site links that will bring you to personality profile Web sites.

Activity 18.1

1. Select one of the personality profile Web sites to visit.

2. Complete the personality questionnaire offered on the Web site you have chosen. You may have to click on several links within the Web site to answer the personality questionnaire.

3. On a sheet of paper, write a paragraph describing whether you think the personality profile is an actual reflection of your personality. You may want to consider the following questions in your paragraph:

    a. What questions may have represented your personality better?

    b. Do you find that answer choices to the questions limit your ability to represent your personality?

    c. Do you think it is possible to characterize your personality into more than one category?

    d. Based on what you learned in this chapter, how do you think this questionnaire could be useful for employers?

4. Write your name on your paper, and hand it in to your instructor.

Activity 18.2

1. Select one of the personality profile Web sites to visit.

2. Print information on understanding personality. This information should be available after you complete an online personality questionnaire. If the Web site you have chosen does not provide a section on understanding personality, visit another personality profile Web site by returning to the *Business Communication at Work* Web site.

3. On the back of your printout, make an outline of the information you learned in the article.

4. On a sheet of paper, write a paragraph describing what you learned from your readings of understanding personality. Your paragraph should be based on your outline.

5. Write your name on your paper and each printout, and hand it in to your instructor.

Selling Yourself to Employers

CHAPTER 18 WORKSHEETS

NAME _____ DATE _____

PRACTICE 1

Proofreading

Instructions: The following cover letter was sent in reply to the advertisement. Read the letter carefully for errors in grammar, spelling, punctuation, format, and content. Circle the spelling errors, and list the other errors below the letter or on a separate sheet of paper.

The Daily News ran the following ad:

Office assistant with excellent telephone skills and experience with payroll, bookkeeping, Excel, Word. Send a résumé to Human Resources, Driscoll Corporation, 750 Commerce Boulevard, Dallas, TX 75205.

Feb. 13, <YEAR>

Human Resource
Driscal Corporation
750 Commercial Boulevard
Dallas, Texas 75205

Dear Gentlemen:

May I trouble you to take a few minutes of your valuable time to read my cover letter, which is attached to my resume? I have just move from Houston to Dallas.

I am very interested in a organization where my book keeping and computer skills will be valued. I am looking for a position with a pleasant working environment.

I can start immediately after my doctor's appointment on January 20. I look forward to receiving a call from you. You can telephone me at the number given on my resume.

Sincerely

Sally Essen

Sally Essen

---

522   Chapter 18

CHAPTER 18 WORKSHEETS

NAME _____ DATE _____

PRACTICE 2

Researching an Organization

Instructions: Clip an employment advertisement from a newspaper or magazine about a position you would like to have. Research the following information about the company:

- products or services the organization offers,
- size of organization,
- the type of ownership (proprietorship, partnership, or corporation), and other relevant information.

Research sources can include:

- company literature,
- a friend or relative, and
- the Internet.

Write a memo addressed to your instructor explaining the results of your research.

Writing a Solicited Cover Letter

Instructions: Prepare a cover letter in reply to the advertisement from Practice 1. Submit the advertisement with your letter to your instructor. Refer to the cover letters of Ricky Lee Santiago and Joyce Benson (pages 501 and 504, respectively) for ideas, but do not copy them. Address your letter to the appropriate person in the organization if you can find out his or her name and official title or position. Otherwise, address it to the human resources manager of the organization. Assume that you will be enclosing your résumé.

Writing an Unsolicited Cover Letter

Instructions: Choose an organization you would like to work for and prepare a cover letter. Assume that you will enclose your résumé. Refer to the letter of Lida Carlton (page 503) for ideas, but do not copy it.

PRACTICE 3

Interviewing

Instructions: Clip an advertisement from a newspaper or magazine or print one from the Internet that describes a position you would like to have. (You may use the same ad you used in Practice 1, or select a new one.)

1. Prepare at least three questions you would like to ask the interviewer.

   _____
   _____
   _____

2. Prepare answers to questions that you believe the interviewer may ask you.

   _____
   _____
   _____

Selling Yourself to Employers

CHAPTER 18 WORKSHEETS

NAME _____ DATE _____

Role Playing

Instructions: Use the questions and answers from the previous question to role-play an interview. Pair up with another student and give your answers orally as your partner asks the questions and makes notes on your answers. Ask your partner to rate your responses using the following checklist:

	Yes	No
Provided good examples	___	___
Emphasized specific skills	___	___
Gave insight into decision-making ability	___	___
Gave insight into self-motivation	___	___
Demonstrated understanding of position and related it to own background	___	___
Showed enthusiasm and confidence	___	___

PRACTICE 4

Follow-Up Letters

Instructions: Respond to the following situations as directed.

1. Assume that you wrote a cover letter to Mr. Thomas Brown, Link Manufacturing, 1901 Main Street, Scranton, PA 18404 and that you interviewed yesterday for a position as a customer service representative in the customer service department. Although you were told that you made a good impression and that you would hear more later, you received no employment offer. Write the thank-you letter to Mr. Brown, Human Resources Manager.

2. Assume you had sent your résumé and cover letter in response to a position advertised about three weeks ago. You may use the advertisement from Practice 3, or you may select a new one. To date, you have not received a response from the organization. Write a follow-up letter inquiring about the status of the opening.

3. Assume that you have been working for a company for the past three years. Your association with the company has been a pleasant one; however, you cannot afford to ignore a job opportunity that offers greater financial benefits and future potential for advancement in your career. Write a resignation letter. Supply an appropriate inside address and salutation, and use an acceptable business letter format as discussed in earlier chapters.

APPENDIX A: REFERENCES

The ability to use the English language competently is an enviable skill in the business world. Studying and practicing the rules of grammar will help you to make fewer errors in your writing—and to recognize and correct your errors **before** you mail a letter or submit a report.

Parts of Speech

Words classified according to their use in the sentence are called parts of speech. The parts of speech are nouns, pronouns, verbs, adjectives, adverbs, prepositions, and conjunctions.

Nouns

A noun is the name of a person *(Vanessa)*, place *(Baltimore)*, thing *(mountain)*, idea *(beauty)*, ability *(talking)*, or quality *(courage)*.

Nouns may be proper *(Rodney)* or common *(book)*, concrete *(tree)* or abstract *(modern)*, or collective *(family)*.

The **gender** of a noun may be masculine *(man)*, feminine *(woman)*, common *(child)*, or neuter *(piano)*.

Plurals of Nouns. The **number** of a noun indicates whether it is singular or plural. To form plurals of most nouns, follow these rules:

1. Add *s* to most singular nouns *(order, orders; decision, decisions; price, prices)*.

2. Add *es* to a singular noun that ends in *s* (or an *s* sound), *sh* or *ch, s, x,* or *z* *(business, businesses; loss, losses; church, churches; tax, taxes)*.

3. Change *y* to *i* and add *es* for nouns ending in *y* preceded by a consonant *(company, companies; copy, copies)*.

4. Add only *s* for nouns ending in *y* preceded by a vowel *(Tuesday, Tuesdays; attorney, attorneys)*.

5. Add only *s* for nouns ending in *o* preceded by a vowel *(ratio, ratios; video, videos; studio, studios; patio, patios)*.

6. Add *es* to most nouns ending in *o* preceded by a consonant *(hero, heroes)*. Some exceptions are *memo, memos; zero, zeros*.

7. Add *s* to the singular of most nouns that end in *f, fe,* or *ff (belief, beliefs; brief, briefs; proof, proofs; plaintiff, plaintiffs)*. For certain other nouns, change the final *f* or *fe* to *v* and add *es (half, halves; self, selves; wife, wives)*.

8. A few plural nouns are formed irregularly *(foot, feet; child, children; woman, women)*. If you are not sure of a plural form, consult a dictionary.

9. For a hyphenated or a two-word compound noun, change the chief word of the compound for a plural form *(account receivable, accounts receivable; brother-in-law, brothers-in-law; notary public, notaries public)*. If the compound is made up of a noun and a preposition, change the noun (not the preposition) to the plural *(passerby, passersby)*. If the compound does not contain a noun, form the plural on the last element of the compound *(trade-in, trade-ins)*.

Compounds written as one word usually form the plural at the end *(letterhead, letterheads)*.

10. Add *s* to most proper nouns *(Buzan, Buzans; Romano, Romanos; Gary, Garys)*. But add *es* to a proper noun ending in *s* or an *s* sound *(James, Jameses)*. Plurals of titles and personal names are formed as follows: *the Misses Shelton* or *the Miss Sheltons; the Doctors Wilson* or *the Doctor Wilsons*.

11. Some nouns have the same form in the singular and the plural *(Japanese; deer; corps; politics)*.

12. Certain nouns are always singular *(athletics; economics; mathematics; news)*.

13. Certain nouns are always plural *(credentials; pants; goods; proceeds; statistics)*.

14. Plurals of words from other languages that have been incorporated into the English language should be looked up in the dictionary *(analysis, analyses; parenthesis, parentheses; criterion, criteria)*. Some of these words have both a foreign and an English plural; in fact, the dictionary may show that there is a difference in the meaning of each plural form.

15. Add *s* to form the plurals of most abbreviations *(Dr., Drs.; no., nos.; dept., depts.)*. The abbreviations of many units of weight and measure, however, are the same in both the singular and the plural *(oz* for both *ounce* and *ounces; ft* for both *foot* and *feet)*. A few single-letter abbreviations form the plural by doubling the same letter *(p.* and *pp.* for *page* and *pages; f.* and *ff.* for *following page* and *following pages)*. The plurals of capital letters, abbreviations ending with capital letters, figures, and symbols are formed by adding *s (Ph.D.s, 3s, &s)* unless the omission of the apostrophe would cause misreading *(A's, I's, U's)*. The plurals of words referred to as words are formed by adding *s* or *es* unless the plural form would be likely to be misread or would be unfamiliar *(ands, dos, don'ts, but which's* and *or's)*. Add an apostrophe plus *s* to form the plural of uncapitalized letters and uncapitalized abbreviations with internal periods *(i's, c.o.d.'s)*.

Possessives of Nouns

1. Add an apostrophe and *s* to form the possessive of most singular nouns *(woman's coat; manager's office; assistant's desk; Charles's vacation)*.

2. For singular nouns that end in *s* if adding the apostrophe and *s* makes the word hard to pronounce, add only the apostrophe *(Ms. Jennings' idea; Achilles' heel)*.

3. Add only an apostrophe to regularly formed plurals *(employees' vacations; ladies' suits; presidents' portraits)*.

4. Add an apostrophe and *s* to irregularly formed plurals *(men's shirts; children's toys)*.

5. Add the apostrophe and *s* to the final member of a compound noun *(her mother-in-law's car; the editor in chief's responsibilities; the secretary-treasurer's report)*. It is usually preferable to rewrite a sentence to avoid the plural possessive of a compound noun *(the decision of all the editors in chief* is better than *all the editors in chief's decision)*.

6. To indicate joint ownership of two or more nouns, form the possessive on the final noun *(MacLaren and MacLaren's clients)*. But if separate ownership is meant, make each noun possessive *(the secretary's and the treasurer's reports)*.

7. To indicate the possessive of a singular abbreviation, add an apostrophe and *s* (*the Harris Co.'s offer; Mr. Hugh Miller, Sr.'s resignation*); of a plural abbreviation, add only an apostrophe (*the M.D.s' diagnoses*).

8. Restrict the use of the possessive to persons and animals. Do not use the possessive form to refer to inanimate things; use an *of* phrase (*the format of the letter; the provisions of the will*). Some exceptions are expressions of time and measure (*today's market; two weeks' vacation; ten dollars' worth of supplies*) and personification (*the company's assets*).

Pronouns

A pronoun is used in place of a noun to avoid repetition.

The chairperson has studied the recommendations and agrees with *them*.

1. A pronoun must agree with its **antecedent** (the word for which it stands) in number, person, and gender.

   One of the men left *his* keys on the desk.

2. Demonstrative pronouns (*this, that, these, those*) should plainly refer to a specific antecedent. Do not use *this* or *that* to refer to the thought of an entire sentence.

   VAGUE: Four people in our word processing department were absent yesterday. *This* accounts for the backlog today.

   CLEAR: Four people in our word processing department were absent yesterday. Their absences account for the backlog today.

3. Relative pronouns (*who, whom*) do not agree in case with their antecedents. Their grammatical function in the sentence determines their case. A relative pronoun usually introduces a clause. To determine the correct case of the pronoun, rearrange the clause in the order of subject, verb, and object. Disregard any parenthetical clauses.

   She is the one whom I believe the committee will choose.
   (Disregard the parenthetical clause *I believe*, and the normal order of the clause is *the committee will choose whom*. The subject is *committee*, the verb is *will choose*, and the object is *whom*.

4. Compound personal pronouns (*yourself, myself,* and so on) have two uses. They may be used for emphasis. They may reflect the action of the verb back upon the subject but are never the subject themselves. A compound personal pronoun should *not* be used in place of a personal pronoun.

   He told me that himself. (Emphasis)

   She gave herself time to get to the airport. (Reflexive)

Verbs

A verb states a condition, implies or shows action, or helps another verb. A sentence must contain a verb to be complete. When the complete verb is a group of words, it is called a verb phrase. A verb phrase has one principal verb and one auxiliary (helping) verb (the auxiliary may include more than one word). The common auxiliary verbs are forms of the verbs *to be* and *to have*.

Marcie *works*. Marcie *has been working*. (Auxiliary: *has been*)

Verb Tenses. The tense of a verb tells when the action of the verb takes place.

>**They want.** (Present)
>**They wanted.** (Past)
>**They will want.** (Future)
>**They have wanted.** (Present perfect)
>**They had wanted.** (Past perfect)
>**They will have wanted.** (Future perfect)

Agreement of Verb With Subject. A verb should agree with its subject in person and number.

>**Three sales representatives complete their new-product training today.**

1. Singular subjects connected by *either... or, neither... nor* require singular verbs.

    Either a refund or a credit memorandum is acceptable.

2. When *either... or, neither... nor* connects subjects differing in number, the verb should agree with that part of the subject that is nearer to the verb.

    Neither the retailers nor the wholesaler *is* liable.

    Neither the wholesaler nor the retailers *are* liable.

3. When such expressions as *together with, as well as, including* separate the subject and the verb, the verb agrees in number with the real subject.

    The catalog, together with the special sales brochures, *is* ready.

4. When the subject is a collective noun that names a group or unit acting as a whole, use a singular verb.

    The organization *is* liberal in its promotion policies.

    But when the members of the group or unit are considered to be acting separately, use a plural verb.

    The jury *were* still deliberating.

5. When a singular noun is used as the subject to indicate quantity *(some, all, none, part)* or when a fraction is the subject, use a singular verb when a singular sense is meant and a plural verb when a plural sense is meant. Whether the plural or the singular sense is meant is usually indicated by the object of the prepositional phrase used with the subject.

    None of the catalogs *were* shipped today.

    All of the event *was* televised.

6. When the subject is *a number,* the verb must be plural. When the subject is *the number,* the verb must be singular.

    A number of students *are* being honored.

    The number of complaints *is* not surprising.

7. When the name of a business firm includes *and Associates* or *and Company,* use a singular verb.

    Boyle, Rickman and Associates *is* opening new offices.

8. When the subject is a group of words, such as a slogan, a title, or a quotation, use a singular verb.

    Sell the sizzle not the steak *is* a well-known saying in the restaurant industry.

Verbal Nouns. Participles ending in *ing* are often used as nouns and are called gerunds. A pronoun modifying a gerund should be in the possessive form.

> I shall appreciate *your* sending the check promptly.

Adjectives

An adjective describes or limits a noun or a pronoun. An adjective construction may be a single word, two or more unrelated words, a compound, a phrase, or a clause. It may either precede or follow the noun or pronoun.

> *Five new portable* dictating machines are needed.

An adjective may be modified only by an adverb, not by another adjective.

> Jonathan is *extremely* (adverb) *agile* (adjective).

Comparison of Adjectives. To express different degrees or qualities, descriptive adjectives may be compared in three forms: positive, comparative (two things compared), and superlative (three or more things compared).

> Shep's grades are *high*. (Positive)
>
> Shep's grades are *higher* than mine. (Comparative)
>
> Shep's grades are the *highest* in the class. (Superlative)

To form the comparative and superlative degrees, follow these rules.

1. To form the comparative of most adjectives, add *er* to the positive: *tall, taller.* To form the superlative, add *est* to the positive: *tall, tallest.*

2. For irregular adjectives, change the form of the word completely *(good, better, best).*

3. For adjectives of two syllables, the comparative is formed by adding *er* or the words *more* or *less* to the positive, and the superlative is formed by adding *est* or the words *most* or *least* to the positive: *likely, likelier, likeliest;* OR *likely, less likely* (or more *likely*), *least likely* (or *most likely*). Adjectives of three or more syllables are always compared by adding *more* or *most, less* or *least* (*more* efficient, *most* efficient).

4. Some adjectives state qualities that cannot be compared *(complete, correct, level, round, perfect, unique).* However, these words may be modified by *more nearly* (or *less nearly*) and similar adverbs to suggest an approach to the absolute.

5. The word *other* must be used in comparing a person or a thing with other members of the group to which it belongs.

> Our new model is selling better than any *other* we have developed.

Compound Adjectives. A compound adjective is made up of two or more words used together as a single thought to modify a noun. A compound adjective should be hyphenated when it precedes the noun if the compound:

1. Is a two-word one-thought modifier (*long-range* goals).

    > **EXCEPTION:** Very commonly used compounds are not hyphenated: *high school* teachers; *real estate* agent.

2. Is a phrase of three or more words (*up-to-date* report).

3. Is a number combined with a noun (*fourteen-day* period).

References

4. Has coequal modifiers (*labor-management* relations).

5. Includes irregularly formed comparatives and superlatives (*better-selling* items; *worst-looking* letter).

6. Combines *well* with a participle (*well-educated* executive).

A compound adjective that follows the noun should also be hyphenated when it:

1. Is a *well* compound that retains its one-thought meaning (*well-read, well-to-do*; BUT NOT: *well known, well managed*).

2. Is made up of an adjective or a noun followed by a noun to which *ed* has been added (*high-priced, left-handed*).

3. Is a noun or an adjective followed by a participle (*time-consuming, factory-installed, strange-looking, ill-advised*).

4. Is formed by joining a noun with an adjective (*fire-resistant, tax-exempt*).

Consult the dictionary for compounds composed of common prefixes and suffixes (*audio*visual, *post*script, *pre*addressed, *inter*office, *mid*-July, business-*like*).

Do not hyphenate a foreign phrase used as a compound modifier (*per capita* consumption, *ad hoc* ruling, *ex officio* member).

Do not hyphenate a two-word proper noun used as an adjective (*Latin American* conference, *Western Union* telegram, *Supreme Court* decision).

Consult a reference manual for compound adjectives that are commonly used without hyphens (*real estate, income tax, social security, life insurance, word processing.*)

Adverbs

An adverb explains, describes, or limits a verb, an adjective, or another adverb.

Does this machine work *efficiently?* (Modifies verb)

It is *very* **efficient.** (Modifies adjective)

We drove *quite* **carefully on the ice.** (Modifies adverb)

1. Place an adverb as close as possible to the word it modifies. Its position may alter the meaning of the sentence.

   He met her *only* **today.**

   He met *only* **her today.**

   Only **he met her today.**

2. Verbs of the senses (*look, taste, feel, smell,* and so on) and linking verbs (forms of *be, become, seem,* and *appear*) are usually followed by an adjective that describes the subject.

   The meat smells *bad.* (Adjective, modifies *meat*)

   He looked *happy.* (Adjective, modifies *He*)

   I feel *bad.* (Adjective, modifies *I*)

   But to describe the action of the verb, use an adverb.

   She looked *happily* **at him.** (Adverb, modifies *looked*)

   He felt *carefully* **for his key.** (Adverb, modifies *felt*)

3. Adverbs that are negative in meaning should not be used with negatives.

   Anne *scarcely* had time to finish the report.

   NOT: Anne *hadn't scarcely* time to finish the report.

Prepositions

A preposition is a word used to connect a noun or a pronoun with some other word in the sentence.

   Jorge asked *about* the current financial condition *of* the store.

1. The noun or pronoun following a preposition is called the **object of the preposition.** A preposition and its object, called a **prepositional phrase,** may be used as a noun, an adjective, or an adverb. The object of a proposition must be in the objective case.

   Trisha sat between *him* and *me*.

2. Do not use superfluous prepositions.

   Where has he gone?

   NOT: Where has he gone *to*?

3. Do not omit necessary prepositions.

   Alex is interested *in* and excited *about* the trip.

   NOT: Alex is interested and excited about the trip.

4. Certain words are always followed by certain prepositions.

   Noah is angry *about* the mix-up. (Angry *about* or *at* something.)

   Noah is angry *with* me. (Angry *with* a person.)

   If you are unsure, look up the word in a dictionary or a reference manual.

5. Ending a sentence with a preposition is acceptable for emphasis. Short questions often end with prepositions.

   These are the questions I want answers *to*.

   Which files are you finished *with*?

Conjunctions

A conjunction is a word that connects words, phrases, or clauses.

1. A conjunction may be coordinate or subordinate. A *coordinate conjunction* connects words, phrases, or clauses of equal grammatical construction. A *subordinate conjunction* connects dependent words, phrases, or clauses to the main, or independent, clause.

   Ten applications have been received, *and* more are still coming in. (Coordinate)

   We have not received the desk, *although* we ordered it six weeks ago. (Subordinate)

2. *Correlative conjunctions* are a type of coordinating conjunctions used in pairs to connect two or more words, phrases, or clauses. They should immediately precede the words, phrases, or clauses that they connect, which should be parallel in form.

References

531

You may order *either* now or when our sales representative calls.

NOT: You may *either* order now or when our sales representative calls.
(Note that *now* and *when* are in parallel form; both are adverbs.)

3. Do not use prepositions such as *without, except,* and *like* to introduce a subordinate clause.

   The package looks as *though* it has been tampered with.

   NOT: The package looks *like* it has been tampered with.

SENTENCES AND PARAGRAPHS

A successful letter is made up of strong, well-constructed sentences and paragraphs.

Kinds of Sentences

A sentence must contain a subject and a verb (predicate) and must express a complete thought.

1. A **simple sentence** contains a subject and a predicate—one independent clause.

2. A **compound sentence** contains two or more independent clauses.

3. A **complex sentence** contains one independent clause and at least one dependent clause in either the subject or the predicate.

4. A **compound-complex sentence** contains two or more independent clauses and one or more dependent clauses.

Sentence Fragments

A group of words that does not express a complete thought is not a sentence. Occasionally such an incomplete thought may stand alone for emphasis. Experienced writers sometimes use this device—but sparingly. In business correspondence, this technique is generally limited to sales writing.

South Padre Island. *The* place to spend your vacation this summer.

Please check these figures carefully and return them to me as soon as you have finished.

NOT: Please check these figures carefully.

Returning them to me as soon as you have finished.

Run-On Sentences

A sentence containing two or more complete thoughts loosely strung together without proper punctuation is called a *run-on* sentence. The remedy for this sentence error is either to place each complete thought in a separate sentence or to retain the several thoughts in a single sentence by the use of proper subordination and punctuation.

RUN-ON: The meeting had to be canceled and the chairperson asked me to notify each of you and she regrets any inconvenience this cancellation may have caused you.

BETTER: The chairperson asked me to notify you that the meeting had to be canceled. She regrets any inconvenience this cancellation may have caused you.

Sentence Length

The length of the sentences in any written message is an important factor in catching and holding the reader's interest. Avoid monotony by varying sentence length. However, very long sentences are suitable for business letters only if they are used sparingly and if they are carefully constructed.

Avoid too many short words, too many short sentences, too many long words, too many long sentences. Avoid also too many similar sounds or too many sentences of similar construction.

Constructing Paragraphs

A paragraph is made up of one or more sentences that together make a single point or relate to one aspect of a central theme.

Topic Sentence

A paragraph should usually contain a topic sentence that summarizes the main idea of the paragraph. The topic sentence is usually at the beginning of the paragraph, but it may be at the end or in the body of the paragraph. In business letters made up of short paragraphs, the topic sentence may be only implied.

Transition

One paragraph should lead naturally into the next, to guide the reader from one central thought or point to the next. To achieve this continuity use transitional words or phrases, such as *however, therefore, for example, in addition, as a result.*

Paragraph Length

A paragraph may be of any length as long as it treats only one point or one aspect of the central thought. Business communications, particularly sales and advertising letters, tend to have fairly short paragraphs so as to keep the reader's interest. Technical communications often contain longer paragraphs.

References

PUNCTUATION

Period

The period is used at the end of a declarative sentence (one that makes a statement) and at the end of an imperative sentence (one that gives a command).

Half a million people are employed by this organization. (Declarative)

Take these books to the library. (Imperative)

Question Mark

The question mark is used at the end of an interrogative sentence (one that asks a question). Even if the question is part of a declarative statement, the question mark is used. Even though a question does not form a complete thought, it may be set off if it logically follows the preceding sentence.

How should we introduce our new product? On a television show? At a press conference?

Do not use a question mark at the end of a courteous request; use a period.

Will you please send us your latest price list.

Exclamation Point

The exclamation point is used at the end of an exclamatory sentence to indicate strong feeling, surprise, or enthusiasm. An exclamatory sentence is seldom appropriate in business messages except in sales and advertising letters.

Comma

A comma indicates a short break in thought within a sentence. Used properly, a comma ensures clarity by conveying the writer's exact meaning. Commas are not, however, to be used in a sentence simply because a speaker might normally pause. Rather, commas are to be used according to well-established rules. For a fuller discussion of comma usage, consult a current reference manual.

1. Separate the principal clauses of a compound sentence by a comma before the coordinate conjunction *(and, but, or)*.

   A new computer will be installed, and a computer programmer will be hired.

2. Set off nonrestrictive elements by commas. A nonrestrictive element is not essential to complete the meaning of the sentence.

   The annual report, *which is published in April,* **shows our financial condition.** (Nonrestrictive)

3. Do not use commas to set off a restrictive element, that is, one which limits the meaning of the sentence.

   The bank cannot honor checks *that are improperly signed.* (Restrictive)

4. Use a comma after an introductory participial phrase. (Avoid overuse of this construction in letters.)

   Having committed ourselves to this plan, we are not backing down now.

5. Use a comma after an introductory inverted phrase or clause.

   Because it was improperly signed, the check was not honored by the bank.

6. Parenthetical (or interrupting) words, phrases, and clauses should be set off by commas.

   We, *like all unions,* must protect the interests of our members. (Interrupting phrase)

   We cannot, *as you will agree,* make such an exception. (Interrupting clause)

7. Transitional words, phrases, and clauses should be set off by commas.

   We must, *therefore,* change our plans.

   Therefore, we must change our plans.

8. Set off appositives by commas. An appositive has the same meaning as the word or phrase it follows.

   Heather Frazee, *the new manager,* telephoned today.

9. A comma is used to set off a direct quotation from the rest of the sentence.

   The speaker said, *"I agree with your recommendation."*

10. Items in a series should be separated by commas. If each member of a series is connected by *and* or *or,* no comma is needed. If a comma is used within any item of a series, a semicolon separates the items.

    The chairs, desks, and tables were all refinished.

    Attending last week's conference in Williamsburg were David Rice, marketing director; Vicki Fuentos, advertising manager; and John Holmes, sales promotion manager.

Dash

A dash is used to indicate a stronger break in thought than is shown by a comma. The word or phrase enclosed in dashes is grammatically separate from the sentence and not necessary to the meaning.

1. A parenthetical expression or an appositive that already contains a comma may be set off by dashes.

   All large appliances—microwave ovens, ranges, refrigerators, washers, dryers—will be drastically reduced this weekend.

2. When an introductory word is only implied, a dash is used to set off a following word or phrase.

   New inventions are patented every month—hundreds of them.

Semicolon

The semicolon indicates a stronger break in thought than the comma.

1. Separate the principal clauses of a compound sentence by a semicolon when no connective is used.

   Meeting notices were sent yesterday; today the agenda was prepared.

2. When the principal clauses of a compound sentence are connected by a conjunctive adverb (such as *consequently, therefore, however*), use a semicolon.

   Budget requests were received late; *therefore,* **the preparation of the final budget was delayed.**

3. When either of the principal clauses in a compound sentence contains one or more commas, use a semicolon to separate the clauses if using a comma before the conjunction would cause the sentence to be misread.

   We ordered letterhead stationery, carbon packs, envelopes, and file guides; but plain paper, carbon paper, and file folders were sent to us instead. (The semicolon is necessary to prevent misreading.)

4. When *for example, that is, namely*, or a similar transitional expression links two independent clauses or introduces words, phrases, or clauses that are added almost as afterthoughts, use a semicolon before the expression and a comma after it.

   Amy K. Shelby is a leader in many professional organizations; for example, she is a member of the board of directors of the Medical Assistants Association and program chairperson of the Business and Professional Women's Club.

Colon

A colon is the strongest mark of punctuation within the sentence.

1. A colon introduces an explanation or an amplification following an independent clause.

   The organization has one objective: to satisfy its customers.

2. A formal listing or an enumeration is introduced by a colon.

   David's qualifications are these: honesty, dependability, and sincerity.

3. If the list or enumeration grammatically completes the sentence, omit the colon.

   David's qualifications are honesty, dependability, and sincerity.

4. A colon introduces a quotation of more than one sentence.

   Dr. Truemper said: "The fate of Velasco's chemical discharges will be determined by the judge. There are, however, two possible alternatives to the procedure now used."

5. A colon follows the salutation in a business letter unless open punctuation is being used.

6. A colon separates hours and minutes *(11:15 a.m.)*.

7. A colon separates the main title of a work from the subtitle *(Africa: Continent in Turmoil)*.

8. At the end of a letter, a colon may separate the dictator's initials from the transcriber's *(HWY:me)*.

Parentheses

Within a sentence, parentheses set off explanatory words, phrases, and clauses that are not essential to the meaning of the sentence. No punctuation is used preceding an opening parenthesis, but the appropriate punctuation follows the closing parenthesis. If the material enclosed in parentheses requires a question mark or an exclamation point, that punctuation should precede the closing parenthesis.

Sales have increased (about 20 percent) **despite the weather.**

He expected to stop overnight in Chicago (or was it Detroit?).

Brackets

Brackets are seldom used in business letters but are sometimes required in formal reports (1) to enclose material in a quotation that was not in the original; (2) to enclose *sic*, which indicates that an error in quoted material was in the original; (3) to enclose material within a parenthesized statement.

Quotation Marks

Quotation marks are used to set off direct quotations. A quotation within a quotation is set off by single quotation marks.

Apostrophe

The apostrophe is used to form the possessive of nouns. The apostrophe also has the following uses:

1. To indicate a missing letter or missing letters in a contraction *(can't, wouldn't)*.

2. To form the plural of letters, figures, and symbols, if the omission of the apostrophe would cause misreading.

3. To indicate the omission of the first part of a date *(class of '86)*.

4. As a single quotation mark.

References

The Quaker Oats Company. 1703 E. Voorhees Street, Danville, IL 61834-4006 (217) 443-3990

August 3, <YEAR>

Mrs. Heather Michaels
Berbaum Corporation
43 Brickyard Road
Fredricksburg, VA 22401

Dear Mrs. Michaels:

The modified-block style is the most frequently used letter style in business today.

The format of this letter style has the date line, complimentary closing, company name, and writer's signature and title beginning at the horizontal center. All other lines begin at the left margin (unless you wish to indent the paragraphs). Enclosed is a sample letter showing indented paragraphs.

The modified-block style usually uses standard (formerly called mixed) punctuation. This means that a colon is typed after the salutation and a comma after the complimentary closing, as illustrated in this letter. The enclosure notation below shows an acceptable style for specifying the items that are enclosed.

Please return the enclosed reply card if you would like to receive one of our Training Department's booklets on letter formats.

Sincerely yours,

QUAKER OATS COMPANY

Dennis R. Lowery

DRL/ism
Enclosures
1. Letter
2. Reply Card

The modified-block-style letter discussed here is the most frequently used letter style. (Courtesy of the Quaker Oats Company.)

KANSAS CITY ROYALS BASEBALL CLUB

February 25, <YEAR>

Mr. Larry Irons
Hutton, Irons & Hesser
Attorneys at Law
102 Ray Court
Hillsboro, TX 76645

Dear Mr. Irons

Subject: Block Letter Style

All lines begin at the left margin with a block-style letter, as shown here. This style has a neat, streamlined appearance and looks very modern. The primary appeal is that it is faster to keyboard than the modified-block style.

This letter also illustrates the open style of punctuation, which means that punctuation is omitted after the salutation and complimentary closing. Standard punctuation, however, may be used if you prefer.

When a subject line is used, it may be keyed as shown in this letter. The word Subject may be omitted, or the entire line may be typed in capital letters. Since the subject line is considered part of the body, it should be typed a double space above the body and a double space below the salutation. In a block-style letter, the subject line begins at the left margin.

The "c" notation below shows an acceptable style for indicating that copies of this letter are being sent to two persons.

Sincerely

Mary L. Carr
Public Relations Director

lk 3/hi&r25
c: Ralph Swanson
     Jim Barnett

P.O. BOX 419969, Kansas City, Missouri 64141-6969 • 816-921-8000 • http://www.kcroyals.com
1985 WORLD CHAMPIONS • 1980 AMERICAN LEAGUE CHAMPIONS • 1976-1977-1978-1984 AMERICAN LEAGUE WESTERN DIVISION CHAMPIONS

The block letter style illustrated here looks streamlined and modern. (Courtesy of Kansas City Royals.)

ILLIANA MEDICAL EQUIPMENT & SUPPLY
912 N. VERMILION
P.O. BOX 1307
DANVILLE, IL 61834-1307

February 25, <YEAR>

Mrs. Janet Payne, Director
Human Resources Department
United Samaritans Medical Center
812 North Logan Avenue
Danville, IL 61832

Dear Janet:

Congratulations on being named to the state of Illinois Occupational Skill Standards and Credentialing Council. I was pleased to read that the governor has chosen you as one of the nine members of this important council.

The development of a statewide system of industry-defined and recognized skill standards and credentials is an important step in the preparation of tomorrow's workforce. I know you will make a great contribution to this council. If any of us at Illiana Medical Equipment & Supply can help you and the other members of the council, please let me know.

Sincerely,

Steve Gulick
Steve Gulick
General Manager

df

PHONE: 217-442-0654 OR 800-252-6008
FAX (217) 442-0022
gu@soltec.net

This letter is illustrated on stationery that has a wider letterhead address. (Courtesy of Illiana Medical Equipment and Supply, Inc.)

CENTRAL STATES
DISTRIBUTION SERVICE
WAREHOUSING • DISTRIBUTION • PACKAGING

September 27, <YEAR>

Mrs. Adrianne Darzinikas
1502 Franklin Street
Rossville, IL 60963

Dear Adrianne:

Congratulations and welcome to the Central States team. We are happy that you are joining our team of friendly people.

The enclosed booklet, *Central States Distribution Service and You*, will answer many of the questions you have about your new job and your new company. The management team, employee programs and benefits, and various company activities are all explained in the booklet.

As an employee of Central States, you will have the opportunity to use your education and your skills. You—and your work—are important to the company and to our customers. We look forward to your starting to work with us.

Sincerely,

Herman Douglas
Herman Douglas
Human Resources Specialist

hsd:tj:378welc
Enclosure

3401 Lynch Creek Dr. • Danville, Illinois 61834   217 442-7302 • FAX 217 442-1115

The block letter style is illustrated in this example with an enclosure notation. (Courtesy of Central States Distribution Service.)

References   539

APPENDIX B: DICTATION TECHNIQUES

Some businesspeople use handheld, portable dictation equipment to record their ideas. By pushing a button, businesspeople can activate marker tones and have quick access to their notes. Some companies encourage their businesspeople to use call-in dictation centers. The dictation can then be transcribed and processed, faxed for review to the person who dictated it, signed, and sent anywhere in the world quickly.

Preparing to Dictate

To dictate a concise, unified message requires a good deal of practice and a working knowledge of the principles of effective communication. The following guidelines will help you prepare to dictate your message:

1. Know how to compose good business messages—follow the seven Cs of effective written communication.

2. Plan your dictation time. Select a quiet location and avoid interruptions to be more productive.

3. Gather all the information and resources you will need for your communication, including any correspondence you are answering (underline the points you will cover) and any enclosures. If you are writing a reply, reread the communication you are answering.

4. Clearly define the purpose of the communication to be dictated. Determine precisely the reaction you want from the reader, and keep that desired reaction uppermost in your mind.

5. Visualize your reader. A communication is always more effective if written with its specific audience in mind.

6. Prepare an outline, decide on the approach, and determine the order in which your facts and ideas should be presented.

7. Plan to dictate a rough draft if you are inexperienced at dictating or if the communication is an especially long or difficult one. If a key phrase or the right way of saying something pops into mind as you plan your dictation, jot it down right then.

8. Before you begin dictating, make certain you know how your recorder operates. Practice speaking into the machine to test the clarity and volume of your voice. In most instances, it is advisable to keep the microphone 2 to 3 inches from your mouth.

Dictating the Message

Before you begin to dictate, you should anticipate what information the transcriptionist will need to produce each document quickly and efficiently. Follow these guidelines when dictating the message:

1. Start your dictation by giving your name, department, and date of recording.

2. Follow with:

    a. The type of document you are dictating—a letter, memo, report, other.

b. Any specific letterhead, form, or paper to be used.

   c. Letter style and punctuation style, if you have a preference.

   d. Your desire for a final copy or rough draft.

   e. The file name to which you want the document stored, if any.

   f. The priority assigned for the transcribed dictation—rush items, 24 hours.

3. Dictate the complete inside address and salutation—spell the names of people and places.

4. Dictate complete phrases or thoughts, and pause at natural points.

5. Indicate special punctuation marks, paragraph breaks, and the placement of tabulations and lists.

6. Spell proper names, technical terms, and similar-sounding words. Say the word first and then spell it.

7. Give corrections clearly and as soon as you are aware of the error.

8. Dictate the closing for a letter, including the complimentary closing and enclosure.

Dictating is a skill that can be developed by applying these guidelines. Developing these skills will enable you and the transcriptionist to produce documents in a most efficient manner. Use the "Dictation Checklist I" below as you prepare to dictate. Then use "Dictation Checklist II" to evaluate your procedures and techniques. The ability to dictate correspondence effectively will become increasingly important as voice-activated computers become more common.

✔ DICTATION CHECKLIST I

Evaluate Your Readiness for Dictation by Reviewing the Following Items to Prepare to Dictate:

- Have I identified the appropriate document (letter, memo, report) style and punctuation style? _____

- Did I use a positive tone? _____

- Did I use the correct approach to writing? _____

- Did I plan my dictation time well? _____

- Did I gather all the information needed before dictating? _____

- Did I clearly define the purpose of the communication? _____

- Did I visualize the reader? _____

- Did I prepare an outline? _____

- Do I know how the recorder operates? _____

Dictation Techniques

✔ DICTATION CHECKLIST II

Evaluate Your Dictating Techniques by Reviewing the Following Items:

- Did I identify the communication as a letter, memo, report, etc.? _____

- Did I specify the letterhead, form, or paper to be used? _____

- Did I indicate the date of dictation? _____

- Did I indicate the letter style and punctuation style preferred? _____

- Did I note whether I wanted a final copy or rough draft? _____

- Did I indicate any documents that were rush documents? _____

- Did I dictate phrases or thoughts, and pause at natural points? _____

- Did I dictate the complete inside address and salutation? _____

- Did I give any special instructions, such as for saving or filing the document? _____

- Did I give corrections clearly and as soon as I was aware of an error? _____

- Did I spell proper names, cities, and any unusual technical terms? _____

- Did I speak naturally, yet distinctly and slowly? _____

- Did I indicate the complimentary closing and any enclosures or copies? _____

INDEX

A

Abbreviations
  in addresses, 172
  in e-mail, 141
Abridged dictionary, 25
Acceptance letters
  adjustment, 273–276
  extending credit, 341–342
  job offer, 517
  order messages, 332–338
  remittances, 235–236, 349
Accurate communication, 311
Acknowledgment forms, 332
Acknowledgments, 232–236
  of gifts and favors, 235
  of information or material, 234–235
  of order messages, 332–338
  of referral letters, 237
  of remittances, 235–236, 349
  stopgap letters, 233–234
  of transmittal letters, 237
Action, in persuasive approach, 115
Active listening, 7
  benefits of, 87
  defining, 83
  environmental preparation for, 93
  mental preparation for, 93
  physical preparation for, 92–93
  process of, 84–87
Active voice, 14–15, 54–55, 69
Adaptation
  of sales letters, 303
  of sayings, in sales letter openings, 307–308
Address books, e-mail, 142–143
Addressee
  address of, 171–173
  envelope format, 183–185
  job title of, 171
  multiple, 173
  name of, 170
Adjustment letters, 268, 273–280
  form letters for, 280
  letters compromising on adjustments, 278–279
  letters denying adjustments, 276–278
  letters granting adjustments, 273–276
  See also Claim letters
Advertisements, in job search, 470, 499
Agendas, 446–450
  components, 448
  distribution, 450
  format of, 448–450
Agreement, subject-verb, 56

AIDA plan, 114–116, 305
Altruism appeal, 300
America Online (AOL), 139
American Psychological Association (APA) documentation style, 419–420
American Society of Corporate Secretaries, 451
Analytical reports, 371–372
and, 62
Anderson, Poul, 410
Anecdotes, in sales letter openings, 308–309
Anger, 204
Announcements, 214
Antecedents, 69–70
Antonyms, 25–26, 33
Apologies, 202
Appeals to reader
  collection letter, 348
  persuasive request, 299–301
  sales letter, 310–311
  See also Attention of reader
Appendix, 428–429
Application for employment
  completing, 484–487
  cover letters, 498–505
Application letters. *See* Cover letters, employment
Appointment requests
  confirming oral appointments, 231
  guidelines for writing, 242
  nature of, 239–240
Appreciation, 276
Appropriate words, 33
Arguing, 203–204
Assumptions, as barrier to listening, 91
Attachment notation, 162
Attachments, e-mail, 142
Attendance reporting forms, 163
Attention lines
  business letter, 173–174
  envelope, 185
Attention of reader
  cover letter, 500–502
  in persuasive approach, 114–115
  in sales letter openings, 306
  See also Appeals to reader
Audience
  identifying, 106–107
  impact of written communication on, 11–13
Audioconferencing, 445
Axtell, Roger, 90

B

Background information, 106–107, 431

"Bad news" situations
  denying adjustments, 276–278
  goodwill in, 206–208
  refusing credit, 343–344
  refusing orders, 335, 337–338
Balance, 14, 68
Bar graphs, 376
Behavioral interviews, 510
Berra, Yogi, 466
Bias-free words, 35–36
Biases, as barrier to listening, 91
Bibliography, formal report, 429, 430, 431
Blame, 105, 197
Blind advertisements, 499
Block style, 179–181
Body
  business letter, 175–176
  formal report, 422–425
  memo, 161–162, 365–366
  persuasive request, 301–302
  press release, 394
  sales letter to individual, 309–313
Body language, 85, 87, 88–90
Bragging, 201
Brainstorming, 3, 133, 145
Brief narrative reports, 373
Brochure, introducing in sales letter, 313
Budget needs, proposal, 431–432
Buffer paragraphs, 111, 249, 277, 279, 337–338
Business letters
  continuation pages, 182–183
  effect on reader, 11–13
  endings, 59–60, 176–179
  folding, 185–186
  parts of, 167–179
  punctuation of, 181
  seven Cs of, 13–17
  style of, 179–181
  techniques for writing, 10–11
  unified message in, 11, 14, 66
  See also specific types
Buying inquiries
  guidelines for writing, 242–244
  nature of, 242

C

Campaign sales series, 319
Career centers, 470
Cartoons, 402
Cause-and-effect pattern, 412–413
Censorship, 3, 133
Central selling point (CSP), 305, 499
Certified mail, 10
Charts, in reports, 433–434
Chicago Manual of Style, The, 420
Chronological pattern, 413, 452

Index 543

Chronological résumé, 473–474
Churchill, Winston, 362
Claim letters, 266–272
　general guidelines, 267–269
　persuasive, 271–272
　routine, 270–271
　value of complaints, 266–267
　See also Adjustment letters
Clarke, Arthur C., 134
Classified advertisements, 470, 499
Clauses, 49
　dependent, 49–51, 62–63
　independent, 49, 50–51
Clear communication, 13–15
Clichés, 32, 401
Closed (directed) questions, 512
Closing
　business letter, 59–60, 176–179
　cover letter, 505
　inquiry, 246–247, 250–251
　interview, 512
　memo, 366
　press release, 394–396
　request, 246–247, 250–251, 302
　sales letter to individual, 314
Coherence, 13, 69–70
Collaboration software, 148
Collaborative approach, 6, 361
Collection messages, 344–349
　objectives, 345
　series, 345–349
Colors, newsletter, 402
Combination résumé, 476
Commas
　misplaced, 57–58
　omission of, 57
　overuse of, 57
Communication skills
　basics of effective, 8–9
　changing workplace
　　environment, 5–6
　developing, 6–7
　importance of, 4–5
　purposes of, 7
　types of, 7–8
Compare-and-contrast pattern, 14, 411
Competence, communication skills and, 4
Complaints
　value of, 266–267
　See also Claim letters
Complete communication, 15
Complex information, 9
Complex sentences, 50
Complex words and phrases, 12, 27–28
Complimentary closing, 176–177
Compound-complex sentences, 50–51
Compound sentences, 12, 50
Compromises, 197

CompuServe, 139
Computers
　applications software, 134–135, 145–147. See also Word processing programs
　history, 134–135
　laptop, 138
　outlining on, 145–146
　See also Internet; Word processing programs
Concentration, lack of, 90–91
Concise communication, 16, 28–30, 58–60
Conclusions section, of formal report, 425–426
Concrete words, 13
Condescending tone, 201
Condolence messages, 216
Confidentiality, 10, 140
Conflict management, 197
Congratulations messages, 210–211
Conjunctions, coordinating, 12, 52
Connectives, 64–65
Connotative meanings, 24–25
　negative, 38–39
　positive, 37–38
Considerate communication, 13
Consistent communication, 14, 17
Constituents, 292
Constructive criticism, 327
Contact information
　in letters to editors, 298
　in letters to lawmakers, 293
　in press releases, 393
Content, 106–116
　negative communications, 107, 110–113
　persuasive communications, 107, 114–116
　positive communications, 107–110
Continuation pages, 182–183
Conversational words, 31, 51
Cooperative approach, 6, 361
Coordinating conjunctions, 12, 52
Copies
　of adjustment letters, 269
　copy notation, 162, 178
Corel® WordPerfect, 145
Correct communication, 16, 36, 37
Cost, in sales letters, 303
Courteous communication, 13, 60, 294
Courtesy titles, 51, 160, 170, 174, 177, 178, 293
Cover letters, 251–254
　employment, 498–505
　　guidelines for effective, 500–501
　　preparation for writing, 498–500
　　purposes, 498
　form letters, 251–253
　guidelines for writing, 253–254
　as sales letters, 318

Covey, Stephen R., 5, 48, 198
Credibility, 201
Credit letters, 339–344
　extending credit, 341–342
　refusing credit, 343–344
　requesting credit, 339–341
Credit rating
　acknowledgment of poor, 335
　evaluating, 341
　four Cs of credit, 341
Credit references, 340
Credit-refusal letter, 343–344
Criticism, 203–204, 327
Cultural diversity, 8–9
　body language and, 88–90
　business cards, 200
　communication styles, 201
　computer software and, 136
　courtesy titles, 51, 178
　credit purchases while traveling, 342
　dates, 169
　forming bonds, 109
　gender gap, 91
　gestures, 36
　gifts, 300
　idioms, 231
　language barriers, 445
　mailing addresses, 171, 173
　negative communications, 113
　punctuality, 241
　response to invitation, 212
　rewards of, 81
　saving face, 7
　24-hour clock, 239
　word meanings, 306, 374
　yes versus no answers, 113, 278
Customer service, 229
Customization, of sales letters, 303

D

Database applications, 146–147
Date line
　business letter, 169–170
　memo, 161
　press release, 393
Deadlines, 298, 465
Dealers
　orders for products sold through, 335
　sales letters to, 315–317
Decision making, 265
Delay in shipment, acknowledgment of, 334
Denotative meanings, 24–25
Dependent clauses, 49–51, 62–63
DePree, Max, 6, 9, 17
Desire, in persuasive approach, 115
Desktop publishing, 403
Dictionary, 25–26
Digital still/video cameras, 138
Diplomacy, 197

Direct approach, 109–110
  for accepting job offer, 517
  in extending credit, 341–342
  for memos, 367
  for reports, 410
  for routine acknowledgments, 335–336
Direct sales letters, 303
Directness, 14
Discontinued items, acknowledgment of, 334
Discounts, in sales letter openings, 306
Discriminatory language, 35
Discussion lists, e-mail, 143
Distractions, 92
Distribution
  agenda, 450
  memo, 159–160
  minutes, 456
  press release, 396
Diversity. *See* Cultural diversity
Docking station, 137
Documenting sources, 409, 419–421
  citations
    APA style, 419–420
    Chicago style, 420
    electronic citations, 418, 421
    MLA style, 419
  endnotes, 419, 420
  footnotes, 419, 420
  plagiarism and, 409
Domain name, 140
Doublet, 29
Doubt, 203
Draft, rough, 119–121
Dress, for interviews, 509

E

E-mail, 139–143
  address books, 142–143
  attachments, 142
  etiquette rules, 140–141
  filters, 142
  formatting, 164
  mailbox feature, 142
E-mail client, 140
Editing, 148, 149
Editors, letters to, 297–298
  characteristics of good, 297
  guidelines for writing, 298
Education
  in résumé, 473, 480
  in self-appraisal inventory, 468
Electronic citations, 418, 421
Electronic meetings, 443, 445
Electronic résumés, 482–483
Emoticons, 141
Emotional appeal, 310–311
Emphasis, methods of, 67–69
Employment agencies, 470
Employment application
  completing, 484–487
  cover letters, 498–505

Enclosure
  introducing in sales letter, 313
  notation concerning, 162, 178
Encrypting, 331–332
Endnotes, 419, 420
Endorsements by users, 312
English language
  grammatically correct, 55–57
  as international business language, 5–6
  as second language, 9
  Standard American English, 23
Enumeration pattern, 413
Envelopes
  addressing, 183–185
  folding messages for, 185–186
Errors, 16
  on incoming correspondence, 231
  taking responsibility for, 148–150
Ethics, 8, 389
Etiquette
  business, 155
  e-mail, 140–141
Exaggeration, 201–202
Excessive humility, 202
Executive summaries, 380–381, 428
Experience
  in résumé, 472–473, 480
  in self-appraisal inventory, 467–468
External goodwill letters, 198
External newsletters, 398
Eye contact, 88

F

Fables, in sales letter openings, 308–309
Facial expressions, 85
Facts, documenting, 401
Fair communication, 297
Favors, acknowledging, 235
Fax machines, 135–136, 164, 331
Federal Express (FedEx), 172
Feedback, in active listening, 86–87
Feelings, in active listening, 85, 87
Fields, database, 147
Fill-in forms, 373
Filler material, 400
Filters, e-mail, 142
Findings section, of formal report, 424–425
First draft, 119–121
First order, acknowledgment of, 334
Five Ws and one H questions, 15, 329, 393–394, 411–412, 452
Flame war, 141
Flattery, 202
FOB destination, 331
FOB shipping point, 331
Folding business messages, 185–186
Follow-up letters
  job search, 515–517
  for letters to lawmakers, 295, 296
  routine, 237–238

Footnotes, 419, 420
Ford, Gerald R., 4
Form(s)/form letters. *See* Preprinted forms
Formal invitations, 212
Formal language, 51
Formal meetings, 444
Formal minutes, 454–455
Formal reports, 370, 416–429
  documenting sources, 419–421
  format of, 423–430
  gathering information, 417–421
  outlines for, 416–417
  parts of, 421–430
Formatting, 154–187
  agendas, 448–450
  business letter, 167–183
  e-mail, 164
  envelope, 183–186
  fax messages, 164
  formal report, 423–430
  informal notes, 164
  meeting notices, 446
  memo-letters, 167
  memos, 156–162, 363, 367
  message-reply forms, 165–166
  minutes, 452–455
    formal, 454–455
    informal, 452–454
  newsletters, 402–403
  outline, 416–417
  preprinted forms, 163–164, 165–166
  press releases, 392–396, 397
  résumé, 482
Fragments, sentence, 52–54
Franklin, Benjamin, 344, 444
Freewriting, 3
Friendliness, 13, 54
Full-block style, 179–181
Functional résumé, 475–476

G

Gender-neutral terms, 35–36, 174
General requests
  guidelines for writing, 242–244
  nature of, 242
Generalization, 68
Generic filler material, 400
Gestures, 36
Get well wishes, 215
Gibaldi, Joseph, 419
Gifts
  acknowledging, 235
  cultural diversity and, 300
Global diversity. *See* Cultural diversity
Goals
  career, 468–469
  press release, 391
Good-news approach. *See* Direct approach

Index   545

Goodwill, 5, 12–13, 105, 229
Goodwill messages, 196–218
  announcements, 214
  "bad news" situations, 206–208
  condolence, 216
  congratulations, 210–211
  get well, 215
  invitations, 212–214
  maintaining/reactivating business, 216–217
  order acknowledgments, 335, 336
  principles of, 198–205, 217
  promptness in sending, 232
  service attitude in, 205–208
  sympathy, 216
  thank-you, 210, 235, 515–516
  types of, 198
  welcome, 215
Grammar checker, 145
Graphics
  in newsletters, 402
  photographs, 402, 434
  for quantitative information, 376
  in reports, 432–434
Group interviews, 510
Grove, Andrew S., 104
Guarantees, 312
Gushiness, 202

H
Halley, Walter, Jr., 498
Heading
  business letter, 167–170
  e-mail, 140
  memo, 159–161
  résumé, 471–472
Headlines, press release, 393
Hearing, listening versus, 83–84
High-pressure selling, 313
Homonyms, 33
Homophones, 33
Honesty, 197
"Hook", press release, 391–392
Hostility, 204
Humanitarianism appeal, 300
Humility, 202

I
Illustrations, 434
Inclusive language, 35–36, 81
Incomplete orders, acknowledgment of, 334
Independent clauses, 49, 50–51
Indifference, 203
Indirect approach, 110–113
  for denying adjustments, 276–278
  for memos, 367–368
  for refusing credit, 343–344
  for refusing job offers, 517
  for refusing orders, 335, 337–338
  for reports, 410
  for special acknowledgments, 336, 337–338

Indirect sales letters, 303–304
Individual responsibility appeal, 300
Individuals, sales letters to, 304–315
Informal invitations, 213
Informal meetings, 444
Informal minutes, 452–454
Informal notes, 164
Informal reports, 370
Informal tone, 54
Information highway, 139
Information letters, 232
Informational reports, 371–372, 374
Inquiry letters, 239–254
  answering *no* to, 247–251
  answering *yes* to, 245–247
  buying inquiries, 242–244
  form replies to, 251–254
  nature of, 239
  replies as sales letters, 246, 317–318
Inside address, business letter, 170–174
Integrated circuits, 135
Integrity, communication skills and, 5
Interest, in persuasive approach, 115
Internal communications, 238–239
  e-mail, 139–143, 164
  envelopes, 185
  informal notes, 164
  memo reports, 370–381
  memos, 156–162, 363–369
  newsletters, 398–399
  See also Preprinted forms; Reports
Internal goodwill letters, 198
Internet, 135, 139–143
  documenting information from, 418, 421
  e-mail, 139–143, 164
  information services and, 139
  in job search, 470
  order placement via, 331–332
Internet Service Provider (ISP), 139, 140
Interpreting meanings, 26
Interviews, 506–514
  follow-up letters, 515–517
  interview process, 511–512
  preparing for, 506–509
  questions, 507–509, 511–512
  self-evaluation after, 514
  traits that influence interviewers, 512–513
  types of, 510
Introduction
  formal report, 422–424
  proposal, 431
Invitations, 212–214
  formal, 212
  informal, 213
  replies to, 212, 213–214
Invited sales letters, 246, 317–318

Invoices, as order acknowledgments, 333
Irritation, 203

J
Jargon, 34–35, 392
Job search
  cover letter, 498–505
  employment application, 484–487, 498–505
  follow-up letters, 515–517
  interviews, 506–514
  networking, 469–470
  portfolio, 487–488
  resignation letters, 518–519
  résumé, 471–483
  self-appraisal inventory, 466–469, 507
Job titles, 171, 175, 293
Johnson, Nancy M., 381
Journalist questions, 15, 329, 393–394, 411–412, 452
Journalistic pattern, 411–412

K
Kennedy, Joyce Lain, 482
Keywords, in scannable résumés, 481–482
Kilbey, Jack, 135
Kipling, Rudyard, 208

L
Laptop computers, 138
Large orders, acknowledgment of, 334
Last call for payment, 348–349
Lawmakers, letters to, 292–296
  characteristics of good, 293–295
  types, 295–296
Lead paragraph, press release, 393–394
Leadership styles, 497
Legislative letters, 295
Length
  of paragraphs, 66–67, 68, 176
  of sentences, 61–63
Letter or memo of authorization (transmittal), 427–428
Letter reports, 414–415
Letterhead, 167–168
Libel, 8
Limitations section, of formal report, 423
Line graphs, 376
Listening skills, 80–94
  active listening, 7, 83, 84–87, 92–94
  barriers to effective listening, 90–92
  hearing versus listening, 83–84
  importance of, 82–84
  nonverbal communication, 7, 85, 87–90
Listing pattern, 413

Local Area Networks (LANs), 135
Lotus cc:Mail®, 140
Lotus Notes®, 135, 147–148

M

Mail lists, e-mail, 143
Mail-order forms, 328
Mail server, 140
Mailbox feature, e-mail, 142
Main clauses, 49, 50–51
Main point, 376
Markup, emphasizing, 316
Meanings
  in active listening, 85
  of words. *See* Word meanings
Mechanical techniques, emphasis through, 68–69
Meetings, 442–457
  agendas, 446–450
  minutes, 451–457
  notices, 445–446, 447
  types, 444–445
Memo(s), 156–162, 363–369
  approaches to writing, 367–368
  format, 156–162, 363, 367
  parts of, 159–162, 364–367
  planning, 364
  purposes of, 363–364
  signing, 162
  tone of, 368–369
  types, 156–159
Memo-letters, 167, 427–428
Memo reports, 370–381
  checklist for, 376
  functions of, 371–372
  gathering information for, 374
  making recommendations in, 376
  nature of, 370–371
  one-page, 380–381
  organizing information for, 374–376
  preparing sample, 377–380
  types of, 373–374
Message
  unified, 10, 14, 66
  See also Body
Message-reply forms, 165–166
Methodology section, of formal report, 424
Microsoft® Excel, 135
Microsoft® Internet Explorer, 139
Microsoft® Outlook, 140, 147–148
Microsoft® PowerPoint, 145, 147
Microsoft® Word, 26, 143–146
Microsoft® Office, 143, 145
Minutes, 451–457
  correction, 456–457
  distribution, 456
  format of
    formal, 454–455
    informal, 452–454
  organization, 452

Minutes summary, 453, 454
Misused words, 34
Mixed punctuation, 181
MLA *Handbook for Writers of Research Papers* (Gibaldi), 419
Modem, 139
Modern Language Association (MLA) documentation style, 419
Modified-block style, 179
Modifiers, misplaced, 69
Money-back guarantees, 312
Moran, Richard A., 364
Mother Teresa, 24
Motions, 455
Multiple addressees, 173

N

Negative communications, 107, 110–113, 203
Negative detail pattern, 413
Negative refusal, 249
Negative words, 38–39
Netscape Navigator®, 139
Networking, 469–470
News releases. *See* Press releases
Newsletters, 398–403
  don'ts, 399–401
  do's, 401
  format of, 402–403
  guidelines for writing, 398–399
Nondirected (open-ended) questions, 511–512
Nonverbal communication, 7, 85, 87–90
  body language, 85, 87, 88–90
  cultural diversity, 36, 88–90
  eye contact, 88
  tone of voice, 85, 88
Notation
  copy, 178
  enclosure, 178
  envelope, 184–185
Note taking, 418
Notes (Chicago style), 419, 420
Notices, meeting, 445–446, 447

O

Objectives
  career, 472
  collection message, 345
Obvious statements, 59–60
Occupational Outlook Handbook, 468–469
On-site interviews, 510
One-on-one interviews, 510
One-page reports, 380–381
Online shopping, 331–332
Open-ended (nondirected) questions, 511–512
Open punctuation, 181
Opening
  business letter, 170–175
  cover letter, 500–502

  interview, 511
  memo, 364–365
  persuasive request, 299–301
  press release, 393–394
  sales letters to individual, 305–309
Optimistic communication, 302
Oral communication, 7, 104, 231
Order acknowledgments, 332–338
  form replies, 332–333
  refusing orders, 335, 337–338
  routine, 335–336
  situations requiring, 334–335
  special, 336–338
Order forms, 328
Order messages, 328–338
  acknowledging, 332–338
  contents of, 328–330
  types, 328–332
Ordinal endings, 171
Organizational name, in closing, 177
Organizational patterns, 411–413
  cause-and-effect pattern, 412–413
  compare-and-contrast pattern, 14, 411
  journalistic pattern, 411–412
  other patterns, 413
Outlines, 47, 120
  on computer, 145–146
  formal report, 416–417
  memo report, 374
Overused expressions, 32

P

Parables, in sales letter openings, 308–309
Paragraphs, 65–70
  buffer, 111, 249, 277, 279, 337–338
  business letter, 176
  closing, 67
  coherence and, 69–70
  emphasis and, 67–69
  length of, 66–67, 68, 176
  opening, 67, 69
  unity of, 66
Parallel construction, 56–57
Paraphrasing, in active listening, 85
Parliamentary procedure, 444
Participial phrase, 14
Passive voice, 15, 54–55, 69
Past tense, in minutes, 452
Payment forms, 330
Performance facts, 312
Periodic reports, 373–374
Personal computer (PC), 135
  See also Computers
Personal digital assistants (PDAs), 103, 135, 137, 148
Personal experience appeal, 301
Personal information applications, 147–148
Persuasive approach, 107, 114–116, 290–319

Index 547

claim letters, 271–272
letters to editors, 297–298
letters to lawmakers, 292–296
for memos, 368
reports, 410
requests, 299–302
sales letters, 303–319
Photocell, 136
Photographs, 402, 434
Phrase, 50
complex, 27–28
participial, 14
trite, 14, 31
Pie graphs, 376
Plagiarism, 409
Planning, 10, 102–121
audience for communication, 106–107
content of communication, 106–116
memo, 364
press release, 390–391
purpose of communication, 105–106
rough draft, 119–121
of sales letters to individuals, 304–305
written plan, 116–118
Portfolios, employment, 487–488
Position, emphasis through, 67–68
Positive communications, 107–110
goodwill messages, 198–205
inquiry and request letters, 245–251
Positive words, 37–38, 61
Post-it® notes, 164
Post office box number, 172
Postal cards, for order acknowledgments, 332, 333
Postscript, 178–179
Prejudice, as barrier to listening, 91
Preliminary interviews, 510
Preprinted forms
for adjustment, 280
attendance reporting, 163
cover letters, 251–254
credit extension, 342
for inquiry and request letters, 251–254
mail-order forms, 328
memo, 158–159
memo-letters, 167
memo reports, 373–374
message-reply, 165–166
order acknowledgments, 332–333
routing, 163
service request, 163
supply request, 163
telephone message, 163
Presentational applications, 145, 147
Press releases, 390–397
distributing, 396

format of, 392–396, 397
guidelines for writing, 391–392
planning, 390–391
Prewriting activities
brainstorming, 3, 133, 145
outlines, 47, 145–146
visualization, 47
Primary sources, 418
Printers, 138
Problem solving, 291
Procedures section, of formal report, 423
Prodigy, 139
Product
analysis in terms of prospects, 305
description of, in sales letter, 311
Programming languages, 134–135
Programs, computer, 134–135, 145–147
See also Word processing programs
Progress/status reports, 373
Promises, 202, 231
Promotion letters. *See* Sales letters
Promptness, importance of, 232, 267, 509
Pronoun pairs, 35
Proof, of communication, 10
Proofreading, 148, 149–150, 232, 401
Proportion, emphasis through, 68
Proposals, 430–432
Proposed plan, 431
Prospects
analyzing, 304
lists of, 304–305
product analysis in terms of, 305
Pseudohomophones, 33
Publication Manual of the American Psychological Association, 420
Punctuation, 57–58
of business letters, 181
e-mail, 141
Purpose of communication, 7, 105–106, 422–423

Q

Questions
closed (directed), 512
five Ws and one H, 15, 329, 393–394, 411–412, 452
interview, 507–509, 511–512
journalist, 15, 329, 393–394, 411–412, 452
open-ended (nondirected), 511–512
in sales letter openings, 307

R

Rapport, in interview process, 511
Rational appeal, 310–311
Rational communication, 294, 297
Reactivating business letters, 216–217

Readability, résumé, 478
Reader-benefit appeal, 300
Reader surveys, 402
Recipient notations, 185
Recommendations section, of formal report, 425–426
Redundant words, 29
Reference initials, 162, 177
Reference line, memo, 162
Reference source errors, 16
References
credit, 340
employment, 480, 483, 518
References list (APA style), 419–420, 429
Referral letters, 237
Refusal letters
adjustment, 276–278
credit refusal, 343–344
job offer, 517
order refusal, 335, 337–338
Registered mail, 10
Release statement, 393
Reminders for payment due
impersonal, 346
personal, 346–347
Remittances, acknowledging, 235–236, 349
Repetition, emphasis through, 68
Repetitiveness, 58–59
Replies, to invitations, 212, 213–214
Reports, 408–435
approaches to writing, 410
formal, 370, 416–429
documenting sources, 419–421
gathering information, 417–421
outlines for, 416–417
parts of, 421–430
guidelines for writing, 414
letter reports, 414–415
organizational patterns, 411–413
types of business, 370–372
visuals in, 432–434
See also Memo reports
Request for approval or authorization, 432
Request for explanation, 347
Request for Proposal (RFP), 431
Request letters, 239–251
answering *no* to, 247–251
answering *yes* to, 245–247
appointment requests, 239–240, 242
form replies to, 251–254
general requests, 242–244
guidelines for writing, 242
letters to editors, 297–298
letters to lawmakers, 292–296
nature of, 239
persuasive requests, 299–302
reservation requests, 241–242
Research reports, 417–421

documenting information for, 419–421
gathering information for, 417–421
Reservation requests
  guidelines for writing, 242
  nature of, 241–242
Resignation letters, 518–519
Respect, in goodwill messages, 200–204
Résumé, 471–483
  caveats, 480
  electronic, 482–483
  parts of, 471–473
  references, 480, 483
  reviewing, 476–479, 509
  scannable, 480–482
  styles of, 473–476
Return address, business letter, 167–168
Robert's Rules of Order, 444
Rough draft, 119–121
Routine correspondence
  acknowledgments, 232–236, 335–336
  claim letters, 270–271
  evaluating, 254–255
  follow-up correspondence, 237–238
  handling, 230–232
  improving, 231–232
  information letters, 232
  internal communications, 238–239
  memos. *See* Memo(s)
  preparing, 232–239
  referral letters, 237
  signing, 230–231
  transmittal letters, 237
  See also Inquiry letters; Request letters
Routing forms, 163
R.S.V.P., 212
Run-on sentences, 52

S

Sales letters, 303–319
  cover letters as, 318
  to dealers, 315–317
  direct, 303
  indirect, 303–304
  to individuals, 304–315
  principles of writing, 304
  replies to inquiries as, 246, 317–318
  reselling in order acknowledgment letters, 336
  series of, 319
Salutation, business letter, 174–175
Sample offers, 312
Sarcasm, 203–204
Scannable résumés, 480–482
Scanners, 136
Scope section, of formal report, 423
Screening interviews, 510

Secondary sources, 417–418
Seconding motions, 455
Section designation, 171–172
Secure Electronic Transactions (SET), 332
Selective listening, 92
Selective targeting, in sales letters, 303
Self-appraisal inventory, 466–469, 507
Semantics, 24–26
Sentence, 48–65
  components of, 49–50
  conversational language in, 51
  guidelines for writing effective, 51–65
  types of, 11–12, 50–51
Sentence fragment, 52–54
Sentence structure, 11–12, 48–51, 63
  components of sentences, 49–50
  emphasis through, 68
  types of sentences, 50–51
Series of letters
  collection, 345–349
  sales promotion, 319
Service attitude, 205–208
Service letters, 296
Service request forms, 163
Shipment instructions, 330–331
Signatures
  on business letters, 177
    letters to lawmakers, 294
    routine letters, 230–231
    of self, 230–231
    signing for employer, 231
  on internal communications, 238–239
  on memos, 162
Simple sentence, 11–12, 50
Simple words, 27–28
Sincere communication
  goodwill messages, 200–204, 208
  sales letter, 311
Skills résumé, 475–476
Slander, 8
Solicited cover letters, 499–501
Solicited sales letters, 246, 317–318
Sources, documenting. *See* Documenting sources
Special features, in sales letter openings, 306
Special mailing notations, 185
Specific instance pattern, 413
Specific words, 36–37, 38
Spell-check program, 26, 144
Spelling, 232
Spreadsheet applications, 135, 146
Staffing needs, proposal, 431–432
Standard American English, 23
Standard punctuation, 181
Standardized outlines, memo report, 374

Statement of account, 345
Status/progress reports, 373
Stereotypes, 35, 81
Stevenson, R. L., 292
Stopgap letters, 233–234
Street address, 171–173
Stress interviews, 510
Stress management, 465
Subject line
  business letter, 175–176
  e-mail, 140
  memo, 161
Subject of sentence, 49, 50–51
Subject-verb agreement, 56
Subordinate clauses, 49–51, 62–63
Summary
  career, 472
  executive, 380–381, 428
  minutes, 453, 454
Supply request forms, 163
Surveys, reader, 402
Sympathy messages, 216
Synonyms, 25–26, 33

T

Table of contents, of formal report, 427
Tables
  database, 147
  in reports, 432, 433
Tasteful communication, 297
Team building, 6, 361
Technical vocabulary, 34–35, 392
Technology
  advances in, 5–6
  See also Computers; Fax machines; Scanners
Telecommuting, 443
Teleconferencing, 443
Telephone calls, 10
  order placement via, 331
  phone interviews, 510
  telephone message forms, 163
  voice mail, 137–138
Templates
  memo, 158
  newsletter, 403
  press release, 397
Thank-you messages, 210, 235, 515–516
Thesaurus, 25–26, 144
Threads, e-mail, 141
Tickler files, 231, 237
Time and timing
  chronological organizational pattern, 413, 452
  cultural attitudes toward, 239, 241
  of letters to editors, 298
  of letters to lawmakers, 294
  of price discussion in sales letter, 313
  of response to sales letter, 311–312

Index 549

Time management, 103, 465
Time wasters/time savers, 30
Title page, of formal report, 426
Titles
  courtesy, 51, 160, 170, 174, 177, 178, 293
  diversity of use, 51, 178
  job, 171, 175, 293
  newsletter, 401
Tone
  of memo, 368–369
  of message, 12, 111
    negative, 38–39
    positive, 37–38, 61, 198–205
  of voice, 85, 88
Topic sentence, 66
Total quality management (TQM), 6
Traits in interview, 512–513
Transistors, 134
Transitional words and phrases, 64–65, 69
Translation, 10
Transmittal letters
  acknowledgment of, 237
  form replies to inquiries and requests, 251–254
  formal report, 427–428
Trial offers, 312
Trite expressions, 14, 31
Trump, Matthew, 230
Trust, 54
Turnover, emphasizing, 316
Typeface
  newsletter, 400
  résumé, 482, 483
Typographical errors, 16

U

Unabridged dictionary, 25
Unclear orders, acknowledgment of, 334
Unified message, 10, 14, 66
United Parcel Service (UPS), 172
University of Chicago Press, 420
Unsolicited cover letters, 499, 501–502
Useless words, 58
Username, 140
USPS mail
  address format, 183–185
  envelope size, 183
  ZIP code, 172–173, 184

V

Vacuum tubes, 134
Vague expressions, 68
Vague words, 12
Variety
  in sentence length, 61–63
  in sentence structure, 63
Verb, 14–15, 49, 50–51
  active voice, 14–15, 54–55, 68
  passive voice, 15, 54–55, 68
  subject-verb agreement, 56
  tense of, in minutes, 452
Videoconferencing, 445
Visualization, 47
Voice
  active, 14–15, 54–55, 69
  passive, 15, 54–55, 69
Voice mail, 137–138

W

Waugh, Evelyn, 390
"We attitude," 200
Wear-out sales series, 319
Welcome messages, 215
which, 63
Window envelopes, 184
Witty comments, in sales letter openings, 307–308
Word banks, 26
Word choice, 26–39
  antonyms, 25–26, 33
  appropriate words, 33
  bias-free language, 35–36
  clichés, 32, 401
  complex words, 12, 27–28
  concise words, 28–30
  concrete words, 12
  conversational words, 31, 51
  correct words, 36, 37
  homonyms, 33
  jargon, 34–35, 392
  misused words, 34
  negative words, 38–39
  positive words, 37–38, 61
  résumé, 477–478
  simple words, 27–28
  specific words, 36–37, 38
  synonyms, 25–26, 33
  trite expressions, 14, 31
  vague words, 12
Word meanings, 24–26
  cultural differences, 113, 278, 306, 374
  interpreting, 26
  types of, 24–25
  word references, 25–26
Word processing programs, 26, 143–146
  envelope feature, 184
  grammar checker, 145
  memo format and, 156–158
  outlining with, 145–146
  spell checker, 26, 144
  templates, 158, 397, 403
  thesaurus, 25–26, 144
Word processors, 143
Word references, 25–26
Wordiness, 58–60, 401
Works Cited list (MLA style), 419, 429, 430
World Wide Web. *See* Internet
Writer's block, 3
Writing process, 24
  computers in, 148–150
  editing, 148, 149
  prewriting, 47, 133, 145
  proofreading, 148, 149–150, 232, 401
  rough draft in, 119–121
  written plan in, 116–117
Written communication, 7, 9–17
  advantages of, 9–10, 104
  effect on audience, 11–13
  meanings of words in, 24–26
  techniques for, 10–11
  tests of effective, 13–17
  unified message in, 11, 14
  writing process, 24
Written plan, 116–117

Y

"You attitude," 12, 13, 84, 121
  in explaining reason for request, 301
  in goodwill messages, 199–200, 206–207
  résumé, 479
  in sales letters, 309–311

Z

ZIP code, 172–173, 184

References

DePree, Max (1989). *Leadership Is an Art*. New York: Dell Publishing.
Covey, Stephen R. (1989). *The 7 Habits of Highly Effective People*. New York: Simon & Schuster.